Strange Writing

SUNY Series in
Chinese Philosophy and Culture

David L. Hall and Roger T. Ames, Editors

Strange Writing

Anomaly Accounts in Early Medieval China

Robert Ford Campany

STATE UNIVERSITY OF NEW YORK PRESS

Cover: the first folio page of the *Shiliju congshu* edition of the *Bowuzhi* by Zhang Hua.

Production by Ruth Fisher
Marketing by Nancy Farrell

Published by
State University of New York Press, Albany

© 1996 State University of New York

For information, address the State University of New York Press,
State University Plaza, Albany, NY 12246

Library of Congress Cataloging-in-Publication Data
Campany, Robert Ford, 1959–
    Strange writing : anomaly accounts in early medieval China /
Robert Ford Campany.
        p.   cm. — (SUNY series in Chinese philosophy and culture)
    Includes bibliographical references and index.
    ISBN 0-7914-2659-9 (acid-free). — ISBN 0-7914-2660-2 (pbk. : acid-
free)
    1. Fantastic fiction, Chinese.   I. Title.   II. Series.
PL2629.F35C36   1996
895.1'30876609—dc20   94-45736
                                                       CIP

10 9 8 7 6 5 4 3 2 1

To my parents

Lawrence Edward Campany

Linda Ford Campany

Robert Carson Sanders

without each of whom not

Contents

Preface

This book is about Chinese texts, written over roughly a seven-century period beginning a little more than two millennia ago, that deal in one way or another with strange events, strange persons, strange places, and strange things. The texts are lists of items, each of which describes an anomalous being or place, or narrates an anomalous event. More than four thousand of these items still exist in some form today. They have yet to be systematically indexed and, with the exception of a few texts, have been translated only piecemeal and in small numbers. At this writing, I am preparing a separate index to the motifs and names in these texts along with a representative set of new translations. In the present book, however, I offer reflections on the larger puzzle of what they all might mean.

Anyone who approaches texts necessarily brings to them certain questions and interests, and it is on these that the kind of significance one finds in the texts largely depends. Most scholars who have written about these particular works—"anomaly accounts," as I will call them—have sought to establish their chronology and textual history, to place them within the larger development of Chinese literature, or to use them to document an early appearance of a particular story-type or cultural custom. These are all important concerns, and I have gratefully and liberally drawn on the fruits of such research in writing this book. But my own interests are somewhat different.

Since beginning to study these texts some eight years ago, I have pondered the ways in which they bear fundamental human significance. The very existence of any genre of writing, after all, cannot be taken for granted; it was not inevitable, but rather contingent, that these works came to be written and read, and this contingence leaves us unable to read them as if they only passively reflected things external to them. Why did their authors—highly literate men, most of whom held important positions in the hierarchy of officialdom—write at all, and at such length, and in these particular veins, about other people's unexpected encounters with denizens of the spirit-world, or startling feats by masters of esoteric arts, or the unusual flora and fauna of distant, inaccessible places? Why, in their world, was this a compelling thing to do? What were the pressing questions to which these writings were urged as answers? What sense can we now make of the portion of them that has reached us across the centuries? What can they be coaxed to tell us about the ideas and values of those who wrote and read them?

Doubtless the answers offered here will bear considerable revision. But I hope this book will at least put the study of these texts on a new footing. They have suffered a bad reputation all along: at first among some contemporaries because of the confusion and moral corruption it was feared they might spread, more recently among some scholars on both sides of the Pacific who—worse yet— have not taken them seriously as the vehicles of cosmological reflection and religious persuasion I believe they were intended to be. If I have succeeded in restoring even a little sense of what and how they might have *meant* in the culture of early medieval China, then I will at least have afforded another glimpse into that fascinating but insufficiently understood chapter of human history.

•

I am indebted to many institutions and individuals who have touched me or this book during the long process of its making. As I complete the project that has been part of almost a fourth of my life so far, it is pleasant to express my gratitude to them, although impossible to thank all who played a role.

I began this work while pursuing my doctorate, although the book that you now hold bears very little resemblance to the dissertation I completed in 1988. A Charlotte Newcombe Dissertation Fellowship afforded me the time to write that dissertation. Later, the American Council of Learned Societies provided a summer's support for work on the book manuscript. A grant from the National Endowment for the Humanities for work on the indexing project mentioned above has also freed up much-needed time for the completion of this book, and I am most grateful for it and for the supplemental funds provided by Indiana University; without them I could not have finished.

I will never forget the stimulating environment at the Divinity School of the University of Chicago, in which I first conceived this project. I owe a vast debt to my teachers at Chicago, especially Anthony Yu, Frank Reynolds, the late Joseph Kitagawa, Wendy Doniger, and Michael Dalby. Jonathan Smith did me the great kindness of carefully reading and commenting on my dissertation as it emerged. Earlier teachers are still part of me as well: Lance Stell, Frank Bliss, Gil Holland at Davidson College; also Jane Moore and Martha Witherspoon; Kung Shu-sen, formerly of Tainan Theological College; and James Pusey and the first-year faculty in the Chinese School at Middlebury College during the unforgettable summer of 1981.

My colleague Stephen Bokenkamp provided invaluable, painstaking comments on the final draft, and I am especially grateful to him for this since my request came in the midst of his mighty labors to finish a major project of his own. Anna Marshall Shields gave insightful critiques of early drafts of some chapters; Julia Luo also helpfully commented on early drafts. Over the years I have also profited from conversations about this subject with Lynn Struve, Ann Waltner, Lisa Raphals, Judith Zeitlin, Robert Eno, and Cathie Brettschneider. Responsibility for any shortcomings and errors in this book is, of course, my own.

I thank my colleagues (past and present) in the Department of Religious Studies at Indiana University for their encouragement and support over the last few years, particularly Stephen Stein (to whom I will always be profoundly grateful), Robert Orsi, Sam Preus, Richard Miller, Luke Johnson, Patrick Olivelle, and Gregory Schopen. I would also like to thank the students from whom I have learned and who showed kindness in often frantic times: they are too many to name, but I must mention Jeff Shirkey, Jason BeDuhn, Matthew Eynon, and Mary Ann Loebker Hatch. The staff at the East Asia Collection of the Indiana University Libraries—Thomas Lee and Ch'en Tung-lan—cheerfully helped track down obscure bibliographic data. Steve Bokenkamp and Lynn Struve have also been bottomless fonts of wisdom and know-how. Jenny Harrell and Jill Rogers have been constant bulwarks of administrative calm in the midst of working confusion.

Three remarkable men have honored me with their continuing friendship over the years and across long distances; with them I have enjoyed stimulating conversations about this project, and from them I have received unspeakable gifts. They are Ed Gilday, Peter Chemery, and Robert Berchman. May they prosper.

It would be impossible to complete this litany of thanks without mentioning the circle of friends and loved ones who have surrounded me as I wrote. John Ebling and the men of Nostos, past, present, and departed, have been rigorously compassionate, and I have learned much from their wisdom: they include Leo, Andy (of fond memory), Joe, Rich, Chris, Charlie, Greg, Harv, Wayne, Justice, and Gary. I couldn't have made it without them, nor without Tip, Nigel, Don, Morris, John, Steve, and Elizabeth, from whom I have also learned much. Thanks to Vicki Lane Marsh for providing seaside accommodations (with card games) during some of the writing, and to Sara Dingfelder for faithful friendship. I am grateful to employees at the Irish Lion, especially J. J., Kirk, Rachel, Denise, and Michelle, for providing what has often been a welcoming haven; as Michelle says, the right ghosts live there. SG has given me the beautiful gifts of her affection, support, and good cheer; to her my heartfelt thanks. To my family—my brother Chris, my mother Linda, my father Lawrence—thanks for encouraging me and putting up with my preoccupation.

Chapter One

Anomaly and Cosmography in Comparative Perspective

All higher knowledge is acquired by comparison, and rests on comparison. . . . The same applies to religion. *He who knows one, knows none.*

Friedrich Max Müller (1873, 9–13)

A pure ethnography or history that is uncontaminated by generalizations based on comparative inquiry is an ideal that cannot exist in practice.

Howard Eilberg-Schwartz (1990, 98)

In this chapter, I will try to articulate in an abstract, programmatic way what seem to me to be the questions and angles of approach most likely to yield fundamental insight into why, in any culture or period, texts about anomalies might come to be written, what and how they might mean, why they are significant, and how they may most fruitfully be read by people of other cultures or periods. These issues transcend cultural, historical, linguistic, and disciplinary bounds. To my mind, they are the issues that make such texts humanly significant, hence worth reading and pondering regardless of one's special area of expertise, disciplinary allegiance, or professional niche.

1

Anomaly and Cosmography

"Cosmography" means, simply, a description of the world. For convenience, I will use it in a not unrelated but much more specific and technical sense to mean the creation, development, and persuasive use (by some particular agent or group of agents) of a discourse concerning anomalies for the purpose of promoting, refining, confirming, or challenging a belief-system, worldview, or ideology. In what follows I will elaborate upon this stipulative and necessarily elaborate definition. Let us begin with "anomalies."

The *Oxford English Dictionary* defines the primary senses of "anomaly" thus:

> **1.** Unevenness, inequality, of condition, motion, etc. **2.** Irregularity, deviation from the common order, exceptional condition or circumstance. . . . A thing exhibiting such irregularity; an anomalous thing or being.

Bound up in its very definition is the fact that anomaly is an essentially taxonomic affair. That is to say, anomaly is inherently a matter of the discrimination of kinds or domains of objects, beings or states, and of the boundaries between them. On the face of it, the anomalous is that which is taken by an observer or speaker as crossing some boundary.

It is also immediately evident that a perception or ascription of anomaly presumes, even if in most cases only tacitly, some *nomos*, some given order of things, a background of what are taken as usual, normal, or expected conditions or objects or beings, including the normal boundaries among these. One cannot speak of the anomalous without assuming and implying some view of the normal against which it appears as such. Or, as Mary Douglas put it, "Where there is dirt there is system."[1] This implied "system" or normal state of affairs can be quite specific or sweepingly general, depending on context; but it can usually be linked in turn, more or less directly, to a larger worldview, belief-system, or ideology of which it forms an explicit part or by which it is entailed.

Any discourse about anomalies is a representation to an audience about things strange. To that extent, even when the discourse is a "memorate" in the first person singular that claims to report personal experience, it reflects conventions and assumptions held by its intended audience; it cannot truly be "people's own, *purely*

---

1. Douglas 1969, 35.

personal experiences,"[2] to cite one famous definition of the memo-rate, for such experiences would be unique and hence culturally unintelligible. It is at the level of these collective conventions and assumptions, then, that I propose to approach cosmographic texts. The notion of anomaly I intend in this chapter is a matter of cultural construction and social discourse, not of individual per-ception, which in any case is hardly accessible through most cosmographic genres. At issue is not the experience of the strange but the how and why of its representation.

For the same reasons, anomaly should be understood strictly as a cultural and not as a natural phenomenon. As Jonathan Z. Smith observes, anomaly is not an ontological but an epistemologi-cal and rhetorical category.

> "Otherness" is not a descriptive category. . . . It is a political and linguistic project, a matter of rhetoric and judgement. It is for this reason that in thinking about the "other," real progress has been made only when the "other" ceases to be an ontological category. . . . Despite its apparent taxonomic exclu-sivity, "otherness" is a transactional matter, an affair of the "in-between."[3]

In the strictest sense, anomalies do not simply happen. Events happen, various people and objects exist, and they are judged and called odd, extraordinary, even contranatural by human agents within communities, who judge and call them so with reference to some reigning worldview, system, or ideology into which they do not readily fit.[4] This judging and calling are the stuff of cosmo-graphy.

When these ascriptions of anomaly cease to be isolated speech-acts and become lasting focal points for social discourse, we can begin to speak of a cosmographic tradition.[5] Over time, such traditions arise, develop, flourish, wither, and die. As they develop and mature, they will necessarily and often quickly become routinized into distinct genres, that is, specific sets of discursive properties codified by society through habitual practice or explicit

---

2. von Sydow 1948, 73, ital. mine; cf. Dégh and Vázsonyi 1974; Honko 1964; Brandes 1974.

3. Smith 1985, 46.

4. Needham 1979, 46; Murray 1983; Lincoln 1989, 165; Humphreys 1968, 18, 20, 33, 90–92; but cf. Hunn 1979.

5. Shils 1981.

principle. Genres set horizons of expectation for the audience and models of performance for contributors. Performers (including but not limited to authors) perform as a function of, though not necessarily in strict accord with, the existing generic conventions. Apparent violations of those conventions help (like any other anomalies) to confirm their existence and make clear—or change—their boundaries. On the other hand, the audience watches, hears, or reads any performance as a function of the relevant generic conventions, though not necessarily consciously and not always passively.[6]

Cosmographic traditions and their genres are rarely born by someone's conscious decision. Traditions and genres take shape by a halting process of comparison, differentiation, and contrast with other traditions and genres. In this process, new channels of discourse are cut, their boundaries with already existing traditions and genres being constantly tested and redefined. The creation of a new tradition or genre of discourse is a matter of carving out a new intellectual, textual, and cultural space or niche in which to work. The new genre is often justified, however, especially in societies that primarily locate authority in an exemplary past, by an appeal to historical precedent, real or imagined.[7] As the genre comes into being, a new set of expectations and models is codified, a new project defined and made available for the participation of agents and audience. This process also results in the creation of a new object of discourse, defined through comparison, differentiation, and contrast with other objects, just as the genre is defined by contrast with other genres.[8]

A complete typology, even an adequate survey, of cosmographic genres is unnecessary here, but I would like in a few sentences to suggest the range of media and genres that have been employed cosmographically. Despite the etymology of the term, a cosmography may be danced, gestured, or sung. Contact cults, including the famous "cargo cults," are the most obvious examples.[9] But any acted-out representation of anomalous others qualifies as cosmographic—consider exorcisms, or certain types of rites for the dead—and we may speak of genres of (cosmographic) ritual action as well as of written literature. Cosmographic work may also be

---

6. Todorov 1975, 1976; Dubrow 1982.

7. Hobsbawm and Ranger 1983.

8. Foucault 1972, 1973.

9. Burridge 1960; Wagner 1979; Sahlins 1981; Schieffelin and Crittenden 1991.

done in visual media. Perhaps the most familiar examples are old mapping traditions such as the medieval European maps that taxonomized the known world into three parts and filled the interstices and *terrae incognitae* with pictures of mythical beasts,[10] but any visual representation of anomalous beings, objects, places, events, perhaps even times carries cosmographic weight. When we come finally to literary genres, the range is enormous. One might begin by distinguishing narrative from non-narrative types. Narrative cosmographic genres are probably almost coextensive with narrative genres, since it is hard to imagine any that may not be used cosmographically; but the most prominent include the epic, exotic travel literature in its various sub-genres including pilgrimage accounts,[11] poetic or scriptural narratives of spirit-travels and dream visions, historical works, folktales, legends, miracle tales, and memorates. The non-narrative genres range from geographic and topographic accounts through ethnographies and "theoretical" treatises of various sorts to sheer taxonomic lists and tables. To speak of a text or performance as cosmographic is to specify nothing concerning its form but rather to characterize its subject matter (anomalies of one or many kinds) and its purpose.

What, then, of its purpose? Cosmographies are sometimes created or invoked in order to support a particular worldview, ideology, or belief-system—often, but not necessarily, the one that is culturally dominant or held by the most powerful elite(s). This support may take the form of confirming a set of beliefs or tenets, thus strengthening the entire ideological system; or of refining the system in some particular respect, enabling it to deal with a new area of experience, a problematic issue, or a nagging exception. In other cases, cosmographic discourse is used to undermine a dominant worldview without necessarily offering a clearly articulated alternative system. In still others, it may be used simultaneously to attack one belief-system and promote another. Furthermore, these and other uses may co-exist within a single cosmographic tradition, genre, or sub-genre. Traditions and genres of cosmographic discourse should not be thought of as rigidly implying commitment to a single, particular worldview, although in any given historical context they may be better suited to some worldviews than to others. Rather, a single tradition or genre more often than not becomes a public field of contention on which individuals or groups play out conflicts and contend for power, using shared conventions of dis-

---

10. Wright 1965 [1925], 65ff. and 121ff.
11. Campbell 1988; Harbsmeier 1985, 1986; Helms 1988.

course about a single object or type of object to advance divergent ends.

Cosmographic performances and/or texts adopt varying stances toward the anomalous.[12] "Anomalies can be ignored, ridiculed, distorted, or suppressed, these all being means whereby they are relegated to the margins and interstices of both a given classificatory system and . . . lived experience. Alternatively, the system under which they are judged anomalous can be modified or abandoned,"[13] as happens in so-called scientific revolutions and paradigm shifts.[14] As Bruce Lincoln notes of the latter case, more is almost always at stake than a mere intellectual change; social and ideological consequences also follow.[15] But we must add that there is no necessary correlation between a dismissive stance toward anomalies and the maintenance of the dominant worldview, nor between recognizing anomalies and rejecting the dominant worldview. In principle, either approach to anomalies can be used to support or to undermine a reigning ideology. Such an ideology might, for example, be based upon not the blanket dismissal but the ongoing recognition and assimilation of anomalies under taxonomic schemes of order. In this latter case, the ongoing micro-revision of the dominant taxonomic system may serve merely to maintain its dominance, not to bring it down, for encounters with anomalies have (in such a system) been portrayed as the very occasions on which the system's power is recreated and displayed. On the other hand, this constant micro-revision may reshape the taxonomic system over time; but again, this reshaping may either challenge or preserve intact the dominant ideology.

In some knowledge systems or historical contexts, such as certain of those in which modern Western scientists work, anomalies are posed chiefly in order to be explained or classified and thus domesticated. Once posed, they may not typically perdure for very long. In other knowledge systems or historical contexts, anomalies may be longstanding and frequently returned to in discourse; the point, for some participants in the discourse, might not be to "solve" them but precisely to keep them around as long as possible.[16] Despite the impression one gets from reading treatments of anomalies in the literature on the philosophy of science and in some anthropo-

---

12. Needham 1979, 46.
13. Lincoln 1989, 165.
14. Kuhn 1970.
15. Cf. Morris 1979.
16. Cf. Needham 1979, 46.

logical works, anomalies are not always and everywhere extremely troubling and domesticated as rapidly as possible; this is only one sort of reaction to anomaly.

Why is cosmographic discourse important in a society or culture? What makes anomalies so "good to think with" and fruitful to talk about, both for the human communities we study and for us who study them?

In the first place, anomalies and incongruities provide occasions for creative thought and action in communities, and so they are good places to observe a human community at work and at play, to note the awakened craft of its response to history. For a good part of the twentieth century, in justifiable reaction to earlier assumptions about the supposed haziness and superstition of non-Westerners' cultures, Western scholars have tended to overemphasize congruity, conformity, repetition, "mechanisms," and the logic of systems. But it is anomalies—the perceived fractures and gaps in such systems, the "perceptions of discrepancy and discord[—] which give rise to the symbolic project that we identify as the very essence of being human."[17] Anomalies stimulate testings, evaluations, modifications, or stretchings of knowledge-systems and action-patterns. In this sense they are grist for a culture's mill. They are the raw material on which a culture works, and although a culture perdures over time by executing an ongoing series of "micro-adjustments" on such material,[18] the creative, ongoing, historical, and processual aspects of these "adjustments" have not always been fully appreciated by structuralists, functionalists, and other such "systematists."

Anomalies also, then, provide a lever for intellectual, ideological, and social change.[19] Anomalies include, but are not limited to, those places where a community's cognitive systems or social structures palpably bump up against a recalcitrant, external reality, giving exponents of internal reform or revolution an opportunity to make their case. Conversely, anomalies are the internal weak points, lines, or fissures that must be defended by exponents of existing systems and structures. Cosmographic discourse can serve both purposes, often simultaneously. The concept of anomaly includes some of what falls under the rubric of "liminality," except that anomaly is not a ritual phase, is usually not ritually constructed, and need not give rise to "danger" in a purely negative

17. Smith 1978a, 297. Cf. Smith 1974.
18. Lévi-Strauss 1966, 10.
19. Kuhn 1970; Ohnuki-Tierney 1990a, 18.

sense.[20] As is true of liminal situations, anomalous events, places, and beings are sometimes fraught with the danger and the power that arise when boundaries are crossed. Anomaly is to ideology or worldview what liminality is to ritual. To deal with anomaly is often to enter an arena charged with danger and to engage issues of power.

Anomalies are "good to think with" in at least one other respect: by their alterity they prompt individual and collective self-reflection. They are thus key vehicles for the collective fashioning of identity and the construction of society. Cultures, groups, religious traditions and sects often indirectly display what they are or hope to be by saying what they are not.[21] Human communities construct themselves as communities by negotiating an ongoing series of resemblances and differences between themselves and all manner of others (not only other human communities) through classificatory, comparative processes.

To this point I have discussed anomaly and cosmography in terms general enough to apply to virtually any society. I now wish to address specifically those modes of cosmography most characteristic of large-scale, urban cultures.

Collecting Curiosities:
Anomalies Bound and Unbound

In traditional societies, the city is typically a sacred zone, a center of ceremony and ritual display. The city can be characterized not only in demographic and socioeconomic terms but also as a center of symbolic action, serving as the exemplar or "style center" for an entire people.[22] The rise of such sacred urban centers is often linked to a characteristic type of worldview, in which the key elements are schemes of spatial-cosmic orientation, "the elevation of leaders to the level of supreme rulers whose actions insured the harmony of heaven and earth,"[23] and calendrical systems which

---

20. van Gennep 1960; Douglas 1969, 1975, 1982; Turner 1969.

21. For salient examples, White 1991; Ohnuki-Tierney 1987, 1990b; Céard 1977; Wright 1947, 1965 [1925]; White 1991; White 1972; Todorov 1984.

22. Wheatley 1969, 1971; Wheatley and See 1978; Geertz 1968, 36–38, and 1980; Tambiah 1976; Smith 1987; Smith and Reynolds 1987; Long 1986, 65–78; Eliade 1959, chap. 1; Eliade 1976, 18–31; Eliade 1961, 37–38.

23. Carrasco 1982, 71.

effect a synchronicity between human life and the rhythms of the cosmos.

In all societies in which sacred centers figure, a dialectical structure is inherent, for a center implies a periphery. Sacred urban centers do not exist in geographical or social vacuums, but depend for their ceremonial status as well as economic subsistence on hierarchically ordered, centripetal and centrifugal interactions with people in the surrounding countryside as well as with itinerant merchants and foreigners. From the point of view of a center of urban culture, the "distance" between the center and its periphery is seldom a matter of mere geographical space, or of the calendrical time required for the journey out and back. The peripheral is, from a centrist perspective, the anomalous—the external other. The distance, then, is also an ontological, moral, taxonomic, and aesthetic distance. Once constructed through discourse, this distance is carefully maintained as a balance or tension across various sorts of taxonomic boundaries and socio-geographic "frontiers."[24]

In centrist ideologies, therefore, the center's interaction with its anomalous periphery often becomes a matter of controlling it by dividing it into parts and assigning these parts distinct places[25] in some hierarchical and taxonomic scheme. The notion of place becomes fundamental, and "the concern to assign every single creature, object or feature to a place within a class"[26] becomes paramount. Agents of the center strive through cosmographic discourse—as well as by other, decidedly more overt and violent means—to "encompass," "domesticate," or somehow "cope with" the periphery and thus subsume anomaly under order.[27] As a general designation for all such acts of emplacement, I propose the term *collection*. Obviously based on the familiar phenomenon of the grouping within a central enclave of objects imported from outside, I will use this term as shorthand to designate the variety of ways in which anomalies are domesticated and re-presented in the interest of, and from the point of view of, the center. "The collection of the world"—the repetitious act, informed by "a structure of desire," of both temporarily closing and ultimately preserving the gap between center and periphery—has been the dominant mode of cos-

---

24. Bohannan and Plog 1967. Cf. Turner 1973; Harbsmeier 1985, 1986.

25. Smith 1987.

26. Lévi-Strauss 1966, 10.

27. "Encompass": Dumont 1980, 239ff.; "domesticate": Goody 1977, chap. 1; "cope with": Barrau 1979. Overall, cf. Todorov 1984.

mography in traditional urban cultures.[28] Expressed through a variety of specific rituals, myths, and institutions, collection has been a fundamental "key scenario"[29] of order in most large-scale, urban societies.

Whatever specific forms it takes, collection entails out-and-back crossings between center and periphery. On leaving the center, the collector—as I will, for brevity's sake, call any collecting agent—enters wild, undomesticated terrain, a country of marvels and wonders. Taxonomically speaking, the space traversed by the collector is not homogeneous; the collector ranges through hierarchically ordered categories of barbarism, finely graded degrees of distance from the center, and his journey—or pilgrimage—recapitulates the taxa of the center's cosmographic map.[30] The collector's journey through space and through categories of "others" is a journey through time as well, as is readily seen when one recalls the longstanding Western discourse on the "primitive."[31]

The collector brings home part of the wilderness, whether it be in the form of stories and reports, objects, or images. What is brought back is displayed, accounted for in some fashion. Four general points about this display should be made here. First, what is brought back has been selected. From a background of commonplace facts, the collector often takes back to the center only those that are noteworthy in the most literal sense, striking, unusual, extraordinary—in a word, anomalous. The collection par excellence thus consists of things that make manifest the difference between the center and the periphery. A fourteenth-century European cosmographic text exemplifies this aspect of collecting in such statements as: "In Greece I neither saw nor heard of aught worth telling, unless it be that . . . ," and "In Armenia the Greater I saw one marvel. . . . But I saw not anything else . . . worth telling as a marvel."[32]

---

28. The first phrase in quotation marks has been taken from the suggestive title of Defert 1982–83; the second, from Clifford 1985, 239. Clifford borrowed it from Stewart 1984, ix: "Narrative is seen in this essay as a structure of desire, a structure that both invents and distances its object and thereby inscribes again and again the gap between signifier and signified that is the place of generation for the symbolic."

29. Ortner 1973.

30. Harbsmeier 1985.

31. Smith 1985; Fabian 1983; Long 1986, chap. 6; Lovejoy and Boas 1935; Boas 1948.

32. Jordanus 1863, 2–7. It is striking that the author, dividing his work by geographical regions, left entire sections empty when he knew nothing "marvelous" to report about certain regions. Thus the section on

Second, to borrow a metaphor from Lévi-Strauss (who borrowed it from tribal societies), collected objects participate in a paradox. On the one hand, they are held to exemplify "raw" wilderness, to emblematize its otherness, yet they can do so only in "cooked" form, divorced from their natural setting and re-presented in a field of other objects arranged by the collector. The objects of collection, like the collector himself, are changed utterly. But collectors often use various devices to mask this mutation. Among these devices is the stereotype: a topos which, because it is constantly returned to in successive collections, gives the illusion that the object out there must be correctly described.[33] Such stereotypes are often remarkably durable. For example, the "marvels of the East," a set of fantastic images of India formed by Greek writers such as Herodotus, Ktesias, and Megasthenes, and passed on to medieval Europe in the works of Pliny, Solinus, Macrobius, and Martianus of Capella, "did not die altogether with the geographical discoveries and a better knowledge of the East, but lived on in pseudo-scientific dress right into the 17th and 18th centuries," and so "determined the western idea of India for almost 2000 years."[34]

Third, collected objects are displayed according to some principle or structure, not randomly. "The good collector (opposed to the obsessive, the miser) is tasteful and systematic. Accumulation unfolds in a pedagogical, edifying manner. The collection itself, its taxonomic, aesthetic structure, is valued."[35] Principles of classification and display may command more attention from cosmographers and their audiences than the anomalous objects themselves.

Finally, in urban traditions the display often aims at a complete *summa* of the cosmos. The taxonomic space of cosmographic display becomes a *plenum* to mirror the world it emblematizes; nothing less is intended than a total re-presentation of the world. A map, for instance, will arrange and divide the entire earth according to the cosmographic principles of its tradition, sometimes filling in the *terrae incognitae* with such place-holders as monstrous creatures and peoples so as to leave no space blank. It will further

---

Aran (a land mentioned in the Bible) consists of the following notice: "Concerning Aran I say nothing at all, seeing that there is nothing worth noting" (50). This paragraph is not to suggest, however, that the only reason things catch travelers' eye is their exotic quality; there are many other criteria, many other agendas that spur collectors on their quest—military, commercial, and so on.

33. Foster 1982–83, 29.

34. Wittkower 1942, 159; cf. Wright 1965 [1925], 274ff.; Lach 1965–1977, 1:3–86.

35. Clifford 1985, 238–39. Cf. Stocking 1983.

express the idea of totality by means of measurement and scale: it represents all of space, whose dimensions can be expressed numerically, by means of correspondingly measured places on its own surface.[36]

In general, then, we may say that the goal of collection is the domestication of that which is dangerously wild, the fixing of anomaly in a stable format, a determinative taxonomic place. But even where collection appears most successful, it is still the anomalous that is collected; and the dialectical structure of collection continually recreates and maintains, even as it also spans, the distance between center and periphery. The anomalous fact or object is emplaced within a cosmographic system, hence domesticated; but the whole point of collecting it is to display its foreignness, and "what is foreign is that which escapes from a place."[37] Even at its most hegemonic, therefore, collection does not permanently destroy the anomalous and the peripheral, but in fact presupposes their existence. Further, the collector's striving toward total representation is of course more a dream than an institutional fact; it is the dream of central elites in most traditional urban societies, but history shows that it is never permanently fulfilled. Collection, essentially an attempt to control reality, is not a uniformly or ultimately successful enterprise, for if one thing is certain it is that reality cannot be fully controlled.

Nor have all urban elites always wanted to control it. Collection is typically tied to what Jonathan Z. Smith has termed a "locative" worldview; but in reaction to this type of worldview there often arises what he terms a "utopian" one. This distinction can form the basis of a useful model for understanding cosmographies.

In a *locative* worldview, the chief preoccupation is the control of reality by means of boundaries. The sacred center is an enclave to be marked off and defended against outsiders. Humanity patterns its life on the fundamental principles of the cosmos. Harmony with cosmic order is paramount; rebellion against cosmic order is a barbaric—and futile—act serving only to highlight order more clearly. Primary, positive religious and cultural value is placed on control and on the mechanisms of control; loss of control, or existence outside the enclave, amount to barbarism at best, ultimate chaos at worst. Historically, utopian worldviews have usually arisen as reactions against locative ones, and they are sometimes,

---

36. Wright 1965 [1925], 65ff. and 121ff.; Wright 1947; Dilke 1985; Harvey 1980, esp. chap. 8; Robinson and Petchenik 1976, chap. 3.

37. de Certeau 1986, 70.

though not necessarily, associated with religions of salvation. In a *utopian* worldview, the limits that are established to confine the sacred come to be felt as oppressing humanity itself. "Man is no longer defined by the degree to which he harmonizes himself and his society to the cosmic patterns of order; but rather by the degree to which he can escape the patterns."[38] Primary value is placed on freedom, and dominant cultural or religious mechanisms of control and order are relativized. Smith's characterization of utopian worldviews is largely based on Hellenistic religions, and in his model a utopian view does not necessarily presuppose a locative view against which it reacts. I propose to use the term *anti-locative* instead of Smith's "utopian," both to emphasize the typically reactional nature of this sort of view and to make the model applicable beyond the Hellenistic context.

The relevant point for our understanding of cosmography is that in any anti-locative view of the world the enterprise of collecting becomes problematic. Either it is left off entirely or its displays become increasingly self-reflexive and self-ironic. People are no longer sure of the value or even the possibility of taxonomically placing anomalies with any finality. The difference between center and periphery, "system" and "dirt," "us" and "them" ceases to be clear, or at least no longer carries much weight. The center as an enclave or hamlet now dissolves into an open space; the preoccupation with emplacing every anomaly into some ordered scheme now gives way to the obliteration of old distinctions. The center itself becomes an other; "what is near masks a foreignness."[39] People begin to speak of the "normal" as including "facts just as wonderful as those that we go collecting in remote countries and centuries," since "it is one and the same nature that rolls its course," to quote Montaigne, a master of anti-locative collecting.[40]

Under these conditions, the project of collecting may continue for a while under its old guises, but it comes to be carried out in an increasingly ironic and acutely self-conscious mode, and is thus slowly altered and ultimately undermined from within. Its political structures of domination, once masked, are now highlighted. The "other out there," often linguistically and metaphorically consigned (as Johannes Fabian has eloquently shown) to a temporal past or an eternal present, now stands as an actual living being among the displayed objects, which are themselves increasingly presented as

---

38. Smith 1978a, 139–40; cf. Smith 1978b, 429.
39. de Certeau 1986, 67.
40. Frame 1958, 342–43.

processes or artifacts "belonging" to (if no longer "owned" by) cultures lying outside the urban center.[41] One might say, as a general rule, that the more anti-locative the setting in which collection is carried out, the more sophisticatedly self-aware collection becomes and the more problematic it is revealed to be. Western academic anthropology over the last century and a quarter is an excellent example of the historical vicissitudes to which a cosmographic tradition is subject: once locative, it is now experiencing an extremely anti-locative moment.[42]

We have to deal, in short, with two modes of cosmography, or perhaps a spectrum of modes. At one end—the locative—ultimate value is given to emplacing anomaly and domesticating the other, for these are the acts by which the cultural center is constructed. At the other end of the spectrum—the anti-locative—value is given to the critique of, or escape from, this emplacement and domestication, for ultimate value is taken to lie elsewhere. At any moment in its history, a cosmographic tradition may tend as a whole toward one or another end of this spectrum; or, more commonly, some authors (for in urban traditions it is almost always a question of written media) will write from a locative, others from an anti-locative viewpoint. Furthermore, within any society a variety of locative and anti-locative views may be advanced simultaneously, and rival versions of the "center" may thus be advanced—for the center of an urban tradition is always constructed and contested. Particular cosmographic genres, media, topics, or motifs may come to be predominantly used by agents of one perspective against others. These may also then be co-opted by opponents, their messages reversed or inverted.

I now wish to attend briefly to one key medium of cosmography, and specifically of the project of "collecting the world," in most urban traditions: the act of writing itself, and the nature of the product. Cosmography means, after all, writing down the cosmos.

Inside and Outside the Cabinet of Writing

For much of its existence, writing has performed the symbolic functions of binding, fixing, delimiting, even coercing.[43] Beyond such

---

41. Clifford 1985, 244–45.

42. Clifford and Marcus 1986; Marcus and Fischer 1986.

43. On the general history and phenomenological and cultural meaning of writing, Danzel 1912; Gelb 1963; Derrida 1976, 1978; de Certeau

media as the display of physical objects in reliquaries, "cabinets of curiosities," museums, zoological and botanical gardens, and the performance of rituals such as triumph, tribute, and obeisance (which enact the periphery's subordination to the center), writing as such has therefore been the chief vehicle of urban centers' cosmographic projects. To collect anomalies has usually meant to write about them: texts have been primary mediators between centers and peripheries, serving, like the cabinet of curiosities (ancestor of the modern public museum),[44] to display the marvels of the periphery. Texts have also been used to alter or undermine projects of collection. The questions are these: Why has writing been such a key cosmographic medium? Is there anything in its nature, beyond its obvious power as a mode of communication, that will shed light on its cosmographic function and thus on the nature of cosmography as a human enterprise? What difference does it make when a cosmographic tradition or genre is not oral or gestural but written?

We may begin to understand the cosmographic value of writing by recalling its nature as a human act. In an age in which words are increasingly stored as electromagnetic bits, we might easily forget that, first and foremost, to write something is to cut, scratch, draw, paint, impress, or otherwise mark a surface. The etymologies of many terms for writing reflect this.[45] But they only confirm a point that seems obvious upon reflection: among ways of communicating, it is peculiar to writing and other graphic and plastic media that they literally embody a message in some physical, external, usually durable form. Unlike speech or gesture or music, whose utterances perdure only as long as the performance continues, writing lifts its message from the flow of time by means of an objectivization in space.[46] My point is not that writing is used exclusively to bind its objects; it is rather that, in the first instance, especially early in its history wherever it has appeared, writing binds. It is therefore no surprise to find that, everywhere it has appeared, writing is used in "magical" practices whose purpose is to bind or

---

1975; Goody 1977, 1987; Diringer 1962; Hooke 1937, 1954; Friedrich 1937, 1938, 1941; Bertholet 1949.

44. von Schlosser 1908; Frese 1960; Lach 1965–1977, v.2, bk.1:7–55; Stocking 1985.

45. Gelb 1963, 7.

46. On the simultaneity of performance, Schutz 1977. On writing's objectifying function, Ong 1981 [1967] and 1982, esp. chaps. 4–5; Ricoeur 1976, 26–29; Gelb 1963, 7–9.

hinder the workings of some power, or to coerce it into effecting specific results.[47] The symbolic binding function of writing in most literate cultures is mirrored in the metaphoric use to which books and other written materials have been put: the image of the book or tablet frequently expresses ideas of fate, destiny, or divine judgment, and writing is a frequent metaphor for the psychological functions of sensory "impressions" and memory.

Ancient views of writing as having the power to bind or fix lie behind more recent and familiar developments. Such momentous events as the standardization of scripts by the state, the emergence of scriptural canons, the invention of the alphabet and (much later) of the printing press, are all complex expressions of the old view of writing as fixing. As scholars including Walter Ong, Jack Goody, Michel de Certeau, and Jacques Derrida have shown, writing lends itself to "fixing" objects of discourse by creating a uniform field of textual space and time in which they assume a definite place. The field of the text may take the form of a manuscript or printed page. It may collect its objects into a table or a list. It may display them in a map or cosmogram, embed them in a historical narrative, or unfold them in ethnographic or geographic formats.[48] Most triumphantly, it may aspire to enclose them once and for all in a complete "circle of knowledge" or *encyclopaedia*. In all these cases, granted the important differences among them, the fundamental act remains one of collecting and binding diverse data into a common and delimited field of display. Almost as long as writing has existed, however, some have resisted this binding function of writing, seeking to preserve or recover the reality that exists prior to or beyond inscription. This nostalgia for the oral is often part of a larger protest against the sort of locative cosmography for which writing had served as a medium.[49] In this sort of context, the unwritten comes to have special integrity as an undomesticated terrain in contrast to the closed, bound display of writing; the collection, once a "cabinet of curiosities" of cosmic import, now itself becomes a curious object; writing is used to undermine its own capacity to bind.

---

47. Audollent 1903, 1904; Naveh and Shaked 1985; Betz 1986; Thorndike 1928–58, v.2; Marquès-Rivière 1938; Piccaluga 1974, 1983.

48. On "field" narratives, Clifford and Marcus 1986; Marcus and Fischer 1986; Stocking 1983.

49. Plato's suspicion of writing: *Republic* 274b–276a; a Japanese parallel, Pollack 1986, 36; a Judaeo-Christian example, Boas 1948, 189, but cf. 191.

The difference between these two broad sorts of attitudes toward writing shows up clearly in traditions of *literary collecting*. In such traditions as folklore, ethnography, certain kinds of geographical writing, and most hagiography or sacred biography—which are not restricted to the Judaeo-Christian and Islamic West but have arisen in most cultures where literacy has developed—writers attempt to capture in writing something that is powerful precisely because of its separateness from writing. Each of these traditions depends on two apparently contradictory assumptions: on the one hand, that the modes of writing it employs constitute an adequate handle to grasp or fix the objects described, or in other words that these objects can be brought under the scope (or into the field) of the particular discipline of writing in question; on the other hand, that the object thus enmeshed in writing merits this attention because it has certain qualities that separate it off from the written tradition and from the ceremonial center, qualities that give it an integrity peculiar to the peripheral and to the unwritten. That which is perceived in the center as "savage," as "peasant," as "holy," as "natural"—whether seen as noble or base—is written about in a text that, displaying these objects for central re-inspection, is at the same time often felt by authors and audience to be palpably distant from and inadequate to its object. "The exotic is always full of surprises; it delights and titilates. To domesticate it exhaustively would neutralize this aspect of its meaning and regretfully integrate it into the humdrum of everyday routines. The ideology of the exotic therefore stops short of an exhaustive interpretation."[50]

These are the sorts of considerations that have framed my inquiry into the Chinese texts introduced in the following chapter.

---

50. Foster 1982–83, 21–22.

PART ONE

The Texts and Their World

Chapter Two

Anomaly Accounts in Early Medieval China: Genre and Texts

The Notion of Genre

During or perhaps even before the Han dynasty, a cosmographic genre—a genre of writing about anomalous phenomena—began to coalesce in China. Its growth accelerated rapidly in the centuries after the fall of the Han. This chapter characterizes the genre in general terms and describes the texts that belonged to it up until the establishment of the Tang dynasty in 618 C.E.

It is first necessary to clarify the way in which I understand "genre," a term of interpretive art. The classical, Aristotelian approach treats genres as formalistically defined textual (or performative) types. On this approach, to define a genre is to list the thematic, stylistic, and compositional features possessed by the texts (or performances) that belong to it. Recently, influenced generally by a Marxist-style turn to historical praxis and more specifically by Bakhtin's "sociological poetics" and Bourdieu's analysis of culture as practice, anthropologists, folklorists, linguists, and historians have developed an alternative approach, in which "genres can be defined as the historically specific conventions and ideals according to which authors compose discourse and audiences receive it. In this view, genres consist of orienting frameworks, interpretive procedures, and sets of expectations that are not part of the

21

discourse structure, but of the ways actors relate to and use language."[1] In short, while the classical approach to genres focuses on properties of texts as finished products extractable from the circumstances and conditions of their production, the comparatively recent practical approach focuses on the extra- and inter-textual assumptions that inform the writing and reading of texts in specific historical and cultural circumstances—on the ways in which people (authors and audience) relate to texts and the ways in which they relate one text to another.[2]

I will use the term genre in a sense that combines both of these approaches, for if the classical approach ignores the expectations shaping the ways in which texts are produced or received, the practical approach at times risks dissolving texts into their contexts. A given set of texts is, to be sure, received differently by different social groups and in different eras (one of those modes of reception being the very notion that they do indeed constitute a "set" in some sense); but it is, after all, the same texts, as modified through time, that are being responded to differently, and if that is so, then a consideration of their intrinsic properties—including the markers to be found in them that signal ways in which their authors (as well as later strata of readers/redactors/commentators) wanted readers to understand them and relate them to other texts—cannot be omitted from analysis. To attend to the properties of texts themselves is particularly important when, as here, one is attempting to "see" a genre from a great historical and cultural distance and to characterize it perhaps a bit more clearly than contemporaries did. Since texts do not come with explicit generic labels affixed to them, classifying texts as belonging to a particular genre, a necessary if preliminary step in understanding the genre in its historical setting, is itself already an interpretive enterprise that must be based on all available evidence, textual, intertextual, and extratextual.

To these so far general considerations I would now like to add further, specific clarifications of the notion of genre as I will use it, in order to match this analytical tool as closely as possible with the manifold complexities of cultural life that it is intended to illuminate.

1. In contrast to some scholars' tendency (Todorov in particu-

---

1. Hanks 1987, 670.
2. My understanding of genre is informed by Todorov 1975, 1976; Bourdieu 1977; Dubrow 1982; Bakhtin 1986; Bakhtin and Medvedev 1985; Hanks 1987; and Briggs and Bauman 1992.

lar) to view genres as totalizing "universes" of thought and discourse that to a large extent determine authors' and readers' mentality, I will assume that, while a given genre may be associated with certain social groups and historical precedents such that "invoking a genre . . . creates indexical connections that extend far beyond the present setting of production or reception, thereby linking a particular act to other times, places, and persons,"[3] authors and audiences may participate in it with sharply different interests. Although to invoke a genre by means of standard framing devices or conventions ("once upon a time . . .") may generate a strongly cohesive set of expectations in an audience, those expectations may be used or played upon through various persuasive rhetorical strategies for various ideological ends.[4] Genres are thus not "transcendental" in the Kantian philosophical sense of constituting a necessary epistemological condition of writing or reading; on the other hand, they are an enabling condition of cultural exchange of ideas and values in the way that a "market"—which is nothing more or less remarkable than the tacit social agreement, grounded in historical precedent, that people will gather at specific periods of time and at the same place—is an enabling condition of other sorts of exchange.

2. While a notion of genres as completely *unconscious* sets of expectations and conventions would make little sense, it must be recognized that authors' and audiences' participation in genres need not be fully conscious to be recognized as such in historical hindsight. Indeed, some measure of historical distance may be required in order to see clearly the pattern of a genre's emergence that was obscured from contemporaries involved in the process. Furthermore, attempts by contemporary theoreticians in a culture to formulate generic classifications or definitions should be read neither as mirror-like, undistorted descriptions of, nor as automatically efficacious prescriptions for, contemporary understandings or practices, but as strategies employed by writers in one genre (the genre of "theoretical writing about genres") to influence the practice of writing in other genres.

3. Genres lack clear boundaries, and when it comes to a text's "membership" in a genre the law of excluded middle most emphatically does not apply. Genres are more like "fuzzy sets" than containers; one may speak of degrees of membership in generic cat-

---

3. Briggs and Bauman 1992, 147–48.

4. Another, possibly more helpful way of putting this is seen in Briggs and Bauman 1992, 148 (middle of page).

egories, and one may speak of particular texts or text-types as "core" versus "marginal" or "peripheral" participants in a genre. Genres are helpfully thought of as analogous to planetary systems: each generic system as a whole stands in specifiable (if complex) relations of proximity/distance to all other systems in a given culture,[5] which as a whole constitute a sort of cultural galaxy of generic systems; any given text may be situated relatively close to or far from the center of its immediately environing planetary-system center, pulled nevertheless (even if only slightly) by gravitational attraction from other systems as well. Authors and redactors use strategies for maximizing or minimizing intertextual gaps between their own and others' texts.[6]

4. One implication of (3) is that genres are not islands unto themselves; rather, they are quintessentially constituted and recognizable as genres by their relationships of difference and similarity (the "gravity" of the galactic system of cultural discourse) to other genres operative in their social-cultural world.

The Genre of Anomaly Accounts: An Initial Characterization

Armed with this preliminary understanding of the concept, it is possible to argue that a genre of anomaly accounts was created in Han China and dramatically developed after the fall of the Han, and to characterize that genre with reference to the following five features of the texts themselves as well as their intertextual relations and their reception among literate Chinese during these centuries.

Form

Anomaly accounts take the form of lists of relatively brief items of narration and/or description. They are thus distinct from continuous narrative texts, and from treatises or essays. In most cases, we do not know with any certainty by what principles these lists were organized in the original texts, since their present arrangement is

---

5. And, potentially, in other cultures as well, to the extent that actors in a given culture are aware of genres and texts operative in other cultures.

6. A notion helpfully explored in Briggs and Bauman 1992, 149–55.

often, even in the case of texts that have survived relatively intact, the work of a redactor standing somewhere between the author's time and our own. But, this having been said, there seem to have been a handful of distinct, routinized formats, including topical organization (Bwz, possibly Ssj, Yy, influenced by and influencing the *leishu* genre which was emerging during the same centuries), geographic or topographic arrangement (Shj, Shenyjing, Szj, and Dmj, borrowing the *dili* format for the description of exclusively anomalous phenomena), annals (*benji*) and "precedent" (*gushi*) formats (the former exemplified in many anomaly accounts, the latter in Hwgs), the biographical or "arrayed lives" (*liezhuan*) format (Lxz, Sxz, and several texts marginal to the genre such as Gshiz and Gsz), and what might be termed the "evidential" arrangement of items to document the truth of religious or moral claims (Xuanyj, Mxj, Jingyj, Gsy, XuGsy, XiGsy, Yhz, Fsty).

Style

Anomaly accounts are written in mostly non-metrical or loosely metrical but non-parallel, non-rhyming, classical prose. They are thus distinct on the one hand from various early combinations of prose and verse, from *fu* ("rhapsodies") and other poetic forms, and on the other hand from later-developing styles of prose that prominently incorporated vernacular forms. Yet, like much other historical writing in the early medieval period, as well as other anecdotal works such as the Ssxy, the anomaly accounts break away from the extreme terseness of earlier classical prose, incorporating grammatically unessential words to a degree that makes their prose seem more relaxed and closer to the patterns of speech than Han works such as the SJ and HS.[7]

Content

Texts of this genre have as their clear and primary focus phenomena that are in some sense (and with respect to some boundary and set of expectations) anomalous. Two caveats are in order here, both made necessary by certain confusions in the Western scholarship on these texts. First, that such texts occasionally mention phenom-

---

7. Yoshikawa 1955 is still one of the most useful works on prose style in this period.

ena not anomalous in any obvious way hardly disqualifies them from being considered participants in the genre; in fact, the juxtaposition of the "ordinary" and the "extraordinary" is a key poetic device of anomaly accounts, as will be seen in Chapter Five. Likewise, to point out that anomalous events are occasionally reported in texts of other genres, including "the most sober-minded official histories,"[8] is hardly to undercut the genre's demarcation from other genres: anomaly accounts were not the *only* texts to mention the sorts of anomalies they focus on, but they *were* the only texts that made anomalousness the central, unifying criterion for their selection of material. Second, and crucially, the characterization of their contents as "anomalous" is most emphatically *not* based on modern Western expectations of what is normal;[9] it is based instead on readily apparent evidence both in the anomaly texts themselves and in their environing social and textual world. Early medieval Chinese anomaly accounts are saturated with indications that their authors and readers themselves judged their contents as "strange" (even if, in many cases, also most certainly "true"), and it is on that judgment alone that my characterization is based. In what sense the contents of these texts were seen as "strange" by contemporary authors and readers, and the variety of perspectives from which phenomena were deemed anomalous and the meaning and function that judgments of anomaly carried, are questions that will be addressed from various angles in this book; but let there be no mistake that the sheer ascription of anomaly is indigenous to the texts themselves and is not in any sense an interpretive overlay created by the disjunction between modern and early medieval worldviews.

Status

Anomaly accounts were, without exception, initially non-canonical, and the vast majority of them remained so. I intend "non-canonical" in a double sense: first, anomaly accounts were generally disapproved by the keepers of the Confucian textual canon identified as such since the Western Han. Not only were they disapproved, but they contained material that was for the most part beyond the

---

8. As argued by Smith 1992, 39.

9. The most proximate stimulus of this caveat is again a passage in Smith 1992, 39.

pale of Confucian classics, and in no sense were they framed as commentaries on those classics. Second, although some "hagiographical" texts—writings about the lives of sacred persons (Daoist transcendents or Buddhist monks and nuns)—as well as sacred geographies were much later incorporated into what are now known as the Daoist and Buddhist canons,[10] these texts were originally understood as historical and not as canonical works, in several senses: they were not revelation texts (direct divine discourse "transcribed" by human hand), nor were they texts whose primary purpose was instruction in the fundamentals of a religious, moral, or philosophical teaching meant for readers who were already religious "insiders," nor were they associated with religious founders. In short, they were not among texts that were deemed *jing* 經 or canonical. These explicitly pro-Daoist and pro-Buddhist works were, in fact, written to be read by religious outsiders as well as insiders; they were polemical, apologetic texts intended to persuade readers that their respective traditions' teachings were true and authoritative.[11] Yet, although they were never considered scripture, all anomaly accounts dealt with matters of the spirit world. The genre's liminal position—betwixt and between ideological persuasions and religious traditions, dealing with the spirit world but from the point of view of ordinary life and in texts deemed noncanonical—is one of the main reasons for its importance for understanding early medieval Chinese religious and cultural history.

Presence of Intertextual Markers

The formal, stylistic, and content features mentioned above were themselves intertextual markers of sorts, in that readers who encountered those features in a text were likely to expect it to resemble other texts of the genre. But several more explicit markers are also evident.

---

10. Even here, they were sub-classified within these canons in a way that clearly marks off their difference from *scriptural* works.

11. Fuzzy in a different way are the biographies of *fangshi* and other religious specialists embedded in official histories. Again, however, they are separated off from other types of figures and are not offered for emulation. The point of view implied in the inclusion of such figures in official histories remains to be uncovered and will be discussed briefly in Chapter Seven.

Structure and content of titles of works. Most of the titles of early works of the genre follow a closely parallel syntactic and semantic structure that subliminally linked one such text with another. That structure consists essentially of: (1) a verb (to use a rough grammatical analogy with Indo-European languages) meaning something like "to set forth, narrate, array, collect, record" (whether orally or in writing),[12] or else related concepts such as "to penetrate comprehensively" (with associations of "to make manifest, to clarify") or "to make an inquest into";[13] (2) a noun usually meaning either roughly "strange events, marvels, anomalies" or something like "spirits, numinous beings, ghosts" or else "broad-ranging";[14] (3) a noun translatable as "records" (most commonly *ji* 記, *lu* 錄, or *zhuan* 傳), always implying written—and, more specifically, historical—documents. This structure already adumbrates

---

12. *Zhi* 志 appears in five titles, *shu* 述 in two, *ji* 集 in two, and *shi* 拾 in one; *lie* 列 appears in two titles; *lu* 錄 (as a verb) appears in one. Similar terms appear in the preserved titles of works now lost.

13. *Dong* 洞, *tong* 通, *jing* 旌, *zhen* 甄 each appears in one title, *sou* 搜 in two.

14. The terms connoting "anomaly" include *yi* 異, *guai* 怪 (both of which as verbs mean "to wonder at"), and *yao* 妖. Traditional dictionaries often gloss *yi* with *guai* and vice versa, as well as with another term, *qi* 奇, which curiously does not appear among the titles to Six Dynasties anomaly accounts, being used only after the beginning of the Tang (hence perhaps its choice as part of the generic compound label *chuanqi* 傳奇 by later critics, on which Adkins 1976, 13; Nienhauser 1986, 356; Chang 1980 [which is largely unhelpful]). Terms connoting "spirits," "ghosts," or "the numinous" include *shen* 神, *gui* 鬼, and *ling* 靈; unlike the above terms, these are rarely used to denote human actions or perceptions, referring instead to types and/or properties of beings. On these terms in general, Hayashi 1970, 1974; Qian Mu 1955; Nagasawa 1964. On the various usages and history of the term *shen*, see *inter alia* Nagasawa 1977, 244–45; Larre 1982; Yu Yingshi 1983; Porkert 1974, passim. On *ling*, Porkert 1974, 193. On *gui*, Nagasawa 1977, 194–97; Shen Chien-shih 1936–37; Ikeda 1953, 2; Ikeda 1956, 1970. Terms connoting "obscurity, darkness" and the "unseen" realm of non-human beings and the arcane workings of the cosmos as opposed to the "bright, clear" (*ming* 明) realm of ordinary human affairs include *you* 幽, *ming* 冥 (these two frequently appear as a compound, as in the title of Yml [which alludes to a passage in the *Yijing Xici shangzhuan*]), and *xuan* 玄, the latter of which has its locus classicus in the first chapter of the *Daodejing*. "Wide-ranging" and "omitted" or "left over"—both of which, I believe, should be read in the sense of including material not found in the official and widely studied canonical texts—are connoted by *bo* 博 and *yi* 遺 respectively.

the cosmographic nature of the genre: if a reader unacquainted with these works encountered only a list of their titles, he or she might already infer that the texts contain "settings forth" or "arrays" or "collections" (or else "manifestations" or reports of "inquests") of phenomena which, while widely varied, share the quality of being anomalous with respect to some implied standard of normality. To contemporaries the titles must have subtly linked the anomaly texts with imperial, centrist traditions of cosmographic collecting to be discussed in the next chapter.

One also notes the frequent recurrence of the term *zhiguai* in the titles, an allusion to a passage in the inner chapters of the *Zhuangzi* (discussed in the next chapter). The repeated use of this term over time by consecutive authors constituted another intertextual link; in fact, usage of this term in the Six Dynasties, Sui, and Tang amounts to a generic label, although the term was not widely used as a designation for a literary genre until the late Ming.[15]

Explicit references in titles to "continuation" of an earlier work. Authors thus sought to link their own text directly to

15. It is often asserted that no attestations of *zhiguai* as a generic designation exist before the late Ming. This is false. Not only, as I have just pointed out, do Six Dynasties authors and critics themselves repeatedly use the term in a way approximating a generic label, but at least one case of its generic usage has been found in a mid-Tang text. The term occurs in the preface by the noted painter, poet, calligrapher, and Daoist Gu Kuang 顧況 (ca. 725–ca. 814, on whom see IC, 486–87) to a once-voluminous collection of anomaly accounts titled *Guangyiji* 廣異記 written by his acquaintance Dai Fu 戴孚. (To my knowledge, only a few fragments of this work now survive; I have seen collections in LWMS and CSJC. Cf. Uchiyama 1979, 14.) Citing precedents for Dai's text, Gu opens by using the pregnant phrase (discussed below in Chapter Seven), "observe the boundary between Heaven and Humanity"; he then argues that Confucian scholiasts' claim that Confucius forbade talk of "anomalies, feats of prodigious strength, natural disorders, and spirits" is a too-restrictive reading of the relevant *Analects* passage. He proceeds to give a long list of many of the works discussed below, also including a few titles which I exclude from the genre's core (such as the *Zhen'gao* and the *Zhoushi mingtongji*); and, most significantly, he prefaces this list by referring to the authors of all such works as *zhiguai zhi shi* 志怪之士, "gentlemen who have recorded anomalies." He thus not only links the major texts of the genre like beads on a single strand, but he also refers to them collectively (if slightly indirectly) as *zhiguai*. The text is anthologized in QTW 528.13b–15a; I am indebted to Stephen Bokenkamp for the reference.

a predecessor's in a line of intellectual and literary filiation. Extant examples include Ren Fang's *Shuyiji* (identified in some bibliographies with the prefix "new" [*xin*]); Tao Qian's *Soushen houji*; the *Xu Qi Xie ji*; the *Xuyiji*; and the *Xu* and *Xi Gsy*.

Explicit references in metatexts or in texts themselves to other anomaly accounts. Quotations in the body of a work, or citations in prefaces or other metatexts of earlier anomaly accounts as precedents, obviously serve as another form of intertextual linkage.

"Silent" quotations or paraphrases from, or allusions to, other anomaly accounts. These can be considered intertextual markers to the extent that literate readers were expected to recognize them as allusions or quotations.

Together, these five criteria yield a "core" of texts that clearly constitute a genre devoted to the cosmographic task of displaying anomalies to their audience. They also allow us to identify certain texts that stand on the margin or periphery of the genre, attracted toward its center of gravity, as it were, by one or another of their characteristics yet markedly different in some way from the core texts. These may be subdivided as follows.

Works Marginal to the Genre by Virtue of Their Form. Although the *Mu Tianzi zhuan* is clearly cosmographic in purpose, and although the Hwdnz has been treated by some scholars as a full-fledged anomaly account and is closely related to works closer to the core of the genre,[16] these works are not lists of discrete items and should not be lumped together with the core texts. Closer to the core of the genre than these texts, yet formally distinct from most other anomaly accounts, are these two: (1) the Hwgs, which is the only anomaly text in the *gushi* format, and which arguably focuses not on the anomalous per se but on a particular ruler around whom many legends of strange events accumulated from early on; and (2) the Szj, which, although comprising a (probably older) core of cosmographic description of distant paradisal realms, stands out in framing that description within a speech delivered by the adviser and master of esoterica Dongfang Shuo to Emperor Wu of the Han.

---

16. Li Jianguo 1984 treats both of these works as generically indistinct from anomaly accounts. On the strong relationship between the Hwdnz and other texts closer to the core of the genre, Smith 1992. On the Hwdnz itself, Schipper 1965; Smith 1994; Li Fengmao 1986, 21–186.

Works Marginal to the Genre by Virtue of Their Content.
Judging from surviving fragments, a number of early gazetteer-like
works on particular regions prominently featured anomalous phenomena; some of them may, in fact, have consisted of virtually
nothing but anomalies of many kinds whose sole unifying quality
was that they emanated from the same area. But, lacking further
evidence, we must assume that these works were not *primarily*
concerned with describing anomalous phenomena, but were rather
accounts of notable aspects of a region; to that extent, although I
believe they were an important source of material for authors of
anomaly accounts closer to the core of the genre, they themselves
hover on its margin. (The same may be concluded concerning the
annotations to the Sjz, which, although heavily weighted toward
anomalous content, seem to be offered simply as more information
about the localities in question and are pegged to a "normal" geographic work.) The same considerations apply to biographical collections on exceptional persons. A primary extant example is
Huangpu Mi's Gshiz, a rather lengthy account of recluses. Despite
the many similarities of form, style, and content between this work
and the Daoist hagiographical anomaly accounts,[17] there is one key
difference: it is evident in reading the text that Huangpu Mi carefully chose his figures and material in such a way as to exclude the
sorts of incursions from the spirit world that are the focus of most
anomaly accounts. This text, then, participates in the anomaly account genre in several respects, but in one key respect its author—
surely not by accident—distanced his text from the genre at the
same time. A related sort of case is that of Buddhist monastic biography or hagiography:[18] while extant narratives of monks' and
nuns' lives do stress the anomalous "responses" associated with
their subjects, their focus is not the documentation of anomalies
per se but of the vicissitudes of the sangha.

Works Marginal to the Genre by Virtue of Their Status.
It is probably both because of his unfamiliarity with the tradition of
religious Daoism and because these texts are included in some Ming
collectanea alongside anomaly accounts that Li Jianguo lists the
Zhoushi mingtongji 周氏冥通記 and the *Zhen'gao* 真誥 as belonging

---

17. I further explore these similarities in a comparative study, now
in preparation, of early medieval hagiographical and biographical works.
18. And one might include the subgenre of Buddhist topographic accounts, the best surviving example of which is the *Luoyang qielanji*.

to the genre.[19] While their content does resemble that of anomaly accounts, in that they document cases in which the spirit world revealed itself in the context of ordinary life (to that extent they may be considered the earliest Daoist "evidentiary" texts), not only their form but most especially their status differs markedly from those of anomaly accounts closer to the core of the genre. These are full-fledged revelation texts; they are scriptural collections central to the Shangqing tradition and are mostly composed of direct divine speech narrated by the human author in first-person discourse.

The Texts

With the above criteria in place and having identified certain groups of works that hover on the fringes of the genre of anomaly accounts, it is now possible to proceed with a list of the works that stand more or less close to the core of the genre, a summary of what is known of their history, and a brief description of them as they have come down to the modern era. First, however, some general comments on the history and current state of these texts are necessary.

Texts of which any trace survives have come down to us in one of three ways (or, in some cases, in a combination of these).[20] (1) Partial or complete early (by which is meant late Tang or later) manuscripts of five anomaly texts have been discovered in this century, two among the Dunhuang manuscripts and three in a Japanese monastery. (2) Seven texts as we now have them are descended in a fairly well documentable, continuous tradition from editions printed during the Sung.[21] (3) The rest have either been recompiled (*ji* 輯) from quotations in early commentaries (notably including the SGZ and the Sjz) and in Tang and Sung collectanea,

---

19. Both are found in DZ (HY 302 and HY 1010 respectively). Recall, however, that Gu Kuang also lumped these texts under *zhiguai* (see n.15 above).

20. For example, in a few cases we have both a continuously transmitted version and a reconstructed version. And we have other versions of texts or of particular items to compare to the texts that survive in manuscript.

21. To avoid confusion, I have romanized the identical names of the two 宋 dynasties differently: "Song" denotes the southern dynasty founded in 420 and replaced by the Qi dynasty in 479; "Sung" denotes the dynasty founded in 960 and effectively ended in 1279.

or else exist only in a small number of as yet unrecompiled quotations dispersed in collectanea and other works, or some combination of these two states. The work of recompilation, begun late in the Yuan period, saw its heyday in the middle and late Ming, a period of intense antiquarian assembling and printing of old texts; it continued throughout the Qing, with gradually improving care in the notation of sources, and culminated early in the Republican period with the completion of Lu Xun's monumental *Guxiaoshuo gouchen*. In addition, for a handful of texts there are now modern, critical editions that compare most or all available versions and note textual variations.

As in the case of all old Chinese texts but particularly pre-Tang ones, then, the textual history of anomaly accounts is extremely complex. To give a complete account of that history, one would have to deal not just with the filiation of the anomaly texts themselves but also with that of the sources for their recompilation. In the comments that follow, I treat almost exclusively of the provenance of the anomaly texts themselves, rarely of the history of the various pre-Tang, Tang, and Sung texts on which their reconstruction must largely be based.[22]

Suoyu 瑣語 *Minor Sayings* (Jzsy)

Alternate title: *Jizhong* 汲冢 *suoyu*, so named because it was found in a burial mound (*zhong*) in Ji commandery. In 281 c.e.,[23] during

---

22. Comments on the editorship and dating of collectanea may be found in the bibliography. One point should be emphasized here, however: although the TPYL was presented to the throne in 983, its contents are now known to have been based not on direct traditions of the works it quotes but on three earlier encyclopaedias, two of which are lost and one of which was the YWLJ—and *the latest of which was compiled in 641*. This means that items attested in the TPYL can be dated back to at least as early as 641, not merely to 983 (see Roth 1992, 54, 91). The textual history of the sources for anomaly accounts (and for many other types of early works) deserves a separate, careful treatment, but here I can only list works I have found especially helpful: Dai Keyu and Tang Jianhua 1981; Hu Daojing 1982; Togawa 1992; Katsumura 1990; Bauer 1965–66; Teiser 1985; Schafer 1980b; Kirkland 1993; Balazs and Hervouet 1978; Shiroki 1953–54; Teng and Biggerstaff 1971; Wang Qiugui and Wang Guoliang 1983.

23. There are small discrepancies in the dating of this event; Li Jianguo 1984, 88.

the reign of Emperor Wu of the Jin dynasty, the ancient tomb of Prince Xiang of Wei, dating from 296 B.C.E., was unearthed. Inside the tomb were found texts written on bamboo strips, including not only the *Mu tianzi zhuan* but also a work titled *Suoyu* in eleven sections (*pian*). It was written in a pre-Qin "old script." Emperor Wu had these texts placed in the imperial library and transcribed into "modern" script, in which form they circulated during the following centuries. The most complete historical passage detailing the text's discovery is embedded in the biography of Shu Xi, one of the scholar-officials charged with studying these precious documents; it describes the Jzsy as "a book of phenomena concerning divinations, dreams, deviations and anomalies, and physiognomic techniques from various [feudal] realms" 諸國卜夢妖怪相書也.[24] At the end of the sixth century, Yan Zhitui saw a copy, noting that some anachronistic elements had crept into the text.[25] Judging from its four-*juan* listing in the SuiS catalogue, over half of the text seems to have perished by the Tang, and later the whole text was lost. Qing scholars recompiled around twenty-six fragments from quotations in collectanea and other works; these are available, with some variations, in four editions.[26]

As in the case of the generic designation *xiaoshuo*, the "small" (*suo*) in the title may refer not only to the supposed insignificance of the contents but also to the format of the text; for, as may be surmised from the sixteen relatively complete-seeming items,[27] the text was a list of tersely worded anecdotal entries concerning efficacious divinations and the prognosticatory interpretation of dreams.

Shanhaijing 山海經 *Classic of Mountains and Seas* (Shj)

Eighteen fascicles. The work is temporally stratified, its oldest parts (thought by many but not all scholars to be *juan* 1–5 of the extant text) having probably been composed sometime in the Warring States period, its latest parts having been written in the Han or even the Wei-Jin eras. There is still no scholarly consensus

---

24. JS 51 (1433).

25. *Yanshi jiaxun* 16 (161); tr. Teng 1968, 177. Teng notes (n. 5) that some have challenged the authenticity of the texts found in this tomb; in that case the date of the Jzsy might lie anywhere from the early Han to 281 C.E.

26. For a list of these eds., Li Jianguo 1984, 89.

27. Ten of the recompiled items seem to be mere fragments of passages.

on dating.[28] The best editions are those prepared by Hao Yixing and by Yuan Ke;[29] there is now a complete translation, and there are indices to the text.[30]

Partly anecdotal in its valuable fragments of ancient myths, partly descriptive in its numerous portrayals of strange peoples and hybrid beasts (thought to have been originally accompanied by pictures), the Shj is the oldest account of anomalies to have survived in something approximating its early arrangement. (It passed under the editorial hands of the Han bibliographer Liu Xin [d. 23 C.E.] and Guo Pu [276–324], a master of esoterica who added a commentary.) That arrangement is topographic; the text moves in apparently systematic fashion across the broad layout of the earth's regions, although the contents of the discrete sections sometimes overlap and do not always match the neatly concentric logic of the section headings: (1) 五藏山經 (*juan* 1–5), the five "classics of mountains," one for each of the five cardinal directions (south, west, north, east, center), covering the wonders at both domestic and foreign mountains. (2) The eight "classics of seas," subdivided into (a) 海外經 (*juan* 6–9 = south, west, north, east) covering areas "beyond the seas," the more distant and exotic countries beyond the ken of the Central Kingdom, and (b) 海內經 (*juan* 10–13, in the same directional sequence) covering areas "within the seas," treating more proximate loci such as rivers on the frontiers of the Central Kingdom or barbarian groups within or near its borders. (3) 大荒經 (*juan* 14–17 = east, south, west, north), the four "classics of the great wastes." Theoretically at least, these tell of marvels beyond even the four regions "beyond the seas," that is, beyond the pale of all civilizing influence; but in fact their contents overlap with those of other sections. (4) 海內經 (*juan* 18), "Classic of [the Area] Within the Seas," covering areas in or immediately surrounding the Central Kingdom.

---

28. For an overview of the major theories, as well as editions, translations, and indices, ECT, 357–67. I have also consulted Yuan Ke 1980, intro. and 337–38; Yuan Xingpei 1979; Gao Quxun 1974; Li Jianguo 1984, 97–111. Meng Wentong 1962 dates all strata improbably early, but he also (mostly on geographic grounds) argues the position, taken by other scholars as well (on linguistic and other grounds), that the text originated in the southwest, so that the "central" regions it describes in fact correspond to ancient Ba, Shu, and Chu.

29. Hao Yixing's is the SBBY ed.; cf. Yuan Ke 1980.

30. Tr. in Mathieu 1983; there is an index to the SBBY ed., and Yuan Ke incorporates this into the index included in his volume.

Not only the dates of origin of the Shj subdivisions but also the interests that shaped their writing vary considerably. There is a marked difference in content between the first five fascicles ((1) above) and the rest of the text. In (1), subdivided into twenty-six sections describing 447 mountains, not only is all material pegged to some particular mountain, but the material itself shows a set of concerns largely absent from (2), (3), and (4): some of the geographical names given may now be identified with relative certainty, flora and fauna are named and described, medical and pharmaceutical information is catalogued along with the meanings of portentous creatures, and ritual prescriptions for the cult of mountain spirits are supplied. In (2)–(4), by contrast, geographical names are largely fanciful; genealogies become prevalent; "botany and zoology give place to fictional ethnology; medical, mantic and ritual prescriptions are no longer found, and mythological accounts become more numerous."[31] In short, no single, guiding set of interests can be discerned in the Shj as we have it; its writing has been not implausibly attributed to masters of esoterica (*fangshi* 方士),[32] but if that attribution is correct then the various "masters" responsible for the knowledge collected in the Shj must have belonged to quite different traditions of learning, and the Shj should then be seen as representing multiple bodies of knowledge and skill in much the same way as the (roughly contemporary?) *Lüshi chunqiu*.

Yu benji 禹本紀 *Annals of Yu*

The sole extant fragment from this pre-Qin text is a quotation in the SJ that briefly describes the wonders of Mount Kunlun. Like the Shj with which it is there mentioned, it was probably a topo-graphically organized book of marvels, perhaps accompanied by pictures. Sima Qian speaks disapprovingly of both texts: "As for

---

31. ECT, 358, on which I have relied for this summary of contents.

32. Thus Gao Quxun 1974. Given the nature of the information in the text as well as its highly schematic organization, this view seems more probable to me than the attribution to "shamans" (as in Lu Xun 1926, 11, 蓋古之巫書也), which I take to mean *mediumistic* specialists (although it is tempting to read some sections as spirit-journey topographies, as in the case of parts of the *Chuci* [Hawkes 1967, 1985]); but Fracasso (ECT, 359) is correct in saying that the Shj "cannot in fact be ascribed in its entirety to any single category of writing."

the anomalous creatures (*guaiwu* 怪物) found in the *Yu benji* and the *Shj,* I dare not even mention them."[33] The implications of the association of the sage-ruler Yu with this type of text will be taken up in the following chapter. This text seems to have been lost before the end of the Han.

Guizang 歸藏 (Guiz)

Named for an ancient commentary to the *Book of Changes,* this text, probably written in the late Warring States period, now exists only in fragments recompiled from collectanea; forty-four items are collected in the JDJL edition.

In his *Xinlun* (ca. 20 C.E.), Huan Tan mentions the Guiz as "containing 4,300 words,"[34] and the late Eastern Han scholar Zheng Xuan refers to it as "an *yinyang* book from the Yin [dynasty]."[35] It is listed in the SuiS bibliographic catalogue (in the section on divination texts) as containing thirteen fascicles. It is hardly as ancient as the Yin, but its contents and language suggest that it did predate the Qin. Judging from surviving fragments, it was not a divination manual on the model of the *Book of Changes* or Yang Xiong's *Canon of Supreme Mystery* but rather a record of divination cases and a description of anomalous phenomena thought to portend a particular type of fortune. The fragments also tersely mention mythological figures and places such as Nü Wa 女娟, Gong Gong 共工, Chi You 蚩尤, and Kongsang 空桑.

The Works Listed under *Xiaoshuo* 小説 in Ban Gu's *Yiwenzhi* 藝文志

Ban Gu included fifteen titles in the *xiaoshuo* section of his "Treatise on Belles Lettres" (*Yiwenzhi*).[36] The import of his remarks on the term *xiaoshuo* will be taken up in the next chapter; our concern here is the nature of the works he listed under this rubric. They are all lost, but judging from their titles and the extremely laconic de-

---

33. SJ 123 (3179); on the text, Li Jianguo 1984, 111–14.
34. Pokora 1975, 90 (he overtranslates the title as "Flow and Return to Womb and Tomb"); Li Jianguo 1984, 115.
35. Li Jianguo 1984, 115.
36. HS 30 (1744–45).

scriptions of their contents, most of them were probably not "core" anomaly accounts. Three of them, however, may have been.[37]

Yi Yin shuo 伊尹説 **Legends of Yi Yin.** A rather euhemerized Yi Yin, sage advisor on politics and morals to the ruler Tang 湯, crops up in many Warring States texts, including *Mencius*, *Mozi*, and *Zhuangzi;* but other early passages suggest that the reason for his skills as an advisor was his *fangshi*-like power.[38] The most detailed early legend about him, in the *Lüshi chunqiu* (discussed further in Chapter Three), says that he was born from a *kongsang* 空桑 tree,[39] and portrays him as having esoteric knowlege of marvelous products from peripheral regions. A fragment from the Jzsy describes him as appearing in a dream to Duke Jing of Qi, extremely bizarre in aspect, as a symbolic discouragement of the Duke's contemplated attack on the state of Song.[40] These portrayals of Yi Yin, when coupled with Ban Gu's disapproving comment on

---

37. I am inclined to follow the general direction of Li Jianguo's conjectures on these texts (1984, 120–25), and to disagree with DeWoskin 1974, 199ff., who says that all the titles in the *xiaoshuo* list "are historical records or philosophical utterances of an ancient sage or a Han court advisor" (200). *Pace* DeWoskin, the *shuo* in some of these titles (especially the three I comment on) probably meant not "sayings *of*" but "sayings (legends) *about*" the figure named. Yi Yin, Shi Kuang, and the Yellow Thearch were the sorts of figures about whom fantastic legends and anomalous material were likely to accumulate. In addition to the three texts discussed here, Ying Shao cites a passage from the *Qingshizi* 青史子 in his Fsty (8, 374); it concerns the reasons for using chickens as sacrificial offerings. It too may have resembled the core anomaly texts, but too little survives to know.

38. As will be noted in the following chapter, Mencius in fact explicitly rejects the tradition that Yi Yin won Tang's favor because of his "culinary skills" (probably a euphemistic reference to his esoteric knowledge). Mencius also at places comments disapprovingly on him because of his shifting loyalties. Note that a text bearing the name Yi Yin heads Ban Gu's list of thirty-seven titles emanating from the "Daoist school" (HS 30, 1729–31).

39. Li Jianguo 1984, 122, points out that a pair of lines from the *Tianwen* 天問 chapter of the *Chuci* 楚辭 also refers obliquely to this tradition. It is repeated, much more clearly, in Sjz 15 (203), and is referred to in Bwz 9.9 (Fan Ning 1980, item 298). Legends of his living to the age of one hundred years and burial in Pei District 沛縣 appear in Sjz 25 (325). Cf. Yuan Ke 1981 [1960], 269ff.

40. Jzsy 13 (TPYL 378); the interpreter of the dream, Yanzi 宴子, is the main figure in the probably pre-Qin text *Yanzi chunqiu* 春秋 (on which

the text—"what it says is superficial" 其語淺薄—make it appear likely that the *Yi Yin shuo* was a list of narratives concerning the strange sayings and doings of Yi Yin.

Shi Kuang 師曠. Ban Gu applies almost exactly the same censure to this text as to the *Yi Yin shuo*: "its sayings are superficial" 其言淺薄. The figure of Shi Kuang appears widely in early texts, particularly in the *Zuozhuan*; the Jzsy depicts him as a dream-interpreter and master of divine esoterica,[41] while the *Huainanzi*, Wang Chong's *Lunheng*, and the anomaly account Syj record various legends about the magical powers possessed by his musical compositions and performances.[42] Sixteen fragments of a *Shi Kuang zhan* 占 (Skz) survive, although these probably do not derive from the text listed by Ban Gu; but one item compiled under this title by Qing scholars is a quotation in the *Shuowen* 説文 about an exotic southern bird called the *qiangjiu*, drawn from a text identified simply as *Shi Kuang*.[43]

Huang Di shuo 黄帝説 *Legends of the Yellow Thearch.* Of this text, too, Ban Gu registers his disapproval, calling it "preposterous" (*yudan* 迂誕). (It is noteworthy that the above three titles are the only ones in this list to which Ban Gu attaches text-specific censure over and above his general reservations about the *xiaoshuo* "school.") The likelihood that it was a list of marvels or strange narratives associated with the Yellow Thearch, and not a Huang-Lao text on philosophy or governance, is supported not only

---

see ECT 483–89), where a variant on this story is given (see Li Jianguo 1984, 122). Another variant of this dream narrative appears in Bwz 7.9 (250), while Yi Yin's birth from the *kongsang* is mentioned in Bwz 9.9 (298).

41. Jzsy 9 (culled from Sjz 6 [83], TPYL 40, and TPGJ 291), 10 (culled from YWLJ 19; TPYL 369, 391), and 11 (culled from TPYL 917).

42. *Huainanzi* 11.1a; *Lunheng jiaozhu* 5 (1:241ff.); Syj 3.3 (8a–b, 9b), 7.1 (6a). See also Li Jianguo 1984, 122–23.

43. Skz 16, note; the eds. comment that they appended this quotation here despite the fact that the *Shuowen* citation made no mention of the word *zhan* in the title. Li Jianguo 1984, 122, reproduces the *Shuowen* passage. The 16 fragments from the Skz fall into two groups: some enunciate general divinatory principles (e.g., what it means when X appears), while others report "cases" of specific divinations performed by Shi Kuang—several of these are in response to inquiries by the Yellow Thearch. Item 16 has Shi Kuang asking for clarification from a figure named Tian Lao 天老.

by the fact that it is listed separately from the "Daoist school" texts but also by two citations of an unidentified text titled *Huang Di shu* 書 in the Fsty—a text that may have been the one listed by Ban Gu, or at least its descendant. The first is a brief anecdote, variants of which appear elsewhere in Han and later writings (including anomaly accounts), that explains the origin of the 25-stringed (as opposed to the originally larger, 50-stringed) musical instrument known as *se* 瑟: the Yellow Thearch once had the Unsullied Woman 素女 play the *se* that had been made (or invented) by Pao Xi (i.e. Fu Xi 伏羲), and the resultant sound triggered such acute sorrow in him and other listeners that he reduced the instrument to 25 strings and a shorter length, presumably to make it less emotionally potent.[44] The second is a longer legend concerning two brothers, Tu and Yulei, who stood beneath a peach tree on Dutuo Mountain, made a register of all spirits (鬼) who wantonly harmed people, tied them up and fed them to tigers (*yang* beasts).[45] Ying uses this citation to explain apotropaic rites performed by local officials; these various contemporary practices "confirm" (*yan* 驗) what the *Huang Di shu* says, while the text makes the practices more intelligible. Nothing about either of these passages cited from the *Huang Di shu* is particularly redolent of Huang-Lao ideology; rather, each narrates an anomalous occurrence in high antiquity.

Liexianzhuan 列仙傳 *Arrayed Lives of Transcendents*
by Liu Xiang 劉向 (ca. 77–6 B.C.E.) (Lxz)

Seventy items in two *juan*. The earliest extant version of the text is that included in the *Zhengtong daozang* (1445 C.E., HY 294);[46]

---

44. Fsty 6 (285–86). Cf. SJ 28 (1396); HS 25A (1232); TPYL 576. Syj 1.1 (1b) has the legend of Pao Xi's making the *se*, as well as other legends about the instrument (1.5b–6a), but at this writing I have not found the story of the Yellow Thearch and the Unsullied Woman in this text, although it is cited by Wang Liqi (Fsty, 286 n.3).

45. Fsty 8 (367). Wang Liqi notes that a number of books in citing this Fsty passage drop the character 書 from the title. This may indicate its absence from some early copies of the Fsty text, and that in turn would further support the possibility that the book cited by Ying Shao is the one listed under *xiaoshuo* by Ban Gu. Tu's name is given in some texts as Shen 神 Tu.

46. For succinct accounts of the history and formation of the Daoist canon, Liu Ts'un-yan 1975; Boltz 1987, 4–9; Roth 1992, 144–47.

several other Ming and Qing editions of the entire text were produced, including two "corrected" (*jiaozheng*) versions.[47] Over four decades ago, Max Kaltenmark published a critical edition and annotated translation.[48] There is an old preface, of uncertain authorship and date; it is not included in the DZ and some other editions.[49]

We can corroborate the early existence of many (but not all) of the extant items not only through citations in Six Dynasties works and early Tang collectanea (including the TPYL)[50] but also through the inclusion of forty-eight of them in *juan* 108 of the Daoist encyclopedia YJQQ, compiled in 1028 or 1029. Internal evidence suggests Liu Xiang wrote the Lxz in the very last years of his life. His authorship has been disputed and the text has been dated later than the late Western Han, but recent scholars have argued cogently for the traditional attribution.[51] Early citations suggest the text originally contained seventy-two items.[52] It is not listed in Ban Gu's HS *Yiwenzhi* but appears in the SuiS, JTS, and XTS bibliographic catalogues.

The text consists of accounts of Daoist transcendents—in particular their special arts and how they acquired them—written in the format of "arrayed lives" (*liezhuan*) as established by Sima Qian.[53] The information on each figure is sparser, the language of the text terser than that in Ge Hong's counterpart text, Sxz, written about three centuries later.

---

47. Some Ming and Qing eds. contain only excerpts; for a listing of two-*juan*, "corrected," and fragmentary eds., Li Jianguo 1984, 192–93. Wang Guoliang 1984 excludes the Lxz and Sxz from his treatment of the genre.

48. Kaltenmark 1953 (26ff. for his comments on eds. used).

49. Reproduced in Li Jianguo 1984, 193–94, and (including tr.) in Kaltenmark 1953, 31–34.

50. For a general discussion of such citations, Li Jianguo 1984, 192. On citations in the CXJ (there are some 48 of them), Xu Yimin 1980, 269. It is curious that the text seems to have been better circulated among the compilers of non-Daoist anomaly account collections and encyclopedias than among Daoists; the Lxz is only scantily quoted, for example, in the late seventh century Daoist compendium SDZN (see Yoshioka 1955, 377).

51. Kaltenmark 1953, 3; Li Jianguo 1984, 188–89.

52. Kaltenmark 1953, 5; Li Jianguo 1984, 191.

53. On Sima Qian's understanding—and the etymology—of *liezhuan*, Ryckmans 1972.

Bozetu 白澤圖 *Charts [Revealed by the] Boze* (Bzt)

Forty fragments of this early work preserved in collectanea are assembled in two similar editions, JDJL and YH.[54] Datable citations begin with Ge Hong's *Baopuzi neipian*[55] and the Ssj (12.4) and continue in later texts including the FYZL, CXJ, TPYL, and TPGJ; a work of this title is listed as containing one *juan* beginning with the SuiS catalogue. Portions of a manuscript titled *Boze jingguai tu* 白澤精怪圖, containing text and nineteen colored drawings, were found at Dunhuang;[56] five parallels between the fragments of the Qing collections and this manuscript have been identified.[57]

Judging from these remnants, the Bzt was a demonography made up of a list of the names and distinctive properties (including appearance, proclivities, preferred habitat, and vulnerabilities) of diverse types of spirits, along with pictures to help the reader identify them.[58]

Guaditu 括地圖 *Comprehensive Charts of Terrestrial Phenomena.* Author unknown. Probably written in late Western or early Eastern Han. (Gdt)

A topographic book of wonders and fragments of ancient mythology, this text is not listed in early bibliographic catalogues but is quoted

---

54. At this writing I have not closely compared the two eds., but according to Lin Congming 1977, 98, they differ only in minor graphic variations and in the sequencing of items. My early dating is a guess based on the style and content of the text, which cannot, of course, be *proven* to have existed before its earliest citation, if then.

55. *Baopuzi neipian* 17.13b–14a; tr. Ware [1966] 1981, 295. This passage in turn formed the basis of Jlz 23 (and Jlz 43 refers to a "White Marsh Earth Mirror"). The Bzt is also alluded to at another point in Ge Hong's text; see Lin Congming 1977, 97 n.7.

56. To my knowledge, at least two Dunhuang manuscripts have been shown to have once constituted part of a copy of this text: on Pelliot 2682 see Chen Pan 1947 and Lin Congming 1977, passim; on Stein 6261 and its relationship to Pelliot 2682, Rao Zongyi 1969, who shows that the former was once part of the latter and somehow became separated; on the text in general see also Harper 1985, 491–93; Kaltenmark 1949, 371; Jiang Shaoyuan 1935, 40ff. and 56ff.; and Seidel 1983, 321.

57. Lin Congming 1977, 100–1.

58. By virtue of its apotropaic function it stands relatively distant from the core of the genre, since anomaly accounts (as I am defining and limning the genre here) typically were not written for this purpose. (The

in early collectanea (including YWLJ, CXJ, and TPYL). Thirty-four items are compiled in HTDL.[59] Some of the material in this work seems to have been drawn from the Shj, although the geographical thought underlying it differs somewhat from that of the Shj.[60]

Yiwenji 異聞記 *Records of Strange Things Heard* by Chen Shi 陳寔 (104–187 C.E.) (Ywj)

Unlisted in early bibliographic catalogues, this work survives in only two quotations, anthologized in LX. Its attribution to Chen Shi, an Eastern Han official,[61] has been questioned by some (Lu Xun, for example, thought the work was a forgery by Ge Hong, presumably because it is quoted in Ge's *Baopuzi neipian*) but has more recently been defended.[62]

Shenyijing 神異經 *Classic of Divine Marvels.* Author unknown (traditionally attributed to Dongfang Shuo, with commentary attributed to Zhang Hua). Probably written in late second century. (Shenyjing)

The Shenyjing is alternately listed in early catalogues beginning with the SuiS as consisting of one or two fascicles. It seems to have been continuously transmitted down to today, albeit with textual losses along the way. There are three versions, all of which arrange the text in a single fascicle. (1) A Ming-period recompiled version containing forty-eight items (HWCS, GZCS, SKQS). (2) A non-recompiled version containing sixty items, descended from an "old version" that was itself presumably descended more or less directly from an early, if not "original," text (ZDHW, CBSF, WCXS, LWMS, BZQS, SK, GJSB eds.). To my knowledge, these sixty-item editions

---

Shj is a difficult case to judge in this regard, but overall seems much less clearly designed for direct apotropaic use in the way that the Bzt—and other, now lost demonographies like it—obviously were.) In terms of its content, form, and style, however, it closely resembles "core" texts.

59. One additional fragment is printed in YHX, 291. Bwz 1.1 quotes a *Hetu guadixiang* 河圖括地象 but I do not know whether this is an alternate title for the same text or a different text.

60. Li Jianguo 1984, 148–51.

61. He has a biography in HHS 62. Significantly, he is also cited as a personal witness to the ascension of a Daoist adept, Shang Chenggong (alias Chenggong), into the clouds as a transcendent (HHS 82B, 2748).

62. Li Jianguo 1984, 213–14.

exhibit identical sequencing of items, with only minor typological variants between them.[63] (3) A modern critical edition that collects ten lost fragments (mostly from TPYL), as well as listing variants between the extant sixty-item text and quotations of matching passages in collectanea.[64]

The Shenyjing was traditionally, from the Six Dynasties on, attributed to Dongfang Shuo, its commentary to Zhang Hua. Both of these men were well known literary figures, and their biographies make no mention of these works (nor do the HS *Yiwenzhi* or Dongfang Shuo's unofficial biography [*biezhuan* 別傳] mention him as having authored a text with this title); for this and other reasons the traditional attributions have rightly been questioned.[65] On the other hand, the work is quoted not only in the Sjz and Pei Songzhi's commentary to the SGZ (presented to the throne in 421 C.E.), where it is attributed to Dongfang Shuo,[66] but also in a commentary to the *Zuozhuan* by Fu Qian 服虔, whose biography puts his death late in the *zhongping* reign period of Emperor Ling (i.e. 184–189 C.E.).[67] The text itself, then, has been surmised by scholars such as Yu Jiaxi and Li Jianguo to have existed by 189, whatever the date of its commentary.[68]

Zhou Ciji, however, argues that Fu Qian's apparent citations of the Shenyjing are in fact citations from the Shj whose resemblance to today's Shenyjing text is due to textual corruption and to its author's borrowing from the Shj. He then concludes, largely on

---

63. The LWMS text, for example, is descended from the ZDHW one, and contains precisely the same number of characters per column (although the two eds. I have consulted were not printed from the same blocks). I have so far found only one typological variation between these two eds., and it is one that does not affect the meaning since it involves substitution of words that are in the context virtually synonymous. Both exhibit the same jumbling of material (obviously due to a pasting error) in the S section on an inexhaustibly combustible wood and a variety of rodent that lives in its fire.

64. Zhou Ciji 1986. An earlier critical edition was prepared by the Qing scholar Tao Xianzeng 陶憲曾, titled *Shenyijing jijiao* 神異經輯校; at this writing I have not yet seen it (cited in Wang Guoliang 1984, 307).

65. Wang Guoliang 1984, 307; Li Jianguo 1984, 151–52.

66. SGZ 4 (118); on the Sjz citation, Li Jianguo 1984, 151.

67. The biography is in HHS 79B. Li Jianguo 1984, 152.

68. But some of its Daoist concepts and general tenor suggest a date not much earlier than this; it speaks, for example, of jade lads and jade maidens organized into nine bureaus (Central sec., item 2, p.13b). Its particular sort of Daoist tenor, along with its reference to concepts such as filiality, resonate with the *Taipingjing*.

the basis of linguistic evidence and mentions of "scriptural piety" (the cultic veneration of sacred texts) in the text, that it cannot have been written earlier than the late Eastern Jin (late fourth or early fifth century).[69] To my mind, his arguments on Fu Qian's citations are forced and unconvincing, as is his argument concerning scriptural piety, which is already attested in the *Taipingjing*; but the reader should note that a late second century date for the Shenyjing has been seriously challenged.

The geographic organization of the sixty-item text is as follows; note that, although the Shj scheme of *hainei* ("within the seas") and *haiwai* ("beyond the seas") is absent in these headings, traces of it do show up in some particular items in the text.[70]

Shenyijing Geographical Headings[71]

東荒經	Classic of the Eastern Barrens	11 items
東南荒經	Classic of the Southeastern Barrens	5 items
南荒經	Classic of the Southern Barrens	11 items
西南荒經	Classic of the Southwestern Barrens	3 items
西荒經	Classic of the Western Barrens	9 items
西北荒經	Classic of the Northwestern Barrens	6 items
北方荒經	Classic of the Northern Barrens	3 items
東北荒經	Classic of the Northeastern Barrens	1 item
中荒經	Classic of the Central Barrens	11 items[72]

69. Zhou Ciji 1986, 80–83; for his arguments on Fu Qian's references, 37–38 n.4, 43–44. Wang Guoliang 1984, 307, also thinks the text is of later provenance but does not mention its apparent citation by Fu Qian; he thinks its earliest quotation is that by Pei Songzhi.

70. E.g., in item 6 of the NW section (p. 11b in the ZDHW and LWMS eds.): 西北海外有人長二千里. Some items also mention locations *beyond* (not simply "in") the barren in question, e.g. item 3 of the E section (p. 1b).

71. The ZDHW ed. gives a table of contents (*mulu*) at the front of the text; this is omitted in the LWMS ed., but the topographic headings are still, as in the ZDHW ed., given in the text. The number of items listed under each heading in the ZDHW table of contents is, incidentally, often incorrect. In addition to the number of items given here under each heading, some of the fragments collected in Zhou Ciji 1986, 75–77, are also explicitly located in one or another geographic zone.

72. Despite its name, this section contains wonders from various quarters. Item 1, however, is truly central in that it concerns Mt. Kunlun (said to be under the jurisdiction of the transcendents of the Nine Bureaus [仙人九府治之]); moreover, a bird that lives atop it, named Rare (希有), is said to face south, and by stretching its left wing it "covers" or "overspreads" (覆) Dongwanggong 東王公, while by stretching its right wing it "covers" Xiwangmu 西王母.

Fengsu tongyi 風俗通義 *A Penetrating Account of Manners and Customs* by Ying Shao 應劭 (140–206 C.E.) (Fsty)

Alternate title: *Fengsutong*. Originally in thirty-two fascicles (so listed in RBG, although the SuiS, JTS and XTS catalogues list it at thirty-one *juan*), its present ten-fascicle length and arrangement stem from the Northern Sung. Wang Liqi's critical edition includes 140 pages of quoted passages recovered from collectanea but not found in the extant text.[73]

Ying Shao probably wrote this book after 194 C.E.[74] Three chapters—2 (debunkings of various "noncanonical sayings" [*sushuo* 俗説] as resulting from erroneous transmissions of fact), 8 (a sorting out of precedents for some popular religious rites and customs), and 9 (a discussion of anomalous transformations, spirits, ghosts, and demons)—are valuable for showing that even very self-consciously Confucian authors (besides those writing about portents such as Dong Zhongshu) did not eschew writing about anomalies. Ying Shao helped to create a Confucian hermeneutics of strange material. He consulted and cited earlier anomaly accounts including the Shj, a text titled *Huang Di shu* (as discussed above, perhaps a variant title of a work listed in the HS *Yiwenzhi* as a *xiaoshuo* text), and a collection titled *Shenxianzhuan*. Cao Pi, Zhang Hua, and Gan Bao incorporated significant amounts of his material into their own collections of anomaly accounts.

Lieyizhuan 列異傳 *Arrayed Marvels* by Cao Pi 曹丕 (Wei Wen Di 魏文帝, 187–226 C.E. [r. 220–226]) (Lyz)

Alternate name: *Lieyiji* 記. Fifty items recompiled by Lu Xun from quotations preserved in Six Dynasties commentaries and Tang and early Sung collectanea; Wang Guoliang has suggested deletions, additions, and other emendations to Lu Xun's listing.[75] The text was lost in the Sung. Its earliest bibliographic listing in the SuiS indicates that it existed in three fascicles in the seventh century, and lists Wei Wen Di as author (as well as mentioning him in the preface to the *zazhuanlei* section). The book catalogues in the JTS

---

73. Wang Liqi, ed., 1981. For comments on other eds. and textual history, ECT, 105–12.

74. Wang Liqi, ed., 1981, pref., 2–3.

75. Wang Guoliang 1988, 52–53.

and XTS also list the text but attribute it to Zhang Hua (author of the Bwz); the latter also gives its length as one *juan*, perhaps reflecting textual loss over the centuries. The SuiS attribution to Cao Pi is broadly though not uniformly supported by citations in Six Dynasties and Tang texts, and Cao is known from other writings (his own and others') to have had a predilection for accounts of transcendents and other "broad learning" topics.[76]

Among the fifty quotations culled by Lu Xun (and the two additional ones located by Wang Guoliang), five contain internal dates later than 226 C.E. This does not prove, as some have claimed, that Cao Pi did not author the Lyz and that it is necessarily a late "forgery"; it does show that, as is the case with most other anomaly accounts, items originally belonging to other texts were at some point misattributed to the Lyz.[77] The items are highly narrativized and concern ghosts, gods, demons, transcendents, and cases of resuscitation and prophetic dreams. Comparison with the contents of preceding and subsequent texts reveals that Cao Pi (or whoever wrote the Lyz) drew on Ying Shao's Fsty for material and on Liu Xiang's Lxz and *Lieshizhuan* 列士傳 for material as well as stylistic models, and that Gan Bao, in turn, incorporated many Lyz items into his Ssj.[78] Several Lyz items have been translated.[79]

Linhai shuitu yiwuzhi 臨海水土異物志 *Treatise on the Anomalous Aquatic and Terrestrial Creatures of Linhai* by Shen Ying 沈瑩 of the Kingdom of Wu 吳 (probably written between 264 and 280) (Lh)

Alternate titles: *Linhai shuitu wuzhi, Linhai shuituzhi, Linhai yiwuzhi, Linhaizhi, Yiwuzhi*. Listed in the SuiS, JTS and XTS

76. Li Jianguo 1984, 245–46, accepts Cao Pi's authorship; so does Wang Guoliang 1988, 45–50, but with more reservation.

77. Another general possibility in such cases is that details in the text, such as place names, were changed by later redactors to conform with contemporary usage.

78. All known overlaps among anomaly accounts will be listed in the index which I am now preparing; but Wang Guoliang 1988, 54–58, includes a useful table on the Lyz. On the author see also Holzman 1974.

79. Lyz 14: Kao 1985, 62–63; 23: Foster 1974, 60–61, and Kao 1985, 56–58; 27: Foster 1974, 28–29; 28 (one of the more famous anomaly tales), Bodde 1941, 351–53, and Kao 1985, 59–61; 31: Campany 1991a, 30–31; 40: Foster 1974, 54; 41: Kao 1985, 58–59; 45: Kao 1985, 61; 47: Foster 1974, 28. Quite a few Lyz items are closely paralleled in other collections.

catalogues (as well as other early bibliographies) as consisting of one *juan*, this work was later lost. It was recompiled in the SF and other Ming and Qing editions, but recently Zhang Chonggen has published an excellent critical edition based on all known quotations in collectanea.[80] The text contains notices of "strange" flora and fauna, both terrestrial and aquatic, of the southeast mainland coast as well as the island now known as Taiwan. Shen Ying, who served as *taishou* of Danyang, is mentioned in the SGZ as having been executed for leading a rebellion against the Sun regime in the state of Wu.[81]

Han Wu [Di] gushi 漢武【帝】故事 *Precedents of Han Emperor Wu*. Author unknown. Probably compiled in third century C.E. (Hwgs)

Long of disputed authorship (the most common traditional attribution to Ban Gu is now almost universally rejected), the Hwgs also has a tangled textual history and is in particularly bad shape. My comments are based on the recent work of Thomas E. Smith.[82] There are now four different versions. (1) The XTZ version contains eighteen items;[83] these match fairly well with Hwgs quotations in *leishu*. This compilation emphasizes passages dealing with Emperor Wu's lavish construction projects. (2) The SF edition became the basis of most other Ming and Qing editions. Its passages emphasize the Emperor's relations with women. Some of its passages appear spurious, but others, including some that are preserved only in this version and are omitted from LX, seem authentic. (3) The JDJL version, like that in LX (but much less useful), is a late recompilation from Sung and earlier collectanea and commentaries. It comprises around seventy-three items, but it often separates clearly overlapping material and some items are extremely brief fragments. (4) Containing fifty-three items, the LX version is the most complete. But it has serious problems, including its omission

---

80. Zhang Chonggen 1980; for dating of the text, see p. 3 of the preface; for history of earlier recompilations, see pp. 9 ff. of the critical introduction.

81. SGZ 48 (1174 ff.).

82. Smith 1992, 101–37; Smith (unpublished); cf. Liu Wenzhong 1984. I am grateful to Tom Smith for making his unpublished paper available to me.

83. XTZ 3.24b–32a.

of SF material likely to be authentic, problems in the edition of the TPGJ (and some other collectanea) on which Lu Xun relied, and its sequencing of items. The last-mentioned problem is perhaps most significant, for Smith argues convincingly that the work was not originally a loose collection of anecdotes (as its now-jumbled arrangement makes it appear) but a tightly structured whole that focused on relations between Emperor Wu and various members of his court.

The argument for a (perhaps early) third-century dating is too complex to summarize here. Suffice it to say that from a citation in Liu Jun's (462–521) commentary to the Ssxy, we know the text must have existed by around 500 C.E., that it shows but few traces of Buddhism or organized religious Daoism, and that its contents seem to reflect the sort of anxiety over how to handle the Han precedent that one would expect during the early or middle Wei period.

I believe Smith is correct as well in his analysis of the term *gushi* in the title:[84] as is clear from a glance at early catalogues, this refers to a sub-genre of literature concerned with procedural, ritual, and quasi-legal precedents from earlier dynasties and reigns, collected for reference and citation by dynastic officials; it has nothing to do with the modern sense of "stories." Partly because of this meaning, the *di* in the title as given in the SuiS catalogue, although dropped from many later citations of the text, is perhaps best restored.

Bowuzhi 博物志 *A Treatise on Curiosities* by Zhang Hua 張華 (232–300 C.E.) (Bwz)

Alternate name: *Bowuji* 記. The received version has 329 items unevenly distributed over ten fascicles; some 212 additional passages have been recovered from collectanea and early commentaries. The text includes commentaries of unknown date by Zhou Riyong 周日用 and an author surnamed Lu (Lushi 盧氏),[85] both of which, like the text itself, seem to have suffered considerable losses. The preface attributed to Zhang Hua that appears at the head of *juan* 1 is in fact a preface to the succeeding geographical chapters, not to the entire work.

---

84. Smith 1992, 102–8; Smith (unpublished), 11–15.

85. The Zhou Riyong commentary dates from at least the second half of the 12th century, when it was seen by Yao Kuan 姚寬; see Fan Ning 1980, 161–62.

There are two versions.[86] Both divide the text into ten fascicles; they are also alike in containing the commentaries and Zhang Hua's preface, and they comprise almost entirely identical material. The differences are (1) variations in the sequence of items, and (2) the presence or absence of thirty-nine topic headings.[87]

The "commonly circulating" or received version (*tongxingben*) contains thirty-nine subject headings (see below). The earliest extant edition containing this version is apparently that of He Zhitong 賀志同, listed in bibliographies at least as early as 1503;[88] there are numerous other editions in this same filiation. Fan Ning has traced this version back to a ten-*juan* abridgment by Chang Jing 常景 as mentioned in his *Weishu* biography (written in mid-sixth century), which seems to have survived alongside Zhang Hua's longer (but also ten-*juan*), autograph text up into the late Sung and early Ming, and which was the initial bearer of the commentaries by Zhou and Lu.[89] This abridgment would not have long postdated Zhang Hua himself. The fate of the non-abridged ten-*juan* autograph text, which there is reason to believe survived at least until the late twelfth century, remains a mystery.

A version without topic headings and with a different sequence of items (but with the same items) surfaced in 1803–1804 with Huang Pilie (in *ce* 26 of his SLJ collection); he says it was based on a copy owned in his family and traceable to the Sung.[90] The ZH and LXJS editions are based on this SLJ edition. The absence of topic headings and non-rational sequencing of items have led some to speculate that the more common received version repre-

---

86. There is apparently a third group of editions that differs simply in lacking items included in the others, but I have not at this writing done a thorough comparison among them individually or between them as a group, on the one hand, and the other versions on the other: these include LeiS, SF, and some lesser known series. The SF text (*juan* 2.17a–19b) seems, as is typical, to be merely a collection of excerpts, running to just over two folio pages and comprising 35 items.

87. Li Jianguo 1984, 263, notes one significant textual variation.

88. Fan Ning 1980, 158, says he has personally seen a copy printed in 1505.

89. Fan Ning 1980, 157–62; his argument, though elegantly concise, is still too complex to be summarized here.

90. Huang's preface dates to 1803 (*jiaqing* 8.1) but his afterword dates to 1804 (*jiaqing* 9.3); both are reprinted in Fan Ning 1980, 152–53. The text is divided into ten fascicles and includes Zhou Riyong's commentary. I can discern no rationale (taxonomic, chronological, or otherwise) for the arrangement of material.

sents a tidying-up of an earlier edition of this one. Because of its supposed Sung ancestry, some scholars have taken this version as a direct, clear descendant of Zhang Hua's original text; but the text Huang had was not necessarily of Sung date (Fan Ning thinks it was not), and even if it was, it is not, by virtue of being a few centuries earlier, necessarily any closer to Zhang's text.

There is a superb modern edition by Fan Ning (1980) that includes not only a critical, annotated edition of the received text but also a collection of 212 additional passages from collectanea, an authoritative discussion of textual history, and reprintings of the prefaces and colophons to major editions. There is a translation.[91]

His JS 36 biography depicts Zhang Hua as a *fangshi* especially skilled at numerological arts and a voracious collector of books, especially ones "strange, secret, and rarely seen." There are in fact many stories in other anomaly accounts about his exploits as a diviner and exorcist. His biography mentions that he wrote a "Bwz in ten chapters" (*pian*), and a text by this title continuously appears (listed as containing ten fascicles) from the SuiS catalogue forward.[92] That catalogue also credits Zhang Hua with annotations to the Shenyjing and a miscellany of essays; these are now lost.

As for the contents of the Bwz, which consist mostly of non-narrative descriptions of various kinds of anomalies (the last two fascicles, corresponding to the last two headings, consisting of short narratives), the thirty-nine topical headings inserted at some point into the received version correspond well to the items arrayed under them:

1 Treatise on the veins of the earth 地理略
2 Land 地
3 Mountains 山
4 Waters 水
5 General discourses on mountains and waters 山水總論
6 Tribes of the five directions 五方人氏
7 Local products 物產
8 Foreign countries 外國
9 Strange peoples 異人
10 Unusual customs 異俗

---

91. Greatrex 1987. At this writing I have not seen this work; it is cited in Birrell 1994, 391–92 (whose translation of *Bowuzhi* as *Treatise on Research into Nature* is inaccurate).

92. In addition to these listings, some catalogues also mentioned a six-*juan* text.

11 Marvelous products 異產
12 Marvelous beasts 異獸
13 Marvelous birds 異鳥
14 Marvelous insects 異蟲
15 Marvelous fish 異魚
16 Marvelous plants 異草木
17 The natures of things 物性
18 The principles of things 物理
19 The categories of things 物類
20 Medicinal products 藥物
21 Discussions on medicine 藥論
22 Food taboos 食忌
23 Pharmaceutical arts 藥術
24 Arts of amusement 戲術
25 Masters of Esoterica 方士
26 Macrobiotics 服食
27 Debates on *fangshi* 辯方士
28 Corrections: of people's names 人名改
29 : of textual records 文籍改
30 : of geography 地理改
31 : of ceremonies and rites 典禮改
32 : of music 樂改
33 : of sumptuary display 服飾改
34 : of the names of implements 器名改
35 : of the names of things 物名改
36 Marvelous things heard 異聞
37 Historical supplements 史補
38 Miscellaneous sayings I 雜説上
39 Miscellaneous sayings II 雜説下

Yilin 異林 *A Forest of Marvels* by a "man of the Lu clan" 陸氏 (text probably written before 303 C.E.) (Yl)

This work, long lost, is not mentioned in early catalogues (except the TPYL book list) but is cited in Pei Songzhi's commentary to the *Weizhi* 魏志—a single tale that was later anthologized in the TPYL and in LX. It appears probable that the author was one of Lu Ji's 陸機's two sons, in which case, according to Lu Ji's JS biography, he would have died in 303 C.E.[93]

---

93. Wang Guoliang 1984, 316.

Shenyiji 神異記 *Records of Spirit-Anomalies* by Wang Fou 王浮 (fl. ca. 300 C.E.) (Shenyj)

A Daoist priest during the reign of Jin Emperor Hui (r. 290-306), Wang Fou is notorious for writing the anti-Buddhist tract *Huahujing* 化胡經. The Shenyj is not mentioned in early catalogues. LX collects eight items, most of which are very short and one of which (item 5) is clearly a misattribution of a Shenyjing fragment.[94]

Shizhouji 十洲記 *Records of the Ten Continents.* Author unknown (traditionally attributed to Dongfang Shuo 東方朔). Probably formed around 300 C.E. (Szj)

Alternate title: *Hainei* 海內 *shizhouji.* The one-*juan* text consists of a brief introduction and conclusion framing a long speech by Dongfang Shuo to Han Emperor Wu, in the course of which this *fangshi*-adviser describes the outlying terrestrial paradises on each of the Ten Continents, four islands, and two mountains (see below). The complicated history of this text has recently been sorted out by Li Fengmao and by Thomas E. Smith, who has also translated it in its entirety;[95] my comments are based on their work. The text was probably at some early stage of its transmission embedded within the Hwdnz. It consists of a core of Han-era material around which later accretions formed; the text as we have it was probably formed around 300 C.E.

There are four groups of editions: (1) An YJQQ version, the end of which is jumbled and the division and arrangement of which reflect post-Tang Daoist cosmological thought.[96] (2) XTZ 1.1a–9b, which, although slightly abridged, preserves important phrases that have dropped out of other editions. Its arrangement, which differs somewhat from that of other editions, is confirmed by a citation in the early Tang CXJ (see table below).[97] It also includes a

---

94. Wang Guoliang 1984, 317.

95. Li Fengmao 1986, 125–85; Smith 1992, 213–26, 379–80, 536–62 (tr.). An earlier but more accessible version of his tr. can be seen in Smith 1990.

96. YJQQ 26. Here the work is titled *Shizhou sandao* 三島, reflecting the amalgamation of "continents" and "islands."

97. CXJ 6 (115–16).

postface by Chao Zaizhi that quotes the introduction supposedly by Dongfang Shuo that stands at the beginning of the text itself in most editions. (3) A DZ edition (HY 598), which is the best preserved of all editions. (4) The commonly circulating edition available in several Ming and Qing collectanea (ZDHW, BZQS, GJYS, LWMS, etc.). These essentially reproduce the DZ text (though with minor graphic variants), adding a table of contents.

The Arrangements of Textual Material in Three Groups of Editions of the Szj

("—" indicates "same as left column")

DZ and *tongxingben*	XTZ	YJQQ
1. Zuzhou 祖洲	1. —	1. —
2. Yingzhou 瀛洲	2. —	2. —
3. Xuanzhou 玄洲	3. —	3. —
4. Yanzhou 炎洲	4. —	4. —
5. Changzhou 長洲	5. —	5. —
6. Yuanzhou 元洲	6. —	6. —
7. Liuzhou 流洲	7. Fenglinzhou	7. —
8. Shengzhou 生洲	8. Jukuzhou	8. —
9. Fenglinzhou 鳳麟洲	9. Liuzhou	9. —
10. Jukuzhou 聚窟洲	10. Shengzhou	10. —
11. Canghaidao 滄海洲	11. Canglang 浪 haidao	11. —
12. Fangzhangzhou 方丈洲	12. —	12. Kunlun[98]
13. Fusang 伕桑	13. Daizhou 帶洲	13. Zhongshan
14. Pengqiu 蓬丘	14. —	14. Fangzhang
15. Kunlun 崑崙	15. Kunjunqiu 崑崚丘	15. Fusang
16. Zhongshan 鍾山[99]	16. —	16. Pengqiu

---

98. Here the YJQQ text inserts a higher-level heading, *sandao*, for the rest of the text, so that the material is divided into ten continents and three islands (even though Canghaidao has already been covered and Fusang below is subsumed under Fangzhang and not, unlike Kunlun, Fangzhang, and Pengqiu, given its own heading). The material on Zhongshan is, as in the other two groups of editions, embedded within the discussion of Kunlun.

99. In all three groups of editions the material on Zhongshan is embedded in the text and appears to be an afterthought; it is not outdented as are the beginnings of the other groups of material. Bokenkamp (1986, 65 n.3) notes that Zhongshan is sometimes an alternate name for Mt. Kunlun; it appears as early as the *Huainanzi* (3.6a.8–10).

Soushenji 搜神記 *Records of an Inquest into the Spirit-Realm* by Gan Bao 干寶 (written between 335–349) (Ssj, Ssj8)

The textual history of the Ssj is among the most complicated of all the anomaly accounts. The following observations are therefore even more tentative than most in this chapter.

We have to deal with two versions of the text, some Dunhuang manuscript material, and (briefly) a text of identical title found in DZ.

Twenty-fascicle version (Ssj). This version contains a total of 464 items unevenly distributed over its twenty fascicles. To my knowledge, its earliest extant edition is that printed in the MCHH series (1603); other editions (presumably descended from this one) include XJTY, JDMS, and BZQS. I know of two modern editions, neither of them critical: one, first printed on the mainland in 1931 by Commercial Press and since reprinted there as well as in Taiwan, is based on the BZQS ed., supplying punctuation; the other, printed on the mainland, is in simplified characters and supplies punctuation, item headings, explanatory notes, and a modern Chinese translation.[100] There is a complete Japanese translation, there is an index to personal names and terms prepared and published in Japan, and many items have, of course, been translated into Western languages, although I know of no complete translation.[101]

In his JS biography, Gan Bao is said to have authored a text titled Ssj in thirty fascicles.[102] A text of this length is listed in the SuiS, JTS, XTS, and RBG catalogues, and is attributed in each case

---

100. These are, respectively, Yang Jialuo, ed., 1982 (1959)a, a photo-reproduction of the 1931 ed. by Hu Huaichen 胡懷琛, and Huang Diming, ed., 1991. A photoreproduced manuscript by Xu Jianxin 許建新 was published as a Masters thesis by Taiwan Shifan University in 1974; this manuscript lists locations where the Ssj is cited in collectanea and notes variant readings, but is not a complete critical edition of the text. A copy is held by the Joseph Regenstein Library, East Asia Collection, University of Chicago.

101. Japanese tr. by Takeda Akira (1964); index, Harada 1983.

102. Some earlier eds. gave a figure of 20 *juan;* DeWoskin 1974, 88 n.39.

to Gan Bao.[103] The Ssj does not, however, appear in some other major but later Sung catalogues in which one would expect it to have been listed if it had been extant.[104] On the other hand, over ninety percent of the 464 items in today's text are attested in extant Six Dynasties commentaries, Tang and early Sung collectanea.[105] Most Chinese scholars who have written on the Ssj, including the SKQS editors, Yu Jiaxi, Fan Ning, Yan Maoyuan, Li Jianguo, and Wang Guoliang, as well as Kenneth DeWoskin, the Western scholar who has researched its history most carefully, have therefore concluded that the Ssj was lost sometime after the early Sung and that the extant twenty-fascicle version is a late Ming reconstruction. This conclusion is further supported by a fairly high degree of correspondence between its sequence of items and the sequence of material in Tang and Sung collectanea, as well as by the following anecdote, which is attested in writings by both of the persons involved. Yao Shuxiang, like Gan Bao and Hu Yinglin a native of Haiyan, and a contemporary of Hu Yinglin's (both were active in the Ming *wanli* period), once visited Hu's library. Noticing a copy of the Ssj, he excitedly insisted on seeing it (which suggests that it had long been lost); but Hu said, "I do not dare trick someone who is knowledgeable. Frankly, it is something copied out of the FYZL and several other collectanea"—in other words, reconstructed.[106] Hu adds to his version of the anecdote the comment that "This is the case with almost all books of strange occurrences which have appeared in later times."

If, as seems likely, the text is a late Ming recompilation, the identities of the compiler(s) and his (or their) methods—but not, in most cases, their sources—remain a mystery, as is the case with most late Ming recompilations. Hu Yinglin died in 1602, so his copy, which he clearly characterized as a reconstruction, was probably in existence by at least the last decade of the sixteenth century; whether it was the basis of the MCHH edition of 1603 is unknown. Fan Ning has proposed Hu Yinglin himself as the

---

103. Quite a few texts with somewhat similar titles and widely variant numbers of fascicles show up in later catalogues (DeWoskin 1974, 88–89). Listings of a *Soushenlu* 錄 probably refer to the Sshj, the relationship of which to the Ssj is discussed below.

104. For a summary, DeWoskin 1974, 90–92. Throughout the ensuing discussion I rely primarily on the thorough treatment in DeWoskin 1974, 55–192.

105. For a list, DeWoskin 1974, 94–111. On the other hand, 49 quotations in collectanea are not to be found in today's Ssj (for a table, DeWoskin 1974, 135–36).

106. DeWoskin 1974, 74–75.

recompiler; DeWoskin rejects this view but considers it likely that Hu's copy—whatever its provenance—was the basis for the MCHH printed text.[107]

Most Japanese scholars who have dealt with the text, by contrast, have clung since the 1940s to the position that the extant twenty-fascicle, 464-item version is descended from some core text continuously transmitted since early times (*how* early varies by scholar), which was then augmented, to be sure, by late Ming editors. In general, the evidence adduced in favor of this position is of two types. (1) Discrepancies between items quoted in collectanea and their parallels in the extant Ssj, particularly where the collectanea items are briefer or less intelligible than their extant-Ssj counterparts, prove (it is argued) that Ming recompilers could not have derived (all of) their text from these sources.[108] (2) The format of the extant text, the uneven lengths of its chapters, and the remnants of what appear to be topical headings and discursive introductions to chapters, all suggest that late (some suggest Tang, some Sung) redactors were striving to preserve an early, transmitted core of which these features are the traces.[109] However, regarding the first point, it must be remembered that the collectanea themselves were as liable to textual deterioration as the Ssj, and such deterioration may suffice to explain most of the discrepancies between collated items. DeWoskin reminds us in this connection that six centuries separate the compilation of the FYZL from its first usable print editions in the Sung, and that six centuries also separate the original TPGJ from its earliest known Ming edition of 1566.[110] And regarding the second point, DeWoskin has mounted a convincing counterargument too complex to be summarized here.[111]

The extant text shows remarkable topical cohesion by fascicle, which itself suggests that it is a late recompilation, since it is

---

107. DeWoskin 1974, 188.

108. Nishitani 1951, passim, on the *wuxingzhi* sections; Takeda 1961, passim, on the relationship between the Ssj and its 98 TPGJ quotations; Kominami 1966, 59–60; cf. DeWoskin 1974, 180, who finds similar results for FYZL and YWLJ parallels. Most scholars agree that *juan* 6–8 were late additions to the Ssj.

109. On the supposed remnant topical headings and discursive introductions, Morino 1965.

110. This counterargument, however, is relevant to our case only insofar as it applies to the deterioration of collectanea *between the time of the Ssj's supposed recompilation (whenever it was) and today;* DeWoskin (1974, 181–82) confuses the issue by discussing the much longer timespan over which these works must surely have dropped material.

111. See DeWoskin 1974, 184–87.

highly unlikely to have survived in such neat form over more than a millennium and a half. The hierarchical ordering of topics, from the august mythical sage-ruler Shen Nong down to the lowest insects, is strongly reminiscent of the organization of the TPGJ.

Ssj Topics by Fascicle

1 Daoist transcendents (31 items)

2 *Fangshi* and shamans (17 items)

3 *Fangshi* adept in divination and medicine (22 items)

4 Encounters with gods (mostly local and regional) and visits to their temples (21 items)

5 Encounters with local gods and accounts of the founding of their shrines; otherworldly messengers and summonses (10 items)

6 Political omens and portents from the Shang period to Sun Hao (77 items)

7 Political omens and portents during the Jin dynasty (48 items)

8 Examples of omens drawn from ancient writings (10 items)

9 Omens pertaining to individuals' fortunes, and their interpretation (14 items)

10 Dreams; their confirmation and real effects in waking life (12 items)

11 Extreme virtue; its power to call forth anomalous responses from Heaven and Earth (37 items)

12 Monstrous creatures (19 items)

13 Marvels at particular places and how places got their names (items 1–12); marvelous creatures (especially lowly ones, 13–17); remarkable objects (18–21)

14 Ancient legends concerning the origins of clans and tribes and their founding ancestors (items 1–10); mythological fragments concerning the origin of sericulture and Chang E (11–12); transformations of humans into plants (13) and animals (14–19)

15 Cases of return from death (items 1–11) and openings of tombs (12–16)

16 Ghost narratives (24 items)

17 Narratives of ghosts and demons (13 items)

18 Spirits of objects (items 1-2), trees (3–6), and mammals (7–26 [26 also features a scorpion-spirit])

19 Snake and fish spirits (items 1–6); miscellaneous tales (7–9)

20 Rewards and retributions (*bao*) by animals (16 items)

Eight-fascicle version (Ssj8). This version, containing forty items, first appeared in the BH series; it was also printed in the ZDHW series as well as in other editions. None of its items is attested in quotations in Six Dynasties commentaries, and all scholars who have dealt with it have commented on the immediately apparent differences of style and emphasis between it and the Ssj. Its many anachronisms have been pointed out, although these exist in almost every anomaly account and do not themselves prove that a text has no relationship to its purported author and era of origin. DeWoskin dismisses it as unrelated to Gan Bao's text due to its heavily "Buddhistic" content, saying that it "contains nothing but the [*yinguo*] type of retribution story."[112] These characterizations are simply wrong, but I do agree that the Ssj8 cannot rival the Ssj as the more representative of Gan Bao's work. It is not impossible, however, that this text preserves items from an early version of Gan Bao's text that are now missing from the Ssj.

Some of the extant Ssj8 items correspond with ones found in the extant Ssj; a list follows, the asterisk (*) marking cases in which the items are clearly related in plot and phrasing but between which there are large differences of character, content, and wording—almost certainly due to reworking of the earlier material represented in the Ssj.

Parallels between Ssj8 and Ssj items

Ssj8	Ssj
1.1	3.6
1.3	16.20

---

112. DeWoskin 1974, 60.

Ssj8	Ssj
2.3	15.1
3.2	20.5
3.3	19.8
3.5	14.2
3.6	18.3*
4.1	18.9
4.2	18.21*
5.4	11.18
5.5	20.9

The Ssj8 is closer to the Dunhuang fragments (on which more shortly) than to the Ssj in its plots and characters, but closer to the Ssj in its diction and linguistic style.[113] Kosugi Ichio argues that it dates from no earlier than 547, the date of Yang Xuanzhi's 楊衒之 trip to Luoyang, because it includes events based on that trip as described in Yang's *Luoyang qielanji*.[114] Certainly its style and religious content agree with this dating. It is risky to date texts by one's subjective impressions of their style, but the style of the Ssj8 combined with the other evidence adduced here suggest that this text originated in the late Six Dynasties or early Tang and that some of its items represent later reworkings of some of Gan Bao's original material into more elaborate narrative form.

Dunhuang fragments. At least five manuscripts found at Dunhuang have been shown to preserve portions of a Tang-period collection of anomaly accounts titled *Soushenji*.[115] Together they amount to thirty-four narrative items. A recension incorporating three of these manuscripts (plus another that has been shown to be a fragment of a work quoting some version of the Ssj) is widely

---

113. Shimizu 1955.

114. Kosugi 1941, 21, cited in DeWoskin 1974, 165. This would probably be the tale of the ghost of Wei Ying 韋英, Ssj8 1.7. It appears in the "Western Suburbs" section of the *Luoyang qielanji;* see Wang Yi-t'ung 1984, 188–89.

115. DeWoskin's discussion (1974, 57ff. and 166) is now superseded by Wang Guoliang 1986, on which the following remarks are based. The Tang dating, on which most scholars concur, is supported not only by the prose style of the texts but by their avoidance of a character tabooed during the Tang. Older discussions of the Dunhuang texts include Nishino 1957 and Giles 1921.

available in a collection of Dunhuang transformation texts.[116] Some of the manuscripts list as their author Ju Daoxing 句道興, about whom nothing more is known. The style and language of the Dunhuang text are far from Gan Bao's, resembling more closely those of Ssj8 but incorporating even more colloquial expressions and more elaborate narrativity than that text.

Fifteen items in the Dunhuang text match relatively well with Ssj8 items. On the other hand, only three Dunhuang items closely correspond to items found in or attributable to the twenty-fascicle Ssj.[117] It seems that either Ssj8 and the Dunhuang Ssj were based, in part, on a common source (which was not a direct descendant of Gan Bao's autograph text, although it presumably bore some indirect relation to it), or else one of these texts incorporated material from the other. Both, in any case, stand at a considerable remove from Gan Bao's Ssj, and are not "versions" of his own writing in any meaningful sense of the word; rather, they represent reworkings of some of his material, intermixed with material from other sources, reflective of the later eras in which they were compiled and aimed at a broader readership.

DZ text titled *Soushenji*. In the Ming Daoist canon there is, finally, a text of the same title, HY 1466, consisting of six fascicles, a table of contents, some small illustrations, and an undated and unsigned preface (presumably by the author of the postscript) that attributes the work to Gan Bao and maintains that this text preserves fragments of his original. The text also bears a postscript dated Ming *wanli* 35 by Zhang Guoxiang. Not a single passage in this text corresponds with any passage in any extant Ssj version or known quotation in commentaries or collectanea. Moreover, its contents clearly belie its utter lack of relation to Gan Bao's work: it opens with a statement on the origins of the three religions, then

---

116. Wang Zhongmin 1984, 865–900, which is based on (1) the Japanese-held manuscript that is most complete, containing a version of all but one of the items found in other manuscripts; (2) Stein 525; (3) Stein 6022; and (4) Pelliot 2656, which Wang Guoliang 1984, 381, convincingly argues is a remnant of another work that was quoting chunks of material from a text titled Ssj (and whose material does overlap with that of other manuscripts). The compilers knew of Pelliot 5545, which has variants of 11 tales, but were unable to incorporate it into their recension; they do not mention Stein 3877, which contains a variant of one item.

117. For tables, Wang Guoliang 1986, 385–87.

presents a Daoist systematic theology, listing deities in hierarchical ranking from major, upper-celestial figures through regional
gods (including their main cult sites) down to "celestial consorts,"
gods of pestilence, and gods of the stove and the latrine. It was
probably written during the Ming.

Shenxianzhuan 神仙傳 *Lives of Divine Transcendents* by Ge Hong 葛洪 (283–343)[118] (Sxz)

The Sxz has come down to us in two versions, both in ten fascicles:
(1) A version containing ninety-two hagiographies, extant in
ZDHW, LWMS, SK, and other Ming and Qing editions, of which
there is now a complete translation.[119] (2) A version containing
eighty-four hagiographies, extant in the SKQS edition (based on a
recension by Mao Jin 毛晉). Other Ming, Qing, and later collectanea
contain excerpts from these.

The text Ge Hong wrote by the year 317 C.E.[120] comprised ten
fascicles, as we know from his JS biography, the autobiographical
statement found at the end of his *Baopuzi waipian* (partially translated in the next chapter), and his preface to the Sxz, which makes
clear that he wrote the text to persuade non-believers of the truth
of Daoist claims to transcendence and to improve upon Liu Xiang's
Lxz.[121] It is also listed at ten fascicles in the SuiS and most subsequent official catalogues. But no extant recension of the text is complete, for a Tang reader records that it had 190 hagiographies,
while the tenth century Daoist hagiographer Wang Songnian mentions that it contained 117.[122] On the other hand, a few among the

---

118. The dates of Ge Hong's birth and death continue to be controversial; compare Li Jianguo 1984, 316 n.1 (he takes Ge's dates to be 284–
364, crediting the reports of Ge's age at death as 81), with Sivin 1969 and
the argument of Hong Ye, which Sivin translates and with which I still
concur.

119. Güntsch 1988; on the eds. used in preparing her trans., p. 18.

120. His *Baopuzi waipian* autobiographical statement lists Sxz
among the works completed by 建武中. In the (possibly inauthentic) Sxz
preface he also mentions his *Neipian* in twenty fascicles, indicating that
that work was completed before the Sxz was written.

121. This preface is not printed in the SK ed.; I have consulted the
SKQS ed., and it is also conveniently accessible in Li Jianguo, 318. See the
translation and discussion in Chapter Seven.

122. Li Jianguo 1984, 317–18; on Wang Songnian, Boltz 1987, 59.

copious citations from the Sxz in early works such as Tao Hongjing's *Zhen'gao* 真誥 and the late seventh century collection SDZN seem to lack analogues in either received version, and probably preserve fragments dropped from the text in the course of its transmission.[123]

Sometime in the late Han, another text of the same title had been written by an unknown author. It is cited in three surviving passages each in the Fsty and the Bwz.[124] In addition to drawing on the Lxz, which he acknowledges in his preface, Ge Hong is also likely to have used the name—and perhaps some surviving contents—of this older text in compiling his own Sxz. Judging from bibliographic catalogues, there were quite a few other Daoist hagiographies in circulation before and after Ge Hong wrote, most of them *biezhuan* 別傳 devoted to a single figure and his or her disciples, now no longer extant (not, at least, as discrete texts);[125] Ge is likely to have drawn on some of these, while others perhaps incorporated material from his text.

Ge Hong's official biography also credits him with a collection of anomaly accounts titled *Jiyizhuan* 集異傳 and a series of biographies of recluses, *Yinyizhuan* 隱逸傳, but these have long since been lost.

Zhiguai 志怪 *Accounts of Anomalies* by Zu Taizhi 祖台之 (fl. ca. 376–410) (Zgz)

Zu Taizhi's official biography (JS 75), which is vague as to the dates of his birth and death, mentions that he "wrote a book of anomaly accounts that was circulated" (撰志怪書行於世). The Zgz is

---

123. For locations of *Zhen'gao* quotations or citations from Sxz, Yoshioka 1955, 353; for SDZN quotations, Yoshioka 1955, 377. At this writing I have not found good analogues in the 92-item version of Sxz for three of these passages, and at least two possible analogues are only approximate, in that there are major differences (so major that I am unsure they are analogues) between the extant Sxz text and the early citation. I have found at least seven Sxz items copied whole or in part into the Ssj. Li Jianguo 1984, 318, reports that there is a collection of lost Sxz fragments in YH, but I find none. YHX does, however, contain three fragments (p. 130).

124. For a list of these, Li Jianguo 1984, 197–98.

125. For a partial list of these titles, Li Jianguo 1984, 320–21. Cf. the list of sources cited by Ge Hong in his *Baopuzi neipian* in Yoshioka 1955, 345–51; several of these were clearly hagiographic texts.

listed in the SuiS and TZ catalogues as containing two fascicles; in the JTS and XTS catalogues it is listed as having four fascicles, probably due to differing divisions of the text. Like many other collections of anomaly accounts, it was lost in the Sung or Yuan, and now exists in two recompiled versions. (1) The GJSB ed. has a version containing nine items. The first seven of these items overlap with the other version of the text; the final two stand a good chance of having been misattributed to the Zgz.[126] (2) LX collects fifteen items but, as is typical, is more cautious in its attributions.

Shiyiji 拾遺記 *Uncollected Records*
by Wang Jia 王嘉 (d. before 393 C.E.) (Syj)

Alternate titles: *Wang Zinian* 王子年 *Shiyiji* (incorporating the author's courtesy name); *Shiyilu* 錄. Extant in three versions: (1) A ten-fascicle text, editions of which are found in several Ming and Qing collectanea, including GJYS, ZDHW, and BZQS (some other editions include only excerpts). All of these stem from the earliest extant printing, done in the late Ming by the Shidetang printing house from a (supposedly) Sung edition. There is a translation of this version, based on a 1970 reprint of the ZDHW edition.[127] The tenth fascicle, a treatise on "noted mountains" (*mingshan* 名山), later circulated as an independent text. (2) A ten-fascicle text in the BH varying significantly enough from (1) to suggest that it stems from a separate tradition.[128] (3) A modern, critical recension, done on the mainland and based on the Shidetang edition.[129]

All of these versions stem from the editorial hand of one Xiao Qi 蕭綺 of the Liang dynasty, of whom nothing more is known. His

---

126. See Wang Guoliang 1984, 319; Li Jianguo 1984, 335.

127. Foster 1974, 123–310; does not include Xiao Qi's *lu*, on which see below. For comments on features of some eds. of the Syj, see pp. 94–99.

128. Qi Zhiping 1981, 17, and Li Jianguo 1984, 325, are of this opinion. Qi notes that the BH text (which is found on pp. 60–105 of v.1 of the 1968 reprint) drops words and phrases found in the other version—but also preserves bits of phrasing not found in the other version. Fortunately, his critical recension incorporates these variations (which are limited to the sort I have indicated). The BH text closely accords with the TPGJ quotations from the work. It sometimes mixes Xiao Qi's comments in with the main text.

129. Qi Zhiping 1981.

preface states that Wang Jia's text, having originally consisted of nineteen fascicles and 220 *pian* 篇,[130] had come down to his time in fragments. These he collected into ten fascicles, adding his own preface and *lu*. The ten-*juan* Syj mentioned in Wang Jia's official biography was, therefore, this recompiled version by Xiao Qi, not the text from Wang's own hand.[131] This filiation also explains why the Sui and Tang official bibliographies list the work twice but at different lengths and under variant titles: the shorter version (or possibly versions), listed as *Shiyilu* 録 in two or three fascicles, must have contained fragments overlooked or excluded by Xiao Qi; it survived independently of his text through the Sung but was afterwards lost, and it may be the source of some quotations in collectanea that cannot be matched with passages in the extant recensions.[132]

On the other hand, that the extant 10-fascicle version is really Xiao Qi's (or anyone else's) assemblage *from fragments* is belied by the tight allegorical structure of the text, which will be analyzed in Chapter Seven. Perhaps Xiao, whoever he was, claimed that the text was fragmentary so as to justify adding his own comments, which constitute a virtual running argument with—and decidedly not a sympathetic elucidation of—the main tenor of the text proper. Given the distanced tone of his remarks, it is also quite possible that Xiao simply did not understand the allegory and hence the persuasive thrust of the text, and so mistook it as being "fragmentary"— that is, a seemingly piecemeal, at best loosely ordered series of items—in much the same way that many other anomaly accounts

---

130. It is unclear in context whether this term means items or topical sections.

131. That either Wang Jia and Xiao Qi had any real connection with the formation of the text has been doubted by Thomas Smith (1992, 288), but the document by Xiao is quite detailed and Smith's argument from silence—that the Syj is not cited in other texts before the BTSC—is unconvincing given the limited circulation of all texts (and especially of anomaly accounts) before the age of printing. Smith is also under the impression that Syj was "influenced" by Dmj; my own view is that the influence, if there was any direct connection between the two, was in the other direction.

132. Li Jianguo 1984, 324. Foster 1974, 93, assumes that there must have been *three versions* in circulation in the Tang and early Sung, since the text is listed as containing two, three, and ten *juan;* but this is not necessarily the case. Foster (p. 97) lists 22 items quoted in the TPYL and TPGJ and attributed to the Syj which he either cannot find in the extant text or which show quite significant variations from it.

are. Xiao would not be alone in so reading the text, since even modern critics have failed to notice its allegorical patterning.[133]

Wang Jia's JS biography appears in the *liezhuan* section on "Arts" (*Yishu* 藝術), here meaning esoteric arts, since the twenty-four individuals to whom biographies are devoted are all Daoist or Buddhist adepts or *fangshi*. The narrative depicts him as a Daoist adept who avoided the five grains, practiced "purity, emptiness, and ingestion of pneumas," taught disciples, lived in reclusion on mountains, could conceal his body, and delivered accurate predictions of future events, one of which angered the commander Yao Chang so much that he had Wang beheaded. Wang was seen at a distant place on the day of his execution, however—a sign that he had achieved "liberation from the corpse" (*shijie* 尸解).[134] He was also given a hagiography in the Daoist collection Dxz (on which more below),[135] and figures prominently in Huijiao's Gsz hagiography of the monk and scholiast Daoan 道安, whom he is said to have met.[136]

The first nine fascicles of the Syj as it has come down to us take the form of a chronologically arranged list of anomalies—mostly marvelous flora, fauna, substances, and products from peripheral realms—each pegged to a ruler, beginning with the mythical sage-ruler Fu Xi at the very beginning of the world and extending to Jin times and the ruler Shi Hu most recently. The text seems to be centrally concerned with the ruler's relationship to these marvelous goods, his response to the presentation of them as tribute or the quest for them on his behalf by an adept; on analysis, however, this theme turns out to be the outer framework for a complex allegory that undermines it (see Chapter Seven). The tenth fascicle is a Daoist sacred geography, its material grouped under "notable mountains" and isles. A table of contents follows.

Syj: Table of Contents

Topic heading	Juan
Pao Xi 庖犧	1
Shen Nong 神農	

---

133. Neither Foster 1974 nor any Chinese or Japanese works of which I am aware mention it.

134. JS 95 (2496–97); for a somewhat problematic tr., Foster 1974, 342–46.

135. YJQQ 110.17b–18b; tr. Foster 1974, 347–49 (this tr. is also somewhat problematic).

136. Tr. Link 1958, 37–39.

Topic heading	Juan
Huang Di 黃帝	
Shao Hao 少昊	
Gao Yang 高陽	
Gao Xin 高辛	
Tang Yao 唐堯	
Yu Shun 虞舜	
Xia 夏	2
Yin 殷	
Zhou 周	
Zhou Mu Wang 周穆王	3
Lu Xi Gong 魯僖公	
Zhou Ling Wang 周靈王	
Yan Shao Wang 燕昭王	4
Qin Shihuang 秦始皇	
Qian Han: shang 前漢上	5
Qian Han: xia 下	6
Hou Han 後漢	
Wei 魏	7
Wu 吳	8
Shu 蜀	
Jin shi shi 晉時事	9
Kunlun shan 崑崙山	10
Penglai shan 蓬萊山	
Fangzhang shan 方丈山	
Yingzhou shan 瀛洲山	
Yuanjiao shan 員嶠山	
Daiyu shan 岱輿山	
Kunwu shan 昆吾山	
Dongting shan 洞庭山	

Zhenyizhuan 甄異傳 *Selected Anomaly Accounts* by Dai Zuo 戴祚 (fl. late Jin) (Zyz)

Alternate title: *Zhenyiji* 記. Listed in Tang and Sung catalogues as containing three fascicles, it now exists in an LX recension of seventeen items (as well as LWMS and other versions that are incomplete and contain misattributed items). Two other items have also been found.[137]

---

137. Wang Guoliang 1984, 321. One of these is found in YWLJ 44, the other in a particular edition (that by Tan Kai 談愷) of the TPGJ.

Dai Zuo served late in the Jin and wrote some minor topographic and annalistic works; no official biography is devoted to him, however, and not much else is known about him. Most of the events in the Zyz are set in the Eastern Jin period.

Guangshiyin yingyanji 光世音應驗記
Responsive Manifestations of Avalokiteśvara
by Xie Fu 謝敷 (fl. mid- to late 4th century C.E.)
and Fu Liang 傅亮 (374–426 C.E.) (Gsy)

A 1943 Japanese report of recent textual discoveries included mention of the discovery at Seiren Monastery 青蓮院 in Kyoto of a Kamakura-period (more specifically, probably early 12th century) manuscript containing three pre-Tang collections of Buddhist miracle tales. The texts were first published by Tsukamoto Zenryū, then republished in 1970 in a careful recension and study by Makita Tairyō. They include Gsy, XuGsy, and XiGsy.

The earliest of the three, the Gsy, was written sometime in the late fourth century by Xie Fu, well known in his day as a Buddhist layman and a close associate of the monk/scholar Zhi Dun 支遁 (314–366), the greatest propagator of Buddhism among the gentry in Jiankang.[138] It originally contained "more than ten" items (十餘事) and was given to a Kuaiji scholar-official named Fu Yuan, from whose household it was lost during Sun En's sack of Kuaiji in 399. Fu Yuan's son Liang rewrote seven of the lost tales from memory (以所憶者更為此記) and collected them to form the seven-item Gsy text. All of this information is given in Fu Liang's brief preface to the work, which survives in manuscript along with the text.[139]

Although brief, this text is extremely important not only because it is the earliest known collection of Buddhist miracle tales, and one of the earliest records in any language of devotion to the

---

138. Xie Fu is given a terse biography in the JS 94 section on recluses (2456–57), but from scattered references in Buddhist literature, it is possible to piece together much more information about him: Makita 1970, 76–79 n.3; Zürcher 1972, 136–37; Tsukamoto 1985, 307 (on his commentary and preface to the *Da anban shouyijing* [T 602]). The key compound *yingyan* in the title of this work and those of XuGsy and XiGsy could equally well be rendered as "evidences of [miraculous] responses"; I discuss the sense of *yingyan* in Chapter Seven.

139. It is printed at the head of the text in Makita 1970, 13.

Bodhisattva Guanshiyin (Avalokiteśvara), but also because it is one of the very few pre-Tang anomaly accounts to have survived in manuscript. It is listed at one *juan* in the SuiS catalogue and the TZ, but had long since vanished until its rediscovery fifty years ago.[140] Wang Yan incorporated five of its seven items into his Mxj, which was in turn drawn upon heavily by Huijiao when compiling his Gsz.

Soushen houji 搜神後記 *Further Records of an Inquest into the Spirit-Realm.* Probably written in late Song or early Qi (Sshj)

Alternate names: *Xu* 續 *Soushenji* (XuSsj); *Soushenlu* 錄. Beginning with the preface to Huijiao's Gsz and continuing through listings in the SuiS and RBG, this work was traditionally attributed to Tao Qian 陶潛 (Tao Yuanming, 365–427 C.E.), and it does contain a version of the haunting "peach blossom spring" story for which Tao is known, as well as several other stories with a similar plot structure. But there are compelling reasons to reject this attribution: not only do any texts before Huijiao fail to mention that Tao wrote a text by any of these titles, and not only does the extant text mention events and reign titles that would have postdated Tao's death; but also, more importantly,[141] most of what is known about Tao makes it seem highly unlikely that he would have written a text stressing the themes and concerns of the Sshj.[142] Based on internal

---

140. In addition to the thorough study in Makita 1970, see Wang Guoliang 1984, 302–3; Gjertson 1989, 16–19; Campany 1993b.

141. Absent other considerations, I am generally not persuaded by arguments from anachronism based on only a few items, since the fact that a few extraneous items may have crept into a text over the centuries hardly by itself invalidates an attribution of authorship; at most, such arguments prove that the items in question were either added to the text after its reputed author could have written it or (minimally) that dates, place names, or reign titles were altered by later redactors.

142. My reasons for saying this will become clear only in Chapter Seven; for now suffice it to say that Tao, who, in his ongoing refusals of office, reclusive life, and in other writings, clearly appears to have been an exponent of the philosophy of "naturalism" (*ziran*)—a philosophy that, admirably expressed in the "peach blossom spring" story and having its roots in Lao-Zhuang-*Liezi* thought, contrasts sharply with the worldview urged in virtually every item in the extant Sshj except 1.5 and a few similar stories.

evidence, the text can reasonably be regarded as having been written in the late Song or early Qi by an unknown person (most likely an official with some connection to the court archives).[143]

After its Tang-period catalogue listings at ten fascicles, and frequent citations (mostly under the title XuSsj) in Tang and early Sung collectanea,[144] the Sshj drops out of sight[145] until Tao Zongyi includes three items from a *Xusoushenji* in *juan* 4 of his SF, compiled at the end of the Yuan or beginning of the Ming. It is possible that he was working from an old copy of the text, but is more likely that he was relying on earlier *leishu*. No Ming bibliographers mention a *Xusoushenji* or Sshj until a ten-*juan* Sshj is included in the MCHH, printed in 1603. (1) This MCHH text, containing 116 items, is the ancestor of one of the two most common versions, forming the basis of the SKQS, CSJC, JDMS, XJTY, and other editions. (2) Two late Ming scholars published a text containing twenty-four items excerpted from the MCHH version; this formed the basis for the LWMS, GJSB, and other editions.[146] (3) In the late *qianlong* period, Wang Mo included another recension in his ZDHW, incorporating the twenty-four items from (2) and adding twenty-four others (al-

---

143. I thus concur with the views set forth in Wang Guoliang 1978, 2–4 and 30. He takes a slightly more cautious tack in 1984, 320–21.

144. BTSC quotes 7 items and YWLJ quotes 17 from a "XuSsj"; CXJ quotes 6, 2 of which are taken from a Sshj, the other 4 from a XuSsj. FYZL, TPYL, and TPGJ all quote from a XuSsj. Given the high proportion of matches between these citations and the Sshj text as we have it today, it is obvious that we are dealing with an older title for this work, not with a different work.

145. It is listed in ten *juan* in the TZ, but, as Wang Guoliang (1978, 5) and others have pointed out, this catalogue was compiled on the basis of previous ones and not from a first-hand inspection of extant texts. It has also been argued by some scholars that mysteriously inflated bibliographic listings (in the SuiS, JTS, XTS, and other catalogues) of the Ssj—at *30 juan*—indicate that these two texts must have been conflated for a time; this is an ingenious but insufficiently supported argument (Wang Guoliang 1978, 4–5, weighs the evidence pro and con and concludes that the argument is "forced").

146. Thus Wang Guoliang 1979, 5. I have examined only the LWMS (*ce* 32) and SF (*juan* 4) eds. The LWMS text conforms to Wang's description, but the SF text—which, in its "revised" (*chongjiao*) version, Wang includes in this filiation—is, at least in the 1927 rept. I have to work with (which is recorded as having been revised [*chongjiao*] by Zhang Zongxiang), even more truncated, collecting only three items under the title *Xu Ssj*.

most certainly from some text in the (1) filiation) to form a forty-eight-item version divided into two fascicles. All but one of the ZDHW items match up with items in the ten-*juan* version (but with graphic variants and altered phrases; see table below). (4) There are two recent critical editions, one done on the mainland by Wang Shaoying, the other on Taiwan by Wang Guoliang.[147]

The 116-item, ten-fascicle text that surfaced in 1603, the sources of which are obscure, probably does not preserve an old, continuously transmitted version of the Sshj traceable back to its author, but was instead recompiled from collectanea in much the same way as subsequent versions of it—and some other prominent texts (notably Ssj, Yy)—were. We know, however, that it was recompiled from early sources and not simply invented from whole cloth since a very high proportion of its items are attested in early collectanea.

An item-by-item comparison between the ten-*juan*, 116-item version and Wang Mo's two-*juan*, forty-eight-item version reveals the extent to which the latter was based in its sequencing on the former. Some items in the ZDHW text are severely truncated, presumably reflecting the quotations in the collectanea (and their editions) on which it was based (such cases are marked with an asterisk *).

CSJC (10-*juan*)	**ZDHW (2-*juan*)**	
1.1	A1	(Complete matches throughout
.	.	the first 11 items of both texts;
.	.	ZDHW *juan* A comprises
.	.	additional items—see below)
1.11	A11	
2.1	B1	(Complete matches through the
.	.	first 14 items of second *juan* of
.	.	both texts; ZDHW *juan* B
.	.	comprises additional items—
2.14	B14	see below)

---

147. Wang Shaoying 1981 includes a critical recension and a small collection of lost passages. Wang Guoliang 1978 includes an introductory discussion of authorship, textual history, and the relationship between the Sshj and Ssj; a listing of citations of the text in collectanea; and a critical recension based on the XJTY ed.

CSJC (10-*juan*)	ZDHW (2-*juan*)
3.4	B20
3.5	B18
3.10	B22*
4.4	B24
5.7	B16
6.3	B19
6.4	B30
6.20	B23
7.1	B17*
7.5	B21
8.6	B25
9.5	B27
9.6	A13
9.7	A14
9.8	A16
9.11	A15
9.12	A12
9.13	B26
9.15	B15*
10.1	B29*
10.2	B28*
10.8	A17
—	A18[148]

Given the high probability that both the extant Ssj and Sshj are late Ming recompilations from pre-Tang commentaries and Tang and Sung collectanea (and not the descendants of independently, continuously transmitted texts), and given the confusion between these two titles in many citations of these two works in those commentaries and collectanea,[149] one wonders several things about the relationship between these two texts as they have come down to us. How much do their contents overlap one another? How many items now in the Sshj (placed there, we are assuming, by late Ming redactors) are likely to have originally been part of the Ssj, and how many items now in the Ssj properly belong to the Sshj? These questions cannot be answered with certainty, but, thanks especially to Wang Guoliang's research, we can go as far as it is possible to go, given our evidence, in answering them.

---

148. I have found no match in the CSJC ed. for ZDHW A18.
149. Cases, that is, in which (for example) the FYZL quotes an item from the "Ssj" but the TPYL quotes the same item from the "XuSsj."

Here, first, is a list of all known overlaps between items in the Sshj and in other anomaly accounts.[150]

Sshj (CSJC ed.)	Other texts
2.5	Yml 108
2.6	Xuanyj 12
2.7	Yml 90; Yslz 13; Gsz *shenyi* A1
2.11	Ssj 3.14
5.4	Ssj 5.4[151]
6.3	Ssj 16.10
6.4	Ssj 16.22
8.2	Yy 6.14

Based on a comparison of all cases in which Tang and early Sung collectanea attribute the same item to both Ssj and Sshj, Wang Guoliang makes a set of principled judgments about the likely provenance of each of these items (many of which are now found in only one or the other text). For convenience I here summarize the results of his and my own research:

Unlikely to have formed part of the original Sshj: 1.1, 2.11, 2.12, 2.13, 5.1, 10.8.

Probably part of the original Sshj: 2.1, 2.9, 3.10, 3.13, 3.15, 5.4, 5.7, 6.3, 6.4, 6.5, 6.12, 7.5, 7.7, 9.4, 9.6, 9.12, 9.15, 10.4, 10.6.

No verdict possible: 7.1, 7.2, 8.2, 8.8.

Likely to have formed part of the original Sshj but **not found in extant versions:**[152]

---

150. Based on my own research and on the data in Wang Guoliang 1978, 19–27. Not included, of course, is the large quantity of data on citations of Sshj items in collectanea, for a list of which see Wang Guoliang 1978, 7–18. No judgment is here implied on the question of whether the overlaps are due to misattributions in collectanea or to genuine borrowing by one anomaly account author from another's work.

151. Wang Guoliang 1978, 22, wrongly says this parallel is found in *juan* 4 of Ssj.

152. Unless otherwise indicated, the source cites XuSsj; † indicates it cites Ssj. Note that Wang does not imply that all of these items should be expunged from the Ssj, merely that they are candidates for inclusion in the Sshj as well.

Identifier	Loc. in Ssj	Source(s)
化鼈	14.17	TPYL 888.5a, TPGJ 471.7, YWLJ 96.1670†[153]
謝奉	10.11	TPYL 400.8a
宗淵	—	TPYL 399.8a, TPGJ 276.33†
猿母	20.12	TPGJ 131.13
施績	16.4[154]	TPYL 396.6b, 884.6a; TPGJ 323.18†[155]
吳猛	1.26	TPYL 736.7a, BTSC 103.5b†
吳猛	1.26[156]	TPYL 702.6a
徐泰	10.12[157]	TPYL 399.8b; TPGJ 161.24,† 276.47†[158]
胡博士	18.16	TPYL 32.3b,[159] 909.7a†
朱恭	—	BZL 7 (540b 1.5)[160]
馬勢婦	15.9	TPGJ 358.2
虞定國	17.4	TPGJ 360.17

With the addition of these latter twelve items and the possible deletion of the six listed above, we are left with a reconstructed text of 122 items.

The writing in Sshj is highly narrativized. No single sectarian affiliation is evident in its contents.[161] The organization of material shows more than a hint of some redactor's topical classification, but on the other hand, these "topics" are not firm, and are often hard to

153. Wang Guoliang 1978, 25, also cites FYZL 42, but I have yet to locate this item there.

154. Wang Guoliang 1978, 26, mistakenly writes that this item is found in Ssj 10.

155. Wang Guoliang 1978, 26, erroneously lists this as TPGJ 322.

156. The collectanea here cite as separate items (or else cite only partially) what now appears as a single Ssj item about Wu Meng.

157. Wang Guoliang erroneously indicates that this item is found in Ssj 18.

158. Both TPGJ quotations give the protagonist's name as Xu Zu 祖.

159. Also cited from XuSsj in *Suishi guangji* 歲時廣記.

160. Cited from *Soushenlu*, another early title of the Sshj.

161. DeWoskin's statement (1974, 169) that "the [Sshj] was apparently compiled by a Buddhist writer after the middle of the Six Dynasties . . . . The 2nd, 3rd, 4th, 5th, and 6th chapters are heavily Buddhistic, relating

discern; some items seem out of place in this scheme, and there are no topic headings nor any signs that the text once had them.

Sshj contents, by *juan*

1. Springs and caves (including several stories exhibiting "discovery of hidden world" motif, of which the "peach blossom spring" story is the most famous [= 1.5])

2. Tales involving masters of esoteric skills (Daoist transcendents, *fangshi*, and Buddhist monks)

3. Mixed: lucky omens telling of prosperity; parasites and their expulsion; bad omens (including cases in which people see the ghost of a family member before news of his/her death arrives)

4. Resuscitation after death (except last item)

5. People's interactions with local or minor deities, some involving "summons" to other world

6. Encounters with ghosts: (a) sexual; (b) involving integrity of the deceased's grave; (c) miscellaneous

7. Encounters with demons

8. Encounters with demons (including some with omen-like signification)

9. Encounters with demons; tales of reciprocity (both positive and negative) involving animals

10. Tales involving dragons, krakens, and large snakes

Youminglu 幽明錄 *Records of the Hidden and the Visible Worlds* by Liu Yiqing 劉義慶 (403–444) (Yml)

Alternate titles: *Youminglu* 幽冥錄, *Youmingji* 幽冥記.[162] Listed at varying lengths in the official Sui and Tang bibliographic cata-

---

exclusively the exploits of early Buddhist heroes . . ." is groundless. But he merely echoes the many Chinese authors who, apparently ignorant of Buddhism, have asserted the "heavily Buddhistic" nature of this text.

162. On the source (in the *Yijing Xici shangzhuan*, 4th sec.) and meaning of Liu's title—which, as its *Xici* context makes very clear, refers to the other- and this-worldly, yin- and yang-realm division among beings—and its variant renditions in later citations, Li Jianguo 1984, 357; Wang Guoliang 1988, 160; and Chapter Seven below.

logues and still extant in the early Sung, the text was lost by the Northern Sung. Expanding upon a Qing recompilation of 158 items, the LX recompilation—the most complete—contains 265 items; Wang Guoliang has suggested corrections to this list that would result in a total of 259 items.[163]

Liu Yiqing, nephew of the military founder of the Song, inheritor of the princedom of Linchuan, and holder of a succession of important regional offices, is perhaps better known as the author of the Ssxy, although the attribution has with good reason been questioned since that book seems to urge the philosophy of "naturalness" over that of "conformity." Liu's SS biography states that he was somewhat wanting in literary talent and summoned to his service men more eloquent than he; Lu Xun proposed long ago that the Ssxy was authored by some of these officials. Kawakatsu Yoshio elaborates on this suggestion in a persuasive argument that the Ssxy was written by this disaffected group, which prominently included He Changyu (who was later banished by the Liu regime to Guangzhou for his mocking verses); these officials, chafing under the new, militaristic Song regime, wrote it as a subtle satire on ignorant strongmen in positions of power, and as a nostalgic lament for the days when the wit and detachment of naturalism counted for something.[164] This theory is quite plausible, although it fails to explain why Liu Yiqing allowed the book to circulate under his name.

However, the Yml would have required some talent to write, and yet it does not advocate the "naturalist" position—quite the opposite, in fact, as we will see in Chapter Seven. And Liu's official biography, as well as the BZL, point out that late in life he displayed conspicuous Buddhist piety.[165] It seems likely that he did in fact author the Yml and Xuanyj himself; these are written in noticeably less elegant prose than that of the Ssxy. He is also said to have authored two collections of biographies of notable worthies, now lost, and a collection of Buddhist miracle tales (see below).

---

163. Wang Guoliang 1988, 158–60. The corrections are of three kinds: (1) elimination of items duplicated because of variations in protagonists' names in different sources (items 4+5, 199+200); (2) elimination or questioning of items probably misattributed to the Yml either by Lu Xun or by his sources (items 32, 63, 64, 217, 257, 258); (3) addition of 2 items (quoted in LeiS 11) missed by LX.

164. Lu Xun 1973, 47; Kawakatsu 1970, 1974; Mather 1976, xvii–xviii. On the Ssxy's naturalist perspective, cf. Spiro 1990, 112–19, who concurs with the revisionist argument regarding authorship.

165. SS 51, NS 13; BZL 3 (504b).

In writing the Yml, Liu, like all authors in the genre, drew liberally on earlier anomaly accounts, although only about thirty-five of the items that have come down to us have so far been traced to other collections.[166] A high proportion of the extant items concerns ghosts, the afterlife, demons, "responsive manifestations" to prayer and recitation, and karmic retribution.

Xuanyanji 宣驗記 *Records in Proclamation of Manifestations* by Liu Yiqing (see above) (Xuanyj)

Alternate title: *Mingyanji* 冥驗記. Listed in the SuiS and other early catalogues as containing thirteen fascicles, the text now survives in thirty-five items recompiled from collectanea in LX, one of which may be misattributed; but at least thirteen other items contained in the extant XiGsy (a text unavailable to Lu Xun) are attributed there to the Xuanyj.[167]

One of the earliest collections of Buddhist miracle tales—the second or third oldest of which we have any record (it is unclear whether it is earlier than the XuGsy)—the Xuanyj was drawn on by later compilers of Buddhist miracle tales, hagiographies, encyclopedias, and polemical treatises.[168]

Xu Guangshiyin yingyanji 續光世音應驗記 *Continued Records of Avalokiteśvara's Responsive Manifestations* by Zhang Yan 張演 (fl. early 5th c. C.E.)[169] (XuGsy)

This is the second text contained in the Kamakura manuscript mentioned above in the discussion of Gsy; it has been published with annotations by Makita Tairyō. It must have been written in the second or third decade of the fifth century. The manuscript text

---

166. Wang Guoliang 1988, 170–71, gives a list; a more complete one will be provided in the index I am preparing.

167. Wang Guoliang 1984, 325–26. It should be noted that Li Jianguo 1984 is much less helpful on both Buddhist and Daoist texts.

168. For a tr. of item 3, Campany 1993b, 242–43; of item 8, Campany 1993b, 241; of item 18, Gjertson 1981, 297, and Gjertson 1989, 20–21; of item 24, Campany 1991b, 51–52.

169. His name is sometimes misprinted as Zhang Yin 寅 (as at Gsz 411a). He is known to have died young and to have preceded his father, Zhang Mao 張茂 (d. 442), in death; the latest mention of him in extant texts

contains ten tales of "responsive manifestations" (*yingyan*) by the Bodhisattva Guanshiyin[170] to pious persons in distress, plus a short preface.[171] Zhang Yan is known from other sources to have been a Buddhist layman. The XuGsy is not listed in official bibliographic catalogues and probably had only very limited circulation.

Yiyuan 異苑 *A Garden of Marvels* by Liu Jingshu 劉敬叔 (fl. early 5th c. C.E.) (Yy)

Extant in a ten-*juan* version comprising 382 items. All complete editions of this version[172] stem from the MCHH edition, which, according to the editor Hu Zhenheng 胡震亨, was based on a copy "on Sung paper" discovered by him and two other scholars in 1588 or 1589. Six Dynasties, Sui, and early Tang texts all cite it as having ten fascicles, and attribute it to Liu Jingshu, and it is so listed in the SuiS catalogue. Some scholars think that the extant version is a Ming recompilation, others that it may be descended from a continuous—but narrow—transmission of the original (or at least a very early) text, albeit with the sorts of textual corruptions ubiquitous among anomaly accounts (and indeed all texts dating from the Six Dynasties period) and even though it does not appear in the JTS and later official catalogues.[173] Comparisons between this re-

---

puts him still alive in the year 428 (cf. the parting scene in the hagiography of the wonder-working monk Bei Du 杯度 [Gsz 10 (392a)] with the mention in the hagiography of the monk Shi Fayi 釋法意 that Zhang Yan was present at this scene [Gsz 13 (411a)]). The discussion of these passages in Makita 1970, 83, contains a typographic error at a key point in the citation.

170. The text's rendering of the Bodhisattva's name as *Guang* 光 shiyin reflects an early transliteration usage later abandoned in favor of the now familiar *Guan* 觀 shiyin.

171. For a tr. of the preface, Campany 1993b, 266–67; for a summary of item 7, Campany 1993b, 252; for a tr. of item 8, Gjertson 1989, 19–20.

172. That is, excluding editions containing only a fraction of the material in the ten-*juan* version. Complete eds. besides the MCHH include JDMS, XJTY (which adds a *mulu* of item titles at the front), SKQS, and SK. This last ed. is apparently based on the XJTY ed. but adds punctuation and deletes the front list of item titles; it contains identical numbers, sequencing, and fascicle division of items, except that it elides 2.32 and 2.33 of the XJTY ed. to form (erroneously) a single item.

173. Even the scrupulous SKQS editors doubted that the text was recompiled by late redactors; most recently, Li Jianguo 1984, 372–73, reaffirms that its "transmission was never broken, although its circulation was extremely small so that it was rarely seen by people in successive

ceived text and its citations in collectanea reveal, not surprisingly, some discrepancies in wording between matching items, at least five items quoted in collectanea but missing from the received version, and many items in the received version that are unattested earlier.[174]

There is no official biography of Liu Jingshu; Hu Zhenheng attached a biographical sketch to his edition of the Yy, but the sources for some of his information are unclear. What information we do have indicates that Liu served under both the Jin and the Song, that (judging from the offices he held) he was a relatively young man during the Jin *yixi* 義熙 era (405–419), and that he may have lived to see the beginning of the Song *taishi* 泰始 era (465).[175] He is also twice mentioned in another collection of anomaly accounts, the Mxj, as a personal witness to events and texts told of there.[176]

The title of the work probably alludes to that of a Han collection of anecdotes by Liu Xiang—the *Shuoyuan* 説苑. Just as Liu Xiang's is a collection of *shuo* or items of discourse, Liu Jingshu's is a collection of *yi* or anomalous phenomena. The contents are remarkably well organized by topic.

Yy Contents by *Juan*

1 (25 items) Anomalous places; "responses" at particular places (especially mountains, rivers, and wells)

2 (37 items) Explanations by *fangshi* of "responses." Anomalous plants. Cases of found valuables transforming into worthless stuff

3 (57 items) Anomalies involving animals, especially:
items 1–12: birds
items 13–17: tigers
items 33–47: dragons and snakes
items 48–52: turtles and fish
items 53–57: shellfish and insects

4 (65 items) Omens, portents, and prognostications

---

generations." Wang Guoliang 1988, 322, however, considers it a Ming recompilation and, given its clear topical organization, I am inclined to agree.

174. For a partial listing and discussion, Morino 1961.

175. Li Jianguo 1984, 374–75.

176. Mxj 20, 56.

5 (38 items) Legends behind the founding of temples, efficacy of offerings to local gods (items 1–19). Encounters between ordinary people and adepts of several sorts (items 20–38)

6 (41 items) Encounters with ghosts

7 (33 items) Dreams: as messages from the dead concerning their graves (items 1–14); as prophetic (items 15, 18–33); as messages from local gods (items 16–17)

8 (46 items) Anomalies involving the taxonomic boundary between humans and animals: demonic transformations of animal spirits into human form (items 1-22); monstrous births (items 26–34); wild men (items 35–36); humans transformed into animals (37–42); warnings against eating meat (items 44–46)

9 (20 items) Divinations and other feats by *fangshi*

10 (21 items) Miscellaneous, including themes of filiality (items 4, 5, 14, 15), automatic, inexorable cosmic reward for virtue and punishment for vice (items 6, 8, 12), and fate (items 2, 21)

Qi Xie ji 齊諧記 *Qi Xie's Records* by Dongyang Wuyi 東陽无疑 (fl. early Song) (Qxj)

This work is listed in the SuiS catalogue as containing seven fascicles. It was lost at some point after the compilation of the TPYL and TPGJ; fifteen items are recompiled in LX from these and from Tang collectanea. One or more of these may originally have belonged to the XuQxj and may have been misattributed to the Qxj due to the similarity of titles. The author's name appears in no official biographies; only thanks to the bibliographic listing do we know that he held the office of *sanji shilang* or Gentleman Cavalier Attendant[177] under the Song. He is probably the character who appears in Mxj 85[178] as the recipient of the (oral?) transmission of the tale in question; this item is set in *yuanjia* 9 (432–433 C.E.). The Dongyang clan originated in Dongyang commandery (in today's

---

177. Hucker 1985, 396.
178. LX 507, drawn from FYZL 62 (760c); both render the name as Dongyang Wu 無 yi.

Zhejiang), and the Qxj often mentions this locale, so it is likely that the author hailed from this area.[179]

Ganyingzhuan 感應傳 *Records of [Divine] Responses to Stimuli* by Wang Yanxiu 王延秀 (fl. mid–5th c. c.e.) (Ganyz)

This collection of Buddhist miracle tales, drawn upon by Huijiao as a source for material for his *Lives of Eminent Monks* (Gsz),[180] is listed in the SuiS, JTS and XTS bibliographies as containing eight fascicles and as authored by Wang Yanxiu, about whom we know only that he participated in an "abstruse learning" (*xuanxue* 玄學) study group in 436 and served the Song as a ritual specialist from 465 to 471.[181] It is now lost. Two brief quotations have been found in collectanea.[182]

Jiyiji 集異記 *Collected Records of Anomalies* by Guo Jichan 郭季產 (fl. during Song) (Jyj)

Alternate title (as cited in TPGJ 276): *Jiyizhuan* 傳. Not recorded in official catalogues, this work is cited in the BTSC, YWLJ, TPGJ, and TPYL, sometimes with the author's name given. There is no official biography of Guo Jichan, but from a bibliographic listing of another of his writings we know that he served under the Song. The work is lost; eleven items are recompiled from collectanea in LX. A story about a prophetic dream (the protagonist is Zhang Tianxi 張天錫) in TPGJ 276, cited as 出李產集異傳, was probably drawn as well from the Jyj by the TPGJ compilers but missed by Lu Xun because of the erroneous citation.[183] Two other TPGJ quotations should probably be ascribed to this text as well.[184]

---

179. Li Jianguo 1984, 388.
180. Gsz 14.418c.
181. SS 66.1734; Wright 1954, 419; Gjertson 1989, 22.
182. Item 1: BZL 7 (537b, third line from end) = TPGJ 111.9; item 2: BZL 7 (537c, line 2) = TPGJ 114.8, tr. Gjertson 1989, 23. Wang Guoliang 1984, 339, doubts that these passages stem from a text by Wang Yanxiu since they both concern events in the Southern Qi dynasty. Gjertson notes that the author is misidentified elsewhere in the SuiS treatise as a Jin official.
183. Following the suggestion of Li Jianguo 1984, 387.
184. Li Jianguo 1984, 387, suggests that the TPGJ 438 story of Zhu Xiuzhi 朱休之 (which also appears as Shuyj 48 [LX 180] and so was either

Guyizhuan 古異傳 *Accounts of Ancient Anomalies* by Yuan Wangshou 袁王壽 (fl. Song) (Gyz)

This text, listed in the SuiS, JTS, XTS, and TZ bibliographic catalogues as extant in three fascicles, is now lost except for one item concerning the Duke of Thunder (Leigong 雷公) recovered from collectanea and printed in LX. Very little is known about the author.[185]

Mingxiangji 冥祥記 *Signs from the Unseen Realm* by Wang Yan 王琰 (b. ca. 454 C.E., fl. late 5th– early 6th centuries) (Mxj)

131 items plus the author's preface have been recompiled from collectanea in LX. The Mxj is listed in official catalogues as having contained ten fascicles; it must have been the largest and (in terms of the types of tales it incorporates) most wide-ranging pre-Tang text devoted exclusively to Buddhist tales of miracles.

　　Much of what we know of Wang Yan stems from his preface to the Mxj.[186] He served under both the Qi and Liang dynasties; part of his youth was spent in northern Vietnam (an area probably more intensely Buddhist than much of China at that time); and he was motivated to write the Mxj by two anomalous events that touched him personally.[187] When he wrote it is unclear, but the extant items contain dates as late as 485,[188] and the text must have been in circulation by 501, since Lu Gao mentions it in the preface to his XiGsy (see below).

　　Wang Yan drew on the Xuanyj for some of his material;[189] the

---

authorially cross-copied or editorially misattributed) and the TPGJ 442 story of Zhang Hua 張華 (which also appears in Ssj 18.9 and XuQxj 5) should be included in the Jyj recompilation. Lu Xun probably withheld these because of a suspicion that they were quoted by the TPGJ eds. from the Tang-period work of the same title by Xue Yongruo 薛用弱.

　　185. Wang Guoliang 1984, 326.

　　186. We also know from the SuiS bibliographic catalogue that he wrote a twenty-*juan* annalistic history of the Song.

　　187. For brief comments on and a partial tr. of his preface, Campany 1993b, 265–66.

　　188. Mxj 124 (LX 532) = FYZL 91.958b–c.

　　189. At this writing, I have found at least 7 matches between Xuanyj and Mxj items. On the sources of the Mxj, Shinohara 1969.

Mxj was heavily drawn on in turn by Lu Gao in his XiGsy and by Huijiao in his Gsz.[190]

Shuyiji 述異記 *Accounts of Strange Things* by Zu Chongzhi 祖沖之 (429–500 C.E.) (Shuyj)

Listed in the SuiS, JTS, and XTS catalogues as containing ten fascicles and as authored by Zu Chongzhi, the text was lost after the compilation of the TPGJ but is fairly well represented in collectanea; LX contains 90 recompiled items. Seven of these also appear in Ren Fang's text by the same title (see below) and so were probably misattributed to Zu Chongzhi's work; of the first four of these items LX notes that this is the case, while of the last three he does not:

Overlapping items in Shuyj and ShuyjRf

Identifier	Shuyj location	ShuyjRf location
夢口穴	6 (139)	1.60 (10b)[191]
朱休之	48 (152)	2.126 (16b)
荀瓖	73 (160-61)	1.78 (13b)
吳龕	86 (164)	2.149 (20a)[192]
歷陽湖	10 (140)	1.75 (13a)
園客	12 (141)	1.72 (12b)[193]
封邵化虎	13 (141)[194]	1.34 (6b)

Zu Chongzhi, a polymath who extensively commented on the classics both Daoist and Confucian and invented the compass, has official biographies in NQS 52 and NS 72. His Shuyj, considering the era in which it was written, contains surprisingly few items on explicitly Daoist or Buddhist themes; instead, Zu seems to have

---

190. As of this writing, I have found at least 32 passages in the Gsz and 16 items in the XiGsy that correspond to extant Mxj items. A complete list will be published in the index currently being prepared.

191. As Lu Xun notes, the ShuyjRf version (which is translated and discussed in Chapter Five) is significantly truncated when compared to its analogue in Shuyj.

192. Cf. Yml 167 (286).

193. Cf. Ssj 1.27.

194. Tr. in Kao, ed., 1985, 156, but without reference to its ShuyjRf analogue.

been particularly interested in portents and transformations. An unusually large percentage of the Shuyj's items are unattested elsewhere, suggesting that, as regards his sources of material, Zu did not rely as heavily as some other authors on previous anomaly collections.

Shuyiji 述異記 *Accounts of Strange Things* by Ren Fang 任昉 (460–508) (ShuyjRf)

Alternate title: *Xin* 新 *Shuyiji*. 283 items in twelve fascicles. The most complete version of the text, available in several editions (ZDHW and its earlier versions, LWMS, BZQS, SK), is traceable to a Sung version in two fascicles; aside from some partial, earlier versions (such as LeiS, SF, WCXS), there is another relatively complete version (in the BH ed.) that differs but slightly from the more common version.[195] The text begins to be listed in catalogues only in the late Tang, and Ren Fang's official biographies in LS 14 and NS 59 do not mention it. Based on these facts, as well as on a glaring anachronism in the received version and the large extent to which the text draws on earlier anomaly accounts, the SKTY editors argued that it was a Tang forgery. Li Jianguo has addressed each of these points: (1) It is not uncommon for minor works to go unlisted in biographies (and Ren Fang was a major literary figure in his day),[196] and the ShuyjRf could well have been included in the large "assorted accounts" (雜傳) mentioned in his biography and in catalogues; it could then have begun to circulate independently during the Sung, accounting for its listings in that period. Early quotations in collectanea also show an awareness by compilers that there were two texts with the same title, one by Ren Fang and one by Zu Chongzhi. (2) There are in fact several anachronisms in the ShuyjRf, not just the one noticed by the SKTY editors (most involve place names), but this does not prove that the text as a whole originated late, only that Sui-Tang editors or copyists took the liberty of changing details in the text to accord with contemporary nomenclature. (3) Many anomaly accounts draw heavily on earlier texts; this is no proof that they were forged.[197]

---

195. For a list of the variations, Li Jianguo 1984, 400.
196. IC, 459–60.
197. For details, Li Jianguo 1984, 396–400.

Morino Shigeo, however, argues that, while the text was indeed a Tang forgery (in the sense that Ren Fang wrote no text by this title in two fascicles), it was assembled by a Tang redactor from another text by Ren Fang that is now lost: his *Diji* 地記, originally a massive work in 252 fascicles. This theory would also explain the large number of borrowings from earlier texts in the ShuyjRf, since Ren Fang's *Diji* was said to be a collection of data from all geographic and topographic books (including a high proportion of anomalous flora and fauna) since the Shj.[198] The ShuyjRf incorporates material from the Shj, Bwz, Ssj, Yy, Shenyjing, Yml, Xuanzj, and Shuyj, as well as from texts outside the genre such as Wang Chong's *Lunheng* and Chang Qu's *Huayang guozhi*.[199]

The text shows signs of a vaguely topical arrangement by some redactor. It also shows the author's special interest in the survival into his own time of various "traces"—not only textual but also archaeological and folkloric—from archaic events and figures, and is in this respect similar to the Fsty.

Xi Guanshiyin yingyanji 繫觀世音應驗記 *More Records of Avalokiteśvara's Responsive Manifestations* by Lu Gao 陸杲 (459–532 C.E.) (XiGsy)

This is the third of the works included in the Kamakura-era manuscript mentioned above and published in Makita 1970. Lu Gao attached his own contributions to the two previous works, to make an omnibus collection of tales involving efficacious responses to devotion by the Bodhisattva Guanshiyin. It was completed in 501 and contains sixty-nine items and a preface.[200] It is listed in both official Tang catalogues as containing one fascicle.

According to his biography in LS 26 and NS 48, Lu Gao also wrote a thirty-fascicle *Lives of Śramaṇas* (*Shamenzhuan* 沙門傳).

---

198. Thus, the fact that the ShuyjRf as we have it borrows material from many earlier works does not indicate that Tang editors pieced together a text of their own (from widely scattered and unrelated passages in other works) and ascribed it to Ren Fang, but rather that they assembled a set of excerpts dealing exclusively with anomalies from a version of Ren Fang's much larger *Diji* (Morino 1960).

199. Wang Guoliang 1984, 313.

200. For a partial tr. of the preface, Campany 1993b, 267.

Zhang Yan, compiler of the XuGsy, was the first cousin of Lu Gao's maternal grandfather, and Wang Yan was an old acquaintance.[201]

The XiGsy is unique among early miracle tales (but similar to the Gsz) in dividing its material according to categories. These eleven rubrics are drawn from two sūtra translations, Kumārajīva's translation of the *Lotus* (T 262, in particular the chapter "Universal Gateway [to Salvation] of the Bodhisattva Guanshiyin," known as *Pumenpin* 普門品 for short) and Nandi's translation of the *Sūtra of Dhāranī Incantations for Imploring the Bodhisattva Guanshiyin to Dissolve and Subdue Maleficent Phenomena* (T 1043).[202] By the very organization of the text we are thus given to understand that the tales collected under each rubric are "manifestations" or "confirmations" (*yan* 驗)—testimonies almost in a legal sense—to the fulfillment on Chinese soil of the sūtras' promises.

Rubrics in the XiGsy

Items	Rubric	Source[203]
1–3	普門品云設入大火火不能燒	56c
4–9	普門品云大水所漂	56c
10	普門品　羅刹之難	56a
11–18	普門品　臨當被害	56c
19–40	普門品云檢繫其身	56c
41–54	普門品云滿中怨賊	56c
55	普門品云設欲求男	57a
56–60	請觀世音經云示其道徑	36a*
61–64	請觀世音　云接還本土	36a
65–67	請觀世音　云遇大惡病	34c
68–69	請觀世音　云惡獸怖畏	35b*

---

201. Gjertson 1989, 27.

202. For general comments on the sources of the rubrics, Campany 1993b, 235 n.6; for specific identifications of passages, I have relied on Makita's annotations.

203. Citations of passages in the *Lotus* (T 262) are to page and register in T vol. 9 (for tr., Hurvitz 1976); of passages in the *Sūtra of Dhāranī Incantations* (T 1043), to page and register in vol. 20. * indicates a slight difference in wording between Lu Gao's phrase and the extant canonical text, probably due simply to the fact that Lu Gao was in these instances paraphrasing.

Xu Qi Xie ji 續齊諧記 More of Qi Xie's Records
by Wu Jun 吳均 (469–520 C.E.) (XuQxj)

Extant in a one-*juan* version, containing seventeen items, that is found in most editions; all but one of these items (item 16 in the ZDHW ed.) are quoted by early Sung or earlier collectanea (or annotations to pre-Tang works) and attributed to the XuQxj. Five additional items, probably once part of the text but not included in this standard version, have been located. Included in most editions, at the end of the text, is a postscript (*ba* 跋) by one Lu You 陸友 of the Yuan era, identifying the source of the titular allusion as the *Zhuangzi* but mistakenly asserting that there was no previous text known as *Qi Xie ji* of which Wu Jun's was the "continuation" (*xu*). The XuQxj is not mentioned in the official biographies of Wu Jun (LS 49/NS 72) but is listed as containing one fascicle in the SuiS, JTS, and XTS catalogues; the latter confuses the author's name with that of a Tang Daoist.

Judging from its quotations in Sung collectanea, a version of the XuQxj containing at least twenty-two items must have been in good circulation during the Southern Sung; whether this text represented a manuscript surviving from Tang (or earlier) times, or was a recompilation by Sung scholars from collectanea, is now impossible to tell, although, as noted above, one item in the received version is not to be found attributed to the XuQxj in early collectanea. In the Yuan, Lu You published an edition, probably based on a Sung copy, that omitted some items extant elsewhere. In the Ming *jiajing* period (1522–1567), Gu Yuanqing put this edition back into circulation in his GSWF; all subsequent editions have either been based directly on the GSWF (GJYS, SF, *Guang* HWCS, others) or on one of these latter (MS21Z and SKQS from GJYS, ZDHW from *Guang* HWCS, WCXS and HKSZ from SF).[204]

The five items which are not included in the standard version are as follows.[205]

---

204. Based largely on Wang Guoliang 1988, 174ff.

205. For complete details on locations in collectanea of these as well as the standard 17 items, including some locations omitted here and recensions of the texts of the five "missing" items, see Wang Guoliang 1988, 177–204. It should be noted, however, that each of these is attributed in some collectanea to other anomaly accounts (and most to more than one); the first item listed, for example, is variously ascribed to Sxz, Ssj, Yml, and Qxj as well as to XuQxj. The ascription of them to the XuQxj is, in other words, hypothetical even if well founded.

Additional XuQxj items

Item no.	Identifier	Places where item is quoted[206]
18	天台遇仙	MQ 中, MQJZ 下, TPYL 862, LeiS 6, GZJ 10
19	王敬伯	ZYJ 12; TPYL 579, 757, 761; SLF 11
20	五色石	TPYL 703, YLDD 2256
21	伍子胥	TPGJ 291[207]
22	萬文娘	CGL 14

Wu Jun, well known in his day as a literary figure and historian, drew liberally and self-consciously on earlier anomaly accounts for material.[208] But the text also shows a high degree of awareness of popular lore and custom. Stylistically, it is one of the most sophisticated and highly developed works of the genre before the Tang.[209]

Shenlu 神録 *A Record of Spirit-Matters* by Liu Zhilin 劉之遴 (477–548 C.E.) (Sl)

Alternate title: *Shenyilu* 神異錄. The Sl is listed in Tang and Sung official as well as private catalogues as containing five fascicles. Three items are collected in LX from commentaries and collectanea, but the attribution of some of these to the Sl is problematic; on the other hand, two other quotations have been located that can reasonably be attributed to the Sl but are not included in the LX recension.[210]

---

206. These are listed in chronological order and represent only a selection of the most accessible locations; for additional ones, Wang Guoliang 1988, 181–82.

207. Wang Guoliang 1988, 183, notes that this item can be found attributed to the XuQxj only in a text titled 五百家音註韓昌黎先生文集, but I have no further information on this text. It is attributed to the Lyz in SLF 6 and to a *Luyiji* 錄異記—presumably the text of this title by Du Guangting (?)—in TZJ 9. The TPGJ gives no attribution. The tale appears in Du Guangting's *Luyiji* (HY 591) 7.1b.

208. Li Jianguo 1984, 407.

209. Translations: XuQxj 17 (8b–9b) in Kao, ed., 1985, 159–61; XuQxj 8 (4b–6a) in Kao, ed., 1985, 161–63; XuQxj 16 (8a–b) in Campany 1991a, 27.

210. Wang Guoliang 1984, 329; cf. Li Jianguo 1984, 424. One of the additional items ascribed to the Sl concerns a Daoist transcendent and is found in TPHY 101; the other concerns a Putiwang Temple 菩提王廟 and is cited in *Liuchao shiji leibian* 六朝事跡類編 *juanxia* 卷下 and in *Quan Sui wen* 全隋文 11 (攝山棲霞寺碑 by Jiang Zong 江總).

Liu Zhilin is given a biography in LS 40 and NS 50. He served under both the Qi and the Liang dynasties and left fifty fascicles of writings at his death.

Xiaoshuo 小説 *Lesser Sayings* by Yin Yun 殷芸 (471-529 C.E.) (Xs)

Listed in the SuiS catalogue as consisting of ten fascicles (and there is some indication that it may originally have been larger), the work now survives only in quotations in collectanea, the vast majority of which are in the XTZ and TPGJ, with three in the TPYL. The first edition of SF contained a recompilation of the text, upon which LX draws liberally in its collection of 135 items. The citations in TPGJ are particularly confused, due partly to frequent variations in the name of the attributed author (despite Yin Yun's relative fame as a Liang writer) and partly to the generic nature of the title.[211] Modern scholars seem reluctant even to discuss the work, presumably because of the messiness of its textual history and the consequent risk of erroneous characterization.[212] The work was frankly derivative; it was itself a kind of *congshu*, not intended as an original work but as a digest of other works.

Jinlouzi zhiguaipian 金樓子志怪篇 *The Golden Tower Master*, chapter "Accounts of Anomalies" by Xiao Yi 蕭繹 (Liang Yuan Di 梁元帝) (508–554 C.E.; r. 552–554) (Jlz)

The *Jinlouzi* as a whole originally contained ten fascicles, of which six survive; they contain fourteen topical sections (*pian*), one of which is devoted exclusively to anomaly accounts. It contains sixty[213] brief items plus a preface. Most of the items concern anomalous

---

211. See the note attached to the first Xs entry in the HY Index to the TPGJ (p. 3 of the index to cited works).

212. One of the few modern discussions is in Lin Chen 1960, 391–92. To my knowledge, neither Wang Guoliang 1984 nor Li Jianguo 1984 discusses the Xs in any detail. On Yin Yun see also IC, 936. Yu Jiaxi's recompilation of the Xs, which I have not seen at this writing, is said to contain two items not in the LX compilation and to be better annotated.

213. Li Jianguo 1984, 425, says that the text contains 54 items; this difference may be due to variations in editions or to different breaks between textual items.

transformations of plants and animals, and most are drawn from earlier accounts. As explained in the preface, the text was written to argue the reality of anomalies independent of human perception of them as such.

Jingyiji 旌異記 *Citations of Marvels* by Hou Bo 侯白 (fl. during Sui) (Jingyj)

Alternate title: *Jingyizhuan* 傳.[214] Listed in various numbers of fascicles in catalogues compiled during the Tang and Southern Sung, the text was lost during the Northern Sung. LX has a recension of ten items; Wang Guoliang has located two additional items not included in LX.[215] There is another version of the text, but much of it duplicates material in Hong Mai's *Yijianzhi* 夷堅志 and seems to have been falsely attributed to Hou Bo.[216]

The extant items are all pro-Buddhist miracle tales, and it is likely that the entire text was made up of such material. Hou Bo was appointed by the Sui Emperor Wen to a post as compiler of history in the imperial archives; he has an official biography in SuiS 58 and BS 83.[217]

Yuanhunzhi 冤魂志 *A Treatise on Cloud-Souls with Grievances* by Yan Zhitui 顏之推 (531–591 C.E.) (Yhz)

Alternate titles: *Bei Qi Huanyuanzhi* 北齊還冤志; *Huanyuanzhi*; *Huanyuanji* 記. Listed in early catalogues as consisting of three fascicles, the work, lost after the Ming, now exists in a reconstructed

---

214. There may have been others: Li Jianguo 1984, 434.

215. Wang Guoliang 1984, 331. One (involving Shi Daolin 釋道琳) is found among the eight items quoted from this text in the section *Lidai zhongjing yinggan xingjinglu* 歷代眾經應感興敬錄 in *Da Tang neidianlu* 大唐內典錄 10; the other (involving the opening by bandits of the tomb of Bo Mao 白茅) is quoted in Duan Chengshi's *Youyang zazu* (前集 13). A tr. of Jingyj item 8 is in Campany 1993b, 249–50; other items are discussed in that article as well as in Campany 1991b; item 3 is tr. in Gjertson 1989, 29–30. For further discussion of the ten-item text, Uchiyama 1979, 52–54.

216. Wang Guoliang 1984, 331; Li Jianguo 1984, 435. On Hong Mai and his work, in addition to the article (and the works cited there) in IC 457–58, Wang Hsiu-huei 1989.

217. He also collected witty sayings from old texts and from his own experience into a text called *Qiyanlu* 啟顏錄, of which some 66 quotations survive in collectanea (Uchiyama 1979, 55).

one-*juan* version published in several editions. This version consists of sixty-two items.[218] Fifteen of these have analogues in a manuscript found at Dunhuang, dated to 882 C.E.;[219] the sequence of items in this manuscript differs from that in the received version. There is a complete translation based on a critical comparison of multiple editions as well as the Dunhuang text.[220]

Perhaps better known for his *Family Instructions* (*Yanshi jiaxun* 顏氏家訓), Yan Zhitui wrote an additional collection of anomaly accounts (see below), a lexicon, and other works. He is given a biography in BQS 45 and BS 83. The Yhz, as its name implies, consists entirely of narratives of cases in which the wrongfully dead appeal to Heaven or the Celestial Thearch 天帝,[221] triggering a cosmic punishment of the perpetrator. The sources of these cases range from ancient writings to apparently oral transmission to the author himself.[222]

Jilingji 集靈記 *Collected Records of Numinous Phenomena* by Yan Zhitui (Jlj)

One item that is relatively certain to have been part of the original Jlj survives, quoted in TPYL 718 and anthologized in LX. There is another, six-item version of the Jlj (GJSB ed.), but aside from the same TPYL quotation incorporated in LX, the other items in this version are misattributed to the Jlj.[223] The text is listed in the SuiS bibliography as containing twenty fascicles, in the JTS and XTS bibliographies as containing ten fascicles; it was lost during the Sung.

---

218. Wang Guoliang 1984, 330, points out that the text of this version corresponds badly with the citations of the work in FYZL and TPGJ, upon which the recompilation was based, and that a new recension is needed. Dien 1968, 218–19, gives the locations of these citations. Kominami 1983, 4–5, points out that the sequence of the first 37 items of the received text corresponds exactly with the order in which these passages are quoted in the FYZL. He also mentions two other, seldom seen versions of the Yhz, both of doubtful tradition. For general discussion of Yhz, Li Jianguo 1984, 442ff.; Uchiyama 1979, 47.
219. Bibliotèque Nationale, Paris, NS #3126.
220. Cohen 1982.
221. Interestingly, the Dunhuang manuscript seems unique in referring to the cosmic appellate specifically as 天帝.
222. For listings of sources, Cohen 1982, 113–16.
223. Wang Guoliang 1984, 330. Li Jianguo 1984, 449, makes no mention of this version.

Guishenlu 鬼神錄 *Records of Ghosts and Spirits*
by Shi Yancong 釋顏琮 (557–610 C.E.) (Gsl)

This work is not listed in bibliographic catalogues, but the author's hagiography in *Xu Gaosengzhuan* 2 mentions that he wrote a work of this title. (Yancong is better known as the compiler of the polemical work BZL, itself a major source of quotations from Six Dynasties anomaly accounts.) Nine quotations appear in the TPGJ from a work of this title or the perhaps merely variant *Shenguilu*; another item appears in a commentary to the *Wenxuan* (*juan* 15).[224]

Dongxianzhuan 洞仙傳 *Lives of Cave-Transcendents.*
Author unknown. (Dxz)

Seventy-seven Daoist hagiographies are contained in the YJQQ edition of this work.[225] It is listed in the SuiS catalogue as comprising ten fascicles; no author's name is given. Only beginning with the listings in the JTS, XTS, and later bibliographies is one Jiansuzi 見素子 ("Master Who Realizes Simplicity") credited with its authorship. In the late Tang, there was a female Daoist adept who went by the same style, but in light of the SuiS listing and the fact that the figures populating the text are all pre-Tang, scholars such as Chen Guofu, Yan Yiping, Li Jianguo, and Li Fengmao have agreed that the text must have been written between the Liang and the Chen dynasties and that, if its real author was in fact styled Jiansuzi, this was not the late Tang woman who went by the same sobriquet.[226]

This collection of hagiographies draws rather heavily on Tao Hongjing's 陶弘景 sixth-century compilations of Shangqing materials revealed to Yang Xi in the mid-fourth century—particularly on his *Zhen'gao* and *Weiyetu* 位業圖:[227] twenty-six of its seventy-seven

---

224. Li Jianguo 1984, 437; whether any of these items is from Yancong's text remains to be seen.
225. YJQQ 110.1a–20a, 111.1a–11a. Yan Yiping 1976, v.1, reprints the YJQQ items with annotations indicating variata from the parallel versions of hagiographies that appear in other extant texts.
226. Chen Guofu 1963, 239–40; Yan Yiping 1976, v.1, preface to Dxz, 1–2; Li Jianguo 1984, 462; Li Fengmao 1986, 187–89.
227. The *Zhen'gao* has been mentioned above; the latter text, whose full title is *Dongxuan lingbao zhenling weiyetu* (Tableau of the Ranks and Functions of the Perfected and Other Powers [thus Strickmann 1977, 5

items incorporate material found in one or both of Tao's works. It also draws on the Szj for three of its items, and doubtless preserves hagiographic legends in circulation during the Six Dynasties but now otherwise lost.[228]

Six Dynasties Works of which the Authorship is Highly Uncertain

Since works are often dated by what is known of their authors, in cases where authorship is especially unclear, dating tends to be difficult; internal evidence alone is rarely a sure guide to date of origin. In this section, I list works that fall into this category but that, having survived in more than one or two items, present a significant body of material for study.[229] They are listed in what seems, for many circumstantial reasons, the most probable chronological order.

Xuanzhongji 玄中記 *Records from Within the Obscure Realm* **(Xuanzj).** Attributed to "a man of the Guo clan" 郭氏; some have taken the author to be the *fangshi* and editor/commentator to the Shj, Guo Pu 郭璞 (276–322 C.E.), but without much basis.[230] Sung catalogues list the text at one *juan*; it was subsequently lost and now exists in various versions and editions, the most complete of which is the seventy-one-item LX recension. The extant text is a list of mythological fragments and anomalies of the periphery (distant lands, mountains, and peoples, rare stones, cross-species transformations of fantastically long-lived plants and animals, demonographic entries), and seems to have emanated from *fangshi* circles.

---

n.5], HY 167), charts the organization of the unseen world as implied in the Perfected Ones' piecemeal revelations to Yang Xi 楊羲. Since this text is a list of names and titles, Dxz textual "overlaps" with it are slight, though correspondences with Yang Xi's scriptures remain to be fully explored.

228. Li Fengmao 1986, 203–4 (regarding borrowings from Szj), 219–24 (a chart that includes listings of overlaps with Tao Hongjing's works), 189–202 (an interpretive discussion of the latter).

229. Not listed here is the Hwgs, which, although of unknown authorship, is, I think, fairly certain to have been written in the third century and was therefore listed above.

230. A few of its items are close if not identical to some of Guo Pu's Shj annotations, a fact which has been taken as lending weight—but, in my view, insufficient weight—to the notion that he authored the Xuanzj as well (Wang Guoliang 1984, 334).

Luyizhuan 錄異傳 *A Record of Anomalies* **(Luyz).** The work is not listed in early catalogues, and citations in collectanea make no attribution of authorship. LX gives a recension of twenty-seven items. Eleven of these duplicate items in other early anomaly accounts, suggesting that the work may itself have been a collectanea-like compendium of items drawn from various earlier texts. One additional item has been located that is omitted from the LX recompilation.[231]

Lingguizhi 靈鬼志 *A Treatise on Spirits and Ghosts* **(Lgz).** Attributed to "a man of the Xun clan" 荀氏, this work appears in Tang and Sung catalogues as consisting of three fascicles but was subsequently lost. There are now two recompilations, one in a supplemented edition of the SF and one in LX; the SF version contains only one item, and it is grossly misattributed. Three of the twenty-four items in LX seem misattributed to the Lgz as well.[232]

Zhiguai 志怪 *Accounts of Anomalies* **(Zgk).** Attributed to "a man of the Kong clan" 孔氏, this text is listed in Tang and Sung catalogues in four fascicles. The LX recension contains ten items, of which at least one is probably misattributed to this text.[233]

Xuyiji 續異記 *Continued Records of Marvels* **(Xuyj).** This work is not listed in bibliographic catalogues, and the eleven quotations from it that have been located in collectanea and recompiled in LX make no attribution of authorship. Its internal dates range from the Han to the Liang; it was probably written in the late Liang or Sui.[234]

Jiuguailu 究怪錄 *A Record of Researches into Anomalies* **(Jgl).** Author unknown; not listed in bibliographic catalogues. But there appear to be a total of ten citations from this work (with some variations in the title) in Tang and Sung collectanea, and

---

231. Wang Guoliang 1984, 336.
232. For details, Wang Guoliang 1984, 332; Li Jianguo 1984, 337.
233. Wang Guoliang 1984, 333; Lin Chen 1960, 396–97. Li Jianguo 1984, 332–33, argues (based largely on a single citation in TPGJ 276) that this "man of the Kong clan" was in fact Kong Yue 約; but no other information on him survives, so the argument is moot when it comes to dating the text. On other grounds, Li reasons that the text is of Eastern Jin date and that it postdates Gan Bao—that is, that it was written between the mid-fourth and the early fifth century.
234. Li Jianguo 1984, 431.

their internal dates suggest the text was probably written in the Sui.[235]

Jishenyiyuan 稽神異苑 *A Garden of Inquests into Spirit-Phenomena and Marvels* **(Jsyy).** First appears in bibliographies in the southern Sung, when it is attributed to Jiao Du 焦度 of the Qi dynasty; later listings do not mention an author's name and the attribution to Jiao Du is probably erroneous. Fourteen quotations have been located in Tang and later collectanea; judging from them, the work was highly derivative, composed perhaps entirely of items drawn from earlier anomaly accounts.[236]

Han Wu bieguo dongmingji 漢武別國洞冥記 *A Record of the Han Emperor Wu's Penetration into the Mysteries of Outlying Realms* **(Dmj).** Alternate titles: *Han Wu dongmingji*; *Dongmingji*. Traditionally attributed to Guo Xian 郭憲, an early Eastern Han *fangshi*, the text was clearly written much later, as it refers to geographic names and textual titles unknown in the Han, and contains apparent allusions to Shangqing scriptural material.[237] It was probably written between the early Liang and the Sui.[238] A version of it was included in the XTZ (1.9b–24a); another, similar (but not identical)[239] one was included in the GSWF collection, and this became the basis of many other Ming and Qing editions (including ZDHW, LWMS). This version divides the text into four fascicles. The Dmj was also included in some early editions of the Daoist canon, and some of its material was incorporated into still-extant Daoist scriptures.[240] There is now a

---

235. Li Jianguo 1984, 452–53.

236. Li Jianguo 1984, 428–29.

237. Smith 1992, 281–82.

238. It is quoted in YWLJ and BTSC, XTZ contains a version of the text, and it is listed at one *juan* in the SuiS bibliographic catalogue (as well as in other early bibliographies, at various lengths—see Smith 1992, 280–81). One theory popular among Qing scholars was that Liang Emperor Yuan wrote it, but the evidence for this is extremely slim (Smith 1992, 287; Li Jianguo 1984, 161). It does, however, seem to be of southern dynasties provenance (Smith 1992, 287). As mentioned above, I believe it to be later than the Syj.

239. The *tongxingben* divide the text into four *juan*, while the XTZ has no such divisions; the XTZ omits two sections of material found in the *tongxingben*, but the latter drop some phrases, as well as including the usual sorts of graphic errors.

240. Liu Ts'un-yan 1975, 115; van der Loon 1984, 61–63, 155; Smith 1992, 291–92.

complete translation based on comparison of all editions and dispersed fragments.[241] The text consists of a report of Daoist knowledge of exotic lands, products, deities, and adepts made available to Emperor Wu of the Han.

Fragmentary Six Dynasties Texts of which the Date is Highly Uncertain

At least seventeen anomaly collections listed in the official catalogues are now completely lost; they are not listed here.[242] The following works, about which we lack sufficient information to date them with much specificity, survive in at least one quotation.

Xiangruiji 祥瑞記 *Record of Auspicious Signs* (Xrj). Listed as consisting of three fascicles in SuiS catalogue, *zazhuan* category, but vanishes from later catalogues. One item is quoted in TPGJ 389.[243]

Guishen liezhuan 鬼神列傳 *Arrayed Accounts of Ghosts and Spirits* (Gslz). The SuiS catalogue, *zazhuan* category, lists it in one *juan* and attributes it to an author "of the Xie clan" 謝氏; the two Tang dynastic catalogues list it in two *juan*. One item is quoted in TPYL 359 and anthologized in LX.[244]

Zhiguaiji 志怪記 *A Record of Anomalies* (Zgj). The SuiS catalogue lists it in three *juan* and gives the author as "of the Zhi clan" 殖氏; by the time the two Tang catalogues were compiled it had apparently disappeared, for it is not listed in those. Two items, one a fragment of only four characters, are quoted in the BTSC and anthologized in LX.

Xushi zhiguai 許氏志怪 *Xu's Accounts of Anomalies.* One item, a tale of an exorcism performed on a girl by an Indian monk named (Seng)yao 僧瑤, is quoted in both TPYL 932 and TPGJ 468. LX anthologizes this item under Zgszg (item 11).

---

241. Smith 1992, 588–652. Eichhorn 1985 is, incidentally, unreliable.

242. They are discussed by Li Jianguo 1984, 458ff.; Wang Guoliang 1984, 337ff. Two of the latest of them are discussed in Uchiyama 1979, 47–51, 56–57.

243. Li Jianguo 1984, 458–59.

244. Li Jianguo 1984, 459–60; Wang Guoliang 1984, 334.

Shenguailu 神怪錄 ***A Record of Spirits and Anomalies*** (Sgl). LX includes two items under this title. One is quoted from a work of the same name in BTSC 136 and TPYL 716; both quotations appear to be incomplete. The other is quoted in two places (MQ and TPYL 559) from a work titled *Shenguaizhi* 志; although this was reasoned by Lu Xun to be a variant title, the same story is quoted without attribution in TPGJ 391, where the protagonist is said to have been a military commander under the Tang, and it probably stemmed from a Tang anomaly-account collection titled *Shenguaizhi*.[245]

Xiangyiji 祥異記 ***A Record of Signs and Marvels*** (Xyj). Two quotations attributed to this work in TPGJ (109, 131) are anthologized in LX; the same two items, however, are attributed by the FYZL (114, 80 respectively) to the Mxj. No work titled Xyj appears in bibliographic catalogues. From internal evidence, the work (or at least these two items) seems likely to be of Liang date.[246]

Zhiguai 志怪 ***Accounts of Anomalies*** by Cao Pi 曹毗 of the Jin (Zgc). Only one item survives, anthologized in LX. The author was an official under the Jin, but his dates are unclear.[247] The Zgc is not listed in early bibliographies, although other works by Cao Pi are.

Zaguishen zhiguai 雜鬼神志怪 (Zgszg). No work by this title is mentioned in early catalogues;[248] it is, in fact, Lu Xun's creation, a sort of "miscellaneous" rubric for some twenty items of whose provenance he was uncertain. These twenty items comprise quotations in collectanea from works of six vague titles (none save the first making any attribution of authorship): *Xushi zhiguai* (see above), *Zaguishenzhi*, *Zhiguai*, *Zhiguaiji* 集, *Zhiguailu* 錄, and *Zhiguaizhuan* 傳.[249]

---

245. Li Jianguo 1984, 469.

246. Li Jianguo 1984, 420–21. Two quotations in TPGJ 342 are also attributed to a work of this title but contain internal dates in the Tang *zhenyuan* period (785–806 C.E.).

247. He is given a biography in JS 92. On the text, Wang Guoliang 1984, 319–20; Lin Chen 1960, 403–4. The author is not to be confused with Cao Pi = Wei Wendi, author of the Lyz.

248. The TPYL list of sources includes a *Zaguishenzhi;* this may have been the basis for Lu Xun's rubric.

249. Lin Chen 1960, 405; Wang Guoliang 1984, 69.

Yindezhuan 陰德傳 *Accounts of Hidden Virtue* **(Ydz) by**
Fan Yan 范晏. Listed in SuiS, JTS, XTS, and TZ catalogues as
consisting of two 卷, this text has since disappeared save for one
quotation in TPYL 556; it concerns the *"gratis* reburial" (in the Han
period) of one Wei Gongqing of Chang'an by one Chen Yi.[250] The
Fan clan had been Buddhist believers for generations; this text
therefore probably consisted of cullings from historical records concerning instances of *yinde* 陰德, which I take to mean "kindnesses
done in secret."[251]

Fragments of Regional Histories and Gazeteers

Quotations in collectanea and commentaries from regional works of
the Six Dynasties period have been recompiled in the SF series;
their provenance is uncertain, and I have not thoroughly checked
the items in the following texts against earlier collectanea. But
these fragments (no set of which, except for 13, runs longer than
three folio pages) will occasionally prove useful to us, especially
since these sorts of works were, I believe, an important source of
material for authors of anomaly accounts, so I list them here with
the authors to whom they are attributed (including the dynasty
during which they lived, where this is given in the SF) and the
abbreviations by which I cite them below.

1. *Jingzhouji* 荊州記 by Sheng Hongzhi (Jin) 盛弘之. (Jzj)
2. *Xiangzhongji* 湘中記 by Luo Han (Jin) 羅含. (Xzj)
3. *Wulingji* 武陵記 by Bao Jian (Jin) 鮑堅. (Wlj)
4. *Nankangji* 南康記 by Deng Deming (Jin) 鄧德明. (Nkj)
5. *Xunyangji* 潯陽記 by Zhang Sengjian (Jin) 張僧鑑. (Xunyj)
6. *Poyangji* 鄱陽記 by Liu Dengzhi (Jin) 劉澄之. (Pyj)
7. *Jiujiangzhi* 九江志 by He Yan (Jin) 何晏. (Jjz)
8. *Danyangji* 丹陽記 by Shan Qianzhi (Jin) 山謙之. (Dyj)
9. *Kuaijiji* 會稽記 by Kong Ye (Jin) 孔曄. (Kjj)
10. *Nanyuezhi* 南越志 by Shen Huaiyuan (Jin) 沈懷遠. (Nyz)
11. *Guangzhouji* 廣州記 by Gu Wei (Jin) 顧微. (Gzj)

---

250. YWLJ 83 and TPYL 811 cite a roughly similar story from a text
called 盧光七賢傳, but the language of TPYL 556 is more detailed. My discussion here is based in part on Wang Guoliang 1984, 339.
251. *Yinde* tales would thus be the moral inverse of cases of
"wronged souls": both cases involve the punishment/reward for behavior
that *goes unseen by other living humans.*

12. *Guangzhi* 廣志 by Guo Yigong (Jin) 郭義恭. (Gz)

13. *Yuzhang gujinji* 豫章古今記 by Lei Cizong 雷次宗. (Yzgjj)

Summary

In conclusion, when considering the anomaly account genre in its formative, pre-Tang period we have to deal with something on the order of sixty-four texts that have survived in some at least minimal, fragmentary form, in addition to which we know of at least seventeen titles of works now completely lost. I have abandoned the attempt to get an exact count of items, but they definitely number over four thousand.[252]

It would be tempting at this point to chart the trajectory of the genre's development over the centuries, counting up the numbers of texts produced in each century or dynasty, changes in format or content, and so on, but enough texts are lost—and enough of extant texts is also lost—to render such an enterprise guesswork at best. Perhaps one can say this much with some confidence:

Originating toward the end of the Warring States period and sustained throughout the Han, early texts of what would soon emerge as a full-fledged genre of anomaly accounts initially focused on two sorts of objects of discourse, and took two forms: (1) descriptions of the anomalous deities, fauna, and flora associated with specific sites on the land (both domestic and distant), arrayed in topographically organized lists, sometimes including narratives of mythical events associated with sites (or associated with divine or human figures associated with a site); (2) narratives of the exploits of mythical figures, sages, rulers, shamans, and specialists in esoteric arts, subdivided into two historiography-based forms: (a) the "annals" form, chronologically listing brief anecdotes of events associated with a single figure, and (b) the "arrayed biographies" form, listing successive entries for multiple persons or figures of a similar type, each entry narrating a string of (usually only loosely interconnected) events. From its earliest appearance in the literary record, the genre already seems to have been participated in with a relatively high degree of self-consciousness.

---

252. This figure is significantly higher than that given in Kao 1985, 48–49 and Foster 1974, 43. It is based on an exact count of all items except those in the following texts, which I have estimated conservatively: Shj, Fsty (the chapters dealing with anomalies that are discussed above and in Chapter Seven), Syj, and Szj.

At the end of the third century a significant addition is made: anomalous material comes to be organized not only geographically or biographically but also topically (the earliest examples being Ying Shao's Fsty, Zhang Hua's Bwz, and perhaps Gan Bao's Ssj). From the fourth century, the "annals" form comes to be only seldom used, except for items concerning omens and portents, and the "arrayed biographies" form comes to be used increasingly for purposes of interreligious polemics and persuasion. But a much more significant shift occurs: a new object of discourse comes into focus, the anomalous *event* per se, and is dealt with in a new textual form—a sheer list of discrete, disjointed narrative items not interconnected by common figures or by any overarching frame or single theme or topic (though sometimes arranged chronologically or topically). Along with this new textual form comes an unprecedented focus on ordinary human protagonists—mostly (but not all) members of the elite, to be sure, but also low- and middle-ranking members, as opposed to divine or legendary figures, rulers, or religious specialists, who had monopolized the pages of most writings in China up until this time.

The period from the early fourth through the first quarter of the sixth century might well be described as the watershed in the development of the genre in pre-Tang times: more texts seem, at least, to have been written, plot structures become increasingly complex, the texts show the deepening self-consciousness of authors and more deliberate intertextual linkages (including richer structures of intertextual irony), and there seems to have been during this period a continuing influx of fresh narrative material, as opposed to the reworking and copying that would mark Liang works, such as the Xs and Jlz, and, to some extent, beyond.[253]

In the next chapter, we turn from this overview of the terrain of anomaly accounts to the sorts of warrants that existed and justifications that were offered for their production.

---

253. The genre continued through the Tang, although it has often been thought rather moribund during that period (when *chuanqi* was in style), and saw a renaissance during the Sung and into the Ming and Qing. The best overall study of it in the Tang period of which I am aware is Uchiyama 1979; for a recent study of its crowning achievement in the Qing, Zeitlin 1993.

Chapter Three

Justifying the Strange:
The Warrant for the Genre of
Anomaly Accounts

子曰, 為政以德, 譬如北辰, 居其所而眾星共之.
The Master said, "The rule of virtue can be compared to the Pole Star which commands the homage of the multitude of stars without leaving its place."

Analects 2.1

子不語怪, 力, 亂, 神.
The Master never talked of prodigies, feats of abnormal strength, natural disorders, or spirits.

Analects 7.20[1]

Often, when a new genre of discourse is in the process of emerging, authors explain and justify it—and their own participation in it—to their audience, contributing to the gradual carving out of a cultural space in which to work. The writing of texts belonging to the genre thus comes to be constructed as a specific type of act informed by certain meanings, associated with certain precedents or

---

1. Tr. of the first passage from Lau 1979, 63; of the second, slightly modified, from Waley 1938, 127.

exemplary figures or historical moments, and presuming a certain ideological and institutional background. This provision of a *warrant* in tradition for a new genre is particularly crucial in cultures, such as that of late classical and early medieval China, that predominantly ground the legitimacy of patterns of action, thought, and discourse in an imagined exemplary past. It is also particularly crucial when the subject matter of the new genre has traditionally been viewed with disapproval, suspicion, or ambivalence.

What, then, was the cultural warrant for the gradual creation, beginning during the Han but climaxing after its fall, of a genre of writing devoted exclusively to the description and narration of anomalies? To what precedents did writers of anomaly accounts appeal? In what tradition of cultural practice did they see—or at least portray—themselves as standing? Who were their exemplars, and what were their models, in that shared (if multivalent) body of extant, recorded textual tradition which was regarded as the locus of authority by almost all literate Chinese, even those who strove to innovate?

In this chapter, I try to answer these questions in two steps. The first step will be to document in Warring States and Han texts a cluster of ideas and practices that together could be seen as a fairly coherent tradition of cosmographic collecting. These ideas and practices were based on a common set of assumptions about the nature of governance and the relation between the royal or (after the establishment of the Qin dynasty in 221 B.C.E.) imperial center and its social, geographic, even cosmological and spiritual periphery. The second step will be to show that, in the face of traditional (and preeminently Confucian) suspicion or ambivalence— if not rigid disapproval—toward discourse on anomalies in general and on the realm of spirits in particular, it was primarily this earlier cosmographic tradition that Han and Six Dynasties writers and readers of anomaly accounts claimed as their precedent.

Part One: The Tradition of Cosmographic Collecting

The Legend of the Nine Tripods

The *Zuozhuan* 左傳[2] tells of nine metal cauldrons, symbolizing the king's virtue (*de* 德). While this passage may not be the oldest of

---

2. The dating of which continues to vex scholars: ECT, 67–71; cf. Watson 1989, xiv.

the ones of interest to us in this chapter, I cite it first because it touches on several themes that will concern us.

Formerly, when the Xia 夏 dynasty had reached the height of its virtue, [people in] the [nine] distant regions made pictures of the strange beings[3] [in their respective areas] (遠方圖物) and presented metal as tribute to the nine governors. With the metal, [the ruler Yu 禹] caused cauldrons to be cast on which these beings were represented (鑄鼎象物); [images of] the hundred strange beings (百物) were prepared. In this way people were made to recognize [all] spirits and evil influences, so that, when they traveled over rivers and marshes and through mountains and forests, they would encounter no adversities, and spirits such as the *chi*, the *mei*, and the *wangliang* could not bother them. By these means concord reigned between those above and those below, and the people received the favor of Heaven.[4]

This is the most detailed of extant early descriptions of the nine tripods (九鼎), royal sacra that, passed down to the Shang and Zhou houses, finally sank into a river at or shortly before the Qin unification.[5] The passage speaks of a distance between the royal

---

3. Scholars have long thought that, in contexts such as this, *wu* 物 does not mean simply "things" or even "beings" but *strange* beings. The Jin commentator on this text, Du Yu 杜預 (222–84), glossed *wu* as "anomalous creatures of the mountains and waters" (山川奇異之物). Jiang 1935, 8–9 (notes 3 and 4), further argues that the term I translate as "the hundred strange beings" (百物), appearing below, is not a synonym for "the myriad things" (萬物) but means some sort of spirit-beings (百物之神 or 精物). Certainly Wang Chong, when commenting sceptically on the apotropaic powers of these pictures (in a passage that closely paraphrases the language of the *Zuozhuan*), seems to have taken it so, or at least as designating anomalous beings, for he glossed *baiwu* as *baiwu zhi qi* 之奇: *Lunheng jiaoshi* 8 (2:375).

4. *Chunqiu Zuozhuan zhengyi* 21 (368, 宣公 year 3). I have consulted but not closely followed the translation in Needham 1954–, 3:503, which freely incorporates Du Yu's commentary, and have benefited from the detailed discussion of this passage in Jiang 1935, 6–12. Cf. the translation in Watson 1989, 82.

5. Wang Chong gives various legends of the later fate of the tripods: *Lunheng jiaoshi* 8 (2:375–80). Here and elsewhere (21 [3:906]) he mentions the belief that they were inhabited by personal deities who, in submerging themselves, were demonstrating their foreknowledge of the demise of the Zhou. Seidel (1981, 238; 1983, 299) cites a brief passage in *Huainanzi* 2 that associates the nine tripods with river charts that appear

center and its periphery, one fraught with cosmic and political import. Across this distance, a symbolic exchange is made: tribute, in
the form of pictures of anomalous creatures and the raw material
with which to fix these images in permanent form, flows into the
royal center; the sovereign's virtue and educative influence radiate
outward. Metal cauldrons, their number symbolizing the totality
of the known, habitable world (for, by the time this text was probably written, the Central Kingdom had begun to be schematically
divided in geographic thought into nine provinces 州), depict the
"strange beings" distinctive of each region, creatures that lurk in
places difficult to traverse, such as mountains and rivers. To represent these beings graphically is to neutralize their danger, allowing safe passage for "civilizers" from the center and thus secur-
ing Heaven's favor for the people of these liminal zones. We note
finally that, although the *Zuozhuan* text itself does not mention
Yu—a figure mythologically associated with the control of disorder
and excess (whether of floodwaters or of unruly spirits)—he was
early on (at least from the early Han [HS 25A, 1225]) identified as
the ruler under whom these image-bearing tripods were forged.[6]

Yu's Tribute

Another, very roughly contemporary text, considered by the Chinese (for reasons we will see later) to be closely related to the story
of the nine cauldrons and also featuring the ruler Yu, is the
Yugong 禹貢 or *Yu's Tribute*.[7] This text depicts Yu as traveling

---

in response to rulers' virtue, but so far I have not located it. SJ 28 (1365)
and HS 25A (1200) record their being "brought into" (入) the state of Qin
after the death of the last Zhou ruler; but the HS also records one legend
that they sank into the Si River beneath the city of Pengcheng 彭城 before
the Zhou fall, and Sima Qian elsewhere speaks of Qin's "seizure" (取) of
"the nine tripods [and other?] precious implements" (SJ 4 [169]). HS 25A
(1225) also mentions the legend of Yu's inscribing images on tripods representing the nine provinces.

6. On Yu's mythological associations, Yuan Ke 1981 [1960], 207–40;
Zhong Likan and Wang Qinggui 1991; Teiser 1985–86.

7. I read the title with a double or perhaps triple meaning: Yu's
land-ordering labors were his "tribute" to the king (he does not seem in
the text to have been elevated yet to the throne, and some traditional
commentators understand the phrase this way); people in outlying regions are described in the text as presenting tribute *to* Yu for conveyance
back to the capital; and the text itself is a record and testimony of his tribute. The text has come down to us as part of the New Text portions of the

through the nine provinces, fixing their borders, clearing and levelling mountains, determining watercourses, and establishing the
tribute which it was appropriate for each "barbarian" group to
present to the ruler. The verbs describing Yu's labors read like a
lexicon of the creation of order from disorder: he regulates, ad-
justs, lays out, measures, fixes. For each province, the text tersely
lists major mountains and waterways, soil types, the quality of
fields and revenues, distinctive tribute goods (sometimes consisting of "strange" 怪 objects[8]), and in most cases the names—and
sometimes an unusual custom or attribute—of the resident barbarian tribes. As a result of Yu's labors, the world was ordered,
made more habitable; and relations between center and periphery
were regularized. In later times, steles were erected on mountains
to commemorate his work.[9]

Attached to this account of the nine provinces, which follows
natural topographic features such as mountains and rivers, is a
schematic, idealized (and probably later) geography, in which the
world "within the four seas" is classified into hierarchically
graded, concentric zones surrounding the exemplary center, the
capital city.[10] This text envisions people's degree of culture (including agriculture) to be directly proportional to their proximity to

---

Shujing 書經 (*Classic of Documents*). Traditionally dated as far back as
the third millennium B.C.E. (Herrmann 1930), the *Yugong* is now usually
placed between the fifth and third centuries B.C.E.—that is, in the late
Warring States or even in the Qin: Needham 1954–, 3:500; Yin Shiji 1957,
5–6; Meng Sen 1974 (in which Ma Peitang argues plausibly that the text
was compiled in the kingdom of Wei to legitimize the continuing division
of China in the face of Qin's growing military might); ECT, 378.

   8. As in *Shangshu zhengyi* 6 (78), the description of Qingzhou,
which mentions "strange stones." The text seems to imply that many
other tribute articles were seen as unusual or rare, even if not explicitly
stated to be so.

   9. Gardner 1873–74.

   10. Chinese commentators have generally assumed the zones were
concentric squares; see the diagrams reproduced in Needham 1954–,
3:502 and Yin Shiji 1957, 52–53. Needham points out that there is nothing in the text to justify this assumption and suggests that it is due to the
cosmological doctrine of the earth's squareness and heaven's roundness.
But John Major has brought forward more cogent reasons why the zones
should be considered square (Major 1984). For a recent discussion of the
shape of cosmos in Shang and early Zhou times, Allan 1991, 74. We must
not overlook the symbolic dimensions of the city itself, a walled enclave of
order amidst relative disorder, laid out according to cosmographic principles: Meyer 1978; Skinner 1977; Smith and Reynolds 1987; Wheatley
1969, 1971; Wheatley and See 1978; Wilhelm 1977, chap. 4; Wright 1977.

the capital. Five hundred *li* in each direction from the capital is the royal domain; the next five hundred *li* is the princes' zone. Outside that is the *suifu* 綏服 or pacification zone, in which the people of the inner three hundred *li* "take measures for culture and instruction," those of the outer two hundred *li* "making exertions for war and defense." Surrounding them is the *yaofu* 要服 or zone of compacts with allied barbarians, the inner three hundred *li* comprising the Yi 夷 barbarians and the outer two hundred *li* the people of the steppes. On the extreme periphery within the four seas is the *huangfu* 荒服, the "wild zone" or "zone of culture-less savagery,"[11] the inner three hundred *li* of which is inhabited by the Man 蠻 barbarians, the rest by nomads, least civilized of all peoples in the author's eyes since they had no fixed abode and practiced no agriculture.

The Tour of Inspection

Perhaps nowhere in early China is cosmographic collecting more explicitly evidenced than in the ideological construct known as *xunshou* 巡守[12] or "tour of inspection." At root an ancient feudal ideal projected onto an increasingly urban, imperial political landscape, the *xunshou* was often recalled and imitated during the Qin, Han, and subsequent dynasties, and was inseparably linked with the system of imperially sponsored local temples and shrines by which the Han and later dynasties sought to implant their authority among the gods and spirits of particular places.[13]

---

11. The former translation is from Karlgren 1950, 18, the latter from Needham 1954–, 3:501.

12. The latter graph in *xunshou* is often written with the dog radical, but appears without it in the early, detailed description of the practice in the *Shundian* 舜典 as well as in a *Zuozhuan* passage (*Chunqiu zuozhuan zhengyi* 9, p. 162, 莊公 year 21) that describes the ruler's visit to the fiefdom of Guo; the syntax of this latter passage suggests that at least one early meaning of the term *xunshou* was a circuitous journey (*xun* 巡) among the various keeps (*shou* 守) of feudal lords in areas at some distance from the king's central domain. Keightley (1979–80, 1983) points out the peripatetic nature of Shang kingship.

13. On the apparently actual performance of *xunshou* before the Han, Creel 1970, 411–13; during the Han, Bielenstein 1979, 41–49; Twitchett and Loewe 1986, 310, 438–40. The SJ "Treatise on the *Feng* and *Shan* Offerings" (*Fengshan shu* 封禪書) and the HS "Treatise on the Suburban Sacrifices" (*Jiaosi zhi* 郊祀志), which is based on it, both open with

The oracle bones already contain records of Shang (12th c. B.C.E. and earlier) kings "hunting" and "inspecting" (the two are often linked) in places outside the core area of their control, and receiving as tribute precious articles such as tortoise shells in those places.[14] But what is probably the earliest fleshed-out, if idealized, account of what such an "inspection" involved comes in the *Shundian* 舜典 or "Canon of Shun," which, like the *Yugong*, is a relatively early (almost certainly pre-Han), New Text document preserved in the *Book of Documents*. Here, the exemplary ruler Shun is said to have made tours of inspection once every five years in each of the cardinal directions: east in the second month of the year, south in the fifth month, west in the eighth, and north in the eleventh, whereupon he returns to the central capital and through sacrificial offerings makes a report to the royal ancestors. In each direction, he journeys as far as the dominant mountain (岳) of the region, where he presents an offering to Heaven and sacrifices to the hills and rivers. Then, granting audience to the nobles of the region, he performs a set of regulative acts: he standardizes their reckoning of seasons, months, and days, thus regulating the calendar; he makes uniform the musical pitchpipes and the standards of length, weight, and capacity; he observes whether ceremonies are being performed as centrally prescribed, or whether they have been locally modified. Finally, he performs a potlatch-like exchange of gifts with the residents.[15]

This tradition is repeated in the *Wangzhi* 王制 ("Royal Regulations") chapter of the *Book of Rites* (*Liji* 禮記), but now in more

---

accounts of the *xunshou* to sacred peaks performed by exemplary rulers of high antiquity and the Qin and Han rulers who followed their example. The famous *feng* and *shan* sacrifices performed on Mount Tai 泰山 in Shandong, first (in legend) by the Yellow Thearch and subsequently by several Han emperors (who sought by their means to obtain immortality), were a special subset of these broader-ranging tours. On the *fengshan* and its links to the immortality quest, cf. also the HHS "Treatise on Sacrifices" (*Jisi zhi* 祭祀志), p. 3163; Chavannes 1910. On *xunshou* performance by Sui Yangdi and the Tang emperors, Wechsler 1985, chap. 8. Cf., in general, Hawkes 1967, esp. 82ff.

14. Keightley 1978, 181; Keightley 1979–80; Keightley 1983.

15. *Shangshu zhengyi* 3 (34–38); Karlgren 1950, 4–5. A remonstrative passage in the *Zuozhuan* (*Chunqiu zuozhuan zhengyi* 10, p. 172, 莊公 year 23) adds a further prescription: since, when the ruler makes a *xunshou*, it must be recorded, strict propriety must be observed in the course of the *xunshou*, lest improper standards creep into the writings handed down to later generations.

detail.[16] The Son of Heaven, in addition to regulating local calendric and measurement standards, inspecting ceremonies, and enforcing sumptuary codes, here orders his ministers to "set forth the songs" sung in each area "so that he might observe the customs of the people" (陳詩以觀民風). He orders other officials to present lists of prices so that he can know what the people like and dislike.[17] We are also told that, in addition to sacrificing to his ancestors upon his return, the Son of Heaven sacrifices to the Supreme Thearch (*shangdi* 上帝) before setting out.[18]

Feudal lords are also described in some early Confucian texts, such as the *Mencius* (6B.7), as making periodic visits to the court to report on customs in their respective domains, in years when the Son of Heaven does not make his tour. Inspecting and reporting on the periphery were thus carried out both centrifugally and centripetally.

The *Bohutong* 白虎通 (*Comprehensive Discussions in the White Tiger Hall*), a text purporting to be a report of a conference of scholar-officials held in 79 C.E., gives the most careful and sustained interpretation by Han Confucian scholars of the meaning of the *xunshou*.[19] It also illustrates the changes that had occurred in the Confucian ideology of the *xunshou* since late Zhou and Qin times. It etymologically links the term *xunshou* with shepherding, and states that the tour is the highest expression of the ruler's "care and esteem for the people."[20] It presents the tour's purpose as circulatory and inquisitory: it is done to assure that the ruler's virtue "transforms" (*hua* 化) the near and the far equally, and to seek out secluded worthies.[21] The *Bohutong* is at special pains to

16. This text, too, is notoriously difficult to date, though there is no reason to assume it is any later than the early or middle Han; ECT 293–97.

17. This moralizing tone echoes the brief discussion of *xunshou* in *Mencius* 6B.7, tr. Lau 1970, 176.

18. *Liji zhengyi* 11 (224ff.); tr. Legge 1926, v.1 [Part 3]:216–18.

19. *Bohu tong* 3.3b–6a; tr. Tjan 1949–52, 2:495–503. On dating and textual history, ECT, 347–56.

20. This emphasis on the *xunshou* as an expression of concern for the common people is echoed in the passage regarding the rite in JS 21 (652–53).

21. I cite a passage illustrating this notion of the ruler's "transformative" capacity, a common theme in classical and Han thought, from the *Chunqiu fanlu*: "The ruler of humanity . . . shares with heaven its transforming power (*bianhua zhi shi* 變化之勢). . . . The ruler, with his likes and dislikes, joy and anger, transforms human habits and customs

say that the *xunshou* is undertaken by the ruler not for his own sake but on behalf of Heaven and his ancestors; that is why the ruler makes annunciatory sacrifices to Heaven before and after the tour, and carries with him an ancestral tablet, jade tokens, and other insignia representing the presence of his ancestors.[22] The text is also at pains to say that a *xunshou* should be performed only after general peace (*taiping* 太平) has been restored; in this respect as in others the *xunshou* resembles the *feng* and *shan* sacrifices, but is more geographically comprehensive. The tour both expresses and effects harmony, stability, and order in the four quarters, in the distant as well as nearer regions. Reflecting the development of cosmological thinking since the era of the texts reviewed above, the *Bohutong* innovates in applying the concepts of *yinyang* and the five phases to the interpretation of the timing and spatial orientation of the *xunshou*; and it correspondingly downplays the cultic function of the tour.

Finally, the third century C.E. text *Kongcongzi* 孔叢子 (*Kong Family Masters' Anthology*) contains a by now acutely and self-consciously Confucian dialogue on the *xunshou* that largely repeats the above traditions but highlights the tour's moral aspects, stressing the ruler's inspection (through the collection of songs) and correction of popular customs: "He commands the scribes to select poems and lyrics from among the people, in order to observe their propensities" (以觀其風).[23]

Meanwhile, practitioners of the schools known as Huanglao 黃老 and the School of the Way (*daojia* 道家) were developing an ideological construct that, while different in some respects from this largely Confucian notion of *xunshou*, closely paralleled it in structure and function: structurally in that it is based on a similarly dynamic, "galactic" interaction between center and periphery, and functionally in that it charts the manner in which the

---

(*bian suxi* 變俗習), just as Heaven, with its warmth and coolness, cold and heat, transforms plants and trees. . . . Heaven, Earth, and the ruler are one" (11 [p. 185]; tr. modified from Fung 1952–53, 2:47–48).

22. The same applies to the triennial tours of inspection to be performed by the emperor's subordinates: regional chiefs inspect their realms and feudal lords inspect their cities *on behalf of* the Son of Heaven; as the ruler stands in the relationship of son to Heaven and to his dynastic ancestors, so these subordinate officials stand in symbolic relation of son to the ruler. They likewise file "reports" (*gao* 告) to him after their centrifugal tours in years when he remains stationary in the center, just as he "reports" to his superiors through sacrificial announcements.

23. *Kongcongzi* 3.1a–2a; Ariel 1986; Ariel 1989, 113–15.

ruler comes to "know" (by a kind of "observation") the outlying reaches of his realm.

The Huanglao silk manuscripts recovered in 1973 from tomb number three at Mawangdui 馬王堆 near Changsha (Hunan Province), while they do not (to my knowledge) mention the term *xunshou*, do explicitly portray the exemplary ruler, the Yellow Thearch 黃帝, as having a sort of panoptical capacity to penetrate to all quarters of the empire from his own still, fixed point in the center;[24] because of his ability to "safeguard unity" (*shouyi* 守一) he is able to oversee and embrace all things within the four seas, each according to its own *dao* or way, while "correcting what is anomalous" (*zhengqi* 正奇).[25] And although he himself seems to remain stationary in the capital, he gains penetrating insight (*guan* 觀) into the state of his realm by sending out emissaries who travel all over the land in disguise to "observe" (in one passage *guan* 觀, in another *shi* 視) the people's doings.[26] While these emissaries do ascertain whether the people are adhering to the "laws and regula-

---

24. From the *Liming* 立命 (Establishing the Mandate) section of the text *Shiliujing* 十六經 (reconstructed in earlier editions as *Shida* 大 *jing*): the Yellow Thearch 方四面, 傅一心, 四達自中. *Jingfa* 45.

25. See the *Chengfa* 成法 section of the *Shiliujing* (*Jingfa* 73–75): having "safeguarded unity," the ruler will be able to 達望四海, 困極上下, 四 嚮 (向) 相抱 (抱), 各以其道. The phrase *zhengqi* appears in this same passage, and also in the *Qiandao* 前道 section of the same text (p. 80, in the phrase [名]正者治, 名奇者亂), and finally near the end of the essay *Yuandao* 原道 in the graphic variants 政畸 (p. 102). Peerenboom 1993, perhaps because of his philosophical preoccupations, is curiously silent on all these counts; for a critique of and alternative to his approach to the Huanglao texts, Defoort 1994. Tu 1979 is still quite helpful. Kang Yunmei 1992 highlights the Legalist character of the silk manuscripts; Yu Mingguang 1989 sets them in context and gives annotated eds. One of the prominent rectifications performed by the Thearch in ancient myth was the pacification of the rebellious man (or, in many texts, monster) Chi You, who was causing drought and bringing disorder on the land; see Lewis 1990a, chap. 5; Karlgren 1946, 283ff.

26. In the first passage, appearing at the head of the *Guan* 觀 section of the *Shiliujing* (p. 48), the emissary Li Hei 力黑 (whose name varies in early texts) is sent; in the second, part of the *Guo Tong* 果童 section of the same text (p. 58), the emissary Guo Tong is similarly dispatched. Both are said to "travel throughout the four [quarters of the] realm" (*zhouliu siguo* 周流四國). On the importance of *guan* (penetrating insight free of the obstruction of preconceived biases) in Huanglao thought, Peerenboom 1993, 70–73, who stresses that the concept is not equivalent to the sort of "mystical" insight taught in the *Laozi*; Tu 1979, 104–5.

tions" (faze 法則) and maintaining the distinctions in social status appropriate to them, the Confucian language of the ruler spreading his virtue to transform the people is absent, as is the potlatch-like exchange between the ruler (or his representatives) and local leaders. The most striking difference from the early (but not later) Confucian descriptions of *xunshou*, however, is the complete absence of the cultic aspects of the tour whereby the ruler, by sacrificing to local mountain and river deities, secures their allegiance in a sort of spiritual feudalism.

The *Huainanzi* 淮南子—a syncretic Daoist text composed by a group of scholars and "masters of esoteric techniques" (方術之士) assembled by the prince Liu An 劉安 at his court in Huainan in the Chu region, and presented to the Han Emperor Wu in 139 B.C.E.[27]—continues the themes of the Mawangdui manuscripts, at least where the ruler's knowledge of the periphery is concerned. The ruler is to remain secluded deep within the palace walls, not travel about through his lands; yet

> even so, he is wholly cognizant of all that goes on within the world because the sources that feed him are immense and those who tap him are numerous. Hence, without going beyond his doors, he knows about the world; without peeping out through his window, he comprehends the heavenly Way.[28]

This is possible because, as adumbrated in the silk manuscripts, the ruler's officials and subjects have become his eyes and ears, affording him a penetrating, panoptical view of the periphery from his quiet center:

> The ruler sees with the eyes of the empire, hears with the ears of the empire, deliberates with the intelligence of the empire, and contends with the strength of the empire behind him. His edicts and commands are able to penetrate to the lowest level and the real condition of his subjects can be known by him above. His bureaucracy has open access to the throne (百官修通), and his various ministers are like spokes

27. For a recent, authoritative discussion of the authorship and dating of the *Huainanzi*, Roth 1992, 12–26. On its thought, I have benefited from, inter alia, Roth 1985, 1991; Howard 1984; Wallacker 1962; Le Blanc 1985; Major 1993, which I unfortunately received too late to make much use of here.

28. *Huainanzi* 14:10b; tr. Ames 1983, 61.

converging at the hub. . . . His sight and hearing being penetrating will not be clouded, and what is actually good and bad being set before him daily, he will not indulge in conjecture.[29]

As will be discussed further below, this Daoist vision of the nation as a true "body politic" wherein the ruler, its metaphoric heart or mind, receives "sensory" reports—communicated in writing—from his peripheral officials and from the people themselves, continued to find expression in the seminal second-century C.E. *Scripture of Great Peace* (*Taipingjing* 太平經).

The Travels of Mu, Son of Heaven, as Cosmic *Xunshou*

The *Mu Tianzi zhuan* 穆天子傳 (*Account of Mu, Son of Heaven*), a fragmentary work in the form of a historical chronicle dating from at least the late fourth century B.C.E., was found on bamboo slips in 280 or 281 C.E. in a tomb dating to 296 B.C.E.[30] It can be read as, among other things, a cosmicization of the idea of the *xunshou*—a tour of inspection writ large. In this text, Mu and his large retinue of officials and soldiers journey to the ends of the earth, crossing desert wildernesses and climbing mountains in the extremities of the four quarters. The Son of Heaven is described as holding audiences with local nobles, many of whom are semi-barbarians of the border states. Such meetings usually include a ceremonial exchange of gifts, the noble prostrating himself to Mu; sometimes Mu bestows a symbolic object, such as a jade disk, and simultaneously grants a noble the right to rule or oversee an area, entailing the obligation to sacrifice to the Zhou ancestors. Mu also collects minerals, flora, and fauna from these outlying lands in order to take them back to his capital for display and reportage: he traps local game, collects gems and the seeds of exotic plants, tastes rare delicacies. At several points in the text, he is described as leaving

---

29. *Huainanzi* 15:3b; tr. Ames 1983, 189. Elsewhere the *Huainanzi* exhorts the ruler to have a mind that is empty and unclouded so that, like a clear mirror, he can respond spontaneously to each situation as it arises: Ames 1983, 180, 188, 192–93.

30. Needham 1954–, 2:355; Mathieu 1978, 101; ECT, 342–46. For a suggestive reading of the text as encoding astronomical observations and mapping mythological details onto these, Porter 1993. For an older, English tr., Cheng 1933–34.

marks or traces of his visit on the landscape: he engraves a message in stone, plants a commemorative tree. And, as in some other texts describing *xunshou*, and as in the ritual system of the Han and subsequent dynasties, there is a pronounced cultic aspect to his activities: he visits the palaces of former semi-divine kings, and sacrifices to the deities of mountains and rivers.

Mu's journey westward beyond the Jade Gate, however, breaks the bounds of the domestic *xunshou*, and announces that the text is concerned with much more than ritual and moral prescription. The western regions, strange and exotic, are also revealed to contain many ancient cultic sites connecting them to Chinese antiquity. And they harbor esoteric knowledge: at Yellow Mountain, "he inspected the charts and the inscriptions on the precious vessels which were stored there for the Son of Heaven"; the vessels were of jade, gems, silver, and gold, and the "charts" inscribed on them recall the images on the nine tripods described in the *Zuozhuan*; Qunyu Mountain, where Mu stops for four days to gather jade and other precious stones, "was the place where ancient kings used to keep their books and scriptures." At Mount Kunlun and at adjoining Chun Mountain, said to be "the highest mountain on earth," he surveys the wilderness stretching in the four directions and visits the ancient palaces of the Yellow Thearch. The journey reaches its western extremity, and the narrative its climax, when the ruler calls on Xiwangmu 西王母, Queen Mother of the West. The pair exchange verses, and Mu promises (vainly, we suspect) to return. Then, moved by compassion for his subjects awaiting his return, he sadly sets off for home, after engraving a record of his visit on the rocks. Back in the capital, he holds a grand audience in the ancestral temple, where he presents an account of his journey containing a list of places, the directions in which they lie, and the distances between them.[31]

The Tributary System

We have already seen, in the *Zuozhuan* legend of the nine tripods, the *Yugong*, and the texts on the tour of inspection, a shared assumption regarding tribute: that the central collection (including the written description) of valuable goods from outlying areas—in

---

31. The predominantly classical-Daoist text *Liezi* 列子 uses the story of Mu's journey as an anti-locative foil for the non-intentional, and therefore superior, sort of travel practiced by the Yellow Thearch 黄帝: *Liezi jishi*, 56ff. and 111ff.; Graham 1990, 33ff. and 61ff.

particular, those goods which are distinctive to each region—is of fundamental importance in ordering the world. The early Chinese tributary system, like the tour of inspection, presupposed hierarchies of center/periphery, giver/receiver, observer/observed, writer/ object. Others have dealt with the economic, social, and political history of the Han tributary system, which, aside from warfare, was the main way in which that dynasty (the first to deploy it as a regular policy) defined its relations with the non-Han others both beyond and within its frontiers to the north, west, and south.[32] For our purposes, it is necessary only to point out briefly the symbolic value of the tributary system and the structuring metaphors it shared with the other institutions under discussion here.

As a mode of cosmography, the tribute system served to emplace peripheral and (from the Han viewpoint) anomalous groups within a centrally determined, hierarchical social—and cosmic— order. To submit tribute was, again from the Han point of view at least, to signal subordination (not necessarily abject submission) to the court. This complex act involved three gestures: periodic homage by the "barbarian" leader (or his representative), including a gesture of prostration beneath the person of the emperor (or his representative); the sending of hostages, often including the heir apparent, to the Chinese court, where they received instruction in Chinese morality and culture; and the presentation of tribute goods. In addition, subordination was encoded in the making of sacrificial offerings to deceased emperors, that is, to the present emperor's ancestors.[33]

Like the *xunshou*, however, the tributary system entailed an economic and ritual exchange between center and periphery; it was not a unilateral appropriation of goods but a two-sided, if asymmetrical, transaction in which the fundamental ethical and ritual structure of *bao* 報 or reciprocity came into play.[34] The Son of Heaven rewarded the tribute-sender with counter gifts (including princesses given in marriage to important figures), as well as

---

32. Yang 1963a and 1968; Yü 1967; Bauer 1980; Twitchett and Loewe 1986, 377–462. Intermixed with the tribute system proper are the subtler aromas of the *exotic* that made goods from distant lands such powerful commodities and palladia in the first place. Although they deal with the Tang period, there are no better ruminations on this theme in Chinese culture than Schafer 1963, 1967, and 1970.

33. Yang 1963a, 1968; Suzuki 1968; Bauer 1980.

34. On this feature of traditional societies in general, Dumont 1980. On *bao*, Yang 1957; Martinson 1973, chap. 2. Cf. Ames 1983, chaps. 5–6, for discussion of related ideas in Han political thought.

with what the Chinese saw as his transformative, enculturating influence.

The symbolic power of collecting at court rare commodities from all quarters of the known world—commodities reflecting the special characteristics of each place, each people,[35] hence embodying their essence—is illustrated in an anecdote preserved most completely in *Master Lü's Spring and Autumn Annals (Lüshi chunqiu* 呂氏春秋), which was clearly intended to argue the benefits of unification. Tang 湯, founder of the Shang dynasty, attains the aid of Yi Yin 伊尹 as his adviser. The next day Yi Yin explains to his patron how to achieve the "perfection of flavor" (至味), an elaborate culinary metaphor for the harmonious unification (調和之事) of the world under Heaven. He lists the far-flung ingredients of this dish, which would consist of tribute articles from various localities, some of them on the extreme periphery of the world (such as a "phoenix egg" from "west of the Floating Sands" and water from "the Kunlun well"), divided into categories for each of which Yi Yin names the most perfect representatives. He further compares the alchemy-like transformations that would have to be worked on these ingredients, balancing their five types of flavor (五味) and three types of material (三材) in one's cauldron, to the cyclical succession of *yin* and *yang* and the four seasons. Only if the ruler is a true Son of Heaven are all of the necessary ingredients attainable, but if he is, then this culinary *summa* of the world may be prepared.[36]

Finally, as the *Zuozhuan* story of the nine cauldrons adumbrated, the tributary system from early on probably included written and pictorial representation of the barbarians and their exotic costumes and products, although no such texts or even titles survive from the Han.[37] Zhuge Liang is said to have written a work

---

35. On the high degree of regional economic specialization evinced in late Zhou texts, Hsu 1965, 119–22.

36. *Lüshi chunqiu jiaoshi* 14 (740–41). Meyer 1994 identifies chapter 14 as Confucian in orientation, but this story, at least, seems equally to reflect the cosmologists' interest in taxonomic resonance. On the politico-cosmic thought in this text, Kalinowski 1980, 1982; Louton 1984. This legend of Yi Yin is alluded to in *Mencius* 5.A7, *Zhuangzi* 23, and other early texts.

37. HS mentions charts (pictures) and texts (*tushu* 圖書) of the recently defeated Xiongnu being made in 35 B.C.E. and exhibited to court women. Some scholars take these to have been diagrams or maps of the hills and rivers of the Xiongnu territories (Enoki 1984, 80 and 102).

entitled *Tupu* 圖譜 on the southern tribes in the third century C.E.; the earliest surviving example of tribute descriptions is the *Liang zhigong tu* 梁職頁圖 (*Pictures of Tribute-Bearing Emissaries [to] the Liang [Court]*), written by the prince Xiao Yi (the future Emperor Yuan) by the year 539 C.E.[38]

The Collection of Portents

In late Warring States times and during the former and later Han, one of the dominant schools of thought was that of the "cosmologists": those who espoused the "doctrine of Heaven and humanity" (*tianrenshuo* 天人説), emphasized classificatory thinking based on the notions of *yinyang* and the five phases, and thought the cosmos to be "a harmoniously functioning organism consisting of multitudinous objects, qualities and forces which, despite their seeming heterogeneity, are integrated into coherent patterns by being subsumed under one or another of many numerical categories," as Derk Bodde inimitably put it.[39] Although the basic idea of omens or portents—that unusual natural events carried messages for humanity—was far older, the rise of cosmological thinking in the late Warring States laid the groundwork for a new systematicity in the interpretation of such events.[40] Not only were Heaven and humanity linked through definite mechanisms of resonance or influence-response (*ganying* 感應), but there were now—with the "monthly ordinance" (*yueling* 月令) essays of the *Lüshi chunqiu*, gathered during the Han into a discrete chapter of the *Book of Rites*, as well as incorporated into the *Huainanzi*

---

38. This work originally consisted of a list of entries on some thirty-five countries. In the extant version, each entry begins with a heading (such as "The Emissary of Gaoli") and continues with information concerning the ancestry of the country's rulers, the country's location, its internal geography, and noteworthy or unusual customs practiced by its people. Each entry includes a picture of the emissary in his native costume. The preface is reprinted in HTDL, 185; Enoki 1984 discusses the text's versions and contents, and reproduces the text and the illustrations. Enoki further compares the text with LS 54, which is obviously based on it. On similar texts in later times, Schmotzer 1973.

39. Bodde 1959, 14.

40. Keightley 1984; Loewe 1982, chap. 8; Maspero 1948–51; Henderson 1984, 75–82; Zheng Zhiming 1986, chaps. 4–5; Powers 1983. On the *fenye* 分野 system in particular, Schafer 1977, 75; Henderson 1984, 68–70.

(*juan* 9–10), and with the *Chunqiu fanlu* 春秋繁露 (ascribed to Dong Zhongshu 董仲舒) and other New Text writings (including divination theories by "masters of esoterica" [*fangshi* 方士])— also increasingly intricate, detailed taxonomic schemes by which to interpret anomalous events observed in the sky or on earth. New Text thought in particular, exemplified by Dong Zhongshu but continuing into the Eastern Han, strove for truly comprehensive classifications of phenomena and exhaustive correlations between taxonomically matching members of different sets of phenomena. Its penchant for anomaly-interpretation has led some scholars to characterize New Text thought as "superstitious," marked by "an appeal to the supernatural rather than to natural explanations of the universe,"[41] but in fact this was a worldview with little room for mystery: anomalies happened for reasons, and the reasons were couched in terms not of miraculous intervention by personal deities but of the essentially taxonomic principle of "like attracts like." As the *Chunqiu fanlu* put it, "All things avoid that from which they differ and cleave to that to which they are similar. . . . There is nothing divine in this" (非有神).[42]

The systematic recording of portents in all parts of the realm likewise became an increasingly important function of government in (and beyond) the late Warring States and Han periods. Since the mandate of Heaven (*tianming* 天命) was one of the things thought to be communicated through portents, much was at stake in their collection and interpretation,[43] which likely explains why a good many portent lists (some with interpretations) have come down to us from the archives compiled by court astronomers and other officials under the Ministry of Sacrifices.[44] Here, too, relations between court and periphery involved an exchange: those reporting favorable portents to the court were frequently rewarded

41. The former phrase is that of Fung 1952–53, 2:7; the latter, that of Loewe 1982, 184.

42. *Chunqiu fanlu* 13 / sec. 57 (p. 206); cf. Fung 1952–53, 2:56. That Dong Zhongshu wrote parts of this text is virtually certain; that he wrote all of it has been questioned for centuries. For recent, somewhat conflicting opinions on the authenticity of the traditional ascription to Dong Zhongshu, Arbuckle 1989; Arbuckle 1992, 215–26; ECT, 80–83.

43. Rubin 1984; Eberhard 1957; de Crespigny 1976; Leban 1978.

44. HS, treatises on astronomy (*Tianwenzhi* 天文志) and the five phases (*wuxingzhi* 五行志), 26 (1273–1314) and 27A, 27B, and 27C (1315–1522) respectively. HHS, treatises on astronomy (3213–3264) and five phases (3265–3383). WS, treatise on "numinous signs" (*lingweizhi* 靈微志), 112A–112B (2893–2969). JS 11–13, 27–29; NQS 18–19.

with goods, cash, or rank; often a general amnesty and distribution of food were declared as well. By the same principle, deities thought responsible for favorable portents were sometimes "rewarded" with sacrifices.[45]

The rise of *chenwei* 讖緯 ("prognosticatory apocypha") literature, near the end of the Western Han and throughout the ensuing reign of Wang Mang and the Eastern Han, represented an attempt, motivated by anxiety over political legitimation, to link the interpretation of portents to the line-by-line (*zhangju* 章句) hermeneutics of classical texts popular in these centuries.[46] Undergirding the production of *chenwei* was a belief that Heaven signals its mandate for political change (and its approval of current policies) by sending not—any longer—just any sort of anomalies but a more specific type: strange texts, charts, talismans, and diagrams, in other words, unusual writings that are revealed spontaneously to humanity. As the roughly contemporaneous *Taipingjing* succinctly put it, "When a great man is about to flourish, strange texts will appear" (*qiwen chu* 奇文出).[47] That scripture, in fact, reveals a central concern with—as well as a detailed social program for—the collection of such "strange texts" and reports of other portents from all corners of the realm. It recommends the establishment of a roadside collection system for reports of portents and all other phenomena revelatory of the "intention of Heaven" (*tianyi* 天意) and the minds of the people, for, once assembled, these will in fact constitute revealed Daoist scriptures, the *Taipingjing* itself being a sort of meta-scripture detailing the way in which scriptures are to be received; it emphasizes the im-

---

45. For a Han example of amnesty and food distribution, Loewe 1982, 83–84; for numerous early Tang examples of rewards to both commoners and deities, Wechsler 1985, 65–66, 71–74; cf. Somers 1986.

46. On *chenwei* I have relied particularly on Itano 1976, 1978; Hihara 1972; Kaltenmark 1949; Fung 1952–53, 2:88–132; Seidel 1981, 1983, where (particularly in the 1983 study) further, thorough bibliographic comments can be found. The texts themselves are available in the monumental Yasui and Nakamura 1971–88. On the relationship between *zhangju* commentary and *chenwei*, and the situation of both within the complexities of "New/Old Text" and "New/Old Study" in the Han and Later Han, Qian Mu 1983, 165–233.

47. *Taipingjing hejiao*, 27. For recent studies of the dating and thought of the *Taipingjing*, Qing Xitai 1988–, 85–123; Lin Fushi 1993; Li Gang 1993; Su Baoyang 1992; Petersen 1989–90; Wang Ming 1984, 99–200; Beck 1980.

portance of circulating written documents as the medium for these reports; and it criticizes those of the Confucian eremetic tradition who shirk this grave social-moral-cosmic responsibility.[48]

The Music Bureau

In discussing the *xunshou,* we saw that when the ruler wished to know the minds of the common people, he or his officials would travel to villages and listen to, observe, and record the words, notes, and gestures of the "music" (*yue* 樂) and "songs" (*shi* 詩) performed by the people, for these, as articulated most famously in the "Great Preface" (*Daxu* 大序) to the *Classic of Odes* 詩經 but also elsewhere, were held to crystallize their thoughts and desires into visible and audible form.[49] More specifically, these odes or "airs" (*feng* 風)[50]—a term also connoting both the ruler's educative influence on his people and the people's critical impact on the ruler, or, in short, almost any linguistically conveyed influence across social levels—were held to be indirect, coded, yet decipherable indices to the moral status of government. And the decipherers of this coded speech were the historians (*shi* 史) who recorded it and made it available to the ruler. In the foundational language of the *Daxu*:

> By *feng* those above transform [*hua* 化] those below; also by *feng* those below criticize those above. When an admonition [to the ruler] is given that is governed by patterning [*wen* 文],

---

48. Injunctions to lower officials and commoners to collect and report portents to the ruler: *Taipingjing hejiao* 25–27, 152, 205, 514. Criticisms of officials who are concealing portents or not participating in their reportage: 313–24 and ff., 335. Collective assemblage of revealed texts by roadside collection and other means: 190–92, 292, 331, 348ff., 415; on this theme cf. Li Gang 1993; Beck 1980, 173–74. The *Xiang'er* commentary to the *Laozi* similarly insists on the need for officials to diligently research anomalous phenomena and pass on these celestial warnings to the ruler: Rao 1991, 44.

49. On early music in general, DeWoskin 1982; on music and odes as outward "crystallizations" of inner states, Liu (James J.Y.) 1975, 67–70; Legge 1926, v.2 [Part 4]:93; and, most recently, the superb discussions in Van Zoeren 1991, 13–15 and 52ff., and Owen 1992, 39ff. The dating of the *Daxu* is the quagmire of all sinological quagmires: ECT, 417; Van Zoeren 1991, 90ff.

50. On the rich semantics of this term, Owen 1992, 39.

the one who speaks it has no culpability. . . . When the royal
Way declined rites and moral principles were abandoned; the
power of government to teach failed; the government of the
states became deviant [*guo yi zheng* 國異政]; the customs of
the family were altered [*jia shu su* 家殊俗]. And at this point
the mutated [*bian* 變] *feng* and the mutated *ya* 雅 [odes] were
written. The historians of the states understood clearly the
marks [*ji* 迹] of success and failure. . . . They sang their feelings to criticize [*feng*] those above, understanding the
changes [*bian*] that had taken place and thinking about
former customs [*huai qi jiusu zhe ye* 懷其舊俗者也].[51]

The people, then, are repositories of memory of how things once
were and still should be; their "mutated" songs, themselves a kind
of portent (note that *bian* "mutation" equally describes natural
and musical aberrations, both encoded with moral meaning), provide "marks" or "traces" of slippage from past ideals to present realities, and are duly noted by historians who, writing them down,
are prompted to ponder the moral devolution they reveal. This
writing is presented as a privileged, protected mode of communication: although it is potentially critical of the ruler or his government, its transmitter is not held culpable.

Although, given this ancient view of their moral importance,
it is quite likely that popular songs had been collected by previous
rulers, a special government bureau was established for this purpose (and others) under the Han Emperor Wu (r. 141–87 B.C.E.),
perhaps around the year 114,[52] as part of his "modernist" expan-

---

51. Following the Chinese text and—with only slight modification—
the translation in Owen 1992, 46–47; cf. Van Zoeren 1991, 95–97.

52. For the most recent studies of the origins of this bureau, Birrell
1988 and 1989; the author is, however, somewhat excessively preoccupied
with the "mythologizing nature" of some historical passages, which, even
if true (cf. Knechtges 1990), does not lessen the ideological importance of
the idea of the Bureau. Still preferable on the establishment of the bureau
and the reasons for its abolition in 70 B.C.E. is Loewe 1973. Important historical passages include HS 22 (1043, 1045), 30 (1756); cf. Xiao 1944, 6ff.
On "Music Bureau poetry" as a genre, Allen 1992. Incidentally, HHS 86
(2842) contains an account of the Han founder hearing a song sung by
Man and Yi tribesmen, recognizing it as the song of King Wu of Zhou
when he attacked the last Shang ruler, and ordering his "musical experts"
(*yueren* 樂人) to learn it—a tale that, in its implication that ancient Chinese songs associated with highly revered figures might have "survived"
in the oral memory of "barbarians," is rather provocative.

sion of the power, grandeur, and ritual and cultic prestige of the empire.[53] The titles and texts of twenty of these Music Bureau (*yuefu* 樂府) songs survive in the HS,[54] and although their popular origins are doubtful, their contents show that they were hymns written as part of the state cults of the Supreme Unity (*taiyi* 太一), the deities of *yin* and *yang* and the five phases, Heaven and Earth, and other recipients of sacrifices. Especially important for our purposes is the fact that most of them commemorate the appearance of auspicious portents indicating Heaven's support for Emperor Wu's policies, such as the emergence from a river (in 120 B.C.E.) of a "heavenly horse" (*tianma* 天馬) and the arrival of others from the northwest; the capture of other rare, auspicious animals; and the appearance of tripods at Fenyin in 112, coinciding with the occurrence of a lunar phenomenon the Chinese called "phosphor star" (*jingxing* 景星) or "star of virtue" (*de* 德 *xing*).[55] Others commemorate the Emperor's performance of *xunshou*.

It remains only to note the reasons why certain reformist officials pressed, beginning in 70 B.C.E., for the curtailment of Music Bureau activities, and why the office was finally abolished in 7 B.C.E. Just as it had been established in a time of "modernist" imperial expansion over the periphery, it was curtailed in a time of retrenchment by members of the official class who wanted to rein in the power of the court; and its reduction and eventual abolishment were part of a general rollback of the huge system of court-sponsored cults, to imperial ancestors as well as a host of local and regional deities.[56] But the ostensive reason given by one of the reformers, the academician Ping Dang 平當, was that the music of the realm of Zheng 鄭, which had been introduced to the capital by the Music Bureau, was morally inappropriate: it was excessively stimulating, it lay outside the old canon of approved tunes (and hence lacked any connection with Confucius and with his tradition

---

53. These expansionist measures also included revival of the *feng* and *shan* sacrifices, the construction of a *mingtang* 明堂 ("bright hall," a liturgical structure keyed to the cosmological and ritual system outlined in the monthly ordinances), and several performances of *xunshou* (Twitchett and Loewe 1986, 664–65). They were linked with Emperor Wu's consolidation of central power through brutal suppression of regionally powerful families and an aggressive military policy in the west and south (Ch'ü 1972, 200–201; Wallacker 1978; Twitchett and Loewe 1986, 770–72).

54. HS 22 (1046–1070); cf. Loewe 1973, 343–44.

55. Schafer 1977, 182–84.

56. Loewe 1971; cf. Twitchett and Loewe 1986, 661–68.

of restrained government), and it issued from a region peripheral to the ancient cultural center of Zhou.[57]

The Symbolic Values of Writing

If the ideas and institutions I have outlined all concerned cosmographic collecting, the *writing down* of what was collected played a key role in each. Let us pause to summarize some key symbolic values with which the very act of writing and the written medium were imbued.[58]

First, as highlighted in the legend of the nine tripods, writing—verbal as well as pictorial representation—served an apotropaic function. Because it fixed and displayed the otherwise shifting and hidden forms of spiritual beings (especially those anomalous beings hovering at the periphery of "normal," state-approved sacrificial cults), it became perhaps the single most important means for controlling spirits, as suggested in the *Huainanzi*'s (13.6b) comment on the invention of writing: "Of old when Cang Jie 蒼頡 [said to have served under the Yellow Thearch] invented writing, Heaven rained down grain and the spirits (*gui* 鬼) howled at night." The lexicographer Xu Shen, compiler of the *Shuowen*, commented around 100 C.E. on this passage as follows: "The spirits feared they might also be engraved in books, and that is why they howled at night."[59]

Hence, there arose not only a genre of demonography—texts depicting the names and forms of usually malevolent, marginal spirit-beings, and the verbal and ritual formulae for protecting oneself from them—but also a genre of "theography" (to which many *chenwei* themselves belong), in which the names and appearances of gods of particular terrestrial and cosmic places were recorded. And these genres served not only apotropaic but also political legitimation functions, as Seidel has shown: the tripods, sacred charts, and other royal/imperial sacra first adumbrated in

---

57. Loewe 1973, 347–51; HS 22 (1070–1076).

58. A more complete treatment of this topic would include analysis of the realia of writing technologies during the relevant centuries in China, on which Tsien 1962; Loewe 1968, chap. 7; Goodman 1989.

59. Acker 1954, 1:63 n.1; Seidel 1983, 322. Wang Chong cites the passage, commenting that while Heaven's raining down grain and the spirits howling might really have occurred, it was a mistake to believe that they occurred in response to Cang Jie's invention (*Lunheng jiaoshi* 5 [*Ganxupian*], p. 249).

pre-Qin texts and later elaborated in *chenwei* were both celestial "responses" to the ruler's virtue and a form of revealed knowledge by which he could protect the people from spiritual attack. As an apocryphon titled *River Chart* (*Hetu* 河圖) puts it, "If the sovereign has the names of the gods of the four seas, the mountains, and the rivers, then he will also be able to invite them, summon them, and employ them to drive off demonic pneumas" (*shi que guiqi* 使卻鬼氣).[60] Aside from the *chenwei*, which in theory at least were exegetically keyed to classics, two such demonographies-cum theographies, fragments of which have survived, are the *Record of the Nine Tripods* (*Jiudingji* 九鼎記) and the *Pictures [Revealed by the] Boze* (Bzt). Both contained descriptions and names of strange spirit-beings from peripheral regions; the *Jiudingji* was purported to be the verbal counterpart of the tripod images Yu had had engraved, and the Bzt was said to have been the Yellow Thearch's record of revelations from an auspicious animal called the *boze*.[61] Both texts are mentioned in a discussion of apotropaic techniques for Daoist adepts in Ge Hong's *Baopuzi neipian*.[62]

But the apotropaic function of writing is not easily separated from its administrative function, as Seidel and other students of the Daoist religion have pointed out; hence the use of tallies (*jie* 契) to make binding contracts with spirits, talismans (*fu* 符) to embody their power, registers (*lu* 籙) to list the ones with which an adept had established official ties. If writing was the key to the increased bureaucratization during this period of human relations with the spiritual forces of the cosmos, it was also the key to the growing unification of the empire, the centralization of decision-

---

60. Yasui and Nakamura 1971–88, 6:140; cf. the comments and tr. in Seidel 1983, 322.

61. I have not located the single fragment from the *Jiudingji* said to be cited in FYZL (Jiang 1935, 40; Seidel 1983, 321 n. 100). There is a Daoist alchemical text which, at least in its title, preserves a memory of this tradition: *Huangdi jiuding shendan jingjue* 黃帝九鼎神丹經訣 (HY 884); cf. Seidel 1983, 312 n. 67, 321 n. 100; a text of the same title (but without the *jue* suffix) is cited in Ge Hong's *Baopuzi neipian* and so existed by the early fourth century. Fragments of the *Bozetu* preserved in collectanea are assembled in the JDJL edition; on this text, Jiang 1935, 40ff. and 56ff.; Harper 1985, 491ff.; Kaltenmark 1949, 371; Seidel 1983, 321. Seidel in fact characterizes the *Bozetu* as a *chenwei* text. There is also a Dunhuang manuscript (Pelliot 2682) titled *Boze jingguai tu* 白澤精怪圖 with text and 19 pictures, on which Lin Congming 1977.

62. *Baopuzi neipian* 17.13b–14a; tr. Ware 1981 [1966], 295; discussed in Jiang 1935, 40–41, 56ff.

making, and an unprecedented degree of bureaucratic surveillance over people's residence, travel, and communication.[63] The Qin "burning of the books" and standardization of script, and the fixing and engraving of an imperially approved canon under the Han, show the rulers' appreciation of the importance of controlling writing as a way of controlling ideology.[64]

Finally, the symbolic capacities of writing lay at the core of cosmological thinking, the goal of which might be summarized as the twin attempts to reduce the observed complexity of all phenomena to a relatively simple set of taxonomic, correlative principles, and to reduce these principles to a diagram, table, or chart. The *loshu*, the *hetu*, the spatial layout of the *mingtang* keyed to the temporal grid of the monthly ordinances, the *fenye* mapping of celestial onto terrestrial zones, the progressive schematization of geography, the rise of systematic cartography: all of these attempts to encapsulate in miniature the articulate structure (the *wen* 文 or pattern) of knowledge and of reality depended on the organization of written signs into a spatial matrix.[65] In turn, writing itself was held to be an imitation of natural patterns; written signs captured the inherent structure of things; their invention was sparked by close observation of bird tracks, markings on turtles or dragons, or patterns in the land or the night sky.[66]

Summary

The ideas and institutions we have surveyed share a set of fundamental features (see Table 1). (1) Each is structured by a graded distinction and a dynamic, often ritualized, exchange-like process between the exemplary center of the world and its periphery. (2) The center's attitude toward the periphery may be summarized as one of collection. Goods and information are gathered from the periphery, either by the ruler's travel outwards or by subordinates'

---

63. Loewe 1967, v. 1; Sage 1992, 134.

64. Bodde 1938; Barnard 1978.

65. On these systems, inter alia, Cammann 1961; Saso 1978; Major 1984. On cartography, Herrmann 1922; Nakamura 1947; Needham 1954–, 3:533ff.; Unno 1983.

66. For a collection of texts on writing's origin, *Shiwu jiyuan*, fasc. 1210, pp. 127ff. On views of writing, Fung 1952–53, 2:92; Acker 1954, 1:61ff.; Gernet 1959, 1963; Shih 1959, 10; Chaves 1977, 203; Robinet 1979a, 29ff.; Hay 1983; Ledderose 1984, 256–57; Lagerwey 1985; Schipper 1974.

Table 1.   Modes of Cosmographic Collecting

	Tribute system	Portents system	Music Bureau	Tour of inspection
Objects collected	valuable, rare, reg-ionally distinctive products	celestial and terrestrial aberrations	popular songs	popular customs, tribute objects
Agents of exchange; "others"	barbarians (ranked by degrees)	Heaven = sender, people = reporters	"folk," officials	"folk," local deities

reporting inwards. Much emphasis is placed on visual, less on au-ral, observation of the periphery;[67] at times, officials and the people are metaphorically assimilated to the role of sense-organs that report to the "mind"-ruler at the center. (3) The goods and information collected, though varied, are mostly anomalous in some way: they deviate from some standard; they are rare or ex-otic or aberrant, weirdly shaped or named, shifting and unstable, mutated, irregular, or encrypted. (4) Knowledge about these anomalous objects, creatures, customs, and events, once garnered through observation, is written down in texts for storage, display, and edification in the center; writers of such texts are classified as historians.

To rule the world was to collect the world. Governance en-tailed a cosmographic enterprise, a placing of the periphery, espe-cially that which was anomalous in the periphery, into some sys-tematic relationship with the center. There was a locative concern to have "a place for everything and everything in its place." Once things were collected, writing enabled them to be situated and de-picted in a unified taxonomic field, a text, table, picture, or chart structured according to proper moral principles and correlative categories.

In late Warring States thought, only a few voices—notably

67. As Marcel Granet remarked, "It is in looking across a long dis-tance [*wang* 望] that the lord [*wang* 王] illumines his domain by means of his bright and pure virtue, and chases off all *ombre de barbarie*" (Granet 1952, 130–31).

that of the inner chapters of the *Zhuangzi*—dissented clearly and strongly from a worldview that included, or at least was compatible with, this cosmographic structure. The *Zhuangzi* inner chapters argued the irrelevance of fixed taxonomies, the danger of clear hierarchies of value, the relativity of cultural judgment, and the limitations of language; they showed delight in the anomalous and the extraordinary as revealing aspects of reality not dreamt of in the received view of things, hence as uncollectable (or, rather, "collection" lost its sense). By the Han, however, this way of thinking about anomalies had gone underground (the Huanglao school favored in the early Han being much more locatively oriented than *Zhuangzi*'s inner chapters and having much more in common with the cosmologists[68]), not to resurface until the third and fourth centuries C.E. in the heady decades of "pure conversation" (*qingtan* 清談) and the writing of the *Liezi*.

Part Two: Justifying the Genre of Anomaly Accounts

The burden of the following is to show how writers and readers of an emergent genre of texts—texts centrally concerned with describing and narrating anomalous phenomena of many kinds—justified their activity during the Han and throughout the Six Dynasties. In particular, I will show that some claimed the cosmographic tradition outlined above as their justifying precedent. At issue here are not the motivations or interests of those who wrote anomaly accounts, but the ways in which they (and their readers) framed the writing and reading of such texts as a meaningful and—more crucially—warranted activity, an activity grounded in ancient, canonical norms. The old, deep ambivalence toward anomalies demanded some such framing.

This ambivalence can already be glimpsed as it runs thread-like through the ideas and institutions discussed above, an uneasy teetering between suspicion of and fascination with things strange. Barbarian ways are just that, yet they are to be observed and accounts of them entered in the historical record; tribute articles from far-flung regions are hoarded in the capital. Popular customs and "mutated" songs are observed, recorded, and reported in

---

68. On similarities—and differences—between Huanglao and various other currents of thought in the period, Peerenboom 1993, 32, 242, 254–55.

order to be "corrected," yet their deviance from the norm is also taken as instructive for the ruler, the privileged basis for historians' remonstrances; transformative influence flows upwards as well as downwards. If auspicious portents are gathered from the periphery to legitimate the ruler's policies, inauspicious portents signal the need for "correction" in the center. The weightiest sacra of cosmo-political power are vessels inscribed not with positive pictures of virtue but with negative pictures (as it were) of that which the ruler's virtue attracts, namely the weird spirit-beings—the cosmo-political equivalent of anti-matter—native to the nine provinces, the fealty of which is thus symbolized.

This same ambivalence toward the strange and the spirit-realm is expressed in the *Analects* list of things Confucius did not speak of, as well as in its admonition to "sacrifice to the spirits *as if* the spirits were present."[69] Note, however, that the Confucian attitude is one not of indifference but rather of studied avoidance. Spirits and the rites for them, shamans, and other such matters obviously formed the locus of a problem for the this-worldly, morality-centered Confucian approach to life. The chapter on rites in the *Xunzi* represents a highly "hermeneutical" approach to this problem, tellingly different from the chapter on ghosts in the *Mozi*, which represents a more pragmatic, less tradition-bound, and unhesitant approach.[70]

The same ambivalence surfaces in early statements on texts belonging to the emergent genre of anomaly accounts. Consider first this account (itself from a collection of anomaly accounts, Wang Jia's Syj) of the third-century writing and reception of Zhang Hua's (232–300 C.E.) Bwz:

> [Zhang Hua] liked to read books dealing with secret and marvelous matters and with charts and prognostications (秘異圖緯之部). He selected various remnant writings from all over the empire, examined records dealing with strange and divine things (神怪) dating from the beginning of writing, and collected things told of in the lanes and hamlets in recent times, and thus created the *Bowuzhi* in four hundred fasci-

---

69. *Analects* 3.12: 祭如在, 祭神如神在, the second clause being a gloss on the first; cf. Waley 1938, 97.

70. Xunzi on the ritual service of spirits: Campany 1992; Graham 1989, 255–61 (cf. 254 for Xunzi on sightings of ghosts). Mozi on spirits: Graham 1989, 38. I mean "hermeneutical" here in the strong sense suggested by Van Zoeren 1991, 25.

cles. He presented it to [Jin] Emperor Wu [r. 265–289 C.E.].
The Emperor summoned him for questioning and said: "Sir,
. . . your broad-ranging learning is without equal. . . . But
your recording of affairs and your choice of words are unsubstantial and exaggerated (浮妄) in many places. . . . Formerly,
when Confucius edited the *Classic of Odes* and the *Classic of
Documents*, he did not include the obscure and dark affairs of
the ghosts and gods (不及鬼神幽昧之事), and thereby did not
speak of 'prodigies, feats of abnormal strength, natural disorders, or spirits.' But in your case, when people read your
Bowuzhi they will be startled by what they have never heard
before and marvel at what they have never seen (驚所未聞，異
所未見). It will only frighten and confuse later generations,
disturbing the eye and ear (將恐惑亂於後生繁蕪於耳目). Therefore, you should remove some of the more unsubstantial and
doubtful (浮疑) material and divide it into [only] ten fascicles."

In the Emperor's presence, Zhang Hua was then granted an
inkstone, a brush, and fine paper—all precious tribute objects
from remote places. The story ends on a perfectly ambivalent note,
for we are told that, after thus cautioning Zhang about his work—
yet also rewarding him for it—"the Emperor always kept the ten-
scroll *Bowuzhi* in his book box and looked on it on his days of lei-
sure."[71] Since this story about an anomaly account occurs in another, later anomaly account, we can assume that it was meant
(among other things) as a persuasive strategy to legitimate the
writing and reading of such accounts, and to offer a model of the
way in which a ruler might respond when presented with one.[72]

Such "meta-texts"—documents *about* texts of a particular
genre and about how others viewed or responded to them—stand
between texts and their readers, forming a frame within which
readers' approach to texts of the genre already begins to be

---

71. Syj 9.7a; my tr. differs somewhat from that of Foster 1974, 279–
80.

72. The ambivalence toward anomalous material as well as the
strategies for addressing it that I am reviewing here seem analogous to
the traditional Confucian ambivalence toward the erotic content of the
Odes and the hermeneutical strategies deployed for neutralizing the danger of that content; cf. Van Zoeren 1991, 8–11. The key difference is, of
course, that anomaly accounts were never canonical in the way that the
Odes were; this explains why they, unlike the Odes, produced no inten-
sive commentarial tradition.

shaped. In early medieval China, this framing was most explicit in prefaces, where authors (or later readers or redactors of the text in question) could establish a warrant for the sort of writing to follow (as well as for the reading of it), and bibliographic treatises, in which scholars could comment on the origin, precedent, and value of particular texts or genres of texts, and could also construct an understanding of their significance by classifying them in relation to other texts, emplacing them in a hierarchical taxonomy that often specified the degree of canonical value possessed by a text or a genre.

There is not as much of this sort of evidence concerning early anomaly accounts as one would like, but what there is suggests three things: an increasingly clear awareness, beginning in the Han but accelerating during the Six Dynasties, of anomaly accounts as a distinct genre of writing; an ongoing uneasiness about anomalous material, manifested in continuing justifications of the genre long after its emergence; and an often explicit, sometimes implicit, appeal to the cosmographic traditions outlined above as the most detailed and forcefully argued strategy of justification.

Let us now review this evidence, beginning with the earliest generic designation for what appear to have been lists of anomalous narrative or descriptive items associated with legendary figures. That designation was *xiaoshuo* 小説, perhaps best translated in this context as "lesser sayings"—"lesser," as we will see, probably both in the size of textual units and the imputed significance of their contents.

"Lesser Sayings" (*xiaoshuo* 小説)

The term *xiaoshuo* first appears in one of the fragmented, miscellaneous chapters of the *Zhuangzi*, in the context (usually overlooked in discussions of the term) of a story about Prince Ren, who fished patiently from atop Mount Kuaiji, using a huge line baited with fifty bulls. After a year, a gargantuan fish swallowed the hook, churning up the sea as it fought the line; having landed it, Prince Ren dried and cut it up, and it sufficed to feed masses of people. "Since then," the text continues,

> the men of later generations who have piddling talents at influence and persuasion (*fengshuo zhi tu* 諷説之徒) all astound (*jing* 驚) each other by repeating the tale. Now if you shoulder your pole and line, march to the ditches and gullies, and

watch for minnows and perch, then you'll have a hard time
ever landing a big fish. If you parade your little theories
(*xiaoshuo* 小説) and fish for the post of district magistrate,
you will be far from the Great Understanding (*dada* 大達). So
if a man has never heard of the style of Prince Ren (*Renshi
zhi fengsu* 任氏之風俗), he's a long way from being able to join
with the men who run the world.[73]

Although the term *xiaoshuo* is here obviously not used in any generic sense to refer to a type of writing, both the point of the passage and the terminology and rhetoric in which it is couched suggest that later writers may have been alluding to this passage
when they used *xiaoshuo* as a label for anomaly accounts.[74] The
term here expresses disdain for the "littleness" of Confucian concerns in contrast to the vast, capacious scale on which Prince Ren
(read: the Daoist) operates, that of "great understanding."[75] It is by
contrast with the extraordinary feat of Prince Ren that this littleness becomes apparent; the feat becomes material for "odd stories"
passed down through "astounded" generations; and it embodies
the "style"—*fengsu*, better translated "custom" were it not used
here to describe an individual (or perhaps the behavior of those of
his ilk [*shi*])—of a man who has great understanding. The very
language of the passage as well as its extraordinary matter and
its contrastive rhetorical strategy all foreshadow later anomaly
accounts.

The earliest known use of *xiaoshuo* to designate a literary
genre occurs in the *Xinlun* 新論 of Huan Tan 桓譚 (ca. 43 B.C.E.–
28 C.E.), an Old Text treatise Huan wrote (probably ca. 26 C.E.) to
criticize the contemporary Confucian fascination with prognostication or *chenwei* texts. Curiously, the passage goes without much
comment in standard studies of the genre, even though it is of crucial importance for piecing together what the earliest texts so
labeled looked like.

---

73. *Zhuangzi* 26/15; tr. slightly modified from Watson 1968, 296.
A. C. Graham (1981) does not include the passage in his collection.

74. Pre-Han "persuaders" often related anecdotes and parables to
make their points. The *chushuo* 儲説 sections of the *Han Fei zi*, for example, are collections of Legalist "persuasions."

75. The "Correcting Names" (*Zhengming* 正名) chapter of the *Xunzi*
uses the related term *xiaojia zhenshuo* 小家珍説, "the idiosyncratic say-
ings/persuasions of lesser schools," to criticize non-standard, hence "disorderly" (*luan* 亂), uses of language, as opposed to the standard, ordering
(*zheng* 正) uses it advocates. *Xunzi jijie* 16 (429).

Those in the tradition of *xiaoshuo* collect fragmentary and petty utterances, and draw analogous discussions from near at hand, to make short books. But [these writings] contain words worth heeding on the subjects of self-control and the regulation of one's family.

小説家合叢殘小語，近取譬論，以作短書，治身理家，有可觀之辭.[76]

We note, first, that *xiaoshuo* texts were "fragmentary" in shape. Huan's description suggests lists of short items—in fact, items written on shorter strips of bamboo than those used to write classics, thus also implying the uncanonical status of these texts.[77] Second, we note Huan's use of the double verb *conghe* 叢合, "to collect," to characterize how these books were assembled; the suggestion is of short, discrete items assembled from different sources into the text. Third, the mention of the metaphoric, indirectly meaningful character of these books is difficult to interpret but may be an attempt by Huan to claim didactic value—usefulness in moral and family cultivation (obviously a key criterion of worth for Confucian readers)—for texts that on their surface had nothing to do with such matters. Finally, Huan registers ambivalence, describing these books in diminutive terms yet also recommending them as being of some limited worth.

Only slightly later is Ban Gu's 班固 (32–92 c.e.) characterization of the "*xiaoshuo* tradition" in his HS "Treatise on Belles Lettres" (*Yiwenzhi* 藝文志). Building on the earlier classificatory efforts of Liu Xiang (79–8 b.c.e.) and his son Liu Xin (d. 23 c.e.), which included seven bibliographic categories (*qilue* 七略), Ban placed *xiaoshuo* last in a list of ten "philosophical traditions" or guilds (*zhuzi jia* 諸子家) and their representative texts held in the imperial library. He describes this tradition and its textual lineage (represented by fifteen titles, as discussed in the previous chapter) as follows:

---

76. Chinese text quoted from Wang Guoliang 1984, 4; my tr. differs from that of Pokora 1975, 212; cf. DeWoskin 1974, 194–95, which is interpolative. On the nature and dating of the *Xinlun*, Pokora 1975; ECT, 158–60. Pokora indicates this fragment survives in a note in *Wenxuan* 31, but I have yet to locate it there.

77. On the double significance of "short books" (*duanshu*), Pokora 1975, 226 n. 43; cf. Forke 1962 [1907–11], 2:77 n. 6, who translates it from Wang Chong as "trivial books"; Tsien 1962, 104–7, on the varying length of bamboo strips and their reflection of the relative value placed on texts.

The *xiaoshuo* tradition probably originated from the "Fine Grain" Office. Its works were created from the "hearing in the highroad and retelling in the lane"[78] of street-conversations and alley-stories. As Confucius said, "Even the minor arts are sure to have their worthwhile aspects. But if pursued too far they tend to prove a hindrance, for which reason the superior man does not practice them."[79] Although that is so, neither are they to be destroyed. Even things touched on by villagers of some little knowledge were collected together and not forgotten, lest they contain just one saying that could be selected out—even though they were [but] the discussions of woodcutters and madmen.

小説家者流, 出於稗官, 街談巷語, 道聽塗説者之所造也, 孔子曰, '雖小道, 必有可觀者焉, 致遠恐泥, 是以君子弗為也,' 然亦弗滅也, 閭里小知者之所及, 亦使綴而不忘, 如或一言可采, 此亦芻蕘狂夫之議也.[80]

Unlike Huan Tan, Ban Gu speculates on the origin of the texts he labels *xiaoshuo*. He speaks of them as emanating from a discrete tradition, guild, or lineage, and hazards a suggestion about the "office" with which this tradition may have been associated—although he may have been shoehorned into this by his scheme of supplying an office for each of his ten categories of texts. The early third century Ru Chun 如淳 glossed Ban's "Fine Grain Office" (*baiguan*) as having been named metaphorically after the way in which "street-conversations and alley-stories" work matters over in detail, the term *bai* meaning a small grain, one of fine consistency. He added: "Kings grew anxious to know the manners and customs (*fengsu*) of the villages, so they established the Fine Grain Office and staff and hence named it thus. Even today, conversations are still called *bai*."[81] Regardless of the accuracy of this etymology, it is crucial to note that the *xiaoshuo*, along with the works in the "Odes" section, are uniquely said to be the work of

---

78. A quotation from *Analects* 17.14: "To tell in the lane what you have heard on the highroad is to throw merit away" (Waley 1938, 213).

79. In the *Analects*, this passage (19.4) is put in the mouth of Zi Xia, one of Confucius' disciples. In translating, I have consulted Waley 1938, 225; DeWoskin 1974, 195–96; and Lau 1979, 146.

80. HS 30 (1745); cf. DeWoskin 1974, 195–96, from whose tr. mine differs; Wang Guoliang 1984, 2.

81. HS 30 (1745); cf. Wang Guoliang 1984, 2; DeWoskin 1974, 195 n.3.

officials who wrote down what they heard among the people and reported it to the ruler. The works of no other school are said to have been produced in this way.

More important is Ban's strong and repeated indication of the rustic and "minor" sources of *xiaoshuo* texts and probably, by extension, of the texts' subject matter as well. His diminutive language echoes Huan Tan's; both suggest *xiaoshuo* were perceived as markedly less significant and less orthodox than any other category of texts, and as decidedly uncanonical. Ban's only comment on the form of these texts is that they were "collected [literally stitched] together" (*zhui* 綴), suggesting, as Huan's characterization affirms, lists of discrete items perhaps not well integrated into textual wholes.

Like Huan, Ban shows ambivalence regarding the value of *xiaoshuo*; yet, in keeping with the Han bibliographic project and his own historiographic aims,[82] he insists on preserving them, since they constitute authentic records of the past and may contain useful nuggets. In the postscript to his section on "philosophers," Ban dismisses this tenth "school," saying that "only nine schools [of the ten] are worth reading" (其可觀者九家而已).

Legends of the Writing of the *Shanhai jing*

Han and later scholars maintained that the *Classic of Mountains and Seas* (Shj) was a direct product of the cosmographic tradition outlined above: it was compiled, they said, as the verbal explanation of the images of strange creatures cast on the nine tripods, both the images and the text having been gathered during Yu's work of ordering the lands and waters. Yu was said to have been accompanied during his labors by a scribal minister named Bo Yi 伯翳 (or two ministers named Bo and Yi);[83] it is this figure (or these figures) who, paralleling Yu's ordering of the land and water through engineering projects, was responsible for simultaneously ordering it through graphic projects—writing down the anomalous phenomena observed at each place.

---

82. On which Shi Ding 1992, who argues that Ban's historiography was "centrist" in the sense that it was motivated by the attempt to enhance cultural and political unity—but through rites more than laws and punishments.

83. Or, as in the Liu Xin passage following, *both* a figure named Yi *and* another named Bo Yi (or *two* others named Bo and Yi).

Thus, the court scholar Liu Xin 劉歆 (d. 23 C.E.),[84] in his "Memorial Submitting the *Classic of Mountains and Seas* [to the Throne]" accompanying the edition of the work he and others had prepared, could write:

The *Classic of Mountains and Seas* originated in the days of [the legendary sage kings] Tang and Yu. In former times floodwaters were inundating the Central Kingdom; the common people had lost their homes and were taking shelter on high ground and in trees. [In dealing with this situation] Gun failed, so the Emperor Yao commissioned Yu [in legend Gun's son] to succeed him. Riding four carriages, Yu traveled along the mountains clearing forest and fixing the tall mountains and the great rivers. Yi 益 and Bo Yi[85] were responsible for arraying[86] the birds and beasts, naming the mountains and rivers, categorizing the herbs and trees, and separating [or distinguishing among the types of] water and land. With help from the [spirits of the] four marchmounts, they made a circuit through the four quarters, reaching places where human tracks rarely had reached and where human conveyances scarcely had penetrated. Within they distinguished [the phenomena of] the mountains of the five regions, without they divided [the phenomena of] the eight seas, recording the rare treasures and anomalous creatures and the things produced in each strange place (紀其珍寶奇物異方之所生), whether it be the waters or lands, flora or fauna, birds, beasts or insects each harbored, or the things of good omen it concealed, or the rare kinds of humans living beyond the four seas in distant realms (及四海之外絕域之國殊類之人).

---

84. Son of Liu Xiang, bibliographer, astrologer, advisor to Wang Mang; his original name was Liu Xiu 秀 but was changed in 6 B.C.E. (see HS 36, 1972). I am not sure from whence Yuan Ke derives this document, which is not quoted in Liu Xin's HS biography; but the ECT accepts it as genuine.

85. It is possible to read this passage to mean three figures, but the syntax supports the interpretation I give here. Han and later scholars obviously differed among themselves over the number of officials involved.

86. This term, *qu* 驅, often means "expel" in such a context and is commonly the verb used when exorcisms of ghosts and demons are described. But it can also mean a drawn-up battle formation, and the context suggests not the expulsion of creatures but their systematic recording—or perhaps both actions, since recording and controlling were virtually inseparable gestures in the Chinese cosmographic tradition.

Yu, then, divided the land into nine provinces and saw that these paid tribute [or took charge of the land to perform his tribute], while Yi and the others categorized creatures into good and pernicious and thus wrote the *Classic of Mountains and Seas*. This work is entirely composed of matters left out of [other accounts of] sages and worthies (皆聖賢之遺事) and is obviously an ancient writing (古文); the matter it contains is clearly reliable.[87]

That this etiology for the *Shanhai jing* is historically inaccurate is of no consequence here; what matters for our purposes is the connection Liu Xin draws between this text—the earliest major account of anomalies to have come down to us in something reasonably close to its probable original form—and the cosmographic tradition of court-sponsored collecting of anomalies from the periphery.

Liu Xin did not stop there, however. To defend the value and integrity of the text he was submitting to the emperor, he cited two instances when advisors to earlier Han emperors—men who were both academically learned and skilled in certain more "occult" arts—drew on this repository of esoteric knowledge to tell their ruler something he did not and could not know from other, orthodox sources, something concerning an anomalous phenomenon with which he had to deal. This passage, too, is laden with significance for us and hence worth quoting at length:

Once when Emperor Xiaowu [Emperor Wu, r. 141–87 B.C.E.] was presented an anomalous bird as tribute, he tried feeding it all manner of creatures; it would eat none of them. When Dongfang Shuo 東方朔[88] saw it, he told not only the bird's name but also what it would eat—and his words proved correct. When Shuo was asked how he knew this, [he said] he had taken it from the *Classic of Mountains and Seas*. During Emperor Xiaoxuan's reign [Emperor Xuan, r. 74–49 B.C.E.], a stone chamber was discovered when the great rock in Shang commandery[89] was shattered; inside was found a man bound and shackled. At that time my father, [Liu] Xiang, who was

---

87. Quoted in Shj, 477.

88. An advisor-adept of whom more will be said in Chapter Seven.

89. This commandery, embracing part of the Ordos chain in modern Inner Mongolia and northern Shensi, figured importantly in Han relations with the Xiongnu and Qiang peoples of the northwest.

serving as Grand Master of Remonstrance, said that this was the vassal Er Fu 貳負. When asked how he knew this, he too gave the *Classic of Mountains and Seas* as his source; for it says: "When Er Fu executed Jie Yu, the Emperor fettered him at Shushu Mountain, shackling his right foot and tying his hands."[90] When he submitted this the Emperor was astounded. From this point on courtiers marveled at the *Classic of Mountains and Seas*, and learned literati and prominent Confucians studied it. For they considered it marvelous that in it could be consulted portentous, mutated, and anomalous creatures (*zhenxiang bianguai zhi wu* 禎祥變怪之物) and in it could be seen the songs and customs of strange peoples from distant realms (*yuanguo yiren zhi yaosu* 遠國異人之謠俗). Thus the *Classic of Changes* says: "[The sages] spoke of the most occulted things under Heaven, yet they cannot be called despicable."[91] Gentlemen of broad-ranging learning (*bowu zhi junzi* 博物之君子) need have no doubts about [the *Classic*]. Respectfully submitted at risk of death by your vassal Xiu.[92]

This is a rich piece of persuasive speech. First of all, we again note the felt need to justify texts about anomalies; Liu Xin is attempting to carve out a cultural niche for texts whose subject matter was evidently frowned upon by some of his contemporaries. Secondly, there is the function of such books depicted here: he who knows their contents is privy to the true names, identities, and histories of anomalous things, and knowing these is, as we have seen, of capital importance within the cosmographic tradition. Correct knowledge of anomalies, though esoteric, thus creates access to political and cultural power; both cases cited by Liu Xin involve courtiers who know something the emperor wants to know, something no other courtiers are in a position to provide. The ability to provide them inspires awe and respect—one becomes something of an anomaly oneself. Liu adroitly clenches both of these points with the *Yijing* quotation, claiming it to be possible, in ef-

---

90. The passage Liu Xiang cited on this occasion is found at the head of the sixth *juan* of today's text (Shj 285–86). Binomial compounds read *jieyu* and written with different graphs appear elsewhere (in the Shj and other early texts) as the names for several hybrid creatures.

91. Liu Xin here quotes from the *Xici* or "Appended Verbalizations" to the *Yijing*; the passage is found in section A8 (corresponding to sec. VI, p. 41 in the HY text) and is further discussed in Chapter Seven.

92. Shj, 477–78.

fect, to journey outward (through the "broad-ranging learning" acquired from such texts) to the anomalous periphery but still safely return to the center, indulge deeply in "the most abstruse things" without losing oneself in "disorder," inspect that which escapes a taxonomic place without surrendering—indeed, while advancing—one's own place at the hub of the world. To paraphrase Zhuangzi, the uselessness of anomalies has its uses.

Other Han authors echo this same tradition of how the *Shanhai jing* was written. Zhao Ye 趙曄, reputed author of the *Wu Yue chunqiu* 吳越春秋 (*Spring and Autumn Annals of Wu and Yue*, mid-1st c. C.E.), wrote:

> Yu . . . toured the four quarters, planning his work with Yi and Kui.[93] When in their travels they reached a famous mountain or great marsh, they summoned the deity of the place and questioned it about the "veins" of the mountains and rivers, whether there was gold or jade to be had, the categories of birds, beasts and insects, and the human tribes of the various strange realms and anomalous territories lying in the eight directions. Yi was ordered to collect and record all this, and [the record] was named the *Classic of Mountains and Seas*.[94]

Wang Chong likewise reports the following legend:

> Yu oversaw the ordering of waters, Yi oversaw the ordering of strange creatures (*yiwu* 異物). Even to the farthest mountains beyond the seas there was no place they did not reach. He [Yi] took what was heard and seen and produced the *Classic of Mountains and Seas*.[95]

In the sixth century, Yan Zhitui again echoed the same idea.[96]

In short, attributing the Shj to Yu and his scribe Yi as they toured and ordered the world served to link a particularly important, early account of anomalies directly to the cosmographic traditions of the *Yugong*, the nine tripods, the tribute system, and the tour of inspection—all of which supplied weighty canonical precedents.

---

93. In legend, Kui was a skilled, shamanic master of music.
94. *Wu Yue chunqiu* 6.2a–b. On authorship and dating, ECT, 474–75.
95. *Lunheng jiaoshi* 13 (597), in the *Bietong pian*.
96. *Yanshi jiaxun* 6 (*Shuzhengpian*, 160); tr. Teng 1968, 176.

Lexicography and Cosmography:
The Making of the *Fangyan*

Yang Xiong 揚雄 (53 B.C.E.–B.C.E. 18), known primarily as a poet
and Old Text author of the *Fayan* 法言 (*Exemplary Sayings*) and
the *Taixuan jing* 太玄經 (*Classic of Supreme Mystery*), also compiled a dictionary of regional and dialect expressions titled
Fangyan 方言 (*Local Sayings*). Although not an account of anomalies in any strict sense, it is a report of linguistic variata from
peripheral regions, and (as will be seen shortly) a late Eastern
Han author such as Ying Shao was likely to lump the recording of
linguistic and other sorts of unusual or anomalous matters into
a single enterprise. The exchange of letters between Yang Xiong
and the court bibliographer Liu Xin concerning this text, as
well as a later author's preface to it, show that Han and early
medieval scholars understood—or at least portrayed—the making
of such a book in the context of the *xunshou* and other cosmographic tropes.

Prompted by an imperial edict, Liu Xin wrote a letter to Yang
inquiring about the dictionary. The edict had expressed the emperor's wish to know more about the "envoys and heralds of the
three eras, the Zhou, and the Qin, who on the eighth month of the
year made a circuit of the highways seeking expressions of various
eras, children's ditties, songs, and skits."[97] In reply, Yang laments
the loss of the ancient records of such envoys, and mentions his
own desire to create a record that would preserve contemporary local speech for inspection by future generations; he also describes
in detail his own method of gathering and recording lexicographic
data.

Three centuries later, Guo Pu 郭璞 (276–322 C.E., on whom
more later), in his preface to Yang Xiong's work, even more explicitly linked Yang's efforts with the inspection tours of the ancients.

I have heard that the making of the *Fangyan* began with the
official tours of the myriad kingdoms by light-charioted envoys. [On these tours] they selected for inspection various
strange sayings (*cailan yiyan* 采覽異言). Whatever their carriage tracks met with, whatever human traces they trod
upon, they recorded them all in writings to be presented [to

---

97. Knechtges 1977–78, 312; the article helpfully sets the exchange
in context and discusses matters of dating. Liu Xin further describes the
present dynasty as "expend[ing] its attention on unusual expressions with
a desire to investigate the affairs of the four directions."

the throne]. In Zhou and Qin times these records were lost, and none [were thought to have] survived. But Yang, being of great singleness of purpose, managed to stitch together this text by working his way through [writings of] many eras. . . . As a result, it is now possible for us to survey what is around us in all directions without passing through our doors. Without troubling ourselves, things come to us to be named. We can investigate the hidden sayings of the nine pacification zones, inspect the rare utterances of the six ages, and categorize the referents and rhymes of linguistic compounds. . . . This work manages to set down folk sayings in regional divisions, comprehending a myriad rarities without confusing these with the truth. It is a strange book (*qishu* 奇書) containing a broad range of data, a work of unacknowledged eminence.[98]

In the early fourth century, then, Guo Pu, a *fangshi* of some repute and editor/commentator of Shj, still felt it necessary to justify the preservation of a work such as Yang's—a "strange book" devoted to "rarities"—by linking it to the ancient cosmographic enterprise.

Ying Shao's Preface to his *Fengsu tongyi*

Ying Shao's (140–203 [?] C.E.) preface to his Fsty similarly attempts to carve out space for a project that, while descended from the exemplary cosmographic acts of the ancient sage kings, is relatively novel in its exclusive application to "strange" objects.

The text opens with a narrative that, reminiscent of Ban Gu's introduction to his bibliographic treatise, reflects this late Eastern Han scholar's sense of distance from the exemplary past. The narrative tells of twin, interlinked devolutions: that of Confucian virtue, and that of the unity of the Confucian intellectual and exegetical tradition. After many exigencies of transmission and the proliferation of commentarial schools and texts, the consensus on the teachings of the Master broke down during the time of the hundred schools. Following the Qin burning of the books, scholars produced a frenzy of new editions and commentaries on the surviving classics, trying, against the odds of centuries, to recover as much as possible of the original texts and their meanings. As for popular sayings and practices, Ying Shao continues, those

---

98. Preface to *Fangyan*.

records of them that survived from ancient times contain matters even more unfamiliar to us today, and their origins are difficult to trace. This fragmentation of virtue and of textual knowledge is mirrored in the current state of the Han realm, of which Ying frankly writes, "The royal house has collapsed, and the nine provinces have been torn apart like a piece of cloth." In an attempt to remedy this situation, Ying submits his rectification of customs (and of records of customs): "I hereby humbly submit to Your Majesty that which I have been able to find out, dividing the material into categories, making up thirty-one chapters in all; and I have titled it *Fengsu tongyi*, meaning that it is comprehensive of the errors and absurdities of popular folkways (言通於流俗之過謬) and corrects each item in accordance with right principles" (而事該之於 義理).

Ying then introduces his subject as follows:

> *Feng* includes such things as the warmth or coldness of the air, the treacherousness or gentleness of the land, the perfection or imperfection of waters and springs, the toughness or suppleness of wood and fibers. *Su* includes those classes of beings with blood in them, which are born in imitation of [the differences in *feng* phenomena]. Therefore speech and song differ in their sounds; drumming and dancing and movements differ in their forms: some turn out straight, others crooked, some good, others vicious. But if there is a holy man who acts so as to measure and equalize them (聖人作而均 齊之), they will all return to correctness (歸於正). Lacking a holy man, they will return to their original coarseness (本俗).

After three brief citations, two from canonical texts—the *Shangshu* on the Son of Heaven's tour of inspection, and the *Classic of Filial Piety* (*Xiaojing*) on music's power to transform customs—and a HS passage on the extreme variation in regional, even local, customs that prevailed at the time of its writing, Ying draws his moral:

> On this basis it can be said that the most crucial thing in governance is to criticize manners and correct customs (辯 風正俗). In Zhou and Qin times it was customary in the eighth month of the year to dispatch Light Carriage emissaries, who would seek out local sayings from different eras and return [to court] where the reports were stored in the Palace Archives. After the downfall of the Ying clan [i.e., the Qin], this practice was abandoned and the ancient records were lost so

that no one saw them. A man of Shu, Yan Junping,[99] had [only] a thousand words or so [of these records? of this sort of record?], and the method used by Linlü Wengru[100] [to compile or arrange such records?] is scarcely a rough outline. Yang Xiong was interested in it, so when the "Filial and Incorrupt" and military officers from the various parts of the empire convened, he would circulate among them asking questions for the purpose of making an arranged and annotated continuation. He labored thus for twenty-seven years before completing the work, and it contains [definitions of?] 9,000 words. Its brilliance and style do not approach that of the *Erya* [an ancient lexicographic work, one of the Confucian classics], but Zhang Song[101] thought it "a book that may hang with the sun the moon and not be outshone." It is with great temerity, then, that I, stupid as I am, dare to submit [another such] work. . . .

[Tradition has it that], in former times, a painter was once at the court of the King of Qi. The king asked him: "What is the most difficult thing to paint, and what the easiest?" The painter replied: "Dogs and horses are hardest, ghosts and demons easiest." Dogs and horses are before people's gaze every day, so if a painting does not resemble them it fails; whereas ghosts and demons are without form, and what is without form is invisible, hence easy to paint.[102] Today, although folk sayings are said to be shallow and trifling, they are nevertheless discussed by the worthy and the stupid alike; and there is that in them which is like the dog and the horse and hence difficult to achieve. So I have assembled together items appropriate for the present times. As Confucius said, "If by chance I make a mistake, people are certain to realize it."[103] I will be fortunate if enlightened thinkers read it carefully.

---

99. A divination expert in Chengdu who honored Lao-Zhuang thought and who was Yang Xiong's teacher; HS 28B (1645), 72 (3057).

100. Mentioned in the *Huayang guozhi*; see Fsty, Pref., 12 n.4, for references.

101. He lived during the Wang Mang era; for details, Fsty, Pref., 14–16 n.10.

102. Ying Shao here refers to an old story found in the eleventh chapter of *Han Fei zi*; see *Han Fei zi jijie*, 202.

103. Fsty, Pref., 1–17. The Confucian quotation is from *Analects* 7.30; see Waley 1938, 129–30, here modified. Confucius' point, and Ying Shao's, is that one is fortunate to receive correction from others. In translating the second paragraph above I have benefited from consulting Knechtges 1977–78, 322.

Ying Shao's appeal to the tradition of cosmographic collecting is direct and clear, as is his placing of Yang Xiong within that tradition.[104] Ying Shao's text will perform a rectification of "manners and customs" similar to the lexicographers' rectification of names—a sorting out of similarities and differences, appearances and realities, and a critique of the present by reference to an exemplary past. The historical oblivion caused by social disorder has left a gap in knowledge and created a dual task to perform: recovery and preservation of fragments of textual tradition, and "correction" of contemporary popular customs which deviate from the norms established in that tradition.

Internal Evidence

We have yet to consider one more type of evidence for authors' attempts to connect their anomaly accounts with the ancient tradition of cosmographic collecting: namely, motifs internal to those accounts themselves. A fair number of items depict in operation the sorts of imperial institutions and ancient royal traditions described above. At least eighty-two items extant in eleven different texts, for example, describe tribute items being brought to the capital or presented to the ruler as he tours outlying areas.[105] There are mentions of privy chambers and storehouses, in which rulers store tribute articles and other marvelous goods.[106] Rulers are also depicted as actively seeking marvels, inviting subjects to submit them to court or traveling to outlying areas in quest of them.[107] Furthermore, more than two hundred items contain reports of portent-events and their interpretations.[108]

---

104. Judging from the similarity of language, Ying obviously had access to Yang's letter about his writing of the *Fangyan*, which was long admired for its style.

105. 41 of these are found sprinkled throughout the Syj; 13 appear in the Dmj, 10 in the Bwz, 7 in the ShuyjRf, and the rest scattered in other works.

106. Szj 5a, 6b; Bwz 2.37, 7.22; Yml 44; ShuyjRf 2.92; Xs 5, 11, 116.

107. For example, Syj passim; Dmj passim, but esp. 1b in the pref., 1.6, 2.3, 2.18, 4.1; Shuyj 18; and XuQxj 4.

108. 132 of these show up in chapters 6, 7, and 9 of Ssj (plus 8.5); 68 others appear in the Yy, particularly in the fourth chapter; 12 portent items are extant from the Shuyj; the rest are scattered throughout other texts. Ssj also contains 5 items in which dreams figure as personal portents and are interpreted (10.1–4, 10.8); cf. Yy 7.15, 7.18–33.

Not only the general fact that anomaly texts contain large amounts of the same sort of material said to have been collected from the periphery in the royal and imperial cosmographic tradition, but more specifically the fact that definite institutions and gestures from that tradition are described in the texts, suggest a high degree of self-consciousness on the part of the authors concerning the primary justification of their genre. Their depictions of rulers seeking marvels, accepting tribute, and (by implication) commissioning interpretations of portents constitute a tacit argument for the legitimacy and usefulness of the genre: past rulers are shown acting the way the present ruler should act.

Other Justifications

Although other meta-texts do not link the writing of anomaly accounts directly to ancient cosmographic precedents, they do attempt to justify it on somewhat similar grounds, usually arguing, as did Ban Gu, Ying Shao, and Guo Pu above, that the sheer preservation of old records and documentation of contemporary customs and sayings are worthy pursuits regardless of the nature of their subject matter. These comments also show an increasing consciousness of anomaly accounts as a distinct genre of writing, and a continuing unease about its legitimacy.

Ge Hong's Literary Taxonomy. Ge Hong, known primarily as the author of an important Daoist hagiographical collection (Sxz) and series of essays (*Baopuzi neipian*), commented as follows on the corpus of his own writings.

> In all, I have composed *neipian* (*Esoteric Writings*) in twenty fascicles [and] *waipian* (*Exoteric Writings*) in fifty. . . . I also compiled a book on those who are not listed in secular [histories] (俗所不列者), which became the S*henxianzhuan* in ten fascicles; I did the same for eminents who do not serve in office, which became the *Yinyizhuan* 隱逸傳 (*Biographies of Recluses*) in ten fascicles. I further extracted from the five classics, the seven histories, and the words of the hundred schools 310 fascicles (plus table of contents) on military matters, esoteric arts (方伎), and short, miscellaneous, extraordinary essentials (短雜奇要). My *Esoteric Writings*, telling of matters concerning spirits and transcendents, esoteric drugs, demonic anomalies, abnormal transformations, nourishing

life, extending one's years, exorcising evil and driving off misfortune, belongs to the Daoist traditions (屬道家). My *Exoteric Writings*, speaking of success and failure in the social realm and of worldly affairs, belongs to the Confucian traditions (屬儒家).[109]

For our purposes, three points in this passage stand out. First, Ge carves out a space for writings dealing with non-political, extraordinary, and frankly religious topics, dubbing them "esoteric," as opposed to the "exoteric," chapters dealing with political and moral issues; and he labels these as belonging to Daoist and Confucian textual traditions respectively. In thus demarcating explicitly Daoist from other concerns, he legitimates them by placing them on their own footing, even as he carefully situates that footing with reference to "exoteric" writings. Second, Ge implies the necessity of new, distinct biographical categories for transcendents as well as recluses, persons not included in "secular" biographical writings, since they typically did not serve the state; this demarcation again legitimizes the writing of hagiographical accounts as an enterprise separable from—and at the same time intelligible in terms of—that of the official historian. And Ge depicts himself culling out of canonical works (the classics, histories, and philosophical schools) passages dealing with esoteric arts and extraordinary phenomena and forming these into a separate, *sui generis* text. In short, this brief passage affords a glimpse of a moment in the process by which the world of thought was being recarved in the early fourth century; texts, and even discrete passages, dealing with (what we would now call) "religious" and "extraordinary" matters are being separated from other materials and assigned to their own bibliographic categories.

The *Dongmingji* Preface. The preface to the Dmj, traditionally attributed to the Eastern Han writer Guo Xian, although certainly later, similarly seeks to justify the preservation of "Daoist" passages on anomalies of various sorts and to argue the importance of the sort of "broad-ranging learning" possessed by Dongfang Shuo in the Han:

> For generations, my family[110] has collected and passed down Daoist books, seeking to analyze the writings of former

---

109. *Baopuzi waipian* 50.11a–b; cf. tr. in Ware 1981 [1966], 17.
110. The ZDHW ed. has "wealthy families" 富家, which makes little

sages and past worthies. The mass of these writings is inexhaustible, more than a thousand chambers could hold or a myriad chariots carry; yet still there are omissions in them. Some charge that these texts are unsubstantial and absurd, that they are not in accord with correct teaching (或言浮誕非政教所同). The canonical texts and the official historians' records of events (經文史官記事) therefore pass over and exclude them.[111] It is probably [for the same reason] that peripheral realms and strange lands (偏國殊方) are also not to be found in the written record.

I maintain that remnant data from ancient times should not be thrown away when obtained. This is even more the case [when one recalls the example of] Han Emperor Wu, a brilliant and singular ruler; for [his advisor] Dongfang Shuo relied on humor and on the "insubstantial and absurd" (因滑稽浮誕) to correct and admonish him. Shuo achieved a penetrating (*dong* 洞) understanding of Daoist teachings, making the depths of obscure (*ming* 冥)[112] traces clearly manifest.

I have herewith compiled what former historians did not record, humbly taking what I have seen and heard to compile the *Dongmingji* in four fascicles, thus making a book representing one [textual] lineage (成一家之書). Many intelligent and broadly learned gentlemen should marvel at its contents. For it was, after all, because Emperor Wu wanted to exhaustively understand the affairs of spirits and transcendents that isolated regions and distant localities made tribute of their rare marvels and strange objects (絕域遐方貢其珍異奇物); and this is furthermore why people skilled in Daoist arts (道術之人) flourished under the Han as never before or since. This is why I have gathered and arranged these materials.[113]

If we were to lay bare the skeletal structure of this piece of persuasive writing, it might look like this. (1) Daoist arts and won-

---

sense here; I follow the trs. of DeWoskin 1977b, 30 ("for generations, my family . . . "), and Eichhorn 1985, 291 (". . . heisst es, dass man in seiner Familie . . . ").

111. The term *yu* 峪, which I translate as "pass over," seems to be extremely rare as a verb; it usually means a valley or level land and occurs as such in place names.

112. The use of these terms is clearly a play on the work's title.

113. Dmj pref.; my tr. differs somewhat from that of DeWoskin 1977b, 30–31; cf. the summary in Eichhorn 1985, 291–92.

ders, as well as marvels reported from distant lands, were passed
over in silence by former official historians and by the classics, despite their quantity. (Implication: opponents' charges of novelty or
fabrication are rendered null; that the contents of anomaly texts
are uncanonical and unattested in old histories is no argument
against their truth or value.) (2) Records of such matters should
rather be collected and preserved, not only because they constitute
records of the past (and hence are intrinsically precious) but more
especially (3) because they are invaluable to advisors and rulers:
to advisors (for whom the exemplar is Dongfang Shuo) because
they provide admonitory and persuasive material, and to rulers
(for whom the exemplar is Han Emperor Wu) because knowledge
of the sorts of affairs they contain (or simply the desire for such
knowledge) attracts the allegiance of distant realms and the aid of
those skilled in Daoist arts.

This preface is an argument for the imperial patronage of
Daoists, and for the legitimacy of anomaly texts, particularly those
that concern gods, transcendents, Daoist arts, and the knowledge
of distant lands accessible, presumably, only to Daoists. In com-
mending Emperor Wu as a model for emperors, the author also (as
had Liu Xin) implicitly likens *himself* to Dongfang Shuo, insofar as
he, like that master of esoterica, is privy to knowledge of things
remote and strange—knowledge transmitted privately, outside the
official histories and palace documents, and hence accessible only
through his own writing.

Gan Bao's Self-Description.   The preface from the brush
of the Eastern Jin historian Gan Bao 干寶, author of the Ssj (written
between 335 and 349), which has won a reputation for being cryptic, is illuminated when read alongside other justications for the
collection of anomaly accounts. As it has come down to us attached
to some editions of the twenty-fascicle text, this preface was
clearly supplied by later editors from its embedded location in Gan
Bao's JS biography (which itself, although of Tang date, was based
on Jin-period documents), and it cannot well be detached from
that context. After telling of his imperial appointment as historian
and his compilation of the well-received *Jin Annals* (*Jinji* 晉紀),
Gan's biography continues:

> By nature [Gan Bao] loved *yinyang* and numerological
> arts, often poring over treatises by Jing Fang 京房, Xiahou
> Sheng 夏侯勝, and others. Bao's father had previously had a
> favorite female servant of whom Bao's mother was extremely

jealous; when the father came to die, the mother pushed the servant alive into the grave. Bao and his siblings were still young at the time and did not know of this. More than ten years later their mother died, and when the grave was opened the female servant was found lying over the coffin as though still alive; so she was taken back, and after several days she revived. She said that their father always brought her food and drink, and had shown affection for her just as when he was alive, and had told her of auspicious and unfortunate events in the household which when checked all proved accurate; and she said she had not found it unpleasant to be underground. They arranged for her marriage, and she bore sons.

In addition, Bao's older brother once stopped breathing due to illness. For several days he did not grow cold, and later he regained consciousness and spoke of seeing the affairs of the ghosts and spirits of Heaven and Earth; he said it felt as though he were in a dream, and he did not know that he was dead.

Because of these [events], Bao compiled and collected [cases of] gods and spirits, numinous anomalies of humans and other creatures, and extraordinary transformations from past and present times (撰集古今神祇靈異人物變化), calling [the work] *An Inquest into the Spirit-Realm* (*Soushenji*), thirty fascicles in all. He showed it to Liu Tan, and Tan responded, "You're what might be called the Dong Hu of the ghostly world."[114]

Now, since Bao had widely selected materials both deviating from and in accordance with [canonical texts?], he had intermixed the spurious with the actual (博採異同遂混虛實); and because of this he wrote a preface to set forth his aims. It read:

"Although we can examine what was formerly set down in records and collect excluded fragments that have come down to the present, I suppose these are not matters which

---

114. The joke turns on an allusion to a *Zuozhuan* passage in which the historian Dong Hu recorded that a certain minister "murdered his lord" because he failed to avenge his lord's death; the passage includes Confucius' praise of Dong Hu as "a good historian; his rule for writing was not to conceal" (*Chunqiu Zuozhuan zhengyi* 21 [p. 366a–b, 宣公 year 2]). This conversational anecdote also appears in Ssxy 25, p. 497; cf. Mather 1976, 409.

were heard and seen with one person's own eyes and ears. Even in these cases, how would one dare say there are no departures from the actual? Consider the case of Wei Shuo losing his sovereignty—the two commentaries on this conflict; or the case of Lü Wang's serving Zhou—[Sima Qian] preserves two versions of this.[115] Cases of this sort abound. Looked at from this viewpoint, the difficulty of unifying [different versions of] things heard and seen has been around since remote antiquity. Even when composing in set phrases a funerary announcement or following the manuals for official history-writing there are cases such as these. How much more, then, when one is peering back to narrate events of a millennium ago, or recording descriptions of unusual customs, or stitching together snippets of words across the fissures and gaps [that separate them], or inquiring of the elderly about how things were done. If one insists that each event be reported only one way and that there be no differences between verbal descriptions of it, or else one will not believe an account, then [by this criterion] former historians will also certainly be found wanting. Yet the state has not seen fit to eliminate offices charged with commenting on historical records, nor have scholars stopped their work of reciting and reading texts. Is this not because that by which [these texts] fall short is slight, while that which they have preserved is great?

"As for what I have herewith collected, when it sets forth what has been received from earlier accounts, any fault that might be found is not my own; if there are vacuous or erroneous places in what has been garnered from inquiries into more recent events, then I would wish to share the ridicule and criticism with former worthies and scholars. Even so, when it comes to what is set down here, it suffices to make clear that the way of spirits is not a fabrication (足以明神道之不誣也).

"The mass of words of the hundred schools are too many to be read in their entirety; what one receives through one's own ears and eyes is too much to be set down completely. What I have roughly chosen herewith will at least satisfy my aim of developing an 'eighth category' even if making only a poor explanation of it (今粗取足以演八略之旨，成其微説而已). I will be fortunate if future curious gentlemen take note of its

---

115. On these cases, see DeWoskin 1974, 260.

basic substance and if there is that in it which sets their minds wandering and captures their attention—and if I am not reproached for this."[116]

The overriding theme of this document is justification for a risky enterprise. Given the fantastic nature of most of his book's contents, Gan Bao clearly feared reproach for departing from actuality, for exaggerating or fabricating the events he reports. The biographical text also clearly portrays him as motivated by unusual occurrences within his immediate family circle to seek out textual precedents for them. The thrust of Gan's argument is that, since historical accounts of events are not eye-witness reports (and since even a first-person narrative must select some features of experience while omitting others), departures from actuality beset all history-writing, not just his own. Hence, unlike the author of the Dmj preface, he downplays the exclusively anomalous content of his text, seeking to minimize the difference between it and any other writings about actual events, past or present. He wants this work to be judged as "history," according to the same standards as any other work of that type. Even his interlocutor's jocular comparison of him to the ancient historian Dong Hu underscores this construction of his authorial role.

Toward the end of the preface, Gan Bao does refer, however, to the special nature of the contents of his book, when portraying his purpose in writing it. The main puzzle of this text is that he seems to state two purposes, both of which are highly ambiguous though not, on their surface, mutually contradictory: "to make clear that the way of spirits is not a fabrication," and to "satisfy my aim of developing an 'eighth category' even if making only a poor explanation of it." What might these mean?

"The way of spirits" (*shendao*) might mean one of two things: (1) the teaching (one meaning of *dao*) that spirits exist and, more specifically, that they have power to reward virtue and piety and punish their opposites, ideas certainly not unheard of in ancient canonical texts and Han-era histories; (2) by analogy with *rendao* (人道, the way of being human, thus the guiding principles of human affairs), the "way of being a spirit," thus the ways in which spirits act and the principles governing their affairs (especially their interactions with human beings). However we understand the term, a mildly polemical or apologetic note in Gan's use of it is

---

116. JS 82 (2150–51); my tr. at points differs considerably from those of DeWoskin 1974, 15–21 and 260–61, and DeWoskin 1977b, 32–33.

unmistakable: Gan portrays himself as trying to counter skepticism regarding the real existence and behavior of spirits. I see no reason, either in the language of this preface or in the actual contents of the Ssj as they have come down to us (analysis of which in later chapters will clarify what Gan may have meant by *shendao*), to doubt the sincerity of this statement.[117]

As for the mysterious *balue*—a term unattested elsewhere—I believe Gan meant to refer, in a way that would probably have been obvious to contemporary readers, to Liu Xin's *Qilue* 七略, a late Western Han treatise setting out a system of seven intellectual and bibliographic categories—a system upon which, as noted above, Ban Gu based the ten-category scheme set forth in his *Yiwenzhi*.[118] Gan Bao portrayed himself as adding an additional category to what remained in his day the canonical way of dividing up books and thought.

Put these two characterizations of purpose together, and one has a coherent and powerful justification of a genre of writing devoted more or less exclusively to accounts of events involving spirits, that is, occasions when the spirit-world and the human realm intersected. The justification builds on well established, indeed canonical foundations, but expands them: the Ssj is another history, to be judged by the same criteria as other works of that type, even though (as distinct from histories) it aims to clear the "way of spirits" from the charge of being a fabrication; its generic place is mapped onto the authoritative *qilue* classification of writing and thought, but it is so mapped by the addition of a new category. In his concern to place his text within an overall classification system, Gan Bao reminds us of Ge Hong, who had similarly attempted (probably only two or three decades earlier) to create a distinct category for his writings on spirits and esoterica, and of the author of the Dmj preface, who spoke of making a book "representing one school of thought."

Other Pre-Tang Gleanings. **1.** In his early-fourth-century preface to his annotated edition of the Shj, Guo Pu begins by noting that readers of that text typically doubted (*yi* 疑) its contents because of "its vast absurdities and twisted exaggerations, its many strange and unconventional words" (閎誕迂誇，多奇怪俶儻之言). He then defends the anomalous matter of the text in a rather

---

117. As has DeWoskin 1974, 260–64.

118. DeWoskin (1974, 261 n.70) hypothetically suggests as much; he also suggests other, to my mind implausible, interpretations.

unusual, Zhuangzian fashion by arguing the relativity of "anomalousness" as a category of judgment:

> What the world calls "anomalous" it does not know by virtue of what it is anomalous; what the world calls "non-anomalous" it does not know by virtue of what it is non-anomalous. How is this so? Things are not intrinsically anomalous; they wait upon a self and only then are "anomalous." "Anomalousness" is therefore located in a self; it is not things themselves that are anomalous.[119]

He goes on to give examples of the culture-bound relativity of judgments of anomaly; he cites the *Mu Tianzi zhuan* as an authoritative precedent for descriptions of distant, weird flora and fauna; and he laments Sima Qian's negative judgment concerning the anomalous beings described in the *Annals of Yu* (*Yu benji* 禹本記) and the Shj.

2. In what were surely allusions to a passage in the "Free and Easy Wandering" (*Xiaoyaoyou* 逍遙遊) chapter of the *Zhuangzi*, authors of anomaly accounts from the Wei Dynasty onward began using the term *zhiguai* 志怪 ("accounts [or records] of anomalies") and the name Qi Xie 齊諧 in their titles. Like the above-discussed *Zhuangzi* passage in which the term *xiaoshuo* appears, the passage that includes the term *zhiguai* is a tale of gigantically proportioned animals—in this case a huge fish, the *kun*, that changes into a huge bird, the *peng* 鵬. The text quotes a passage about the *peng*: "Qi Xie was [is?] a recorder of anomalies (齊諧者志怪者也); according to him (諧之言曰), 'When the Peng travels to the South Ocean, the wake it thrashes on the water is three thousand miles long, it mounts spiralling on the whirlwind ninety thousand miles high, and is gone six months before it is out of breath.'"[120] Whether we take this cryptic passage to refer to an author or a text, we can assume that some early medieval (but not Han) authors of anomaly accounts meant to suggest this passage as a precedent for

---

119. Shj, 478. The Chinese text is given in the epigraph to Chapter Seven below.

120. *Zhuangzi* 1/1–4; tr. modified from Graham 1981, 43. Both Graham and Watson (1968, 29) take *qixie* to be the name of a book, not an author; Graham's "Tall Stories of Qi" is much preferable to Watson's "Universal Harmony." The phrase *qixie* certainly lends itself to this interpretation, but the syntax of 諧之言曰 supports the alternate view that an author's name, not a title, is meant, and I translate accordingly.

their work since at least two titles of tale-collections incorporate *qixie* and five contain *zhiguai*.[121] Neither was a set term until these titles were crafted. To my knowledge, the earliest use of the term *zhiguai* as a clear generic designation for anomaly accounts (and their authors) occurs in the Tang, but it was not widely used in this way until the late Ming scholar Hu Yinglin (1551–1602) worked it into his six-part classification of *xiaoshuo*.[122]

3. In Liu Xie's 劉勰 (ca. 465–ca. 520 C.E.) *Wenxin diaolong* 文心 調龍 is found a passage decrying the quest for novelty that, according to Liu, impelled the production of anomaly accounts. The passage reflects (though it obviously disapproves) a by now familiar "functional" strategy of justification: namely, that anomaly accounts preserved textual fragments otherwise in danger of oblivion, and thus supplemented the historical record.

> In recapitulating the life of the distant past, the farther back the past is, the more chances there will be that the reports are unreliable. . . . Common people love what is strange (俗皆 愛奇), and pay no attention either to facts or to what ought to be. In transmitting what they hear, they magnify it in pompous style, and in recording the distant past, they describe it in detail. They throw out what is commonplace and pick out what is unusual (棄通即異), boring and digging to find support for unwarranted views, bragging that "in my book is recorded what cannot be found in earlier histories." This is the source of all error and exaggerations, the greatest of poisonous influences in writing about the past.[123]

Most telling is that nowhere does Liu accuse these authors of inventing their material outright, although he does accuse them of

---

121. Incorporating "Qi Xie": Qxj, XuQxj; incorporating *zhiguai*: Zgc, Zgj, Zgk, Zgszg, Zgz.

122. Hu Yinglin 1958 [1590], *juan* 36 (for a salient passage on "discourse on anomalies" [變異之談] to be discussed below) and *juan* 29 (for his six-part sub-classification of *xiaoshuo*). For brief discussions, DeWoskin 1974, 188–90; IC, 440. On the Tang-era generic usage of *zhiguai*, see the discussion in Chapter Two, note 15.

123. *Wenxin diaolong*, 286–87; tr. modified from Shih 1959, 92. Liu Xie's opposition to writings in the anomaly account vein is particularly significant when coupled with his known Buddhist sympathies (Gibbs 1970–71); nowhere in this passage do his objections to records of *past* anomalies take a form that would have undermined the justification for Buddhist miracle tales which were being written and circulated in his day, and which mostly concerned recent events.

embellishing accounts of events heard from others or read elsewhere. He seems to view anomaly accounts as a faulty, low-class sort of history.

4. Xiao Yi 蕭繹 (508–554), later Emperor Yuan of the Liang (r. 552–554), included a chapter of anomalous items (based on earlier accounts by other authors) in his Jlz. He implies in the chapter preface that he wrote the *Zhiguai pian* to argue that there are transformations that are intrinsically anomalous, independent of any human observer's perception of them as such—a position so closely contrary to Guo Pu's that it was probably formulated in deliberate opposition to his. The Emperor opens with his thesis— "Now as for the view that outside the ears and eyes there is no 'anomalousness,' I consider it not so" (夫耳目之外無有怪者余以為不然也)—and follows it with a series of examples, first of natural transformations from one extreme to another or exceptions to apparent regularities of nature (e.g., "heavy things should sink, but there is a 'Floating Stone Mountain'"), then of cross-species transformations. He concludes by saying "On account of this I have made a chapter on anomalies" (故作志怪篇), although quite a few of the sixty items comprised in the chapter do not concern transformations.[124] His is, then, a metaphysical justification for anomaly accounts: certain types of strange events, at least, are not only real but also intrinsically anomalous, so writing about them is permissible.

5. A major Liang-period collection of anomaly accounts, the Xs by Yin Yun 殷芸, by its title obviously alludes to the Han-period bibliographic rubric, fitting itself snugly into a venerable niche. By its contents we know that Liang authors and readers, at least, saw the term *xiaoshuo* as fitting the same sorts of anomaly-items found in works such as the Ssj and the Yml (since both the material and the form of Yin Yun's book parallel the material and form of those).

6. Xiao Qi 蕭綺, of whom we know nothing more than that he lived during the Liang (and may have been related to the imperial house), claims to have found a copy of Wang Jia's fourth-century Syj (which had already been lost by that time), added his own comments in a *lu* 錄 ("Record"), and put the text back into circulation. His last entry, although rather cryptic, is noteworthy for our purposes because it mentions as precedents for the Syj itself the descriptions of "noted mountains and great marshes" found in the *Yugong*, the Shj, and the official histories, to the variations in which the tenth and final chapter of the Syj is offered as a corrective. Xiao thus implies that the Syj (or at least its tenth chapter)

---

124. Jlz *pian* 12 (*juan* 5.14b–27a).

stands in direct and unproblematic filiation with those texts and helpfully sorts out the confusions found in them.[125]

Anomaly Accounts in Post-Han Bibliographic Rubrics

Having already examined the place of *xiaoshuo* in Ban Gu's *Yiwenzhi*—a taxonomy of writings and thought that retained considerable authority during ensuing centuries, not least because of its sheer connection with the prestigious name of Han—let us now summarize the ways in which bibliographers after Ban Gu classified anomaly accounts. Doing so will yield further insight into how early medieval men of letters viewed—and justified—the genre of anomaly accounts in relation to other genres.

Unfortunately, bibliographic catalogues compiled at the Wei and Jin courts have not survived. But from the preface by Wei Zheng 魏徵 to his SuiS *Jingjizhi* 經籍志 (presented to the throne in 656), we know that their compilers developed the now familiar four-part classification to replace the seven-part Han system; and it is these four rubrics—classics (*jing* 經), histories (*shi* 史), philosophers (*zi* 子), and collections (*ji* 集)—that Wei Zheng uses.[126]

A shift has occurred since Ban Gu's classification: with very few exceptions,[127] anomaly accounts of all kinds are now categorized as histories, not philosophies; meanwhile, they have disappeared from under the *xiaoshuo* rubric (a subcategory of philosophers) except for Yin Yun's Liang-period work Xs, which was obviously so classified by virtue of its title and not its contents.[128] Wei Zheng distributed the anomaly accounts among several subcategories of history.

---

125. Syj 10.10a–b; on Xiao Qi's "Record," Foster 1974, 92, and below, Chapter Seven.

126. On the pre-Tang origins of this system, Togawa 1992.

127. Fsty and Bwz are listed as philosophies (SuiS 34 [1006]); they are subclassified as 雜者 "miscellaneous" because they are taken as representing multiple perspectives (通眾家之意, p. 1010). The other exception involving a "core" anomaly account, Xs, is discussed immediately below. A large proportion of the texts grouped under the "five phase school" of the philosophy division (SuiS 34 [1026–40]) are portent-lists and methods for the interpretation of portents; they could be considered closely related to anomaly accounts.

128. *Xiaoshuo* are listed in SuiS 34, 1011–12; a prominent member of this category is Liu Yiqing's Ssxy, here simply listed as *Shishuo*. On Wei Zheng's classification, cf. DeWoskin 1977b, 45–47.

1. Under "mixed histories" (*zashi* 雜史), we find one "core" anomaly text that is organized in chronological fashion, Wang Jia's (*zi* Zinian) *Shiyiji*,[129] as well as several collections of narratives with a high proportion of "strange" content, particularly concerning southern regions, including *Yuejueji* 越絕記, *Wuyue chunqiu* 吳越春秋 (in two versions), and *Nanyuezhi* 南越志. Echoing themes discussed above, Wei Zheng comments on the older of these "mixed histories" that their authors were motivated by fear of losing even scraps of ancient lore; but he disapproves of authors since the Eastern Han who "culled and selected from ancient histories to make a book of their own. . . . In both content and form they are non-canonical" (體制不經). Even more suspect are histories that exhibit "casual alley-talk, preposterous anomalies and irresponsible absurdities, with no thought of what is true or false" (委巷之説, 迂怪妄誕, 真虛莫測). They all merit preservation, however, because they contain matters pertaining to rulers.

2. Under "former affairs" (*jiushi* 舊事), a category of writings used as administrative precedents (many of whose titles end in the suffix *gushi* 故事), we find the Hwdgs heading the list of texts.[130]

3. Under "mixed accounts" (*zazhuanlei* 雜傳類) falls the bulk of "core" anomaly accounts. Their order of listing suggests a yet finer, if implicit, division between biographical and other texts: collected narratives on Confucian recluses, Buddhist monks, masters of esoterica, and Daoist transcendents are grouped together and precede non-biographical tale-collections, the list of which begins with the Xuanyj and includes thirty-six titles.[131] The "mixed accounts" category overall boasts the largest number of titles (217) and the second-largest number of fascicles (1,286) in Wei Zheng's history division. In his comments on this category, Wei Zheng refers explicitly to the ancient cosmographic tradition of peripheral reports to the center, and traces the origin of these texts to "lesser affairs of the Offices of Historians" (史官之末事); but he disapproves of authors whose ambition drove them to include affairs "not in the canonical histories" (不在正史), as well as of texts that "are laced with false, absurd, aberrant sayings" (雜以虛誕怪妄之説). Thus, while Wei Zheng is willing to trace "mixed accounts" to an-

---

129. Listed in two versions (p. 961), one (titled 拾遺錄) in two *juan* and attributed to "the *fangshi* Wang Zinian," the other (titled 王子年拾遺記) attributed to the Liang author of the *lu* attached to it, Xiao Qi.

130. SuiS 33, 966–67; on the notion of *gushi* and how the Hwdgs exemplifies it, Smith (unpublished).

131. SuiS 33, 974–82.

cient precedents, he also seems acutely conscious of—and troubled by—the "expansion" (*guang* 廣, used twice) of this category of writing into increasingly anomalous subject matter since the Han.[132]

4. Under "geographical records" (*diliji* 地理記) fall geographically arranged anomaly accounts, as well as regional histories with a high proportion of "strange" (異) and "peripheral" (方) content. Heading the list is the Shj. This category comprises the second largest number of titles (139) and the largest number of fascicles (1,432) in the history division. In his gloss, Wei Zheng again refers to the ancient cosmographic tradition, citing the *Yugong* and describing the collection of information on peripheral lands, flora and fauna, products, and unusual popular customs from which these geographical writings were thought to have emanated.

For Wei Zheng, then, as for most of his predecessors (and for Tang scholars of later generations such as Liu Zhiji [661–721], author of the *Shitong* 史通), collections of anomaly reports formed a sub-branch of history, albeit one of questionable value and status; they were understood and explained as stemming from the ancient traditions of cosmographic collecting.

The early Sung JTS (compiled between 940 and 945) treated anomaly accounts in much the same way as had Wei Zheng in the seventh century. Only during the Northern Sung in the eleventh century, with Ouyang Xiu's XTS, were anomaly accounts systematically split off from history and relegated to the *xiaoshuo* category of the philosophy division; at the same time, many of these works, by now fragmented, were collected in the TPGJ. The "broad" (*guang*) in this title reflects a narrowed sense of "history," from which anomaly accounts were increasingly expunged.

Conclusion

Historians of Chinese literature have often viewed the rise of the genre of anomaly accounts teleologically, seeing it as the "origin" of a mode of writing that would later "develop" into "fiction" or "the novel." In Western scholarship, Kenneth DeWoskin's argument—reflective of most recent Western writings on the genre—that early anomaly accounts represent "the birth of fiction" and that late Six Dynasties texts belonging to the genre show "conscious fictionalizing," is perhaps the best known example of an approach

---

132. SuiS 33, 981–82.

shared by many Asian scholars.[133] His argument seems to rest on an ambiguous and simplistic definition of fiction as "something made up or imagined,"[134] but that, to my mind, is the least of its problems. I have argued in this chapter for a very different understanding of the rise of the genre. To view the earliest anomaly accounts as the locus of the "birth of fiction" is, I believe, to misapprehend them on several counts.

1. It is anachronistic as a portrayal of how contemporaries saw and represented this sort of writing. They saw it as a branch of history, dedicated to preserving endangered fragments of historical accounts and recording (and sometimes "correcting") popular customs, justified by appeal to ancient cosmographic precedent. Even critics of anomaly accounts—and there were many—charged their authors with "absurdity" and "falsehood," with misrepresenting events, even with uncultivated taste, but not with simply "making up" their narratives out of whole cloth.[135]

2. It is an inaccurate picture of how anomaly texts were actu-

---

133. Representative of some Chinese scholars' views: Lu Xun 1926 (and Lu Hsun 1976); Guo Zhenyi 1961; Liu Yeqiu 1959. Representative of some Japanese scholars' views: Maeno 1969; Takeda 1967, 1992; Shimura 1968. On the "birth of fiction," DeWoskin 1977b; he speaks of "conscious fictionalizing" in "late Six Dynasties *chih-kuai*" (49) and of the genre "maturing quickly with genuine fictive qualities" (45) but cites no specific texts in support of these characterizations. DeWoskin also categorizes the persuasive aims of texts in peculiar ways, claiming, for example, that the Yy and Jlz are among "Buddhist *chih-kuai*" and "helped to form the narrative core of the Buddhist canon" (50).

134. DeWoskin 1977b, 25.

135. Ming scholar Hu Yinglin recognized this distinction when he noted that Six Dynasties "discourses on abnormal transformations and anomalies" (變異之談) were "in most cases transmitted records of confusions and errors; they were not necessarily completely fictive [illusory] or invented discourse" (多是傳錄舛訛, 末必盡幻設語); Hu 1958 [1590], *juan* 36 (p. 486). Mair 1983 argues (citing several modern Chinese scholars' views as support) that there was essentially no such thing as "fiction" in any strong, self-conscious sense in China before the Tang, and that the very idea of fiction, presupposing certain ontological and epistemological structures, only became possible with the introduction of Buddhism—a thesis with which I agree, though I do not agree with several of Mair's specific assertions about pre-Tang *xiaoshuo*. On the intimate relationship between "fiction" and "historiography" in traditional China—which long perdured after Buddhism's introduction, despite Mair's use of the term "narrative revolution"—Yu 1988 is enlightening; Lu 1987, however, perpetuates rather than resolves traditional confusions.

ally produced. As will be seen in Chapter Four, preliminary source analysis of the contents of texts show them to be what their authors said they were: compilations of items drawn from older texts, combined with both oral and written reports of events "heard and seen" more recently.

3. It embodies a misunderstanding of anomaly texts themselves as finished, independently existing pieces of discourse—a misunderstanding, more specifically, of the poetics of these texts, of *how they mean*, an analysis of which is presented in Chapter Five.

4. It cannot account for the variety of persuasive uses to which the genre was put (a topic taken up in Chapters Seven and Eight), all of which rested on contemporaries' assumption that, whatever else could be said about them, these texts were purported to contain reports of actual events.

Viewing these texts as "made up" in any sense much stronger than "compiled," then, fits neither their authors' intentions (both stated in prefaces and, arguably, implied in the texts themselves) nor their readers' perception and reception of them. Contemporaries saw and portrayed the genre—whatever their particular and varied persuasive *uses* of it—as an extension of old cosmographic and historiographic traditions into the territory of the more or less exclusively "strange." Liu Tan's characterization of Gan Bao as "the Dong Hu of the ghostly world" nicely captures the point: at bottom, anomaly accounts were new wine in old bottles; they were a casting of familiar nets of historical, geographical, and biographical writing over an ever more demarcated, isolated, and articulated domain of objects that shared the fundamental taxonomic marker of being anomalous—most of them anomalous in some "dark" or "hidden" (*ming* 冥, *you* 幽) way. The story of the early development of the genre is unhelpfully told as one of "the birth of fiction," for the term "fiction" and all that it entails only obfuscates the case. The story is rather one of gradual isolation and spiritualization of the genre's anomalous subject matter, and regularization of the tropes and motifs under which authors explored it. Authors carried the old project of collecting the world into territory more and more exclusively populated not with all anomalies per se but with those anomalies revelatory of the spirit-world, the unseen but palpable strands that connected Heaven, Earth, gods, ghosts, demons, transcendents, animals, plants, and humans all into one vibrant, cosmic web, whose structive and active principles or veins (*li* 理), though mostly mysterious, might be disclosed inductively by a sufficient collection of cases, thus establishing the author as one possessed of knowledge hidden from most readers. This was a terrain of which Confucius had not spoken, and concerning which the time-honored classics had remained mostly silent. Authors of anomaly accounts ventured into this breach, daring to report "feats of abnormal strength, natural disorders," and, most especially, "prodigies" and "spirits."

Chapter Four

The Making of the Texts: Who, How, Why

Every genre has its own orientation in life.

M. M. Bakhtin and P. N. Medvedev[1]

There may be some views of the world and how one should live in it—views, especially, that emphasize the world's surprising variety, its complexity and mysteriousness, its flawed and imperfect beauty—that cannot be fully and adequately stated in the language of conventional philosophical prose, a style remarkably flat and lacking in wonder—but only in a language and in forms themselves more complex, more allusive, more attentive to particulars. Not perhaps, either, in the expositional structure conventional to philosophy, which sets out to establish something and then does so, without surprise, without incident—but only in a form that itself implies that life contains significant surprises, that our task, as agents, is to live as good characters in a story do, caring about what happens, resourcefully confronting each new thing.

Martha C. Nussbaum[2]

---

1. Bakhtin and Medvedev 1985, 131.
2. Nussbaum 1990, 3–4.

161

Like the preceding chapter, this one views the formation of the genre of anomaly accounts against its social, religious, and intellectual background. Here, however, we turn from the precedents appealed to by shapers of the young genre to its place in the culture of its own time. Our questions, at their simplest, are these: What sorts of persons wrote these texts? How did they write them? And why did they come to write this *sort* of text? Before taking up these questions, we must unravel a knot of assumptions that has long hindered scholars' attempts to answer them.

Prevailing Explanations of the Rise of the Genre

As we have seen, some highly literate Chinese have shown disdain for writings about things deemed "strange" almost since their inception and, in fact, right up into this century. For these writers, things or events that cross proper boundaries and ingress on proper order are, in the best of cases, annoying and hence ought to be ignored; in the worst of cases, they bring dangerous disorder and should be rectified. The subject matter of anomaly accounts largely consists of things long dismissed by some literati with words constituting a concise but vivid lexicon of distaste: in general the "vulgar" (*su* 俗) and the "disorderly" (*luan* 亂), in cultic matters the "impure," "licentious," or "illicit" (*yin* 淫), in matters of belief the "superstitious" (*mixin* 迷信) or "deluded" (*huo* 惑), and in overall significance the "lesser" or "minor" (*xiao* 小). The longstanding attitudes bound up in these terms tally remarkably closely with an almost equally old set of Western assumptions (classically set down in David Hume's *The Natural History of Religion*), characterized by the social and religious historian Peter Brown as a "'two-tiered' model" of culture—a model that is all the more powerfully determinative of the assumptions we bring to the study of culture for being mostly unconscious.[3] Modern Chinese scholars who have written on the earliest anomaly accounts have therefore done so under the influence of mutually reinforcing two-tier models, stemming from both Chinese and Western traditions; likewise, Western scholars trained in classical Chinese language and culture have often absorbed the tacit model of culture held by some traditional Chinese elite, reinforcing a tendency already prevalent in their own traditions of scholarship.

"Model" captures the powerful internal coherence of this view

---

3. Brown 1981, chap. 1; Hume 1957.

of culture but perhaps is too suggestive of a carefully worked out systematicity. For the "two-tier model" is essentially a chain of subliminal associations that comes into play when scholars seek to describe, interpret, and explain cultural phenomena—most especially cultural change. Usually presuming, first of all, a sharp bifurcation between "elite" (literate) and "popular" (illiterate) social strata, the model then posits an extremely tight correlation between persons' social level and their type of worldview (and even, in the model's crudest forms, their basic intelligence). Literate elites, particularly in the Chinese case, are assumed to hold rationalistic, often naturalistic (as distinct from otherworldly or explicitly religious)[4] worldviews, or else their religion will be of a "pure," contemplative, highly orthodox sort; the masses are assumed to be "superstitious" and to prefer their religion in impure, that is to say *mixed*, form. Given these initial assumptions, any cultural or religious change that can be characterized as a move toward or away from "rationalism" or "naturalism" (whatever these turn out to mean for a particular writer) can be ascribed to the waning or waxing, respectively, of the constant downward tug—a sort of cultural gravity—of "the popular." It is then a matter of filling in the evidential details.

This picture of cultural dynamics is so numbingly familiar as to need no further description; let us proceed directly to how it has framed scholars' views of early Chinese anomaly accounts. There are three prevailing sets of terms ("theories" would suggest an elaborateness that is missing from most attempts) in which the origin of the genre has been described, interpreted, explained, or some combination of these. In my view, none is adequate, but the first two in particular are so powerfully driven by a two-tier model of culture that they have led to serious misreadings of the historical facts. The third set of terms is the most helpful as far as it goes, but does not explain quite enough. For brevity's sake, I will summarize without doing full justice to the complexities of the cited individual authors' arguments.

The Genre as the Locus of the "Birth of Fiction"

I have already discussed this view in the previous chapter. Expressed most recently by DeWoskin and Karl S. Y. Kao, and earlier

---

4. The extreme vagueness of such terms naturally only perpetuates the model, since it accommodates a huge range of actual cultural phenomena.

by Japanese scholars including Maeno Naoaki and Takeda Akira,[5] it is a product of the attempt to portray early medieval anomaly accounts as the beginning of a process of linear development whose termini include the modern Chinese novel, novella, and short story—an attempt already evident in the twenties with Lu Xun's *Brief History of Chinese Fiction*. It partakes of two-tier assumptions in this way: the authors of anomaly accounts (note that, in DeWoskin's case, the prime example is the "Confucian" historian Gan Bao) were highly literate members of the ruling class, yet the contents of the texts betray "superstitious" mindsets and "folk materials";[6] therefore the authors (who, since they were literati, must have been "rationalist") must not have meant for the texts to be taken seriously and straightforwardly—the texts must be pulling our leg in something like the way that a late traditional allegorical novel does, for their authors could not have believed that the events they narrate may actually have happened. Or else the authors wrote of "folk" beliefs[7] as cognitively distant "ethnographers" and "folklorists" interested solely in documenting folkways for their own sake (or in exploiting their sheer literary value), while bracketing the actual contents of their documents.

This view hollows out the genre's significance to its contemporary authors and readers in a way that strains credibility. It is hard to believe that people wrote so many hundreds of textual items—indeed thousands, if we imagine the size of many anomaly accounts (as reflected in early listings) before they suffered their considerable losses—as an amusing pastime, a purely literary exercise with little or no concern for the specific contents of their texts.

The Genre as the Creation of Masters of Esoterica (*Fangshi* 方士)

Originally suggested by Qing scholars, developed by Lu Xun and greatly elaborated since mid–century by scholars such as Wang

---

5. Takeda 1967 (the same viewpoint informs his collections of essays in Takeda 1980 and 1992); Shimura 1968; Maeno 1969.

6. The latter phrase is found in the discussion in Kao 1985, 21, which draws on DeWoskin.

7. Such a view, of course, presumes that the contents of anomaly accounts are made up mostly of "folklore," a presumption that many scholars have been quite comfortable with (Foster 1974, 87; Kao 1985, 21; etc.).

Yao and Fan Ning, and supported to some extent even more recently by Li Jianguo, Wu Hongyi, and Karl S. Y. Kao, the *fangshi* thesis (as I will refer to it) essentially runs as follows.[8] The *fangshi* were men who, while originating from more than one region and learned in more than one tradition, shared two fundamental characteristics: first, though literate and in some cases highly learned, they held relatively lowly status among the *shi* or upper classes as a whole, and were, almost by definition, at a considerable remove from positions of significant political power and economic wealth; second, since they occupied a social level closer to the "popular," they were (so the theory goes) more apt than most literate persons of their day to "believe in" the realm of spirits and the efficacy of esoteric arts for supplicating and controlling them, as well as for foretelling the future and prolonging life. During the Han, they began to circulate stories, in historiographic format, documenting the truth of these beliefs and the efficacy of their own arts. These collections of stories, the earliest of which being those listed in Ban Gu's bibliography under the rubric *xiaoshuo*, were thus essentially a sort of advertisement—a way of "proclaiming the divine efficacy of their own arts" (*zishen qi shu* 自神其術), as the stock phrase of modern scholarship has it—for a group of men desiring to secure the notice and the patronage of those in higher positions. In its most extreme Hegelian–Marxist formulations by Fan Ning and Li Jianguo, this thesis is shaped by classical deprivation theory: socioeconomic disaffection in this world generates compensatory fantasizing about the unseen world; these fantasies are *written down*, since writing is a gateway to social prestige (and because it is a gateway to prestige it is also a powerful marketing[9] medium); and so a genre is born.

A natural, indeed necessary, corollary of the *fangshi* thesis is that, since mainstream, well known authors in positions of relative importance would have had neither the economic motivation nor the mentality to write anomaly accounts (and since their role was restricted to that of the sceptical, rationalist readership the lowly *fangshi* hoped to persuade), authorial attributions to them must be proven false no matter what the earliest citations and catalogue listings say. Proponents have therefore tended to place great

8. See, *inter alia*, Wang Yao 1951; Fan Ning 1957; Wu Hongyi 1979; Kao 1985, intro.

9. The most crassly commercial language in this literature is to be found in Fan Ning 1957.

weight on textual evidence when it corroborates their thesis but to discount it when it does not; thus the attributions to Liu Xiang (to whom early texts attribute the Lxz), Cao Pi or Wei Wendi (to whom the Lyz is attributed), and Tao Qian (credited with the Sshj) have been treated until recently in this century as highly suspect, despite ample and (in some cases) early textual evidence to support them,[10] and later Six Dynasties works attributed to high officials and even princes and rulers are typically ignored entirely. Furthermore, proponents defend the thesis by circular arguments: noted authors who rose from relatively humble stock but whose biographies lack the slightest suggestion of *fangshi* learning or activities—who present an apparent, glaring exception to the thesis, and of whom the prime example is Gan Bao—are said (simply *because* their origins were relatively lowly and *because* they wrote of anomalies) to have been heavily "influenced" by *fangshi*. Finally, proponents of this thesis generally lump *fangshu*, religious Daoism, and early Buddhism together: since they are all "religious" or "superstitious," they are all alike *ipso facto* "popular," as were (again by circular logic) the authors who wrote anomaly accounts in order to advance them.

This thesis is fraught with problems. (1) It separates "religion" from the rest of the culture of educated persons in early medieval times in a way that does not fit the historical facts. Major doctrinal, scriptural, and cultic developments within the Buddhist and Daoist traditions were the work of literati; Daoism in particular has often been misportrayed by those who know little about it as an exclusively popular, mass movement, so that the very word "Daoist" comes to connote "popular."[11] On the other hand, the supposedly rational, sceptical "Confucian" official, particularly at the

---

10. I, too, suspect that Tao Qian was not the author of the Sshj, but not for the reasons these scholars have advanced; see the discussions of this text in Chapters Two and Seven.

11. Or else the religion of the literati is taken not as really "religious" but as a sort of philosophy which, even then, is not taken seriously in its own right but as a source of concepts to be discussed in detached fashion in salons—as is the case in some portrayals of Buddhist circles during this period. "Gentry Buddhism" (with both its discussions of *xuan* and emptiness and its notions of karmic retribution and lay vows) and the sort of Buddhism that prompted literate authors to write miracle tales were one and the same thing, and the people engaged in these two spheres of activity were the same people.

commandery and district levels, functioned as among other things a *ritual* representative of the central administration; governance was always partly a cultic affair, and officials functioned as ritual legates. (2) The thesis reflects a misunderstanding of the social category of *fangshi* and the nature of *fangshu*, on several counts: historical records do not support the view that *fangshi* were uniformly any "closer to the people" than other literati (though they do support the view that *fangshi* was a *relatively* disparaged social designation);[12] given the cosmological assumptions that seem to have held sway throughout large segments of early medieval society, *fangshu* were highly rational, systematic, perhaps proto-scientific traditions of knowledge, not "superstitious";[13] and writers such as Fan Ning use the term *fangshi* so loosely that it comes to mean just about anyone who had some education but left writings that evinced any attitude toward the spirit world other than that of Wang Chong–like scepticism. Most importantly, however, (3) the *fangshi* thesis does not explain the variety of viewpoints actually found, on analysis, in the texts, and (4) it does not square with what we know of the authors of many anomaly accounts: not only were very few identifiable authors of anomaly texts *fangshi* in any meaningful sense of that word, but also many authors belonged to high-status families and achieved high court positions—some were even rulers.

The *fangshi* thesis works best as a hypothetical explanation of the raison d'être of the very earliest strata of texts, on the authorship of which we have no information. It also helpfully focuses attention on the question of the rhetorical and persuasive uses of anomaly accounts. And there *are* anomaly accounts that emanated from *fangshi* circles; their implied perspectives will be analyzed in Chapter Seven. But the *fangshi* thesis does not explain the development of the genre as a whole; its relevance recedes sharply as we move from the Han and Wei into the Jin and subsequent eras. And its proponents' tendency to debunk all authorial attributions that do not fit the theory—spurred by the two-tier model, which makes it hard to imagine anyone other than *fangshi* as having a reason to write anomaly accounts—undermines its credibility.

---

12. The term itself is probably diminutive, suggesting *merely* "angular," that is, narrowly limited (issuing from and/or relevant to only one *fang* or spatial quarter) and overly technical, approaches to life.

13. On *fangshu*, see Ngo 1976; DeWoskin 1981, 1983.

The Genre as the Result of a Complex Convergence of Religious, Literary, Intellectual, and Socioeconomic Factors

Wang Guoliang, Wu Hongyi, Li Jianguo, and other scholars in recent decades have tried to explain the rise of the genre by listing the social and cultural trends of the time that seem related to it. These include the influx of Buddhism and the rise of religious Daoism, the increasing privatization of writing, the exclusion from office of some literati of low-status families (spurring them to write as a way of attracting attention and thus gaining appointment), and—often—sweeping characterizations of the age as one of "superstition" and "faith." Such discussions may aid us somewhat as general portrayals of the era, but they do not really explain why these particular sorts of texts came to be written during these centuries; they do not explain why this genre was "good to think with" in a way that other genres were not. The question of why the genre arose, then, needs to be sharpened: what we want to know is, what work the new genre allowed writers to do that they were not sufficiently able to do in the other genres available at the time. I will address this question at the end of this chapter.

Let us turn now to the authors themselves. What sorts of persons wrote anomaly accounts? Does any of our information about the authors yield clues to their reasons for, or methods of, writing them?

The Authors

If we eliminate the attributions seen in Chapter Two to be clearly fictive or otherwise problematic, and if we include persons known to have written an anomaly account even when only scant fragments of it survive, we have to deal with a group of slightly fewer than forty identifiable authors.[14] The available evidence on these individuals belies any account of the origin of the genre that bases itself on two–tier models of culture. It also undercuts any notion

---

14. "Identifiable" in the sense that we have their full name; mere surname attributions are excluded. Included among these figures are Liu Xin and Guo Pu, who probably did not write anomaly accounts themselves but compiled, edited, and (in Guo Pu's case) commented on (and quite possibly added to) the Shj.

that the authors formed a unified group within early medieval society or occupied a single social niche.

Region of Origin, Family Background, and Official Status

First of all, was the writing of anomaly accounts from the Han to the Sui a regional or a truly national phenomenon? Did authors or their clans tend to originate from a particular area, or are they well distributed over the lands significantly populated by Han Chinese during these centuries? In brief, the answer is that the genre drew a geographically rather limited—not truly national—participation. The geographic distribution of authors' places of origin, however, to some extent reflects that of the bulk of the literate Chinese population from the first decade of the fourth century onward, making its significance uncertain.

If one arranges on a north–south axis the authors' places of origin that are known (some are unknown), the line stretches from Fanyang 范陽 (in modern Hebei province, about 50 km. south of modern Beijing) in the north to Le'an 樂安 (in east-central Zhejiang, the modern city of Xianju 仙居, about 35 km. west of medieval and modern Linhai 臨海) in the south. As one would expect, given the largescale southward migration of Han people after the beginning of the fourth century, however, this axis swells toward the southern end: fewer than half a dozen authors hailed from points north of the Yellow River, confirming the overall impression one gets from reading these texts that they were predominantly written and circulated (at least before the Sui) in the areas controlled by the southern dynasties. The bulk of authors came from the post-311 heartland of Han culture, with Jiankang (modern Nanjing, capital of the Wu kingdom and of the southern dynasties after ca. 311) roughly at its midpoint, including southeastern Henan, Jiangsu, Anhui, and Zhejiang. Our picture is unavoidably skewed by the significant number of texts with no known author; I suspect that many of the anonymous early texts (excepting the Shj, which many believe to reflect southern—Chu—origins) emanated from the northeast areas of Yan and Qi (modern Hebei and Shandong). Strikingly few, at any rate, were authors from points west of roughly 115° longitude—that is, west of Wuchang on the Yangzi River, Xincai 新蔡 (home of Gan Bao) on the Yi 澺 River, Chen 陳 Commandery on the Ying River, and Dunqiu 頓丘 Commandery just north of the Yellow River. Relatively numerous, on the other hand, are authors from two rather large and adjoining regions now counted as southeastern (but not, of course, the extreme southeast of Fujian and Guangdong, which were only sparsely populated by Han Chinese even after the fourth century migrations):[15] the upper reaches of the Huai River basin (including southeastern Henan and northwestern Anhui), known during the Song as Yuzhou 豫州 and (mostly western) Xuzhou 徐州, and the political and economic heart of the kingdom of Wu, extending from Jiankang southeast across the Hangzhou Bay and through the region known as Kuaiji 會稽.

The question of region can also be asked concerning the settings of anomaly account items: do phenomena reported in the texts (excepting for the moment those texts specializing in distant lands and peoples) show a regional bias? They do—toward south-central locations. In one respect, this bias merely reflects the geographic zone most heavily populated by Han Chinese during these centuries (especially after the early fourth century). Additionally, however, given that the center of southern intellectual and religious culture lay at Jiankang, it is significant that a large proportion of anomalous events are set in outlying, culturally more marginal areas west and southwest of the southern capital, and that they are much more widely distributed than the authors' places of origin themselves. True to the old cosmographic tradition, the texts report untoward events in areas far removed from the political, cultural, and ritual center at Jiankang.

When it comes to authors' family background, the *fangshi* thesis prompts us to expect the authors of anomaly accounts to have stemmed from the "cold" or "elite mean" lineages (*hanmen* 寒門) that, although containing literate sons, were frozen out of positions of real power and confined to relatively low-ranking positions in the official hierarchy. One also wonders whether the anomaly-account authors were predominantly from families of originally northern or southern ancestry. These questions are to some extent answerable by consulting the historical data on known authors, but again it must be remembered that many texts are of unknown or uncertain authorship. Furthermore, the longstanding picture of the southern dynasties as marked by an extremely rigid social hierarchy dominated throughout by a small handful of "great families" has been seriously qualified by recent scholarship. This scholarship has demonstrated that real "great family" control of southern society ended as early as 385, that men from mean elite (*hanmen*) and even non-elite (i.e., non-*shi* or *hanren* 寒人) families gained control

---

15. Bielenstein 1959; Wiens 1954.

of many appointments in the central government and the military by the mid-fifth century, and that the real determinant of young men's reputations and "local ranks" (establishing the level of office for which they were deemed qualified) was less their heredity than their recognition by senior members of the hierarchy, based on literary ability and an aesthetic of social deportment centered on a complex cultural code, evolved since the late Eastern Han, built upon a delicate dialectic between engagement and withdrawal.[16] For our purposes, the net effect of this new picture of early medieval society is double-sided: on the one hand, literary ability is confirmed as having been, throughout the period, a way especially for young individuals from lesser-known families to attract the notice of well placed officials; on the other hand, it no longer appears as the desperate gesture of last resort it was once assumed to be—one cannot always take non-official writing as a sign of social disgruntlement.

All known authors of anomaly accounts were of *shi* status. Most belonged to families that had long been among those from which important officers were drawn; but the prominence of such families waxed and waned over time, depending on their success in placing their members in high posts, and several authors, particularly early on, are described as originating from "poor" families of lesser status.[17] Until the fifth century, with the exception of Cao Pi, author of the Lyz, who became Emperor Wen of the Wei dynasty, no known authors of anomaly texts were connected with the small handful of families represented at the central court; from the Song onward, however, more and more powerful officials wrote such texts, perhaps a sign that such writings had shaken some of the moral stigma formerly attached to them. Liu Yiqing was a nephew of the military founder of the Song; Xiao Ziliang was a southern Qi

---

16. Kawakatsu 1974a, 1974b, 1982; Mather 1969–1970; de Crespigny 1980; Grafflin 1981, 1990; Holcombe 1989, 1992; Spiro 1990; Mao Han-kuang 1990. On the general social history of the period, I have also consulted Ebrey 1978, 1990; Eberhard 1977; Crowell 1983, 1990; Chin 1964; Balazs 1964; Gernet 1956, 1982; Holzman 1956, 1957, 1976; Mather 1968; Honey 1990; Johnson 1977; Miyakawa 1964, 1974; Zhou Yiliang 1963; Shryock 1963; Yang 1963b.

17. These include Chen Shi, Zhang Hua, Gan Bao, Tao Qian, Ren Fang, Wu Jun, and Wang Manying. "Poverty" in such contexts is, of course, a relative term. It also should not be taken as a necessary sign of low hereditary or cultural status among the elite; indeed, at certain points in their careers it served some aspirants well as a self-consciously adapted pose in an elite culture favoring decorous reserve over too-blatant lunging for wealth and power (Holcombe 1989).

prince, second son of Qi Wu Di; Xiao Yi of the ruling family of the Liang regime became Emperor Yuan of that dynasty in 552.

It is usually difficult to determine whether authors were of northern emigré families or belonged to old southern lineages. Most, however, seem to have belonged to the former group, with the known exceptions of Ge Hong, Dongyang Wuyi, Zhang Yan, Wu Jun, and Lu Gao, who were of families long established in the Wu region.

One may also ask after the authors' levels of official status. This question differs from that of family background in that we are asking in this case after the highest office to which authors were able to rise, regardless of their origins. The answer is that, with few exceptions, the authors of anomaly accounts, whatever their origin may have been, held positions of central—not just local or even regional—eminence by the time of their death, though not necessarily positions affording wealth or the ability to shape policy. Even a man such as Zhang Hua, who according to his biography tended sheep when young, and who was widely known for excelling in supposedly lowly *fangshu*, rose through a series of important regional offices to be appointed Chamberlain for Ceremonials (*taichang* 太常), in charge of great state sacrificial ceremonies at the imperial ancestral temple and elsewhere, foremost of the Nine Chamberlains (*jiuqing* 九卿) in prestige; because of this high court appointment he was involved in intrigues among the innermost core of Jin elite.[18] Most of the exceptions to the rule were men who declined most official appointments (or else resigned after a short stint), preferring to remain in stylish reclusion, sometimes in order to pursue religious avocations: these include Ge Hong, who requested postings to the extreme south of the Jin empire because he heard that cinnabar was available there;[19] Wang Jia, who practiced Daoist techniques in reclusion in the mountains;[20] and Xie Fu, who, a high-profile Buddhist layman, declined appointments.[21]

---

18. JS 36 (1068–78); on the office, Hucker 1985, 476.

19. JS 72 (1911–14).

20. JS 95 (2496–97).

21. JS 94 (2456–57); other sources of information about him are cited in Chapter Two. Two other possible cases are Guo Jichan, whose highest recorded office is that of *taishou* of Xinxing (but who may have held higher offices); and Wu Jun, who, despite his historiographic efforts to gain renown, seems never to have secured an appointment at court (though he did hold minor offices at the commandery level, LS 49 [698–99]). In addition, if Tao Qian were to be considered the real author of the Sshj (which I contend he cannot have been), he would be included in this group, for he

The *fangshi* thesis and the frequent mention (in discussions of the genre) of the "privatization" of writing during the early medieval centuries also lead us to expect that the writing of anomaly accounts was motivated in part by the desire to advance up the ladder of official rank. But there is no evidence whatsoever that writing anomaly accounts—as distinct from literary talent displayed in poems and *pianwen*—actually helped any of these men advance their career. Given the genre's marginal status in the eyes of some literati (judging by its reflection in the defensive tone of authors' prefaces and the sneering tone adopted by bibliographers), one may wonder if in fact the opposite is not the case: that circulating such a text with one's name attached as author was a luxury that one could afford only after obtaining high office or only if one's family was well established. Clearly this sort of writing was on the lower end of the prestige scale, valued for its content and not its "pattern" (*wen* 文), unlike poetry.[22] We would be helped here by knowing more about just how such works were received and discussed, evidence for which is unfortunately lacking.[23]

It is not so much authors' rank and status as their public identities in a world of gestural and discursive signs, and the particular offices they held (because these often determined what sorts of books they had access to), that is informative as to why and how they wrote anomaly accounts.

The Religious-Sectarian Personae of Anomaly Account Authors

Half of the known authors of anomaly accounts were men who explicitly took up a publicly expressed and recognized religious vocation, or adopted a public stance as a master of some sort of esoterica. This proportion of half includes authors who are known

---

was a classic "recluse" who preferred a life of rustic simplicity to officialdom, declined most appointments and resigned the ones he briefly accepted, and was said to have made only one trip (a sightseeing excursion to Lushan) outside his home area: JS 94 (2460–63); NS 75; IC, 766–69.

22. On the other hand, in an age when a show of aloof disinterest in the petty affairs of officialdom and an expansive transcendence of Confucian anxieties were sometimes routes to higher social status, perhaps writing an anomaly account was just the thing to demonstrate one's insouciance.

23. One thinks of the anecdote concerning the reception of Gan Bao's Ssj discussed in the previous chapter.

to have been Buddhist laymen or to have written Buddhist evidential tales, since—by the fifth century at least—to take the lay vows
and to write such tales was to take a clear, definite public stance
"for" Buddhism, as against its detractors. It also includes pro-
Daoist writers, from priests to possessors of and writers about revealed texts. My criterion for inclusion in this group is not mere
private preference or fideistic commitment, which would in any
case remain unknowable to us unless they had been expressed; it is
rather the construction or adoption of a public persona that was
clearly if complexly expressed through recognized cultural gestures.

Masters of esoterica. Again despite what the *fangshi* thesis leads us to expect, only two known authors are men explicitly
identified as *fangshi*; both lived after the Han. Zhang Hua (232–
300), author of the Bwz,[24] and Guo Pu (276–324), editor of and commentator on (and possibly contributor to) the Shj,[25] were both
widely known for their prowess in esoteric skills (*fangshu*). One
other author who may be included in this group, though perhaps
marginally, is Zu Chongzhi (429–500), author of the Shuyj, a polymath and master of calendrics and other technical arts during the
Song and southern Qi dynasties; he was also the great-grandson of
Zu Taizhi, author of another anomaly account. He is credited with
several mechanical inventions, although no supernormal feats are
ascribed to him. Most of his offices were at the regional or district
levels. He wrote commentaries to Daoist as well as Confucian
classics.[26]

Daoist practitioners and exponents. If the Han court
bibliographer Liu Xiang was indeed the author of the Lxz, then he
must be numbered at least among exponents, if not practitioners,
of a tradition of thought and practice directed toward the goal of
"transcendence" that would soon be retrospectively merged into the
full-fledged Daoist religion as developed by the Celestial Master,
Shangqing, and Lingbao traditions. This historico-hagiographical
work seems to have been the earliest to apply the conventions of
the *liezhuan* format to transcendents as a distinct *type* of person or
social persona, and was clearly intended to promote the various
cults of these figures mentioned in the text, if not to extol in detail

---

24. JS 36 (1068–78).
25. JS 72 (1899–1910). He is said to have been personally acquainted with Gan Bao (1905).
26. NQS 52 (903–6).

the practices its subjects are depicted as following. The cases of the three other known Daoist authors are more straightforward. Wang Fou (fl. ca. 300), reputed author of the Shenyj, is better known for his anti–Buddhist polemics, carried on in debates with Buddhist exponents and in his famous treatise "On the Conversion of the Barbarians" (*Huahujing* 化胡經), which is said to have maintained that the "Buddha" who taught in India was in fact an avatar of Laozi.[27] Ge Hong (283–343) belonged to a lineage of transmission of Daoist texts and techniques, to whatever extent he practiced these himself; his Sxz is a major pro-Daoist apology.[28] Wang Jia (d. before 393), author of the more subtly though no less profoundly pro-Daoist work Syj, is depicted in his official biography (which places him in the company of a miscellaneous assortment of Daoist, Buddhist, and *fangshi* practitioners and wonder-workers) as a Daoist-style adept who himself mastered some of the techniques and powers ascribed to transcendents; indeed he was eulogized in the third extant Daoist hagiography (Dxz), probably compiled two centuries later.[29]

Buddhist lay exponents and monks. From the middle or late fourth century into the Sui, nearly a dozen members of the official class who were not ordained monks—but some or all of whom may have formally taken the five lay vows—are known to have written pro-Buddhist evidential accounts, that is, texts that report events corroborating the general authority of Buddhist teachings and sacred personages or the specific assertions of certain Buddhist

---

27. Zürcher 1972, 293 ff.

28. His official biography appears in JS 72 (1910–13); his own auto-biographical statements—both prefaces and the comments sprinkled throughout his *Baopuzi*—also contain invaluable information about his life and outlook. See also Sivin 1969.

29. His official biography is at JS 95 (2496–97); his hagiography, in YJQQ 110.17b–18b. Neither mentions any formal lineage or even a teacher; both portray him as simply retiring to the mountains to practice respiration and meditative techniques, and as taking a small number of students. Both place his origin in Anyang in Longxi, and both mention that he resided in seclusion at Dongyang (in today's Zhejiang); but the Dxz hagiography adds narrative material concerning Fu Jian's inquiries of him, in which Wang Jia displays his prognosticatory prowess. This material is consistent with Wang Jia's death date in 393; Fu Jian's southern offensive culminated in 383, when he was repulsed at the Fei River (Gernet 1982, 182), and the text is careful to say that Fu Jian sent a messenger to interview Wang Jia—it was not a face to face exchange.

scriptures. The earliest of these, Xie Fu (fl. mid-late 4th c.), is characterized in his official biography as a recluse, based in part on his refusal of an appointment to a low-rung position; he is also known, from Buddhist sources, to have been active in the Buddhist study circles of his day in the capital.[30] Liu Yiqing was related to the founder of the Song, and held important offices under that dynasty; his official biography, as well as the pro-Buddhist polemical work BZL, mention his Buddhist piety.[31] The layman Zhang Yan, descended from an old southern clan in Wu commandery 吳郡, died young but served as a retainer to the Song crown prince.[32] Wang Yanxiu, author of the Ganyz (now lost), took part in "abstruse learning" circles in the capital and served the Song as a ritual specialist.[33] Wang Yan, an official under both the Qi and Liang dynasties, spent time in Jiaozhou (northern Vietnam), an intensely Buddhist area; his preface to the Mxj tells of two miraculous events in his own life that spurred him to collect evidential accounts of similar events elsewhere. Xiao Ziliang, author of a lost collection of pro-Buddhist evidential tales (the *Mingyanji* 冥驗記) and the second son of Emperor Wu of the Qi, was known for inviting Buddhist monks to court; his literary salon was populated by monks as well as pious Buddhist laymen.[34] Lu Gao was related to Zhang Yan, and was, like him, a native of the city of Wu 吳 in Wu commandery; he was also a close acquaintance of Wang Yan. He held very high positions at the Liang court, as well as serving as *taishou* of Yixing commandery. His biography tells us that, in addition to his XiGsy, he also wrote a thirty-*juan* biography of monks, now lost.[35] Wang Manying, author of a *Buxu mingxiangji* 補續冥祥記 (now lost), came from a "poor" family native to Taiyuan, extensively studied both Confucian and Buddhist texts, and once exchanged letters with the monk Huijiao, author of the Gsz.[36] Hou Bo was appointed by Sui

---

30. JS 94 (2456–57); Makita 1970, 76–79 n.3; Zürcher 1972, 136–37; Tsukamoto 1985, 307. Not much information survives concerning the official who rewrote Xie's tales after they were lost, Fu Liang, a native of Kuaiji.

31. SS 51, 1474–77; BZL 3 (504b).

32. SS 53 (1511); Gsz 10 (392a), 13 (411a); Makita 1970, 83.

33. SS 66 (1734); Wright 1954, 419; Gjertson 1989, 22.

34. Mather 1986, 1987, 1988.

35. LS 26 (398–99); NS 48.

36. LS 22 (348); NS 52; Wang Guoliang 1984, 341. For his correspondence with Huijiao, which concerns the latter's Gsz (of which Manying had recently seen a copy) and which shows the layman's rather detailed knowledge of Chinese Buddhist history, *Guang hongmingji* 廣弘明集 (T 2103) 24.275a–b.

Emperor Wen to a post as official historian.[37] The author of the Gsl, Shi Yancong, better known for the polemical work BZL, was a monk.[38]

The fact that half of the identifiable authors of anomaly accounts were explicitly and publicly aligned with a particular religio-cultural tradition, or wrote to support the cause of such a tradition, signals the large extent to which the genre was turned to sectarian uses, at least from the fourth century on. Yet *fangshi* are the least numerous of such authors, and none of these writers seems to have been socioeconomically deprived or culturally marginalized to any great extent.

Historians, Bibliographers, and Academicians

At least fifteen identifiable authors—over a third of the persons known with reasonable probability to have written anomaly accounts—served at some point in their careers as historian, librarian, archivist, or in positions requiring the handling of large numbers of official documents. The records to which these officials had access doubtless served as a major source of materials for the compilation of their anomaly accounts. A number of authors— among them Liu Yiqing, Ren Fang,[39] Lu Gao, Liu Zhilin,[40] and Yin Yun[41]—at some time held the important post of Director of the Palace Library (*bishujian* 秘書監). Others held the post of Editorial Director (*zhuzuolang* 著作郎) or Assistant (佐) Editorial Director; attached to the palace library, they were responsible for compiling imperial diaries and other documents, and included Cao Pi (author of Zgc) and Zhang Hua.[42] Some authors, including Liu Xin, Ren Fang, and Yan Zhitui, undertook major bibliographic projects in

---

37. SuiS 58 (1421); BS 83; *Xu Gaosengzhuan* 2; Lin Chen 1960, 406–7; Li Jianguo 1984, 434. One might also mention Fan Yan among Buddhist authors, since his lost collection of tales, the *Yindezhuan*, is likely to have been pro-Buddhist, and since his clan had been Buddhist believers for generations. He was descended from a Jin general, and his father, Fan Tai, had served under Xie An's military command and was awarded high posts at the Song court (SS 60 [1616–23]).

38. His lengthy hagiography appears in *Xu Gaosengzhuan* (T 2060) 2.436b–439c.

39. LS 14 (251–58); NS 59.

40. LS 40 (572–74); NS 50.

41. LS 41 (596); Lin Chen 1960, 391–92; IC, 936.

42. Also in this category are authors of two lost texts, Gu Yewang and Xu Shanxin; see Wang Guoliang 1984, 42–43.

the palace archives.[43] At least two of our authors—Gan Bao and Hou Bo—held imperial commissions to write dynastic histories;[44] Guo Jichan privately wrote a history of the Jin,[45] Dai Zuo also wrote some private annals, and Wu Jun wrote a history of the Qi— which was rejected as "inaccurate" by the Liang emperor—and at his death left behind (among other writings) an almost-completed comprehensive history (*tongshi* 通史), annotations to Fan Ye's *Hou Han shu*, a ten-*juan Miaoji* 廟記 (*Records of Temples*), a sixteen-*juan Shi'erzhouji* 十二州記 (*Records of Twelve Regions*), and a five-*juan Qiantang xianxianzhuan* 錢唐先賢傳 (*Traditions Concerning the Former Worthies of Qiantang*).[46] Liu Zhilin was imperially commissioned (along with others) to edit an "original copy" of Ban Gu's *Hanshu* that had been discovered.[47] Liu Jingshu, although not a historian, apparently served as a Supervising Secretary (*jishizhong* 給事中) under the Song, and, in that capacity, may have had access to the imperial archives.[48] Cao Pi (the author of *Zhiguai*), Yin Yun, Ren Fang, and Liu Zhilin held national academic posts.

Judging solely from the texts themselves, we can conclude that the large majority of anomaly account items containing any specific temporal setting are set in periods predating the author of the text in question, not in the author's own day. Anomaly accounts are predominantly, then, in their prose style, format, and temporal setting, historical—not "ethnographic"—writings; their authors, with few exceptions, must have drawn mostly on written documents as opposed to oral sources, and the bulk of these documents must have been historical (including geographical and biographical) records of one or another sort.[49] This impression, derived from

---

43. Yan Zhitui's biography: BQS 45 (617–26) and BS 83; cf. Teng 1968.

44. On Hou Bo, SuiS 58 (1421), BS 83.

45. See SuiS 33 (958); since there is no record of an official assignment to write this *Further Annals of the Jin*, we can only assume it was a private work.

46. LS 49 (698–99); cf. NS 72. He seems never to have garnered a court appointment.

47. LS 40 (572–74).

48. On the office, Hucker 1985, 132.

49. This *pace* DeWoskin (1977b, 37–38), who makes much of Gan Bao's role as a sort of proto-ethnographer. (For another critique of the "ethnography" view of anomaly accounts, see Bokenkamp 1986, 70.) There are oral-based items, as will be seen below, but they account for only a small fraction of the total corpus.

a study of the texts, finds confirmation in the fact that so many authors held offices that afforded them access to the largest collections of texts available in their time.

But the question of the authors' sources of material lends itself to more detailed consideration.

The Sources of Anomaly Accounts

It is impossible to trace most anomaly account items to earlier sources. Not only do authors fail to cite their sources, except in rare instances, but, more crucially, given the nature of the contents of these texts and the low esteem in which they were apparently held by many literati, most of the sorts of texts on which anomaly accounts were probably based have long since disappeared.[50] One can, however, reconstruct some probable routes by which they were compiled.

We can begin by drawing a hypothetical distinction between two large groups of sources. One group comprises written documents likely to have been accessible in central archives. These would have included not only classics, histories, annals, biographies, and various types of reports from or concerning outlying regions (including Music Bureau and tribute records), but also records of portents observed across the land (which would have been carefully collected by court officials seeking signs of dynastic legitimacy), and all manner of old, rare texts scarcely available elsewhere and therefore valuable. The other group comprises documents and narratives that, local in nature, were only spottily available (if at all) in central archives—things that would have been knowable only to persons travelling through, or holding office in, the places in question, or else through personal contacts such as conversations and private correspondence.[51] These would have included purely oral narratives; local, perhaps family-held, records of such narratives, and other sorts of documents concerning sayings and customs in particular areas, such as local gazeteers of extremely narrow circulation, perhaps prepared for and preserved by

---

50. Cf. the caveats issued in Bokenkamp 1986, 74.

51. In theory, of course, any of the following sorts of records, in transcribed form, could have reached the imperial archives; but it seems likely that, in practice, large numbers of them would never have been submitted to or collected by the court and so would have been accessible only through private, personal channels.

officials serving at particular regional or local posts; family histories containing clan legends; stone inscriptions (some of them
closely related to images[52]) on stelae (*bei* 碑) at family shrines
(*ci* 祠),[53] at non-family shrines to officials and other locally or
regionally notable personages, and at family and public temples
(*miao* 廟);[54] other paper or bamboo documents available at temples
and shrines, and oral recitations by temple caretakers (including
the "shamans" occasionally mentioned in the anomaly accounts as
residing or working at local temples); and inscriptions, paper or
bamboo records, and oral narratives associated with Buddhist
monasteries and Daoist abbeys.

Histories and Palace Archives as Sources

Chapters Six and Seven of the Ssj are prime examples of material
drawn by a court historian from palace archives. These chapters
consist of a more or less chronologically arranged list of portents
concerning the fortunes of the Han, Eastern Han, Wei (and Three
Kingdoms), and Jin dynasties and their rulers. They correlate well
with similar lists in the relevant dynastic histories themselves.[55]
Chapter Four of the Yy similarly consists of narratives of political
portents interspersed with tales of omens concerning individuals'
fortunes; most of these events are set in the Jin period and a few
are set in the Song, and it is reasonable to suppose that Liu
Jingshu gleaned this material, in particular, from documents to

---

52. Wu Hung 1987 is thoughtful on the relationship between tales of
a certain type and a group of Sichuan stone carvings, including the question of how the transformation across media might have affected plots and
thematic emphases. For other treatments of funerary shrine art and its relationship to verbal media: Wu Hung 1989; Powers 1981, 1984; Delahaye
1983; Kominami 1984, 13–94; Sofukawa 1993; Till and Swart 1979–80;
Hou 1981; Sahara 1991.

53. These, however, were not likely to be many, given the interdic-
tions on family-shrine (i.e., funerary) stelae during many reign periods after the Eastern Han (K. Ch'en 1975).

54. A recent study of one of the few records on temples to have survived is Lai 1990.

55. Whether these chapters are (directly descended) from Gan Bao's
own hand, or imported into the text by later redactors and lacking any relationship to Gan Bao's autograph text, has been disputed back and forth
for decades: DeWoskin 1974, 72–87, 319–28; Nishitani 1951; Yu Jiaxi
1974 [1937], chap. 18 (pp. 1131ff.).

which he had access in his capacity as Supervising Secretary under the Song.[56]

A significant number of items in anomaly accounts, particularly narrative items, are likely to have been based on histories both officially commissioned or adopted and unofficial. In most cases, these sources are impossible to detect, since the unofficial histories have largely disappeared.[57] In the case of official histories, there are not as many overlaps with extant anomaly accounts as one might expect; but this might be explained by one old and, as far as it goes, valid theory that some anomaly collections—most notably the Ssj—were compiled from materials omitted because of their suspect content by their historian-authors from their standard-format histories, and so constitute a sort of "left-over history."[58] It should also be pointed out that several important dynastic histories covering this period drew on anomaly accounts for material.

Palace collections were not the only places where authors could gain access to old, relatively rare documents such as unofficial biographies and histories (as well as demonographies, descriptions of flora and fauna, and perhaps all sorts of preexistent anomaly accounts that were lost before the compilation of the SuiS bibliographic catalogue). Several authors' biographies make a point of mentioning their extensive antiquarian book collections. Of Ren Fang, we read that, "although his family was poor, he collected books amounting to over ten thousand fascicles, including many unusual titles" (*yiben* 異本); after his death the Liang Emperor Wu sent two highly regarded scholar-officials, Shen Yue and Jia Zong, to Ren Fang's home to gather from his library all titles not already

---

56. A cursory check in the indices to the *chenwei* texts published in Yasui and Nakamura 1971–88 has not turned up much evidence of borrowing from these works by anomaly account authors, but a more careful study might reveal that they were an important source of material. Even if they were, however, this will be hard to prove, since so many of them have perished.

57. One documented case is that of the story involving Ganjiang 干將 and Moye 莫耶, makers of magic swords for the King of Chu. Found in variant versions in Lyz 6 (TPYL 343), Ssj 11.4 (tr. DeWoskin 1974, 286–88, and Kao 1985, 73–76), and (*very* variant) Syj 10.8b, this legend goes back in its fullest form to the *Wu Yue chunqiu* (4.1b.10–3b.1), although allusions to it occur in earlier texts. Although it does not directly involve anomaly accounts, an instructive analysis of how authors in our period reworked earlier material into new narrative forms is to be found in Riegel 1986.

58. Takeda 1965.

possessed in the palace collection.[59] Zhang Hua is said to have collected "thirty cartloads" of books; upon death he left few valuable possessions other than his library, which, like that of Ren Fang, was partially appropriated by imperial librarians and contained large numbers of rare, strange texts.[60] Liu Zhilin's notable collection of "several thousand" old, curious artifacts may have included books.[61] We have from Ge Hong's own hand a remarkable account of his efforts to find literary "rarities" and to "browse widely in everything written."[62]

Sacred Texts as Sources

It is also likely that sacred texts, emanating from the several Daoist traditions and from the circles in which Buddhist scriptures were translated and circulated, formed the basis of a fair number of anomaly accounts. Only a few instances have so far been documented, but more will doubtless come to light—although I suspect that sacred texts were not, numerically speaking, a major source of material.

Stephen Bokenkamp has demonstrated that the famous peach blossom spring story, a version of which is found in today's Sshj (1.5),[63] has its source in Daoist scriptural material perhaps dating back to the Han and incorporated at some point in an important Lingbao scripture.[64] Although the respective wording of these two passages is not closely similar, they share a common plot

---

59. LS 14 (254); Wu 1937, 252.

60. JS 36 (1074): 天下奇秘, 世所希有者, 悉在華所. Cf. Wu 1937, 248–49.

61. LS 40 (572–74).

62. *Baopuzi waipian* 50; tr. Ware 1981 [1966], 9–10, 15.

63. For discussions of this story, including both the religious ideas that informed it and the realities of fourth-fifth century society that it may reflect, Chen Yinke 1936; Kawakatsu 1974a, 33–43; Bauer 1976, ch.3 (esp. 190–91). For translations of Tao Qian's tale, Birch 1965, 167–68; Hightower 1970, 254–58.

64. Bokenkamp 1986. The scripture in question is *Lingbao wufujing xu* 靈寶五符經序 (HY 388); the narrative in question appears at 1.1a.1–11b.4. It is known to have existed by the first half of the fourth century since it is cited in both Ge Hong's *Baopuzi* and the Yang Xi revelation texts collected in *Zhen'gao* 真誥 (HY 1010); HY 388 probably consists of a core Han or older material surrounded by layers of later accretions, but there is no scholarly consensus on dating. On the Lingbao corpus, Bokenkamp 1983.

structure much too closely for the resemblance to have been accidental. I quote Bokenkamp's summary of it:

In both cases, the search into the "cave" begins as a quest for the source of a spring 源; the cave entrance is first narrow and dark, then broad and filled with light; and there is a grove of remarkable trees (T'ao has placed them outside of the grotto). Both interlopers come upon a place of habitation, but, while the Recluse finds only footprints and cart tracks, the fisherman of T'ao's account meets the cavern residents. Both men report their finds to the proper authorities, though the cavern paradise is inaccessible to the less worthy, regardless of rank and status.[65]

Exactly what text(s) formed the basis for the Sshj narrative is, however, impossible to determine; the texts are not so close as to require us to conclude that the Sshj author must have had before him a copy of the scripture. And the picture is complicated by the existence of more than a dozen other anomaly account items with a somewhat similar plot—many of them predating the Sshj, especially if my dating of it in the late Song or Qi periods is correct.[66] Were it not for the attested early date of the scriptural narrative, one might even say that the opposite scenario is equally possible— that the author of this portion of the scripture could have built it around an already existent anomaly account item. In any case, Bokenkamp perceptively notes that Tao Qian's version of the tale and the scriptural text urge similar conclusions on the reader: the

---

65. Bokenkamp 1986, 69. The quotation marks around "cave" are not in the published passage but have been added (to fit his original intention) at Stephen Bokenkamp's request.

66. I here list closely similar, as well as more vaguely analogous, items (the latter indicated with "cf."), all of which share what I call the motif or theme of the "hidden world discovered": Zgk 2; Shuyj 4; Yy 1.24 (the protagonist is a Man tribesman), 5.29 (cf.); ShuyjRf 2.29; Yml 4, 39, 63, 64, 252 (cf.: an example of the motif of a miniature hidden world, in this case the world inside a cypress pillow), 253; Wlj 2a (which explicitly refers to Tao Qian's Taohuayuan ji); Pyj 1b (cf.); Syj 10.9b–10a, tr. in Foster 1974, 305–6, and Bokenkamp 1986, 75; Sshj 1.2, 1.3, 1.4, 1.6, 1.7; XuQxj 8 (cf.: here an adept spits out and re-swallows entire internal "worlds"); Lxz 46 (cf.), 68; Jyj 6 (a Buddhist variation on the motif); Fslz 25 and Sxz 28 (cf.: an adept disguised as a common street merchant habitually leaps into a gourd at the end of each day, and upon entering one discovers that the gourd contains huge jade palaces).

scriptural tale warns against illicit bestowal of the sacred text in which it is embedded, while Tao's story "criticizes the single-minded pursuit of Daoist wonders, probably on the part of some acquaintance of his among the Nanyang Liu family."[67] He says further that while the symbolism of Tao's story is Daoist, "the moral decidedly is not," for the story ends: "Liu Ziji 劉子驥, an exalted gentleman, heard of the grotto and went off joyfully to see it—without result. [In fact,] he became ill and died. After this, no one inquired after the passage into the grotto." This Liu Ziji, who is recorded in his biography as having had an adventure similar to the one recounted in Tao's tale, was the ancestor of one Liu Dan 馼, an acquaintance of Tao's.[68]

Buddhist texts, particularly collections of *avadāna* tales (which began to be translated into Chinese in the middle of the third century, although most became available only from the fifth century on), also furnished material for some anomaly account items. Some students of the genre have created the impression that large numbers of items were probably derived from *avadāna* collections; I suspect, on the contrary, that those scriptures were at best a minor source of material for our authors, which would explain why scholars who have discussed *avadāna* tales as sources unfailingly cite the same small number of "examples."[69]

The best documented case—and the only one I have been able thus far to confirm—is the story, occurring twice in extant texts,[70] of a compassionate parrot that exhausts itself attempting to save

---

67. Bokenkamp 1986, 69, romanization altered for consistency.

68. Bokenkamp 1986, 69 (including n. 23). Liu Ziji (a.k.a. Liu Linzhi 驎之) has a biography in JS 94 (2447–48), among the lives of recluses. Significantly, it contains a version of the story Tao is telling, so Tao's telling may not simply have been a satire, as Bokenkamp suggests, but may also have referred to a (supposed) real event in the life of his contemporary's ancestor. (Or else the JS compilers drew on Tao's account in writing Liu's biography.) In another sense, of course, Tao Qian's purpose in writing differs from the scriptural author's, since Tao's story can be read as undermining the entire Daoist quest for esoterica (including scriptures!), whereas the scripture warns only against illicit transmission of texts whose aura of mystery and sacrality it seeks to enhance.

69. I have not undertaken a thorough study of the voluminous Chinese *avadāna* texts, but a cursory examination of them suggests to me that they were unlikely candidates for borrowing by our authors. Furthermore, a search through Chavannes 1910–34 has turned up no overlaps with anomaly account material.

70. (1) Xuanyj 15, based on YWLJ 91; CXJ 30; TPYL 924; BKLT 94. (2) Yy 3.4. Wang Guoliang 1988, 9, incidentally, gives erroneous informa-

its fellow creatures from a forest fire and is rewarded by *devas*. Various scholars claim to have found this tale in numerous *avadāna* texts, but at this writing I have found it only in two: (1) T 203 (4:455a–b), *Za baozangjing* 雜寶藏經 (*Mahāratnakūta*), which would seem to have been translated in the early or middle sixth century and is therefore not the source of the tale as it appears in the Xuanyj or the Yy; and (2) T 206 (4:515a.1–9), *Jiuza piyujing* 舊 雜譬喻經 (*The "Old" Assorted Avadānas Sūtra*),[71] translated by the Sogdian Kang Senghui, active in Jiankang from the fourth through the sixth decades of the third century. Some version of Kang Senghui's text was most likely our authors' source. To anyone acquainted with the entire corpus of anomaly accounts, this particular item stands out from most, and is in fact almost unique, because its only characters are animals and spirits; no human beings are involved.[72]

There are, furthermore, two unusual tales featuring foreign adepts who produce whole sets of cooking utensils and other persons from their mouths; they seem to be experts at miniaturization.[73] Lu Xun says that a version of this tale is found in the *Jiuza piyujing* (T 206), but I am unable to locate it there.[74] However,

---

tion on the location of the parrot story. It is also discussed in Chi 1958, 125; Schafer 1959, 280.

71. No Sanskrit analogue is known; the work was presumably so titled to distinguish it from the "new" work of the same title (T 207), apparently translated in the early fifth century.

72. Only a very small handful of items share this feature, and they, too, are likely to have been based on *avadāna* texts: Xuanyj 16 (TPYL 917, occurring in fuller form in the *Da Tang xiyuji*), quite similar in plot to Xuanyj 15; Yy 3.8, in which a flock of birds avenges the killing of one of its members by a dog; Yy 3.46, in which a snake heals itself with herbs. Although it involves a human character in a minor capacity, Xuanyj 14 (TPYL 900) is also likely to have been based on an *avadāna* tale: in it, a cow tells of its former life as a slave.

73. (1) Lgz 17, based on FYZL 61; TPYL 359, 737; tr. Kao 1985, 121. (2) XuQxj 8. These seem to be the same basic tale, but there are a great many differences of detail and wording. The Lgz version, for example, provides a Chinese date but no proper names; the XuQxj version provides proper names but no date.

74. Lu Xun 1973, 35–37; as is typical of many Chinese literature scholars' citation methods, Lu does not mention the fascicle or page number where he saw the tale. The same needle-in-the-haystack problem arises with regard to Wang Guoliang's statement (1988, 9–10) that the story of Yang (var. Tang) Lin (Yml 252, tr. Kao 1985, 149) is based on a passage in another *avadāna* collection, Kumārajīva's *Da zhuangyan lunjing* (T 201), which runs to 92 triple-register pages in the Taishō edition.

already in the Tang, Duan Chengshi noticed that the XuQxj version was based on what he simply termed "a Buddhist *avadāna sūtra*" (釋氏譬喻經).[75]

Local Sources: Oral Narratives

When it comes to local sources,[76] first of all, a significant number of items pointedly mention the folkloric (and therefore usually local) nature of information they transmit, using such phrases as "the common people [there] say" ([*qi*] *minyue* 其民曰, *suyue* 俗曰) or "the folk call it . . . " (*suwei zhi* 俗謂之 . . .). Such items need not have been directly derived by the author himself from oral sources; they could have been based on local topographies or other written records, but an ultimate oral source is nevertheless clearly implied.[77]

---

75. *Youyang zazu* (*Xuji* 續集 4.7a.7–8a.2); he quotes the XuQxj text. Chen Yinke 1930 demonstrates a clear borrowing from an *avadāna* source in a SGZ biography (cf. SGZ 20 [p. 580] and T 240 [449b.20–25]). He also suggests that the name of the healer-adept, Hua Tuo 華佗, the subject of SGZ (29 [799–806]) and HHS (82B [2736–39]) biographies, is derived from the Sanskrit [*a*]*gada* (medicine, antidote) and that some of the exploits attributed to him were loosely based on *avadāna* sources, including T 553.

76. It should be pointed out here that anomaly texts vary widely in their inclusion of items likely to have been based on such sources; some are heavily weighted toward central, dynastic figures or are almost entirely derived from earlier anomaly accounts, and so could have been compiled without reference to any local documents or oral transmissions whatsoever.

77. These items include but are not limited to: Jlz 34; Ssj 1.8, 11.32, 16.8; Yml 11, 70, 170; Yy 1.1, 3.21, 3.28, 3.34, 3.51, 3.56, 3.57, 5.3, 10.2; Sxz 20, 32 (an especially clear case), 45 (implied); Gsz wangshen 1 = Mxj 6; Fslz 1; Lyz 49; XuQxj 15; ShuyjRf (many instances, including 1.28 and 2.144); Nkj 2a; Fslz 3, 9. In sectarian contexts, these phrases could be taken to mean not a "popular" but a "vulgar" (in the sense of heterodox, erroneous) statement, but this connotation is not to the fore in the above passages. Despite the "folkloric" sources of some items, one has only to sample folkloric narratives and folklore studies to sense the difference between them and our texts; see, e.g., Eberhard 1937, 1942, 1958, 1965, 1968. While Eberhard and others (e.g. Ting 1970; Liu 1932) sometimes cite early medieval anomaly accounts for early occurrences of later "motifs," there are significant problems when these accounts are placed alongside later types of texts as more or less equivalent witnesses to a constant body of motifs and narrative patterns.

A relatively small number of items go so far as to specify the person(s) from whom the author heard the story in question, sometimes even telling where *that* person heard it or citing other, corroborating witnesses.[78] Others indicate that a narrative was drawn from living members of a particular family, who told it as a story about one of their ancestors.[79] And a few narratives are told in first person.[80]

Local Sources: Inscriptions: the Case of Tang Gongfang

There is evidence that writers of anomaly accounts drew—either directly or through circulated topographies or other works—on inscriptions from stelae at shrines and temples, and more such evidence will doubtless be uncovered with continued research.[81] The best documented case I have found so far is that of Tang Gongfang 唐公房, noted for taking his entire family with him when he ascended into the heavens as an elixir-ingesting Daoist transcendent. A stele erected during the Eastern Han to commemorate the refurbishing of a temple to Tang in his native Chenggu 城固 (in Hanzhong 漢中 commandery, modern Shanxi province) survived at least into the late Qing; Ouyang Xiu and many others left descriptions of it down through the centuries.[82] The Sjz describes a shrine

---

78. These are most prevalent in Buddhist texts, suggesting the importance in mixed lay-and-monastic Buddhist circles of shared networks of informal discourse about the religion. Perhaps such narratives also formed sermon material—oral as well as written apologetics. They include but are not limited to: Gsy 2–7; XuGsy 1, 5, 9; XiGsy 13, 16, 33, 34, 38, 40, 47, 49, 53, 62, 63; Mxj 20, 27, 30 (= Gsy 5), 31 (= Gsy 6), 32, 56, 77, 85, 90, 110, 115, 120, 121; Gsz, *wangshen* 7; Fslz 30; Fjz 3, 5 (tr. DeWoskin 1983); Sxz 59; Ssj 20.11. Cf. Bwz 7.20 (Fan Ning 1980, item 261), where the author says he heard this story from others (not named) but did not personally see the events in question.

79. E.g. Sshj 1.1, 1.4; Ssj 20.11.

80. Among them are: Ssj 12.17; Sshj 4.2; Yy 3.22; Jlz 17, 18.

81. I am working on a systematic study of the Sjz and its relationship to the anomaly account corpus, and hope to publish the results reasonably soon.

82. Ouyang Xiu saw the stone in 1064 (*Ouyang Xiu quanji* 5: *Guji lubawei* 古集錄跋尾, pp. 178–79). Curiously (perhaps due to a taboo)—especially since he mentions that the stone was in excellent condition—he uses the graph 昉 instead of 房 in recording the transcendent's name, a usage also evident in the Sxz and Yy passages discussed below. A more useful

(also mentioned in the *Huayang guozhi* and in another early topography)[83] built at the very spot from which Tang was said to have ascended; the shrine included a stele erected "to mark and record [this] numinous anomaly" (表述靈異)—doubtless the same stele seen by later generations of visitors.[84] On the back of the stele were recorded the names of fifteen officials in the area who contributed to the work on the shrine; on its front was carved a detailed narrative of Tang's ascension and the circumstances preceding it, followed by the name of the principal donor for the temple's repair (*shanguang* 繕廣) and sponsor of the stele, one Guo Zhi 郭芝, governor of Hanzhong commandery.[85] The core of the narrative runs as follows:[86]

The old people say that in the second year of Wang Mang's *jushe* reign period [7 or 8 C.E.] the Lord [君, i.e., Tang Gongfang] was a subofficial functionary for the commandery. {He grew} edible melons on {his} land. Nearby, unbeknownst to others in the area, there lived a Perfected Man (真人); only

---

transcription (indicating lacunae) may be found in Wang Chang 1985 [1805], *juan* 19:1b–2b (it clearly gives 房). Chen Yuan 1988, 5–7, reproduces the text on the back (陰) of the stone as well as the front. For a listing of other descriptions, Yang Dianxun 1957, 22, col. a. I do not know whether this stone still exists today; a comment by Chen Yuan suggests that it does, and Wang Chang says that in his day it could be seen in Xingyuan.

83. Hygz 2 (124–25). YWLJ 95 (1658–59) quotes a *Liangzhouji* 梁州 記 passage describing a temple (the text uses both *miao* and *ci* to designate it) on Mt. Xuxiang north of the Xu River (in Hanzhong); the text says that there was a stele on the site proclaiming it as Tang's residence, but does not appear to be quoting the stele (hence, it is likely referring to the same one described in other texts). It also mentions a variety of mouse on the mountain called "changing-innards mouse," so called because it disgorges its old guts (to replace them with new) three times each month. (It is also here that an early commentary to the YWLJ cites the Bwz passage discussed below.)

84. Sjz 27 (353). Tang's story is here paraphrased, not copied verbatim from the stele text.

85. That the stele was originally on the grounds of the temple is indicated not only by early records concerning the site but also by the stele text itself: it clearly says that Guo Zhi and others contributed toward "the refurbishing of *this* temple" (*simiao* 斯廟). Guo Zhi does not seem to be mentioned in HHS, and I have no other information about him.

86. At points, I offer conjecture about the probable contents of lacunae in the text; these are indicated by placement in braces { }. Empty braces indicate a one-graph lacuna.

the Lord offered him his finest melons, and also became his follower and treated him with utmost deference. The Perfected Man was pleased, and so he agreed to meet {the Lord} on top of the mountain at Gukou.[87] [There] he gave the Lord a divinely efficacious drug (神藥), saying that after ingesting it he could extend his awareness across ten thousand *li* and understand the speech of birds and beasts. Now at that time the commandery headquarters was at West City, over seven hundred *li* away from his home; [but] in his comings and goings during his times off and between [official] visits he would arrive as fast as one could turn one's shadow. People all over the commandery were amazed at this and reported it to the governor, who promptly [?] promoted him to Director of Functionaries.

Now a mouse had eaten some provisions in a cart. The Lord drew a picture of a prison on the ground, summoned the mouse [into it], and executed it; then, looking inside its belly, he found it did indeed contain the [missing] provisions. The commandery governor { } treated him as a guest and feasted him, wishing to follow him in studying the Way, but Gongfang suddenly vanished from his presence.[88] The commandery governor grew angry and ordered his guards to seize Gongfang's wife and children. At this Gongfang returned to Gukou and called upon his teacher, telling him of the imminent danger. His teacher went back [to the headquarters] with him and gave the drug to Gongfang's wife and children to drink, then said, "Now you can go." But the wife and children were attached to their home and could not bear to leave it. [The teacher] again spoke: "How can you desire to take all your household belongings with you?" The wife replied, "I insist on

---

87. The phrase is difficult, and scholars have offered various suggestions about the troublesome graph *xu* 婿. I suspect it was meant to refer to the river that joins the Mian River at the point where the ancient city of Chenggu was located, and I might therefore be tempted to translate as follows: "he agreed to meet {the Lord} on top of the mountain *at the mouth of the Xu valley*." But there was also a town—and presumably also a mountain—northeast of Hanzhong and Chenggu called Gukou 谷口, and I have opted to translate as though the meeting were taking place there; my translation is, however, tentative. One of the recluses Huangpu Mi wrote about, one Zheng Pu, was a native of Gukou (Gshiz 2.20a).

88. Or perhaps: had nothing with which to advance him, that is, had nothing to teach him. Or, reading the phrase less literally: (temporarily?) put him off.

it." So he daubed the drug on the walls and columns of the house and fed it to the oxen, horses, and other domestic animals. In a moment a great wind and a dark cloud arrived to welcome Gongfang, and in an instant he, along with his wife and children, his house, and his domestic animals, departed.

In former times Qiao Song and Cui Bo each attained the Way by himself, but Gongfang, in managing to save his entire household, was superior to them![89]

There is no knowing how many anomaly accounts once incorporated this story, but three versions of it or allusions to it survive in extant texts.

1. The earliest is a brief quotation (or summary or paraphrase?) from the Bwz that is more a folk etymology for the name of the variety of mouse associated with Tang than a narrative of Tang's achievement of transcendence: "When Tang Fang [sic] ascended to [become a] transcendent, his chickens and dogs went with him. He left behind only a mouse, because it was despicable. Out of regret, the mouse emptied out its guts three times a month. [This variety of rodent] is called the Tang mouse."[90]

2. The latest mention of Tang in the extant anomaly accounts—written about a century and a half after the above Bwz item—similarly focuses on a mouse.

The "Tang mouse" is shaped like a mouse but is slightly longer. It is blue-green and black. On the side of its underbelly there is a protrusion like an intestinal tract; at times waste is even passed through it. [This animal] is also called "changing-innards mouse." In former times the transcendent Tang Fang took his household with him and ascended to Heaven. All of his chickens and dogs went along. Only a mouse fell back down; it did not die but its innards protruded several inches, and every three years it would exchange them. The people call it "Tang mouse." It lives in the rivers around Chenggu.[91]

3. A version of the Tang Gongfang story is embedded in Ge Hong's hagiography of the transcendent Li Babai 李八百 ("Li Eight-

---

89. Tr. based on the text and notes in Wang Chang 1985 [1805], 19:1b–2b, and Chen Yuan 1988, 5–7.

90. Fan Ning, ed., 1980, 125 (fragment 80); YWLJ 95 (1659). This passage does not appear in the common ten-*juan* version of the Bwz.

91. Yy 3.29; TPGJ 440.13 cites this item from Yy. The graph used for Fang is 眆.

hundred"), a native of Shu—hence roughly of the same region as Tang.

Summary: Li Babai (personal name unknown), a native of Shu, was sighted throughout many generations; someone once calculated his age to be 800, hence his nickname. Sometimes he hid himself in mountain forests, other times he appeared in city markets. Knowing that Tang Gongfang[92] of Hanzhong had the aim [to become a transcendent], Li decided to teach him, but first tested him. Disguised as a messenger, he worked for Tang for a while; Tang wondered at his speedy deliveries. Li then feigned serious illness; Tang did not balk at calling in expensive physicians and purchasing all necessary prescriptions. Li then made smelly, pus- and blood-oozing sores appear all over his body. At a loss, Tang asked what else he should do to help Li recover, and Li said that it only required that someone lick his sores. First three maids were sent to lick them; then, at Li's request, Tang himself and finally his wife licked them as well. Li then proclaimed his sores would heal if he obtained thirty hu[93] of fine wine for his bath. Tang provided both wine and tub; on being bathed, Li's sores healed at once, and his body shone like congealed fat, bearing no trace of illness. Li then said to Tang: "I am a transcendent. You have the aim [to become one]; that is why I have tested you, and you are worthy to be taught. I will now bestow on you the secret of transcending the world." Gongfang, his wife, and the three maids all reverted to youth, their countenances again beautiful. Li then bestowed a one-fascicle scripture on elixirs (丹經) on Tang, who entered Cloud Terrace Mountain to synthesize an elixir. When it was complete he consumed it and departed as a transcendent.[94]

Without lingering over the many specific differences and similarities among these four texts, what, in general, can we learn from them as examples of the ways in which authors may have used in-

---

92. The graph used is 昉.

93. A *hu* is ten times the volume of a *dou* (roughly equivalent to a peck?); this is, therefore, a very large quantity of wine.

94. Sxz 10. YJQQ (28.8b, note) quotes a work on the twenty-eight parishes (治) of the Celestial Master religion as mentioning that "Babai was Tang Gongfang's teacher." Given its location, the cult of Tang Gongfang was almost certainly connected in some formal way with a Way of the Celestial Master parish.

scriptional sources in the process of writing? Obviously, each of the three anomaly items was composed, in part, from material *not* included in the stele inscription at the temple, and none comes close to quoting it. Yet each shows a familiarity with the story carved on the stone, however that familiarity was acquired. Ge Hong's text, like the stele text, focuses on the attainment of transcendence, but differs in stressing the nature of the teacher–disciple relationship. It downplays Tang's success in transporting his entire household into the heavens, although in mentioning the reversion to youth of Tang's wife and servants it does make a concession to that element of the story as displayed at the temple. The stele, for its part, mentions a drug-dispensing teacher but does not bother with his name, nor does it mention a transmission of scripture; instead, it seems intent on promoting the unique significance of the figure worshipped at the shrine. The interest of the inscription text is local, that of Ge Hong is trans-local: he seeks to document an ongoing, effective quest for transcendence by various means, and so appropriates the Tang Gongfang story as one among many examples of the themes he explores throughout his text (teacher–disciple relations, scriptural filiation, the importance of "aim" and firm resolve in the face of difficulty, the teacher's initial occlusion—this last also apparent in the stele text, however).

The connection of the Bwz and Yy items with the stele text is more oblique, but the stele *does* mention a mouse—rather abruptly, as though there had been a legend of a mouse connected with Tang (and hence with his temple) that the author of the stele text felt obliged to work, however awkwardly, into the narrative—and the mouse *does* provoke Tang's ire and *does* have its belly cut open as a result. It is not that the Bwz and Yy show no interest in accounts of transcendents;[95] but each uses the story of Tang Gongfang not to illustrate the quest for ascension but to explain the name and unusual physiology of a local variety of rodent.

Other Cases of Local Inscriptions as Sources

Other cases in which anomaly account items and stele inscriptions at temples and shrines (as recorded in the Sjz) probably bore some relationship to each other—though in no case a direct relation-

---

95. It is telling, however, that both of these texts promote the more loosely defined *fangshi* as a type of adept; neither shows the sort of sectarian interest in transcendents displayed by Ge Hong.

ship—include the following. Again, further research will probably turn up more cases:[96]

1. The first appears to be an instance of a body of legend attached to one place—and recorded, in part, in at least one early anomaly account—crystallizing at a different location, thanks to the enterprising spiritual hermeneutics of a district magistrate; we have to deal with local officials vying to attach the names of former worthies and numinous men and women (in this case, a transcendent) to new cults in their districts in order to attract pilgrims—and doing so by means of the interpretation of local anomalies. The Lxz contains a hagiography of Wangzi Qiao 王子喬; it states that he was a sixth-century B.C.E. crown prince of Zhou who departed on a white crane from atop Mt. Goushi 緱氏山 (in the vicinity of Luoyang, east-southeast of that city), and concludes by noting that shrines were built for him at the foot of that mountain and on the summit of nearby Mt. Songgao 嵩高山 (perhaps a dozen kilometers further southeast).[97] Other anomaly accounts contain additional, vaguely related bits of legend about Qiao: the Ssj tells of how he transformed into a white bow of light and bestowed divine drugs on his disciple Cui Wenzi 崔文子, who, thinking the light an evil apparition, struck it down, only to see Qiao's corpse—which then transformed into a large white bird and flew away;[98] the Xs tells of a

---

96. Even in cases where the Sjz does not indicate that it is explicitly quoting a stele, wherever it reports a shrine as being dedicated to a particular figure we can assume that a stele of some sort was probably on the site (this would, of course, have been a primary way of identifying the figure to whom the shrine was dedicated); and where an anomaly account item exists featuring the same figure—and most especially where that item mentions the establishment of a shrine for him or her—we can assume that there must have been some relationship between the contents of the anomaly account item and the contents of the stele. Another area where further research might turn up parallels between surviving inscription texts and anomaly accounts is that of Buddhist miracle tales and hagiographies. Shinohara 1988, 119–27 and 183–87, details 25 cases of verbatim parallels between lives of Tang monks in Zanning's *Song Gaosengzhuan* and surviving inscriptions (at least 21 of which were clearly placed at the stūpa in which the remains of the monk in question were housed). He relies on Kasuga 1936 to identify the texts of stūpa inscriptions contained in the QTW. Similar work on Huijiao's and Daoxuan's hagiographies might show a similar picture for hagiographies of pre-Tang figures.

97. Lxz 28 (1.13b–14a); tr. Kaltenmark 1953, 109–14.

98. Ssj 1.9. Cui is said to have been a native of Taishan. More of his exploits are narrated in Ssj 1.17. He is mentioned in the pref. to Jlz.

grave robber being terrified by finding only a sword (emitting roars like those of tigers and dragons) in Qiao's tomb, suspended in midair—and the grave is said to have been in Maoling 茂陵, about twenty-five kilometers west of Chang'an, far west of the places mentioned in the Lxz account.[99]

Meanwhile, in Meng district, Liang commandery (well east of Goushi and Songgao), a temple to "the transcendent Wangzi Qiao" had been founded during the Eastern Han.[100] Cai Yong 蔡邕 (133–192 C.E.), known for his literary talent and particularly for his stele and *ming* 銘 (funerary stone) compositions,[101] wrote the text of a stele erected there sometime shortly after 165 C.E.;[102] judging from its verbatim quotation in the Sjz, it was probably still intact in the early sixth century.[103] The inscription reflects considerable uncertainty about the identity of Wangzi Qiao, saying only that "he must

---

99. Xs 31 (based on XTZ 4.11a–b). During the Qi, there was a district of this name in northern Yizhou (modern Sichuan), but the Xs text clearly specifies "the Maoling in the [vicinity of the] capital city" (京茂陵). Given this and the next item discussed, we could speculate that Qiao's cult over the centuries from the Han to the Liang moved both up and down the Yellow River system, at least as far west as Maoling (at approximately 108.5° longitude) and as far east as Meng district (at approximately 115.6° longitude)—some 600 km. apart. Wangzi Qiao is also mentioned in Fslz 5 (HHS 82A [2712]) as the possible identity of one Wang Qiao who possessed "divine arts"; but their biographies are not at all similar.

100. Perhaps this is related to the stele seen by Yan Zhitui some four centuries later, although the location he mentions seems to have been somewhat north of Meng district. He mentions seeing a stele inside the west gate of Boren City 柏人城 (in some periods this *ren* was apparently written 仁)—located (and so called in both the Eastern Han and the Sui) in southwestern Hebei just west of the Dalu Marsh 大陸澤. He notes that the stele was erected by the people of the city in honor of their district magistrate, Xu Zheng 徐整, during the reign of Han Emperor Huan (r. 147–167), and quotes it as saying: "This is Quanwu Hill, where Wang Qiao became a transcendent." *Yanshi jiaxun* 6 (163); cf. tr. (from which mine differs) in Teng 1968, 179–80.

101. On *ming* as a literary genre, Kamatani 1989.

102. The date of the anomalous incidents at the grave mentioned in the stele text is *yonghe* 1 (136 C.E.); the date of the imperial ritual legation is the eighth month of *yanxi* 8 (165 C.E.).

103. Sjz 23 (299). The Sjz text closely matches that preserved in the collected works of Cai Yong (which I have consulted in Chen Yuan 1988, 2), which is tr. in Ebrey 1980, 337, with some small variations. It explicitly indicates that it is quoting the stele. On the Sjz in general, I have benefited from Yan Gengwang 1985; Zheng Dekun 1974.

have been a Perfected Man of a former age; one hears that he became a transcendent, but in what era is unclear. If one asks Daoist experts, some say he came from Yingchuan, others that he was born [here] in Meng and first founded this city and that that is why his tumulus is here." But it narrates in detail the events leading up to the temple's founding: first, a man who lived near the old burial mound heard a crying sound coming from the top of it one winter night; the next morning he made an offering there and, looking about, noticed that there were no human footprints in the freshly fallen snow, but in the place where he made the offering he noticed the tracks of a large bird. "Everyone nearby thought it must have been a spirit." These events were followed by the appearance of a red–gowned spirit who clearly identified himself as Wangzi Qiao and warned a woodcutter not to take any more trees from atop his tumulus. The district magistrate, one Wan Xi, "investigated what the elders said [about the gravesite] and, moved by these numinous and auspicious responses, inquired whether they could be confirmed. He concluded that they were trustworthy and correct, and so he built a spirit-housing temple (靈廟) in order to put this spirit to rest (以休厥神)."[104] The inscription goes on to tell of how Daoist pilgrims subsequently began to arrive from afar at the temple, strumming lutes while chanting of the Grand Unity 太一, meditating in order to reach the "cinnabar mound" 丹丘;[105] the sick also traveled there to be instantly cured. It also mentions a ritual legation sent by the Han emperor in 165 to perform sacrificial offerings. Clearly, Wan Xi's efforts to promote this cult—and thereby enhance the prestige and welfare of his district—had succeeded.

    2. The Sjz mentions the legend of Wu Zixu 伍子胥 drowning himself in Wu; the people there took pity on him and founded several shrines along the river Jiang.[106] The gist of this material is also found in an anomaly item.[107]

---

104. The Sjz text omits two very suggestive phrases describing Wan's investigation; I have translated directly from Cai Yong's text (and my tr. differs from that of Ebrey 1980, 337).

105. Thus the Sjz text; Cai Yong's inscription (as reproduced in Chen Yuan 1988, 2) has "cinnabar field" 田.

106. Sjz 40 (497–98); it is difficult to tell whether the text is here quoting the *Wuyue chunqiu* or has simply referred to it in passing. A temple to Wu Zixu (at a different location), with a stele, is mentioned elsewhere in the text as well (5, p. 61).

107. Luyz 5 (based on quotation in SLFZ 6). On this figure, Johnson 1980. He is also mentioned in passing in Sxz 46 and Bwz fragment 82 (quoted in CXJ 6; Fan Ning 1980, 125).

3. The Lxz has a hagiography of the Warring States era transcendent Qin Gao 琴高;[108] the same material reappears in the Ssj, but with a different place name.[109] The hagiography mentions a shrine to him, established by his disciples, in Tang 碭 commandery.[110] The Sjz repeats the same narrative without citing a source (the author Li Daoyuan could have simply been quoting a copy of the Lxz), and locates it at Mt. Tang.[111]

4. The Lxz hagiography of Gu Chun 谷春, a transcendent who lived during the reign of Han emperor Cheng and who achieved corpse liberation, says that a shrine was built for him atop Mt. Taibo 大白, also known as Mt. Taiyi 太一 (west-southwest of Chang'an), which is where Gu Chun is said to have gone to dwell after his liberation.[112] The Sjz repeats the legend, and reports that there was indeed a shrine to Gu Chun atop the mountain.[113]

5. The Sjz reports that in Taiyuan commandery there had once been a shrine (now destroyed) to Jie Zitui 介子推; in front of the spot where it once stood there was a stele, but the words were effaced.[114] Jie Zitui is given a hagiography in the Lxz.[115]

6. Master Redpine 赤松子, reputedly one of the most ancient of all transcendents, is given a hagiography in the Lxz (largely repeated in the Ssj) and is mentioned in the Sxz.[116] The Sjz mentions

---

108. Lxz 26 (1.13a) (also attested in YJQQ 108.5b); tr. Kaltenmark 1953, 104–7.

109. Ssj 1.11 mentions Zhuo 涿 commandery, but this placename was quite possibly inserted in the text at some point well after the Six Dynasties.

110. This presumably would have been the town (and mountain of the same name) upriver from Pengcheng.

111. Sjz 23 (300); the text does not describe a temple or shrine at the site, although it does include the legend's mention of the establishment of a shrine by Qin Gao's disciples.

112. Lxz 52 (2.6b–7a) (also attested in YJQQ 108.12a); tr. Kaltenmark 1953, 157–58. Gu Chun also appears in the hagiography of Mao Nü ("the Hairy Woman") as her teacher (Lxz 54).

113. Sjz 18 (232).

114. Sjz 6 (75); no narrative is given.

115. Lxz 19 (1.9b–10a); tr. Kaltenmark 1953, 86–90. No specific place is mentioned, nor is a shrine to him. He also appears in Syj 3.4a and Xs 30.

116. Lxz 1 (1.1a) (also attested in YJQQ 108.1a); tr. Kaltenmark 1953, 35–42. Cf. Ssj 1.2. Sxz 6 mentions him as the namesake of the transcendent Huang Chuping 黃初平. In later Daoist theology he was the Perfected Man of the Southern Marchmount (*Wushang biyao* [HY 1130] 87.11a–b).

a temple erected at the spot (in northern Changshan 長山 district) where he is said to have transformed into a feathered being; it also says that he was chased by Yan Di's daughter, who also thus managed to achieve transcendence—a detail included in the Lxz and Ssj narratives.[117]

7. Fei Changfang 費長房, featured in several anomaly account items,[118] is also mentioned in the Sjz, where elements of his story are repeated in connection with a shrine, in front of which there was a stele with the words effaced.[119]

8. Gui Fu 桂父 ("Old Man Cinnamon") receives a short hagiography in the Lxz, where he is said to have fed on cinnamon and achieved extraordinary longevity.[120] The cassia grove where he was said to have lived is mentioned in the Sjz, which adds details not found in the Lxz entry.[121]

9. The Lyz and Ssj tell of a man from Chencang 陳倉 who, during the reign of Duke Mu of Qin, found a strange creature underground and submitted it to the throne as a portent; this led to the capture of two marvelous fowl (male and female), possession of which guaranteed rulership. A shrine was established for them, and they were called the Chen Treasures (陳寶).[122] The Sjz reports that a shrine to them existed on Chencang Mountain and gives a version of the narrative.[123]

---

117. Sjz 40 (497).

118. Lyz 15 (based on quotation in TPGJ 466), 16 (based on TPYL 882, TPGJ 393), and 17 (based on YWLJ 72, TPYL 862), all narrate incidents involving Fei Changfang, as does XuQxj 9. He appears as a skilled reader of an otherworldly letter in Ssj 15.4; receives a biography in Fslz (HHS 82B [2743]); is a major character in Ge Hong's hagiography of Hu Gong (Sxz 28); and is among the *fangshi* who appeared at the Wei court in Bwz 5.2.

119. Sjz 21 (269). The shrine is not clearly dedicated to Fei Changfang; the text says rather cryptically that "for generations it has been called Zhang Mingfu's shrine," but the shrine is mentioned in the context of a discussion of Fei Changfang and may originally have been his, the local people's understanding of the identity of its occupant having changed over time.

120. Lxz 31 (1.15a–b) (cf. YJQQ 108.6b); tr. Kaltenmark 1953, 118–20.

121. Sjz 37 (454); no shrine or stele is mentioned.

122. Lyz 2 (based on quotations in TPYL 375, 917, 954; YWLJ 90; BTSC 89), Lyz 3 (based on citation in a commentary to the SJ *Fengshanshu*); Ssj 8.7. These items are all apparently based on a SJ passage (28 [1359]).

123. Sjz 17 (230).

10. The Ssj tells of a pair of shamans or *fangshi* with magical abilities "in Min" (modern Fujian)—Xu Deng 徐登, a woman who changed into a man, and Zhao Bing 趙昞. They were killed by a district magistrate. The Sjz tells of a shrine to them in Yongning (on the coast, in modern Guangxi autonomous region) and recounts closely similar events.[124]

11. The Bwz and Ssj narrate the old legend of Lord Lone Bamboo (孤竹君), the self-claimed title of the spirit of a man (younger brother of Bo Yi, one of the two hermits who starved themselves in protest at Shouyang Mountain in ancient times) whose coffin floated onto a riverbank in Liaoxi 遼西 (in what is now eastern Hebei) and for whom the local people built a temple and named a walled city. Whoever tried to open his coffin and peer inside died without any signs of prior illness.[125] The Sjz tells of a temple to him overlooking a walled town bearing his name.[126]

12. The Sjz mentions a stele to the official Fan Ning 范寧; the Mxj contains a narrative about the auspicious appearance of a spirit-monk during Fan's construction of what was presumably a Buddhist *vihara*.[127]

13. The Syj and ShuyjRf narrate the wonders worked by a *fangshi* named Fan Li 范蠡 who served the king of Yue in ancient times; the Sjz mentions a shrine and stele to him in Li 酈 district (northwestern Hebei).[128]

The upshot of this discussion of sources is that the picture gleaned from prefaces and other meta-documents about how anomaly accounts were composed is essentially confirmed. They were assembled item by item from a large range of documentary sources and, to a much smaller extent, some oral sources as well.

---

124. Ssj 2.3–5; Sjz 40 (497). The two sets of narratives are nearly identical, so either both were derived from a common source, or one was derived from the other. Zhao Bing is also mentioned in the Shuis (LX p. 108).

125. Bwz 7.18 (Fan Ning 1980, item 259); Ssj 16.6. The Sjz cites a SJ passage, corresponding to SJ 61 (2123); Lone Bamboo is also mentioned in SJ as the name of a territory (SJ 4 [116], 5 [185]).

126. Sjz 14 (189).

127. Sjz 40 (496)—but no narrative of the event is given here and the stele is mentioned only in passing; Mxj 39 (based on quotation in FYZL 19).

128. Sjz 31 (395); this seems an unlikely location for a shrine to this figure. Cf. Syj 3.12a; Sxz 2, 57; ShuyjRf 1.38, 1.40. The Fan Li cycle in the anomaly accounts seems to be based, however, not (primarily at least) on inscriptional sources but on passages in SJ (129 [3256ff.]) and *Wu Yue chunqiu* (7.1a ff.).

They were evidential, not fictional, works. Their authors selected materials that, amassed together, would constitute formidable bodies of evidence concerning the topics with which they dealt; and this points us toward the next and final question we have to deal with in this chapter.

Why Anomaly Accounts?

If we want to understand why the genre of anomaly accounts was created, we are left with this important and as yet unanswered question: why were texts of this genre good to think with and good to write (and, by extension, good to read)? As we have seen, the *fangshi* thesis does not convincingly answer this question except for a handful of texts. Explanations of the genre's rise that point to general conditions of the time cut too broad a swath, for they do not tell us why this *kind* of text (in these forms of discourse and about these objects of discourse) came to be written in relatively large numbers during this period; they tend to assume text-writing to be a sort of passive mirroring of whatever was on people's minds in a given era, whereas I am assuming that it is likely to be much more complex than that. Whenever a new *genre* is created—usually a momentous event in the history of a culture's literature—we should suspect that the new genre must have allowed some sort of cultural work to get done that was not getting done in the genres already available. The question then is: what work were anomaly accounts *distinctive* in allowing in early medieval China?

I believe the answer to be twofold. Anomaly accounts allowed writers to deal with a certain rather large but, so far (at least in any written form), scantily treated subject matter; and they allowed writers to take a certain previously untaken approach to that subject matter. The subject itself was twofold, but each aspect overlapped to a large extent with the other: on the one hand, the "unseen and hidden" (*youming* etc.) world alluded to in the titles of many works—gods, ghosts, spirits, demons, the afterlife; on the other hand, anomalies of all other sorts, but most especially the *su* or "vulgar" (vertically anomalous in terms of the hierarchy of status, authority, and knowledge) and the *fang* or "peripheral" (horizontally anomalous in terms of the ideology of the sacred center). The approach was inductive and evidential, that is to say, historical. Both this subject area and this approach to it were justified by appeal to the mandates of the old cosmographic tradition, which had helped to create the constellation of ideas and values in which writers and readers could think of such writing about such subjects as contributing to the ordering of the world and society—and this despite all the talk of this genre's "minor" status relative to others.

The subjects on which anomaly accounts focused had simply not been explored at any length in written forms. Their closest predecessors were Sima Qian's *Fengshanshu* and the HS *Jisizhi*, but even these constituted only marginal precedent for the new genre; for the anomaly accounts, unlike these treatises, were not tied to the history of specific dynasties—or indeed to political history in any but the broadest and loosest sense. They were historically more comprehensive, unbound from the rigidly dynastic (and to that extent exemplar-focused) framework of official historiography. Their authors did not confine themselves to specific periods but ranged widely over materials from all periods, selecting cases that fit their interests.[129]

As for the evidential, historiographic form of the anomaly accounts, it constituted an alternative to the only others that had been used—and to only a slight degree—to explore these subjects: the *lun* 論 or treatise (one thinks of Mozi's treatise on ghosts, or Wang Chong's essays), the *fu* 賦 or rhapsody (one thinks of rhapsodies on theophanies), and the *ci* 辭 or songs contained in the *Chuci* 楚辭. What, then, did the historiographic form allow authors to do that these other forms did not allow? It provided a distinctive medium in which to explore the impress of the unseen but sometimes tangible world on ordinary life in this world. It allowed scope for the portrayal—inductively, just as in the historiography of dynasties—of the hidden yet inexorable principles on which the unseen world and our relations with it were structured. It even offered a permissible forum for the depiction of the day to day workings of that—to us, here—extraordinary world, so that it might be seen for the first time *as if* ordinary: how the dead behaved and what they were interested in, what the topography and society of the realm of the dead were like, how gods comported themselves, and the full range of possible relationships and interactions between living humans on the one hand and dead humans, former humans, transcendents, spirits of all kinds, on the other. By this new sort of writing, the dark world was brought to light, made visible, if only piecemeal in the item-by-item searchlight of historically specific narratives and

---

129. An exception is the Hwgs, which for this reason (and others) should be understood as standing at some remove from the core texts of the genre.

descriptions, which, while incapable of showing the overall lay of the otherworldly land, was uniquely capable of showing the intricate detail of each particular topos it shone upon.

And it is in that detail, that narrative and descriptive specificity, as well as in the moral complexity (and hence the unpredictability) of the interactions between humans and Others depicted in the texts, that the other world came, in the anomaly accounts, to take on a recognizably human aspect—to be domesticated, which is not to say (fully) controlled but merely rendered familiar. More often than not in these works, a character's interaction with a spirit no longer consisted of fight or flight, or the unilateral hurling of formulaic imprecations (as in demonographies), but took on the character of a negotiation—complex, fraught with danger yet also with opportunity, much as are negotiations between living people. Similarly, interactions with animals were revealed to be morally complex in ways hitherto unimagined. In the process, authors rendered the other world less mysterious while rendering this world more so. And, above all, the anomaly accounts made the seen and the unseen worlds seem closely knit together into a single cosmo-moral patchwork fabric, even if, like any patchwork, this one too had its highly prominent seams and borders. I suggest that, at bottom, it is this sense of the mutual implication of taxonomically (hence hierarchically) distinct orders of being that the authors of anomaly accounts developed their genre to convey. For this vision of distinct yet radically co-implicated orders of being was a worldview of the sort Martha Nussbaum describes in the second epigraph to this chapter, amenable to being captured neither in the marching logic of the essay nor in the prosody-driven formality of the pre-Tang poem, but only in the detailed specificity of a new sort of "history," one cut loose from its political moorings and hence free to focus on the anomalous as its unifying *topic*.

In the chapters to follow I explore the ways in which—and ends to which—authors approached this topic.

PART TWO

Interpretive Perspectives

Chapter Five

The Description and Narration of Anomaly: Cosmographic Poetics

A likely impossibility is always preferable to an unconvincing possibility.

Aristotle, *Poetics* 1460a27

Tant le fantastique est rupture de l'ordre reconnu, irruption de l'inadmissible au sein de l'inaltérable légalité quotidienne, et non substitution totale à l'universe réel d'un univers exclusivement miraculeux.

Roger Caillois (1965, 161)

In his *Guide to Supernatural Fiction*, subtitled *A full description of 1,775 books from 1750 to 1960, including ghost stories, weird fiction, stories of supernatural horror, fantasy, Gothic novels, occult fiction, and similar literature*, Everett F. Bleiler warns that the word "supernatural" does not fit some of the works described in his book.

In the late eighteenth and early nineteenth centuries, supernatural fiction dealt very largely with beings that were in some sense superior to mortals or living men. Today, it is much less concerned with such beings than with a world view

205

that is in direct opposition to that of materialism. It is "contrary" rather than "above," "contra" rather than "super." . . . My thesis is that modern fiction has erected a mirror world based on direct contradiction to what most of us believe, related through the strong principle of positive negation.[1]

When it comes to "the fantastic" as a literary type, we are dealing with writing whose crucial trait is not that it contains gods or ghosts or demons—which are in any event characterizable as "supernatural" only in the context of the traditional Western cosmology, with its dichotomy between matter and spirit and their respective realms—but that it plays upon a difference between "what most of us believe" and another view that is momentarily entertained as a possibility. In this sort of writing, "things are added to, subtracted from, and modified away from reality," to quote Bleiler again; which is to say that, in playing upon the difference between the ordinary and the extraordinary, fantastic writing both presupposes and challenges a prior structure of expectation. What counts as ordinary may be a "materialistic" worldview, as Bleiler thinks, and this worldview may have arisen from an earlier, "non-materialistic" one, making the assertions of "contranatural fiction" seem archaic; but it need not always be so. Let us start with the less restrictive view that the fantastic is that kind of "contra"-writing that plays parasitically upon the difference between a received worldview—"what most of us [or them] believe"—and its own partially different but not "wholly other" view of things.

Taking this notion of the fantastic as my point of departure, in this chapter I will explore the literary shape of individual textual items in anomaly accounts, guided by the overarching question of how their language and verbal structure communicate meaning— how the medium itself delivers a message. I want to show that anomaly accounts of all kinds do not simply represent phenomena that are anomalous, but that a structure of anomaly is built into their very representations, that is, into the nature of their language and into the shape and structure of how they say what they say. The objects of which any cosmographic discourse speaks—the "contents," as we metaphorically say, as if texts were containers holding objects we could take out and describe independently—certainly hold keys to understanding that discourse, but so, obviously, do the ways in which they are spoken about. This chapter contributes to something scholars of religion, culture, and literature do not

---

1. Bleiler 1983, 553.

presently have but ought to develop: a comparative cosmographic poetics.[2]

The Fantastic

We can first refine our notion of the fantastic as "contra"-writing by drawing on a few other Western critics' treatments of literature and art.

Gilbert Lascault pinpoints the nature of the monstrous in Western art by way of a meditation on sameness and difference. The monstrous, he says, arises not in art that seeks to imitate reality through representation, nor in art that simply differs from reality through its abstract, non-figurative forms, but in art that plays upon both sameness with and difference from reality as people ordinarily perceive it. Monstrous forms are those that are seen as deviating from nature in ways predicated on a partial similarity with nature. In other words, the extraordinary is necessarily defined in relation to the ordinary (whether that relation be the "strong principle of positive negation" or some more subtle mode); deviance, or the contra-natural, is a form of relation, not the absence of relation, with the natural.[3]

Similarly, Roger Caillois has argued that the essence of the "fantastic" in literature lies not in the presence of "supernatural" beings (fairies, demons, and so on), but in a specific type of relation between the events narrated in the text and the worldview the text presupposes its readers to have. Once again, that relation is a contra-relation: beings appear or events occur that are out of place in what is otherwise an ordinary world. In a fairy tale, for instance, the setting is such that anything can happen, and anything does in fact happen; but in a fantastic tale, the setting is such that X is impossible or highly unlikely, and then it is precisely X which occurs.[4]

Tzvetan Todorov has expanded such thinking into a sophisticated work on the fantastic as a distinct genre in Western literature. He begins by pointing out a specific process of decision by both the reader (outside the text) and the protagonist (inside it). Confronted with ambiguous events which seem supernatural and yet which may be amenable after all to natural explanation,

---

2. Cf. Harbsmeier 1985.
3. Lascault 1973.
4. Caillois 1966; cf. Caillois 1965, 161.

both reader and protagonist hesitate. This hesitation, drawn out suspensefully until the story's end or (less often) left unresolved, defines the fantastic. But

> at the story's end, the reader makes a decision even if the character does not; he opts for one solution or the other, and thereby emerges from the fantastic.[5] If he decides that the laws of reality remain intact and permit an explanation of the phenomena described, we say that the work belongs to another genre: the uncanny [*l'étrange*]. If, on the contrary, he decides that new laws of nature must be entertained to account for the phenomena, we enter the genre of the marvelous [*le merveilleux*].[6]

Todorov goes on to draw a five-part map or spectrum of what we might term the terrain of "extraordinary" literature—literature which works upon the space between the ordinary and the extraordinary: (1) uncanny → (2) fantastic-uncanny → (3) fantastic → (4) fantastic-marvelous → (5) marvelous. Immediately to one side of the fantastic itself is the genre "fantastic-uncanny," in which events that seem supernatural throughout the story are rationally explained in the end; the causal "machinery" that was at work all along is finally revealed.[7] Immediately to the other side is the genre "fantastic-marvelous," in which events that have an ambiguous aura of the supernatural throughout the story are confirmed as supernatural at the end. On the two outer extremes are the pure uncanny, essentially an attitude toward narrated events (usually one of fear or horror), and the pure marvelous, which is characterized not by an attitude but by the strange nature of narrated events themselves.[8] In the middle is the pure fantastic itself, in which the decision between two potential solutions to the narrative's ambiguity is left unresolved.[9] Paradoxically, one of these solutions (the marvelous) is relatively probable yet supernatural, while the other (the uncanny) is relatively improbable yet natural.

---

5. Although it is not crucial to my argument, I differ here from Todorov: there is no reason why the reader may not suspend judgment and thereby remain poised in the zone of the fantastic.

6. Todorov 1975, 41.

7. Todorov 1975, 45.

8. Todorov 1975, 54ff.

9. Todorov significantly adds that this impossibility of resolution "in itself suggests the existence of the supernatural" (1975, 52).

Three features, then, characterize the fantastic as a type of writing. (1) It is "contranatural," defined not by the presence of beings who are "above" nature but by the fact that the narrative goes against the "ordinary" worldview. This worldview is not only the one held by most readers; it is also set up by the text itself as the background to the more "extraordinary" features of the plot. Fantastic writing therefore presupposes some notion of regularity, some order of expectation, perhaps some view of causation, though not necessarily a rigid law of "mechanistic" necessity—in short, some boundary or limit of what is possible, normal, natural, or expected. (2) It may be further classified according to whether, in the end, the ordinary features of the world suffice to explain and thus contain the irruption of the extraordinary and the anomalous, or whether, on the contrary, the boundaries of the ordinary world must be enlarged to encompass the new phenomena. (3) It sometimes deliberately evokes an older or "archaic" worldview, in which the sorts of things now outside the limits of the possible or the expected were once inside. Fantastic literature often constructs itself as a survival from older, wiser times, and thus implies that there exists an important difference between the past and the present (often accompanied by nostalgia for the past).

I now turn to the Chinese texts, beginning with brief comments on the nature of the language in which they are written (and what that tells us), then analyzing the fundamental modes of writing about anomalies in late Han and early medieval China.

The Language of Anomaly Accounts

Without exception, early medieval anomaly accounts are written in classical language. Unlike the Tang transformation texts (*bianwen*) or later tale literature,[10] they are not vernacular texts, and even though the material for some of them was undoubtedly derived from oral sources, very few traces of orality remain in the language into which that material was transposed. Nor were they written as prompts or scripts for oral storytelling. They were clearly meant to be read in the same manner that histories and similar works from the period were read—not surprisingly since, as we have seen, they were thought of as a branch of history.

Furthermore, except on the rare occasions when they quote folksongs or reproduce poems uttered during a reported dialogue,

---

10. Mair 1989; Hanan 1981.

early anomaly accounts are completely written in prose; they seldom use the regularized meter or rhyme structure characteristic of parallel prose (*pianwen*). In this respect as well, their closest literary analogue is the historical writing designated by the suffixes *ji* 記, *ji* 紀, *zhuan* 傳, and *zhi* 志—suffixes carried in the titles of most anomaly accounts themselves. Yet their language is not as formal as that of the histories; it is slightly more colloquial, and is noticeably less laconic in its wording.

The texts therefore present anomalous material in quite ordinary, if literary (as opposed to oral-like), language. This impression is most striking when one reads them against contemporary Daoist scriptures (particularly those describing divine revelations) or Buddhist canonical texts (particularly *sūtras*). Next to the special terminology often invoked in scriptural texts, their technical descriptions of and prescriptions for internal states of mind and body, and their dazzling depictions of celestial scenes and cosmic light-rays—or, for that matter, next to the ornate poetry of contemporary rhapsodies (*fu*) or Music Bureau poems[11]—the language of the anomaly texts seems relatively pedestrian. Authors of those texts did not choose uncanny, theological, esoteric, or archaicizing language to convey their messages, despite the fact that they dealt with uncanny, theological, esoteric, and archaic phenomena. They couched accounts of extraordinary things in ordinary writing. The very language of the texts, therefore, exhibits the structure of the fantastic: the literary ordinariness of the prose itself already helps to form the backdrop of the "normal," in relation to which the anomalous event or object appears all the more so.

The Three Modes

Next we have to distinguish three fundamental modes[12] of written discourse in the genre; for, despite the fact that anomaly accounts

---

11. Knechtges 1976, 1982; Allen 1992.

12. By "mode," I simply mean a fundamentally distinct type of writing, one which textually orders its objects and (to some extent) portrays human subjectivity in ways distinct from other types. I am aware that literary critics such as Northrop Frye and Hayden White have used the term "mode" in more specific and sophisticated ways than are intended here. Their uses of the term are, however, closely tied to the Western literary tradition in ways that render them unhelpful for analyzing Chinese poetics.

in general are often characterized as "tales," they are hardly all narrative texts. The first of these modes can be quickly disposed of; the other two deserve more detailed analyses.

First, there is what I term the *theoretical* mode. One occasionally finds passages that do not concern specific objects or events but are statements in discursive meta-language of general laws or principles abstracted from particular cases. Many such passages read like—and probably were originally—introductions to chapters or sections dealing with specific topics. They were doubtless intended as a kind of frame for the items that followed. Others seem to have been authorial asides. The large majority of "theoretical" passages that have come down to us occur in two of the earliest texts of the genre, Zhang Hua's Bwz and Gan Bao's Ssj. In comparison to the vast majority of surviving items, such passages are rare. What importance they have lies in the fact that they constitute possible clues to the sorts of points their authors wished to impress upon readers through the amassing of particular instances—a topic taken up in Chapter Seven.

The Ssj, for instance, contains four discursive passages on the theory of how things transform across taxonomic categories and how anomalous creatures come to exist. One of them (12.1) heads a chapter comprising eighteen examples of mostly demonic metamorphoses. Long enough to constitute an essay of its own, and based on similar passages in such earlier texts as the *Yueling*, *Zhuangzi*, *Liezi*, and HS, this item explains such changes (along with human character traits, the effects of certain diets, and other phenomena) with reference to the recombinatory potency of the five types of pneuma (*qi* 氣).[13] A similar, but much shorter, passage appears elsewhere in the same chapter as a general gloss on an item describing dangerous creatures dwelling in the hills around Linchuan, which the people called "*daolao* demons" (刀勞鬼). It seems to deny the possibility of the sorts of transformations documented elsewhere in the same chapter, while asserting a version of the principle that ontogeny recapitulates phylogeny:

> The demons and spirits (*guishen* 鬼神) of Heaven and Earth are produced just as we are. It is [simply] because their pneumas are distinct that their inner natures (性) are anomalous (異) [with respect to that of other, "normal" creatures]; it is simply because their environment is different that their outward forms (形) are unusual (殊). No beings are inter-

13. DeWoskin 1974, 180–82.

changeable.[14] Their birth is controlled by *yang* and their death by *yin*; they are each produced in a manner in accordance with the inner nature they receive. In the midst of the great *yin* (*taiyin* 太陰) is where anomalous creatures (*guaiwu* 怪物) dwell.[15]

The other two Ssj discourses on transformation theory are placed in the mouths of well known figures: Guan Lu, a *fangshi* expert in many kinds of divination who is given a biography in the "esoteric arts" section of the SGZ,[16] gives one, Confucius the other.[17]

One also finds several discursive passages (often quite brief) on the theory of cosmological resonance or influence-response (*ganying* 感應), including in some cases the relationship between it and the theory of portents and omens.[18] Some of these discourses are again placed in the mouths of skilled masters such as Zhang Hua.[19] There are similar passages on the theory of the five phases, dietary practices, portent-interpretation, dreams, disease, soil types, animal reproduction, ethnological traits, and demons.[20]

The other two modes, *descriptive* and *narrative*—together accounting for the vast majority of anomaly text items—differ from the theoretical in that they make no general statements of

---

14. I take this to mean that, because the nature and form of each creature—anomalous or not—are radically conditioned by *qi* (pneuma) and *yu* (environment), none can take the place of another; each is unique. This might be taken (among other things) as an argument against any theory of classes or species (*lei* 類), but I interpret it as a foregrounding of the notion of *fen* 分—"allotment," or the specific place and nature assigned to each being, according to fixed principles, in the cosmological thinking that (as I argue in Chapter Seven) the Ssj seeks to defend.

15. Ssj 12.10; earlier in this item two texts are cited, one a passage from *Laozi* 39, the other a passage from a so-called "heterodox book" (*waishu* 外書), a general designation for *chenwei* texts.

16. SGZ 29 (811 ff.); tr. DeWoskin 1983, 91 ff.

17. The first is in Ssj 3.5; the second is in Ssj 19.6 (tr. de Groot 1982 [1892–1910], 5:644).

18. Bwz 1.32, 1.44, 4.18–20; Ssj 6.1, 6.2 [cf. DeWoskin 1974, 283], 7.7, 11.14–15.

19. E.g. Yy 2.3.

20. On the five phases: Bwz 1.24, Ssj 13.19. On dietary practices: Bwz 4.18–25, 4.40–49, 5.12, 5.14. On portent-interpretation: Bwz 9.16, Ssj 6.52. On dreams and their causes: Bwz 10.7. On disease: Bwz 1.41–42. On soil types: Bwz 1.43. On animal reproduction: Bwz 4.1. On ethnological traits: Bwz 1.34–42. On demons: Yy 3.32, XuQxj 5, Yml 31.

principle, but instead deal with specific events, persons, beings, objects, or places. They do so in different ways, however. Most descriptive items are not stories; they rarely have a protagonist. They often seem timeless, not essentially bound to any temporal or historical framework. As I will show, the descriptive items that do take a seemingly narrative form (in the sense that they report events more or less sequential in time) can be seen on closer inspection to use this device to *describe* an object of discourse among others of the same class. The key medium in which items in the descriptive mode unfold is space or place—either geographic or taxonomic (or both). By contrast, narrative items tell a story that unfolds in time as its key medium and that is also often set in a particular historical period. At the center of most narrative items is a human protagonist, whose relationship to other beings and whose reactions to the narrated events form the crux of the tale.

The Descriptive Mode

I begin with the following item from the Ssj:

In the south there is an insect called *dunyu*; another name for it is *zeshu*, another is *qingfu*. In form it resembles a cicada but is slightly larger. It has a fine flavor and is edible. It hatches its young onto grasses or leaves; they are about as big as silkworms. If you take its hatchlings, the mother will fly to you no matter how great the distance; and even if you hide them, the mother will know where they are. If you take the mother's blood and smear it on coins in an "eighty-one pattern,"[21] and do the same with the hatchlings' blood on another set of coins, then when you buy things in the market, whether you use the mother-coins or the hatchling-coins, the counterparts will return at once. Without fail they will roll back to you. This is why the "*Huainanzi* 'Arts'"[22] mentions "returning coins" 還錢; it uses the term *qingfu* (Ssj 13.14).

---

21. I do not know what this pattern was; it probably incorporated the graphs for "eight" and "one."

22. This reference to *Huainanzi shu* 術 is probably short for a now-fragmentary collection of alchemical practices known as *Huainan wanbishu* 萬畢術 that was originally part of the *Huainanzi* collection but later became separated from it. Huang Diming 1991, 373; Roth 1992, 16, 24–25.

This passage has all the hallmarks of the descriptive mode. First is often given a place or region ("in the south"); sometimes, when the item concerns an ancient topic, a time marker is initially given instead, locating the item in a particular reign. Second, the object of discourse is introduced, often by the mention of the general type or class to which it belongs ("an insect"). Third, the proper, specific, or technical name of the object is given, including multiple names where applicable (*dunyu, zeshu, qingfu*). Fourth, relevant and identifying properties are listed, including both ordinary and exceptional features ("resembles a cicada," "has a fine flavor and is edible," "hatches its young onto grasses or leaves," etc.). Fifth, the special uses or functions of the object—what it is good for—are indicated ("without fail . . . "). Sixth, corroborative passages in other texts are sometimes cited, variant versions of the description are provided, or explanations of certain features are given (here a *Huainanzi* passage is mentioned).

These discursive features can be summarized as follows:

1. Spatial (and/or sometimes temporal) and taxonomic mapping: (A) Place (and/or time) marker; (B) Type or class marker.

2. Nomenclature.

3. Identifying features, including: (A) Relevant but unremarkable features; (B) Remarkable, exceptional, anomalous features.

4. Uses or functions.

5. Variata.

These elements do not always appear in precisely this order, and many items lack one or more of them, particularly the last. Furthermore, some items combine two or more of these sorts of information in a single comment. And some items are relatively fleshed out, others relatively laconic. But this discursive structure is implicit in most descriptive items.

Take, for instance, the following item from the Bwz, in which all except the last discursive element listed above also appear, but in much more telescoped form:

In the Realm of White People 白民國 there is [a creature called] *chenghuang* 乘黃. It is shaped like a fox and has flesh on its back. He who rides it will live for three thousand years (Bwz 2.2).

Here we find a place marker ("the Realm of White People"); a class marker combined with a description of relevant but unremarkable features ("shaped like a fox ... flesh on its back"); nomenclature ("*chenghuang*"); and an account of the uses or functions of the object combined with a description of its anomalous features ("he who rides it will ... ").

In the section on "amusing arts" in the same text can be found this concise item:

On the fifth day of the fifth month, bury the head of a dragonfly beneath a west-facing door. Leave it buried three days without eating it and it will transform into a *qingzhen* pearl. Other recipes say to bury it under the main door.[23]

Here, as in the many comparable accounts of esoteric procedures and recipes for attaining extraordinary results, the description is stripped down to a statement of uses or functions and—in this case—a mention of variata ("other recipes ... "). The day on which the procedure is to be performed, a day of note in the popular Chinese calendar, might be read as a temporal marker ("things to be done on the fifth day of the fifth lunar month"). In the following item from Ren Fang's ShuyjRf, apparently based on a passage in the Syj, the initial marker is a place marker and is more pronounced:

To the east of Yuanjiao Mountain 員嶠山, also known as Ring Hill, is a cloud stone some five hundred *li* across. On it live seven-inch-long, black silkworms with scales and horns. If covered with frost and snow they will produce foot-long, five-colored cocoons. These may be woven into patterned brocades which, if dipped in water, will not get wet.[24]

Unusual plants and plant products are also often treated under the descriptive mode. Here is an example from Ren Fang's text:

From Nanhai comes "thousand-pace fragrance" 千步香: if you wear it, its scent can be detected from a thousand paces away. Today at Haiyu there exists a "thousand-pace herb"; this is one variety of it. Its leaves resemble those of crabapple trees only they are red and green. The *Records of Miscellaneous*

---

23. Bwz 4.59 (50); cf. TPYL 888, TPGJ 473.
24. ShuyjRf 1.71 [12b]; cf. Syj 10.5b, tr. Foster 1974, 298–99.

Tributes 雜貢籍 [25] mentions that "the Southern District Commandery submitted as tribute 'thousand-pace fragrance'" (ShuyjRf 2.51 [5b-6a]).

As is his wont, Ren Fang here pays much attention to variata; under a single rubric he tries to link together as many pieces of contemporary folklore and historical record as possible.[26]

Aside from using it to describe anomalous animals, plants, and insects, authors of anomaly accounts turned to the descriptive mode when they wanted to characterize particular places on the landscape. They applied this mode to distant, mythical lands as much as to domestic places.

For example, some Daoist-inclined texts take the form of what might be termed mythical-visionary geography. They constitute a textual tour of fantastic places—mostly distant mountains and isles—accessible, it would seem, only to spiritual travelers. Most of the information provided about each place consists of the marvels to be found at and around it.

Hook Shadow Mountain 鉤[27] 影山 is 30,000 *li* from the Shining River. The vapors which form around it when viewed from a distance look like the shadow of a mountain. Cinnabar pulse[28] grows in its shadow; its leaves float in water. [Beside the mountain] is the Purple River, ten thousand *li* long and a hundred feet deep; in it grows Cold Lotus, which blossoms and is fragrant only after a frost. There is also an altar for the descent of spirits, a pond for the cultivation of spirituality, a Palace of Apportioned Light with five rooms, a House of Quick Thunder with seven rooms, and a [Lunar] Toad-Gazing Tower one hundred and twenty feet high on top of which are golden bells four feet wide.[29]

---

25. To my knowledge, this is an otherwise completely lost text; it is not cited in the CXJ, TPYL, or TPGJ.

26. Campany 1990b.

27. Reading 鉤 for the text's 釣.

28. Clearly a medicinal herb of some sort, this term may refer to "bean-leaf aromatic" or patchouli; Schafer 1963, 172–73.

29. Dmj 1.4 [2b]. There directly follows an entry on mirrors sent as tribute from the Realm of Qi, which seems to be a misplaced fragment. I have translated from the ZDHW text; for a different tr., which incorporates fragments from other sources, cf. Smith 1992, 595–96.

In this passage, replete with lunar imagery, we find the expected place and class markers, a metaphorically and metaphysically elaborate nomenclature (typical of Daoist texts), and lists of identifying features both remarkable (the Cold Lotus, the extraordinarily high tower and deep river) and relatively unremarkable (the vapors). Absent are functional comments and variata.

Some mythical places become anchors for detached bits of mythology, as in this item from one of the later sections (perhaps added by Guo Pu) of the Shj (*Dahuang nanjing*):

> Beyond the Eastern Sea[30] in the vicinity of Sweet Water is the Realm of Xi He 羲和之國. There is a woman [there] named Xi He who bathes the sun in the Sweet Gulf. Xi He was the wife of Thearch Jun 帝俊; she gave birth to ten suns (Shj 381).

Place ("Beyond the Eastern Sea") and class ("Realm") markers, nomenclature, and ordinary and extraordinary features are all in evidence here. The third sentence can be read as a notation on variata, as it supplements the main point of the item with background information on the ancient myth of Thearch Jun and of Xi He's birth of ten suns, which lies behind the description of this place.[31] This last sentence seems a sort of tag, added to the description of a place in order to link that description explicitly with, or map it onto, the terrain of ancient mythology.

Anomalies connected with domestic places are described in much the same format:

> At Billow Mountain in Yongning District there is a river whose water is a deep red color. A natural stone bridge crosses it; there are many fish, otters, and strange birds. At times when it is cloudy and rainy, the sound of drums and horns can be heard quite clearly (Yy 1.14).

Although the assertion sounds strange, *events* are sometimes treated in anomaly texts in the descriptive as opposed to the narrative mode. This is best seen in the lists of portents that appear prominently in some collections:

---

30. Emending the text's "Southeastern Sea" as suggested by Yuan Ke.

31. On the myth, see Yuan Ke 1981 [1960], 173ff.; Mitarai 1984, 477–505; Bodde 1961, 394ff.; Karlgren 1946, 262ff.

On the first day of the eighth month of the first year of the Great Prime reign-period [251] of the Wu ruler Sun Quan 孫權, there was a great wind and the rivers and seas rose. Water covered level ground to a depth of eight feet. Two thousand trees on high places were uprooted, stone steles were knocked down, and two gates in the city wall of the Wu capital were blown off [their hinges]. In the next year Quan died (Ssj 6.73).

This is not the narrative of a storm; there is no plot unfolding in time and (despite the prominent mention of Sun Quan) no protagonist. It is a list of events that were seen in retrospect as having portended a specific outcome with political consequences. It takes its place among similar items in a list (in this case, 125 such items), and the details that make up this item are what mark it as a specific instance of the general type, "portent-description." The text unfolds, therefore, by locating successive list-items in taxonomic space, even when those items consist of events precisely placed in historical time and concerning historical personages.

Finally, some "biographical" or "hagiographical" items in the anomaly-account corpus are better seen as descriptions—in precisely the sense characterized here—of a person than as narrative histories of a life, even though they may contain narrative elements. Take, for instance, this item, which is typical of Liu Xiang's Lxz:

Ning Fengzi 寧封子 was a man of the Yellow Thearch's era; legend has it that he was the Yellow Thearch's master potter. A person came to visit him who could cause his palm to burst into flames and emit five-colored smoke. After a long time this person taught the art to Fengzi. Fengzi then started a fire and burned himself: he ascended and descended following the smoke from the fire. When the remaining ashes were examined, his bones were found among them. These the people of the time agreed to bury on a mountain north of Ning. This is why he came to be called Ning Fengzi (Master of the Tumulus at Ning).[32]

Every discursive element of the descriptive mode is present in this item, although, as we have seen in the case of other descriptive items, some of them overlap. The passage opens with time ("Yellow

---

32. Lxz 2 (HY 294 1.1b); cf. the tr. in Kaltenmark 1953, 43–47.

Thearch's era") and type ("man . . . master potter") markers and no-menclature. It gives the unusual features that identify this particu-lar transcendent as an individual—his special abilities with fire; it also mentions a relatively unremarkable feature, namely his occu-pation as potter. What in the case of an object, animal, plant, or place might come under "uses or functions" finds its equivalent here and in other biographical items as a list of anomalous capaci-ties—again (in this case) his ability to summon fire. Finally, the closing comment about the reason for his retrospectively applied name—"Master of the Tumulus at Ning"—falls under the category of variata, since it supplements the account with an explanation.

This hardly constitutes a "biography" in any familiar sense of that term. It more closely approximates a descriptive item in an in-ventory of men and women, all of whom are anomalous with re-spect to ordinary persons but each of whom is so by virtue of a distinct combination of features. (As a man of the "Yellow Thearch's era," Ning Fengzi is also here *ipso facto* presented as the original and the prototypical potter.) This text's predominant medium is not the passage of time but the unfolding of graphic space as the reader moves down the inventory. For it must not be forgotten that each descriptive item takes its place in a surrounding list of items with which it is usually connected (if indeed its juxtaposition is not merely random, as seems to be the case with some texts in their present form) by a common topic or taxon, seldom if ever by any temporal or causal link.[33]

In the descriptive mode, we have to deal most directly, in short, with *Listenwissenschaft*, characterized by Jonathan Z. Smith as "a science which takes as its prime intellectual activity the pro-duction and reflection on lists, catalogs, and classifications, which progresses by establishing precedents, by observing patterns, simi-larities, and conjunctions, by noting repetitions."[34] Of an enumera-tion of items taken from a member of the Iatmul people of New Guinea, Smith says:

It . . . represents a map of a particular culture's selection, out of the multitude of elements which make up their common life, those which are capable of bearing obsession, those which

---

33. Thus, even in the case of chronologically arranged portent-lists, the links between discrete items are not causal or historical in nature in the way that entries in historical annals are; temporal sequence is simply used as the ordering principle.

34. Smith 1982, 47.

are understood as significant. Properly interpreted, it is a diagram of the characteristic preoccupations (as well as the occupations) of the Iatmul.[35]

Furthermore, Jack Goody has shown the etymological and conceptual connections between matters of "list" and matters of "boundary." The list, he reminds us,

> depends on discontinuity rather than continuity; it depends on physical placement, on location. . . . It has a clear-cut beginning and a precise end, that is, a boundary. . . . And the existence of boundaries, external and internal, brings greater visibility to categories, at the same time as making them more abstract.[36]

We must add to Smith's characterization, in the case of anomaly items in the descriptive mode, that the "selection" in question is controlled by a special cosmographic interest in anomaly; authors selected *for* the exceptional, the odd, those phenomena which by their anomalous nature highlighted the boundaries between categories. Furthermore, it is a question not of "a particular culture's selection" but of a particular author's, an author who works within a particular tradition (while often working against another) that is not co-extensive with the entire surrounding culture, but rather represents a specific configuration of cultural and social interests. Finally, as Goody says of lists in general, central to the descriptive mode is the question of location, in the following sense. Each animal, each plant, each place, each event, each person "covered" (as we metaphorically say) by the fabric of the text is one animal, plant, place, event, or person among all others. And, more narrowly, each is one anomalous case of its category among other known anomalous cases. The individual item first maps its particular case onto the appropriate taxonomic location by making clear what general class of phenomena it belongs to; then it proceeds to specify the features that make this particular case both anomalous (with respect to "ordinary" cases of the same class) and *distinctively* anomalous (with respect to other anomalous cases of the same class), and that thus warrant a discrete item in the list.

But what of the notion of the fantastic with which we began? Is it exclusively a feature of narrative discourse, or is it helpful in

---

35. Smith 1982, 46.
36. Goody 1977, 81.

characterizing the poetics of descriptive items as well? If we speak not of "narrative" and "plot" but of "description" and "text," we find at once that two of the three key features of fantastic narrative identified above apply with equal force to the descriptive items under discussion here.[37] To begin with the first of those features, descriptive items are contranatural in that they go against fundamental aspects of the worldview of most readers; this trait arises already from the fact that they deal with anomalies. More to the point, like fantastic narratives these descriptions begin by setting up ordinary expectations in the reader, which they then undercut as reading proceeds. But they do so even more subtly than many narratives. Here, not only in its everyday quality of language but also simply by mentioning either the main taxon to which the object of discourse belongs ("In the south there is an insect") or its relatively unremarkable features ("In form it resembles a cicada . . . [and] has a fine flavor"), or both, the descriptive text lays a foundation of ordinariness and naturalness on which it then constructs the surprising, anomalous features which are its focal points. By virtue of the worldview presumptively held by the reader and apparently (initially at least) shared by the implied author—a worldview containing a set of taxa and expectations about the basic properties members of each taxon possess—the reader, unless already versed in the lore about to be presented (in cases of stereotypes and intertextual borrowings, for instance), does not expect an object of the type and with the properties initially mentioned to be described as having the further properties listed. In presenting these surprising features and thus frustrating the reader's expectation, descriptive items execute a "contra" move that is structurally indistinct from the "pivot" in fantastic narratives (on which see below). The descriptive mode differs from the narrative only in deploying its anomalous turn while moving not through the processual time of successive events but through the textually unfolding depiction of taxonomic space and of an anomalous object (or fact) inhabiting that space.

---

37. The second feature—the classification of fantastic narratives according to whether they end by allowing the reader to explain the portrayed anomalies within the parameters of the received worldview, or by pressuring the reader to alter that worldview to encompass the new phenomena—does not really figure at the level of the individual item in the descriptive mode. One must look at the entire text to gain a sense of its overall locative or anti-locative orientation. Only in the case of single *narrative* items can one sometimes discern one or the other approach to anomaly.

Descriptive items further share with many fantastic narratives a taste for the archaic (as well as the folkloric) as exotic. Not only do some of them focus on figures and events of the mythical or legendary past, as in the item on the Realm of Xi He above;[38] some also attempt to trace the mythical past into the folkloric present by interpreting folk sayings and customs as survivals from former times, as does Ren Fang in his item on "thousand-pace fragrance" and elsewhere.[39]

In sum, we may speak of fantastic descriptions as well as fantastic narratives. Items in these two modes share essentially the same structure of the fantastic outlined above.

The Narrative Mode

I begin with the following tale:

Beside the river in the western part of Ailanthus City District in Nankang there is a stone chamber called Mengkou Cave 夢口穴. Once there was a boatman [in the area] who chanced upon a man who was completely clad in yellow and was carrying two baskets of yellow melons. He asked for a ride. As the boat pulled up to the bank, the man spat into the till, disembarked, and directly entered the cave. At first the boatman was very angry at the man, but when he saw him enter the cave he began to realize that something strange was afoot (始知異). Looking at the spittle in his till, he saw it had turned completely into gold (ShuyjRf 1.60 [10b]).[40]

---

38. Examples include a host of items concerning the Queen Mother of the West (Yy 1.5; XuQxj 3; Yml 30; Szj 1a, 10b; Dmj 1.2, 1.7, 2.1, 2.17; Syj 3.3a, 4.4b, 6.6b; Ssj 1.2, 6.43, 14.12, 20.4; Bwz 8.23, 9.1; Sshj 5.8; Lxz 1) and the Yellow Thearch (Lyz 1; Lxz 2–5, 7; ShuyjRf 1.4, 1.20, 1.44; Dmj 3.9; Syj 1.3b, 1.12b, 9.7b; Bwz 8.1, 9.2; Yy 7.14; Sxz 1), and a handful each concerning a great many other figures such as the creatrix Nü Wa (Syj 5.3a; Bwz 1.17), the Divine Husbandman 神農 (Yy 2.36; ShuyjRf 2.44–45; Jzj 1b; Ssj 1.1–2; Lxz 1), the ruler Shun 舜 (Yy 1.5; Ssj 8.1; Syj 1.11a), Yu the Great 大禹 (Szj 12b; Dmj 2.14; Syj 2.1a; Bwz 2.10, 2.14, 7.1, 8.3), the monstrous rebels Chi You (ShuyjRf 1.4; Syj 1.7a, 1.8a, 1.12b, 9.7b) and Gong Gong (Shenyjing nw 2; Bwz 1.17), the charioteer Kua Fu who raced the sun (Bwz 7.11), the cosmic progenitor Pan Gu (ShuyjRf 1.1), and the tribal progenitor Pan Hu (Ssj 14.2, Wlj 1a).

39. Campany 1990b, 1991c.

40. Shuyj 6 gives a more complete version of this tale, in which we are *first* told of the divine resident of the cave and *then* read the part of the

Let us now analyze this narrative into its component parts. Like most anomaly items, this one starts by laying an ordinary-enough foundation: an unremarkable geographic area, a river, a cave. And in its first sentence there is nothing so far that is distinctively narrative in nature; we would not be surprised to see this sentence at the head of a descriptive item. With the word "once" (*chang* 嘗), however, the text enters the narrative mode: we now expect an account of a particular event. And we expect that event to happen to the protagonist supplied in the ensuing phrase ("there was a boatman who . . . "). The text then drops an advance hint that something anomalous is about to occur—a detail the perceptive reader is invited and perhaps expected to notice, but one which the character inside the tale apparently does not notice. This hint consists of the fact that the passenger is not only completely dressed in yellow—not an ordinary attire at the time (as even a reader unfamiliar with the history of Chinese costume might surmise from the fact that the story is at pains to mention this detail)—but, as if to emphasize his own extraordinariness (and to set up his secret association with gold which will be revealed at the end), is also carrying melons of the same color. (Many contemporary Chinese readers would probably have further associated the color yellow with Daoist masters and esoteric arts.) Following this, the text sets in motion a normal and familiar cultural process governed by certain customs and expectations: that of hiring a ride on a boat. A second wave of anomaly then comes when this strange passenger spits instead of paying the boatman, violating the custom he is expected by the reader to follow in the normal process of getting a boat ride. (His entrance into a cave—a third wave of anomaly—would have confirmed his association with Daoist esotericism for most readers.) It is this violation that finally alerts the protagonist or "straight" character that "something strange was afoot," and the climax then comes swiftly as the text reports the contranatural transformation of saliva into gold.

Comparison with the following tale will further illuminate some of the shared structural features of anomaly narratives:

During the Han period, a lictor for the Zhuji District[41] office named Wu Xiang 吳詳, because he feared being sent on a difficult mission, set out to escape into the deep mountains.

---

story told in ShuyjRf. Interestingly, not only does the ShuyjRf version stand on its own, but the structure of expectation on which it plays is quite different.

41. Located in today's Zhejiang Province.

While walking along, he came to a stream and the sun was about to set when he saw a young woman dressed in very formal, brightly colored clothes. She said: "I live all alone, and I have no neighbors except for one old widow. [My home] is nearby." When Xiang heard this he was very pleased, and so he followed her. They walked about half a mile, then reached the woman's home, which was quite modest.

She set out a meal for Xiang. At the end of the first watch he heard an old woman call out, "Miss Zhang?" The young woman replied, "Yes." Xiang asked who it was and the young woman said, "That was the old widow I told you about earlier." The two of them then slept together.

When dawn arrived and the cock crowed, Xiang departed. The two of them had some feelings for each other; she gave him a purple handkerchief as a gift, and for his part he gave her one of cloth. He walked to the place where they had met the day before. He tried to re-cross the stream, but the water had risen overnight and he could no longer wade across. So he turned back toward the woman's home. But nothing he saw corresponded to what he had seen the day before; there was only a tomb there.[42]

For the sake of clarity, I now lay out and name certain elements shared by the narrative structure of both tales, followed in parentheses by the relevant phrases from each (**A** designating the first tale, **B** the second):

(1) **Setting.** A particular place or geographical region, as well as a more or less specific time period, are given (sometimes only one of these, as in the first tale). (**A:** "Beside the river . . . there is a stone chamber"; **B:** "During the Han period . . . Zhuji District.")

(2) **Specifier.** Some indication is given next of the specific situation or string of events narrated by the tale, so that the focus is narrowed to a particular occasion when an event happened. This focusing is usually accomplished in part by introducing a protagonist (usually but not always identified by surname and given name,

---

42. Sshj 6.2 (68–69); TPGJ 317.1. The TPGJ version gives a different graph for Wu's given name of Xiang and varies in other minor details; I have consulted both texts in translating. The TPGJ cites the FYZL as its source, but I have yet to locate this tale in that collection.

sometimes by surname only, sometimes unnamed).[43] (**A:** "Once there was a boatman who chanced upon a man"; **B:** "A lictor . . . because he feared . . . set out to escape.")

(**3**) **Process.** Some sort of familiar process or type of interaction is set underway—some human activity with a predictable sequence, even if it is not an everyday activity. (**A:** "He asked for a ride"; **B:** "While walking along.")[44]

(**4**) **Hints.** Advance signals are often given that something anomalous is about to occur; these are detectable by the reader but often go unnoticed by the protagonist. (**A:** "completely clad in yellow . . . carrying two baskets of yellow melons"; **B:** "a young woman dressed in very formal, brightly colored clothes. She said: 'I live all alone.' ")[45]

(**5**) **Limen.** Often (not always) a liminal marker is now introduced. An incomplete list of such markers mentioned in the anomaly accounts might include the following: almost any sort of travel, especially on rivers and lakes or through mountains; sunset, midnight or early morning, sunrise; the approach of a storm; a death; an illness; a dream; drunkenness; a doorway or gate; a shore or bank; a distant land. (**A:** "As the boat pulled up to the bank"; **B:** "deep mountains . . . he came to a stream and the sun was about to set.")

(**6**) **Pivot.** Something distinctly odd now happens and the reader—usually joined at this point (if not earlier) by the protago-

---

43. Sometimes the introduction of the protagonist is better understood as forming part of the "setting." Since the analytical framework I am developing here is only intended heuristically to make manifest the fantastic structure of the narratives, the exact placement of the mention of the protagonist in any particular item makes little difference to my analysis.

44. It should be noted that elements 1–5 do not always appear in the order indicated here; this is a frequent but not a necessary ordering.

45. Perhaps some comment is needed on these details. In Chinese culture at the time, it would have been highly unusual to find a beautiful young woman who lived alone, not to mention one who lived alone in the deep mountains and who in that setting wore formal clothing. This formalness is a foreshadowing of the fact that she is dead: these are her burial garments, and the "old widow" is doubtless another dead person buried in the same grave or else nearby. Hilly and mountainous areas were—and still are—commonly used as burial sites.

nist—becomes unmistakably aware of the strangeness of the situation. The text enters the zone of the fantastic proper.[46] As we will see below, the pivot is often marked by a characteristic cluster of phenomenological terms describing the protagonist's sudden sensory perception of and affective reaction to the anomalous event. (**A:** "the man spat into [the boatman's] till, disembarked, and directly entered the cave. ... Looking at the spittle in his till, he saw ..."; **B:** "Nothing he saw corresponded to what he had seen the day before; there was ....")

(7) Climax. The full force of the anomaly hits home to both protagonist and reader. (**A:** "it had turned completely into gold"; **B:** " ... only a tomb there.")

The following story well illustrates the sixth and seventh structural elements, not only because it contains the frequently occurring phenomenological phrase "suddenly saw" or "suddenly appeared" (*hujian* 忽見), but also because it has what might be characterized as a slow, sweeping pivot and a delayed climax. The numbers in parentheses mark the appearance of each element in the text following:

> **(1)** During the Jin period, the wife of one Yan Meng 嚴猛 of Kuaiji went out to gather firewood and was killed by a tiger.[47] **(2)** A year later **(3)** [Yan Meng] was walking past **(5)** her tomb when he **(6)** suddenly saw his wife, who said, "On your goings about today you will certainly meet with something bad. I am here to prevent it." So **(3 and 5 again)** they set out together. **(6 again)** Suddenly they encountered a tiger. It leapt toward Meng, but his wife raised her hand as if holding it at bay. At that moment a westerner (*huren* 胡人) carrying a spear passed by. Meng's wife pointed to him, **(7)** and so the tiger seized the westerner and Meng was spared.[48]

In this tale, the pivot into the anomalous zone merely begins when the protagonist "suddenly sees" his dead wife. That would be

---

46. Compare Todorov's remark on one of his stories: "At this moment there occurs an event which causes the narrative to swerve" (Todorov 1975, 53). This "swerving" is what I term "pivot."

47. The wife's sudden and violent death might be read as a "hint" (4), since many Chinese readers would probably have expected someone killed in this manner to return as a spectre.

48. Yy 6.11; cf. TPGJ 426.6, FYZL 65 (78c).

anomaly enough, and in some stories might constitute the climax, but this is no simple ghost tale, and the true climax comes only when the ghost of the protagonist's wife succeeds in saving his life, as she promised. Meanwhile, we have a second round of the "process" and "limen" elements, as Meng and his wife's ghost start walking together.[49] The climactic anomaly of the tale is not the appearance of Meng's wife's ghost but her success in warding off the tiger, combined with her apparent foreknowledge of the event.

The semantically related cluster of terms used in the pivot constitute an implicit phenomenology of the perception of anomaly, and are hence worth mentioning.[50] In its fullest form[51] this cluster contains three sorts of expressions, and hence depicts three moments in a phenomenological process: (a) "Suddenly" (usually *hu*). This term in anomaly narratives almost always introduces a break or swerve in the course of events. (b) A verb either of perception (most often "saw") or of occurrence (often "appeared," or simply "there was"), followed by the anomalous object or event. In both cases, the protagonist's point of view is usually implied by the verb, but more directly in the first sort of case. (c) An expression indicating the protagonist's affective or psychological reaction, usually fear, surprise, shock, or wonder.

Here is a tale illustrating the first two sorts of expressions. The true protagonist—the person who primarily experiences an encounter with anomaly—is not the first but the second man mentioned.

> Li Jing 李經, a native of Guiyang, was being chased around by one Zhu Ping 朱平, who was armed with a spear. Ping ran about a hundred paces when he suddenly saw (*hujian*) a demon (鬼) over ten feet tall stop him and say: "Li Jing has an allotted lifespan (*ming* 命). How can you kill him? If you don't stop, I'll hurt your hand." But Ping was drunk, so he continued on to Jing's house, the demon following. When Ping saw Jing and was about to stab him, he suddenly (*hu*) stood straight up and did not move, as if someone were holding him. As a result, his left hand and fingers were injured. He

---

49. Their walking along constitutes "process," while the mere fact that Meng is walking with the spirit of a dead person—let alone the fact that they are presumably in the mountains and are also awaiting some unknown, unpleasant event—constitutes a definite "limen."

50. Jones 1987.

51. Again, not every pivot passage contains all three sorts of expression; some contain only two or one sort.

stood there in the courtyard till dusk. When he finally sobered up, he left. The demon said to him, "I warned you. Why didn't you comply?" When it had said these words it vanished.[52]

The following tale contains two pivots; in the first, all three sorts of expressions occur, while in the second we find the anomalous creature "suddenly appear[ing]."

> Wang Zhongwen 王仲文 served as Assistant Magistrate of Henan. His residence was in Goushi District, and he was returning there one evening on a road that passed by a marsh. Glancing behind his carriage, he saw a very lovable white dog. He thought to call it and take it, but suddenly it changed into a human form, five or six feet long, with the appearance of a *fangxiang* 方相.[53] It alternately approached and fell back, and seemed intent on mounting the carriage. Zhongwen was terrified (*bu* 怖). On arriving home he ran inside, got a torch, and returned to look around, but the creature had disappeared.
>
> A month or more later, Zhongwen was transporting a slave along the same road when suddenly it appeared again. Both men were captured by it and killed.[54]

Elsewhere, only the term "suddenly" marks the pivot into the fantastic:

> In the first year of the Primordial Felicity period [of the Song, 424 C.E.], a gang of over a hundred thieves in Jian'an Commandery raided the official headquarters and robbed the commoners. The daughter of Zi Chanzi 資產子 fled into a Buddhist stupa 佛圖, where many donated treasures had been carefully stored in a separate room. The thieves had just broken the door down when suddenly several myriads of bees

---

52. Yml 211 (LX 299); cf. TPGJ 318.16.
53. The *fangxiang* was a masked dancer who, said by some authors to imitate the mythical, theriomorphic figure Chi You (a monster later domesticated by the Yellow Thearch and who in this form later became the Han god of war and also a deity prayed to for rain in times of drought [Karlgren 1946, 285]), went at the head of exorcistic processions and imperial tours (Bodde 1975, chap. 4 passim; Knechtges 1982, 1:217). *Fangxiang* are mentioned at several points in anomaly texts, and demons are sometimes described as "looking like a *fangxiang*" (Zyz 4; Yml 23, 161, 163; Sshj 7.9; Ssj 9.13, 15.4, 16.1, 17.9; Yy 4.2).
54. Yml 161 (LX 285); cf. TPGJ 141.6.

emerged from a garment trunk and all at once stung them. Each of them was covered with a hundred stings; their eyes were injured and they were blinded. They each dropped the items they had pilfered and fled (Sshj 3.6 [38]).

However the narrative pivot is marked, the point for our purposes is that it *is* clearly marked by some device such as the ones I have described. The language of the tale itself expresses the crossing of a boundary—a boundary of expectation, a boundary separating normal from abnormal sequences of events. And central to that pivot-language is the depiction of a more or less ordinary person's reactions to the abnormality in question. This person—no deity, transcendent, spirit, or animal—is one with whom the reader can identify. His or her reactions to anomaly provide a textual mirror for the reader's own sequence of reactions, from initial suspicion (at the hint stage) to sudden awareness and recognition with its attendant shock (at the pivot and climax stages). This focus on a textually portrayed human subject who undergoes the encounter with anomaly—along with the fact that we have to deal in every case with a specific *event* in time—is the most important respect in which the narrative mode differs from the descriptive.

To this point I have identified seven elements that make up the structure of anomaly narratives. But some tales add two or three additional elements, which I will first list and then illustrate with examples:

(8) Response. Some tales do not end with the climax of the anomalous event; they continue by reporting the protagonist's response to it, which varies widely. The protagonist *does* something that constitutes a sort of answer to what has befallen him or her. This response provides an important key to the persuasive intent of the tale; the full range of such responses will be examined in Chapters Seven and Eight.

(9) Outcome. In tales in which there is some response by the protagonist, comment is usually made on how things worked out. Chains of events set in motion by the anomalous event and the protagonist's subsequent response are brought to a conclusion.

(10) Impact. Very occasionally—especially in Buddhist miracle tales and in stories concerning the origins of cults and temples—further comment is made on reactions by persons other than the protagonist, or on some later situation relevant to the tale. In every case these comments concern the lasting impact made by the narrated event on a person or group of people or on the landscape.

One sort of tale in which these elements often appear recounts the founding of a temple or shrine. An example follows, with the narrative elements indicated:

> **(1)** The most outlying district in the southwestern part of Yi 夷 territory is called Yelang 夜郎 District. **(2)** Once before it was established, a woman was **(3)** washing clothes there[55] when **(6)** suddenly a piece of bamboo with three nodes floated up between her legs. Hearing sounds coming from inside it, she cut open the bamboo and looked inside, **(7)** only to find a baby boy. **(8)** She took him home and raised him. **(9)** He grew up to become a warrior, setting himself up as the Marquis of Yelang and taking Bamboo (Zhu 竹) as his clan name.
>
> **(10a)**　In the sixth year of his Primordial Tripod reign period [111 B.C.E.], Emperor Wu of the Han mounted an expedition into the southwestern Yi territory, changing this area's name to Yangke Commandery. The Marquis of Yelang submitted to him, and so the Son of Heaven bestowed on him a jade seal of office.[56] Later he died.
>
> **(10b)**　When the Yi and the Liao flourished, because the Bamboo King [as they called him] had not been born of blood, they established a temple (*miao* 廟) to him.
>
> **(10c)**　Today in Yelang District there is a "Bamboo King Deity" (竹王神); this is he (ShuyjRf 2.153 [20b-21a]).[57]

Here, it is the woman's response to an anomalous occurrence that sets up the most important point of the tale, which is to document the historical links between a cult still existing in the sixth century and the legend of its founding many centuries earlier. The author, Ren Fang, makes three distinct remarks on the "impact" of the woman's response at successively later points in historical time.

In many cases the later impact is of a more graphic sort, as in the following tale of an encounter with an unexpectedly visible deity.

---

55. A "limen" (5) is implied since she is standing in the shallows of a river. There are no "hints" (4), however.

56. Twitchett and Loewe 1986, 158.

57. On the Bamboo King and his temple, Wang Jiayou 1987, 116–30. This is thought to be the basis of the famous Japanese tale of Momotarō ("Peach-boy"), attested in Heian texts.

(1, 2) One Wang Gengsheng 王更生 was Governor of a commandery during the Han. Within his jurisdiction there was a temple to members of the Yuan clan which was (4) quite efficacious (*lingxiang* 靈響). (3, 5) Passing by the temple [on one occasion], Gengsheng made an offering and then left without taking his knife. He sent one of his lictors, named Li Gao, back to fetch it. Gao saw the knife atop the temple altar, but when he went forward to take it, (6) looking up he saw a lord 君 sitting there dressed in a large cap and a gown, his hair half white. (7) This lord told Gao, "You may take it and go. If you say nothing of this, I will bless you in times to come." (8) So Gao returned and, as instructed, said nothing.[58]

(9) Later Gao was appointed to serve at a commandery headquarters, and was due to be promoted to a governorship. By now he was over sixty years old and his descendants numbered over one hundred. So he said to someone, "Long ago, when I served as a lictor under Gengsheng, I was dispatched to a temple to fetch a knife that had been left there. I saw the temple god. He told me not to speak of it, and down to today I have not dared to do so, but in my heart I have long been ashamed of witholding [this incident] from my superior." (10) When he had spoken these words, that same knife rose up and pierced Gao beneath the heart, and soon he was dead.[59]

Like other tales in which a promise or conditional agreement is established, this one creates an expectation in us as we read, or at least a series of questions: Will Gao be able to keep silent? If he is able, will the god keep his promise, and what will the "blessings" be? The final "outcome" and "impact" elements are set up by, and answer, the questions posed by the cross-boundary agreement that constitutes the "response" element.

My final example of the response, outcome, and impact elements of anomaly narratives illustrates the frequent use of these devices in Buddhist miracle tales:

(1, 2) The Jin-period [monk] Shi Fa'an 釋法安 was a disciple of the Dharma Master [Hui]yuan of Lushan. Toward the end of the Flourishing of Righteousness reign period [ca. 415–

---

58. The text later seems to imply that he not only said nothing but also kept the knife in his possession.

59. Luyz 19 (LX 415); cf. TPYL 345.9b.

419 C.E.], there was an acute outbreak of tiger attacks in Yangxin District. In that district there was an earth god shrine (*she* 社) with a large tree, beneath which had been constructed a temple to the god (*shenmiao* 神廟). Over a hundred families lived near it. Every night one or two people there were attacked and killed by a tiger.

(2, 3) Once Fa'an was passing through this district and **(5)** arrived at this hamlet toward evening. Because of their fear of tigers the villagers had shut up their doors early, and since they did not know Fa'an they were unwilling to receive him. So Fa'an went beneath the tree [in the earth god shrine] and sat in meditation the whole night.

(6) Toward dawn there came a tiger carrying a person.[60] It was heading to the north of the tree, but **(7)** seeing An it seemed to leap with delight and crouched down in front of him. **(8a)** An expounded the Dharma and transmitted the precepts to the tiger, during which time the tiger remained motionless on the ground. **(8b)** After a while it departed.

(9a) At daybreak, people from the village looking for the dead person arrived at the tree. Seeing An they were greatly shocked 大驚; they said he must be a divine man 神人 since he had not been harmed by the tiger. **(9b)** And from this time on there were no more tiger attacks. **(10a)** This filled the people with even more awe and wonder 益敬異. **(10b)** Almost all the people of that district, of both the official and commoner classes, converted to the Dharma.[61]

In this tale the response, outcome, and impact elements have a two-part, exchange-like structure the significance of which will form the subject of Chapter Eight. After the climax of the narrative—the meeting between tiger and monk—the monk's response is to preach the Dharma, while the tiger's is to listen receptively and depart without harming him. This event generates a dual outcome: the people are "greatly shocked" (*dajing*) and attribute divinity to the

---

60. The Gsz text, which differs somewhat in wording from that of the Fyzl version, gives the perceptual verb *wen* 聞, to hear: "Toward dawn he heard a tiger. . . . " It is thus closer to the typical semantic structure of the pivot element.

61. Mxj 55 (LX 488); cf. Gsz 362b–c, FYZL 19 (428c–429a). The item continues with more miraculous episodes from the life of Fa'an not translated here. Huiyuan was a well known intellectual, literary, and spiritual figure; see, *inter alia*, Zürcher 1972, 204–53; Tsukamoto 1985, chap. 8.

monk, while the marauding tiger (or perhaps tigers) of the area ceases its attacks on humans. This entire complex of events then has two final impacts on the surrounding people, the first immediate, the second more permanent: the cessation of tiger attacks inspires them with another wave of "awe and wonder" (*jingyi*), which in turn moves them to "convert to the Dharma" in large numbers. Like most Buddhist-oriented tales, therefore, this one does not stop at simply reporting an anomalous occurrence; it devotes almost equal attention to the aftermath of that occurrence—that is, to the power of such miracles to affect people by turning them toward Buddhist faith and practice.

Meta-anomaly

I close this analysis by pointing out a type of tale which, though it occurs infrequently in the corpus of anomaly narratives, reveals much about their poetics. This tale-type involves what I term "meta-anomaly," and the briefest way to characterize it is again by examining a particular example and then expanding on that analysis.

> There was a Director of Convict Labor named Lai Jide 來 季德, a native of Nanyang. While his funeral services were underway his form suddenly appeared sitting on the altar for offerings. His face, expressions, clothing, voice, and mannerisms were all quite familiar. One by one his sons, grandsons, wife, and daughters received instruction from him, and in each case what was said corresponded with the facts.[62] He then whipped his slaves and servants each according to their faults. When he was done eating and drinking he bade them farewell and departed. Old and young, all the members of his family were able to stop their feelings of grief and bereavement.
>
> [But] this went on for several years, and the family began to suffer hardship.[63] On one later occasion he drank too

---

62. This depiction mirrors the conversations that have long occurred in ritual contexts in Chinese society—and may still be observed today in Taiwan (I have seen them in the Temple to the Great Thearch of the Eastern Marchmount 東嶽大帝 in Tainan)—between living and dead relatives through a spirit-medium.

63. Due, no doubt, to their "ancestor's" excessive consumption of their resources.

much wine, became drunk, and thus revealed his form, which turned out to be that of an old dog. The family members then together beat it to death. An inquiry ascertained that it was a dog belonging to the brewer family in the village.[64]

What occupies the first paragraph of my translation has all the marks of a "standard" ghost narrative: a dead family member or friend temporarily reappears, visibly consumes offerings, dispenses moral instruction, and departs.[65] This part of the item, furthermore, has the usual sequence of narrative elements. The reader (at least one acquainted with traditional Chinese ghost tales) is *led to expect* that, after its anomalous appearance, this ghost will go away quietly as do ghosts in other, so far similar tales. But this tale does not end that way; with "[but] this went on for several years," it executes a second pivot, after which yet another anomalous appearance reveals this tale to be not a case of ghostly apparition but one of demonic disguise. The narrative structure is thus one of meta-anomaly: the expected sequence of events established early in the tale is itself a sequence involving a type of anomaly; the latter portion of the tale then frustrates the reader's expectations of one sort of anomaly and replaces them with another sort of anomaly.[66]

This type of tale depends for its effect on a readership for whom the narration of a certain type of anomaly is already a partly customary cultural act. In other words, it depends on an intertextual network in which certain conventions (even conventions in the narration of anomalies) have been established and certain expectations set up. Familiar patterns of narration about types of interactions with beings stereotypically familiar in their unfamiliarity then become the "normal" foundation on which the tale builds its fantastic structure.

The lesson we learn from meta-anomaly tales is that the poetics of cosmographic discourse is driven primarily by structures of expectation. At bottom, discourse about anomalies is discourse that presumes as well as sets up certain expectations in its audience, so that it may then contradict them in some way. Those expectations may take almost any shape, including even an expected type or

---

64. Ssj 18.21; I have not found this item elsewhere.

65. See, for example, Yy 6.2 (and cf. 6.30) and Mxj 67, 101, 114, and 123; cf. Campany 1991a.

66. Another excellent example of a meta-anomaly is Yml 213, in which a pack of demons, after initiating an assault on a man, is persuaded by one of its members to desist on account of the man's virtue.

pattern of anomaly which is then itself contradicted at the meta-level.

Conclusion

It should not be forgotten, in reducing the rich texture of discourse on anomalies to some bare bones, that the point of that discourse was to move readers in and through its very richness of texture. Its structural bones were clothed in the luxuriant flesh of detailed description and narration. I have tried to delineate certain features of that structure in order to clarify *how* the texts mean. The value of these labors lies solely in their fruits—the extent to which they help us to see how the texts mean and, in turn, perhaps to be in a better position ultimately to say *what* they mean.

I have here shown, first, that three modes of discourse within the genre ought to be distinguished. Anomaly accounts are sometimes referred to collectively as "tales" or "stories," but many of them are not narrative in nature, and the ones that are display varying degrees of narrativity. It might be argued in response that all of these texts should not, for this very reason, be construed as belonging to the same genre. I would answer that they do constitute different modes of writing but within a common genre of writing—not only because they belong to the same historical tradition of cosmographic discourse (as seen by contemporaries) and share many features of cosmographic and cosmological thought, but also, more cogently, because my analysis has shown that they exhibit a fundamental similarity at the level of poetics.

I began by characterizing that similarity in terms of "the fantastic," an inherently contrastive mode of writing in which objects or events linked to distinct worldviews are juxtaposed. The fantastic has often been understood as a type of narrative, but I have shown it at work in anomaly texts of both the descriptive and the narrative modes. The defining properties of fantastic literature, I would therefore maintain, have to do not with structures of narrative but with structures of expectation.

I have gone on to show in detail how each mode of writing within the genre creates, and then violates, these structures of expectation. This construction and violation are accomplished at every level: first and most basically, through the nature of the very language in which the texts were written; then, in the individual item, through a series of elements that succeed one another either in the medium of taxonomic and/or textual space (in the descriptive mode) or in that of processual time (in the narrative); next, at the intratextual level (in some texts at least), through the relations between one item and another; and finally, at the intertextual level, through the invocation and subsequent modification or violation of generic and thematic conventions (especially evident in meta-anomalous accounts). I have worked mostly with an eye to the poetics of the individual item (and secondarily to its intratextual surroundings). At this level, the succession of structural elements—as well as the patterned, repetitive regularity of that succession from one textual item to another—is a fundamental way in which the texts mean. In each case, and at every level, the poetic structure is built on the device of the "contra"—the contrast, or more strongly the contra-diction, between what is expected of the text (based on what the text itself as well as its intra- and intertextual environment present) and what is subsequently found in it.[67]

In short, the very medium of anomaly texts bespeaks their contents and, to that extent at least, their message. Their very nature as texts—from the sort of language in which they are written to the relations among the elements they contain—partakes of, indeed creates, anomaly. Another way of putting this is that anomaly texts do not simply represent phenomena that are judged to be in themselves anomalous. The texts also re-create or re-enact anomaly in their very textuality, and in this chapter I have tried to show just how. The question of *why* their authors thus manipulated readers' expectations—that is, to what end—forms the focus of Chapters Seven and Eight.

---

67. This way of putting it is from the reader's point of view; but the same "contra" movement is mirrored within the text by the narrated events and the protagonist's reactions to them.

Chapter Six

Modes of Anomaly:
Cosmographic Logic

人多奇巧奇物滋起.
The more clever skills people have, the more strange things spring
up.

Daodejing 57[1]

Like texts of any cosmographic genre, early medieval Chinese accounts of anomalies test and probe culturally constructed boundaries. They contain so many examples of boundary-stretching,
boundary-straddling, and boundary-crossing beings and phenomena that a reader confronting the entirety of these texts can only
assume that issues concerning boundaries lie at the very heart of
the genre—the nature of boundaries, their fixity or fluidity, the precise location of certain boundaries, the ways in which they may be
crossed or blurred, and the consequences of crossings and
blurrings. Yet authors of anomaly accounts rarely address these issues explicitly, that is, in the declarative modes of philosophical or
cosmological discourse. Rather, through conventions dictated by
older cosmographic traditions of collecting and reporting—by displaying the picked-up pieces of "historical" reports or local narratives—anomaly accounts approach the question of boundaries

---

1. Based on the trs. of Lau 1963, 118, and Mair 1990, 26.

through piecemeal description and narration of "things heard" and "things seen." They constitute an almost casuistic mode of taxonomic thinking and writing—"almost" because they seldom draw explicit conclusions from the cases they present, leaving these for the reader to infer but also pointing the reader toward them.

Studies of taxonomic systems and their roles in culture typically focus on the systems of categories themselves—their inner logic and the principles of classification,[2] the nature of particular categories or the rationale behind specific taxonomic decisions in a system, or the system's connections with aspects of the environing culture,[3] most prominently its social structure,[4] also its physical habitat.[5] But in any cosmographic discourse, the modes of anomaly—the variety of logical or structural ways in which anomaly can happen, or in which incongruity is (or can be) constructed as a phenomenon—are at least as important as the modes of classificatory congruity, and indeed probably more important. The logical structure of anomaly in a particular cosmographic discourse or classification system is seldom studied, however.[6] Anomalies are usually treated as piecemeal, isolated events, and things are assumed to be anomalous in more or less the same way. This may work well enough for understanding some taxonomic systems, but when one has to deal with a cosmographic discourse, one quickly finds that not every anomaly is anomalous in the same respect, and that the differences in modes of anomaly sometimes themselves bear crucial implications. To ignore these implications is to ignore a key vehicle of meaning in cosmographic discourse.

The anomaly accounts presume, but rarely discuss, the principles and categories of "normal" classificatory systems and laws of regularity. They assume a world—or at least a reader's view of the world—that is basically ordered, and against that backdrop they highlight data that seem to violate order. It is against this background assumption of congruity that the incongruities they point out become noteworthy.

---

2. Berlin, Breedlove, and Raven 1974; Hunn 1977; Brown 1984.

3. Bulmer 1967, 1979; Kesby 1979; Granet 1973 [1953]; Tambiah 1985, 169–211.

4. Durkheim and Mauss 1963 (cf. Bloor 1984); most studies of "totemism" down through Lévi-Strauss 1963 and 1966; Douglas 1969, 1975, 1982; cf. Beidelman 1973.

5. Hunn 1979.

6. An exception in the visual-perceptual realm is Shepard's subtle nine-part analysis of the differing modes in which his drawings are visually anomalous (1990, 42ff.).

In keeping with the nature of the anomaly accounts themselves, my task in this chapter is to map the dominant modes of anomaly evidenced in the texts behind and amid the vast profusion of particular cases. It is not my purpose to list all of the *types of objects or beings* that count as anomalous nor all of the specific types of boundaries in question, though many of these will be touched on as examples.[7] Rather, this chapter charts the main ways in which persons, things, or phenomena are represented as being or becoming anomalous, as a way of explicating the taxonomic and cosmographic thinking embedded in the anomaly accounts. This explication—itself a taxonomic exercise, a sort of categorization of the ways in which categories are broken (and hence liable to the sorts of boundary-fuzziness endemic to all taxonomies)—will do two things. It will reveal aspects of a philosophy of categories and category-membership that is implicit in the texts, and it will show which specific sorts of taxonomic boundaries were of most concern to the authors. The question of point of view and of implication—whether, that is, particular accounts of anomalies should be read as challenging or reinforcing certain boundaries (or both)—is not at issue here, but will be dealt with in the following two chapters. Here, I deal with the prior issue of the logic of anomaly itself as played out in the texts.

Anomaly by Taxonomic Location

In this first category are phenomena that count as anomalous by virtue of their location within an implicit taxonomic structure. These include three subcategories. First of all, there are anomalies of degree: things that belong to a certain "normal" category, but are anomalous because positioned at its outer edge or limit due to some special feature. Secondly, there are hybrids and cross-boundary-behaving beings: things that by their combination of properties or behaviors straddle one or more taxonomic boundaries. Finally, there are anomalies of kind: whole categories that, relative to others in the system (a crucial qualifier), are marked as anomalous as such or filled with members that count as anomalous simply by belonging to the category.

To speak abstractly, these three sorts of anomaly by taxo-

---

7. So that the reader need not constantly be reminded of the fact, it should be understood at the outset that the specific items cited are given as examples and do not constitute complete listings of relevant passages.

nomic location cut against the implicit, received, "normal" taxonomy in different ways. Anomalies of degree challenge it by seemingly requiring an enlargement or bulging of the extension of the
category they inhabit—perhaps in some cases stretching it to such
an extent that the category seems pointless or obsolete. Hybrids
challenge the received taxonomy by seemingly requiring a redrawing of the boundaries between categories. Anomalies of kind challenge it by suggesting that the taxonomic system should be revised
or extended to include whole new categories of beings not sufficiently accounted for; on the other hand, they are, perhaps for this
reason, the least challenging, since adding a category allows the existing ones to be left intact.

Anomalies of Degree

Anomalies of degree include beings or phenomena which, due to
some special trait, are located at the edge or limit of a category
populated with otherwise normal beings or phenomena.

Size. Echoing the *Zhuangzi*'s use of the gigantic and the
miniature as rhetorical strategies for relativizing the reader's sense
of the ordinary—particularly in the *Xiaoyaoyou* ("Rambling Without a Destination") chapter—creatures of odd size figure among the
anomalies of degree mentioned in anomaly accounts. Of these, human pygmies and giants are the most common. Their anomalous
size is often embellished with other strange traits such as hollow
chests and large ears[8] or, in Daoist texts, longevity-related features;[9] but they are implicitly understood to be exceptional human
beings, not a separate species or class of being. Many are assigned a
"country" or "realm": the Realm of Pygmies is often located in the
north or northeast;[10] that of giants, in the extreme east.[11] Both
pygmy and giant races are also placed in the extreme northwest[12]
or in other distant lands.[13] The sudden appearance of giant or mini-

---

8. E.g., Bwz 2.18.
9. Shenyjing nw 5, 6.
10. Shj 342; cf. *Liezi jishi* 5 (97); Graham 1990, 98.
11. Bwz 2.16, 2.17, 2.18; Shj 341. The anomaly accounts here as in
many other places reflect older traditions; see Yuan Ke 1981 [1960], 252,
on classical and Han passages regarding the Realm of Giants.
12. Shenyjing nw 5, 6.
13. Jlz 4, 11; Bwz 2.13.

ature humans within the Central Kingdom was sometimes taken as a political portent;[14] but this attention to anomalous features also grew out of the ancient tradition of physiognomy, and many of these traits are somatic signs of extraordinary longevity or of sagehood.

Shape. Things shaped differently in some way than other members of their class (but not so differently as to be classified in a distinct species) are another frequently mentioned type of anomaly of degree. There is a type of fish "shaped like an ox";[15] there is another shaped like a blob of congealed blood, lacking a head, eye sockets, or internal organs.[16] In a certain country there is a type of fox with nine tails;[17] in another, a type of bird with six heads.[18] People in distant lands are described as having a dizzying variety of anomalous shapes: the people of Zili have one arm and two legs, which are turned backwards;[19] those of the Pierced Chest Realm are shaped accordingly, and can thus be conveniently carried on shoulder-borne poles;[20] those of Earth Lungs Realm lack joints;[21] members of a certain tribe in the "great western waste," descendants of the ancient sage Zhuan Xu (grandfather to the Yellow Thearch), have three faces and one arm, and live forever.[22]

Composition. Things shaped the same as other members of their class but made of (or eating and excreting) different stuff fall under this category. A prominent motif is that of living animals made of precious metal or stone. Golden silkworms and jade swallows are listed among the marvels of Mount Jiyang;[23] a golden bird that spit out gold pellets was sent as tribute to the Wei kingdom from Kunming.[24] Golden and bronze oxen and horses are mentioned.[25] According to a Daoist topographic anomaly text, on the

---

14. Ssj 6.16 [cf. Shj 341 n.1]; Ssj 6.59.
15. Bwz 3.21; Jlz 51.
16. Bwz 3.25.
17. Shj 347.
18. Shj 417.
19. Bwz 2.19.
20. Bwz 2.10; Shj 194; Guo Pu's commentary cites a lost *Yiwuzhi* 異
物志.
21. Jlz 32.
22. Shj 413.
23. ShuyjRf 1.36.
24. ShuyjRf 2.111; Syj 7.5a [tr. Foster 1974, 248].
25. Yml 14; Yy 2.7, 2.17.

distant Cowering Continent in the Western Sea are beasts with bronze heads and iron foreheads.[26] Atop certain numinous mountains are golden or stone roosters; in some cases, their crowing at dawn is said to be the signal for all ordinary roosters to crow.[27] Other animals eat or excrete metal: an animal "like an ox" eats iron and produces manure that can be used for weapons;[28] a hare is found with metal in its guts;[29] a snake disgorges a golden kettle to thank its human benefactor.[30]

Excess. Things normal except for one disproportionate trait constitute anomalies of excess. One prominent topos is extreme virtue, especially that of filiality, as shown in mourning and parental caretaking;[31] other virtues include faithfulness in conjugal love[32] and mildness or selflessness in office.[33] A sub-topos here is that of bereaved persons who sacrifice their lives to recover their relative's missing body.[34] There is a distant Country of Gentlemen in which people are extraordinarily polite.[35] Plants that grow abnormally fast or in extraordinary abundance are anomalies of excess that are sometimes taken as portending political fortune.[36] Abnormal swarming and voraciousness are other types of anomalous excess, as in a type of flying insect that struck during an epidemic and rapidly devoured new corpses.[37]

Behavior. Things which act differently from other members of their class or show different interactive properties, or natural events out of synch with normal patterns, account for a wide variety of items that, for lack of a better term, might be grouped together as "behavioral" anomalies of degree.[38] There are a great

---

26. Szj 6a; Smith 1990, 100.
27. ShuyjRf 1.36; cf. Yml 15, Jlz 9.
28. Shenyjing center 6.
29. Yy 3.25.
30. ShuyjRf 1.96.
31. Sshj 2.1; Ssj 1.28, 11.14–31; Yml 155, 180, 184; Yy 10.15.
32. Ssj 11.32–35.
33. Yy 10.16; Yml 57; Xs 62.
34. Ssj 11.29; Yy 10.14.
35. Bwz 2.3; Shj 345–46.
36. Ssj 6.27, 6.32, 6.41; Sshj 3.4.
37. Bwz 2.34.
38. These are to be distinguished from the cases of cross-species behavior discussed below under "hybrids" in this respect: in the present cases, it is a matter of a difference from behaviors and patterns of interac-

many accounts of strange, inexplicable behaviors in animals,[39] many of them portents.[40] There are also anomalous properties, such as a variety of ox from which meat can be continually cut without killing the animal.[41] Stones are described as producing heat,[42] standing on end,[43] and floating on water.[44] Wood and cloth (asbestos) that do not burn are also mentioned.[45] Human behavioral anomalies—some of which, again, are interpreted as political portents—include cannibalism by both Chinese and non-Chinese peoples,[46] bizarre social mores,[47] odd fashions in clothing,[48] and a host of curious customs of non-Chinese peoples, either idealized as residents of fanciful lands[49] or simply recorded, in the case of groups within and around China.[50] Anomalous natural phenomena—the classic sort of political portent—include events occurring out of season and cases in which heaven rained down things other than some form of water.[51]

Source and locale. Things originating from an exotic, distant source, things produced in strange ways, and things distinctive of one particular region or locality are all anomalies of source and locale. Exotic items include stones, minerals, metals, herbs, fragrances and other products imported from peripheral and dis-

---

tion "normal" to the class in question; in the "hybrid" cases, by contrast, the behavior is such as to suggest that the being or object in fact straddles the boundary between two particular classes. In other words, the present "behavioral" anomalies are, categorically speaking, "inward"-looking (with the focus on difference from other members of the "own class"), while those discussed below are "outward"-looking (with the focus on the boundary between two distinct classes).

39. Yy 3.27; Yml 111.
40. Ssj 6.33, 6.34, 6.35, 7.8.
41. Bwz 3.5; Jlz 8.
42. Jlz 16.
43. Ssj 6.26, 6.75.
44. Ssj 7.24; Yml 167.
45. Jlz 34; Ssj 10.6, 13.18; Sshj 5.8.
46. Chinese: Ssj 6.54; non-Chinese: Shenyjing w 3; Lyz 18; Bwz 2.27; Yml 254.
47. Ssj 6.30, 6.43, 6.50, 6.53, 6.63, 7.17, 7.23, 7.25.
48. Ssj 6.77 and 7 passim.
49. Dmj 2.2, 2.5, 2.13, 2.16, 2.18, 3.4; Xuanzj passim.
50. Bwz 2.27–30, 2.32–33; Ssj 12 passim.
51. Yy 2.27, 4.10, 4.61; ShuyjRf 2.7–27; Bwz 7.23; Ssj 6.31, 6.36, 6.49.

tant regions,[52] medicinal substances obtainable only from mountain areas (many of them southern) difficult of access,[53] and marvelous products available only on the isles of transcendents.[54] Things produced in anomalous ways include stones, such as agate, thought to be formed from the congealed blood of demons,[55] or plants produced from concentrated human emotion or from human secretions,[56] as well as the many portent-notices of monstrous births.[57] Things distinctive of particular locales include most notably the customs and sayings of people in the various regions of China,[58] and special physical landmarks or "traces" of past events.[59]

Frequency. Things which are extremely rare or scarce (often therefore perceived as being of high quality) constitute anomalies of frequency. These include rare animal and plant species,[60] and particular animals of unusual quality or ability,[61] a large subcategory of which comprises stories of faithful dogs.[62]

Refinement. Things which, though in the same class, differ in being more or less refined in some respect include most notably the many accounts of human beings (not hybrids) taken to be less civilized or cultured than the Han Chinese. A large proportion of such peoples mentioned in anomaly accounts are southern tribes— the Yi 夷,[63] Man 蠻,[64] and Yue 越.[65] One could also place in this cat-

---

52. Xuanzj 64–69; ShuyjRf 1.59, 2.51, 2.53–54; Shenyj and Lh passim.

53. ShuyjRf 2.42–48, 2.71–81.

54. Szj, Dmj, and Shenyjing passim.

55. Syj 1.7b–8b, 3.7a.

56. ShuyjRf 1.23–24; Bwz 8.2, 9.9; Jlz 40; Ssj 11.32.

57. Ssj 6 and 7 passim.

58. Yy 1.1, 3.21, 3.28, 3.34, 3.51, 3.56–57, 5.3, 10.2; XuQxj 15; ShuyjRf passim; Nkj 2a; see Campany 1990b.

59. ShuyjRf passim; Yml 3–5, 19–23; Jzj 1b, 3a–b; Lyz 2; Lgz 22; Sl 1; Lxz 18; Sshj 6.3, 6.5.

60. Yy 3.20; Bwz 5.3.

61. Szj 7b; Bwz 3.1–2; Yy 3.23.

62. Xuyj 1; Qxj 15; Shuyj 15, 43–44; Yy 3.24; Ssj 9.10, 20.9–10. This story-type (instances of which are only partially listed here) is classified thus, instead of under behavioral anomalies, because of the emphasis on quality.

63. ShuyjRf 1.86, 2.127, 2.153; Gzj; Lh passim; Ssj 14.2.

64. Lgz 15, Xs 29; Yy 1.24, 3.13, 6.21; Gzj; Sshj 4.7.

65. ShuyjRf 1 passim; Kjj; Lh passim; Nyz; Bwz 3.14; Ssj 12.11.

egory the many accounts of specific individuals more refined than ordinary people, which are treated in the next two chapters; these accounts span the Confucian, Buddhist, and Daoist traditions as well as shamans and *fangshi* 方士 ("masters of esoterica") expert in one or more esoteric arts.

Hybrids and Cross-Boundary-Behaving Beings

Hybrids—beings that by attribute, origin, gender, or in other ways mix and conjoin classes of beings usually distinguished within a given taxonomic system—straddle (or, more accurately, are deemed to straddle) the boundaries constructed by cultures. So also do beings that cross boundaries not by having any special physical feature but by behaving in ways seen as characteristic of members of a category not their own. Authors of anomaly accounts continued the old cosmographic practice of making lists of hybrid animals and spirits that dates back to at least the late Warring States and the Han periods,[66] but they were innovative in that they wrote of such beings in more elaborate, more narratively specific, and more comprehensive ways.

I organize the following summary around the main boundaries straddled.

Divine/human/animal. Certain local deities and spirits are described as having forms that combine human and animal characteristics; the Shj, in both its earlier and later sections, abounds in these.[67] They are not to be confused with spirits that temporarily assume human or animal form, for such cases are better understood as anomalies of transformation. The hybrid character of these gods was doubtless intended in part to enhance their aura of sacrality.

Distinct animal species. The corpus of anomaly accounts contains an array of beings that straddle distinct animal categories. Authors drew many of these items from the same portent lists that appear in dynastic histories of the period as well (perhaps) as from *chenwei* texts. One type consists of an animal growing a part not normal to its own kind—for instance, dogs, horses, and rabbits

---

66. Loewe 1978; Harper 1985.
67. Shj 343, 348, 350, 355, 370, 401, etc.

growing horns.[68] Another consists of cross-species resemblance, such as a mollusk that resembles a bird.[69] A third includes cross-species mating and reproduction.[70]

Distinct plant species. These are relatively rare; they include two species of tree growing from one root and one tree producing several species of fruit.[71]

Nature/culture. The most numerous examples of this type of anomaly are natural objects or beings found to bear written characters of apparently spontaneous origin. These traverse the plant, animal, and mineral kingdoms. A willow tree sprouted and grew to maturity in a single day; then caterpillars ate its leaves so as to form the words of a portentous message.[72] Echoing the well known legends of the origins of the River Chart and Luo Writing (*hetu* 河圖 and *luoshu* 洛書), several items tell of animals discovered to bear graphic signs or messages.[73] Stones are found to contain characters, often upon cracking apart; these are sometimes termed *kaishi* 開石 or "opened stones."[74]

Animate/inanimate. This is a more fluid boundary in Chinese than in traditional Western thought, since all things are made of the same substratum of pneuma (*qi* 氣) differing only in degree of refinement. But many anomaly accounts work across it quite deliberately, by describing human-made objects that spontaneously move or come to life. This is a frequent motif in Buddhist miracle tales of images of Gautama Buddha or a bodhisattva (predominantly Guanyin) miraculously appearing, moving, or touching the protagonist; such anomalies are always triggered by the devotion—and often by the urgent need—of a Buddhist devotee who is in many cases the maker of the image.[75] In a related motif, the

---

68. Ssj 6.3, 6.18–19.
69. Yy 3.54.
70. Ssj 6.21.
71. Jlz 31 and Yy 2.26, respectively.
72. Ssj 6.27.
73. Yy 4.26; Yml 149, 154, 236; Lxz 11. On these charts, see Itano 1976, 1978; Saso 1978; Seidel 1981, 1983.
74. Yml 44; Bwz 7.15–7.17, 7.22; Jlz 43; Ssj 7.1, 9.3 [= Yml 44], 11.21–22.
75. Xyj 3, 29, 33; Mxj preface, 1, 97, 111, 129; Jyj 2; XiGsy 22 [= Mxj 129], 66.

image receives executioner's blows on its wearer's behalf—and the number and location of dents in the metal image correspond exactly to the number of times and the places the sword fell on its human wearer's body.[76] Monastery images weep upon recognizing long-absent visitors;[77] likewise, non-Buddhist temple images are described as drawing their bow and shooting intruders,[78] or moving with apparent spontaneity to indicate messages to their human audience,[79] and wooden animals come to life.[80] Grave figurines (*tongren* 桐人) buried with the dead emerge from graves to disturb the living.[81] There are accounts of automata that, though not actually alive, so closely resemble living persons or animals that they inspire wonder and are treated by people as if alive; these tales echo depictions in classical texts of the carpenter Lu Ban and his automatic marvels, as well as of a lifelike automaton in the *Liezi*.[82]

Plant/human. Plants closely resembling humans are a type of portent.[83] One item records the discovery of a miniature human being inside a bamboo stalk.[84] Others tell of the birth of future heroes or deities from women impregnated by floating pieces of wood or bamboo.[85] Several tales recount the sprouting of plants from human tears,[86] and the expression of human emotion through the shape of trees growing over graves.[87]

Animal/human. This boundary must have been of acute interest to anomaly account authors, for they left behind a wealth of tale-types in which it is straddled or blurred.

There are, first, hybrids and monsters that by their very makeup bestraddle the boundary: mermaids and mermen, bird-

---

76. XiGsy 13, 14; Xyj 7; Jyj 8.
77. Yml 134.
78. Sshj 5.5 = Yml 150.
79. Yy 5.16; see Jordan and Overmyer 1986, 38.
80. Lxz 23; Ssj 16.17.
81. Zgz 14; Lgz 20; Ssj 16.15, tr. Kao 1985, 92; Yml 183. For examples of *tongren* from this period, Capon 1975–77.
82. Shuis; Xs 5, 8; Syj 3.7a, 5.4b, 7.4b, 8.7b; ShuyjRf 2.57; Jlz 2; Sshj 2.4; Yy 10.3. On the lifelike automaton, *Liezi jishi* 5 (111–13), tr. Graham 1990, 110–111.
83. Ssj 6.37, 6.56, 6.60; cf. 17.12.
84. Yy 2.29.
85. Yy 5.4.
86. Bwz 8.2; ShuyjRf 1.23.
87. ShuyjRf 1.24; Ssj 11.32; Jlz 40.

people, dog-people, people furry from the knees down and hoofed, to name a few.[88]

Next are animals shaped like or resembling humans and, just over the boundary from these, "hairy people" (people who in this respect resemble animals) encountered in the wilds outside cities and cultivated lands—the Chinese "wild man," sometimes noble in his behavior, which only increases his oddity.[89]

Then there are a great many stories of cross-taxonomic modes of birth. These break down into, first, the birth of future human heroes and clan-ancestors from eggs;[90] and second, the simultaneous birth from the same human mother of human and animal offspring,[91] including the sub-motif of a snake—twin of a human being—who returns for its human mother's funeral and mourns by wrapping itself around her coffin.[92]

This last example leads us to instances of cross-boundary behavior, predominantly the human-like behavior of animals. There are over two dozen mentions of animals—birds, fowl, dogs, oxen, turtles—that can talk or at least understand and respond intelligently to human speech;[93] one tale even explores the legal ramifications of this ability.[94] Such anomalies are sometimes listed among portents.[95] On the other side of this boundary are persons who understand animal speech.[96] But the vast majority of cases that test the animal/human boundary consist of tales of other human-like—and often distinctly moral—animal behavior; and the majority of these tales in turn explore the issue of moral reciprocity between people and animals. They will be dealt with in Chapter Eight.

---

88. Mermaids and -men: Zgz 7; Yy 1.25. Bird-people: Bwz 2.5, 2.12. Dog-people: Bwz 3.10; see White 1991. People furry from the knees down and hoofed: Shj 463.

89. Animals resembling humans: Ssj 12.14; Yml 257; Lh 16. Wild men: Sshj 7.5; Yy 3.32, 8.36; Lh 4, 8; Ssj 14.19; cf. White 1978, 150; White 1972.

90. Bwz 7.10; Ssj 14.4, = ShuyjRf 2.136 [cf. White 1991, 140–71]; cf. Ssj 14.9.

91. Sshj 9.5; Yy 8.31 (boy, tiger, and fox born as triplets), 8.33; Ssj 6 and 7 passim.

92. Ssj 14.8; Yml 198.

93. Shuyj 41; Yy 3.10, 3.38, 3.39; Ssj 18.25; Yml 53, 96, 97, 118, 228; Xuanyj 14.

94. Yml 96.

95. Yy 4.59; Ssj 7.26, 7.31.

96. Shenyjing sw 1; Yy 9.7–8.

Anomalous Kinds

In a certain sense, this phrase is oxymoronic, since the anomalous is that which escapes any determinate taxonomic place; if a thing can be categorized, it is *ipso facto* no longer anomalous. But taxonomic systems can contain categories that by their intension or extension are themselves anomalous relative to all other categories in the system. Such categories are likely to have fuzzy boundaries, and their individual members are likely to be blurry or protean as well.

The best and most ubiquitous example in the anomaly accounts—and of course in many other traditional Chinese writings—is the "dragon." At once we note that this single English term papers over a multitude of Chinese terms and an even greater variety of descriptions and anecdotes.[97] Taxonomically, dragons—covered with scales and of an elongated, tailed shape—as a group are close to snakes, yet they are also associated with water, often living in ponds, rivers, and wells, and so border on the fish classes; again, some are described as having wings, as flying,[98] and as bringing thunder and rain, often appearing as rainbows; and they are often depicted as legged, which sets them apart from both snakes and fish and juxtaposes them to lizards and crocodiles, and as horned, which sets them apart from all of these classes. They sometimes received cults even at the highest levels of society, were of semi-divine status, were often depicted as the beasts of burden of Daoist transcendents and deities, and were associated with royalty, yet their flesh was also consumed as a rare delicacy.[99] They are depicted in anomaly accounts as morally ambivalent, sometimes helping the needy or protecting monasteries,[100] sometimes (as the bodily form of a local deity) submitting to the superior authority of Buddhist monks[101]—in all of these cases displaying an amalgamation with the Indian and Southeast Asian figure of the *naga*[102]—sometimes appearing as portents,[103] but sometimes eating human

---

97. Other, less ubiquitous categories of this sort include that of the *lin* 鱗 or kirin (Bwz 8.12–13; Lxz 70), often misleadingly translated as "unicorn," and that of the *boze* 白澤 (Jlz 43; Ssj 12.4, 18.6).

98. Thus associated with large birds—Yy 3.32–34.

99. Yy 3.33; Bwz 4.24, 5.11.

100. Yy 3.37, 3.40.

101. Yml 134, 255.

102. Bloss 1971, 1973; Rawlinson 1986.

103. Ssj 6.10–12, 6.17, 6.48, 7.5, 7.19.

victims, lying in wait for them under bridges[104] or in the roofbeams of buildings,[105] or demanding them as temple sacrifices.[106] They are sources of wisdom and power—one item claims that consuming their flesh allows one to write inspired prose.[107] Like the pangolin (a scaly ant-eater) in the taxonomic system of the Lele people, therefore, the dragon seems to inhabit an anomalous class of its own yet one that borders on many surrounding classes—a node-category through which many distinguishing lines pass.[108] It is not a hybrid, because it is rarely described in terms suggesting its combination of attributes of other species (such as "half-snake, half-fish"), nor do its various names suggest a hybrid nature; it is a type unto itself.

Moreover, the anomaly accounts depict dragons as extremely protean in character. They are constantly changing into something else or are themselves the result of a transformation from another kind of creature,[109] suddenly appearing or disappearing,[110] or flying off into the sky.[111]

Finally, the usual subcategories within the dragon class show up in the accounts: there are *long* 龍 or dragons proper; *yinglong* 應龍, a special type of winged dragon responsible in archaic times for slaying the monster Chi You and thus restoring rainfall, now dwelling in the extreme south;[112] *jiao* 蛟 or "krakens";[113] *mang* 蟒 and other huge serpentine beasts;[114] and a variety of other related reptilian creatures, many with cognate names. The boundaries of these subcategories are themselves fuzzy, which is not surprising in light of these beings' protean nature.

Anomaly by Transformation

We turn now to things anomalous not by their spatial location in the taxonomic field but by their temporal transformation across the boundary separating one category from another. These are no ordinary transformations of birth, maturation, and decay; they are the

---

104. Zgk 5; Zgz 5; Xunyj 1b.
105. Ssj 19.2.
106. Ssj 19.1.
107. Bwz 4.24.
108. Douglas 1975, 33–46.
109. ShuyjRf 1.15.
110. Yy 3.42.
111. Yy 3.34.
112. Shj 359, 427, 430; ShuyjRf 1.4.
113. Schafer 1980a [1973], 25; XuQxj 13; ShuyjRf 1.6–10.
114. Bwz 10.13.

extraordinary transformation of one *kind* of thing into a different kind. Such transformations pose a different sort of problem for any system of boundaries than the problems posed by locational anomalies. They do not merely question the placement of a specific being or phenomenon in one or another category. Enlarging or redefining a category, or redrawing its boundaries, do not address the issues raised when one kind of thing changes into a different kind. This process of becoming seems to suggest more radically that the particular boundaries of the system, or perhaps even any taxonomic boundaries in principle, are merely arbitrary, clumsy, contingent, or too-rigid cultural overlays upon an infinitesimally various and ever-changing field of natural objects and events.

Not only do many hundreds of anomaly account items describe anomalous transformations; these transformations also cross a great many kinds of boundaries. Below, I focus on those boundaries to which authors seem, based on the surviving corpus of texts, to have paid most attention.

Divine/human and transcendent/mortal persons. Many items effectively describe the transformation of human beings into local deities by recounting the founding legends of specific temples and shrines and the origins of cults to specific individuals.[115] In most but not all cases, this transformation of status includes the death of the cult recipient. Many other items—Daoist-inspired, but not exclusively in texts of predominantly Daoist orientation—depict human beings becoming transcendents (*xian* 仙), often completing the process by disappearing, visibly flying into the sky, or rising from their apparent death to live on through the technique of *shijie* 尸解 or "liberation from the corpse."[116]

Human/animal. As in the case of hybrids and anomalies of cross-boundary behavior, so also by transformation this is a boundary frequently crossed—most often by people becoming tigers[117] or other animals,[118] sometimes by animals becoming people.[119]

---

115. Ssj 5 passim; Yy 5 passim; ShuyjRf 1.21, 1.48, 1.130, 2.66–67, 2.119, 2.138, 2.146, 2.153; Lyz 2–4, 21, 39; Luyz 5; Zgszg 19–20; Gshiz 2.17a.

116. Lxz passim; Sxz passim; Bwz 7.2, 8.1; Yml 197; ShuyjRf 1.78, 2.55, 2.63, 2.119, 2.137–139; Ssj 1 and 2 passim; Dmj 2.4, 2.19–22, 3.1, 3.14, 3.16, 4.1.

117. Qxj 2, 5; Shuyj 13, 88; Yy 3.15, 5.3, 8.38–40; ShuyjRf 1.34; Bwz 2.25; Sshj 4.7; Ssj 12.8.

118. Ssj 14.16–18, 19.4; Yy 3.51, 8.42; Yml 166.

119. Xuanzj 47; Ssj 20.1.

Human/mineral. Several items recount the transformation of persons into stone or describe unusual rock formations said by local tradition to be transformed humans.[120]

Spirit/animal, spirit/plant, and spirit/mineral. In keeping with an already established cosmological principle, anomaly accounts describe animals, plants, minerals, and other things (including mountains and bodies of water) transforming into or producing—usually due to extreme longevity—"spirits" (*shen* 神), "sprites" or "emanations" (*jing* 精), or "numina" (*ling* 靈).[121] As one text states, "Every rare and precious thing after a long time produces sprites and numina."[122]

Distinct animal and plant species. Also sometimes ascribed to longevity are transformations of one kind of animal into another.[123] Such transformations are not always due to aging, however.[124] Some are listed as portents.[125] Long-lived and other plants are described as changing into other plant species.[126]

Plant/animal and plant/mineral. Instances include the transformation of a tree into a bird, of bamboo into snakes, of ferns into parasitic worms, and of mapleseeds into a type of amber.[127]

---

120. Lyz 48; Pyj 1b–2a; Luyz 25; Sshj 1.10; Ssj 8.7, 11.1; ShuyjRf 2.117; Yml 11–12; Jlz 41; cf. Ssj 11.7. Much less frequently are people described as changing into plants (Bwz 3.29; Ssj 14.13).

121. These events are to be distinguished from spirits' "possession" of, and also from their temporary disguise in the forms of, animals and other objects. The mechanisms of boundary-crossing are different in each type of case. In transformation proper, a thing of one class becomes a member of another. In "disguise," a thing of one class temporarily takes on the form typical of another class. In possession, one thing "borrows" the body or faculties of an actual, already-existing member of another class—even in some cases of ordinary objects such as tools (Ssj 18.1–2; Yml 187, 231; Yy 8.9).

122. Syj 7.6a; cf. Xuanzj 48, 61; Ssj 12 passim; Yml 31= ShuyjRf 2.92.

123. ShuyjRf 1.26, 1.30–33, 2.121; Xuanzj 49.

124. ShuyjRf 1.28; Ssj 13.15–16, 14.4, 14.11; Yy 3.42–44, 3.52–53.

125. Ssj 6.4, 6.29, 6.57, 7.4.

126. Long-lived plants changing: Bwz 4.34; Jlz 10; Xuanzj 62. Other plants changing: Bwz 4.16; Ssj 6.74.

127. Tree into bird: Gyz 1. Bamboo into snakes: Yy 3.44. Ferns into worms: Sshj 3.9. Mapleseeds into amber: Xuanzj 63.

Parts/whole. Discarded pieces of meat are said to transform into whole animals, often of a different species.[128] Similarly, of certain foreign peoples it is said that the hearts or livers of their dead, after lying buried for a hundred years, transform into whole human beings.[129]

Female/male. The anomaly accounts mention instances of women changing into men, men into women, and male and female twins changing into androgynes; most of these cases are laconically listed as portents.[130] Much less is made of this boundary in the anomaly accounts than in certain other cultures' cosmographic discourses, however.[131]

Apparent/real. Under this large and final category I group all items that share one important feature, namely, that things appearing to some human perceiver to be one sort of thing turn out in fact to be another sort—due not to any error on the perceiver's part but to a change in the object of perception itself. Such cases differ from other transformation accounts in that the changes here described are primarily changes of form, shape, or appearance and are also of relatively short duration. In other words, we have, in many of these cases, to deal with tales in which beings of one class *disguise* themselves as (or temporarily change into) beings of another class, often for purposes of deception. Such tales contain not one but two transformations: the initial one of disguise, implied but not normally described in the narrative, and the final one of retransformation, which is often the climax of the narrative and the moment when the true taxonomic identity of the creature is revealed.

In several tales, for instance—all variations on the same plot—a man crossing the Yellow River finds a floating stone, the oddity of which catches his attention. He takes it home and places it at the head of his bed. It then transforms into a woman; in one version she identifies herself as the daughter of Hebo 河伯, the divine River Uncle.[132]

Much more common is the motif of an apparent woman or

---

128. Ssj 13.12; Yml 152; Yy 2.24.
129. Bwz 2.20.
130. Ssj 2.3, 6.14, 6.44, 6.66, 7.18, 14.1, 14.10.
131. O'Flaherty 1980, 281–334; Lincoln 1989, 166.
132. Shuyj 86; ShuyjRf 2.149; Yy 2.23; Yml 167.

man who seduces or attempts to seduce the opposite-sex protagonist of the tale, then transforms into her or his "true form"—some
species of animal.[133] The best known of such tales involve women
who change into foxes,[134] but there are also items in which men who
seek sex later change into foxes, or in which male foxes are found
with lists of human women's names, wearing fragrance, or with
other similar evidence of cross-boundary philandery.[135] And there
are many similar tales involving other kinds of animals of both
sexes, including birds, monkeys, otters, roosters, rodents, pigs,
dogs, turtles, and even insects and animated broomsticks.[136] Furthermore, there are many stories of foxes disguised as people that
do not involve sexual pursuit; oddly, several of these occur in
academic settings, the fox appearing as a student or a teacher.[137]

In other tales, animals disguised as humans appear seeking
something other than sex—usually food or information—and later
transform again into their animal shapes.[138] In some cases, animals
even disguise themselves as temple deities, as family members, or
as deceased members of the protagonist's family temporarily returned from the dead.[139]

Many of these items use death as the mechanism of re-trans-
formation into animal form: that is, it is upon being killed that the
true identity of the disguised creature is revealed.[140] In other tales,
the mechanism is sunrise: only on the next day, after the liminal
period of night has ended, can the protagonist discern the true form
of the being he or she has just made contact with. This pattern

---

133. On such beings in general, Campany 1985, 1986, and the works
cited there; Harper 1985; de Groot 1982 [1892–1910], passim.

134. Shuyj 87; Ssj 18.11, 18.13; Yml 127, 181; Yy 8.10; cf. Yml 105;
Uchida 1961; Nishioka 1968.

135. Sshj 9.13–14; Yml 110, 196; cf. Yy 8.41.

136. Birds: Sshj 9.1; Yy 8.3; Yml 80, 148. Monkeys: Yy 8.8. Otters:
Zyz 16; Ssj 18.24, tr. de Groot 1982 [1892–1910], 5:608; Yml 170, 171 [= Yy
8.16], 250; Yy 8.18. Roosters: Yml 262. Rodents: Yml 229. Pigs: Zgz 11; Ssj
18.18. Dogs: Ssj 18.20; Sshj 9.10. Turtles: Zgk 9; Yy 8.14; Ssj 19.4, tr. in
three places: de Groot 1982 [1892–1910], 5:625; DeWoskin 1977a, 106; Kao
1985, 107. Insects: Yy 8.15, 8.17. Broomstick: Yml 231. Note that these are
mostly domestic animals.

137. XuQxj 5; Ssj 18.8–9, 18.16; Yml 33.

138. Sshj 9.2; Ssj 19.3, tr. de Groot 1982 [1892–1910], 4:216; Ssj
18.17, tr. de Groot 1982 [1892–1910], 5:602.

139. Deities: Ssj 19.5. Family members: Ssj 16.15; tr. Kao 1985, 92.
Deceased members of the protagonist's family: Yml 160; Ssj 18.21.

140. E.g. Yy 8 passim.

occurs in a related and well known motif, that of the traveler (usually male) who stops for the night at a wayside inn—often sleeping with the lonely innkeeper (usually female)—only to look back on his way out the next morning to see a tomb where he had slept.[141]

The transformation of apparent objects of one sort into real objects of another is also seen in tales in which money or valuables found by accident or gotten by trickery later transform into dust, ashes, or other useless things.[142]

Finally, it should be noted that anomalies of transformation in anomaly narratives are not restricted to tales of unexpected events that simply happen. Transformation (*hua* 化, *bianhua* 變化) is also one of the esoteric arts acquired by *fangshi*, Daoist adepts, and Buddhist monks, allowing them to transform themselves into animal shapes and other forms.[143] A similar art is that of "illusion" (*huan* 幻, also *hua*), by which adepts can transform things into different shapes and create alternative "virtual realities."[144] And one might include under this category Daoist tales of the transformation of mortals into transcendents.

Anomaly by Causation

Some types of anomalies dealt with in the anomaly accounts are matters not primarily of taxonomic membership but of causation. They differ from anomalies of transformation in that they consist not in one kind of thing changing into another kind but in one state of affairs resulting from—or being mysteriously connected to—another. The specific boundaries thus crossed vary enormously, but the mode of crossing is always a transition over time.

Under the broad category of anomalies of causation, we have to deal with two large sub-categories. In one of these, the focus is on the fact that some hidden, mysterious causal process is at work behind certain phenomena. The specific causal agent is not discussed in detail; rather, the main point is often a hermeneutical one: how are the phenomena to be interpreted, and what do they mean? The anomaly usually lies both in the mysterious nature of the causal

---

141. Luyz 24; Sshj 5.7, 6.1–2; Ssj 16.20; Yy 6.5, 6.20; cf. Yml 46.

142. Yy 2.8–13, and cf. 6.19; Yml 127, 152.

143. Jlz 41; Sshj 1.1; Ssj 1.9, 1.15, 1.21, 1.23, 2.3; Lxz 38.

144. Yy 9.17–18; Yml 102; Jlz 3; Ssj 2.10; cf. Bwz 5.2. A prominent, probably roughly contemporary passage on "illusion" appears in *Liezi jishi* 3 (56ff.), tr. Graham 1990, 61ff.

agent or process (how did things get from point X to point Y?) and in the surprisingly meaningful and "legible" nature of the outcome (how comes it that a message is so clearly and forcefully signified by this event?). We might for convenience term these anomalies of "mysterious causes and significations." In the other subcategory, the focus is on agents or processes that produce surprising, marvelous, even apparently contranatural effects, usually of a beneficial nature. At issue in these cases is not the hermeneutics of outcomes but the demonstration of efficacy. The anomaly in question is usually one of degree—a matter not of taxonomic location but of causal potency. Such cases might be termed anomalies of "marvelous effects."

In a sense, anomaly by causation is just the opposite of a true anomaly: events are described for which there is in fact a "rational" or "principled," if arcane, explanation. But the point of most such items is that such events are anomalous only from the perspective of one who refuses to take seriously the causal processes and agents described—one whose world has no room for such arts. These items urge on their readers an expanded perspective.

Mysterious Causes and Significations

Omens and portents. As has been noted above, the anomaly accounts prominently contain lists of anomalous events that were interpreted by contemporary court specialists as carrying indirect or symbolic messages concerning the impending fortunes of the ruler or reigning dynasty. In many cases, this mode of interpretation is quite explicit, and many of these cases also appear in dynastic histories.[145] In others, it is implied in the narrative structure: a strange event is described, then we are told that after a certain length of time something happened, with a causal—or, more precisely, confirmatory—connection implied.[146] Rather than narrating a particular portentous event, some items consist of a general statement (sometimes couched in a reported speech or conversation) on the nature of omens and portents or on the meaning of a certain type of occurrence.[147]

An important sub-class is that of ominous dreams and visions. Typically, a ruler, official, or ordinary person is depicted as contem-

---

145. Ssj 6 and 7, passim; Yy 4 passim; Nishitani 1951.
146. Xs 7; Shuyj 28–30, 32, 59–60, 62; Ssj 9.7–14.
147. Xs 9, 43; Bwz 1.32; Ssj 6.2; Yy 3.45.

plating some course of action when he or she has a dream that is taken—often after consulting a professional dream-interpreter—as either promising success or warning of failure. The dream is almost always a symbolic code requiring interpretation. The tale usually ends by noting that things turned out as predicted,[148] which leads us to the next point.

The efficacy of esoteric arts. Aside from dream-interpretation, several other esoteric methods for predicting future events, assessing human character, and finding lost objects are featured in anomaly accounts. Each of these methods is, in a sense, based on both the positing and crossing of a specific distance between two areas of life—the "micro"-area manipulated or "read" by the diviner and the "macro"-area in which the referred-to events or objects have their seemingly independent yet tacitly connected existence. These techniques were based on elaborate metaphysical systems of correspondence, but the anomaly accounts rarely discuss the rationales or cosmological principles underlying them; instead, they seek to impress upon the reader the reality of the hidden connections of cosmic correspondence, by illustrating the striking efficacy of the arts concerned.

Among the arts highlighted are several styles of divination,[149] physiognomy,[150] and the observation and interpretation of folk songs and sayings.[151] There is also an important story-motif consisting of predictions made by various means—none of which, again, are explained in any detail—coming true with convincing specificity.[152]

Spontaneous "responses" to morality or piety. The anomaly accounts contain many stories illustrating what might be termed moral causation: the apparently spontaneous or natural

---

148. Ssj 10.1–4, 10.8; Yml 51, 119; Shuyj 78; Yy 7.30–33.

149. Zgz 3; Shuyj 36; Yy 4.34–36, 4.39, 5.16, 5.21–22 [concerning the origin of certain techniques], 7.9, 7.23, 7.31–32, 9 passim; Yml 90, 122, 256; Bwz 9.3, 9.13–16; Sshj 2.12–14, 9.2, 9.15; Ssj 1.31, 3 passim, 7.26, 8.3, 9.1–2, 9.7, 11.34, 14.12, 15.7, 15.10, 17.10.

150. Yy 4.34, 5.26; Yml 122; Jlz 22.

151. Ssj 6.64, 6.67, 7.11–13, 13.8; Yy 4.8, 4.15, 4.53.

152. Shuyj 10; Xs 54, 61, 79, 80; Yy 1.17, 4 passim, 6.21, 7.15, 7.20, 7.31; Luyz 20, tr. Kao 1985, 152; Sshj 2.12–14, 3.3; Ssj 2.7, 3 passim, 4.17, 4.21, 5.1, 9.1–2, 9.6, 19.9 [= Yml 42]; Yml 49–50, 55, 75, 122, 129, 153, 240; Lxz 12; Syj 7.7a, 8.1a, 8.5a (all prophecies made at the birth of a future mythical hero).

(in the sense of not humanly applied) reward of human virtue or punishment of vice. In the classical phrasing, the cosmos—whether through the impersonal agency of "Heaven" or through the action of a particular spirit—is depicted as "responding" (*ying* 應) to the "stimulus" (*gan* 感) provided by human action and intention. Buddhist karma theory, as well as accounts of bodhisattvas' responsiveness to human need, fit readily with this complex of ideas.[153]

Many tales thus depict Heaven as responding to human virtue or vice, or imply in their narrative structure—without claiming explicitly—that events in the tale are due to the hidden causal forces of cosmic reward and retribution.[154] Some tales make this point more straightforwardly, by placing a speech about retribution in the mouth of a deceased person temporarily returned to the realm of the living, or in that of a person who died and subsequently returned to life. Such persons are narratively construed as being in a position to discuss authoritatively the workings of spontaneous retribution because they have been on the other side of the boundary separating this world from the "dark realm" to which the dead go, and from which the destinies of the living are silently but inexorably controlled.[155] Reflecting the Buddhist emphasis on nonviolence, some tales outside of Buddhist contexts directly or implicitly warn against taking life and eating meat;[156] some protagonists even suffer the same fate as the animals they consume,[157] or mistakenly kill their own relative while hunting as punishment for killing animals in the same fashion.[158] Naturally, these themes are even more heavily emphasized in tale-collections explicitly designed to promote the Buddhist cause.[159]

Also in this category of anomalies are springs and wells that automatically adjust their flow or temperature to particular persons' wishes, usually as a response to their virtue or piety.[160]

---

153. Campany 1993a.
154. Bwz 7.3–8, 8.5; Jlz 60; Luyz 1; Sshj 2.6, 5.1,10.4; Ssj 1.28, 8.1–4, 8.6, 9.4–5, 10.4, 11 passim; Yml 155, 168, 178, 194, 207; Yy 2.27, 5.33, 5.38, 10.4, 10.6, 10.8.
155. Sshj 6.19; Yml 83, 126, 248 [= Mxj 4, tr. Kao 1985, 166]; Yy 5.32.
156. Yy 4.27, 5.38, 8.44–45.
157. Sshj 9.12; Yy 5.32.
158. Yy 8.37.
159. Xyj 2 (in which even the killing of lice is forbidden), 10, 12–13, 24; Mxj 6, 21, 33, 38, 54, 67, 114.
160. Ssj 13.1, 13.5; Yml 8, 18.

Marvelous Effects

Not surprisingly, the type of marvelous effect in which authors show by far the most interest is unusual—sometimes contranatural —longevity. This theme is naturally prominent in Daoist hagiographies and topographies, but it appears widely in other texts as well. Certain rare animals and animal products are described as inducing extreme longevity if consumed or ridden.[161] Herbs which if consumed prolong one's lifespan or enable one to avoid death altogether are mentioned more frequently,[162] as are nuts and fruits, minerals including but not limited to cinnabar, water from particular springs and wells, and a special type of wine.[163]

Other extraordinary effects are noted. The unusually powerful curative properties of certain herbs are described in several tales.[164] Some objects if ingested bring unusual linguistic facility;[165] certain herbs induce quick and easy seduction;[166] certain wines produce extraordinarily long or deep states of intoxication.[167] One tale recounts a woman's conception after she drank a man's bath water.[168]

Anomaly by Contact

The final mode of anomaly explored in the anomaly accounts consists of contact—usually brief—across some important boundary. The key conditions of anomaly by contact are two: that beings on either side of this boundary do not, under ordinary circumstances, have direct, unmediated dealings with one another, but rather exist at a considerable distance (whether ontological or epistemological); and that the boundary is sufficiently firm, and important enough in the reigning cosmology or worldview, that mere contact across it is an event sufficiently irregular to merit recording as an anomaly. From the sheer number of tales of unusual contacts as well as the

---

161. Consumed: ShuyjRf 1.28; Xuanzj 50–51. Ridden: Bwz 2.2, 3.11.

162. Shuyj 3, 12; ShuyjRf 1.62, 1.77, 1.109, 2.29; Yml 77; Bwz 1.43, 2.21, 5.9; Jlz 13; Ssj 14.1, 14.12.

163. Nuts and fruits: Ssj 1.5, 1.10. Minerals: Ssj 13.11. Waters: Bwz 1.46, 1.48; Ssj 13.11; Yy 2.20. Wine: Bwz 8.24.

164. Bwz 4.37–39; Ssj 12.17; Yy 2.33, 2.36, 3.46; Xuanzj 71.

165. Jlz 38; Shenyjing nw 5.

166. Bwz 3.29; Ssj 14.13.

167. Bwz 5.13, 10.10; Ssj 19.8; Yy 5.28.

168. Ssj 11.33.

variety of sub-motifs, it is evident that authors—and presumably, their audience as well—were keenly interested in this mode of anomaly.

Contact with the realm of the dead. One of the primary boundaries across which anomalous contact is made in the texts is that separating the dead from the living. Authors developed several major narrative motifs in which to explore the implications and meanings of such incidents of contact.

One of these motifs is that of return from death or, in recent North American parlance, tales of "near-death experiences." The protagonist dies, then revives to tell what he or she saw while among the dead. Most such tales emphasize the scenery glimpsed by the mortal traveler while on the other side of the boundary. Some present that scenery in mostly non-sectarian terms;[169] others portray a decidedly Buddhist afterlife realm.[170] A few tales emphasize not the protagonist's vision of the other world but the means by which the resuscitation was accomplished,[171] or else the mere fact that it occurred.[172]

The other prevalent type of tale involving contact with the dead is the ghost story, in which a dead person temporarily returns in spectral form to visit the living.[173] There are many sub-types. One of the most ubiquitous is that of the vengeful ghost, returned to seek revenge on some living person for an unpunished wrong.[174] Another is that of the grateful dead, who appear to thank living, non-kin persons for a favor, often the reburial of their corpse.[175] But

---

169. Campany 1990a; Zyz 9, 11, 13–15; Luyz 16; Sshj 4.2–5; Ssj 15.1–8, 15.10, 15.12–14, cf. 18.21; Yml 132, 199, 206, 221, 241, 248 [= Mxj 4]; Yy 8.24–25.

170. Yml 248, 264–266; Xyj 1; Mxj 4–5, 21–22, 29, 34, 44–45, 58, 64–65, 71, 76, 103, 109, 117–118, 124. I am preparing an article on these tales.

171. Sshj 4.1, 4.2 [= Yy 8.23 = Yml 206], tr. Kao 1985, 130; ShuyjRf 1.90, 1.102; Bwz 5.8, 10.10; Ssj 1.10, 1.20, 15.1–2; Lxz 21, 27, 32, 52; Yml 176, 204.

172. Ssj 7.27. These accounts are not to be confused with stories concerning the sheer survival of persons mistakenly buried alive—a motif perhaps better interpreted as involving an anomaly of transformation from apparent death to actual life (Ssj 15.5, 15.10, 15.12–14).

173. Yu 1987; Campany 1991a.

174. Yhz passim [see Cohen 1982]; Shuyj 53, 61, 67; XuQxj 6; Yml 99, 107, 121, 166, 219, 232–233; Sshj 5.9, 6.8, 6.12, 6.16–17; Ssj 1.7, 3.8, 10.9, 16.9; Yy 5.1, 6.1–2, 6.23, 6.27.

175. Jlz 58; Yml 147, 165, 185, 235, 261; Yy 7.5, 7.11, 7.14, 7.28; XuQxj 16; Sgl 2.

other stories lack such obvious didactic intent: in some, ghosts harm living people for no apparent reason;[176] in others, they steal food or implements from the living;[177] elsewhere, they are depicted as gratuitously helping living strangers.[178] Many stories emphasize the reality of contact with revenants by mentioning tangible or visual details—an object figuring in the interaction between ghost and living protagonist later discovered missing from the dead person's grave, for example—that are meant to confirm that the narrated event actually happened.[179] Others portray contact by telling of otherwise ordinary people who have the special power to see ghosts.[180] There are also tales of dead ancestors appearing briefly to help their living relatives[181] or, in a few cases, to harm them.[182]

In all of these tales, the most important vehicle of contact with the dead is vision; the protagonist first and foremost *sees* the dead person or the realm of the dead, whatever other interactions may occur.

Contact with deities, spirits, and demons. This emphasis on seeing beings normally invisible to the human eye also characterizes the many tales of contact with other spiritual beings, ranging from celestial deities to local gods, tree-spirits, and demons and emanations of various types.

Influenced by Daoist scriptural texts and legends are the tales of ordinary people's encounters with jade maidens 玉女 and with transcendents who return their kindnesses.[183] A related theme is that of Daoist transcendents or advanced adepts who appear to be ordinary persons and who for a long time keep their special abilities secret, often by taking on the guise of commoners and selling wares in a market;[184] sometimes these figures' true identities are revealed only when neighbors notice that they do not age.[185]

---

176. Zgz 12; Gslz 1; Luyz 11; Sshj 6.10; Yml 213.
177. Sshj 6.20; Ssj 16.11; Yml 256; Yy 6.22.
178. Sshj 6.9; Ssj 17.2; Yml 173; Yy 6.32.
179. Zgz 2; Lyz 31; Shuyj 82; Luyz 9; Ssj 16.19–22; Yy 6.2, 6.30, 7.1, 7.4, 7.11; Yml 124.
180. Sshj 6.13–18; Ssj 16.11–12; Yml 67, 137, 214, 224.
181. Lyz 42; Yml 103–104, 115, 124–126, 169, 176, 216, 239, 260; Jlj 1; Luyz 23; Ssj 17.3; Yy 6.11, 6.25 [= Yml 103].
182. Shuyj 58, 66; Yml 89; cf. Ssj 3.8, 16.11.
183. Jade maiden contacts: ShuyjRf 1.66–67, 2.140; Yml 29; Jzj 3a–b. Transcendents repaying favors: Zyz 3; ShuyjRf 1.60 (translated in the previous chapter); Shenyj 3; Yml 131.
184. Lxz 4, 9–10, 19, 23, 25, 27, etc.; Ssj 1.10.
185. As in Lxz 13, 16.

Spirits, too, are frequently depicted as revealing or concealing their true forms.[186] In a few humorous cases, the spirit reveals its form to a person by mistake, sometimes due to drunkenness.[187]

Contact with the spirits of particular places is a prominent motif in the anomaly accounts. Many of these are the local deities of mountains, rivers, lakes, and other territories, who receive offerings in temples and shrines. Some tales simply describe routine offerings or recount the founding legends of particular cult sites, but many tell of more direct, visual contact with these deities and often rather complex interactions between them and the human protagonists of the tales.[188] These interactions vary widely, and will be treated more closely in Chapter Eight; they include, for example, gods' rewarding of humans who make generous temple offerings or show unusual respect when passing their temple,[189] gods' coveting of human possessions,[190] and gods' jealous protection of their temple precincts from even casual defacement, poaching, or removal of produce.[191]

Particular deities well known from other textual genres also show up in the anomaly accounts: the (Yellow) River God, for example, figures in many tales,[192] as do the gods of Mt. Lu near Lake Gongting.[193]

Other spirits of places with whom human protagonists make direct contact are not gods worshipped in temples but free-floating beings that usually appear to travelers in animal or human disguise, only later to be revealed for what they are. These include the mountain spirits of whom Ge Hong famously warned his readers in Chapter Seventeen of his *Baopuzi neipian*, who appear disguised as women, boys, or pieces of wood.[194] They also include arboreal spirits, often recognized when the trees they inhabit emit blood upon

---

186. Ssj 18 passim; Sshj 8.1–3; Jlz 23; Luyz 12.

187. Ssj 18.12, 18.21; Yml 160 [cf. Yml 37].

188. Yy 5 passim.

189. Yy 1.2, 1.18, 4.11, 5.2; Yml 57, 61, 84, 179, 210; Luyz 17 [tr. Kao 1985, 151; = Ssj 4.13], 21; Ssj 4 passim, 18.4.

190. Zgk 7; Shuyj 83; Yml 54, 76, 162; Bwz 7.12.

191. Zgz 1; Lgz 13; Shuyj 4–5, 8; Yy 2.22, 4.27, 5.10, 5.19.

192. Shenyjing w 7; Zgk 7; Lyz 20–21; Xs 115 [= Yy 2.3]; Yy 2.15, 5.3, 6.9, 10.13; ShuyjRf 1.123 (cf.), 2.92, 2.135; Szj 9b; Luyz 21; Ssj 4.4–6, 11.3; Bwz 7.1–2, 7.12; Yml 167, 253.

193. Zgz 8, 9 [= Ssj 4.9]; Lyz 38, 49; Shuyj 1–3, 18; ShuyjRf 1.47–48; Yml 54; Zgszg 8; Ssj 4.8–13; cf. Miyakawa 1979.

194. ShuyjRf 2.145, Jlz 21, and Sshj 7.2, respectively.

being cut[195] and appearing either in human form or as animals.[196] The mere sighting of these beings was an anomaly worth recording, since they are rarely visible to the human eye;[197] sometimes they are invisible but audible, and people who happen to overhear their conversations with each other learn their secret weakness, and are thus able to expel or kill them.[198] However, contact with such spirits is often depicted as having ill effects, usually sickness and death.[199]

Sexual contact with non-human (or non-living human) beings. The authors' treatment of this most intimate mode of contact between humans and other beings can be subdivided into three types of tales.

First, deities of various kinds and levels are sometimes depicted as choosing human sexual partners. A few such cases involve celestial and astral deities such as rainbows and star-spirits;[200] many more involve terrestrial deities[201] or, in rare cases, transcendents.[202] Marriages are depicted between mortal men and local goddesses or daughters of local gods.[203] In some of these tales, the divine woman bears a child whom the mortal man is permitted to visit periodically.

Second, sexual encounters are depicted between various non-divine spiritual beings and humans. These tales were discussed above as a type of anomaly by transformation, since these spirits usually initially appear as humans to their human partners, and only later re-transform into their true forms.

Third, sexual contact and marriage occur in the tales between

---

195. Ssj 6.68, 18.6–7; Yml 140; Yy 8.11; Sshj 8.8.

196. Human form: Yml 227; Ssj 18.4. Animal form: Ssj 18.3.

197. Sshj 7.4, 7.6, 8.6, 9.8; Ssj 12 passim; Yml 23, 151, 225; Yy 6.3.

198. Luyz 3; Sshj 6.11; Yy 3.48; Ssj 16.18 [= Lyz 28], 17.5, 18.3, 18.26.

199. Shuyj 38; Sshj 7.7–9, 8.2, 8.4, 9.1; Ssj 9.13, 11.34, 15.17; Yml 144, 161, 193, 211, 225; Yy 6.14, 6.33, 6.37, 7.19.

200. Sshj 3.2 [cf. Yml 109], 7.1; Syj 3.5a.

201. Sshj 5.4, 5.7–8, 6.4; Ssj 1.30–31, 4.6, 4.8, 5.3–4; Yml 167, 199, 207.

202. Yml 69. In this tale, the spirit-lover is not explicitly identified as a Daoist transcendent; but he is suggestively styled "Changsheng" 長生 (long life). Such a case is distinct from that of Daoist adepts with spouses or families, whose hagiographies end with their achievement of transcendence.

203. Ssj 4.6, 4.9; Yml 209, 253.

living and dead human beings. In some of these tales, the ghosts of the dead seduce the living by posing as living persons themselves; in others, marital relations established during life continue after death.[204] Pregnancy and childbirth resulting from such unions are occasionally described.[205]

Revelation. Another form of contact between humans and spiritual beings that goes beyond a mere vision involves the revelation of some esoteric text or skill. Anomaly tales recount the transmission to humans by deities, spirits, or ghosts of magical seals and sacred texts.[206] They also tell of the similar transmission of divine medicines and curative techniques.[207]

Miraculous intervention. Buddhist tale-collections abound in accounts of beneficent intervention by superior beings—most commonly the Bodhisattva Guanyin—in human affairs. Such intervention usually follows a pious request for salvation from imminent danger.[208] It is "miraculous" in that it is taken as a confirmation of certain religious teachings, is often strikingly contranatural (a clear departure from what would have happened without intervention), and is a deliberate act by a personal being (see Chapter Seven).

Journey to distant regions. As already glimpsed in the case of return-from-death accounts, anomalies of contact include not only events that occur "here" but also encounters "out there." Some human protagonists journey out into the eastern ocean, where they meet with various strange beings and locales.[209] Others make excursions up to the astral regions,[210] into the precincts of divine palaces,[211] or into the realm of transcendents or of the dead.

---

204. Zgk 2; Lyz 40; Shuyj 81–82, 84–85; Luyz 4 [= Ssj 16.19, tr. Kao 1985, 93]; Sshj 4.6, 6.1; Ssj 16.19–24; Yml 52, 113, 226, 238; Yy 6.19–20.

205. Luyz 10; Yy 6.10; Yml 176.

206. Ssj 1.25, 1.31, 4.6, 8.6, 15.4; Yml 140, 193, 222, 253, 259; Yy 5.7, 5.14, 5.22, 6.40; Lyz 26; Campany 1993a.

207. Ssj 15.4; Yml 155, 188 [cf.], 253; Yy 6.19.

208. Campany 1993a; Gsy, XuGsy, and XiGsy, passim.

209. Xs 1; ShuyjRf 1.70, 2.4–5; Szj 2b; Kjj 1a; Lh passim; Bwz 2.31; Jlz 14–15.

210. Bwz 10.11; Yml 155.

211. Yy 5.20–21, 7.18, 7.30.

Discovery of hidden worlds. The mirror image of such accounts can be seen in those tales—familiar to students of Chinese literature from the famous exemplar of Tao Qian's "Peach Blossom Spring" 桃花源記—in which a person happens upon an entire microcosm or territory hidden in the midst of the Central Kingdom and normally inaccessible. Examples among anomaly accounts are numerous.[212]

Contact through dreams. Finally, in Chinese theory of the time, dream-states constituted a sort of spiritual journey outward into realms not normally contacted.[213] Things occur in dreams that do not occur in normal, waking life, such as images moving or coming to life.[214] The accounts are often at pains to demonstrate that dream-encouters are no mere mental figments but are real; they do so by presenting some tangible evidence or definite change that carries over from the dreaming into the waking state and confirms the reality of what happened in the protagonist's dream.[215]

Conclusions

This analysis has revealed at least two aspects of the taxonomic, as well as cosmological, thinking embodied in the anomaly accounts. First, it has uncovered views of the nature of boundaries and categories implied in the texts, as well as a logical structure of anomaly. Second, it has shown which particular boundaries anomaly account authors were most concerned to probe. I conclude this chapter by summarizing these findings and reflecting on their significance.

---

212. Zgk 2; Shuyj 4; Yy 1.24, 5.29 [cf.]; ShuyjRf 2.29; Yml 4, 39, 63–64, 252–253; Wlj 2a; Pyj 1b; Syj 10.9b–10a; Sshj 1.2–7; Lxz 68; and cf. XuQxj 8 in which an adept disgorges and re-swallows whole internal "worlds."

213. Strickmann 1988.

214. Ssj 4.8, 5.3.

215. Bwz 7.8; Luyz 9, 13; Ssj 5.10, 10.6–7, 10.9 [cf.], 11.6; Yml 116, 141, 195, 243; Yy 6.15, 7.4, 7.11, 7.18, 7.21, 7.23, 7.26, 7.31–33. Compare the theme of the confirmation of real contacts with souls of the dead discussed above. In this period and genre at least, the predominant Chinese interest in confirming the "reality" of dream-events contrasts with the more complex and ambivalent Indian ontologies (and anti-ontologies) of dreaming (O'Flaherty 1984).

The Nature of Boundaries

Most (but not all) anomalies represented in the anomaly accounts occur at or across boundaries. The texts make implicit assertions about the nature of taxonomic boundaries, and they do so at several levels. Individual tales or descriptions comment on the nature of specific boundaries; groups of tales exhibiting common motifs or themes can be read as commenting in general on certain types of boundaries. At the highest level of generality, it is tempting to read the genre as a whole as arguing some definite case about boundaries, but, as I will show in detail in the next chapter, the picture is more complex than that, since different authors can be shown to have used the genre to assert quite different things about boundaries, and thus advance their respective—divergent—interests.

It is enough here to note that, in general, boundaries between categories of beings (and realms of being) are suggested in many anomaly items to be negotiable, flexible, indeterminate, porous, or relative. In short, anomaly accounts portray a world in which boundaries between kinds and realms are less like walls in a building than like cell membranes in an organism. On the other hand, the membrane-like porousness of boundaries does not entail their complete absence. The description of a hybrid or cross-boundary-behaving being, for instance, does not imply the non-existence or destruction of the boundary separating its constituent kinds; on the contrary, the very cognitive and emotive force of the hybrid, its shock-value or capacity to inspire wonder, depends on a taxonomic boundary that is normally and otherwise intact. Further, accounts of hybrids in fact heighten awareness of the boundaries they straddle. Hybrid beings function as boundary-markers, as do texts about them.

Similarly, anomalies of transformation do not obliterate boundaries; they show their porousness under certain special conditions or on certain exceptional occasions. In anomalies of contact, something usually hidden becomes manifest; something, the existence of which is doubtful or non-evident, reveals itself to someone, affecting that human subject in some marked way. Anomalies of causation do not suggest that the cosmos works randomly; rather, they suggest the silent working of certain causal principles that are not commonly known or understood but are no less effective for that.

Furthermore, in tales falling under each of these types of anomaly there are usually two sorts of boundaries in question, one of *being* and one of *knowing*, but different tales or tale-types may highlight one or the other sort. A sheer physical description of a hybrid, for example, highlights the ontological boundary between two or more kinds of creatures at the same time that it assumes (but does not emphasize) an epistemological boundary between the reader and the strange being described. The latter boundary is crossed in the very depiction of the hybrid: it makes the reader aware of something of which he or she is presumed unaware. A tale of anomalous causation, by contrast, highlights the epistemological boundary between a described set of causes or conditions and a narrated—but, to the reader, unexpected or unexplainable—effect or outcome; it also assumes (but does not emphasize) an ontological boundary between two spheres of actions or events, improbably crossed by the causal link posited in the tale.

And in each of these types of account, definite implications usually follow from the demonstration of the porousness of a boundary. These groups of implications—concerning the capacities of certain persons or types of people, the truth or power of certain ideologies, the cross-boundary obligations human beings may have—are the subject of the next two chapters.

The Structure of Anomaly and the Nature of Categories

Aside from what they imply concerning the nature of boundaries, the anomaly accounts, taken as a whole, also reveal a logical structure of anomaly—a set of structural ways in which anomalies may occur with respect to any given taxonomic system. Those four ways include anomaly by taxonomic location, by transformation, by causation, and by contact. Existing studies of taxonomic systems not only pay little attention to anomalies in general, they pay virtually no attention at all to variations in the modes of anomaly and to the significance these variations might have.

The most important exception of which I am aware is Rodney Needham's elegant, if briefly set forth, typology of the "transformations" to which the categories comprised within a system of boundaries can be subjected.[216] These are not transformations of beings from one category to another, as discussed above, but temporary or partial transformations in the relationships between categories (most often social categories), ritually enacted to mark the boundaries between sub-groups, genders, stages of growth or identity, and

216. Needham 1979, 38–43.

so on. Needham speaks of three logically distinct types of transformation: inversion or reversal (transvestism, for example), disruption (as in the saturnalia and other temporary periods of stipulated behavioral license), and nullification (the temporary negation or destruction of any status whatsoever attaching to a person normally assigned certain attributes, as in the isolation, denuding, washing, and public appearance of a new king during coronation ceremonies or of neophytes during initiation). This typology applies well to, and was clearly developed for, the analysis of ritual enactments of social categories and the symbolic marking of social boundaries through collective action; it describes anomaly in a ritual key, anomaly in the realm of "things done" as opposed to "things said." The fourfold typology I have developed lends itself more readily to the analysis of texts and of taxonomic thinking as embedded in verbal (as opposed to ritual or gestural) social discourse.[217]

Although derived solely from the anomaly accounts, my typology also to some extent resembles—and its formulation may have been unconsciously influenced by—the British empiricists' attempts to describe and prescribe modes of thought in terms of "laws of association." The *locus classicus* is Hume's discussion (in *Treatise of Human Nature*) of resemblance, contiguity, and cause and effect as the fundamental modes in which the human mind connects or associates ideas with one another.[218] In somewhat garbled form, these "laws" made their way into comparative studies through the writings of Victorian ethnologists such as E. B. Tylor and J. G. Frazer, who (unlike Hume) took cause and effect to be the true, scientifically verifiable mode of relation and the other two as characterizing pre-scientific thought. Frazer opens his *Golden Bough* with an account of how "sympathetic magic" is subdivided into "homeopathic magic," based on the law of similarity ("like produces like"), and "contagious magic," based on the law of contact ("things which have once been in contact with each other continue to act on each other at a distance after the physical contact has been severed").[219]

The various types of anomaly by location imagined in the anomaly accounts, especially anomalies of degree, also constitute a way of thinking about the nature of categories that is noteworthy in its own right. George Lakoff has identified the three key features of the classical Western view of categories (from Aristotle to Kant and

---

217. Fernandez's analysis of the modes of transformation of metaphors is also very suggestive in this regard (1986, chap. 2).

218. Hume 1888, 10–13.

219. Frazer 1951, 14.

beyond) thus: (1) categories are exercises in abstraction, and are like containers in which particular objects are placed, such that any particular thing is either inside or outside the category; (2) things are in a certain category if and only if they have certain properties; (3) these properties define the category.[220] The twentieth century has seen many revisions of this notion of the category; among them are the concepts of family resemblance, centrality and gradience of traits among category members, and membership gradience or fuzzy sets. Although expressed in the quasi-casuistic form of piecemeal items, the anomaly accounts seem to imply something like this more realistic and nuanced (if less locatively satisfying) understanding of the nature of categories.

The Busiest Boundaries

Finally, if the anomaly accounts are centrally concerned with the boundaries between categories and realms, not every boundary held equal interest for their authors. It takes nothing more sophisticated than a count of how many tales exhibit which motifs and themes to show without the slightest doubt that the authors were overwhelmingly concerned to address two boundaries in particular: that between animals and human beings, and that between humans and spirit beings of all kinds. These are the boundaries that bear by far the heaviest traffic in the texts. The human/animal boundary is most often explored in accounts of hybrids and cross-boundary behavior, secondarily in transformation accounts. The human/spirit boundary is predominantly explored in accounts of cross-boundary contact, secondarily in tales of transformation.

Consider now the following additional facts. First, in the hierarchy of taxa common to most Chinese classification systems and "category books" (*leishu*), traces of which are evident in some anomaly accounts, though probably thanks to Tang and Sung (or later) redactors' hands, and which was becoming firmly established during this same period, these are the two boundaries that separate humankind from its nearest upward and downward neighbors in the system.[221] Furthermore, among animals there is more attention in the texts to the higher forms (primates, simians, mammals) than to the lower, whereas among spirits there is more attention to the borderline and lower ranks (transcendents, local gods, demons,

---

220. Lakoff 1987, 12.
221. Bauer 1965–66; Schafer 1980b; Teiser 1985.

ghosts, active bodhisattvas) than to the higher. Finally, the implied taxonomic "vector," or motion across categories, is significantly imbalanced in each case: in items dealing with the animal/human boundary, there are far more tales of animals who act like (or turn into) humans than there are of humans who act like (or turn into) animals; in items dealing with the human/spirit boundary there are far more tales of spirits who (through whatever means) make contact with humans here on earth than there are of humans who journey downward to the underworld or upward into the heavens.[222]

What do these combined facts tell us about the overall nature and purpose of the genre? One thing is clear: for all their fantastic narrative structure and for all their attention to what seem to most modern readers to be fanciful beings and improbable events, the early anomaly account genre as a whole remains fundamentally humanistic in nature. The overridingly, if not exclusively, important concern addressed in the texts is humankind's place in the cosmos and among the other kinds of beings who inhabit the cosmos above and below us (taxonomically speaking). The texts show relatively slight interest in the nature or workings of the cosmos per se when compared to their great interest in human encounters with other beings. To be sure, the fantastic character of the events and beings described in the texts have led some scholars to emphasize the "cosmological" nature of the genre; "nature, not history," maintains one critic, is their dominant concern.[223] Anomaly accounts certainly show more interest than the dynastic histories in natural and cosmological phenomena, but such characterizations miss the fundamental point that it is the nature of the human being that remains at the center of the genre. And the human "nature" in question is not the "inner" nature (*xing* 性) of intellectual and emotional disposition, nor the structure of the self's ascent toward perfection through self-cultivation, but precisely humankind's *taxonomic*

---

222. However, as regards transformation in one direction or the other the vector remains upward: not surprisingly, given the ancestor cult, the lore of transcendents, etc., people are much more often described as changing "upwards" into spirits than spirits are described as changing "downwards" into people. These hierarchical vectors must also be qualified by reference to the traditional Buddhist system of rebirth, which places humans above hungry ghosts and often above lesser spirits or *asuras* in the five- or six-rung ladder of beings. The actual figures to substantiate the above claims will be made apparent in my forthcoming index.

223. Jones 1987, 8.

place among other kinds of beings, the nature of its *relationships* to other kinds. To paraphrase William James, the axis of concern manifest in the anomaly accounts runs predominantly through human places; "they are strung upon it like so many beads."[224]

---

224. James 1902, 490.

Chapter Seven

Strange Persuasions: Cosmographic Rhetoric

What the world calls "anomalous" it does not know by virtue of what
it is anomalous; what the world calls "non-anomalous" it does not
know by virtue of what it is non-anomalous. How is this so? Things
are not intrinsically anomalous; they wait upon a self and only then
are "anomalous." "Anomalousness" is therefore located in a self; it is
not things themselves that are anomalous.

世之所謂異，未知其所以異，世之所謂不異，未知其所以不異，何者，物不自
異，待我而後異，異果在我，非物異也.

Guo Pu, "Preface to a *Shanhaijing* Commentary"

"Otherness" is not a descriptive category. . . . It is a political and linguistic project, a matter of rhetoric and judgement.

Jonathan Z. Smith[1]

Performers and writers in most cultures have turned to cosmography as a powerful medium of persuasion. Discourse about anomalies can be a winning vehicle for revising or replacing a dominant
worldview, or for exploring the finer implications of one already
largely accepted—and for persuading one's audience of the truth or

---

1. Smith 1985, 46. The Guo Pu epigraph was cited and discussed in
Chapter Three.

worth of one's expressed or implied stance toward it. Things out of place have a way of clarifying people's perception of the taxonomic space they stand out against; characterizing a range of Others can throw readers' views of themselves and of their place in the large scheme of things into sharp relief. But being "out of place" or "other" is a human-made property of phenomena, and in the choices cosmographers make in constructing and representing that so far rather abstract property—in the specific types of language and discourse they use, the specific metaphoric modes and tropes, the techniques they employ for linking or distancing their own from others' texts, the structures of plot and patterns of characterization—there lies a formidable repertoire of rhetorical techniques, strategies of persuasion that shape the text and move the reader of the text in a thousand subtle ways.[2]

In early medieval China, various authors wrote anomaly accounts to various persuasive ends. The genre provided a common arena of contention between proponents of divergent—and sometimes directly competing—perspectives on the nature of the world and humanity's place in it, the relationship between what we would call "religion" and "culture," the scope of the ruler's authority, and the nature of certain taxonomic boundaries. Our task in this chapter is to disclose those perspectives: to see if we can sort the profusion of texts into the relatively small number of cultural and religious persuasions they were arguably designed to advance, as well as to say with as much precision as possible just what those persuasions were, and how authors sought through their texts to render them plausible and compelling.

This task is complex in ways that the adjective "didactic," which students of "literature" often apply to this sort of writing, will never begin to adumbrate. Our texts do not come with sectarian labels attached, nor do most of their authors. Furthermore, whatever it is that authors wanted their readers to conclude from their texts is not always what it appears, is rarely obvious (these are not transparent, Aesop's-fables-like tales with "morals" attached), and so requires analysis to be uncovered—analysis more discriminating than that which many have applied, since it must include sensitivity to the full range of ways in which the texts carry meaning, as well as familiarity with the historical trajectories and

---

2. Highly polemical, suasively overdetermined representations of anomalies—that is, "miracle tales"—take on particular importance in situations involving intense inter-religious or sectarian conflict, which obtained not only in China during these centuries and beyond (see Verellen 1992) but also, for example, in the early centuries of the Christian tradition (Remus 1983; Kee 1983) as well as in the Reformation era (Soergel 1993).

the range of options within as well as between the dominant religious and ideological traditions of the era.[3] All previous attempts of
which I am aware to come to grips with this task have proceeded in
one of four ways, none of which I regard as satisfactory: (1) by simply separating off the obviously pro-Buddhist sectarian texts from
the rest, and mentioning in the latter texts only a few themes, such
as afterlife and debates over the real existence of spirits of the
dead;[4] (2) by repeating the procedure in (1), only adding a "Daoist"
category and (often) including under "Buddhist" any texts that deal
with moral reciprocity, since this theme is conceived to be a version
of "karma" and therefore makes the texts in question "Buddhist"
texts (which here becomes a large category);[5] (3) avoiding sectarian
labels, except for obviously sectarian texts such as the pro-Buddhist
miracle tale collections and the two most often studied pro-Daoist
hagiographies, while proceeding to classify all others as "syncretic"
(typically in this approach the largest category), which is to say
miscellaneous (which is to abandon the attempt to identify any
more specific persuasive intent), often while adding a "content
analysis" that ignores the persuasive ends for which these texts
were written, and merely categorizes their subject matter;[6] or (4) by

---

3. This sort of familiarity (not to speak of thorough knowledge) has
only become possible in the last twenty years or less, as our understanding
of the Daoist tradition, in particular, has been deepened by the labors of
scholars in that field.

4. As in Takeda 1992, 98–123.

5. This is presumably the rationale behind the inclusion of Sshj,
Yml, Yy, Jlz, XuQxj, and Yhz in the "Buddhist" category in Yan Maoyuan
1940. What rationale might have informed his inclusion of Syj in this category is a mystery. So far as I am able to discern his views on the subject
through his laconic treatment, Lu Xun seems also to have inclined to this
approach, using the label "Buddhist" to include obviously sectarian, pro-
Buddhist texts, and "Daoist" for just about everything else. DeWoskin at
points tends in this direction (e.g., 1977b, 50); at times he has more provocative, but unfortunately not well founded, speculations (e.g., 1977b, 37,
"anti-establishment bias"), but mostly he is distracted from the question of
rhetorical persuasion by his attempt—which I have argued is misguided—
to demonstrate "conscious fictionalizing" (1977b, 49).

6. Variations of this approach occur in Yan Maoyuan 1940, whose
"Daoist" category oddly includes Bwz, Qxj, and Shuyj, and who at least
names his third category something more specific than "miscellaneous"
(viz. "yin-yang and five phases," a heading that would include all of his
"Daoist" and some of his "Buddhist" texts as well); Foster 1974, chap. 2,
whose "syncretic" category includes 37 of the 45 texts he deals with; Wang
Guoliang (the scholar most inclined toward "content analysis") 1978, 27–
30; 1984, 119–291; 1988, 14–34; and Kao 1985, 16–21.

splitting the entire genre into two camps, works by "literate *fang-shi*" and by "*fangshi*-influenced literati," an approach favored by those who, as discussed in Chapter Four, explain the genre as the attempt by masters of esoterica to legitimate their skills and worldview.[7]

A fresh approach is called for, one that (1) attends to the rhetorical subtleties of the texts, (2) takes them seriously as attempts to shape readers' views of the world, and does not dismiss them as "fiction" or as "disinterested" historiographic exercises[8] (is any writing "disinterested"?), (3) works with a palette of perspectives more variegated than the "explicitly sectarian-religious/other" scheme presupposed by all of the above approaches, and hence one that matches more closely the richness and complexity of religious, cosmological, and moral thinking in the period, and (4) one that, even in the case of clearly sectarian texts, goes beyond getting them in the correct pigeonhole, toward specifying more clearly just *how* they urge perspectives that are "Buddhist" or "Daoist," and just what, for their authors, those perspectives entailed. Saying that a work "is Buddhist" or "is Daoist" is where interpretation should begin, not stop. Put succinctly, what we want to know is this: what does each text, and each group of texts sharing similar rhetorical aims, suggest the world and humanity's place in it to be? What are the implied worldviews and values that the authors, through their texts, strove to render plausible? And what strategies of persuasion are deployed toward those ends?

One caveat is necessary. Since I proceed by comparing item with item, text with text, and (finally) perspective with perspective, texts from which only a small handful of items survives are difficult and risky to interpret. I have abandoned the quest to fit every text into the analysis, opting instead for a reading of the lay of the generic land that accounts for the texts that are of significant size but does so in a newly detailed, documented way.

The Early Medieval Grain of Thought: A Digression

In the following analysis, I seek not only to disclose the perspectives implied in particular groups of texts, but also to situate these

---

7. Wang Yao 1951; Fan Ning 1957.
8. Thus Kao 1985, 20.

within the larger grain of early medieval thought within which authors worked—something of which I cannot here attempt even a summary, but about which it is necessary to make two points that bear directly on the task at hand.

First, in the foreground of thought during these centuries were, of course, the explicit "isms": sectarian traditions which, precisely during this period and largely due to the pressure toward self-definition brought by the importation of a foreign, complex religion, came to be increasingly self-conscious stances within the larger culture. For all their bluntness (especially when reified as monolithic agents, and when conceived of on the model of Protestant Christian denominations) as tools of historical understanding, and for all the fuzziness and porousness of the boundaries between them, the cluster of Chinese terms translatable as "Daoist," "Buddhist," and "Confucian" *meant* something to contemporaries; however much common ground existed between them, each of these cultural identities was *marked* as distinctive in certain ways. Proponents of each stance were clearly engaged in a constant struggle for cultural authority, measured in ways as tangible as favored positions at court[9] and the imperial sponsoring—or else the imperially mandated destruction—of local religious establishments. Even local shrines to figures including Confucian-style worthies could be targeted for destruction, as they were under the Daoism-influenced Later Han Emperor Huan in the mid-second century and also under the Wei,[10] but Buddhist monasteries and Daoist abbeys and their residents were more frequent targets for secularization if not outright destruction—the earliest anti-Buddhist persecution occurring in the mid-third century in the Wu state.[11] Buddhists in particular, due to the foreign provenance of their religion, had to

---

9. As perhaps the paramount Daoist case, one thinks of Kou Qianzhi and the Northern Wei, on which Mather 1979; as perhaps the paramount Buddhist case, one thinks of the Liang Emperor Wu's heavy sponsorship of the sangha and suppression of Daoism, on which Strickmann 1978 (but cf. Strickmann 1979 for examples of simultaneous if limited sponsorship of Daoist pursuits); Ch'en 1973, 10–11. In general, I have benefited from the following works (in addition to the others cited elsewhere): Hurvitz and Link 1974; Robinet 1984, 1985–86; Strickmann 1977; Mather 1992.

10. de Crespigny 1980; Tsukamoto 1985, 119–23.

11. On the Wu persecution, part of a general campaign against "impure cults," Zürcher 1972, 52; Tsukamoto 1985, 156–59. For an example of the suppression of Daoism—which, to my knowledge, was rarer during these centuries—Strickmann 1978.

struggle to win a hearing for their views;[12] the historical record suggests that only beginning ca. 300 C.E. did Buddhism begin to win serious consideration as a worldview on the part of Chinese literati, and that even in 400, its serious practice by Chinese (as opposed to resident foreign monks) was a very recent phenomenon.[13] From 340 onward there was periodic debate, carried out at court and through correspondence, over the exemption of members of the sangha from the duty to pay gestural homage to the ruler—a symbolic focal point for the larger issue of the extent to which the sangha was to remain a largely autonomous body.[14] One fear on the part of the ruling classes that doubtless underlay all of these debates was of the mass movements that broke out regularly during these centuries (beginning even before the Daoist movements of 189), of a sort unprecedented in China, fomented by the eschatological, utopian elements of Buddhist and Daoist preaching and piety.[15] These sectarian clashes on the levels of both ideology and social institutions must be borne in mind as we consider the persuasive ends to which the anomaly accounts were written, for much was at stake in the outcome of those clashes.

Second, beneath these highly visible sectarian struggles was a deeper current of thought and discourse, summed up in the opposition between "conformity" or "the moral teaching" (*mingjiao* 名教, literally "the teaching of names") and "naturalism" or "naturalness" (*ziran* 自然).[16] And this opposition is a classic case of the tension between locative and anti-locative worldviews, respectively, as discussed in Chapter One. At its most fundamental, the issue was this: is humanity's place in the world paramount, central, necessary, and cosmically ordained, such that the structures of human knowledge and society correspond necessarily to structures in the world out there (the *mingjiao* position)? Or is it relatively paltry,

---

12. Important studies of Buddhist exegesis and apologetic include (aside from those cited above and below) Pelliot 1920; Ch'en 1952, 1973; Liebenthal 1952; Hurvitz 1957; Link 1961; Link and Lee 1966; Schmidt-Glinzer 1976.

13. Zürcher 1972, 72–73.

14. Hurvitz 1957; Zürcher 1972, 106–10, 160–63, 214, 259ff.; Ch'en 1973, 69–77; Michihata 1980; Tsukamoto 1985, 823–44.

15. Eichhorn 1954; Levy 1956; Michaud 1958; Seidel 1969–70; Sunayama 1975; Overmyer 1976, 73–75, 80–83; Zürcher 1982; Crowell 1983; Lewis 1990b.

16. The best general discussions include Fung 1952–53, 133–292; Mather 1969–70; Hsiao 1979, 484–674; Henricks 1983; Spiro 1990.

marginal, accidental, and a merely human conceit, such that the structures of human knowledge and society, cut loose from their moorings in objective reality, become subject to adjudication on more pragmatic grounds (the *ziran* position)? Each side in this debate had its venerable textual authorities: partisans of the moral teaching could point to both classical and Han-period Confucian texts, while proponents of naturalism cited Laozi and Zhuangzi as their main authorities.[17] But, once again, this perennial issue from the Han to the Tang was no mere scholastic concern. Positions taken on it set the tone for state policies: the Cao clan of the Wei favored naturalism, since its metaphysics of "the obscure" (*xuan* 玄) and its epistemology of relativism and ineffability cleared the way for a pragmatist, absolutist regime, allowing government to bypass Han traditions, and to assume greater central control of appointments to office; the Sima clan of the Jin favored the moral teaching which, associated with Confucian and Han traditionalism, allowed them to tap discontent among the elite over the policies of the Wei. And closely bound up with this tension between conformity and naturalness was that between the obligation to serve the state— that is, the obligation of loyalty (*zhong* 忠), next to filiality the most fundamental of Confucian virtues—and the posture of "reclusion," immensely popular in some circles from the third century on, and imaged most famously by the free-spirited "seven sages of the bamboo grove."[18] The tensions between conformity/official service, on the one hand, and naturalism/reclusion on the other, cut across the religious-sectarian divisions discussed above; Buddhism, Daoism, and even Confucianism each had their *mingjiao* and their *ziran* aspects, their activist and eremetic wings.[19]

---

17. The writings attributed to Laozi and—especially—to Zhuangzi enjoyed a renaissance, beginning in the third century, after a period of relative neglect: Arendrup 1974; Robinet 1981; Knaul 1985a, 1985b; Chan 1991. The contrast between locative and anti-locative views shows up especially clearly in the wide disparity between competing interpretations of the *Daodejing*, ranging from views of it as a locative mapping of bodily functions and cultivational techniques, as in the *Xiang'er* commentary (Qing Xitai 1988, 146–91; Rao Zongyi 1991), to views of it as the expression par excellence of *xuanxue* anti-locativism, as in the Wang Bi commentary.

18. This is, of course, a huge topic in its own right; the reader who wishes to pursue it may consult, *inter alia*, Holzman 1956, 1957, 1976; Li 1963 (not terribly useful); Balazs 1964; Mather 1983, 1985, 1988; Bauer 1985; Holcombe 1989, 1992; Pearson 1989; Spiro 1990, an especially admirable work; Berkowitz 1991; Yu Yingshi 1985.

19. As noted in the Buddhist case in Zürcher 1972, 136–37.

These tensions, too, of which a fuller discussion is not possible here, must be kept in mind as we return to the anomaly accounts, for we will see that those texts play upon them in complex, subtle ways.

The *Fangshi* Perspective: Knowledge and Mastery

This is the earliest attested perspective in anomaly accounts. Texts advancing it include the Shj, the Shenyjing, the Xuanzj, and the Bwz; tentatively (since so little of these texts survives), I also include in this group the *Yu benji*, Guiz, Gdt, *Shi Kuang* and Skz, Bzt, *Jiudingji*, *Yi Yin shuo*, and *Huang Di shuo*.

The fundamental trope of texts urging the *fangshi* perspective is the display of knowledge of the periphery and the demonstration of mastery of esoteric skills. This display and demonstration—which are tacit, rarely explicit (at least in the earlier texts) claims to power and authority—are primarily accomplished on a horizontal grid of space and time. That is to say, the main metaphoric or symbolic register of power in these texts[20] is not ascension but rather outward movement from the center toward things undreamt of there—spatially, knowledge of the periphery; temporally, knowledge of both future and distant past events.

Geographically organized texts display the *fangshi*'s knowledge of anomalous, peripheral places and beings on a spatial grid. These texts include the Shj, Shenyjing, Gdt, and probably also the *Yu benji*. The geographical schemata of the Shj and the Shenyjing were summarized in Chapter Two; here, it is only necessary to comment on the rhetorical strategies used in this group of texts. Since the Shj is better known and available in translation, and since the *Yu benji* survives in only one quotation, I will focus for a moment on the Shenyjing; much of what is said here also applies to the Gdt insofar as it is known to us.

The implied author[21] of the Shenyjing (and, for that matter, of the Gdt and much of the Shj) writes as a *direct* reporter of phe-

---

20. My thinking on which notions has been shaped especially by Lakoff and Johnson 1980.

21. On the notions of implied author and implied reader, Chatman 1978. My approach to the texts in this chapter and in Chapter Five, in particular, is greatly indebted to Chatman and could certainly stand to pay even closer attention to his distinctions and terminology.

nomena that are extremely—in some cases, indeed, cosmically—distant. He is a "direct" reporter in that he cites no intermediate sources of his knowledge—no texts, for he does not write as an ordinary sort of scholar or historian, and no teachers, for he does not write as a member of any explicit filiation of teaching. The text reads almost as if he knew of the matters related in it from personal experience; the implied author shows no sceptical distance from his material but instead relates it with a sense of immediacy. This directness of voice creates an aura of authorial mastery, which is enhanced above all by the *inaccessibility* of the places described. The text is a display, in this ordinary part of the world, of things extraordinary to it and fantastically distant from it—the rare, the esoteric, the scarcely obtainable yet (on that account as well as for their intrinsic properties) immensely valuable.

The prestige of the distant and the extraordinary—and hence the prestige of the author-specialist who displays his knowledge of them—is further enhanced by the geographical, cultural, and moral decentering accomplished in the text. At the center of the implied cosmology of the Shenyjing is not the Central Kingdom—indeed, its familiar mountains and rivers are not even mentioned—but Mt. Kunlun.[22] In view of the cosmic vistas and gigantic proportions unrolled in the text, the familiar geography of the nine provinces all but disappears, paltry in comparison to the majestic palaces at Kunlun and at the far-flung corners of the cosmos.[23] Furthermore, the text mentions a tribe of giants in the extreme southwest who know the properties of all mountains and minerals, birds and

---

22. Kunlun and its wonders seem to have bulked large in the Gdt as well; several of the surviving items concern Kunlun and Zhongshan and their environs.

23. And there is an implied mythico-ritual scenario of hierogamy in the text, with its structuring around the east-west (but the "west" as cosmic center) polarity of Xiwangmu and Dongwanggong (on which Kominami 1984, 13–94; Loewe 1979; Fracasso 1988; Smith 1992), its "jade lads" and "jade maidens" who dwell at Kunlun, and the nomenclature of the palaces that stand at the extreme quarters of the world—all but the northeast and southwest corners, that is, which are occupied by gates. In addition there is a statement in the description of Kunlun that "the jade lads and jade maidens of the nine bureaus become dormant [only] when Heaven and Earth do; they do not pair and mate as male and female, yet they achieve the way of transcendence by themselves" (C2; ZDHW 13b; Zhou Ciji 1986, 67). This comment rather strongly suggests Daoist attitudes toward the role of sexuality in the quest for transcendence and perfection (found, for instance, in the *Xiang'er* commentary to the *Laozi* and some Shangqing writings).

beasts, who know the speech of animals and the ways of all human beings. The variant names of this tribe are "Sage" (*sheng* 聖), "Wise" (*zhe* 哲), "Worthy" (*xian* 賢), and "All-Comprehending" (*wubuda* 無不達). "Whoever sees them and does obeisance to them will be granted the intelligence of gods; such a person will become a sage to all the world."[24] A fragment dropped from the common version of the text describes a people in the extreme west in equally utopian terms:

> In the western barrens there is a people who, although they do not read the five classics, think in their terms; although they do not observe the patterns of Heaven, their minds are in touch with them; although they do not recite the rites and ordinances, their spirits match them. Heaven grants them their clothing. . . .[25]

The notions that sagehood was obtainable by bowing to a foreign people and that foreigners were naturally equipped with the moral and cultural training most highly prized in China—deployed here as decentering devices, much as they are in the *Zhuangzi* and the *Liezi*—would have struck the more conservative among contemporary readers as outlandish.

By all of these devices the text of the Shenyjing constitutes a tacit but clear claim to cultural power based on knowledge of the secrets of the inaccessible, yet value-drenched, periphery. But no explicit apologetic is in evidence. Terms for religious specialists— "earth-transcendent" (*dixian* 地仙) and "transcendent" (*xian*)—are used only occasionally and in passing, and the text narrates no interactions between rulers and *fangshi* that might model how the former are to treat the latter.[26]

Much the same may be said of the rhetorical strategies deployed in predominantly apotropaic texts, particularly the Bzt; they, too, display the implied author's mastery of horizontally peripheral beings—only here, the beings do not live on cosmically distant mountains but in places that, while removed from ordinary life, are much nearer to hand. If the Shj and Shenyjing chart the numinous barrens on a macrocosmic scale, the Bzt seems to have presented a microcosmic demonography—and garbology. For some

---

24. SW 1 (ZDHW ed. 7b; Zhou Ciji 1986, 35).

25. Zhou Ciji 1986, 75, fragment 4; based on TPYL 685.4a. The item continues by briefly describing the attire worn by the men and women of this race.

26. E5 (ZDHW 2a; Zhou Ciji 1986, 12) mentions that one becomes a *dixian* upon eating the fruit of the *li* tree; C1 (ZDHW 13a–b; Zhou Ciji 1986, 66–67) mentions "nine bureaus of transcendent persons" 仙人九府.

of its demons are waste-dump denizens, infesting the old, discarded places among humans—old gates and houses, old towers and wells, old ponds, markets, and grave mounds; others simply dwell in wood, water, fire, jade, and, of course, mountains.

Texts recording successful or noteworthy divinations—primarily the Skz and Guiz, possibly also the three texts in Ban Gu's list discussed in Chapter Two (*Yi Yin shuo, Shi Kuang,* and *Huang Di shuo*)—employ essentially the same strategy, only in the temporal mode: the implied author reveals his seemingly direct knowledge of the prognosticatory import of certain events, thus demonstrating his knowledge of distant—here, temporally distant—phenomena, as in the Skz; or else he documents the reliance on divination of well known figures of ancient history and legend, as in the Guiz. The Skz also records instances in which the Yellow Thearch asks Shi Kuang about future events or other esoteric topics; and Shi Kuang himself is depicted as asking a question of a figure called simply "the Celestial Elder" (天老).[27]

The Xuanzj, like the Shenyjing and the Bwz, lists peripheral marvels in direct (but not first-person) speech. It displays a list of strange phenomena that stand distant from the court center in both space (the wonders of various outlying mountains and peoples) and time (fragments of mythological knowledge set in the archaic past). It also displays its author's demonological knowledge by recounting the properties of marvelous creatures such as mountain spirits and "water pigs," as well as what extremely aged things metamorphose into. The Xuanzj, like other texts of this persuasion, thus implicitly represents the author-*fangshi* as one who knows the world's secrets and could, if requested, set forth more than are recorded in this open-ended list.

Written in what I believe were the latter days of the *fangshi* tradition as a separate cultural stance (as distinct from a sheer historiographic convention)—shortly before its final absorption into the Daoist religion—Zhang Hua's Bwz amounted to a sort of summation of the *fangshi* perspective, even as it reflected new, third-century currents of thought in its sharper apologetic edge and its incorporation of themes that appear to us in hindsight as Daoist.

Let us first recall that Zhang Hua himself was noted as a *fangshi* practitioner who achieved high position in the Western Jin court. Quite a few tales depict him as knowledgeable of all sorts of

27. Bwz 5.9 (Fan Ning 1980, item 186) has the Yellow Thearch asking a question of the same figure regarding why certain natural substances induce longevity in those who eat them.

products and creatures from remote regions, and as a diviner and exorcist. He is often represented as serving the same function during the Jin that Dongfang Shuo served in the Han court, that of explainer of anomalies, only—and the difference is crucial—without the strong trickster-like character shown by Shuo. I here summarize these tales, roughly grouped by theme.

Items involving Zhang Hua as a Character (Zhang Hua abbreviated as ZH)

His knowledge of unusual and/or distant flora, fauna, and minerals

(a) ZH bursts into tears upon recognizing the meat served at a banquet given by Lu Ji as dragon flesh (Yy 3.33).

(b) ZH identifies a tree that flourishes and withers on alternating sides in alternating years as a "Mutual Concession Tree" (ShuyjRf 1.105 [18a]).

(c) ZH identifies on sight a type of rock from Yuzhang that turns hot when bathed in water (Jlz 16).

(d) ZH uses plant products from distant lands and peoples to make "nine-brewed wine" (Syj 9.3b).

His knowledge of subterranean and remote realms

(a) On request, ZH interprets the six month cave-journey accidentally undertaken by an ordinary man who fell into a deep cave north of Mount Songgao (the Central Marchmount): ZH explains that what the man visited was a Transcendents' Hall, what he drank was Jade Liquor, and what he ate was Dragon Cave Stone Marrow (Sshj 1.2, Yml 64, Xs 118).

(b) A man pushed into a deep cave by his wife survives the fall and discovers a subterranean world consisting (among other things) of nine interlinked palaces inhabited by giants who wear feathery garments and pluck otherworldly tunes. In the last palace, famished, he is told to stroke the beard of a goat under a cypress tree; in doing so he obtains three pearls, the first two of which are confiscated by one of the giants, the last of which he is instructed to consume to satisfy his hunger. Asking the names of the palaces, he is told that his destiny does not permit him to stay there but, upon returning, he should ask ZH, who will know where he has been. Years later, he interviews ZH, who explains that one sort of dust he brought back was dragon saliva from beneath the Yellow River, that another was mud from beneath Mount Kunlun, that the nine palaces were the offices of earth-transcendents (*dixian* 地仙), and that the "goat" was the Fool-Dragon; the first pearl he obtained would, if consumed, have brought him longevity equal to that of Heaven and Earth, while the second would have lengthened his lifespan significantly. The pearl he was given to eat was good only for satiating hunger (Yml 63[28]).

(c) ZH is shown maps and pictures of the land and strange products of the distant realm of Pinsi; he says that the country is "divine and marvelous" (*shenyi*) and that its marvels cannot be verified (implying he has no knowledge of this distant realm— nothing against which to check these foreign envoys' reports) (Syj 9.6b).

His skills as diviner of future events and as interpreter of portents

(a) ZH is asked to interpret natural "responses" to distant stimuli, and does so successfully (Yy 2.1–4; cf. Xs 114, 115, 117).

(b) ZH is asked about the meaning of obscure writing on a bamboo strip found on Mount Songgao. He in turn asks a *boshi* about it, and thus identifies it (Yy 2.5).

(c) Someone obtains an extremely long feather and shows it to ZH; he sighs, identifies the type of bird that is its source, and says that its appearance portends landslides. Subsequent events prove him correct (Yy 4.17).

(d) Although said to be expert at hexagram divination, ZH is outwitted by a thief who, scheduled for execution, is granted tempo-rary leave to bid his parents farewell; the convict follows the advice of one Zhao Shuo, who prescribes a set of actions designed to thwart ZH's ability to locate him by divination (Ssj8 4.5).[29]

His knowledge of spirits and exorcistic techniques

(a) ZH recognizes an elegant and knowledgeable "student" to be an ancient fox spirit in disguise; he unmasks and destroys it in the light of a tree that had been impregnated with another ancient

---

28. Tr. in Foster 1974, 37–38.

29. I interpret the main point of this item to be not the inadequacy of Zhang's skills but the amazing skill of the other party—he is so skilled he can beat out even Zhang Hua.

spirit, commenting that if these creatures had not run into him they would not have met their match for another millennium (Ssj 18.9,[30] XuQxj 5, Ssj8 4.1).

(b) A pair of pheasants suddenly appears inside a tightly enclosed military storehouse; ZH says they must be transformed snakes. A search of the storehouse turns up two shed snakeskins (Yy 3.42, Xs 116).

His cosmographic collecting activities

(a) ZH presents his Bwz to the ruler, who requests that he trim its size and downplay its anomalous content, then rewards him with scholars' implements imported from distant lands (Syj 9.7a–b; this item was translated in Chapter Three).

(b) ZH comes into possession of one of the magical swords commissioned in ancient times by the king of Wu (Syj 10.8b).[31]

Divine, cosmic, and natural recognitions of his special status

(a) A military commander is upbraided and threatened by a spirit-official for submitting a memorial recommending ZH's execution (Ssj 9.12).

(b) Anecdotes about ZH's conversations and dealings with his pet parrot, showing his rapport with the bird and his knowledge of how to win its release by a bird of prey (Yy 3.3, Xs 119).

(c) An omen precedes ZH's death (Yml 65).[32]

Like other texts advancing the *fangshi* perspective, the Bwz embodies a horizontal mode of cultural power based on knowledge of the geographic, ethnic, cultural, and technical periphery. Its displays of knowledge of arcane matters cover foreign lands and peoples and their products,[33] little known macrobiotic techniques

---

30. This version is tr. in Kao 1985, 101–3.

31. These are the swords Gan Jiang and Mo Ye; this legend, which appears in other anomaly accounts, is briefly discussed in Chapter Four.

32. He shows up in a few other contexts; e.g., in Ssj 1.31 his "Rhapsody on a Divine Woman" (*Shennüfu*) is cited; Xs 86 quotes from the Sxy his witty comment on a certain social relationship.

33. There are sections on tribes of the five directions (1.34–42), local products (1.43–48), foreign countries (2.1–12), anomalous peoples (2.13–26), the unusual customs of distant lands (2.27–34), marvelous products as tribute (2.35–39).

and the names and properties of rare medicinal substances,[34] the names and appearances of anomalous flora and fauna,[35] and a series of "corrections" (*gai* 改) to names and terms in canonical texts and "supplements" (*bu* 補) to received historical accounts.[36] All of these topics allow for demonstration of the author's mastery of esoterica; the last-mentioned category is particularly bold in venturing to expand and correct even the five classics and the histories. These items imply a certain authorial stance: the *fangshi*-author has access to independent sources of information, beyond the pale of—yet applicable to—more canonical versions of the past.

The text shows a systematizing, correlative bent; some items subsume phenomena under the five phases, and attention is paid to categorizing things according to their diverse, inborn natures. Chapter Seven of the text comprises twenty-four narratives, most of which illustrate the responsiveness (*ying* 應) of the cosmos to human stimuli (*gan* 感) or, conversely, people's responses to the anomalous stimuli generated by the vibrant cosmos. These strands of the sort of correlative cosmological thinking that originated in the pre-Han period, however, do not amount to a full-blown centrist argument for the all-pervasive power of the emperor and his court, since it is now the *fangshi*-author, not the ruler directly, who wields the knowledge of the periphery needed to subsume it under centripetal order.

The authorial voice in the Bwz is sometimes direct and authoritative in the ways described above; but sometimes it is tempered by the citation of textual sources. The "Zhang Hua" implied in the text combines the personae of ("direct") master of esoterica, one confident in his personal knowledge of distant phenomena and his competence in marvelous skills, and ("indirect") historian of anomalies, one who transmits things found in old texts or, in a few cases, gathered from local speech—and is therefore less confident. For all the legends of his marvelous exploits, his text portrays Zhang Hua as somewhat distanced from the tradition he claims to represent.

In striking contrast to earlier texts promoting the *fangshi* perspective, however, the Bwz is more explicitly apologetic, seeming to anticipate the reader's scepticism and quickly offering antidotes, reporting cases in which masters' esoteric skills were tested and

---

34. 4.29–54, 5.10–14.

35. 3.1–31. As in other texts of the *fangshi* persuasion, emphasis is on the uses to which they may be put by people.

36. 6.1–47.

proved effective. Here are summaries of the most notable examples of this rhetorical strategy, with my interpretive comments placed in braces { }.

5.1/178   Emperor Wu of Wei, fond of methods for nourishing life and rather knowledgable of esoteric drugs, summoned *fangshi* from all over the realm. {Zhou Riyong's commentary adds, based on other sources, that he did so in order to test their powers.}

5.2/179   The names of sixteen *fangshi* who responded to this summons from the Wei court are listed, along with their unusual abilities: all eschewed cereals,[37] could divide and conceal their bodies, and could enter and leave enclosed areas without using doors; Zuo Ci exhibited still other abilities.

5.3/180   Another description of the abilities of the most notable *fangshi* collected at the Wei court.

5.4/181   The adept Feng Junda set forth his essential methods; Emperor Wu of Wei tried some of them and got good results.

5.5/182   Quotation of a first-person account by Cao Zhi, in his "Disputations of the Way" (*Biandaolun* 辯道論), of his initial scepticism concerning esoteric arts and the trials to which the adepts gathered at court were subjected. The adept Chi Jian was denied cereals for one hundred days but remained in excellent health; Gan Shi was very old but had the face of a youth.

5.6/183   During the reign of Emperor Ming of Wei, the adept Jiao Sheng was summoned and his abilities tested by a governor; his abilities were all confirmed as real (皆有實事).

5.7/184   Chen Yuanfang and Han Yuanchang, among the most talented men of their era, both believed in the reality of transcendents because of a story one of their fathers told of watching as an adept named Cheng Gong, after announcing that "I have attained transcendence," gradually ascended into the sky until he was out of sight.

5.8/185   Citation of an account in Huan Tan's *Xinlun* of Dong Zhongshu's (?) feigning death in prison, then returning to life after his burial (i.e., his achievement of liberation from the corpse).

5.9/186   An explanation of why it is reasonable to believe that certain herbs induce longevity, relayed in the context of a dialogue between the Yellow Thearch and the Celestial Elder.

5.15/192   Although Liu An, the Han Prince of Huainan, is said to have been executed for plotting rebellion, there is also a legend that he achieved the Way.

---

37. A prominent feat of Daoist adepts as well, not surprisingly given Daoist teachings on the harms of eating grains (Lévi 1983).

5.16/193   Although Consort Gou Yi was killed at Yunyang, it is said that she attained corpse-liberation and that her coffin was opened and found empty. {Though rulers may execute skilled adepts, adepts' esoteric skills enable them to transcend this ultimate form of central control.}

5.17/194   Quotation from the *Dianlun* by Emperor Wen of the Wei concerning the esoteric abilities of various *fangshi*.

5.18/195   More of the same, including the statement that [Wei] Emperor Wu personally tried some of the drugs in question.

5.19/196   The remarkable abilities of Liu Gen and Wang Zhongdu are described.

5.20/197   Doubts on the part of Sima Qian, Yang Xiong, and Huan Tan concerning the possibility of transcendence are recorded. {Probably part of this item has dropped out and some statement of refutation followed.}

8.10/275   Confucius is stumped trying to adjudicate between two differing explanations—offered by boys—of the sun's apparent motion across the sky. {Lacking the knowledge a proper *fangshi* would surely be able to bring to the subject, he is unable to decide the matter.}

8.17/282   Marquis Wen of Wei, having heard about a mountain-dwelling man who, caught in the fires set by a large hunting expedition, seemed quite unperturbed by the smoke and flames, asks Zixia (Confucius' disciple) about it. Zixia replies: "According to what I heard from the Master, one who harmonizes with things cannot be harmed by things. For this sort of man, to sojourn in metal or rock or tread through water or fire are all possible." When asked by the Marquis whether he, Zixia, could do this, Zixia gives an evasive answer that suggests that although he could do it, he has not, preferring to increase his knowledge. When asked whether his Master (Confucius) could do it, Zixia replied that he, too, was capable of doing it, yet never did. "The Marquis was not pleased." {There are levels of mastery higher than those obtained by Confucius and his followers, accessible through esoteric arts.}

8.23/288   Embedded in a relatively lengthy narrative of the visitation by the Queen Mother of the West to Han Emperor Wu is a scene in which she catches Dongfang Shuo peering in at them and says to the ruler, "This little boy peeking through the window has come and stolen my peaches three times." "The Emperor thought this very strange. From this time on, people called Shuo a divine transcendent." {The reality of Shuo's claims to cosmic travel are "confirmed" by the Queen Mother's independent testimony.}

8.24/289   Dongfang Shuo demonstrates his knowledge of the periphery by instantly recognizing the immortality-inducing wine procured at great length from atop Mt. Wubao. {He also demonstrates his autonomy by gulping the wine down himself, thus denying the ruler its benefits.}

9.11/300   Auspicious omens were frequent during the Han, culminating in the reign of Emperor Wu; under Wang Mang the commanderies and kingdoms also reported many auspicious omens, but this was due to their desire for a stable rule and their flattery, and many were unfounded, causing people to begin mistrusting omens. {The implication is that auspicious omens are real but only appear when conditions warrant; false cases are due to human error and do not invalidate the reality of omens.}

9.14/303   A list of accurate divinations involving famous, ancient rulers. {Readers could be presumed to know from history that the predictions proved accurate.}

In the considerable overlap between Bwz items on adepts and Daoist hagiographies (see table below), we see evidence of the process of absorption of *fangshu* traditions into a "Daoism" increasingly conscious of itself as a distinct, alternative cultural and religious tradition. There are three important differences, however, between Zhang Hua's uses of this material and the uses made of it by Daoist hagiographers. First, the theme of *autonomy*—the adept's utter freedom from, if not superiority over, the ruler's power and influence—is, although detectable, quite muted in the Bwz when compared with its prominence in the Daoist texts, a point to which I will return below.[38] Second, we will shortly see that the hagiographies play largely upon the vertical mode of *ascension*; while this mode is also evident in the Bwz, the same adepts are there presented under the rubric of *fangshi*, and the whole metaphoric structure of the *fang* is built around a horizontal mode of contrast between center and periphery. Third, although these figures clearly served Zhang Hua as exemplars of the perspective he sought to promote, he would probably not have identified that perspective as "Daoist" in any sectarian or filiational sense; I suggest that he was appropriating these adepts as exemplary masters of esoteric techniques, whereas the Daoist hagiographers appropriated them as links in the chain of filiation constituting a tradition dedicated to transcending the world. Zhang Hua's transcendents and Ge Hong's

---

38. Certain items in the Bwz do, however, suggest a political ideology of *wuwei*-like, limited state power: 7.10, 9.2, 9.3, 9.6. This is in line with the change of political climate between the authoritarian Wei and the (in name at least) more traditionally Confucian Jin.

transcendents are arrayed as exemplars of two different, if increasingly convergent, cultural traditions.[39]

Adepts in the Bwz vis-à-vis Daoist Hagiographies and the HHS *Fangshu liezhuan*

Bwz Location[40]		Location in Daoist Hagiographies (and HHS)
5.1/178	etc.[41] Zuo Ci 左慈	Sxz 27; HHS 82B (2747)
5.2/179	Wang Zhen 王真	Sxz 84; HHS 82B (2750)
„	Lu Nüsheng 魯女生	Sxz 90
„	Hua Tuo 華佗	HHS 82B (2736)
„	Zhang Diao 張貂	HHS 82B (2749)
„	Leng Shouguang 冷壽光	Sxz 78 Ling 靈 Shouguang; HHS 82B (2740) Leng Shouguang
„	Ji Zixun 薊子訓	Sxz 29; HHS 82B (2745)
„	Fei Changfang 費長房	Sxz 28; HHS 82B (2743)
„	Xian Nugu 鮮奴辜	HHS 82B (2749) Jie 解 Nugu
„	Chi Jian 郗儉 (*zi* Mengjie 孟節)	HHS 82B (2750) Hao 郝 Mengjie
5.4/181	Feng Junda 封君達	Sxz 92; HHS 82B (2750)
5.6/183	Jiao Sheng 焦生	Sxz 33 Jiao Xian 先[42]
5.7/184	Cheng Gong 成公	Sxz 61 Cheng Xian 仙 gong; HHS 82B (2748) Shang 上 Chenggong

---

39. Note too that several figures—including the healer Hua Tuo, of whom much is made in the Bwz and the HHS—are not to be found in the Sxz.

40. Bwz passages are here, as in the list above, cited by fascicle and item number in the ZDHW ed. and (after stroke /) by item number in Fan Ning 1980. Variations in the names of adepts are indicated; this type of variation is extremely common in hagiographic literature (particularly Daoist) of the period. Sixteen adepts who were summoned to the Wei court are listed in Bwz 5.2/179, but very little in the way of narrative is given on most of them, and in cases where the same figure appears in more detail in a subsequent Bwz item, I list only that occurrence. In all cases these figures receive much more thorough hagiographies in the Sxz.

41. Zuo Ci (*zi* Yuanfang 元放) is the most often mentioned *fangshi* in the Bwz, figuring in the following items: 5.1, 5.2, 5.3, 5.5, 5.10, 5.17, 5.18.

42. DeWoskin 1981, 89, says he also shows up in SGZ 56 but so far I have not located the passage.

5.15/192	Liu An 劉安	Sxz 20[43]
5.16/193	Consort Gou Yi 鉤弋	Lxz 43 Consort Gou Yi 翼[44]
5.18/195	Liu Jing 劉景	Sxz 75 Liu Jing 京
„	Gan Shi 甘始[45]	Sxz 88; HHS 82B (2750)
„	Dongguo Yannian 東郭延年	Sxz 88 Dongguo Yan; HHS 82B (2750) Dongguo Yannian
„	Rong Cheng 容成	Lxz 7 Rong Chenggong 公
5.19/196	Liu Gen 劉根	Sxz 13; HHS 82B (2746)
„	Wang Zhongdu 王仲都	Sxz 73
8.1/266	Yellow Thearch 黃帝	Lxz 5[46]
Fragment 29	Du Jiang 杜姜	Sxz 45 (= Dongling Shengmu 東陵聖母)[47]

Now, Ge Hong does not cite the Bwz in his *Baopuzi neipian*; the overlaps between his Sxz (which was completed by 317) and Zhang Hua's text probably result not from his having borrowed from the Bwz, but rather from the fact that both authors drew on some of the same hagiographical material circulating in the late third and early fourth centuries—material evidenced by the titles of works cited by Ge Hong, which include four general hagiographies (including the Lxz and three lost works) and a multitude of works by or on individuals on whom there is a hagiography in his Sxz. Similarly, Fan Ye is likely to have drawn his HHS material not from either of

---

43. The Bwz item is extremely terse—hardly more than a mention that the Prince of Huainan was said to have attained transcendence; the Sxz hagiography, by contrast, is rather long and detailed. There is probably no direct relationship between the texts here, whereas in most of the other cases listed there surely must have been.

44. The Lxz item explains that her name was changed due to a taboo.

45. Gan Shi is also prominently mentioned in several other items as one of the three "star" *fangshi* under the Wei (Bwz 5.2, 5.3, 5.5).

46. The Bwz item focuses, however, not on the Thearch's own achievement of transcendence but on that of his vassal, Zuo Che 左徹, who, placing a wooden image of the Thearch on the throne after his ascension and waiting seven years, passed on the throne to the Thearch's grandson, Zhuan Xu, and proceeded to become a transcendent himself. This figure is not mentioned in the Lxz account.

47. She shows up in *Zhen'gao* (HY 1010) 10.24a.2; other Sxz adepts show up in this *juan* and elsewhere in the *Zhen'gao*, although the relationship between the two texts has yet to be fully explored.

these texts but from the same sources they drew on or—yet more likely—on other, historico-biographical texts, roughly contemporary with and slightly later than the Bwz and Sxz, that drew on those sources. More than twenty histories of the Later Han had been compiled, after all, by the time Fan Ye wrote his in the fifth century.

The persuasive structure of Fan Ye's biographies of those skilled in esoteric arts *(fangshu liezhuan)* differs yet again from both the *fangshi* and the Daoist perspectives, though it draws on the same material. The tension between "conformity" and "naturalism," between service to the state and reclusion, is not to the fore in Zhang Hua's text; it is, however, perhaps the major leitmotiv in the HHS biographies.[48] I reserve further discussion of Fan Ye's text, which makes for an illuminating comparison with Zhang Hua's tales of adepts and Ge Hong's hagiographies, for the section below on the Confucian perspective.

What, then, are the most fundamental views to which *fangshi*-oriented anomaly accounts seek to persuade the reader? (1) Esoteric arts, *fangshu*, are indeed efficacious. (2) The *fangshi*, as well as the author who writes in that persona, uniquely possesses broad-ranging knowledge of peripheral, distant, anomalous matters. On its surface, the world is a vast, mysterious, extremely various place; its marvels, displayed in cosmographic texts, dazzle the eyes and stun the mind. But the *fangshi*-author has the know-how to explain the existence of all manner of seemingly bizarre, contranatural, and countercultural phenomena, as well as to interpret their portentous significance. This is possible because there is a small set of principles or veins (*li* 理) underneath everything, although it takes a skilled specialist—a *fangshi*, a *bowu junzi*—to discern their workings in the messy skein of events. (3) The rhythms of the cosmos are intertwined with those of humanity; each influence in the human sphere has its response in the natural, and vice versa. In this locative worldview, rooted in the pre-Han thought of the cosmologists and developed throughout the Han as reflected in its increasingly elaborate correlative schemes,

---

48. In the form of the Daoist's autonomy with respect to the ruler (but compassionate engagement with common people), this tension also bulks large in Liu Xiang's and Ge Hong's hagiographies—on which more shortly. On the tension as it runs through Fan Ye's biographies, Ngo 1976, 67–72.

numerologies, and *chenwei* texts, anomalies are radically interpretable *signs*, messages from the thinking, speaking interlocutor of humanity, the cosmos itself. And *fangshi* are the ones who hold the keys to that crucial task of interpretation, readers par excellence of the language of the anomalous.

Daoist Perspectives: Ascension, Mediation, and Autonomy

One might subdivide texts of pro-Daoist persuasion in several ways: hagiographical collections (Lxz, Sxz, Dxz) versus other texts, allegorical works (Syj, Dmj) versus the rest, works that embed their descriptions of distant lands and their strange products within the "frame" of a report of an adept-advisor's speech to the ruler (Szj, Dmj) versus "unframed" texts, or texts centering on Emperor Wu of the Han and his advisor Dongfang Shuo—a group of texts that includes one (Hwgs) rather marginal and another (Hwdnz) quite marginal to the genre (also Szj, Dmj)—versus the others. All of these texts claim authority for the Daoist tradition as it was coalescing during these centuries; they seek to persuade the reader that Daoist adepts have keys to transcending the limitations of the ordinary world, most especially the ultimate limitation of death. But they claim more than that, and the different types of texts do so in different ways. I will discuss the hagiographies first, then the other texts, because, as I will show, the dominant tropes and metaphoric modes divide along this line.

The Hagiographies (Lxz, Sxz, Dxz): Ascension and Autonomy

The dominant trope of these texts, particularly the Lxz and Sxz,[49] is the arraying of a gallery of named individuals, each of whom exemplifies in a particular way the attainment of transcendence. The mode of writing is "biographical"—a subset of historiographic writing—but with the note of the anomalous distinctly sounded.

---

49. In fact, most of the comments in this section apply more to the Lxz and Sxz than to the Dxz, which, true to its name, is much more an "insider's" text and focuses on techniques, not on the evidentiary display of transcendents' deeds.

These texts therefore work intertextually with and against the more canonical historiographic mode of *liezhuan* introduced by Sima Qian—against it in that, by their very subject matter, their "arrays" are faux-historical: these authors chart the recurrent, if infrequent, intersection of two planes, the historical (horizontal) and, slashing through it in every item, the trans-historical (vertical). Daoist hagiographies are arrayed histories of persons said to have transcended history as it is understood in this world.

The persuasive strategy of these texts turns on the nature of their implied author and the authorial voice. The hagiographer writes not as a transcendent but as a reliable recorder of cases; his persona is that of historian and apologete, which is, at bottom, incompatible with that of the distant, inscrutable transcendent. These texts' claim to authority is based precisely, therefore, on their distance from their subject. By their very format, as well as their implied author's stance toward the material as a transmitter of things read and heard, these "biographies" claim an intertextual place among very different (because more or less "ordinary," non-world-transcending) others of the same format, and hence strive to be read on the same footing as other *liezhuan*. Ge Hong's comment on his Sxz makes this quite clear: "I also compiled a book on those who are not listed in secular [histories] (俗所不列者), which became the *Shenxianzhuan* in ten fascicles."[50]

The hagiographic rhetoric deployed in these works also plays on an identity or close similarity between implied author and implied audience. Although to some extent knowledgeable, presumably, of the techniques of transcendence, the author does not write as a practitioner of them, merely as a reporter of their results in specific cases. To that extent he is, relative to the matters he narrates, an outsider, standing in this world with the implied reader, even though closer than the reader to the "traces" (*ji* 跡 or 迹, literally "footprints") his distant subjects left behind. He is a compiler of records about practitioners, not a discussant or revealer of practices; likewise, the reader's interest is assumed to revolve around whether or not such feats are possible, not how to do them.[51] The distance from his subject that the implied hagiographer shares

---

50. See the tr. and discussion of this document in Chapter Three.

51. Many techniques, medicinal substances, and elixir ingredients are mentioned, and the names of a few revealed texts are given, but such information is never given in detail sufficient to engage in the practices in question.

with his reader constitutes his pledge of veracity: he is a relatively (but indirectly) knowledgeable, reasonable outsider writing for the edification of other, less well informed outsiders.[52]

These authors' distance from their subject must not, however, be construed as disinterest, any more than the canonical historian lacks a definite (if subtle and complex) moral interest in setting out his biographical "arrays." Already with the Lxz, the intent of the text is clearly, if only implicitly, apologetic; Liu Xiang's very adoption of the *liezhuan* format implies that he was concerned to substantiate Daoist claims to longevity and transcendence. Three centuries later (after many intervening hagiographies, now lost, had been written), Ge Hong not only took an even more directly apologetic tack in his writing, he also (apparently) left a preface stating his aims quite clearly along with the sources—and the limitations—of his work.[53]

When I wrote my *Inner Chapters* in twenty fascicles, discussing matters pertaining to divine transcendents, my student Teng Sheng asked me: "Master has said that the metamorphosis into transcendence (*xianhua* 仙化) can be attained and that deathlessness can be studied. But as for 'the ancients who achieved transcendence,' did such people really exist?"

52. Perhaps it is necessary to point out again that Ge Hong, while no mere dilettante, was known more for his collection of Daoist books than for his practicing of their techniques; he himself wrote that he could not afford the materials for elixirs. The point was made long ago in Sivin 1969. Lest students of literature be misled by a *tongxingben* available in Ming and Qing editions such as ZDHW, ascribed to Ge Hong and titled *Zhenzhongshu* 枕中書 ("Pillow Book"), which is a first-person record of a direct divine revelation to its author, I should mention that there is no evidence whatsoever that Ge wrote a book of this title, and, given its contents, it is clearly either a forgery or simply misattributed to Ge Hong. Books of similar but not identical title appear in the list of texts he collected (*not* written by himself) in *Baopuzi neipian* 19 (see 4a.2, 5a.2, 5b.3–4, 6b.4), for trs. of which Yoshioka 1955, 49–61; Ware 1981 [1966], 309–17 and 379–85. Some of these may be the ancestors of two texts with similar titles now preserved in the DZ (HY 863, which contains a rather cryptic statement regarding the source of part of the scripture at 11a.2, and HY 1411), neither of which bears the slightest resemblance to the *tongxingben*. For recent discussions of Ge Hong and his thought, Wang Ming 1984, 55–79; Tang Yijie 1988, 169–217; Qing Xitai 1988, 1:301–35; Hu Fuchen 1989, 77–122, 186–308.

53. Whether this document flowed from Ge Hong's own brush has been questioned. I translate from the text in the LWMS ed., consulting Güntsch 1988, 21–30, and the partial tr. in DeWoskin 1977b, 30.

I replied: "Those recorded by the Qin grandee Ruan Cang numbered in the hundreds,[54] and those written about by Liu Xiang made up a further seventy-odd persons. But divine transcendents are hidden and obscure, of a different ilk than the world (然神仙幽隱與世異流), and those of whom the world has heard do not amount to even a thousandth [of actual cases]."

Ge Hong proceeds to list some thirty of these ancient transcendents, summarizing the feats of each one; they are all figures eulogized in the extant Lxz.[55] He then continues:

I am now engaged in another copying and collecting of [records of] ancient transcendents, such as they appear in canons on transcendents (*xianjing* 仙經) and macrobiotic methods (*fushifang* 服食方) as well as in books of the hundred schools, the sayings of former masters,[56] and the discussions of aged scholars. I am arranging them in ten fascicles so as to transmit them to those gentlemen who recognize the truth and who would know what is distant.[57] I would hardly insist on showing them to those who are entangled in worldly affairs (*fansu zhi tu* 繁[58]俗之徒) [or] who would think them unorthodox and trivial (*si bujing wei zhe* 思不經微者).

It will now be realized how brief and truncated Liu Xiang's accounts are, how many compelling matters they omit (美事不舉). My own accounts, although they cannot completely record things that are deeply wondrous and strange (雖深妙奇異不可盡載), still preserve the essentials. I would say that they surpass Liu Xiang's, which omit much.

But the apologetic, polemical aims of the texts would be quite evident without such meta-documents, for their "distanced" mode

---

54. I have no information on this author or his text.

55. Ge Hong's order of listing and that in the extant Lxz do not entirely match, but there is a surprisingly high degree of correspondence.

56. Or, as Güntsch reasonably understands this: the sayings of *my* former teacher(s).

57. This phrase is (perhaps deliberately) ambiguous and could perhaps as well be translated: to record (reading 傳 as *zhuan* and not as *chuan*, "to transmit") those masters who realized perfection and knew of remote things.

58. Reading *fan* 繁 instead of the LWMS's *xi* 繋. This entire sentence is difficult; if I understand Güntsch's tr. correctly, we read it similarly.

of writing itself already constructs a view of adepts as seen through non-adept onlookers' eyes. This mode of writing is inherently evidentiary, in the sense that adepts' wondrous deeds and abilities, culminating in their climactic ascension into the heavens, are all *confirmatory signs* of the reality of their powers and the efficacy of their techniques.[59]

This "confirmatory" or "evidential," and hence implicitly apologetic, mode, which is at work throughout the hagiographies, is foregrounded in certain particular narrative motifs that present the reader with a sort of built-in confirmation carried out by the characters in the text. A complete survey of these motifs is impossible here and will be given elsewhere, but a partial list of the most salient ones—above and beyond the many records of sheer supernormal feats—follows.[60]

1. Witnesses notice that the adept has not aged over many years; or, successive generations of neighbors or family testify to seeing the adept alive.[61]

2. Non-practitioners doubt or test—and confirm—the adept's special abilities.[62]

3. The adept's corpse does not decay after his or her (feigned) "death."[63]

4. Although the term is seldom used, the adept achieves one or another type of "liberation from the corpse" (*shijie* 尸解): the adept seems to die, but the coffin or tomb is found to be empty, or the corpse has been replaced by belongings such as shoes or clothes. Often the burial site is checked because the supposedly dead adept has been sighted alive.[64]

---

59. For an analysis of Du Guangting's late- or post-Tang pro-Daoist collection along these lines, Verellen 1992; I disagree, however, with his claim that Du was "inverting" a Buddhist strategy, since I see a similar strategy already at work in the Sxz and even, to some extent, the Lxz.

60. On the transcendent in general as a hagiographic type, Robinet 1985–86.

61. Lxz 13, 16, 32, 34; Sxz 9–11, 13, 16, 19, 29, 30, 32, 34, 37, 90.

62. Sxz 56, 59.

63. Lxz 43, 52. As will be seen below, this motif is even more prevalent in pro-Buddhist texts.

64. Lxz 5 (Yellow Thearch), 12 (body replaced by text), 43 (female adept, body replaced by slippers), 52 (body replaced by clothing); Sxz 7, 19, 28 (the latter two instances done on behalf of disciples by an adept so that they can escape their home to study the arts of transcendence), 29 (cf.: adept substitutes mud baby for real baby in coffin, thus apparently resuscitating dead child), 29 (body replaced by shoes), 30 (cf.: clothes remain

5. In a related motif of post-"mortem" sightings, adepts thought to be dead are glimpsed alive, often soon after their apparent decease at places improbably distant.[65]

6. Adepts' predictions of future events, or else their descriptions of distant events happening simultaneously, prove accurate.[66] This demonstration of accuracy is often quite detailed: for example, after Luan Ba magically extinguished a fire in distant Chengdu by spitting a mouthful of wine toward the southwest at a banquet on New Year's Day, and was accused of impropriety for what seemed to the banqueters an act of rudeness, he explained the reason for his action. A rider, dispatched to Chengdu to check his story, returned to report that a fire had broken out in the city after the hour of New Year's banquets there; a great storm had then rolled in from the northeast, putting out the fire, and those who had got wet from the rain smelled of wine.[67]

7. If the sum total of adepts' deeds, as well as records and narratives of those deeds, are their "traces," adepts sometimes leave literal "traces" behind, marks of their former presence that can still be viewed or experienced "today": marks on the landscape (footprints in rock at the mountain peak where Liu An and company ascended into Heaven, Qiong Shu's stone bed and pillow inside his former cave dwelling[68]), personal belongings (a family still has the letter and talisman given by the transcendent Wang Yuan to their ancestor Chen Wei[69]), or, more figuratively, traces of influence in others' behavior (for example, offerings at a shrine dedicated to

---

behind like a sloughed-off shell, body disappears; later in story another character exhibits a "purer" form of *shijie*—the coffin, opened, is found to contain only a bamboo pail), 37 (a drawing on cloth of a human being and, on reverse, a talisman design, replace body), 45 (cf.: in a play on the motif, the coffin is replaced by a jail cell which a female adept escapes by flying through its window, leaving her shoes behind), 46 (clothes remain behind as sloughed-off shell, the sash remains untied), 59 (talisman replaces body), 61 (bamboo staff replaces body), 62 (no replacement; this is *bingjie* or "liberation by martial [execution]"), 78 (coffin nails remain intact; pair of shoes replaces body). For canonical discussions of *shijie* see *Wushang biyao* (HY 1130) 87, on which cf. Lagerwey 1981, 185; YJQQ 84. Cf. Robinet 1979b; Seidel 1987; Pokora 1985.

65. Sxz 18, 19, 34, 46, 59, 61, 62, 78, 90.

66. Sxz 7, 8, 11, 15, 26, 34, 39, 52, 56, 58, 61, 63, 75.

67. Sxz 26. He, too, was later canonized in the *Zhen'gao* (10.23b.2), where his exorcistic powers are stressed.

68. Sxz 20 and Lxz 18, respectively.

69. Sxz 7.

an adept—there are many such cases, and they will be discussed below—or a cultic or cultural practice initiated by him or her).[70] These traces are place-holders in this world of persons now gone beyond it, signs of the former, real presence of someone now distant; when adepts are done with the world entirely, they "cut off their traces" (*jueji* 絕跡).[71]

8. Ge Hong at points deploys a polemic against certain historians as well as against "Confucians" (*ruzhe* 儒者), perhaps intending this term not in a sectarian sense but simply as designating sceptical, narrow-minded, bookish, hidebound scholar-officials caught up in the pursuit of petty goals and fixated on a too-narrow understanding. He complains that the *ruzhe* of the world, not knowing of the wonders of divine elixirs (*shendan* 神丹), write misguided interpretations of Wei Boyang's commentary on the *Book of Changes*, causing its real message—an encrypted alchemical method for producing an elixir—to be lost.[72] He also subtly criticizes those *daru* 大儒 who stop at learning about distant esoterica and do not master the arts of true transcendence, and he attacks the "Han historians" who kept secret Liu An's attainment of transcendence for fear later rulers would shirk their duties in pursuit of his methods, instead fabricating the story that he had killed himself as a way of explaining his disappearance.[73] Recall in this context his comment on his own corpus of writings (discussed in Chapter Three), which, seen in this light, looks more clearly

---

70. Cf. the burning of incense on *jiazi* days, a "trace" of the "Xian Gong" 仙公 eulogized in Sxz 60. Other instances of the "survival" of Daoist adepts' traces include: Lxz 31 (cassia pellets left behind by adept); Sxz 31 (people still alive who knew an adept and his family), 44 (a "transcendent's tower" at a spot where an adept who became a *dixian* retired).

71. As does Shen Jian in Sxz 36. By contrast, the current locations of at least two adepts in this world are given (Sxz 82, 85). Incidentally, *dixian* is a term of mild intra-Daoist polemic; as in his *Baopuzi neipian*, Ge Hong is here too concerned to differentiate between "higher" and "lower" modes of practice, the lower ones leading "only" to *dixian*. (His "higher" modes of practice—uniquely allowing the adept to *ascend to Heaven* rather than remaining here *below on Earth*—typically involve ingestion of elixirs; his "lower" modes involve consumption of special natural substances, avoidance of grain, *qi*-control, gymnastics, and sexual arts.) For such "rankings" within the Daoist tradition (not all, but most, of them using the term *dixian*), see in particular Sxz 5, 7, 9, 13, 18, 20 (an especially clear case), 21, 30, 44, 49, 53, 57, 61, 62, 77, 79, 80.

72. Sxz 4.

73. Both of these critiques show up in Sxz 20.

polemical: "My *Esoteric Writings*, telling of matters concerning spirits and transcendents, esoteric drugs, demonic anomalies, abnormal transformations, nourishing life, extending one's years, exorcising evil and driving off misfortune, belongs to the Daoist School (屬道家). My *Exoteric Writings*, speaking of success and failure in the social realm and of worldly affairs, belongs to the Confucian School (屬儒家)."

9. Ge Hong's reference to *daru*, however, comes in the context of what may be another subtle polemic: Ge Hong seems concerned to promote the goal of transcendence over what he sees as the less exalted (though still valuable) arts of *fangshi*. This may be seen in his puzzlingly ambivalent hagiography of the *fangshi* Guo Pu, noted for his prognosticatory prowess. Although Guo Pu is there said to have "possessed the way of leaving the world behind" (有出世之道), and to have been seen alive three days after his execution at the hands of the commander Wang Dun (who, on hearing the report, had his coffin opened, only to find it empty), his stated current rank among transcendents—that of "Earl of Water Transcendents" (*shuixianbo* 水仙伯)—would seem to place him lowest in Ge's entire gallery of transcendents, beneath even "earth-transcendents."[74] Again, Ge's hagiography of Liu An begins by detailing this prince's quest for *fangshu* and (in the same breath) his fondness for "Confucian studies" (*ruxue*)—clearly the Han "Confucian" persuasion and the quest for mastery of the peripheral are linked in Ge's view—but then goes on to undermine the importance of such pursuits in a narrative of the visit paid to Liu An's court (in response to his call for Daoist books and *fangshu zhi shi*) by "eight gentlemen" whose astonishing powers eclipse the prince's comparatively paltry "desire to obtain great scholars/Confucians who have broad-ranging knowledge of essential, arcane matters" (欲得博物精義入妙之大儒).[75] Realizing he has set his sights too low, the prince drops to his knees in submission to these gentlemen, who then teach him their superior arts of transcendence.

10. The Lxz and Sxz both often mention shrines and temples to departed or still-present adepts, as well as depicting rulers and officials making offerings and otherwise showing deference to them. These items model the appropriate response to Daoist adepts by

---

74. Sxz 62; Guo's mode of liberation is termed *bingjie* 兵解 or "liberation by martial execution."

75. Sxz 20; this "desire" is ranked in the text *between* the prince's quest for knowledge of the arts of longevity (on the uppermost tier) and his quest for esoteric martial techniques (on the lowest tier).

readers.[76] Their contents also in some cases probably derive from legends promulgated at the cult sites in question.

11. A variety of other "confirmation" strategies are used. For example, Jie Xiang 介象 magically sends a rider to Shu 蜀 on a bamboo cane to buy some Shu ginger for the fresh fish he has just obtained (also magically) for the ruler of Wu. While in Shu, the rider meets an Wu envoy who happens to be there at the time, and this envoy gives a letter to the rider to carry back home to his family. In moments, the rider returns not only with the ginger (which readers might otherwise suspect could have been secretly purchased closer by) but also with a letter from a countryman known to have been in Shu at that time.[77] This detail acts as a sort of tally of authenticity.[78]

12. Ge Hong, in particular, portrays some Daoist adepts as far superior in skills and power to the gods of local cults. These items reflect attempts on the part of various Daoist writers and practitioners to distance their tradition from the temple worship of gods, which prominently featured meat offerings and shamanic possession.[79]

In the Daoist hagiographies, the main metaphoric and symbolic registers of power are *ascension*—visually and etymologically implied, of course, in the very term *xian*, but expressed more richly through narrative themes—and *autonomy* with respect to the world in general and rulers and officials in particular.

To begin with, a great many hagiographies end by saying that their subject ascended a mountain or rose up into the clouds—so

---

76. Temples and shrines to adepts are mentioned in: Lxz 26, 27, 28, 30, 35, 39, 43, 47, 48 (cf.), 52, 55 (cf.), 63, 65, 68; Sxz 45, 56, 59. People (other than rulers) are depicted in the following items (among others) as making offerings to adepts: Lxz 20, 21, 26, 27, 28, 39, 49, 52, 55, 65, 68; Sxz 7, 19 (implied), 22, 25, 26, 35, 36, 56, 85. Rulers make offerings or establish shrines to adepts in: Lxz 14, 16, 39; Sxz 30.

77. Sxz 59.

78. Other items using strong "confirmatory" strategies include Sxz 20, 21, 27, 30, 60, 61, and 88.

79. One prominent case concerns the official-adept Luan Ba's extermination of local cults and their shamans under his jurisdiction: Sxz 26; HHS 57 (1841); *Zhen'gao* 10.23b.2–7; Miyakawa 1979, 92; Lévi 1986, 100. Another concerns Ge Hong's own ancestor, Ge Xuan: Sxz 46 (cf. Ssj 1.25). There is record of a stele text on him written by Tao Hongjing (Chen Yuan 1988, 21–22). On Daoist attitudes toward local cults, Stein 1979 (other works cited below). Shamans and their activities as portrayed in our texts form a subtopic of their own, on which I am preparing further research; on the ancient background, Schafer 1951; Zhou Cezong 1979; Hawkes 1967.

many that some sort of final ascension as the climax of the adept's earthly career comes to seem formulaic. Many of these climactic ascensions are said to have occurred "in broad daylight," implying that witnesses were on hand to confirm the event; a common formula is "he (or she) ascended into Heaven in broad daylight and so departed" (白日昇天而去).[80] But the Daoist's metaphoric association with height extends to other motifs: some adepts possess the ability to fly from one place to another or float in midair, some appear in feathery garb, some are able to cover vast distances in marvelously short amounts of time, some can scale mountains and cliffs with unnatural ease.[81] Whatever its particular narrative expression, the same basic metaphoric equation holds: moving "up" amounts to gaining in power, purity, rank, and celestial-bureaucratic prestige. Daoist texts emphasize this vertical movement upward, where texts of the *fangshi* perspective emphasize horizontal movement outward.

To move up is also to win autonomy, freedom from constraint, and authority, on a number of fronts. Adepts advancing toward final transcendence are portrayed as free from normal spatio-temporal limitations: through "body division" (*fenshen* 分身), they

---

80. Cases where the adept's career ends in explicit ascension into the heavens and/or into mountains include the following (ascensions done "in broad daylight" marked with *, those done with mate and/or family in tow marked with †, those done on a dragon marked with ‡): Lxz 3‡, 5†‡, 13, 17, 28, 35†, 36, 62, 63, 67, 68; Sxz 9*, 10†, 13–15, 17, 20*, 21†, 24, 31†, 37, 38*, 39, 41–45, 42, 47, 51, 52*, 53† (cf.), 54*, 56, 60, 68, 81, 82*, 83, 84, 86, 88, 90–92. In many other cases, one of three simpler, less dramatic endings is resorted to in order to solve the paradoxical problem of depicting (in this temporal world where things, including narratives, must end) the adept's entrance into a non-ending, trans-temporal state: (1) the adept is said to have "departed as a transcendent" (*xianqu* 仙去), as in Sxz 4, 7, 10, 13, 20, 27, 43, 47, 48, 50, 58, 61, 66, 67, 69, 71, 73, 81, 83, 84, 86 (some of these overlap with more explicit ascension scenes since the phrase *xianqu* or its variant caps the narration of the ascension scene); (2) the adept "departed and never returned," "was never seen again," etc., almost always after entering a mountain, as in Sxz 11, 14, 15, 23, 29, 57, 70, 72, 76, 92 (again some of these cases combine with other closing formulae); (3) the adept simply "attained transcendence" (*dexian* 得仙), as in Sxz 48, 57, 64, 74, 80 (cf.: adept obtains *changsheng zhi dao*), 87 (adept "transcended the world").
81. Flying and floating in air: Lxz 2, 4, 6, 20, 46, 50 (cf.: "running as if flying"), 54; Sxz 20, 37 ("seemed to fly"), 45, 86 (sits in midair). Feather-clothes: Sxz 47, 60 (cf.: adept appears as a crane after his ascension), 61 (transcendents again appear as white cranes). Fast locomotion: Lxz 65; Sxz 5, 14 (?), 15 (cf.), 17, 23, 27, 29, 32, 36, 46, 52, 55, 59, 60, 70, 75, 84, 86, 90. Easy scaling of heights: Sxz 32.

are able to be at several places at once, they disappear at will, they transform their appearance into that of other persons or species, pass through walls and rocks, slip into tiny spaces as well as across dimensions of time, enter water without getting wet and pass through fire without burning, walk on water, secure fruits out of season, and magically produce foods, water sources, and fire.[82] This freedom from limitations also results in mastery over other creatures and elements—over many ranks of denizens of the spirit-world, over animals, over rain.[83] These wonders all constitute visible signs of the efficacy of Daoist arts, but the nature of these feats also symbolizes more specifically the freedom from ordinary limitations acquired by adepts in their special, disciplined practices, as well as the *power in and over* elements of the world that their *freedom from* the world makes possible. The freedom most prized in these texts, of course, next to the freedom from death that many achieve only at the very end of the narrative, is freedom from aging;[84] the two are not the same, since the ascent into transcendence caps the adept's career as an event quite separate from his or her long lifespan and youthful appearance while preparing for final upward departure.

But the most telling sort of autonomy adepts are portrayed as

---

82. *Fenshen*: Sxz 14, 20, 22, 27, 29, 46, 52. Disappearance: Lxz 20; Sxz 12, 20, 27, 45, 48, 71 (cf.), 79. Self-transformation: Lxz 31; Sxz 13, 14, 26, 27, 38, 39, 45, 55, 59, 60, 61, 79; changing objects into likenesses of themselves or others: Sxz 27, 55. Passing through obstructions: Sxz 26, 38, 50, 59. Slipping into small spaces and across time: Sxz 28, 35. Immaculate passage through fire: Sxz 20, 33, 38, 46, 50, 59, 79; through water: Sxz 18, 38, 46, 55, 79 (cf.). Walking on water: Sxz 20, 46, 50, 52, 55. Fruits out of season: Lxz 44; Sxz 46, 55, 59, 69. Magical production of food, sometimes by summoning the "traveling canteen": Sxz 7, 27, 38, 40, 41, 46, 55, 56, 69, 79; of water sources: Sxz 55, 86; of fire: Lxz 13, 14; Sxz 38, 46, 50, 55, 59.

83. General mastery of spirits: Lxz 5; Sxz 13, 17, 20, 25–28, 42, 62, 66, 80, 90. Exorcism: Sxz 18, 25, 28, 37, 46. Ghosts fear Daoist adept: Sxz 92. Daoist adept exterminates or tames false, extortionist local god: Sxz 25, 26, 28 (cf.), 46, 92 (cf.). Magical mastery over animals: Lxz 35, 36; Sxz 20, 22, 46, 52, 55, 58, 66, 70; cf. understanding the speech of animals, Sxz 61. Production of rain: Lxz 11, 17; Sxz 28, 37, 42, 46, 52, 70. Control over other meteorological phenomena: Sxz 25, 52, 55.

84. Here is a list simply of those items where extraordinary longevity is more or less explicitly said to have been achieved (many others hint at this): Lxz 11, 12, 15, 17, 18, 22, 25, 26, 27, 29–34, 36, 39–41, 44, 48, 49, 50, 54, 57, 58, 59, 61, 65, 67; Sxz 1, 5, 6, 7, 8, 9, 10, 12, 13 (promised), 14, 16, 17, 19, 20, 21, 23, 24, 25, 30, 32, 33, 35, 36, 37, 39, 51, 57, 58, 66 (promised), 70, 72, 73, 74, 75, 76, 77, 78, 79, 80, 81, 83, 85–87, 90, 91, 92.

enjoying is with respect to the normal nexus of social relations, and it is here that the Daoist diverges from the *fangshi* perspective most clearly. Where the implied-authorial Zhang Hua and the *fangshi* he depicts in his text (who all appear at court when summoned) tend toward at least relative "conformity" (*mingjiao*) in their more or less dutiful service to the ruler and in the scholasticism of some, most Daoist adepts of the hagiographies tend toward a naturalism that claims authority higher than—or at least free from—that of emperors, kings, and officials, as well as a higher calling that loosens and sometimes severs their family ties.[85] As Ge Hong makes Peng Zu proclaim, "This way is the greatest of all; it is not something that lords and kings can accomplish."[86] To be sure, Daoists (or, more accurately, various adepts who are being retrospectively co-opted by the pro-Daoist hagiographers as exemplars of their own traditions[87]) in these texts are depicted as assisting rulers as their advisors or as serving the state in some official capacity—although this is more the case in Liu Xiang's than in Ge Hong's text, perhaps reflecting the growing prestige of withdrawal from official life as a cultural stance by Ge Hong's time.[88] But they do so on their own terms: some refuse court summonses, others refuse to answer when asked to reveal their methods, and when rulers grow exasperated enough to order their arrest or execution, such measures always at best prove futile (the adept eludes capture or only feigns death at the executioner's hands, often mocking the ruler's attempt), and at worst they rebound to the ruler's detriment.[89] In other cases the Daoist's autonomy is ex-

---

85. There is not sufficient space to discuss issues of family and filiality here, but Ge Hong, in particular, was clearly wrestling with the problem of world-transcending adepts' place in the ancestral lineage and their role in the nuclear family; many of his hagiographies explore these issues and present varying perspectives on them. I hope to treat this question in a future monograph on Buddhist, Daoist, and Confucian hagiographies in early medieval times.

86. Sxz 3 (1.4a.5 in the SK ed.). Peng Zu is speaking here specifically of *his* "way" or method, which is alchemical in nature.

87. An example of this process is discussed in Durrant 1977; more study is needed of Daoist hagiographers' co-optations of historical, pre-Daoist figures as a legitimating strategy.

88. Adepts as advisors: Lxz 12, 20, 25, 26; Sxz 12 (bestowal of text on ruler), 20, 24, 62, 92. Adepts as officials or as aiding government: Lxz 25, 26, 32, 33, 35 (cf.: adept marries princess), 39 (cf.), 40–42; Sxz 26, 37, 62.

89. The following contain variations on this theme: Lxz 8, 14, 27, 38, 43, 53; Sxz 27, 34, 62.

pressed more metaphorically: when officials try to impose a levy on a cinnabar harvest, the mineral flows away from them so that they cannot impound it; when a Han emperor declares to a visiting adept that "You are my subject," the adept promptly vanishes.[90] Adepts have secret knowledge that rulers want; rulers can get it only by the adepts' consent; and rulers are by and large—seemingly by the simple fact of their office—unfit to receive any but the least potent methods.[91]

The Syj: A Naturalist Allegory

The Syj is an allegorical tapestry woven on a simple framework of dynastic succession from the warp threads of cosmographic collecting (tribute, center/periphery) and the weft strands of *yin-yang* and five phases symbolism. That tapestry shows a pattern of persuasion that, while not opposed in any explicit way to the quest for transcendence or the exercise of esoteric skills, is primarily pro-Daoist in the classical, naturalist sense. It is much too rich to be analyzed here in the detail and complexity it deserves; I must content myself with a summary analysis.[92]

On first reading, the Syj appears to be a straightforward instantiation of the old cosmographic tradition—a chronologically organized record of the marvels attracted from the periphery by the virtue of rulers and dynasties, with emphasis on exotic, numinous tribute items from distant, fantastic lands, as well as on the deities and spirits who visited rulers. Read in this way, the text seems loose and disjointed; but since many anomaly accounts read this way, the Syj hardly seems unusual in this respect. The more closely one reads the text, however, the more one realizes that it is a tightly woven allegory in which almost every seemingly insignificant detail of description and narration is overdetermined by an elaborate symbolic code. Its appearance of haphazardness only testifies to the artfulness of its allegorical construction.[93]

---

90. Lxz 46, Sxz 48 respectively.

91. Rulers or high officials ask Daoists for their "way" in Lxz 27; Sxz 1, 12, 13, 20, 59, 92. Rulers or officials cannot understand texts intelligible only to adepts in Lxz 11 and Sxz 41. Rich reflections on the ruler/adept dyad may be found in Seidel 1969–70, 1978, 1981, and 1983.

92. A separate study of the Syj will be published elsewhere.

93. To my knowledge, no one who has previously published on this text has commented on its allegorical nature. Smith 1992, 275, rightly

The succession of rulers and dynasties on which the text is structured is, first of all, keyed to the mutual production sequence of the five phases.[94] Here is the sequence in its bare form, with only a very partial list of the textual evidence for the phasal identifications. When placed in parentheses, the phasal identification is my own inference from the symbolism; the other cases are ones where the identification is explicitly made in the text at the point indicated.

Phasal code for the succession of rulers and dynasties in Syj

hundun: non-differentiation	[Pao Xi] . . . 變混沌之質文 1.1b.8
Pao Xi (Fu Xi)	Wood 春皇 1.1a.4; 木德 1b.9, 2a.2
Yan Di (Shen Nong)	(Fire) 炎; 丹渠 1.2a.5; 朱草 2a.6; 丹雀 2b.2
Huang Di	Earth 黃; 土德 1.3b.4
Shao Hao	Metal 金德 1.4b.7
Zhuan Xu	(Water) *Grandson of Huang Di*; 黑龍 1.6a.3; 天北辰 6a.6[95]
Gao Xin	(Wood) His mother dreams of swallowing *8* suns, gives birth to *8* sons.[96]

points out the similarity of its "imagery" to that of the Dmj, although I believe he is mistaken in attributing it to the "influence" of the latter on the former. The traditional scholars he cites in support of his view, from Tang (Liu Zhiji) to Qing (Yu Jiaxi), were all working on the now discredited assumption (rejected, too, by Smith himself) that the author of the Dmj was Guo Xian and that it was therefore an Eastern Han text.

94. The author's phasal associations of particular dynasties differ from those reported in histories to have been claimed by their founders. Here, as in other ways, the author is recasting familiar associations and inverting traditions in ways designed to further his suasive ends.

95. Also: 冥海之北 1.6b.6; 黑河水 6b.7; 黑玉 6b.9; 闇河之北 7a.3; etc.

96. 8 is the number assigned to the northeast quadrant of the *Luoshu* diagram (Cammann 1961); east is the locus of the wood phase, and northeast is situated "on the way to" wood from the phase that produces it, namely water, the phase of the previous ruler in the Syj's scheme. Similarly, 5 (seen below with the ruler Shun) is the number assigned to the center, the locus of the earth phase, which is often a sort of substratum where the other phases conjoin and harmonize.

Yao

Fire 火德 1.10b.1

Shun

(Earth) 5 star-spirits visit court; copious images of 5-phase harmony

Yu of Xia

(Metal) Casts metal tripods; creates water channels[97]

Tang of Shang

Water 湯; 以繼金德 2.3b.8; 殷湯水德 3.5a.7

Zhou

Wood 水將滅, 木方盛 2.4b.1; attacks last Shang ruler in east

Qin

? Consumes wood to build tower (hence fire?)[98]

Han

Fire 木衰火盛 5.1a.9 (cf. 7.2a.5)

Wei

Earth 魏土德王 7.2a.5

Jin

Metal 土上出金是 . . . 晉興 7.2a.6; 金德 9.1a.6

Shi Hu

(Water) Copious water imagery (ponds, baths, etc.)

The text is built around the locative, centripetal values of the tribute system in several ways. It makes much, for example, of the worldwide diffusion (the verb is usually qia 洽) of the ruler's virtue, which provides the stimulus (gan) for outlying realms' responses (ying) in the form of tribute and emissaries. It also highlights the

---

97. In addition, he is commissioned (hence "produced") by Shun (earth), who cedes the throne to him (and from whose court, when he does so, the five incarnate star-spirits vanish).

98. Or, since white tigers and a western tribute-bearing country figure prominently, Qin could represent metal; the ruler's destruction of wood can be read as fitting metal too. This would, however, destroy the production sequence. I prefer to read the Qin as either "fiery" like the Han, such that the Han merely continues the phase of the Qin, or "woody" like the Zhou, so that it continues the sign of that "dynasty." Note that further in the sequence, when describing the Han, the text mentions that "wood is extinguished, fire flourishes"; wood is quite explicitly the phase of Zhou, fire is explicitly that of Han, so the Qin must arguably be subsumed under one or the other of these. One other possibility is that Qin is not a legitimate part of the production sequence at all but merely acts as a catalyst, a metallic influence to spur the destruction of the wood (Zhou) phase, thus clearing the way for the rise of (Han) fire.

vicissitudes of certain royal palladia, not only the famous nine tri-pods (and other sacred objects linked to dynastic legitimacy) but also a certain agate urn, to be discussed shortly. But the Syj plays upon the locative structure of the tribute system in an ironic, sub-versive, decidedly anti-locative fashion. Its persuasive intent is not pro-center but pro-periphery, and like some parts of the *Zhuangzi* and *Liezi* it envisions the periphery as the locus of the simple, the natural, and thus by implication the *primordial* condition that has been progressively lost in the Central Kingdom. The author deploys several strategies toward this end; again, their complexity can only be hinted at here.

1. A scheme of devolution pervades the work. The statement near the beginning of the text that Pao Xi "altered the simple pat-terns of *hundun*" (變混沌之質文) might seem innocuous enough, but to readers familiar with the standard Daoist cosmogonic scenario of a progressive "fall" from primordial simplicity to the manifold (and, for Daoists, undesirable) forms of cultural complexity—ornate language, elaborate ritual, political coercion—it carries ominous allusive force.[99] The early rulers introduce successive cultural inno-vations: Pao Xi introduces rites, Yan Di the plow and music, Huang Di writing and books, boats and hierarchical social distinctions; and although no harm is explicitly said to have come from these in-ventions, the reader is given to feel the increasing weight of down-ward-spiraling history in other, subtle ways.

One of them is the lengthy story of the agate jar or "precious urn" (*baoweng* 寶甕, the term *bao* resonating with the symbolism of other numinous palladia such as the nine tripods) containing "sweet dew," presented by the Cinnabar Mound Realm as tribute to Gao Xin, the second "wood" ruler in history. After being told that the dew in the urn varies in depth according to the quality of the ruler and his age, we read that it diminished significantly under Yao (= fire), was honored and put to good use (and presumably replenished) by Shun (= earth), and sank into the ground when Shun died. It was unearthed during a Qin (= wood?) canal-digging project; "later" (Han = fire) people obtained it, but did not know what it was, except for Dongfang Shuo, who recognized it and wrote an inscription about it—the text of which is laden with gourd im-agery as well as with the Daoist names for certain outlying conti-nents associated with deathless, primordial simplicity. We have to deal, then, with a watery palladium presented to a wood-ruler, which declines in the subsequent fire phase and is briefly revived

---

99. Girardot 1983; cf. Lévi 1977.

under the ensuing earth phase, at the end of which it falls into oblivion until being unearthed under a subsequent wood-dynasty; later (fire-period) people do not even recognize its value, until it is interpreted for them by a sort of adept-archaeologist of primordiality whose very name (both parts of it, in fact) connotes the east and, therefore, wood.

Similar comments regarding the loss or oblivion over time of auspicious earlier objects or skills are made throughout the text. For example, of the music of the southern realm of Fulou (whose emissaries appeared at the court of King Cheng of Zhou [= wood]), the text says that although it has been continuously studied over the ages since then, "we have retained its dregs but lost its essence," and what has come down to today is erroneous.[100] While studying his books one night in the palace archival tower (itself, as we will see below, a symbol of imperial excess as well as of fruitless learning of esoterica), Liu Xiang is blessed with a visitation by a spirit announcing himself as "the Essence of the Grand Unity" 太一之精, who speaks to him of "matters before the [cosmogonic] Opening and Division" 開闢之前, and bestows on him texts containing "celestial patterns and terrestrial charts." Liu Xiang receives these books, later passing on the skills in them to his son, Liu Xin; but the entry concludes by noting sourly, "And Xiang did not even realize who this person was."[101] But a more complex way in which the text speaks of losses over time as we recede from the original condition of non-differentiation is in its language of "remnant simulacra" (yixiang 遺象), a term that may shed light on the work's title. Throughout the early chapters are sprinkled comments, following the description of a rare tribute object or narration of an adept's deeds, to the effect that "down to today, its remnant simulacra still exist"—cultural and physical "survivals" from earlier times, which can still be accessed as precious remnants of the simpler, purer past. (The text itself, then, is in part a "gathering" [shi 拾] of these "remnants" [yi 遺], sparks of the Dao scattered out through time and in danger of being extinguished.) Late in the text, however, such comments, with few exceptions, take the form of "today no traces of it remain."[102] This shift implies a gradual deterioration of the capacity for survival of "remnant simulacra" as we move farther down in time. It is probably no accident that the final comments of

---

100. Syj 2.8b.2–4.

101. Syj 6.11b.6–12a.4.

102. On the larger themes surrounding "traces" and memory, Owen 1986.

the last three chapters all concern the erroneous transmission or outright destruction or forgetting of traces of former events.

2. Within this overall structure of devolution, however, there are also epicycles of relative proximity to and distance from the condition of primordial simplicity. All of the wood-phase rulers and dynasties receive relatively positive description; the fire-phase periods, by contrast, unfailingly come in for the harshest critique (along lines elaborated below). Yan Di is said to have "changed the simplicity of Pao Xi"; Yao, as we have seen, depletes the sweet dew in the agate urn presented to Gao Xin, and during the ensuing reign of Shun (= earth), it is revealed that during Yao's reign there was catastrophic flooding in a certain extreme northern realm—an omen of imbalance and excess;[103] and during the Han an unusually large number of heavily *yin*-natured, metallic and watery tribute articles are presented, as are repeated depictions of rulers lost in sexual desire (often consummated near pools) and of watery and metallic omens, as if the cosmos was responding with extra *yin* to offset the empire's excess of *yang*.

In this light, the historical terminus of the text at the end of Chapter Nine is extremely significant. The last ruler to be included in the series is Shi Hu, whose reign, following the metal phase of Jin, is imaged in clearly watery terms. This terminus suggests that the author was setting the stage for the reappearance in history of the relatively desirable wood phase; the text implies both a critique of the reigning watery powers and a legitimation of the woody forces waiting in the wings. Wang Jia, the purported author of the text, died sometime before 393; Shi Hu reigned under various titles from 334 to 349, but only in his last year did he proclaim himself emperor; at one point the text mentions the "end of the Jin,"[104] and although the Song was not installed by the Liu clan until 420, the author of the Syj could have understood Shi Hu's self-proclamation in 349 as the effective end of the Jin. Seeing his own age as one dominated by the water phase, his text encodes a suasive mandate directed at those who will usher in the coming era of wood.

3. The text mounts a persistent if subtle critique of a cluster of centrist pursuits and values, including the rites, centrist expansion (including the lavish construction of towers and palaces and the too-active search for anomalies), narrowly Confucian as well as "broad-ranging" learning, and excessive desire, particularly sexual desire, on the ruler's part. Devoted students of the classics receive

---

103. Syj 1.11a.5–11b.2.
104. Syj 9.10a.5.

revelations of higher orders of knowledge.[105] Rulers who build too many towers (some with hubristic names like "Cloud-Transgressing Tower") in quest of encounters with goddesses, or devote themselves too zealously to the search for exotica with which to stock their palaces, receive—and often heed—cosmic warnings, in the form of portents, and human responses, in the form of remonstrances from ministers.[106]

A series of rulers are reprimanded for their excessive desires and frustrated in their quest for complete union with divine women. (1) King Zhao of Zhou dreams of a feathered male figure who, at his request, magically aids him in purging his heart of the lust that blocks his quest for long life.[107] (2) King Zhao of Yan asks an official about the arts of transcendence and, after being told of a transcendent the official once met who had "rid himself of the impediments of desire and distanced himself from sensual love, cleansed his spirit and eliminated his thoughts," is pronounced incapable of practicing the necessary methods because his eyes, mouth, and heart are corrupted by his luxurious, overstimulating surroundings of rich foods and beautiful women.[108] This king reduces his desires, simplifies his life, and as a result is granted (after five years) a visit from the Queen Mother of the West; the description of her visit is laden with images of *yin*-forces bringing forth *yang*-forces, the last of which is a moth which appears carrying in its mouth fire from a cave that reaches the Nine Heavens. Being told that this moth can be used to prepare certain elixirs, the king asks for it, wishing to make a "ninefold-reverted divine elixir" (九轉 神丹), but the Queen Mother does not grant his request—an indication that his progress is still insufficient to practice the higher arts of transcendence.[109] (3) A version of the story of Han Emperor Wu's fervent desire for his deceased Consort Li is told. Li Shaojun, the

---

105. Syj 4.7a.8, story of Zhang Yi and Su Qin (cf. SJ 70 & 69); and cf. the story of Liu Xiang's revelation mentioned above.

106. As does Emperor Ming of the Wei (Syj 7.3a.2–3b.7); cf. 4.4b.8; 4.7a.1. The author of the Syj is in agreement here with Confucian criticisms of imperial excess: see Knechtges 1982, 2:1 and 16ff., for an example.

107. Syj 2.8b.5–9a.5; the king obtains medicines from this figure but is not said to have attained the long life that was his goal, only the ability to fly—or seem to fly—over vast distances.

108. Syj 4.2a.4–4b.4.

109. Syj 4.4a.8–4b.7. The Queen Mother's impending visit is announced in advance by an adept named Gujiangzi (on whom I have no further information), who says that she will speak to the king of "arts of emptiness" (*xuwu zhi shu* 虛無之術).

adept who arranges for the emperor to meet a stone simulacrum of his favorite (the stone for which is obtained from beneath the Sea of Darkness), reproaches the ruler for his desire to draw close to the stone image, which he is allowed to view only through a curtain; when the "interview" is concluded, the adept grinds the stone into powder, which he forms into a pill and administers to the ruler, who as a result no longer dreams of his consort. This whole magical display is patently designed not to satisfy but to uproot the ruler's longing.[110]

The lone counterinstance to this pattern of warnings is King Mu of Zhou's apparently successful meeting with the Queen Mother. But this ruler is portrayed in ways tellingly different from the ones above: he tours the world (travel is a symbol of non-attachment, as discussed below), in the process gaining *personal* knowledge of esoteric, distant phenomena (instead of relying on the knowledge of an adept); it is because of his knowledge that "beings of the most extreme rarity *submitted themselves* to him *unexpectedly*" (絕異之物不期而自服焉)—the language powerfully suggesting that this ruler, unlike the others, did not grasp too much after rare things; and just before the Queen Mother's approach he travels *east* to a *valley* where he visits the Spring Night 春宵 Palace—all of which are symbols of his association with the birth of the wood phase, as well as his receptiveness to the nourishing influence of *yin*. The Queen Mother comes textually bedecked with symbols of the union of *yin* and *yang*, and bestows on Mu gifts suggesting the completion of the phasal cycle and harmony of the five phases.[111]

But the Syj's most direct attack on centrist values comes in a speech delivered by emissaries from the "Realm Separate from Defilement" 泥離之國, located even farther east than Fusang. These persons were horned, fanged, "covered in their own numinous hair" (靈毛), dwelt in deep caves, and lived to an "incalculable" age—traits which announce their proximity to the condition of primordial simplicity. Their foreign speech required interpretation by the *fangshi* Han Zhi 韓稚, who, descended from Han Zhong (who had

---

110. Syj 5.3b.3–5a.3. Li Shaojun is well attested in other accounts, including SJ 28 (1385), HS 25A, and a hagiography in Sxz 30. In addition to these unions with spirit-women, there are numerous episodes of excessive devotion to living, human women, one of the most striking of which is the Wei Emperor Wen's lavish pursuit and reception of Xue Lingyun, generating a "dust" (symbol of worldliness) that obscures the moon, as well as inauspicious folksongs foretelling the fall of the Wei (Syj 7.1a ff.).

111. Syj 3.2b.8 ff.

been commissioned by the First Emperor of Qin to put to sea in quest of herbs of immortality),[112] had recently appeared at court, purportedly as a response to the ruler's penetrating virtue and the establishment of the utopian condition of Great Peace (*taiping*), declaring himself an emissary of the God of the Eastern Sea. On being asked about how things were prior to the age of Nü Wa, the visitors from the Realm Separate from Defilement replied through him:

"Upward [in time] from the Snake-Bodied One [Nü Wa],[113] the eight winds were regular and the four seasons orderly. Neither punishments nor rewards were used to try to take possession of the subtle changes of things." [The emperor] asked further about how things were prior to the Flintman.[114] They answered, "Once people started to bore wood to make fire and cook raw meat, fathers when old became 'compassionate,' sons when old became 'filial.' From the time of August Xuan [the Yellow Thearch] forward people fussed over those things to the point of wiping each other out. Their lives became fleeting and over-agitated. Corrupted by 'rites,' thrown into confusion by 'music,' the 'virtue' of successive generations grew ever more perfidious and false, and the pure manners [of old] declined."

When [Han] Zhi had made their answer known to the emperor, the emperor said: "How remote are these deep, obscure matters![115] Only someone who penetrated the spirit-realm and comprehended the deepest principles of things could speak with [these people] about their Way!"

At this, [Han] Zhi withdrew from court and no one knew where he had gone. The emperor had all his *fangshi* erect a Transcendent's Altar to him north of the city wall of

---

112. On Han Zhong, Ngo 1976, 18. He may be the figure mentioned in Sxz 13 as the teacher of Liu Gen.

113. Foster 1974, 203, translates: "When the snake-bodied [Nü Wa] was already on high," and understands "on high" to mean "on the throne." But the question concerned affairs before her time. I read 已 as 以 and translate accordingly. My tr. below differs in other ways as well from Foster's.

114. Suiren 燧人, the sage responsible for the introduction of fire and hence of cooking: *Han Fei zi jijie* 19, p. 339 (sec. 49, *Wudu* [The Five Robberies]).

115. Given the text's allegorical patterning, it is probably not accidental that the locution chosen here, *yaomei* 杳昧, graphically suggests an eastern orientation in its combination of sunny and woody emblems.

Chang'an, and named it Hall for Offerings to Han [Zhi]. Commoners say [Han Zhi] is the Divine Overseer of the Cold 司寒 之神 and sacrifice to him north of city walls.[116]

This passage is notable not only for the foreign envoys' eyewitness reports of primordial simplicity and subsequent decline, but also for the aftermath of their speech: the ruler responds in what the text argues is the only way possible for one in his position, amazement and incomprehension; then, dropping his pretended response to the ruler's virtue, the interpreter-adept—acting in the role of mediator between ruler and strange periphery—vanishes from the scene. To this event, too, the ruler responds in the only way he can, by establishing a cult. "Commoners" (su) worship the departed one as a functional deity in the bureaucratic pantheon, but the implied reader is let in on his true identity as an adept conversant in the simple but now forgotten language spoken in the times before humankind's gradual fall into "civilization."

4. The text presents a clear alternative to the excesses of the imperial center in its depiction of extremely distant lands as paradisically simple and harmonious. Supposedly—on the centripetal model of the tribute system—moved to present tribute by the virtue of the ruler at the world's center, these fantastically distant lands in fact embody naturalistic modes of life much closer to the primordium of hundun. The farther out they are in space from the Central Kingdom, the closer these lands are to the primordial condition of simplicity. A corollary to the naturalistic lives of people in these lands is their extreme longevity.[117]

5. Most adepts in the Syj—about three dozen are mentioned—are either recluses or, if they do act as advisors to rulers, use that capacity to criticize the ruler's preoccupations, while all the while maintaining their own absolute autonomy, symbolized by their coming and going as they please, their sudden disappearances, and their free-spirited roamings about the cosmos. Han Zhi, as we have seen, comes to the Han court of his own accord, saying he was sent as an emissary from the god of the Eastern Sea as a response to the emperor's virtue; but soon he vanishes, leaving the emperor to regret his departure and found a shrine for him.[118] During the Zhou,

---

116. Syj 5.2b–3a, also consulting Qi Zhiping 1981, 114, and following his emendations.

117. See, for example, Syj 1.6b.6, 1.7a.3–5, 4.3b.1, 4.6a.4, 5.7b.1, 6.3b.4–7.

118. Syj 5.2b.3–3b.2.

Duke Wen of Jin hunts down the reclusive adept Jie Zitui the way hunters pursued wild game, setting fire to a mountain forest in order to force his prey into the open, but white ravens (*yang* creatures in an *yin* color) circle about the adept and protect him from the fire, inspiring the local people to build a tower to commemorate the event.[119]

6. The term *you* 遊, "wandering" or "travelling" but with specific allusive resonance with the *Zhuangzi* chapter *Xiaoyaoyou*, is used so often that one cannot but conclude it is meant to emphasize the condition of unattached, spontaneous freedom imaged in the *Zhuangzi* chapter and elsewhere in classical Daoist texts.

7. Finally, the text narrates several penetrations by adepts into deep caves; again, it is the repetition of this motif that alerts us to ask after its allegorical significance, which at the most basic level seems to be the need of *yang*-forces to seek wisdom and power in the depths of *yin*-forces. The first figure to play out this action-pattern is Yu, who, in the process of ordering the floods, bores his way into a mountain and discovers a cave; lighting his way with an *yin*-fire (a "Night Bright Pearl, bright as a candle"), he finds in its bright depths a snake-bodied deity (later revealed by the text to be Fu Xi) who points out to him a chart of the eight trigrams and bestows on him a jade measuring rod with which to order both time and space.[120] Then, Fu Yue (= the shaman-adept Yi Yin discussed in Chapter Three) hires himself out as a laborer, and grinds grain deep in a cave to support himself; the verb for this "grinding" (*chong* 舂, EMC *cuawn*) may be a graphic and phonetic pun on "spring" (*chun* 春, EMC *tchwin*), which would tie this episode into the repeated pattern of *yang* entering *yin*.[121] Later in the text, the adept Wangzi Qiao peers into a well beside a cave containing mysterious writings in undecipherable, archaic script; from a *black* (*yin*) sparrow he obtains a ladle filled with well-water, upon drinking which the sky fills with clouds and snow.[122] And the very last passage of the text proper narrates the entrance into a cave-realm

---

119. Syj 3.4a.1–7. Jie Zitui's hagiography is in Lxz 19 (1.9b–10a), where a less violent version of the Duke's attempts to cajole him is given; the Syj author seems to have rewritten the legend to emphasize this violence.

120. Syj 2.2b.5–3a.4.

121. Syj 2.4a.2 ff. Fu Yue figures prominently in the *Zhuangzi's* lyrical list of persons who attained the Way; see *Zhuangzi* 16.6.29–35, tr. in Watson 1968, 81–82.

122. Syj 9.6a.4–6b.9; the text gives his name as Wangzi Jin, and the well and cave are located in the Realm of Pinsi, of which Zhang Hua is said to have no knowledge.

of an herb- and stone-collector who experiences his trip—which features a sojourn among beautiful but reserved maidens who give him various hunger-allaying elixirs to drink—as brief, but discovers on returning home that he has been gone for three hundred years. This instantiation of the "hidden world discovered" motif ends, like the famous Sshj tale, by saying that the location of the cave was spoken about but—or perhaps I should write *therefore*—soon forgotten.[123]

Overall, then, the perspective advanced in the Syj is pronaturalist, yet is set forth in an allegory based on the locative systems of phasal correspondences and *yin-yang* classifications; it is a critique of "worldly" sensuality (particularly on the part of the ruler and when linked to desire for other sorts of power), yet is developed in imagery rich in sexual overtones (cave-penetrations and *yin-yang* interplays). In this last respect it is strongly reminiscent of the *Zhen'gao* narrative of Yang Xi's encounter with his divine consort. And, if we take the text to have been written in the latter half of the fourth century, then its lofty critique of rulers' desire and seeming indifference to imperial patronage of Daoist establishments can be seen as exactly fitting the spirit of the age, in which to seem to be above the concerns of officialdom was an effective means of official advancement.

The implied author's viewpoint throughout is that of the court, in the sense that peripheral lands and peoples are described through their centripetal appearances at the capital; as readers we are invited to stand with the implied author at the center, looking out. Yet the author of the text clearly adopted this trope in order to undermine the centrist values of the tradition of cosmographic collecting, for it is the fantastically distant periphery that is the locus of the utopian conditions advanced in the text. An ironic mode therefore pervades the allegory developed as the text unfolds: the Syj is one of the most explicit manipulations of the tradition of cosmographic collecting in its structuring around tribute reports and rulers, yet it is certainly the most powerful attack on that tradition to be found in the extant corpus of anomaly accounts.

Ultimately, the Syj plays ironically upon the genre of anomaly accounts itself, for in reality it contains no anomalies, only phenomena that seem anomalous to the reader entranced by its veneer of tribute accounts. To the reader attuned to the allegorical code woven into its language, it presents a quite different picture of the world, one unfailingly structured according to the fixed principles of *yin-yang* dialectic and five-phases cyclicity. The only real anomaly

---

123. Syj 10.10a.6–10b.5.

in the Syj is Confucius' untimely appearance, a water-phase figure
in a wood-phase time—an odd episode which only demotes his significance, since his untimeliness, his lack of harmony with the
rhythm of the cosmos, renders him completely ineffective.

The Han Wu Di Cycle: Adepts as Autonomous Mediators

In the core anomaly accounts Szj and Dmj, combined with two texts
marginal to the genre—the Hwgs and (even more marginal) the
Hwdnz—we have a cycle of narrative material centering on the
figure of Emperor Wu of the Han, as well as on others active at his
court, the most crucial of whom for our purposes is the adept
Dongfang Shuo. Thomas E. Smith has effectively demonstrated the
original unity of these texts and analyzed the perspectives they
seek to advance. My comments will take the form of addenda to
Smith's analyses—as well as some slight revisions from the van-
tage point of the present book.

Overall, the perspectives advanced in these texts resemble
those of the Syj to the extent that they present Daoist adepts—
imaged in the central figure of Dongfang Shuo—as autonomous mediators between the ruler at the center, on the one hand, and the
esoteric methods and peripheral marvels he seeks, on the other.
The texts repeatedly insist that those methods and marvels will
elude the ruler's grasp unless made available to him by the adept.
We find in all of these texts, but especially in the Hwdnz, a critique
of rulers' lust for sensuality and control that is reminiscent of the
Syj. And in the Szj and Dmj we find a similar use of the tribute system as the dominant, structuring trope. But none of these texts is
nearly as naturalistic in its values as is the Syj; here, the emphasis
falls more on the adept, as one privy to esoterica and hence able to
work wonders and travel magically about the cosmos, and these
texts more directly promote the ruler's quest for esoterica, even as
they insist on the necessity of adepts' mediation if that quest is to
enjoy success.

Smith is justly concerned to document a "ritual pattern" in the
texts involving the ruler's quest for "renewal" through contact with
spirit-beings, usually of the opposite sex. But in doing so, he risks
underemphasizing that it is the adept who is key in orchestrating
this quest. Without the adept's help, the ruler would ultimately fail
to achieve renewal; and he ends up failing anyway, but the texts
are at pains to say that this is because of his own inevitable limita-

tions, not the adept's. Furthermore, I would insist that the tribute system forms an additional "ritual pattern" essential to the meanings these texts convey. And although Smith persuasively argues the thematic and ideological unity of these texts, they must also (particularly the Szj and Dmj) be understood in the context of the anomaly account genre, the coherence of which Smith seems to want to dissolve.

The format of the Szj is that of a geographic description of outlying continents framed as a speech by Dongfang Shuo to the emperor, which is in turn framed by a brief narrative setting for this discourse, including an introduction that sets up the occasion for it and a conclusion emphasizing Dongfang Shuo's complete autonomy with respect to his imperial patron. The implied author of the text therefore adopts the persona of a "historian" passing on a record concerning a particular ruler. Yet most of the text is the direct speech of the (secretly divine) adept-advisor Shuo, and the dominant trope of this "inner" portion, at least, thus approximates the display of marvels in direct discourse seen in some texts of the *fangshi* persuasion.

More powerfully than any other text of this group, the Szj extols the divine knowledge, and hence the key advisory role, of the adept-advisor Dongfang Shuo. He emerges as a virtual deity or transcendent at court, but one who here conceals his identity (revealed in other texts of the cycle and likely to have been known to many readers) as the incarnate spirit of Venus while displaying his knowledge of the marvels of outlying realms. This knowledge has very clearly been gained first-hand; the text uses the first person and narrates Shuo's personal experience in these realms. He has visited them all, something no ruler could ever hope to do, since they are reachable only by a kind of spirit-travel. Emperor Wu, for his part, is here put in a bad light for not following his adepts' advice more closely—not just Shuo's but that of Lijun and of foreign envoys bringing marvelous objects of tribute.

The preface to the Dmj, translated and discussed in Chapter Three, sets up the implied author of that work as a historian who, coming after Emperor Wu and Dongfang Shuo in time, wants to extol the glorious reign they together achieved. But the text itself again clearly emphasizes the need for any ruler who would "exhaust the affairs of gods and transcendents" to rely on help from an adept-advisor such as Dongfang Shuo, through whom—and *only* through whom—he can hope for success. The text models the way in which rulers should become patrons for knowledgeable Daoist adepts.

Smith shows that the Dmj is structured allegorically, much as is the Syj; but in the case of the Dmj the allegory seems to control only the descriptions of individual marvels, not the overall progression of the work. The text works its way, in a sequence of no apparent design, through a description of the wonders of fantastically distant regions, as well as those presented as tribute to Emperor Wu. Always in the foreground, however, stands the dyad of Ruler/ Advisor-Adept. Thus the text begins by narrating the legend of the miraculous birth of Emperor Wu, but, immediately afterwards, it narrates at greater length the noticeably more miraculous birth of Dongfang Shuo, leading on to anecdotes of his cosmic wanderings as a boy. The third item then brings together these two main characters, as Dongfang Shuo, already implied to be in the ruler's employ, bows and tells him of his journey to the extreme east. Thus begins a series of cases in which the emperor summons the adept to explain a strange tribute object or answer a question about esoteric matters. These exchanges are interspersed with sheer descriptions of exotica. When asked a question, Shuo more often than not answers in elliptical, cagey fashion. Moreover, not only does Emperor Wu have the unfortunate habit of giving away, releasing, or losing the marvels to which he is afforded access; sometimes Dongfang Shuo even seems implicated in these losses. A number of other adepts (many of them figures mentioned in the Lxz) pass through court, and the emperor honors them all but seems to gain nothing of substance from them; and the entries on them typically end by saying that they left and their whereabouts are unknown.

All of these features of the text suggest that the Advisor-Adept, he who knows esoterica, has personally wandered the far reaches of the cosmos, and as a virtual deity (not virtual but actual in the case of Dongfang Shuo, whom the reader of, but not the characters in, the text know to be the incarnate spirit of Venus) performs an ambivalent function with respect to the Ruler, and that it is this function that the text is centrally concerned to highlight. As the mediating gateway between the Ruler and what the Ruler wants (to wit, knowledge of esoterica, most especially life-preserving substances and hierogamic contact with goddesses), the Advisor-Adept never simply opens the gate to afford the Ruler full access to the marvels he knows. Rather, he reveals his secrets only piecemeal if at all, couching them in indirect, personal narratives. He answers each of the Ruler's direct questions about esoterica with a story about his own wanderings, as if putting off the Ruler's request, and yet the Ruler almost always replies as if perfectly satisfied with this elliptical "answer."[124] Although we witness Emperor Wu enjoying a great many peripheral products, and even having direct encounters with the Queen Mother of the West and other divine women, it seems, in the end, as if the utterly autonomous Dongfang Shuo—who comes and goes freely and changes form at will—has served not so much to open as to guard and perhaps ultimately shut the gate to the esoterica Emperor Wu ardently desires.

The Buddhist Perspective: Manifestation and Cultural Legitimation

By the late fourth century, authors concerned to promote the initial acceptance and deeper enculturation of Buddhist traditions in China began turning to the anomaly account genre as a persuasive medium.[125] Extant pro-Buddhist texts that are of appreciable size include, in chronological order, Gsy, Xuanyj, XuGsy, Mxj, Jingyj, and XiGsy. A handful of items each survive from Xyj, Ganyz, Xrj, and Zyz, which seem to have closely resembled the larger texts. In addition, the overall perspective of the Yml is not, in my view, accurately described as Buddhist, and this text will be analyzed in a subsequent section; but certain of its items are explicitly pro-Buddhist, and these will be included where relevant in the following analysis. I will deal here with extant Buddhist hagiographical texts from the period—the Bqnz and Gsz—only in passing, deferring a thorough comparison of Buddhist and Daoist (as well as other) hagiographical traditions to another occasion. Although one could divide off those texts that exclusively concern miracles involving the Bodhisattva Guanshiyin (He Who Observes the Sounds of the World),[126] this entire group of pro-Buddhist texts can conveniently

---

124. The clearest example of this pattern comes in Shuo's response to the emperor's direct request for a method for preventing his favorite concubine from aging. Shuo answers with a series of anecdotes about himself, and the item ends without any helpful knowledge or substance having changed hands; in fact, all Shuo really says is that he himself has eaten immortality-inducing foods. He flatly declares himself able to keep the young from growing old, but he does not do so (Smith 1992, 645–46).

125. On these texts, see esp. Gjertson 1978, 1981, 1989; Campany 1991b, 1993a, 1993b, and Forthcoming (a), and the other works cited therein.

126. On which, see the more detailed interpretive study (with selective trs.) in Campany 1993b. Such tales also bulked large in Japanese Buddhist piety: e.g. Dykstra 1976 (see my article for other references).

be discussed together, since (unlike the Daoist texts we have just reviewed) in their style, format, and persuasive messages they closely resemble one another.

The fundamental trope of all these texts can be summed up in two words, *yan* 驗 and *ying* 應. Each of these terms signals a particular sort of dyadic relationship, and the relationships are of an identical, one-two structure that I call "manifestation": *yan* denotes manifestation in the realm of knowledge, *ying* denotes it in the realm of action and event. *Yan* is essentially a hermeneutical term, denoting a particular function in the evaluation of data. In the juridical field, *yan* means confirming evidence or proof; to *yan* is to take up a claim and, based on an examination of the evidence, find it true. In the divinatory field, *yan* means a "sign," something by which fortunes or the trend of events can be judged, known, or recognized. Only by extension does *yan* also carry into the moral field, meaning the "fitting answer" or response (*ying*) to an agent's actions.[127] Like *yan*, *ying* carries hermeneutical force, in that it is a mode of interpreting events (such that Y is to be seen not as a random event but as a specific response to X); but its scope primarily resides in the realm of things agents do (including things they do in speech and in thought) and things that happen as a result. *Ying*, meaning here the necessarily just or fitting "response" called forth virtually automatically by an action, has resonances that are both moral and metaphysical in nature. Common metaphors emphasize its automaticity ("as an echo follows a sound," "as a shadow follows a body"). It is often paired with the term *gan* 感 (here "stimulus"), and as a compound, *ganying* refers to the notion of "resonance" that is the metaphysical, moral, and taxonomic foundation of the correlative cosmological thinking that arose in the late Warring States period and flourished during the Han and, in fact, throughout our period.

The pro-Buddhist texts are therefore just what their titles, by playing heavily upon these terms, announce them to be: records of confirming evidences, proofs, or signs, or else of responses.[128] And the "manifestation" trope is the key to the persuasive strategies deployed in these texts. For they all turn on the documentation of *striking responses* to stimuli of various religiously "marked" kinds, each response furnishing a piece of *evidence or proof* which it is the author's purpose to gather, in order to compile a persuasive brief

---

127. DKW 45024 (12.556d–557d).

128. Pro-Daoist writers would later adopt this set of strategies to answer their pro-Buddhist opponents (Verellen 1992).

for the truth and efficacy of Buddhist teachings and the authority of bodhisattvas, buddhas, monks and nuns, and even pious laypersons. Just the inverse of the *fangshi* and pro-Daoist texts that display the marvels of the peripheral and the esoteric, these texts stress above all the ordinariness of context within which the extraordinary "manifestations" of their religion unfold. Events occur at named, familiar places and in recent or contemporary times; they involve and are witnessed by named, often independently attested individuals—individuals much like the implied reader in predilection and social station. Presenting the results of the implied author's work of *yan*, the texts thus invite the reader to *yan* these reports as well. This overriding concern to display evidentiary responses *occurring in China* mirrors the Buddhist community's characteric anxiety during this period—its continuing status as a relative outsider, a still-foreign religion striving for widespread acceptance. These texts aim to domesticate Buddhist tradition in China, to weave it tightly into the fabric of Chinese society and implant it into the very landscape of local cultic sites and official posts, demonstrating its efficacy on Chinese soil despite its foreign provenance.

Even more than the Daoist hagiographer (and like the implied "Gan Bao" of the Ssj preface in this respect), and strikingly unlike the author-adept of *fangshi* texts, the implied author of Buddhist miracle tales completely resembles his implied reader. As both the prefaces and the texts proper show, the author writes in an informal, intimate vein, presenting himself as an ordinary if official-class person essentially like the reader except, perhaps, in his Buddhist conviction (which in some cases has been shaped by miracles that touched him personally and of which we are informed). His claim to knowledge of that of which he writes is based not on any esoteric tradition but only on a social network (itself also made up of persons like the implied reader), through which narratives of events are transmitted, and of which he takes care to leave a textual trail throughout his work, citing eyewitnesses or intermediate sources.[129]

---

129. Authors cite personal witnesses of events (as well as of independent confirmations) in: Gsy 3–7; XiGsy 13 (?), 38, 40, 49; Mxj 20, 27, 31 (= Gsy 6), 56, 77, 85, 90, 110, 115, 120, 121; Gsz wangshen 7. They specify the individuals who were the sources of stories in: Xugsy 9; XiGsy 16, 33, 34, 38, 40, 47, 53, 62, 63; Mxj 27, 30 (= Gsy 5), 31 (= Gsy 6), 32. They mention named individuals (whom, it is implied, they know personally) who knew someone involved in a miracle in: Gsy 2, 7; Xugsy 1, 5; XiGsy 13, 38, 53, 63; Mxj 27, 30 (= Gsy 5), 31 (= Gsy 6).

What, then, were the perspectives of which these authors sought to persuade readers? One can readily explicate them by simply asking: What sorts of phenomena counted as proofs, signs, and responses? What claims were being examined and found true, or attested by evidence? Of what were the reported phenomena the signs, and to what were they the responses?

These questions can be answered, in turn, by charting the structure of "manifestation"—that is, the action-pattern defined by the intersection of *yan* and *ying* motifs—revealed in the corpus of Buddhist narratives. This single structure informs both tales of the responses of powerful, personal beings to devotional acts (most of which in this period feature Guanshiyin) and tales illustrating the impersonal mechanisms of karmic reward and retribution.[130] What is perhaps most crucial about it is that it is a causal chain looping back on itself; the fifth moment (as analyzed below) collapses into the first, and the very writing and reading of the miracle tale are actions that become implicated in an ever-widening series of karmic connections.[131]

A seed of religious instruction or pious habit is planted in the protagonist. In many tales, this is only implied, but some make a point of noting that the protagonist received Buddhist instruction as a youth or had been otherwise exposed to habits of piety or cultivation (such as making offerings to monks, reciting scriptures, venerating images, or meditation) prior to the time of the focal events of the story.[132]

The protagonist does something that is "marked," positively or negatively, in the field of specific Buddhist values or precepts. (A) Positively marked deeds prominently include devotions to powerful beings (mostly Guanshiyin) in supplication for protection or salvation; such devotional acts include

---

130. One of the major exceptions to this pattern runs the temporal/ causal/narrative sequence in reverse, beginning with a present misfortune and working backwards in time and karmic causality, to explain its roots in a past misdeed, much as a *jātaka* or *avadāna* tale would do. Such narratives of "karmic hermeneutics" are the temporal inverse of "accurate divination" narratives. Examples include Xuanyj 3; Mxj 6 (= Gsz wangshen 1), 66, 82, 100; and, for cases where this karmic mechanism is confirmed by ones returned from death to life, Yml 83, 126, 248 (= Mxj 4).

131. As argued and further explained in Campany 1993b.

132. Notably Gsy 4 (= Mxj 27); XuGsy 1; XiGsy 3, 4, 6, 7, 9, 15, 18, 27, 29, 30–34, 38–40, 46, 48, 50, 57, 61–62, 64, 68; Xuanyj 3, 8; Mxj 72.

repeated acts of mental concentration on, vocalizing the name of, or reciting *sūtra* texts about the supplicated figure.[133] Other positively marked actions include donating to the sangha, confessing misdeeds (*huiguo* 悔過), releasing living creatures (*fangsheng* 放生), fasting, performing Buddhist rites for the dead (often consisting of an assembly and banquet for monks and laity alike, or of a scripture recitation), making or commissioning or venerating Buddhist images, and sponsoring the construction of temples or the erection of stelae.[134]

(B) **Negatively marked** deeds prominently include the taking of animal life, eating meat, and stealing or destroying or desecrating images or *sūtras*.[135]

There occurs an anomalous—often strikingly contranatural—response to the protagonist's act; details are frequently supplied to persuade the reader to see the occurrence as a response to the specific act in question and not an accident. An extremely broad range of events occur as re-

---

133. Mental concentration: Gsy 4, 7; XuGsy 1, 5, 7; XiGsy 1, 5, 16, 19, 22, 24, 28, 32, 33, 38; Xuanyj 3, 23; Gsz shenyi B8. Repeated recitations of scripture as devotional acts: XiGsy 27, 34–37, 39, 40, 62, 67; Xyj 2; Mxj 96, 102, 119; Jyj 8; Gsz, *songjing* section *passim*, but esp. 6, 13, 17.

134. Confession: Mxj 2, 6, 11, 115; Gsz shenyi B8; Gsz wangshen 3. *Fangsheng*: Xuanyj 31, Mxj 77. Rites for the dead (including *daosu dahui*): Mxj 15, 17, 67, 106, 123; Jyj 4; Gsz songjing 10. Reciting scriptures on behalf of the dead: Mxj 21, 63, 80. Other scripture recitations as acts of merit: Mxj 13, 17, 23, 24, 56, 71, 89, 108. Recitations during self-immolation: Gsz wangshen 5–8. Fasting: Mxj 22–24, 43, 56, 75, 84, 97, 115; Xuanyj 30–31; Jyj 8. Feeding the sangha: XuGsy 6; XiGsy 43, 62; Xuanyj 3, 18; Mxj 10, 28, 43, 97. Building temples: Xuanyj 18, 19. Making, commissioning, seeking images: XiGsy 14, 17, 21, 22, 29, 32; Xuanyj 7, 9, 29; Mxj 1, 14, 18, 43, 55, 107, 108, 113, 129, 130. Wearing images: XiGsy 13, 14, 17, 21. Venerating images: XiGsy 13, 17, 43, 63, 65; Xuanyj 6, 32; Mxj pref., 74, 116; Gsz shenyi B11 (by monk); Gsz wangshen 9 (the offering consists of the offerer himself, burned). Veneration of the Buddhas of the ten directions: XiGsy 49.

135. Images stolen, destroyed or desecrated: Xuanyj 4, 9, 18, 34, 35; Mxj pref., 74, 78, 110, 115; Jyj 1; Gsz shenyi B8. Sūtra texts desecrated: Mxj 82, 120. Taking animal life (including eating meat): Xuanyj 2 (lice!), 10, 12, 13, 24; Mxj 6 (= Gsz wangshen 1), 21, 33 (protagonist while hunting kills piglet which turns out to be his own deceased and reborn relative), 38 (?), 54, 67, 114 (the last two are warnings by dead persons against meat-eating).

sponses;[136] the more significant rhetorical problem faced in these texts, however, is how to convince the reader not only that the untoward events really occurred but also, even more importantly, that they *are responses* triggered by the protagonist's actions, and are not simply fortuitous. Or, to use the indigenous language of divination, how is the "sign" to be brought within the new, specifically Buddhist hermeneutical framework? The answer lies in six sorts of persuasive strategies used by the authors of these narratives. **(A)** The contranatural quality of the event is emphasized with such phrases as "when there was no way out . . . " or "when escape was impossible . . . "[137] **(B)** An "interpretation" of the event is provided in its very narration: a mysteriously appearing figure clearly identifies himself as Guanshiyin, or a clairvoyant monk identifies a layperson's present misfortune as the karmic result of a specific past misdeed, or the protagonist recognizes an anomalous event as a direct response to his or her act.[138] **(C)** An explicit "pre-condi-

---

136. Here is a list simply of the types of responses granted to those who, in dire straits, appeal through their devotional acts to Guanshiyin for swift relief. Pardon from criminal charges: XuGsy 2, 4; XiGsy 22, 23, 43. Escape from prison: Gsy 4 (= Mxj 27); XuGsy 1, 7, 9; XiGsy 15, 19, 20, 21, 23 (= Mxj 84), 25–40; Xuanyj 8, 23; Mxj 72, 119; Jyj 8. Salvation from executioner's blade: XiGsy 13, 15–18; Xuanyj 7, 8; Jyj 8. Orientation when lost: Gsy 5, 6; XiGsy 56–58, 60, 61. Healing: Gsy 7; XiGsy 65–68; Xyj 2 (cf. Mxj 125, Gsz songjing 13); Xuanyj 9; Mxj 32; Gsz shenyi B8. Rescue from animal attack: XiGsy 68, 69; Mxj 73. Rescue from fire: Gsy 1 (= Mxj 12); XiGsy 1–3; Mxj 128. Rescue from bandit attack: Gsy 3; XiGsy 11, 12, 14, 41, 42, 44–47, 50, 64. Rescue from attack by hostile, invading troops: XuGsy 8; XiGsy 25, 48, 51–54, 56, 59; Xuanyj 21, 22; Mxj 61. Protection from demon: XuGsy 3. Reunification of separated relatives: XiGsy 62–63; Xuanyj 6. Birth of son: XiGsy 55; Mxj 69, 102. Rescue from drowning: XuGsy 10; XiGsy 4–9, 45 (XiGsy 6 = Gsz songjing 6 [407a]); Xuanyj 26; Mxj 87, 96; Gsz songjing 7 (407b).

137. As in Gsy 1 = Mxj 12; Gsy 3, 6; XuGsy 7–9; XiGsy 1, 2, 4, 6, 8, 25, 45, 49, 52, 54, 59, 67; Xuanyj 21; Mxj 43, 119.

138. Protagonist recognizes that he or she has been granted a miraculous response: Gsy 2; XiGsy 23, 51, 53, 59, 64; Xuanyj 3, 6. Direct visions of bodhisattvas or buddhas: XuGsy 5, XiGsy 19–21, 24, 34, 47, 61 (of Guanshiyin); Gsz songjing 7 (407b, of Maitreya); Mxj 81, 83, 86, 88–89, 121, 129 (cf.). Karmic "diagnoses" can be done not only for others (as in Xuanyj 3), but also in one's own case: in Gsz shenyi B3, one monk tells another that he once broke a chicken's leg and will soon suffer retribution for this; someone then attacks this monk and injures his leg. In Mxj 6 (= Gsz wangshen 1), a monk diagnoses his own impending death as due to having destroyed a bird nest when young; he is now dying because birds have built

tional" device is inserted into the narrative; for example, the protagonist states that she is seeking a sign, and then a sign appears, or, even more explicitly, the protagonist makes a vow of the form "if saved I will do Y" or a statement of the form "only if X happens will I consider myself to have received a sign," so that when the protagonist is saved or when precisely X happens the reader is preconditioned to view these events as responses.[139] **(D)** Similarly, a "postconditional" device is inserted whereby the effects of a miraculous event are quite strikingly limited to the object or area "protected" by karmic or devotional provisions; for example, in a fire only the *sūtras* and images remain intact, or in a shipwreck only the persons who call on Guanshiyin for help are saved.[140] **(E)** Ghostly apparitions and temporary trips to the unseen world afford a sort of X-ray glimpse—painfully clear—of what in this world is normally invisible, namely the karmic effects of behavior counter to the fundamental Buddhist precepts.[141] **(F)** Scriptural passages—often containing vows made by bodhisattvas—are cited, and events are explicitly identified as instantiations of the fulfillments of these vows or other scriptural statements on Chinese soil.[142]

Others react with amazement to the response, or else with scepticism; in the latter case, further anomalies occur or an inquest (*yan*) is conducted, often by a ruler or official, and the sceptic is convinced. Onlookers react with "shock" (*jing* 驚) or "wonder" (*yi* 異, *guai* 怪) at the anomalous event;[143] they

---

a nest on the bridge to his only water source and he is unwilling to disturb them to get a drink. Other, even more direct "internal confirmations" of a bodhisattva's intervention as the explanation for the anomalous event: Gsy 6; XiGsy 7–9, 32–33, 38, 67.

139. "Only if X happens . . .": Gsy 2; XiGsy 46, 49, 55; Xuanyj 3; Gsz shenyi B6 (cf.); Gsz wangshen 7. Other, similar requests for signs: Mxj 13, 74, 81, 90, 116. Sign indicating that protagonist's wish has been granted: XiGsy 49. Vows by devotee ("if saved I will . . ."): Xuanyj 8, 23 (an item which also elucidates the consequences of breaking such a vow); XiGsy 6, 15, 24, 48, 49, 68; Mxj 90; Jyj 8; Xyj 2 (cf.); Gsz songjing 13.

140. Gsy 4; XiGsy 2, 3; Xuanyj 5, 28; Mxj 20, 35, 85, 127; Gsz shenyi B4.

141. There are many examples; among the most salient are Mxj 21, 22.

142. Gsy 7; XuGsy 6; Mxj 32; and, as noted in Chapter Two, the entirety of XiGsy is structured this way, each anomalous event grouped under the scriptural rubric of which it is a fulfillment.

143. Gsy 1 (= Mxj 12), 6; XuGsy 4; XiGsy 3, 34, 38, 61, 62; Xuanyj 28.

or the protagonist (or both) extol the divine power of the unseen being responsible, and some witnesses ask how to perform the devotional acts by which this response was secured, or imitate the protagonist's performance.[144] Rulers and officials, perhaps weary of claimed anomalies, typically react with caution, launching an investigation that confirms the event as real;[145] in a variation on this motif, officials or prison wardens recognize anomalies as miraculous signs of the innocence of their pious prisoner and grant a pardon.[146] Other disputers are silenced by a second wave of anomaly.[147]

These events in turn stimulate (*gan*) positively marked Buddhist acts by others. The protagonist, witnesses of the response, or those who hear of it secondhand are moved to convert to Buddhism, take monastic vows, redouble their spiritual efforts, give up hunting or fishing, assume a vegetarian diet, perform periodic fasts, feed the sangha, or build a temple.[148] Very occasionally, there is also a natural response to the anomalous stimuli, as if to emphasize that the natural, as well as the human, world bows to the authority of Buddhism.[149]

Although I am here eschewing a fullscale treatment of Buddhist hagiographies, a few remarks are in order concerning the treatment of wonderworking Buddhist monk- and nun-adepts in the texts under consideration. At the most obvious level, first of all, such figures and their wondrous deeds themselves constitute signs of the truth and efficacy of Buddhism in the same way that Daoist adepts signal the authority of Daoist teachings. More significantly, the reader familiar with Daoist hagiography immediately intuits a large and quite specific overlap of themes and motifs in narratives concerning Buddhist adepts, and a systematic theme- and motif-index such as the one I am preparing for publication confirms this

---

144. Gsy 1, 3; XiGsy 13, 31, 41, 54; Xuanyj 5; Mxj 26, 55, 84, 108, 112, 128; Jyj 8. Asking or imitating protagonist: XuGsy 4; XiGsy 3, 10, 15, 24, 58.

145. XiGsy 3; Xuanyj 19; Mxj 3, 9, 36, 74; Gsz shenyi B6, B16 (cf.).

146. Gsy 3; XiGsy 15, 17, 18, 20, 26, 32, 33, 37–39, 43; Mxj 119.

147. Gsy 1 (= Mxj 12); Mxj 8 (= Gsz shenyi A3) (cf.).

148. Join sangha: XiGsy 4, 13, 16, 18, 35, 48, 51, 54, 63, 69; Xuanyj 3; Mxj 24, 99. Redouble spiritual efforts: XiGsy 14, 23, 61, 63; Xuanyj 28, 32; Mxj 43, 121. Give up hunting or fishing: XiGsy 37. Assume vegetarian diet: XiGsy 21. Fast: Xuanyj 1. Feed sangha: XiGsy 6, 7, 38, 60. Build temple: Mxj 2. Conversion and miscellaneous: Gsy 4; Mxj 24, 55, 83, 88.

149. Gsz wangshen 6, 7, in both of which items a pair of paulownia trees grows at the spot where a monk has immolated himself.

intuition in precise terms. It would be possible, in fact, to plug our Buddhist material into the rhetorical analysis of Daoist hagiographies above, for all of these pro-Buddhist authors, not just the great hagiographer Huijiao, made sure that the extraordinary champions of their faith matched the Daoists feat for feat and skill for skill, right down to such supposedly distinctive Daoist wonders as liberation from the corpse (*shijie*) and flying and floating in midair;[150] and their tales matched the Daoists', confirmation device for confirmation device, so as not to seem any less plausible. Were we to overlay the motifs and themes of these two bodies of hagiographic material, there would be surprisingly little residue;[151] but, on the other hand, what residue there was would tell us much about the differences in the zones and levels at which these religions made themselves felt in the culture and society of the time. Three such differences deserve comment here.

First, we have seen that the Daoist hagiographies are built around metaphors of ascension; the Buddhist authors' textual images of their adepts are not. Rather—and somewhat ironically—the Buddhist emphasis (when it comes to the ultimate fate of the adept as seen from *this* world) is on the incorruptibility and the perdurance of the very body of the holy one.[152] To put it differently,

---

150. *Shijie* by Buddhist monk-adepts (partial listing): Gsz shenyi A1 (387a, only almsbowl and staff are found, no corpse); cf. A2 (= Mxj 59, cicada metaphor used); A3 (= Mxj 8, only robe and shoes are found); B5 (only burial shroud); B8 (only shoes); B11 (cf.: monk is not encoffined, but his body, laid out in temple, disappears and he is later seen at a distant place); B12 (similar); Mxj 16 (cf.: holy one simply disappears, so the left-behind robe and alms bowl are buried beside the temple); Mxj 17 (cf.: "both of them [foreign monks] sloughed off their skeletons so as not to die"). Related but not identical is the motif of deathlessness, as (e.g.) when the monk is sighted after his supposed death: Gsz shenyi B15, Mxj 106. Airborne Buddhists: Gsz songjing 2 (406c, = Mxj 41: monk floats his way out of prison); shenyi B7; Mxj 15 (monk levitates), 39. Buddhists with the skill of marvelously fast locomotion: Gsz shenyi A1; A2 (cf. Mxj 59); A4 (= Mxj 7); B1 (= Mxj 9), B5, B6, B8.

151. One of the most rhetorically important of these was the theme of Buddhist monks' and nuns' autonomy with respect to rulers, graphically illustrated, for example, in Gsz shenyi A1, B7, B16; wangshen 1 (cf. Mxj 6).

152. *Stūpas* for monks are mentioned, e.g., in: Xyj 1; Xuanyj 4, 18; Mxj 11, 19, 59, 94, 106. Relics: Xuanyj 30 (granted as response to a woman who fasts); Mxj 20; Jyj 7. A holy monk is buried beside his temple in Mxj 16. In Mxj 59, an official venerates the corpse of a holy monk (and cf. Mxj 106, 123). The burial sites of monk-adepts are noted in Gsz songjing 20, Gsz shenyi A1 (386c), A2 (= Mxj 59), B8, B16; Gsz wangshen 3; Mxj 16. Adept's corpse does not decay in Jyj 4, 7, 9; Gsz shenyi A2 (= Mxj 59), B2

Buddhists' "traces" consist (in addition to other, less tangible legacies) of corporeal relics (*sheli* 舍利, from Sanskrit *śarīra*), permanently accessible to the worshipper through stūpas and occasionally more directly accessible when removed and carried in procession; by contrast, Daoists' traces could not be corporeal since they in effect took their body with them upon ascending into the heavens, so their traces consisted of such things as personal belongings, places and marks on the landscape, narratives about their exploits (but so far their Buddhist counterparts left similar marks behind), and, most importantly and most distinctively, newly available sacred texts and bodies of esoteric knowledge they transmitted before departing.

Second, Buddhist texts stress even more than Daoist the religious adept's authority over the spirits and shamans of local cults. Sometimes a struggle is necessary to establish the priority of the newly arrived religion; in other cases, the local spirit submits voluntarily to what it at once recognizes as a superior teaching, asking to be taught the Dharma.[153] Even a Buddhist layman is able

---

(despite cremation; corpse is placed in mountain cavern where it is seen intact more than 30 years later), B12 (cf.); Gsz wangshen 2, 3 (and cf. 6, 11); *but* also in Lxz 43, 52, this early Daoist text reflecting values on corporeality that later changed (note that this motif is entirely absent from Sxz). Monks' corpses are strangely (and pleasantly) fragrant in Gsz shenyi B8, B13, B16.

153. Locally worshipped gods and spirits (as opposed to garden variety, non-localized demons) are subdued by Buddhist monks in: XuGsy 3, 6 (monk destroys temple outright); XiGsy 10; Xuanyj 1, 17; Mxj 59; Jyj 3 (a beautiful example in which a lake god, the shamans [called followers of the "Way of the Left"] attached to his temple, and the Buddhist "Lesser Vehicle" are all trumped by the higher authority of the Greater Vehicle), 10; Gsz songjing 1 (406b), in which a specialist in recitation is requested to explain the *Lotus* to a local god in his shrine; Gsz songjing 2 (406c, = Mxj 41), in which a monk is instructed by dark-clad figure to open a stone vault in a shrine on Mt. Tai, inside of which he finds treasure, which he distributes to the poor); Yml 83 (tr. Kao 1985, 147), 134, 255. Local spirits test the wits of monk-adepts in Mxj 59; Gsz songjing 14, shenyi A2 (cf. Mxj 59). Gsz songjing 8 (407b) is telling: shamans at a shrine notice (presumably in visionary trance) that the gods who reside there scatter when a monk approaches; songjing 21 is similar. On the tension between the new religion and the old temple cults, cf. Mxj 85, in which a layman burns his image of a god to display his conversion to Buddhism. Notably eloquent examples of this theme are also found in non-Buddhist texts, e.g., Shuyj 9, which is almost touching in its sad depiction of the ancient god's departure from the mountain where a monk has for the first time taken up residence. Cf. Miyakawa 1979; Faure 1987.

to stop the predations of a pack of local demons "using the power of the sūtras and the precepts"; his recitations of the *Śuramgama-[samādhi]sūtra* compel them to come in (in human form) for an interview, during which both parties agree to establish a boundary that neither side will henceforth cross.[154] There are obvious echoes here of old Indian Buddhist themes of the submission of *nagas* to the Buddha and his followers—reflections of the Buddhist conquest-by-assimilation of ancient, local cults. In the ongoing "Buddhist conquest of China," similarly, there was not only the air war among intellectuals and officials and the strategic-level "matching of concepts" (*geyi* 格義),[155] but also an infantry war on the ground, a guerilla warfare of the spirit (complete with minefields),[156] to which these narratives bear rich testimony.

Third, there is in Buddhist texts a levelling of the playing field when it comes to the abilities of adepts versus those of ordinary persons; these texts seem to open the terrain of wonders to anyone willing to undertake fervent Buddhist devotional practice—something scarcely imaginable in any of the types of pro-Daoist texts in our genre. If the feats of Buddhist monk- and nun-adepts can be mapped with surprisingly little remainder onto those of Daoist adepts, the feats accomplished by pious Buddhist laity can also be so mapped onto those of the Buddhist spiritual elite. Particularly in the tales of Guanshiyin's salvific interventions, monks and nuns are in no special position to request aid; the Bodhisattva of Universal Compassion is available to all equally, and all can access his power through identical channels. Even more strikingly, though, unusually pious laypersons are depicted—especially in the Mxj—as gaining the special powers normally reserved for monastic adepts, yet without performing the austerities wonder-working monks

---

154. Mxj 23, the first half of which (but not the part discussed here) is tr. and discussed in Campany 1991b, 48–49.

155. Lai 1979; Zürcher 1972, 184, 187, 404 n.18; Tsukamoto 1985, 248 (as a "stage"), 284–85, 291 (as an "age"), 293–97, 309–10, etc.; Link 1958, 2; Link 1969–70; Hurvitz and Link 1974; Wright 1990, 40, 130n.19, 131n.22.

156. In this war, the Chinese battlefield was "mined" by the Buddhists: one of the cleverer motifs of prolepsis was that of the ancient *stūpa* (especially, but not limited to, the "Aśokan *stūpa*"), temple, or stele which, unearthed in an ongoing archaeology of Chinese religious prehistory, was supposed to prove the ancient presence of Buddhism on Chinese soil. Examples include Mxj 9, 55; Jyj 1, 7; Gsz shenyi A1, B1 (= Mxj 9), in both of which a monk tells where to dig to find an ancient *stūpa* or temple; B14 (similar, with two stelae unearthed); and cf. Yml 263. On this theme, Zürcher 1972, 243–44, 277–80.

subjected themselves to. The same can be said of ordinary persons who die, see the true (and, in these cases, Buddhist) nature of the other world, and then return, speaking of what they witnessed: through the mechanism of the return-from-death tale these protagonists step into a role reserved to spirit-traveling shamans in ancient times.[157]

Finally, I summarize examples of pro-Buddhist items that stand out in the directness of their attacks on opponents of and alternatives to the Buddhist religion, or else in their ingenious arguments for the antiquity of Buddhism on Chinese soil.

Warnings against irreverence toward images

1. The bandit Ding Ling, "perverse by nature and lacking a faithful heart," shot the face of a large, bronze Buddha image with an arrow. The statue ran blood, which remained visible despite people's efforts to wipe it off. Ding ordered five hundred of his strongest men to topple the statue so that it could be melted down for weapons. But a noise like a peal of thunder issued from the statue's mouth, and the men all fell terrified to the ground. Many afterwards converted to Buddhism. As for Ding Ling, he later grew ill, then was executed.[158]

2. The Wu ruler Sun Hao, violent by nature and disrespectful of human feelings (so we are told), had a metal Buddha image tossed into his latrine. On the Buddha's birthday he urinated on its head, joking to his women that he was performing the ceremonial bath of the Buddha. Soon afterwards his penis swelled and was so painful that he could not sleep. A diviner concluded it was due to having offended some great deity, but none of the court physicians or other specialists knew what to do. One woman, who was a pious Buddhist, recommended that Sun perform an offering to the image in the latrine, and his pain was so severe that he complied, personally washing the image in the palace, prostrating himself

---

157. The same holds for protagonists of return-from-death tales of the Heaven and Humanity perspective discussed below; the motif is not at all distinctly Buddhist. But Buddhist authors used it to good effect, in, for example, Yml 248, 264–266; Xyj 1; Mxj 4, 5, 21, 22, 29, 34, 44, 45, 58, 64, 65, 71, 76, 101 (cf.), 103, 104 (cf.), 109, 114 (cf.), 115 (cf,), 117, 118, 123 (cf.), 124.

158. Xuanyj 35, based on BZL 540a. There was also a northern tribe known as the Dingling, but this item clearly refers to an individual.

before it, and begging forgiveness. The same night the swelling and pain subsided; Sun received the five lay precepts from the well known monk Kang Senghui, built a monastery, and nourished the sangha.[159]

Superiority of Buddhism over Daoism and shamanic cults

1. In the year 313, fishermen in the coastal Wu district saw two human-shaped figures floating offshore at the mouth of the Yangzi River. Taking them for gods of the ocean, the fishermen invited shamanic invocators (巫祝) and set out meat sacrifices by the water, in order to welcome the gods ashore. But the wind freshened and the waves swelled, so the fishermen grew frightened and withdrew. Then a follower of the "Way of the Five Pecks of Rice and of Huang-Lao" said the figures were Celestial Masters. Again the fishermen attempted to welcome them, this time accompanied by the Daoist, and again the wind and waves rose. Now among them was a Buddhist layman who suggested they might be a "compassionate manifestation of great *bodhi*." So they prepared a vegetarian meal and, together with monks and nuns from Dongling Temple 東靈寺 and other believers, returned to the shore. When they bowed in reverence, the wind and waves subsided and the two floating figures approached. As they drew near, it became apparent that they were stone statues. The people tried to lift them up but they could not be moved by human strength; when they gave up, the images floated up on their own and mounted the carriages. The little crowd carried them back in procession to the Mystic Temple 玄寺. The statues bore inscriptions on their backs: one was named Vipaśyin, the other Kāśyapa. No one could tell in what era the images had been made, but the inscriptions were quite clear. They were each seven feet tall. Dharma-seats were prepared for them, but several dozen men could not budge them; when they were once more simply invited, they floated up to their seats. The incident was reported to the court and, because of it, nine out of ten households, both aristocrats and commoners, converted. The monk Shi Fakai, who had come from the West, said that a *sūtra* spoke of the East having "two stone images as well as Aśokan *stūpas*" and said that whoever

---

159. Jyj 1, based on FYZL 13 (53.383b); Xuanyj 18, based on BZL 540a. The Jyj version gives more background on the image, which was said to have been an ancient one created by King Aśoka.

made offerings to and revered them would expunge his evil
karma.[160]

2. An official who "loved the teachings of Lao and Zhuang, did
not believe in the Buddha, and devoted himself entirely to animal
sacrifices" dreamed that one of his pet geese was carrying a scroll in
its bill; when, in the dream, he examined the text, he found that it
contained matters of sin and merit. On awakening he found the
text in his chambers. It was a Buddhist *sūtra*. From that moment
he ceased killing and converted; later he became wealthy and
prominent.[161]

3. Cheng Daohui 程道慧, a fervent upholder of the Way of the
Five Pecks of Rice, a believer in Laozi, and a notorious maligner of
Buddhism, died and then returned to life. He told of seeing the
Buddha's disciples in charge of the underworld, headed by King
Yama, and countless sinners receiving tortuous retribution. Cheng
learned that he had been mistakenly summoned and hence was
allowed to return to life; he also recalled while "dead" that in a
former life he had honored the Buddha. Having rediscovered his true
religious identity, he returned to life only with regret, jostled by the
crowd at his funeral and disgusted at the stench of his own corpse.[162]

4. Shi Jun upheld Daoism and maligned Buddhism, calling
the Buddha "a minor deity not worth serving." Every time he saw a
Buddha image he would disparage it. Later he grew ill. A friend
advised him to make an image of Guanyin, and, because of the
seriousness of his illness, he complied. When he had completed the
image, he dreamt of the bodhisattva and was cured.[163]

---

160. Jyj 2, based on FYZL 13 (383b.26–c16). I have omitted a variant
version of how the images were transported to the temple. The two inscriptions are names of ancient Buddhas; I have no further information on the
monk Fakai, whose "interpretation" of the event with reference to a *sūtra*
marks it as a "confirmation" (*yan*) of the text while at the same time con-
ferring scriptural authority on the images and their cultic veneration. The
reference to Aśokan *stūpas* is an example of a familiar "proleptical" strategy by Buddhist apologists—the attempt to ferret out traces of ancient
Buddhism in Chinese texts and to argue that unearthed objects were Zhou-
era remnants of "Aśokan *stūpas*" (Zürcher 1972, 269ff.; on Aśoka, Przyluski
1923; Strong 1983).

161. Xuanyj 24, based on BZL 539a; a full tr. may be found in
Campany 1991b, 51–52.

162. Mxj 44, based on FYZL 55 (709a), tr. Gjertson 1978, 10–13, and
Kao 1985, 172–75. A truncated version of the story appears as Xuanyj 27,
based on BZL 539a–b.

163. Xuanyj 9, based on TPGJ 111 and BZL 539c; Mxj 130, also
based on the BZL passage (which quotes both works).

Confucian Perspectives: Canonical Authority, Cultural Rectification, Official Service

When it comes to designating early medieval tendencies of thought or the perspectives of texts or their authors, the adjective "Confucian" is no less ambiguous than "Daoist" or "Buddhist." In the broadest sense, of course, almost all scholar-officials and other educated persons were "Confucians." Here, I use the term more narrowly to designate authors who self-consciously aimed to advance a perspective that clearly aligned itself with what had been identified since the second century B.C.E. as a Confucian textual canon.

The classical Confucian attitude toward anomalies, enunciated by the Master himself, was a studied indifference, but in the first and second centuries the cloak of indifference began to slip from even the most dedicatedly Confucian writers. One late Han Confucian work that approaches indifference yet still betrays the felt need at least to respond to others' extravagant claims is the *Shenjian* 申鑑 (*Extended Reflections*) of Xun Yue 荀悦 (148–209), which, in a discussion of "Common Superstitions," attempts to translate divinatory and self-cultivational terms into the language of Confucian virtues.[164] Then there is the famous *Lunheng* (*Arguments Weighed in the Balance*) by Wang Chong (27–97), which deploys a critical, reductionist hermeneutic—but one based on rational and cosmological principles, not on the classics—to "strange" material such as ghosts, demons, portents, and divination. Unlike Xun Yue, Wang Chong is hardly indifferent to topics in the realm of the anomalous, and he seeks to *explain* strange, seemingly otherworldly phenomena with reference to known, this-worldly principles, not merely to translate them into Confucian categories. But Wang's critique is not at all "Confucian" in the sense I am developing here, for his ultimate standard is not the Confucian textual canon.

It is in Ying Shao's Fsty, probably written between 194 and 206, that we find the centerpiece of a truly Confucian perspective on the cosmographic task. His preface, which was discussed and partially translated in Chapter Three, clearly shows the ambivalence that is the hallmark of centrist, Confucian-leaning discussions of the genre: matters of the "common" and the "strange" deserve scrutiny but not fascination; they warrant attention because they are useful barometers of social sentiment and public vir-

---

164. *Shenjian* 3.1a–5a, tr. Ch'en 1980, 150–62; cf. C.-y. Ch'en 1975, 144–46.

tue, but too much attention to them is a waste of time at best, corruptive at worst. For Ying Shao, however, writing as the last remnants of Han central order crumbled into a chaos of regional warring factions, the zone of the anomalous was important for another reason. Preoccupied as he was with the decline in knowledge and virtue from the era of Confucius to his own day, he saw anomalous beliefs and customs as holding twin keys to the exemplary past: if they provided an objective measure of the degree to which culture had degenerated since antiquity, they also, for that same reason, constituted a real if distorted link with the past; they served as so many confirmations, in actual popular practice and discourse, of the contents of the classics. Once subjected to a corrective hermeneutic, they could be read as gateways to an otherwise quickly and disturbingly receding past.

Three of the extant chapters of this work concern us here. Each takes the form of an essay, opening with a general topic (framed by quotations from Confucian classics[165]) and followed by a series of items illustrating the topic. The dominant trope throughout is one of critical comparison of more recent cultural phenomena with early, canonical standards. The implied author writes as one thoroughly grounded in texts the authority of which he sees no need to defend, since the implied reader is assumed to revere them as well.

Chapter Two, titled "Rectifying Errors" (*Zhengshi* 正失), opens with a disquisition on the ways in which old traditions become garbled in transmission and on the consequent need for ongoing "rectification of names."[166] Eleven such "errors" are then discussed. In

---

165. The work most frequently cited in the Fsty is a book titled *Sushuo* 俗説 ("Common Sayings") that must have served Ying Shao as a key source on customs (50 citations); but the list of other texts he most often cites clearly reveals where he saw cultural authority to lie: *Odes*, 48 citations; *Zuo Commentary*, 27; *Analects*, 25; *Book of Documents*, 23; *Changes* and a work simply titled *Commentary* (*Zhuan*), perhaps the *Yijing* commentaries, 22 citations each; *Zhouli*, 17; *Guoyu* and SJ, 11 each; *Liji* and HS, 8 each; *Records on Rites and Music* (*Liyueji*), 7; *Erya* and *Xiaojing*, 6 each. Conspicuously absent is Wang Chong's *Lunheng*, of which Ying Shao seems to have been unaware.

166. Among the authorities quoted are the *Analects*, *Book of Changes*, and *Mencius*. This attempt to reconstruct an exemplary but increasingly remote past, and its attendant anxiety over present deviance from past, scarcely knowable standards, is typical of Han (and most especially of later Han) writing. Compare Ban Gu's HS 25, which recounts a history of sacrificial offerings since ancient times so as to define (and

each case, Ying Shao first relates a legend current in his day (seemingly based on texts, not on oral sources), then gives reasons for thinking it ill-founded and, in some cases, his opinion as to the cause of the error in transmission. I list a few here as examples.

1. A cluster of legends surrounding the *feng* and *shan* sacrifices on Mount Tai, with emphasis on the ones maintaining that the Yellow Thearch ascended into the heavens from the top of the mountain: Ying Shao argues that the Yellow Thearch was actually mortal, citing texts that give the location of his tomb and reminding the reader (citing the *Chunqiu* as his authority) of the unreliability of transmitted tales.[167]

2. Legends concerning Wangzi Qiao's attainment of transcendence: Ying Shao, citing ancient texts about this figure, argues that the legends of his transcendence are due merely to his prediction of the time of his own death, and cites Yang Xiong on the mortality of various former sages.[168]

3. Legends concerning celestial responses (including a "rain" of grain kernels) to Dan, Prince of Yan, in the time of Qin Shi Huang: Ying Shao dismisses the reality of these contranatural responses and suggests that because of Dan's popularity, his followers fabricated these stories.[169]

4. The elaborate claims regarding Dongfang Shuo, including the claims that he was the incarnate spirit of the Taibo star (the planet Venus), that this star-spirit had transformed himself into a series of ancient ministers including Lao Dan (= Laozi), and that he could cause the flourishing of any ruler he served: Ying Shao debunks all these legends. He cites Liu Xiang's supposed questioning of elderly people who had been alive during Shuo's tenure at court and their reports that he was nothing but a slick self-promoter; he also quotes Yang Xiong, who similarly dismisses the reports. He concludes that the whole Dongfang Shuo cycle is due to "later novelty-seekers who augmented the accounts of him with deviant sayings and strange statements."[170]

5. The story of the attainment of transcendence of Liu An, Prince of Huainan: Ying Shao points to historical accounts of the

---

implicitly to criticize) present ritual usages, and Cai Yong's (133–92) *Duduan* 獨斷 (on which see ECT, 467–70), which attempts to sort out the confusing nomenclature and the plethora of offerings appropriate to various classes of officially worshipped deities.

167. Fsty 65–80; this is the third in the chap. 2 series of cases.
168. Fsty 81–89; this the fourth in the series.
169. Fsty 90–92; this is the fifth in the series.
170. Fsty 108–14; this is the seventh in the series.

prince's suicide due to his implication in a failed seditious plot. He attributes the legends of Liu's transcendence to his followers' shame at his ignominious end and their desire to promote a favorable memory of him.[171]

Chapter Eight, titled "The Canons of Sacrificial Offerings" (*Sidian* 祀典), is an attempt to trace the authentic origins of around sixteen widespread cults, apotropaic practices, and seasonal observances. The introduction quotes classics such as the *Book of Rites, Discourses of the States* (*Guoyu*), and *Analects* on the impropriety of sacrificing to spirits outside one's lineage or otherwise straying "outside the canon of sacrificial offerings."[172] In particular, it seems to be the ever-expanding range of cults introduced during the Han that Ying Shao targets. The chapter does not unfold as a direct attack on these cults and practices; perhaps that would have seemed too blatant an assault on the Han system. It does, however, constitute a subtle critique, for as it sorts out the true origins of these practices and cult figures, distinguishing these either from the "common sayings" (*sushuo* 俗說) about them or what one or another old text says about them, this "return to the origins" (*fanben* 反本) discloses the cultural and moral distance that has been travelled since pre-Han times, revealing the latent extent of degeneration. Ying Shao does not urge that these practices be abandoned, only that the original reasons for them be understood correctly.

Here again, then, Ying Shao rectifies a series of slippages in the transmission of knowledge over time—in this case, slippages that affect contemporaries' understanding of certain of their religious observances.[173] It is crucial to note two assumptions he makes: that dubious cults and improbable stories are actually linked with the past as reported in old texts, thus constituting invaluable keys to the past, *and* that they do not reflect the past clearly but distort it, necessitating a decoding.

Chapter Nine, titled "Deviant Spirits" (*Guaishen* 怪神), rectifies errors in a closely related area of cultural practice: namely,

---

171. Fsty 115–18; this is the eighth in the series. Note that Ying Shao does not debunk Liu An's supervision of the compiling of the *Huainanzi*, only his personal attainment of transcendence.

172. This phrase, which furnishes the title of the chapter, is quoted here from the *Guoyu*.

173. Fsty chap. 3, "Mistaken Rites" (*Qianli*), similarly points out lapses from canonical standards—in this case, in the performance of family rites and the maintenance of proper family relations. Here too, Ying compares recent practice with classical texts and finds the practices wanting.

stories of encounters with spirits, including, in some cases, the founding of unauthorized cults to them. This chapter is distinctive in that it quotes at length, mostly from unnamed sources (so that they seem to be orally circulating stories which Ying Shao had heard), narratives of recent, named individuals' anomalous experiences. These narratives may be divided into two types: in one, the intent is to argue that mistaken beliefs, though unfounded, can cause real harm—hence the need for ongoing rectification;[174] in the other, the intent is to show that an attitude of cool composure and a trust in the Confucian classics in the face of (real) demonic incursions will lead to success.[175] Examples of the first type include the story (which involves Ying Shao's own ancestor and must have been passed down in his family) of how an acquaintance is frightened when he sees what he takes to be the apparition of a spirit-snake in his wine cup; his fright brings on a serious illness. Ying Shao's ancestor, noticing that a bow hung on a wall caused a serpentine reflection in a cup on the table where his acquaintance saw the apparition, has the sick man carried in and demonstrates to him that what he saw was no snake-spirit, and so he recovers.[176] Other examples include fervently practiced cults that suddenly spring up due to someone's noticing an object left by accident at an unexpected place: a fish dropped in a field that is taken to be the embodiment of a god, a plum pit left in the hollow of a mulberry tree that sprouts and is taken as a sign of the presence of a divine "Lord of Plums,"[177] or a cake left by a traveller beneath a human-shaped stone, taken by other travellers to be an offering to the stone in repayment for a cure it effected. The harms in these cases are worshippers' extravagant expenditures of resources and energy.

Each of the stories of the second type narrates the exemplary behavior of a scholar-official in the face of an anomalous occurrence that terrifies others: the official merely continues his ordinary routine, or dons his official attire and chants classics such as the *Classic of Filial Piety* or the *Book of Changes* during the night; the offensive creature dies, revealing itself to be a spirit-possessed dog, fox, or other beast, and the official is later promoted to high office. Tellingly, one of the heroes here is Dong Zhongshu, whose "way" is

---

174. These are grouped in the first half of the chapter and take up Fsty, 388–417.

175. Fsty, 418–44.

176. Fsty, 388–91.

177. A version of this story reappears in Ssj 5.9, tr. DeWoskin 1977a, 104.

tested by the Han Emperor Wu: the ruler commands a shamaness from Yue to place a curse on him; Zhongshu "donned his court gowns and faced south, chanting classics and treatises; he could not be harmed, and the shamaness suddenly died."[178] The moral of all of these stories, which is drawn explicitly several times, is, as one formulation has it, "How can anomalous creatures possibly harm a man?" or, in another, "Those who are like Shu Jian [the protagonist of the just-told story], with hearts harder than metal or stone so as to have no fear when demons arrive, so as to take their good fortune into their own hands—are they not strong?"[179]

The upshot of the combination of these two story-types in chapter 9 is that humanity's place in the cosmos is privileged, protected by Heaven; a cultivated person need not follow uncanonical apotropaic practices but only act in the way proper to a human being—maintaining customary decorum, reciting texts transmitted from antiquity—to avoid harm from lesser beings in the cosmic hierarchy. It is only fear of such beings that brings calamity, and that fear arises when one *forgets* the sure ground of (Confucian) tradition, with its canonical texts and its canons of proper behavior.

Overall we may conclude that, in Ying Shao's humanity-centered worldview, the anomalies that are of significance are human beliefs and practices anomalous with respect to a cultural, not a cosmological, taxonomic field. His approach to anomalies is historical, not cosmological, since his concern as rectifier of culture is to take the measure of contemporaries' distance from past, canonical norms. The extent of this gradual slippage in manners over time is the criterion of anomalousness in which he is most interested.

I conclude this section by commenting on the discrete sections in the HHS and SGZ that deal with masters of various esoteric skills, for these, too, reveal a type of Confucian perspective. Chen Shou's Fjz contains biographies of five individuals, each of whom possessed wondrous esoteric skills in a particular area: Hua Tuo, a physician; Du Kuei, skilled at musical tones and pitches; Zhu Jianping, a physiognomist; Zhou Xuan, an interpreter of dreams; and Guan Lu, a famed diviner and interpreter of omens.[180] The

---

178. Fsty, 423.

179. The first quotation is at Fsty, 434; the second, at Fsty, 418.

180. SGZ 29 (799–830); DeWoskin 1983 translates four of the five biographies.

historian's brief concluding assessment (*ping* 評) merely emphasizes the extraordinariness of their talents. We note, however, that
two of the figures included in this section (Hua Tuo and Guan Lu)
were clients of high-status patrons, that the other three held official
appointments in which they exercised their skills, that all practiced
arts utilizing the locative cosmology and numerology developed
during the Han, and that none are described as shamans (or otherwise in direct touch with spirits) or, for that matter, as Daoist practitioners.

Fan Ye's Fslz, by contrast, contains biographies of some forty-
four individuals of various persuasions, some *fangshi*, some Daoist
(at least eleven of his subjects are included in Daoist hagiographies
as well), and some shamanic. In keeping with the times, a major
theme of this text is the tension between *ziran* and *mingjiao*, between the purported autonomy of the adept and the mandate to
serve the state. An excellent case in point is the treatment given
the adept Zuo Ci in this text as opposed to his depiction in the Bwz
and the Sxz. In Zhang Hua's Bwz, Zuo Ci appears as an adept who,
appearing at the Wei court after being summoned, exhibits skills in
abstention from grain and other macrobiotic regimens; body division, concealment, and switching; passing through obstructions;
illusion; sexual techniques; and exorcism. Narratives about him
are slender, however, and one is left simply with the impression
that he was tested and ended up impressing those in power with
his skills. He does not exhibit the trickster-like nature of a
Dongfang Shuo, who is the Bwz's most autonomous adept.[181] In Fan
Ye's biography, by contrast, he depletes the supply of meat and
wine in the city market and otherwise toys with Cao Cao, enraging
the commander enough to order his execution, at which point Zuo Ci
uses his technique of body switching to blend into a flock of sheep
and elude capture.[182] But the context suggests that Zuo Ci's tricks
were not, on the whole, necessarily salutary, whereas in Ge Hong's
Sxz hagiography, in which Zuo Ci is portrayed in even more trickster-like terms, the context clearly allows us to read the author's
treatment of him as an argument for the autonomy of the adept.[183]

In the descriptions and ordering of individuals there is a clear,
if silent, demarcation between two groups: those who gained their

---

181. Bwz 8.23, 8.24, 9.7 (the last item relates the legend that he was
the Year Star in human form).

182. Fslz 27 (2747), tr. in Ngo 1976, 138–40, and DeWoskin 1983,
83–86.

183. Sxz 27. Zuo Ci also shows up in Ssj 1.21 and 1.25.

skills (all of which are in this case based on manipulations of the Han locative cosmology) from the study of texts of some sort, often sitting at the feet of named teachers or studying at named academies, on the one hand, and on the other hand those whose powers derived from contact with spirits or else from no specified source.[184] In the ordering of these two groups is implied a hierarchy of status, and most members of the first group serve the state or rulers in one capacity or another, while most members of the second group wander about or live in reclusion, thus serving no useful political or moral purpose. Quite significantly, all of the figures who are also the subject of extant Daoist hagiographies belong to the second group, none to the first.

Fan Ye's preface and postscript to this group of biographies are perfect studies in ambivalence. It is clear that he writes not as a proponent of the *fangshi* or a Daoist perspective, nor as their opponent, and certainly not as a practitioner of either, but as an outsider—a historian, writing from the perspective not of the periphery but of the center—trying to sort out what is valuable and useful, and what dangerous, in these strange arts. "At times they prove useful in actual affairs, but these methods (*dao*) are hidden and distant (*yinyuan* 隱遠), shrouded in mystery and difficult to get to the bottom of (*xuan'ao nanyuan* 玄奧難原), and that is why the Sage [Confucius] did not speak of anomalies and spirits and rarely spoke of human nature and destiny."[185] After recounting the struggle between Old Text Confucians such as Huan Tan and the New Text and *fangshi* fascination with esoterica and *chenwei*, showing his sympathy for the former camp, Fan Ye nevertheless adds (rather defensively, it seems) that anything—even the so-called "broad Way" of study of the classics—if pursued one-sidedly can prove a hindrance; partiality and obsession, whether in the study of esoteric arts or of the *Odes* and *Documents*, lead to error. The closing encomium (*zan* 贊) echoes the themes of the mysteriousness of these skills, the difficulty of verifying them, and the need nevertheless to consult them; it grants that some may be genuine, while warning against deliberate deceptions.[186]

---

184. Hua Tuo (HHS 82B, 2736–41) is the last of the former group; the latter group begins with Xu Deng (HHS 82B, 2741) and extends through the last figure in the list, Wang Heping (HHS 82B, 2751).

185. HHS 82A (2703); cf. the trs. of this preface in Ngo 1976, 73–79, and DeWoskin 1983, 43–46.

186. HHS 82B (2751); Ngo's tr. (1976, 148) is excellent, DeWoskin's (1983, 89) is somewhat off the mark.

The Perspective of "Heaven and Humanity": Humanity's Place in a Responsive, Crowded Cosmos

We come now to one of the greatest unsolved problems in the study of the early anomaly accounts: namely, that the worldview implied in some of the most prototypical texts of the genre—the Ssj, Sshj, Yml, Yy, Qxj, and others—has yet to be satisfactorily illuminated *as* a coherent worldview and not a "miscellaneous" jumble of "superstitions" recorded from "popular" sources by proto-ethnographers. The words in inverted commas have peppered most discussions of these texts, but they are substitutes for, not terms of, analysis. If we are to take the genre seriously as a vehicle of moral, religious, and ideological suasion, then we must come to terms with the implied rhetorical aims of these admittedly wide-ranging and variegated writings; but, unlike the groups of texts we have analyzed so far, these bear no clear sectarian affiliation, often treating of Buddhist and Daoist adepts, *fangshi*, and upright Confucians alike. Is it possible to arrive at any more nuanced understanding of these texts' aims than the often-repeated one that they seek to show that spirits really exist (or, even more minimally, that many people so believed)?

I believe that it is, and I will elucidate here and in the following chapter what I take to be the specific, coherent, and principled, if multi-faceted, perspective to which the authors of these texts sought to persuade readers. That perspective had no name in its day, principally because it cut across distinct traditions and even religions; yet it was not "syncretic," which would imply a joining together of ideas and values from diverse sources to form a new combination, because it was in fact a morally and religiously conservative (yet also, as we will see, in some respects quite innovative) continuation and modification of a unified, indigenous set of Han-era values. Over fifty years ago, the term *tianrenshuo* 天人説— "the teaching [or persuasive stance] of Heaven and Humanity"— was proposed as a characterization of Gan Bao's thought, and that term will, with some explication, serve as well as any to designate this set of emphases.[187]

---

187. Nishino 1943 first proposed the term; DeWoskin 1974, 33ff. and 1977b, 41–42, adopts it, citing this article. But the following explication of the term and development of its aptness as a designation for this group of texts are my own.

Attestations of the phrasal pairing of *tian* and *ren*, in this sense at least, begin with the *Xici* appendix to the *Book of Changes*.[188] The "Heaven-and-Humanity tradition" (*tianrenjia* 家) is mentioned in the SJ as one among many guilds of divination. The cognate expression *tianren [zhi] ji* [之] 際, literally "the boundary of Heaven and humanity"—the border or frontier where they meet—shows up in several early contexts,[189] the most instructive of which occurs in the HS biography of Dong Zhongshu. In the context of his ongoing argument with Han Emperor Wu, in which he deployed New Text, locative ideology to try to check the ruler's expansionist and centrist policies, Dong is recorded as having written to him: "Your servant cautiously studies what is in the *Springs and Autumns* and scrutinizes the precedents set by the actions of former generations, in order to observe the mutual boundary between Heaven and humanity, which is much to be revered 以觀天人相與之際，甚可畏也. When the nation is about to undergo the misfortune of losing the Way, Heaven first produces catastrophic anomalies as a warning. . . ."[190]

The connections of these phrasal variations on *tianren* with divination, the *Xici*, and Dong Zhongshu's description of his study of historical texts as a way to "observe the mutual boundary between Heaven and humanity" are hardly fortuitous and bear directly on our own interest. Gan Bao left an important commentary on the *Changes*; what remains of it indicates that he interpreted that classic by assimilating historical examples to each of its hexagrams.[191] Moreover, Gan Bao (like Zhang Hua but even more promi-

---

188. The *Xici* was found with the *Yijing* in a Mawangdui manuscript and so dates at least to 168 B.C.E.: ECT, 221. Peterson 1982 accurately but awkwardly translates *Xicizhuan* as "Commentary on the Attached Verbalizations"; I will simply refer to this text as the *Xici*. Some of the following comments on *tianren*, *tianrenji*, and *tianrenjia* are based on DKW 5833.856, 860, and 857 (3:491d–492b) respectively. In the late fifth century C.E., the inverted term *rentianjiao* was used to designate a particular form of lay Buddhism emphasizing similar locative values (good deeds leading to better rebirth as a human or in the heavens); Lai 1987, 12–17.

189. Others: (1) SJ biography of Sima Xiangru: 天人之際已交; (2) Ssxy, "Wenxue" chap., used by He Yan to praise the superiority of Wang Bi's *Laozi* commentary over his own: "With such a person one may discuss the frontier between Heaven and Man!" (Mather 1976, 95); (3) cf. *tianren zhi he* 和, HS 23 (1112) and elsewhere. The phrase "Heaven and humanity are one body" 天人一體 appears in the *Taipingjing*: Wang Ming 1960, 16.

190. HS 56, 2498.

191. Nishino 1943; DeWoskin 1974, 34. His commentary, fragments

nently) interpreted portents at the Jin court; no Jin figure is cited more often in the JS "Treatise on the Five Phases" as a commentator on recent anomalous events as auspices.[192] Note, too, that Liu Yiqing drew the title for his Yml directly from the *Xici*, and that the term *youming* 幽明 is used at one point in the Yy to designate the relations between the seen and unseen worlds: "The *you* and the *ming* are separate paths," a dream-figure tells a man who had rudely peered down by torchlight on the strange creatures cavorting beneath the surface of a river; "why did you shine your light on us?"[193]

The common thread linking these observations is the *Xici* as, it seems, a Confucian warrant for the study of anomalies both contemporary (for prognosticatory and admonitory purposes) and historical (for "observing the mutual boundary between Heaven and humanity"). Perhaps the *Xici* was written as a buffer around the ancient *Changes* to legitimate its appropriation as a canonical text; this might have been seen as necessary since prodigies—implying techniques of divination—were among the things of which the Master did not speak,[194] and the text has the sort of defensive tone which is the mark of anxiety over legitimacy. Whatever the origins of this obscure but rich text, the worldview set forth in it, to the extent that we can grasp it, and most especially the role it constructs for the *Changes* as a text, are crucial clues to the perspective that seems to inform and to be urged in the Ssj, Yml, Yy, and similar anomaly accounts.

---

of which are scattered throughout *Zhouyi jijie*, is said to be in the tradition of the diviner Jing Fang, who shows up as a character in a number of anomaly account narratives.

192. Gan Bao is quoted as an interpreter of anomalies on at least the following pages of JS 27–29 (I may have missed others): 805 (where he cites Dong Zhongshu as an authority), 806, 820 (Liu Jingshu, another anomaly account author, is also mentioned here, but not as an interpreter of portents), 822, 824, 827, 850, 853, 858, 880, 896, 906—in all, 12 cases. DeWoskin 1983, 169n.40, says he is mentioned in "over twenty" cases.

193. Yy 7.19; the man was punished for his brazen curiosity with a swift death. Cf. the paired usage of these terms in the postscript to Fan Ye's biographies of adepts (HHS 82B, 2751), the language of which is strongly reminiscent of the *Xici*. The homophonous *youming* 冥 which also appears in texts of this era designates the "dark" side of the border exclusively: e.g. Gsz 368c.26; T 2102 (52.18a.8); Sxz 80.

194. Self-consciously Confucian writers long remained uneasy about the *Changes* (Peterson 1982, 77–78).

In a provocative article, Willard Peterson has pointed out that the *Xici* speaks of the *Changes* in terms appropriate to a spirit-medium; the text itself steps into the archaic but still active (throughout Han and early medieval times) role of the one who channels communication between the separate realms of the seen and the unseen.

> The *Change* in effect will be our *wu* 巫, a shaman or diviner . . .
> who puts us in touch with *shen* [spirits, or the numinous]. . . .
> The *Change* is [a] medium also in the sense of being the
> means of passing from the realm of what is intelligible to us to
> the realm of what is not directly or only imperfectly knowable.
> . . . The technique and text of the *Change* include, and mediate
> between, the unknown and the known, both in the present
> moment, with phenomena as known and numinosity [*shen*] as
> what is not directly knowable, and over time, with the past as
> known and the future as unknown.[195]

According to the *Xici*, the *Changes* can perform this function because it was created by sages who, seeing what remains obscure to ordinary people, and thus knowing what would otherwise remain unknowable, stored in it various mimetic graphs and writings including "symbols," "images," "simulacra," or "figures"—all possible translations of the key term *xiang* 象—which captured both the visible and the normally invisible aspects of reality, and which more-over captured them indirectly or symbolically yet totally, without remainder. Both the mediatory function and the mimetic activities of the sages (and, by extension, of the book they bequeathed to later ages) are emphasized in the following passage among others:

A8.1   As for the figures (*xiang*), the sages, having the means to see [things that are] occulted in the world (有以見天下之賾),[196] created analogues to their form and characteristics and fig-

---

195. Peterson 1982, 107–9; I have taken the liberty of stringing together three successive comments.

196. The term Graham translates as "occulted," *ze*, was glossed in some early texts (including a comment on the *Xici* passage at hand) with the phrase "that which is obscure and deep, hard to see" 幽深難見也 (DKW 36887 [10.797c]). For the reader's convenience, numbering of passages follows that in Peterson 1982, except for the passage translated next, which he omits; his numbering does not, however, match the ed. of the *Yijing* which I have also consulted.

uratively represented them according to their [features as]
beings; this is why they are called "figures."[197]

Later in A8 we read:

[The sages, by means of figures and other graphs,] spoke of
the most occulted things under Heaven, yet they cannot be
called despicable; they spoke of the most active things under
Heaven, yet they cannot be called disordered.

But earlier there occurs a passage which, even if standing
alone, could almost serve as a blueprint for the writing of anomaly
accounts, particularly those of the Heaven and Earth persuasion. I
first translate, then explicate, this seminal discussion:

A4.1–4 The *Changes* is on a level with Heaven and Earth,
therefore it is able to remain in alignment with the courses
of Heaven and Earth. [The sages] looked up to observe the
patternings of Heaven and looked down to examine the
veinings of Earth; this is how they knew the causes of what is
hidden (*you*) and what is manifest (*ming*) (仰以觀於天文俯以察於
地理是故知幽明之故). They returned to the beginnings of things
and went back to the endings of things; this is how they knew
the explanations of death and birth. They [understood that]
essence and pneuma [combine to] form strange creatures[198]
and that wandering cloud-souls are responsible for anomalies;
this is how they knew the actual circumstances of ghosts and
spirits (精氣為物游魂為變是故知鬼神之情狀).
    A4.5–8 They [accurately] mimicked [what is in] Heaven
and Earth; this is why they did not go astray. They possessed
all-encompassing knowledge of the myriad things, yet in their
courses they succored the world; this is why they did not
transgress. They acted with detachment, not as most did, and
they delighted in Heaven and knew its decrees; this is why
they had no anxiety. They brought security to their domain
and remained strong in their humanity; this is why they were
capable of loving others.

---

197. This is my own tr., consulting Peterson 1982, 114, and Graham
1989, 362. I have greatly benefited from both of these discussions of the
Xici as well as that in Schwartz 1985, 396.
    198. Reading *wu* here (given what follows in this context) as ex-
plained in Chapter Three.

A4.9–12   [The *Changes*] is modeled on and embraces the transformations in Heaven and Earth yet does not transgress; it bends with and brings to completion the myriad things yet leaves nothing out; it penetrates the courses of both day and night yet still has knowledge. Therefore, just as the numinous has no location, the *Changes* has no embodiment.[199]

In brief, the *Changes* is here maintained to be a text that: (1) thanks to the gnosis of bygone sages is able to speak of things that would otherwise remain invisible, unknowable, hidden from our view; (2) does so through a mediatory graphic mimesis, such that the writing of and in the text shows to us what the "occulted" showed to the sages; (3) completely maintains its own correctness, fixity, and legibility, not transgressing or going astray, despite daring to speak of things bent, dark, shifting, and numinous. To these points we must add one other: that, although the *Changes* began as a book for divination, the *Xici* maintains that it encompasses not only future but also past configurations of events, that its function is not just prognosticatory but also historical:

A11.7   [The sages,] being numinous [themselves], knew what was to come; being knowledgeable, they stored up what had passed (神以知來知以藏往).

What, then, of the anomaly accounts? To put as briefly as possible a series of points that will be further elaborated in the following analysis, one can see the authors of the Heaven and Humanity persuasion as, in effect, transposing the above three characteristics of the *Changes* as portrayed by the *Xici* into a different

---

199. This section, too, is my own tr., consulting that in Peterson 1982, 99ff. The corresponding location in *Yijing* is p. 40, cols. a–b. Regarding A4.9–12 in particular, I believe that Peterson misses the *tension* that the text is wrestling with in order to urge the canonicity of the *Changes* despite its (from a narrowly Confucian standpoint) suspect subject matter and purpose: on the one hand, it argues that the *Changes* is modeled on and even embodies flux and transformation, that is, prodigies, as well as the numinous (*shen* 神); hence the *Changes* necessarily "bends" (deviates from what is *zheng* 正 or upright), delves into matters of both day and night, and even lacks embodiment—an unusual claim to make for a book. Yet on the other hand it argues that the *Changes* remains a steady, reliable guide; it mirrors change but in a fixed, constant, hence "safe" way, and it encompasses "bent," dark, and numinous things without itself transgressing, omitting, or lacking in knowledge.

key, keeping the relationship between parts but changing the notes. In the anomaly accounts, the role of "sage" as seer, as one with gnosis, is now played on a much humbler scale by the textually posited experiencer or witness of the recorded event, the one who "sees" the phenomenon in question. The nature of the text has shifted from systematic and "figurative" to piecemeal, historical, and (as befits the post-Han age of distance from origins and from canonical standards) necessarily incomplete, open-ended like any list of particulars. But the function of the text, as well as that of its author, remains mediatory, in the sense that direct vision on the part of the implied reader of that which was seen is presumed impossible or unlikely, but is described and reported from someone else's experience (someone, as we will see, on a par with the implied reader), and thus made accessible through the text. The purpose of the text remains that of limning (but now case by reported historical case) the structure of both the seen and the unseen worlds and, most especially, the shape of the boundary where they meet. And the warrant remains similar: that it is possible for the text to speak of unfathomables and of anomalous transformations without becoming lost in these, and that doing so serves an instructive purpose. If this latter point reminds us of the sorts of justificatory statements made about the new genre of anomaly accounts that were surveyed in Chapter Three, it does not, I believe, do so by accident.[200]

In short, given the evident interest of our authors in the *Changes* and their allusions specifically to the language of the *Xici* appendix, and given the parallelism between the role carved out by the *Xici* for the *Changes* and the role that our texts want us to

---

200. The implied worldviews of the *Xici* and this group of anomaly accounts are also similar: both seek to chart not only abnormal transformations (*bianhua* 變化), which occur in the visible realm between Heaven and Earth and are messages from the cosmos to humanity, but also the numinously indeterminate (*shen* 神), defined in the *Xici* as simply "that which is not encompassed in *yin* and *yang*," the latter being aspects of the mutable world which, in contrast to *shen*, generates more commonly visible and directly knowable phenomena. But *shen*, too, are ultimately knowable (for the *Xici*) through figures. The combination of *bianhua* and *shen* (in the broadest sense) would not be an inaccurate summary of the contents of this group of anomaly accounts; as explained momentarily, they simply replace the figures of the *Yijing* with narrative "traces" of the moments in time and points in space at which the *shen* (that is, the *you* 幽) has manifested itself in some concrete relation to the realm structured by *yin* and *yang* (that is, the *ming* 明).

read them as playing, one could do much worse than to view the anomaly accounts of the Heaven and Humanity persuasion as constituting a sort of supplement, in the historiographic key, to the *Changes*. Like the *Changes* (as portrayed in the *Xici*), they operate in the zone between Heaven and Earth. They focus not (as the *Changes* do) on the numinous itself but on its points of intersection with humanity. Their "figures" are not all-encompassing, systematically arranged series of graphic patterns but records of specific historical incidents. Sacrificing the efficiency of the hexagrams but gaining the fleshed-out concreteness of narrative and the verisimilitude of the historically "confirmable," they afford glimpses of the patternings of that which is normally invisible, like tracks left by subatomic particles in a cloud chamber, "history" being, in the post-sage, post-Han era, perhaps the only remaining—or else the only trustworthy—medium for this purpose. And let us not neglect the historian-author's claim to cultural authority that is latent in his subliminal appeal to this august precedent: if not himself a seer of things unseen, he nevertheless transmits to the implied reader "figures" or representations of what is numinous and occulted. At the same time, his closer proximity to the implied reader—he is no remote sage, simply a historian passing on cases discovered through research—renders him more believable and his text more accessible.

But the texts we are about to examine share not simply this view of their task but also a common vision of what the unseen world and its boundary with this world were like; and that vision went beyond the generalities of the *Xici* to explore the finer ramifications of Han cosmological thinking in the full range of human relations with beings and forces "not encompassed by *yin* and *yang*."

The major texts with which we have to deal are the Ssj, Yml, Yy, and Sshj, together accounting for more than 1,200 items; to these I add at least the following texts as sharing essentially the same perspective, although since relatively few items survive from these texts their inclusion is necessarily tentative: Lyz, Shuyj, Luyz, Qxj, XuQxj, Xs, and Jlz. I also include the Yhz in this group since, although it exclusively narrates cases of revenge exacted by the dead on the living, its perspective closely resembles that of the other texts discussed here; ghostly vengeance is, in fact, a prototypical Heaven and Humanity theme. I will cite other texts when their story-types overlap with those just listed; I will also cite corresponding items from the ShuyjRf, although, as I will explain at the end of the chapter, that text in fact represents a "hybrid" mixture of the Heaven and Humanity persuasion with another set of interests.[201]

When one charts the themes and motifs prevalent across these texts, it becomes evident that their authors were concerned to urge something approximating the following views. My discussion here will be somewhat limited since it is largely these same texts that I take up again in the next chapter.

Humanity is inexorably connected to (although not indistinct from) all other species of beings between Heaven and Earth, both visible and invisible. These connections are not simply metaphysical but are also moral and ritual in nature; the lives and welfare of humanity are intertwined with those of all other classes of beings. These texts do not stop at urging that unseen beings of many kinds really exist; they further urge that humans impact and are impacted by them in ways to which they seek to draw attention, and which they urge the reader to take seriously. They do so through narrative portrayals of human protagonists surrounded by and implicated—in many surprising and intimate ways—in a teeming network of beings not of our own kind.

Most of the story-types that implicitly argue this thesis explore some sort of *moral* connection between humans and others, and such connections are the focus of the following chapter. But other story-types emphasize the sheer ontological connectedness of taxonomically distinct beings. Chief among these are tales depicting cross-species or cross-class *transformations* of one or another sort.

There are, first of all, a few theoretical discussions of cross-species transformations, some of which may have once been "frames" for subsequent lists of narrative items; these were briefly

---

201. Some of the remaining texts are simply too fragmentary to yield to analysis. The Lgz, for example, shows a marked heterogeneity of themes: six of its 24 extant items are explicitly pro-Buddhist; two seem strongly pro-Confucian (in the sense outlined above), since upright officials successfully ward off demonic attacks; four narrate demonic attacks unsuccessfully warded off by ordinary persons (including one home-grown attempt at exorcism that fails miserably); and two warn against *gu* or black magic (on which see Feng and Shryock 1935). On balance, the only message extractable from this assortment is something like "rely on trained specialists to do your spirit-related work, and do not attempt low-class techniques yourself—but do get help, since demons do real harm"; but 24 items is not much to go on, and one senses that if more of the Lgz had survived we would not be so easily thrown off its rhetorical trail.

dealt with in Chapter Five.[202] But there are many more narratives of purported actual cases of transformation. Some of them state or imply that a person is transformed into an animal as a divine punishment for misdeeds;[203] even here, despite the moral overlay, the sheer ontological possibility of such an event is stressed, but it is emphasized more strongly in items that simply narrate such a transformation without giving a moral etiology for it. People metamorphose into a wide variety of animal species, into stones, even into water or rainbows.[204] In some cases the implied (or occasionally explicit) etiology for such events involves the power of emotional bonds between people (often designated *xiangsi* 相思): for example, a woman who climbs to a mountaintop to steadfastly watch for her husband's return changes into stone.[205] (The same principle applies in tales of filial sons who sacrifice themselves to locate their parent's missing corpse: the son leaps into the water where his parent was lost, and soon the two corpses appear, hand in hand, as if bonded by their mutually resonant sympathy, allowing for proper burial.[206]) And many tales feature transformations from one animal or plant species to another, or cross-kingdom transformations (plants changing into animals, etc.).[207]

Working from the opposite side of the ontological/taxonomic equation, other tale-types depict animals as behaving in human-

---

202. Ssj 3.5, 12.1, 12.10, 19.6.

203. People divinely changed into tigers (noted in anomaly accounts for their marauding attacks on human communities) as punishment: Yy 5.3, 8,38, 8.40; into "a horse or ox," Yml 166; into a bear, Yy 8.42.

204. People transformed into tigers: Qxj 2, 5; Shuyj 13, 88; Yy 3.13 (cf.), 3.15, 8.39; Sshj 4.7; Ssj 12.8. Into dragons or snakes: ShuyjRf 1.15; Ssj 14.9. Fish: ShuyjRf 1.25; Yy 3.51 (cf.). Birds: Ssj 13.2, 14.14. Turtles: Ssj 14.16, 14.17, 14.18, 19.4. Foxes: Ssj 18.13, 18.16 (?). Deer: Yy 8.37. Stone: Lyz 48; ShuyjRf 2.117; Yml 11 (implied), 12, 70 (cf.); Pyj; Jlz 41 (via sheep form); Luyz 25; Sshj 1.10; Ssj 8.7 (via bird form), 11.1 (cf.) 11.34 (cf.). Water: Ssj 11.33. Rainbow: Yy 1.3. Yy 10.17 envisions such transformations as due in some cases to intoxication.

205. "Looking for husband stone": e.g. Yml 12. Similar cases: Ssj 11.1, 11.14, 11.15, 11.32, 11.37; ShuyjRf 1.23, 24; Jlz 40; Yml 11.

206. Ssj 11.29; Yy 10.14.

207. One type of animal into another (sometimes as portent): ShuyjRf 1.28; Ssj 6.4, 6.29, 6.57, 7.4, 14.4, 14.11 (sericulture myth); Yy 3.42–44 (all snake/pheasant), 3.52, 3.53. One animal-type into another due to extreme longevity: ShuyjRf 1.26, 1.30, 1.31, 1.32, 1.33, 2.121; Yy 8.14 (cf.). One kind of plant into another: Jlz 10, Ssj 6.74. Plants into animals: Sshj 3.9; Yy 3.44; Gyz 1. Mineral/vegetable: Jlz 30. Other cases: Ssj 11.7, 11.26, 13.2; Yy 2.24, 4.57; Yml 152.

like ways—walking upright, talking,[208] and, most importantly, showing through their actions a seeming awareness of moral principles (a theme which will be taken up in Chapter Eight).

All such episodes tend to emphasize humanity's metaphysical connectedness with other species, and subtly suggest that the differences between humans and others may stop at distinctions in form and station and may not extend to morality or even to "nature" (*xing* 性).

These connections pervade the entire human species, and are not modulated solely through the ruler or the adept. It is perhaps one of the most distinctive and momentous innovations of these works that, along with the Buddhist tale-collections discussed above, they urged readers to imagine ordinary people as capable of visionary encounters and other spirit-world contacts formerly reserved to shamans and religious adepts. Where ancient divination traditions and the Han systems of correlative cosmology made the ruler and his adept-advisors uniquely able to access the unseen world—a value preserved in most *fang-shi* and Daoist anomaly accounts, which strove to maintain specialists' monopoly of such skills—texts advancing the Heaven and Humanity perspective sought to portray this privilege as no longer fit exclusively for emperors and kings and their special servants.

Thus, while in temple religion of the time it was shamans who could see and report the doings of spirits, these anomaly accounts tell of ordinary men and women, persons who have received no esoteric training, who can see ghosts and demons (sometimes on a regular basis).[209] While some tales depict people commissioning specialists to perform exorcisms on their behalf, many others show laypersons successfully dealing with spirits—noxious or otherwise—on their own.[210]

---

208. Animals knowing human speech: Shuyj 41, 48; Yy 3.1, 3.4–6, 3.10, 3.13, 3.48, 4.59; ShuyjRf 2.131; Jlz 59; Ssj 7.26, 7.31, 18.25, 20.15; Yml 53, 96, 97, 157, 195 (in dream), 258.

209. The following items emphasize visionary skills, but dozens more could be cited as documenting protagonists' visions (and many will be cited below in other contexts): Sshj 6.13–15, 6.17–18; Ssj 2.17, 16.11–12; Yml 67, 137, 214, 224.

210. Successful exorcisms by ordinary people: Sshj 7.2; Ssj 14.19, 16.13, 16.15 (but the exorcism later goes bad), 18.11, 18.14–15, 18.17, 18.19–22, 18.26–27, 19.1; Yml 80, 160, 163, 181, 182, 227, 230, 262; Yy 8.5–6, 8.8–10, 8.19–21. Other successful dealings with spirits by ordinary characters (in addition to the many specific motifs illustrating this point that

Anomalies are meaningful messages; visions of the "hidden realm" are real and should be heeded; those who heed them benefit. Several themes bearing on this proposition are closely intertwined.

First of all, the unseen world in general is such that it constantly speaks to humanity through the code of anomalies. This attitude simply continues the familiar worldview underlying divination and, more specifically, the locative cosmology developed by Dong Zhongshu and many others, in which every untoward occurrence, in principle, *means* something. Not surprisingly, anomaly accounts of the Heaven and Humanity persuasion incorporate many reports of omens and portents, almost always including a note confirming that, in retrospect, the anomalous event was in fact an accurate auspice.[211] But they also report cases of more direct cosmic "speech" to humans, such as stones found to contain written messages.[212] And they expand such cross-boundary communications in several ways, among them the fact that Heaven is no longer their sole or even the primary sender, nor the ruler their sole or primary recipient.

Dreams—which are understood to be not merely mental states but real contacts with normally unseen beings (gods, the human dead) or journeys to distant places—are described in ways that emphasize their reliability as auspices of future events[213] or accuracy as symbolizations of current situations.[214] The reality of experiences undergone by protagonists while dreaming is confirmed when they awaken by the tangible presence in this world of some object seen in the other world, or else by some other real change in state.[215]

Such confirmable visions of things normally invisible are described as occurring not only in dreams but also in the waking state. Living people do not simply "see" the souls of the dead, for

are cited below and in Chapter Eight): Zgk 8; Lgz 7–9; Lyz 43, 47; Shuyj 23, 41, 45, 47, 55, 57, 61, 65; Xs 55, 101; Zyz 2, 7; Yy 6.6; XuQxj 16; Yml 60, 67, 80, 146, 173; Sshj 9.10–11; Ssj 17.10 (with help from diviner), 18.1–2, 18.24–25.

211. Shuyj 17, 25, 28–30, 32, 33, 59, 60, 62–64; Xs 2, 7, 9, 43; Yy 2.25, 2.26, 3.45, 4.1–65; XuQxj 2; Yml 50, 51, 65, 75, 91, 119 (dream-warning to ruler); Sshj 2.5, 8.5, 8.7, 9.9; Ssj 6 and 7 passim, 8.5, 9.7–14.

212. Yml 44; Jlz 43; Ssj 7.1, 9.3, 11.21–22; Yy 1.13 (cf.).

213. Sshj 3.1, 3.11, 5.3; Ssj 8.10, 9.12, 10.1–4, 10.8, 10.10–11; Yml 43, 51, 86, 123, 195; Yy 1.17, 5.15.

214. Ssj 9.12; Yy 4.4.

215. Luyz 9, 13; Ssj 5.10, 10.6, 10.7, 10.9 (cf.), 11.6; Yml 116, 141, 195, 243; Yy 6.15, 7.4, 7.11, 7.18, 7.21, 7.23, 7.26, 7.31, 7.32–33 (cf.).

example, but some further, tangible evidence is added to confirm the reality of this visual contact.[216] But these tales, with their emphasis on the *confirmation* of vision, are merely a rhetorically intensified subset of a much larger theme: that of the visionary or (more rarely) auditory experience that reveals, to an ordinary protagonist, some scene in a world normally invisible and inaudible. When massed together in these collections, these tales create the impression of a vast, bustling, teeming world that carries on its affairs in our very midst at all times—a world of which we are normally unaware, but by which we might be overwhelmed if we had the eyes to see it with and the ears to hear it with, and of which we would be more respectful if only we could see and hear it.[217] The souls of dead humans are normally invisible, but on rare occasions their consumption of food offerings is plainly visible,[218] or they are glimpsed at their own funeral,[219] proving, in the face of Confucian disdain for such discussions, that spirits really receive ritual offerings. Normally inaudible sounds made by spirits are by chance overheard.[220] Even objects close to home—tools, broomsticks—can be inhabited by spirits which on rare occasions manifest their presence;[221] how much the more, then, the trees in liminal, forested areas, which bleed when cut and thus reveal the presence of an indwelling spirit,[222] or other mountain-dwelling spirits (often ini-

---

216. Objects left behind or missing from the grave as tangible evidence of contact between living and dead characters: Zgz 2; Lyz 31; Shuyj 82; Luyz 9; Sshj 4.6; Ssj 2.14, 15.4, 16.19–22; Yml 124; Yy 7.1, 7.4, 7.11. Other tangible or visual evidence of reality of contact with the dead: Sshj 3.14; Ssj 11.6, 15.4, 16.12, 16.24; Yml 46, 123, 147, 177, 186, 214 (cf.), 215 (cf.), 219 (cf.), 242, 251; Yy 6.15, 6.18, 6.36, 8.25.

217. This attitude does not extend to *all* spirit-manifestations: certain narratives portray a studied indifference to unauthorized, overweening spirits (usually animal-spirits making extortionist threats) as the best response, as exemplified, for instance, by the story of Zhou Nan and the rat spirit (Lyz 47, Yml 53).

218. Yy 6.2, 6.30.

219. As in Yml 78, 98.

220. Strange drumming sounds stated or implied to be the work of spirits: Lyz 15, 31; Yy 1.15, 7.6; XuQxj 7; Yml 81, 98, 156. Human overhears conversation among spirits, often thereby learning their secret weaknesses: Luyz 3; Sshj 6.11; Ssj 16.18 (= Lyz 28), 17.5, 18.1 (cf.), 18.2 (?), 18.3, 18.26; Yy 3.48.

221. Ssj 18.1 (tools), 18.2 (rice pestle); Yml 187 (fencepost), 231 (broomsticks); Yy 7.29 (cf.), 8.9 (broomstick).

222. Luyz 3; Ssj 2.1, 5.9, 6.68, 18.3–7; Yml 140, 162, 200, 201, 227; Yy 7.29, 8.11; Sshj 8.8.

tially manifesting themselves in disguise).[223] These tale-collections are at pains to point out the rewards that can result from such sightings, as well as the dangers of neglecting them; truths, from the relatively trivial (the location of hidden treasure)[224] to the morally vital (the reality of otherworldly punishment for this-worldly misdeeds) are revealed.

The most numerous of tale-types featuring *vision* of the unseen realm are the ghostly apparition and the return from death. Little need be said here on these narratives, since they have been relatively often studied.[225] I would here emphasize these points: (1) Such tales stress the sheer reality of the spirit world and afterlife existence by exposing them to a sort of textual X-ray. They do so most especially in two motifs: that of tangible evidence of travel to the realm of the dead (an object brought back that is recognized by a living relative of a dead person, for example), and that of the "ghostly apologue," in which a ghost manifests itself to refute and punish an eloquent sceptic.[226] (2) But they go farther, exploring the range of obligations that obtain between the living and the dead, particularly where the parties are not related by kinship. What they have to say on this score will be discussed in the following chapter. (3) They do not merely reinforce the reality of the afterlife (and of reward and retribution there for deeds done in this life), but also chart the details of its bureaucratic (sometimes almost absurdly bureaucratic) workings. These tales create the impression that, as a marvelously apt phrase has it, "the other world will be admirable for congruities"[227]—that it surprises not by its strangeness but by its resemblance to this world even at its most mundane.

Morality and piety—no matter of what kind—are unfailingly rewarded; immorality and impiety are unfailingly punished. One of the themes through which this group of authors urged this view is that of the celestial response to the moral

---

223. Mountain-dwelling spirits in disguise: ShuyjRf 2.145; Jlz 21, 23, 24; Sshj 7.2, 7.4 (implied); Ssj 12.4, 12.10, 12.14, 18.13; Yy 3.32, 6.38.

224. Lyz 27, 44; Luyz 25, 26.

225. Yu 1987; Campany 1990a, 1991a, Forthcoming (b).

226. Arguments for the non-existence of ghosts (*wuguilun*) refuted— often by the actual appearance of a ghost to the proponent of their non-existence (marked by *): Yml 68*, 214*, 260*; Xs 130, 131; Ssj 16.3*, 16.4*, 16.8.

227. This phrase of Benjamin Whichcote's serves as the epigraph to Yu 1987; I do not know its source.

quality of individuals' (not just rulers' or dynasties') deeds.[228] Another is that of springs and wells that automatically adjust their temperature or flow to match virtuous pilgrims' desires.[229] Illnesses, furthermore, are sometimes claimed through narrative to be the somatic manifestations of their sufferers' previous misdeeds.[230] Ghosts or living humans who temporarily visited the other world also confirm the reality of afterlife rewards and punishments—and not all such tales are explicitly pro-Buddhist.[231] The upshot of all these tale-types is that the universe itself is not morally neutral or inert, but rather responds with sensitivity to the quality of people's actions and intentions, particularly where it is a question of deeds done in secret, or where the victims are persons otherwise without sufficient protection in the social system.

The way the world looks to us fluctuates between an anti-locative, mysterious, surprising jumble of events and a locative, rule-governed network of stable relationships and patterns. These texts grant the seeming truth of the former view but uphold the latter as ultimately true. Texts of the Heaven and Humanity persuasion, in other words, play upon the tension bound up in the phrase *mingli* 冥理,[232] the "unseen principles" or "principles of the unseen world": some story-types stress the mystery of things, their quality of being hidden or occulted (*ming*), and therefore surprising; others stress that even these *ming* aspects of the world are, at some higher or ultimate level, subject to *li*, to an implicate order that obtains even in the unseen realm, although not immediately evident to ordinary humans. This tension is closely homologous to that between *mingjiao* and *ziran*: these texts grant the *ziran*-seeming quality of phenomena but ultimately come down on the side of *mingjiao*, since they remain willing to take the measure of the unseen world according to familiar, human standards.

---

228. Jlz 60; Luyz 1 (implied); Sshj 5.1 (implied), 10.4; Ssj 1.28, 8.1–4, 8.6, 9.4–5, 10.4, 11.9–12, 11.15, 11.17–18, 11.20–28; Yml 155, 168 (implied), 178 (implied), 194, 207 (implied); Yy 2.27, 4.2, 5.33 (implied), 10.4, 10.6 (punishment for vice), 10.8 (celestial punishment implied for male infanticide by mother). Cf. stories in which treasure proves inaccessible to immoral persons: Sshj 3.5, 3.6; Yy 10.21.

229. Ssj 13.1, 13.5; Yml 8, 18.

230. Sshj 2.6; Yy 5.38, 10.6.

231. Sshj 6.19; Yml 83, 103, 126, 248 (= Mxj 4); Yy 5.32, 6.25, 6.28; Shuyj 34, 37; Zyz 14.

232. Occurring in Yy 7.27 and elsewhere.

Hence it does not surprise us to learn of Gan Bao's distate for Pure Conversation, the excessive study of Laozi and Zhuangzi to the neglect of the classics, the discussion of empty, abstract points at the expense of those of substance, and the glorification of social detachment at the expense of honest industriousness in office; and his attaching the name Ruan Ji to this entire bundle of mores— which he cites as the cause of the failure of the Jin—leaves us no room to doubt that it was the *ziran* perspective that he saw as most dangerous and to which he expressed his opposition through his writings.[233] Nor need it any longer surprise us that Liu Yiqing authored a work such as the Yml. By the same token, however, Tao Qian's authorship of the Sshj looks highly suspect when one exposes the views to which that work seeks to persuade readers and—even more—their resemblance to the views advanced by staunchly pro-*mingjiao* men such as Gan Bao and Liu Yiqing.

I take each of these emphases by turn, dwelling on the locative, *mingjiao* side since it is the one these authors wanted, in the final analysis, to advocate.

1. Although events may seem to occur at random, there are principles that inexorably govern the world's workings—principles which normally remain obscured by the jumble of events but which occasionally are revealed with particular clarity by certain types of anomalous occurrences. It is crucial to note that these texts use reports of anomalies to paint a locative portrait of the world as an interlocking system of categories of beings, governed by fixed if implicit principles of moral resonance. In these texts, things are temporarily moved out of place, normally invisible beings become visible, in order to illuminate the unexpectedly long reach of what a character in one item calls "the unseen principles" (*mingli* 冥理) which are "hard to dodge" (*nantao* 難逃); or, as another asks, "How could the retribution for good and evil possibly be avoided?" (*shan'e zhi bao qi neng mian hu* 善惡之報其能免乎).[234] After the revelation of principles, things are put back in their normal places again: when the narrative ends, the window onto the other world closes, and both the characters in the story and the implied reader return to the world as it is normally experienced. In this respect, too, we are shown a

---

233. Takeda 1965; DeWoskin 1974, 32. These views surface in an extant fragment of the "summation" to his *Annals of Jin*.

234. Yy 7.27 and Yml 165, respectively.

world surprising in its occasional revelations not of the ultimate incongruities but of the ultimate congruities of things.

Thus, prognostication works; people make specific predictions that are indeed confirmed by subsequent events.[235] While in texts of other perspectives this is a prominent motif for displaying the special power of adepts, in these tales it becomes a statement not so much of the prowess of specially trained individuals as of the amenability of events to prediction due to the law-governed nature of the universe itself; what matters is not who does the predicting or how they do it but its sheer success. Thus, the temporal vector can be reversed: old objects are found that self-referentially depict an event that just happened, including their own discovery at the time in question.[236] Or the specialist can be omitted entirely and, in a direct continuation of the old cosmographic tradition, prophetic folk songs that turned out in retrospect to be true are incorporated into narratives, or prognisticatory texts are mentioned.[237] Although not always explicitly mentioned,[238] the concept of personal destiny, or *ming* 命, is in silent operation throughout these texts, and the lawlike and predictable nature of events is sometimes symbolized by texts and registers in which people's fortunes and lifespans can be consulted.[239] The world seems to have the regularity of a great text, even if its grammar remains, under normal circumstances and to ordinary people, illegible; demons, ghosts, and gods are almost always depicted as knowing of future events as a matter of course. But the more that is revealed of this grammar, the more it is clear that its principles match those of this world point for point; the other world is made to seem less mysterious, as fundamentally like this world, perhaps nowhere as much as in those return-from-death tales that expose the absurdly mundane, error-prone bureaucratic

---

235. Shuyj 10; Xs 54, 61, 79, 80; Yy 1.17, 4 passim (65 items), 6.21, 7.15, 7.20, 7.31; Luyz 20 (tr. Kao 1985, 152–53); Sshj 2.12–14, 3.3; Ssj 2.17, 3 passim, 4.17, 4.21, 5.1 (both predictions by protagonists of their own elevation to divine status after death), 8.8 (contra), 9.1–2, 9.6, 19.9 (= Yml 42); Yml 49–50, 55, 75, 122, 129, 153, 240.

236. Yy 4.3, 7.11; Ssj 3.1.

237. Ssj 6.64, 6.67, 7.11–13, 13.8; Yy 4.8, 4.15, 4.53. Prognosticatory texts (excluding inscriptions): Yy 4.7, 4.22, 4.23 (cf.).

238. People's destiny, including predictions of it: Sshj 3.12, 5.3; Yml 42, 162, 211; Ssj 3.5, 3.6, 9.6, 19.9. Characters foretell their own deaths: Sshj 2.13, 5.2; Ssj 4.21 (cf.), 8.8, 10.10; Yy 7.31–33.

239. Register of destinies or of the dead: Ssj 3.6, 10.12; Yml 124, 125, 165; Yy 8.23 (= Sshj 4.2).

workings of the realm of the dead.[240] The more the other world's
working principles are assimilated to those of the familiar world,
the greater the possibility of various types of negotiations with
denizens of the other world, and of various bendings of its supposedly inexorable principles.

Aside from such themes surrounding the *knowability* of things
from the perspective of the *ming* side of reality, the other group of
themes underscoring the locative, *mingjiao* worldview advanced in
these texts concerns the inexorability of reward for good deeds and
retribution for bad. But I reserve discussion of those themes until
the following chapter.

**2. Things are not always as they seem; the seen world
remains on its surface mysterious, even if the episodic
glimpses of the unseen world afforded through the texts reveal it to be ultimately rule-governed.** Taken as a whole, this
group of texts embodies a sort of rhetorical paradox: its piecemeal
revelations of *mingli*, of implicate order in the unseen realm, come
at the price of repeated ruptures of regularity in the seen realm of
everyday life. *This* world comes to seem *more* mysterious the more
the other world is limned. Appearances on this side of reality are
sometimes deceptive (though not, as would be the case in a Platonic
or an Indian Mahāyānist worldview, by any necessary cause or any
inherent defect in the faculties of perception or judgment); one's
bed partner could turn out to be a fox or a stone or a corpse, and
last night's cozy inn a cold tomb.

Hence a famous story-type: a weary traveler far from any
town gratefully stumbles across a lonely inn, where he receives the
favors of an ardent young woman; next day he looks back to see
only a grave.[241] But such stories can be seen as a small subset of a
much larger class: namely, tales in which the central event is the
deception of the human protagonist by some sort of spirit-being

---

240. On which, in general and also on this specific theme, Campany
1990a. In the following tales, temporarily dead protagonists manage to exchange destinies with another soul or substitute another's name for their
own in the "register of the dead": Yml 71, 130; Ssj 10.12, 16.4, 17.10 (cf.);
Yy 5.23, 6.11 (cf.). There is also the motif of the "mistaken summons," in
which otherworldly officials cause the "wrong" person to die (i.e., their con-
duct varies from the register-ordained "script" or timetable they are supposed to follow): Ssj 15.4, 15.10 (cf.); Yml 71, 74, 206; Yy 5.20 (cf.), 6.16.

241. Luyz 24; Sshj 5.7, 6.1 (implied), 6.2; Ssj 16.20; Yml 46 (cf.); Yy
6.5, 6.20.

who pretends to be a fellow human in order to draw close. A man finds a stone and places it at the head of his bed; at night it changes into a beautiful woman, with whom he has intercourse; next day he discards the stone.[242] More commonly the metamorphosis works in the opposite direction: the protagonist encounters what seems to be a person, some interaction takes place, an anomaly tips off the protagonist (or another character, sometimes an adept wise to the ways of such beings) that something is amiss, and then the climax—the unmasking of the disguised being, entailing a revelation of its "true form," commonly that of a mammal, reptile, or bird.[243] Besides such tales, much attention is paid in general to the revelation or occultation of the "true form" of spirits.[244] The most ubiquitous and famous of such trickster-spirits is that of the fox. Many fox-spirit narratives depict these beings as interested primarily in sex with humans, in which role they appear disguised in both human genders.[245] In others, they pose as students or teachers, in order to gain entrance to academies (perhaps to further their sexual conquest among the young men concentrated there),[246] haunt inns or government offices,[247] or otherwise try to insinuate themselves into relationships with humans.[248]

---

242. Shuyj 86; ShuyjRf 2.149; Yy 2.23; Yml 167.

243. Yy 8 is entirely taken up with such tales; in addition, see the following: apparent people into real tigers: Sshj 9.2; Yy 3.15 (?). Into otters: Zyz 16; Ssj 18.24; Yml 170, 171, 250. Into deer: Ssj 18.17. Into pig: Zgz 11; Ssj 18.18. Into turtles: Zgk 9; Ssj 19.4. Into snakes: Ssj 19.3; Yml 134 (cf.). Into birds: Ssj 8.7; Sshj 9.1; Yml 148. Into apes: Sshj 9.5 (cf. Wu Hung 1987). Into dogs: Sshj 9.10–11; Ssj 18.21–22.

244. Some of these may overlap with above listings: Jlz 23; Luyz 12; Sshj 5.1, 7.9, 8.1, 8.2, 8.3, 9.4, 9.10; Ssj 18.8 and 18 passim, 19.3, 19.4, 2.15; Yml 69 (?), 105, 134, 143, 170, 171; Yy 6.3, 6.38, 8.22. In a few cases the spirit humorously reveals its true form due to drunkenness or some sort of mistake: Ssj 18.12, 18.21; Yml 160.

245. Fox-spirits disguised as women have sex with men or attempt to: Shuyj 87; Ssj 18.11 (cf.), 18.13; Yml 127, 181; Yy 8.10. Lecherous male foxes: Sshj 9.13, 9.14 (implied); Yml 110 (implied), 196; Ssj 18.8 (cf.).

246. As in XuQxj 5; Ssj 18.8, 18.9, 18.16; Yml 33. Cf. Sxz 26.

247. Lodge: Ssj 18.14, 18.15, 18.27. Office: Yy 8.2; cf. Yml 230. Cf. Yml 105, in which a fox-spirit in female disguise seeks lodging; the male protagonist kills the creature but is charged with murder by the "husband" of the woman who is finally—fortunately for the man in question—revealed to be a fox as well.

248. Xs 85; Sshj 9.15; Ssj 18.10 (disguised as family member), 18.11, 18.12; Yml 92 (but no disguise here); cf. Yy 8.19, 8.41.

The proximate unruliness of the ultimately rule-governed world also reveals itself in tales of spirits' misbehavior. Most of these will be dealt with in Chapter Eight, but I mention here the fact that, although most ghost stories emphasize the workings of the law of reward or retribution between the living and the dead, a few portray ghosts as essentially just like living persons, liable to the same faults and defects of character. Some attack people for no apparent reason; others steal food or offerings, usually doing little harm.[249] A few items even portray dead ancestors as hostile toward their living kin.[250] The net effect of all these tales is to close the moral and psychological gap between living and dead persons, to emphasize their common moral nature and, hence, the continuing "humanity" of the dead.

A Hybrid Text: The ShuyjRf

Ren Fang's two-fascicle text to some extent shares the persuasion I have just outlined. But it seems markedly less anxious to make the claims advanced in these other texts; its implied author speaks in a slightly more detached voice. This detached effect is due, in part, to the prevalence in this work of an additional interest essentially unrelated to that of the Heaven and Humanity standpoint: namely, the documentation of survivals of practices and events from ancient times in contemporary, largely rural legend and custom. Ren Fang's interest in this enterprise reminds us of Ying Shao's, except for its conspicuous lack of any discernible agenda for the critique of contemporary culture. In fact, Ren's inverts Ying's approach: where Ying sought to rectify customs with reference to canonical texts, Ren seems to take customs as his baseline in reality, and to try to salvage the credibility of ancient texts with reference to these social "traces" of the events they report. The ShuyjRf is, with the exception of local histories and topographies (which participate only marginally in the genre), the only anomaly account from this period that I believe fully warrants the characterizations "antiquarian" and "folkloric," because, unlike most of our other authors, Ren Fang

---

249. Apparently unmotivated ghostly attacks: Zgz 12; Lyz 45 (?); Luyz 11; Sshj 6.10; Ssj 15.9 (?); Yml 213. Ghost steals offerings: Yml 93, 94. Disrupts funeral: Sshj 6.10. Steals food and otherwise freeloads among the living: Sshj 6.20; Ssj 16.11 (a mild case), 16.16 (cf.); Yml 256; Yy 6.22 (cf.).

250. Ancestors hostile toward own kin: Shuyj 58, 66; Yml 89 (?); Ssj 3.8 (?), 16.11 (?); cf. Sxz 13.

seems to have taken such keen interest in local narratives and folk etymologies that he recorded them not for any extrinsic, persuasive purpose (none that is evident, at least) but simply for their own sake.

Of its 286 extant items, at least fifty-four are explicitly concerned to link an ancient legend or figure with a particular place on the contemporary landscape and, in some cases, a particular saying or custom preserved by commoners (usually termed *su* 俗) there; many more do so implicitly.[251] At least as many again cite folk etymologies, explanations (usually by reference to a more or less fantastic narrative) of how places, animals, or plants got their names. When combined, these two sorts of antiquarian material take up the majority of items. The rest of the text is made up of two sorts of items: (1) narratives stressing Heaven and Humanity themes (although even in these Ren Fang often adds an antiquarian note[252]); (2) descriptions of sheer exotica such as one would find in a *fangshi* text or in some Daoist works—indeed many of the ShuyjRf's descriptions of distant lands are quotations of material also found in the Szj, Syj, and Dmj, although it is difficult to tell whether Ren Fang had direct access to these texts. Again, no clear rhetorical point underlies his inclusion of the latter items; he claims no special mastery (at least no extra-textual mastery) of the geographic periphery and does not tout the skills of any set of adepts. He simply seems to have found such material curious. The most we can say about his suasive aims is that he sought to show that the world is vast and wondrous.

---

251. Examples are translated and discussed in Campany 1990b.

252. An example: 1.76 tells of a girl who made her living by harvesting mollusks and was subsequently devoured in the place where she was lodging by a horde of them. In a Buddhist or straightforwardly Heaven and Humanity text, this tale would probably be left at that and would exemplify the theme of retribution even across species. But Ren Fang adds that this incident accounts for the name of the place in question, Mollusk Lodge; he thereby transforms a cautionary tale into a record of folk etymology.

Chapter Eight

Reciprocity across Boundaries: Cosmographic Ethics

The parrot can speak, and yet is nothing more than a bird; the ape can speak, and yet is nothing more than a beast. Here now is a man who observes no propriety [*li* 禮]; is not his heart that of a beast? But if men were as beasts, and without propriety, father and son might have the same mate. Therefore, when the sages arose, they framed the rules of propriety in order to teach men, and cause them, by their possession of them, to make a distinction between themselves and the brutes.

The Book of Rites[1]

Tian of Qi was going on a journey; he sacrificed in his courtyard to the god of the roads, and banqueted a thousand guests. Someone was serving fish and geese at the seat of honor. Tian looked at them; then he sighed and said: "How generous Heaven is to mankind! It grows the five grains and breeds the fish and birds for the use of man."

All the guests answered like his echo. But a twelve-year-old boy of the Bao family, who had a seat among the guests, came forward and said: "It is not as your lordship says. The myriad things between Heaven and Earth, born in the same way that we are, do not differ from us in kind. One kind is no nobler than another; it is simply that the stronger and cleverer rule the weaker and sillier. Things take it in turn to eat each other, but they are not bred for each other's sake.

---

1. *Liji zhengyi* 1A (p. 16); tr. slightly modified from Legge 1926, 1:64–65.

Men take the things which are edible and eat them, but how can it be
claimed that Heaven bred them originally for the sake of man? Besides, mosquitoes and gnats bite our skin, tigers and wolves eat our
flesh; did Heaven originally breed man for the sake of mosquitoes
and gnats, and his flesh for the sake of tigers and wolves?"

The Book of Liezi[2]

Two attitudes toward humankind's place among other species are
exemplified in these epigraphs: the one, characteristic of classical
Confucianism and found in one of its canonical texts, confident of
the human species' superiority to others by virtue of its unique possession of the rules of propriety; the other, characteristic of classical Daoism, expounding—in explicit opposition to what is portrayed
even in this little anecdote as the majority view—a radical naturalism unwilling to privilege humankind on moral grounds, levelling
all kinds to the same quest for self-preservation.

From the fourth through the sixth centuries, some writers of
anomaly accounts—particularly those concerned to advance the
Buddhist and the Heaven and Humanity persuasions—urged a
middle position in which humans on the one hand, and other species, ranks, and realms of beings on the other, are interlinked by
some of the same moral principles as those encoded in the sage-
given rites. This position differed from both classical Confucian and
naturalist views in imagining non-human beings other than ancestral spirits to have moral dispositions and to act according to moral
principles.

In this chapter, I will show how some authors of anomaly
accounts pushed the boundaries of the moral sphere outward to
encompass more types of beings than ever before, as well as to
envision more complex and finely grained structures of obligation
with beings that had long been part of the indigenous ritual and
moral system. Specifically, I will show in this chapter how the plot-
structures of many tales imply that the community of beings to
whom the basic ritual and moral principles apply go far beyond humanity to include beings both above and below us in the cosmic hierarchy: above, spirits of various sorts, most especially local deities;
below, souls of the non-kin human dead, animals, and even some
animal-spirits or demons.

---

2. *Liezi jishi* 8 (p. 296); tr. slightly modified from Graham 1990, 178–
79.

After brief introductory comments on the ideas being explored by our authors, I will proceed to analyze the ways in which their texts highlight the nature of human interactions with three particular classes of beings. In each of these three cases, I will not only explicate the anomaly texts themselves but will also juxtapose them with certain contemporaneous social and religious trends; this will allow us to see the significance of our texts more clearly.

Notions of Moral-Ritual Reciprocity: A Digression

Naturally, it is neither necessary nor possible to do more here than review a few aspects of this topic that are directly relevant to our interests.

The single most fundamental item in the moral and ritual lexicon that concerns us is *bao* 報, which, in simplest terms, means the repayment of a debt (whether positive or negative), the restoration of moral and ritual equilibrium. *Bao* is often translated as "revenge" or (verbally) "avenge," but just as frequently—particularly in ritual contexts—*bao* means a repayment or reward for a previously received benefit. I therefore render the term as "reciprocity," understood as negative (retribution for a wrong suffered) or positive (reward for a benefit conferred) according to context. Its early attestations fall into two groups: verb-object compounds such as *baoyou* 祐 , *baoen* 恩 , *baogong* 功 , all of which connote positive reciprocity, the making of some counter-gift in response to a gift received; and verb-verb compounds, some of which (as *baoying* 應, "reciprocating response") occur in moral, others (as *baoji* 祭 , "reciprocating offering," thank-offering—specifically, the autumn harvest ritual) in ritual, contexts. Originally grounded in ritual practice, *bao* and its surrounding complex of compounds later developed into formal moral and legal concepts that persisted until the present century.[3]

During the Han, the concept of reciprocity was assimilated into correlative cosmological thinking; *bao* and *baoying* named in the moral sphere what *ganying* named in the metaphysical: each connoted a measured, resonant response across some taxonomic boundary. The only new element added in the Han was the notion that an agent's actions might somehow receive an *automatic* response, if not from other human agents then from Heaven or the

---

3. This discussion is based on DKW 5275 (3.216d); Yang 1957; Martinson 1973; Dalby 1982.

cosmos itself, since all levels of being were interwoven into a single, if hierarchically tiered, web of resonant connections.

Given this foundation, early Buddhist proponents found it easy to introduce the idea of karma, which, especially early on, they glossed as *baoying*; the Buddha, for his part, took on in some proselytizing writings the familiar role of Heaven or the Way, responding (*ying*) to every stimulus (*gan*) yet himself empty, quiescent, and "natural" or self-so (*ziran*).[4] Reward and retribution come as certainly in the Buddhist as in the correlative cosmology; as Sun Chuo 孫綽 put it in his mid-fourth century "Clarification of the Way" (*Yudaolun* 喻道論):

> If it is [already, under the social-moral system instituted by the former sages] possible for the good and wicked to get their dues and for justice not to be perverted when the ruler is discerning, the ministers impartial, and the world at peace and well governed—then how much the more under the rule of the [new] spirits who, regardless of distance or nearness, darkness or depth (況神明所蒞無遠近幽深), are intelligent and upright in their punishment of the wicked and their blessing of the good. Because of them, even the slightest merit or the most trifling defect cannot miss its timely repayment in kind (報應之期).[5]

What struck the Chinese as newest and strangest in the doctrine of karma was the associated idea of rebirth. To be sure, good analogues lay ready to hand in such old texts as the *Zhuangzi*, with its vision of death as just another in a series of changes, and in its depiction of human decease as simply a change in form. But rebirth was, in turn, part and parcel of a larger complex of ethical and soteriological concerns that were new mostly in their radically universal scope, breaking the bounds of the Confucian emphasis on kinship. Buddhist texts and their expounders introduced activist notions of social welfare, the bodhisattva goal of salvation for all

---

4. As in the treatise by Sun Chuo cited immediately below; also in Daoan's writings (Link 1969–70, 204–10; Hurvitz and Link 1974, 411–21). On the general topic of the overlap between indigenous and Buddhist notions of resonant reciprocity, see the thorough treatment in Scharf 1991, ch. 3.

5. T 2102 (52.16b–c), tr. modifying Link and Lee 1966, 179–80. The reference to "spirits" (*shen*) is either simply metaphoric for the numinosity of the workings of karma or means the *devas* and *apsaras* or *tianshen* 天神 who populate the heavens and sometimes visit the sub-celestial realms in Buddhist cosmology. For more on Sun Chuo, Mather 1961.

beings, and the cultivation of compassion and non-violence toward all living creatures coupled with the abandonment of special attachment to one's own kin. These values made the as yet undomesticated new religion, particularly in its earliest periods but continuing to some extent almost until the Tang, a "tiny exotic plant flowering on the ruins of the Han empire."[6]

Local Gods are People Too

The notion that human and divine beings are mutually implicated in a relationship of moral-ritual reciprocity was an ancient one in China. And, after all, most of the beings who received worshippers' offerings in temples and shrines, particularly at the local and regional levels, had themselves been human beings prior to their elevation to a niche in the divine hierarchy. But the early medieval anomaly accounts were innovative in their explorations of the range of obligations on both sides, and in their depiction of the human-divine relationship as mimicking everyday interactions between living persons, so that one's dealings with the gods could seem (in these narratives at least) to be carried out in the common coinage of more mundane relationships. In these stories, low-level gods and goddesses, the spirits of particular places, or even high-ranking deities unexpectedly become visible or audible (either in person or through their subfunctionaries)—and when they do, it is usually in order to assert their claims in the very midst of ordinary human life, to make known their potency as moral agents sensitive to insult, appreciative of piety, and to whom certain gestures of respect are due.

One of these gestures is respect for the sanctity of temple grounds, as well as of uncultivated areas—any site belonging to a god. A group of items depicts local gods and the spirits of particular places responding protectively to even slight violation of their domain, challenging people's right to harvest its goods. One of the most explicit of these items follows:

In Yuzhang commandery there is a village called Lusong. A man of the commandery named Luo Gensheng cleared an area in the uncultivated land outside the village in order to raise melons. He set up an altar to the gods there. At first the melons put forth tendrils, which the man cultivated every morning. But one day he suddenly saw a newly-inscribed

---

6. Zürcher 1991, 293.

plaque with black characters set up on the altar. It read: "This is a place set aside for the pleasure of the gods. You may not stay here. Remove your plantings at once." Luo knelt down and apologized, saying, "I stupidly thought it permissible for us villagers to propagate crops on this land. If by chance someone is forging this divine directive, let them be speedily condemned. If, on the other hand, this is an authentic divine directive, I humbly ask that you change the characters to red as a sign." The next morning when he went to look, he found that the placard was still there, but now the black characters had all been changed to red. So Luo again apologized and departed.[7]

I summarize as examples four other items that depict local gods in this fashion:

1. Travelers who climb to the top of a mountain find there a lake with a grove of fruit trees carefully planted in orderly rows, as if by human labor. The fruit is perfectly ripe. They eat some of it, then decide to take some back home to show others (*wairen* 外人). But they lose their way, searching in vain for the path home. Suddenly a voice from midair says, "Drop the fruits and depart immediately, and I will allow you to go." Having done as instructed, they turn and see the path leading home, and hastily leave the mountain.[8] The protagonists' entry into a sacrosanct area, their attempt to take home something forbidden to show to "outsiders" (*wairen*), and their consequent inability to find their way home echo stories of the "discovery of hidden worlds," of which the most famous example is that of the peach blossom spring.

2. At a certain spot on the Yangzi River there is a sunken boat said by locals to have belonged to Cao Cao, the famous military commander. Once, a fisherman spending the night near it struck it with his own boat. On doing so he heard the sound of pipes and stringed instruments and smelled a rare, powerful fragrance. Falling asleep then, he dreamed that a man chased him off, warning him not to approach "the official's" (*guan* 官) boat and singing girls. For legend has it that Cao Cao had on board a group of geisha when his boat capsized and sank at this spot, and they are still there under the water.[9]

---

7. Shuyj 8.

8. Attested in Ssj 17.12 and Shuyj 4; I suspect Yy 2.22 is a garbled version of the same story.

9. Somewhat variant versions of this tale appear in Ssj 16.10, Sshj 6.3 (CSJC ed.), and Sshj B19 (ZDHW ed.).

3. A man spies a monkey in the top of a tree on the grounds of an earth god shrine (*she* 社). He climbs the tree, seizes the monkey, redescends, and cuts open his prey to find a foetus inside. That night he dreams of a man calling himself the local earth god and blaming him for committing this act. Soon the monkey-killer grows ill, first acting like a madman, then metamorphosing into a tiger and wandering into the mountains never to be seen again.[10]

4. A well known protagonist—Xie Qing, father of Xie Ling-yun—while passing by on horseback shoots some birds roosting in a temple to the goddess of the "Temple of the Young Maiden," identified as the younger sister of the god Jiang Hou 蔣侯 or Marquis Jiang, whom we will meet again shortly. Immediately upon shooting the sacred birds he feels an odd sensation; that same night he dreams of a girl, her sleeves shaking with anger, who upbraids him: "Those birds were raised by me. Why did you harm them?" Within a day he was dead.[11]

In other cases, human protagonists have the opportunity to respond respectfully and gratefully to a divine offer, but instead they act with irreverence. That most such stories end with the protagonist's swift demise implies that the god in question has punished them for their hubris. Thus the earth god of the area offers his daughter in marriage to a local official, but the official stubbornly refuses the god's advances, dying soon thereafter.[12] The son of a poor family is offered the hand of a celestial maiden (*tiannü* 天女) in marriage but is too shy to consummate the nuptial ceremony on his wedding night; the rejected bride sends messengers to retrieve her gifts and clothes, and withdraws from the household, whose members furiously upbraid the son for his stupidity. The boy dies of embarassment.[13] A girl who temporarily acts as a celestial messenger (*tianshi* 天使) declares to the governor of her commandery that he should rise and greet her; he is promised wealth and rank if he does, misfortune if he does not. The governor's only response is scepticism—he asks where she is from—and he is executed three weeks later.[14]

As in the just-mentioned cases, so in other tales deities show themselves just as prone to suffer effrontery as people are, and they use their superhuman power to exact revenge (negative *bao*) for insults to their dignity. A man slaughters a dog as an offering to the

---

10. Shuyj 88.
11. Yy 5.10.
12. Yml 209, tr. Kao 1985, 141–43.
13. Yml 207.
14. Yml 194.

local god at the time of the village festival, but the meat is not fully cooked; the angry god responds through a temple shaman that this man "has insulted me by offering raw meat. He must make recompense by eating raw meat himself," and later that year the offending villager metamorphoses into a tiger.[15] The divine warrior Xiang Yu kills a governor brash enough to enter the official chamber dedicated to him at commandery headquarters, where the god was reputed to personally attend to commandery affairs with regularity—this despite the governor's respectful setting out of offerings as if anticipating a guest.[16] Even rulers are not immune from punishment for insulting the gods of the places occupied by their palaces: tales of divine chastisements on Emperor Wu of the Han and Emperor Wu of the Jin, in particular, circulated widely.[17] Nor were adepts of the higher religions necessarily always the masters of gods, for, although unusual, there are tales that narrate the victory of local gods over Daoists and Buddhists who attempt to supplant them or extinguish their cults—a striking reversal of the more common outcome of such spiritual clashes.[18] Similarly, over-zealous officials attempting to wipe out unauthorized but otherwise effective cults are depicted in a few items as being divinely punished.[19]

---

15. Yy 8.40.

16. Yy 5.19. Xiang Yu seems to have been one of a large class of military heroes who graduated to divine status after death and were installed as guardians of government bureaus (Maspero 1981, 108); here, he does his job all too well. He is elsewhere reported to have done similar deeds: TPYL 882.1a, citing a now non-extant passage in the (or a) *Qishu*, also set in Wuxing (the protagonist here is a Buddhist-inclined official named An Ren, who does not appear in today's NQS—he perishes for refusing the god his customary offering of an ox upon taking office); tr. Lévi 1986, 92.

17. Yml 135 = Xs 27 contain the tale of the Jin emperor's insult to the god of the pond in an imperial park, for which he paid with his death (but cf. Yml 133 for a conflicting etiology of this ruler's death, also due to insulting a god). Versions of the story of a local spirit's complaint about the encroachments by Han Wudi's extensive construction projects appear in Yml 31, ShuyjRf 2.92 (10b–11b), and Zgz 1.

18. Telling examples include Yy 5.18, in which a god whose temple is burned by a Daoist libationer—and whose fan is confiscated by another man present at the time—requites at least the theft of his fan with death to its possessor, and ShuyjRf 2.67 (8a), in which the deceased commander Fu Jian (not known during life for his Buddhist sympathies) succeeds by dint of violent threats in converting the Buddhist monastery where he was killed into his own personal temple, where he is presented every month with offerings of oxen by the local people.

19. E.g., Yml 121.

Surveying the entire assemblage of tales concerning people's interactions with local gods, one finds that the authors of anomaly accounts portrayed them in no single, simple light; instead, they explored the moral complexities of these interactions, as well as the ambivalent nature of the gods themselves, who as a group seem no more or less virtuous than their living human counterparts. On the one hand, many tales feature divine rewards for rich offerings or otherwise pious treatment on the part of worshippers—a straightforward application of the principle of *bao* by deities in response to gifts from humans. Examples:

1. A lake god rewards fishermen's ample offerings by allowing a large catch—although only after they grow resentful of his delay in responding.[20]

2. The god of Lake Gongting divides wind and water currents to reward traveling merchants for their offerings.[21]

3. The father and son of a poor family encounter the lengthy train of a nobleman in the mountains. Realizing he is the god of the mountain, they prostrate themselves and request a blessing, whereupon they re-enter the mountain and find a piece of jade. Thenceforth all their affairs turn out as they wish and they become wealthy.[22]

4. The resident deity of a local temple at Wuchang heals with utmost effectiveness a sick worshipper who requests divine aid.[23]

5. Local residents, noticing the constant yellow pneuma around a tall tree beside a nearby inn, speculate that it may have divine efficacy, and present offerings of wine and meat to it during a drought. That night, a poor woman of the village receives a visit from a divine woman, the resident of the tree, who calls herself the Yellow Ancestress and announces her ability to summon rain. Citing the offering performed that morning by the local elders, she says that she has already petitioned the (Celestial) Thearch for a heavy rain to arrive at noon the following day. The rain arrives on schedule, and the people establish a shrine for the goddess, whose continued bestowals of blessings on the poor woman are also narrated.[24]

6. In front of a temple and grave mound in Chengyang district

---

20. Yy 1.18. Cf. Luyz 17, in which a lake god offers gifts to an individual who always makes generous offerings when crossing the lake (tr. Kao 1985, 151–52); this tale is also found in Ssj 4.13.

21. Yy 5.2; cf. Miyakawa 1979.

22. Yml 179.

23. Luyz 21.

24. Ssj 18.4. Similar items include Yml 84, 210; Sshj 5.7; Ssj 4.8, 4.10, 4.18–20.

is a fish pool. Visitors who fail to make offerings never catch any fish there; those who do make offerings are duly rewarded.[25]

On the other hand, some local gods are portrayed as extorting lavish sacrifices from the surrounding populace in exchange for services. In one such narrative, people build a temple to a spirit inhabiting a raft in a river in Hengyang commandery in order to appease it; it would sink beneath the water and allow to pass any travelers who made sufficient offerings at its temple, but would rise up to break the boats of those who neglected this duty. The virtuous governor, Ge Zuo, assembles a group of men and prepares to go and destroy the raft with axes; his resolve forces the spirit to move its obstruction downstream without a struggle.[26] An even more striking case follows:

Summary: Behind the home of Chen Qingsun of Yinchuan was a divine tree. Many people went there seeking blessings, so a temple was built, called "Temple to the Celestial Spirit" 天神廟.[27] Now Qingsun had a black ox. The god said to him from midair: "I am a celestial spirit and I like your ox. Unless you give it to me, I will kill your son on the twentieth day of the coming month." Qingsun said, "Human life is determined by destiny (*ming* 命), and destiny does not depend on you." But the boy indeed died on the predicted day. The god then announced, "If you do not give the ox to me, I will kill your wife in the fifth month." Still Qingsun did not sacrifice the ox; his wife died in the fifth month. Again the god spoke: "If you do not give me the ox, I will kill you in the autumn." Still Qingsun could not be moved. When autumn arrived, however, he did not die. The spirit (*gui* 鬼) then came and apologized, saying: "Sir, you have a correct heart. You will soon receive much wealth. I hope you will not mention this affair, for if Heaven and Earth should hear of it, my guilt will not be light. Look on this minor spirit (*xiaogui* 小鬼) with pity. I had managed to get appointed as "treetrunk in charge of [soul]-ferryings" under the Director of Destinies (司命度事幹),[28] and,

---

25. ShuyjRf 2.103 (13a).

26. Ssj 11.13, Yml 57 (based on TPGJ 293); tr. Lévi 1986, 83.

27. Ordinarily a mere tree spirit would not rank as "celestial"; this is an example of the sort of flattery through grandiose titles that can still be observed in Chinese popular religion today.

28. The final two graphs, *shigan*, are a pun on *ganshi*, a generic term for subofficial clerks in local adminstrative bureaus, often abbreviated to *gan* (Hucker 1985, 276), which also means treetrunk.

since it was your wife's and son's time to go anyhow, I only said that to get food from you. I hope you will forgive me. You will receive rank and salary, live to the age of 83, and have a happy household. The spirits (*guishen*) will assist you, and I myself will be your servant." Then could be heard the sound of someone knocking his head on the ground.[29]

This item's change in nomenclature, from *shen* to *gui*, reinforces the sense that this spirit-being has crossed the fine line dividing the "normal" relationship of reciprocal exchange on which local cults are based from the making of excessive demands backed by threats. Other items document similarly greedy, excessive demands by local spirits for particular goods or services.[30] A few portray gods demanding sex and even human sacrifice; some do so with impunity, others are eventually punished for their violations of the implicit code of reciprocity.[31]

---

29. Yml 162, based on TPGJ 318.

30. In one, a river god covets a horse presented as tribute to Emperor Ming of the Jin, constantly appearing in the ruler's dreams to ask him for it (Yy 7.17, Zgk 7 [TPGJ 276]); in another, a spirit attaching itself to the district headquarters demands an ox from the functionaries every year, and appears to angrily (and successfully) demand the reinstatement of this practice after a new prefect tries to discontinue it (Yml 208 [TPGJ 294]). Other examples: Ssj 5.1 (the story of Jiang Hou's theogony: in life, he was a man who overindulged in drink and sex, and who claimed that after his death he would become a god; he died violently, then appeared and began demanding that a temple be established to him, and he inflicted plagues on the people of the area until they finally relented and established a temple to appease his appetite for sacrifices); Yml 54 (but in this case the god later returns the item, a fancy hairpin being carried from "the south" as tribute to the Wu ruler Sun Quan, cf. Ssj 4.11), 135; Ssj 2.17 (another horse story—but in this case the horse's return is negotiated by a man who can see spirits); Yy 5.3, 5.9.

31. Shuyj 83 (TPGJ 294), god demands girl for sex; Ssj 5.4, the god Jiang Hou has a sexual affair with a girl, but she is able later to break it off; Ssj 5.3, three goddesses (probably Jiang Hou's daughters) along with their divine father require the death of three men who irreverently and jestingly discuss marriage in front of their temple images, in order to fulfill the marriage agreement (tr. DeWoskin 1977a, 104; Kao 1985, 72); Ssj 5.2, Jiang Hou summons a man to serve as his subordinate official; the man tries to excuse himself but to no avail, and he soon dies; Yml 76 (TPYL 400), god demands worshipper's son, for what purpose is unclear; Ssj 19.1, local deity (who takes the form of a giant serpent) demands human sacrifice (tr. DeWoskin 1974, 269; 1977a, 106; Kao 1985, 105).

Between the moral poles of divine reward for offerings and divine extortion, a number of other unusual dealings between gods and people are depicted. A man whose wife is seized alive by a tiger first sacrifices to the god Jiang Hou and prays for his help, then hunts down the tiger and rescues his wife; that night he dreams of a figure who gently reminds him that Jiang Hou's envoys aided him—a decorous if thinly veiled request for a thank-offering, which the man duly provides (in the form of a pig) upon arriving home.[32] A traveler encounters two goddesses whose temple residence is beside Lake Gongting; they ask him to buy them some silk shoes, which he does, taking the trouble to wrap the gifts carefully. He mistakenly leaves his book knife inside one of the parcels. After leaving them at the goddesses' temple, he continues his homeward journey when a fish suddenly leaps into his boat, carrying his knife inside its belly.[33] People deliver letters for gods, give them rides, or loan them objects such as talismans or knives, for which services they are rewarded.[34] People and gods enter into agreements, often involving secrecy; most such items end with the human party later assuming it safe to break the agreement, whereupon punishment (or at least the promised outcome of failure to keep the agreement) comes swiftly.[35]

One gains the impression from these narratives about local deities that even the self-aggrandizing ones may, according to these texts, have the right to exist and receive *some* offerings, and not all of them are exterminable by representatives of the state or of higher religions. On the other hand, most such gods, although they may temporarily succeed in enforcing their demands, eventually meet their match, and the proper balance of reciprocity is restored. These texts portray local gods as essentially like us in character. Moreover, the same codes govern our interactions with them as with each other. And even though these gods are more powerful than we, they are not ultimately powerful. Therefore, the same sorts of subtleties and complexities that characterize human relationships also characterize human relations with the gods. These gods act like people, except that they stand on the other side of the veil separating the seen from the unseen; they command respect

---

32. Ssj 5.5.

33. Ssj 4.10.

34. Ssj 4.7, 4.11; Yy 5.3, 5.11, 5.13, 7.16, 7.29; Yml 61.

35. E.g. Luyz 19 (TPYL 345); Yml 49, 259; Shuyj 37 (tr. Kao 1985, 156). Yml 34 is a case where the man honors the agreement and is rewarded.

despite their usual inertness and invisibility. They are really there and they notice and respond. Like us, some of them are not above overstepping their bounds out of greediness.

This collage of portraits of local gods is significant in light of contemporaneous Daoist and Buddhist efforts to curtail or supplant local cults, evidences of which we saw in Chapter Seven.[36] The view presented in those documents is one-sided: local gods more often than not appear as subhuman, bloodthirsty monsters (albeit also, especially in the Buddhist case, amenable to "conversion"). It is particularly in anomaly accounts of the Heaven and Humanity perspective that one glimpses the other side of this inter-religious struggle, for our view here is from the ground up, as it were, and conditions on the ground appear messier and more complicated, even morally so. In these texts, local gods are not monochromatically predatory; human relations with them are colored in subtler hues. They, too, have certain rights and prerogatives, and cannot be hastily strong-armed out of existence by imprecation-wielding Daoist adepts and Buddhist monks or by canon-reciting Confucian officials, for they are part of the same cosmic-moral fabric in which humanity, too, finds its place.

The Vengeful and the Grateful Dead

In the representation of relations between living and dead persons in the anomaly accounts we have a set of themes quite similar to those seen in depictions of interactions between humans and local gods. Here, too, the anomaly accounts innovate not in their positing of mutual obligation between the living and the dead—this much is as old as any records we have of human culture in the geographic area now known as China—but in three other ways: the range of situations in which such obligations apply, mimicking that among living persons; the vividness and force with which the dead assert their claims and repay their debts in the world of the living; and, most especially, in the extension of structures of obligation, as well as a sheer sense of fellow-feeling and community outside the bounds of kinship, so that living persons are depicted as interacting with the non-kin dead in ways formerly rare or unattested.

We have to deal, first of all, with the well known motif of the

---

36. Miyakawa 1964, chs. 13–14; Miyakawa 1979; Stein 1979; Lévi 1986; Faure 1987; Campany 1994; Campany [unpublished], where other works on this topic are cited.

vengeful dead, in which a person wrongfully killed (or else wronged in life and dead before gaining the chance to seek redress) returns in spectral form to punish the living party responsible. Such tales are the special subject of Yan Zhitui's Yhz but are also well documented in other texts, predominantly those urging the perspective of Heaven and Humanity.[37] Their basic action pattern is an exact playing out of the principle of reciprocity, only, in this type of case, across the boundary that normally and rightfully separates the living from the dead. All narratives of ghostly vengeance can be seen as arguing, in effect, that the dead, although they are ontologically liminal beings normally removed from the realm of the living, are still not without some power of appeal and redress of grievances—that they are not *morally* liminal, not outside the network of obligation. Such cautionary narratives argue that the dead have rights and the wherewithal to stake their just claims; if unable to reach satisfaction themselves, they are not without recourse, for they are often depicted as appealing to the Celestial Thearch for justice.[38] These victims prominently include women, orphans, even servants and slaves: although denied power in the society of the living, they do not remain downtrodden once they cross over into the unseen world. Similarly, even rulers and high officials cannot by their office escape ghostly vengeance.[39] These tales emphasize the com-

---

37. Yhz passim; Shuyj 53, 61, 67; XuQxj 6; Yml 121, 166, 219 (perhaps a case of jealousy more than injustice), 232, 233; Sshj 5.9 (an apparent case); Ssj 1.7 (implied), 3.8, 10.9 (cf.: dead emperor in dream reproaches current emperor for killings, and the dreamer soon dies), 11.6 (cf.), 11.36 (cf.), 16.9; Yy 5.1 (the Daoist goddess Ma Gu as a vengeful ghost, since she was killed by husband), 6.1 (see note below), 6.2, 6.23 (cf. Yml 219: dead wife castrates husband for remarrying), 6.26 (cf.), 6.27. Compare Sshj 4.3 and Yml 132, in each of which the wronged, deceased party first revives, then prosecutes his murderer; Sshj 6.8 and 6.17, in which ghosts seek revenge for shabby treatment after their death, not while living (a qualifier which also applies to a few of the above-listed items); and Sshj 6.12 (dead father returns to protest shabby treatment of his orphaned daughter) and 6.16 (a ghostly subpoena). On this theme, cf. Cohen 1979, 1982.

38. Tiandi 天帝 or simply Di often plays this role in the Yhz narratives; he does so also in Xs 1; Ssj 4.16; Yy 6.2.

39. In Yml 107 (TPYL 812), a high military officer under Huan Xuan sexually violates the corpse of a drowned woman; her ghost appears, accusing him, then a tiger bites off his penis and he dies. Yy 6.1 narrates the haunting of Jin Emperor Xuan by Wang Ling, whom the ruler had executed; he is aided by the god to whom he shouts his protest while passing his temple after being arrested.

monality of moral principles across social as well as ontological boundaries.

Another theme is that of the dead person's protection of his or her bodily remains and of the precincts of the tomb. The implication of these narratives is that the tomb is the active, vital home of the dead person, not (as it appears to the eyes of the living) a chamber full of lifeless remains and useless objects. It may not be violated with impunity; if it must be disturbed, an offering and reburial are required to compensate the occupant (who sometimes responds with a counter-gift). Examples follow:

1. One Wang Boyang buries his wife in the old tomb of another, unrelated man, only to be visited afterwards in a daytime reverie by a nobleman, mounted on a carriage and followed by several hundred retainers, who declares, "My tomb here had been peaceful for over two hundred years. Why did you destroy it?" His retainers then beat Wang and depart. Wang awakens to find that the places where he had been struck in the reverie have broken out in sores; he dies soon afterwards.[40]

2. A grave robber named Wang opens an old tomb and finds that the grave goods have all rotted away; there is only a white fox, which runs off; he chases it and wounds its left leg with a spear before it escapes. That night Wang dreams of a white-haired, formidable man who curses Wang for wounding him and strikes Wang on the left leg with his staff. When Wang awakens, his left leg is sore; later it develops sores that never heal as long as he lives.[41]

3. A late Han tomb was known to emit strange vapors long into the Jin period. During the Jin, one Wen Fangzhi was hunting near the tomb and opened it. As he was riding home he fell off his horse and died.[42]

4. A merchant traveling by night encounters a ghostly figure who accuses him of violating the precincts of his home. The merchant retreats and asks a local elder about the place; the elder confirms that it has long been haunted. The next day the merchant returns to the spot and finds a grave there.[43]

5. Yan Zong, having recently built a new house, dreams of a man who accuses him of destroying his grave. Next day, he digs beneath the head of his bed and unearths a coffin, whereupon he sets out an offering and announces, "I will move you to

---

40. Sshj 6.5 (70–72).
41. Ssj 15.17.
42. Yy 7.3.
43. Yml 59 (TPGJ 317).

a better place and will make another small grave for you." The next morning a stranger calls at his home, introduces himself, and says, "I lived here for forty years. Yesterday I received rich offerings, for which I am grateful. Today is an auspicious day, so you may exhume my coffin, inside of which you will find a box containing gold mirrors, which I hereby give you." Yan Zong retrieves the mirrors as directed, at which point the guest suddenly vanishes.[44]

6. The widow of Chen Wu and her two sons live over an old grave. She likes to drink tea, and whenever she drinks any she always offers a measure to the grave's occupant. Her sons mock her, saying, "What knowledge could the occupant of an old grave have? Why bother making the offering?" They try to dig it up, but their mother insistently forbids them. The same night she dreams of a man who says, "I have been fortunate to live in this grave for over two hundred years. Your sons would have destroyed my dwelling, but you prevented it; moreover, you present me with fragrant tea. Although I am only a rotten skeleton, I will not neglect to repay (*bao*) you." She awakens next morning to find ten thousand pieces of cash in her home. The coins look as though they have been long buried, but the holes through which they are strung are all newly drilled. She shows them to her sons and tells them of her dream, which causes them to wear sobered looks. From this time forward, salary and rank flow to the family.[45]

It is not simply the grave itself but any goods surrounding it which are the property of the deceased occupant, as shown in the following examples:

1. Travelers take fish from a reservoir below a tomb. On the road they meet the tomb's occupant, who challenges them, "How dare you take my fish?" The ghostly interlocutor then seizes several measures of fish and departs.[46]

2. Once some villagers were passing by an old tomb said to date from the Han and happened to notice several dozen millstones on the ground. They took one home with them. That night someone pounded on their door and urgently requested that his millstone be returned. The next morning they took it back and laid it where they had found it.[47]

---

44. Yml 147 (BTSC 135); cf. Yy 7.5, the ending of which is more intact.

45. Yy 7.4.

46. Yml 21 (TPYL 936).

47. Yml 22 (TPYL 762).

In many stories, protagonists who respond to non-kin ghosts with decency and compassion, doing some at least of what they would do for their own dead kinsman, are thanked and sometimes materially rewarded by the spectral recipient of their kindness. Ghosts, for their part, need help from the living; some ask for it, others are spontaneously helped by the living, but both afterwards make their gratitude known in some clear way.

The help most often requested by ghosts is reburial of their disinterred or uninterred corpse, or relocation of it from a damaged grave. I summarize two examples; note the grounds on which the spirit bases its appeal.

1. An official while traveling by boat "suddenly dreams" of a man who says he is dead and is floating in the river; tomorrow, he says, the official will have the chance to save him, and should do so, since humanity and kindness (*ren'en* 仁恩) extend to the dead. The next day the official sees a coffin float up to the place where he is sitting. He has it pulled out of the water and it is just as he dreamed. He takes it up to a high point and (presumably after burying it) makes a small offering. That night he dreams that the dead man returns to thank him for his kindness (*xie'en* 謝恩).[48]

2. During the Han, the official Wen Ying stayed overnight during a trip outside his jurisdiction when, at the third drum, he dreamt of a man kneeling before him and saying: "Formerly my relatives buried me here, but water has disturbed my grave; the wood of my coffin is wet, the coffin is half full of water, and I have no way to get warm. Hearing that you are here, I have come to request your help and would like to trouble you to stay a little longer tomorrow and move me to a high, dry place." He then spread open his clothes to show Wen Ying, and they were soaking wet. Wen Ying felt sorrow in his heart; then he awoke. He told his companions, but they said, "Dreams are empty. What is there in it to wonder at?" Wen Ying then went back to sleep at the same spot. He dreamed of the same man saying, "I have already pleaded with you desperately; if you have no compassion, what am I to do?" In the dream Wen Ying asked him who he was, and the man replied, "I was originally from Zhao and am now a spirit in the Wangmang lineage." Ying asked, "Where is your coffin?" The spirit replied, "Under the withered willow tree beside the stream, a dozen paces north of your tent. It is almost dawn; I cannot see you again, so you must remember." Wen Ying agreed. Suddenly he awoke. At dawn the others were about to set out, but Wen Ying persuaded them to

---

48. Sshj 6.7 (73–74).

stay a bit longer, and they agreed to test out (*yan* 驗) his dream. They found the withered willow and, beneath it, a coffin, rotten and half filled with water. Wen Ying then declared: "What is false is what I heard from you fellows; what has been passed down for generations among the folk cannot be without confirmation." He relocated the coffin, buried it, and departed.[49]

Other tales tell of such reburials, undertaken either spontaneously by the living upon encountering a corpse or coffin or at the dream-request of the needy spirit; most (but not all) of these, unlike the last example (which stresses the reality of dream-messages from the dead in the face of scepticism), emphasize the spirit's repayment of the favor, often in the form of grave goods found by the compassionate protagonist.[50] In addition, other tales portray the dead as requesting food and drink from the living,[51] or else the delivery of a message, the exaction of revenge, the protection of the deceased's endangered grave, or even healing or resuscitation.[52]

Yet there are plot-structures that, precisely because they do not partake of the clear-cut principle of reciprocity, illustrate even more plainly that, for these authors, the living and the dead form a single moral community, divided by visibility and frequency of contact, perhaps, but not by obligation, affection, emotion, or even aesthetic taste. We read of learned discussions between living and dead scholars—typically when a dead commentator appears in response to a living commentators' appraisal of his work.[53] We see friendships between living persons continued or renewed after

---

49. Ssj 16.8. Similar tales (in which a ghost requests reburial): Yml 115, 185; Yy 6.4, 7.14, 7.28.

50. Sgl 2 (includes the detail of a self-fulfilling prediction attached to the coffin, presumably made at the time of burial 300 years earlier, that the protagonist will find the coffin at the time in question); Jlz 58; Yml 147, 185, 261; Yy 6.4, 7.5, 7.11 (here a living couple uses money found in an ancient, rich tomb for reburying the corpse), 7.14 (ghost repays with an ancient *sanqu* instrument and high rank for his benefactor), 7.28 (this ghost has no possessions with which to repay his benefactor but makes a helpful prediction instead).

51. Yml 165, 235; Yy 6.6.

52. XuQxj 16 (healing, tr. Campany 1991a, 27); Sshj 4.1 (resuscitation and marriage); Yml 165 (food), 235 (food); Yy 6.6 (food), 6.8 (message delivered), 6.25 (merit to be transferred to the dead); Ssj 16.14 (boatride).

53. Qxj 11; Lgz 9; Yy 6.5 (Wang Bi and Lu Ji); Yml 99 (ghost of Zheng Xuan scolds young scholar for laughing at his comments on the *Yijing*).

the death of one member of the pair.[54] Dead and living together enjoy musical performances.[55] Ghosts pretend to be living persons in order to enjoy wine in wineshops or—a famous motif—sex in a roadside inn (or elsewhere) with a living person.[56] We read of how "old" ghosts introduce "new" ghosts to their condition; and even stories in which a living person pretends to be a ghost— sometimes involving trickery—create a sense of shared humanity between the two parties.[57] A crowd of ghosts, among them a young man recently deceased, visit the home of his bereaved father to comfort him.[58]

In sum, if one surveys the entire body of anomaly account narratives depicting interactions between living and dead persons, one's deepest impression will be a sense of sympathy, community, and fellow-feeling across the boundary between the "light" and "dark" realms. Seen against the background of contemporaneous efforts in the Daoist and Buddhist communities to extend solicitude for the welfare of the dead beyond the circle of kinship,[59] these texts appear as part of a much larger social and religious trend. Abandoning old Confucian strictures against the making of offerings to non-kin spirits as "impure" and "of no benefit," many authors of anomaly accounts, as if in support of changes being slowly enacted elsewhere in their society, portrayed for their

---

54. Yml 203 (cf.: repayment of favor done while the deceased person was still alive), 212, 221; Yy 6.12, 7.8.

55. Yml 46, 113, 222; Yy 6.3, 6.7, 6.24; Ssj 16.14 (cf.: here the ghost frightens its human audience after performing on the *pipa* for him).

56. Wine: Ssj 16.16. Cross-boundary love (most by trickery and between strangers, some by agreement between spouses): Zgk 2; Lyz 40; Shuyj 81, 82, 84, 85; Luyz 4, 10; Sshj 4.6, 6.1; Ssj 16.19–24; Yml 52, 113, 186 (cf.), 221 (cf.), 226, 238; Yy 6.10 (dead husband gets wife pregnant, but she bears only water because of breaking pregnancy tabu), 6.13 (implied), 6.19–20, 6.29 (cf.).

57. Lyz 28 = Ssj 16.18, story of Song Dingbo, who pretends to be a ghost (tr. Kao 1985, 59; Bodde 1941, 351); Yml 215, in which a man sees a lame ghost and imitates its limp for fun; Yml 256, in which an old ghost teaches a newcomer the ropes.

58. Yml 98.

59. See, *inter alia*, 1987; Seidel 1982, 1985, 1987; Teiser 1986, 1988a, 1988b; Sawada 1968; Xiao Dengfu 1989; Yu Yingshi 1964–65, 1981, 1983, 1987. Much more work needs to be done, however, on the relationship between the universalization of death rites and the indigenous kinship structure.

readers a wide variety of situations in which living and dead individuals who began as strangers ended up, through some particular conjunction of events, bound to one another with moral and, often, emotional cords, despite the chasm that still separated them.

Animal Rites

In anomaly accounts of the *fangshi* persuasion, strange animals are usually strange by virtue of their anomalous shape, their cross-species combination of traits, or their propensity (especially when long-lived) to change into other species. And these texts usually note some use to which they may be put by persons knowing their secret properties; for example, eating them allows one to live longer, or seeing them allows one to become ruler. This set of attitudes contrasts sharply with that revealed in texts of the Buddhist and Heaven and Humanity persuasions; for, in these texts, humans are depicted as standing in moral relationships with animals, and animals find their way into the stories as anomalous creatures not, typically, because of their hybrid quality but because of human-like behavior that seemingly suggests their membership, with humans, in a single moral community.

The plot structures here are many and varied. I simply list, first of all, examples of stories in which animals behave as though they possessed human-like dispositions.

1. A virtuous parrot saves other animals from wildfire (Yy 3.4; this tale comes straight from a Buddhist *avadāna* collection, as discussed in Chapter Four).

2. A flock of birds avenges the killing of one of its members (Yy 3.8).

3. A tiger attacks a lodge, but takes only the official there, leaving the commoners alone (Yy 3.14).

4. A tigress carries off a man, but returns him intact after a week (Yy 3.15).

5. An elephant carries off a man, but treats him well while he is in captivity (Yy 3.21).

6. An ox grows sick as its master prepares to sell it for slaughter (Yy 3.22).

7. A mother-kracken appears in human form and reprimands the man who killed her son; he dies (Yy 3.38).

8. A kracken listens to reason when appealed to by a human (Yy 3.39).

9. A monstrously born rat mourns its human mother and jumps into her coffin (Yy 8.33).

10. A monstrously born snake mourns at the funeral of its human mother (Ssj 14.8, Yml 198).

11. A dog walks like a person and wears its master's clothes (Ssj 18.23).

12. A rat speaks and wears clothing (Ssj 18.25).

13. An ox about to be slaughtered pleads for its life (Yml 97).

14. A rat predicts a monk's death (Yml 118).

15. A man grieving over a dead relative sees fish grieving over *their* relative and releases a fish he has just caught (Yml 169).

16. An ox mourns the death of its owner (Yml 246).

17. An ox speaks of its former lives (Xuanyj 14).

18. Birds extinguish a wildfire on a mountain to save the creatures there (Xuanyj 15, 16).

19. Turtles or other animals orient themselves to point out to lost human travelers the direction home (Sshj A18, Ssj 13.7, Yml 172, Yy 3.49).

20. An animal understands, and sometimes can produce, human speech, *except* where this is simply a portent (Shuyj 41, 48; Yy 3.1, 3.4–6, 3.10, 3.13, 3.48; ShuyjRf 2.131; Jlz 59; Ssj 18.25, 20.15; Yml 53, 96 [legal ramifications of this ability], 97, 157, 195 [in dream], 258; Xuanzj 54, 55).

21. An animal responds to human virtue (Ssj 11.11–12; Yy 10.4).

Aside from the above examples, we have also to deal with a large group of stories illustrating more specifically a relationship of moral-ritual reciprocity—both positive and negative—between humans and members of the animal kingdom. I list here only the most salient story-types, with a few examples of each.

(1) A human being helps an animal and is later helped (or at least thanked) by it (or its kind) in return. **(a)** There is the story of the King of Ants, in which a man traveling by boat plucks a struggling ant out of the water, then takes special pains to save it from other passengers who curse him for bringing a "poisonous creature" aboard, setting it free on reaching shore. The same night, he dreams that the ant appears to him as a black-clad man, introducing itself as the King of Ants and promising to help him if he is ever in need. Over a decade later the man is held prisoner by bandits and whispers of his plight to some ants; he then dreams of the black-clad figure again, who instructs him on where to go to avoid further danger, and when he awakens, ants have gnawed through the cage in which he is being held.[60] **(b)** A man was jailed for a crime he did not commit. As his execution date neared, he noticed crickets crawling on the ground nearby and sprinkled some rice on the ground for them, saying, "If you are divine and have the power to save my life, should I not go on living?" They ate it and departed. Soon they returned but were much larger; he thought it strange, so he fed them some more. After a week of this, they were as large as pigs. To repay (*bao*) him they dug a large hole and broke his fetters, enabling him to escape. Later, there was an amnesty, and so he was able to live. For generations this man's descendants made offerings to crickets in the city streets once each season, and they continue to do so today.[61] **(c)** A man buys four black ducks for an offering. His son dreams of four black-clad persons begging for their lives; awakening, the first thing he sees is the four ducks about to be slaughtered. He saves them, buying meat in the market as a substitute offering. Then he dreams of the four figures again; they thank him, then depart.[62] **(d)** A high official named Kong, when young, once saw a turtle in a market, bought and released it in a stream called Drink-Not Creek. As it swam away, the turtle looked back at him several times over its left shoulder. Later in life, because of his merits Kong was enfeoffed as "Marquis of Drink-Not Pavilion"; but when his seal of office was cast, the turtle in the design unexpectedly came out looking to the left. It was cast three times with the same result. The metalsmith told Kong about it, and Kong then realized this was the turtle's reward (*bao*) to him, so he took it and wore it at his belt. He was then promoted through a succession of high offices.[63]

(2) An animal exacts revenge for being wrongly harmed or killed by a human. **(a)** Ssj, Yml, and Yy each contains a story with roughly the following plot (each with different protagonist and details): a man traveling in the countryside beside or on a body of water kills or wounds a large serpentine creature. He feels uneasy about having done so, leaves the carcass behind and tells no one. A year or more later he returns to the spot with friends and, recalling

---

60. Ssj 20.8; Qxj 1; the latter version is tr. in Kao 1985, 134.

61. Yml 159 (CXJ 20, TPYL 643); Ssj 20.11. The Ssj version is more complete.

62. Yml 164 (TPGJ 276).

63. Ssj 20.6. Other items exhibiting this theme include XuQxj 3 and Sshj 10.8, which also involves a turtle that conspicuously looks back over its shoulder at its human benefactor.

his earlier deed, tells them about it. That night the spirit of the slain serpent appears in his dream, announcing it has been waiting for him to return so it can exact its revenge. The man subsequently dies.[64] **(b)** A man kills his family dog for food. The following year he and his entire family die.[65] **(c)** A man sees two krackens sporting in water; he shoots and hits one. Later he sees a woman weeping in the marketplace and holding his arrow. Thinking it strange, he questions her; she says only that he is cruel, then hands him the arrow and disappears. The man flees in terror but dies before reaching home.[66]

(3) Story-types (1) and (2) combined. **(a)** Three men lost in mountains happen upon a group of turtles, to whom they do obeisance, asking directions. The turtles extend their necks in a certain direction "as if by human intention"; the men walk that way and so find their way out. But one man takes one of the turtles with him, and he later cuts it up and eats it. Soon he dies a painful death; the other two men are not injured.[67] This tale combines positive and negative reciprocity: two imbalances are created, the first as a "credit" to the men (due to their bowing), the second as a "debit" to the man who kills the turtle, and each imbalance is righted. **(b)** After a river crests, a large fish is trapped in a pool, dying after three days. Everyone in the city eats of it except for one old woman. Suddenly she sees an old gentleman say to her: "It was my son who met this unfortunate end. You alone did not eat him; I will richly reward (*bao*) you. When the eyes of the stone tortoise at the eastern gate turn red, the city will be about to perish." She speaks of this to a young boy; he colors the tortoise's eyes red in order to fool her. Seeing them, the old woman immediately leaves the city. On her way out she sees a green-clad youth who says, "I am a dragon's

---

64. Ssj 20.14; Yml 145 (TPYL 930, TPGJ 131); Yy 7.25, which is the most dramatic, putting a speech in the mouth of the dream-figure.

65. ShuyjRf 2.126 (16b).

66. Yy 3.38. Other items on this theme include Yy 3.39 (but in the opposite direction: a man seeks revenge against *jiao* who kill people—but he merely remonstrates with them, and they stop their predations), 3.41, 4.27; ShuyjRf 1.76; Yml 97; XuQxj 6 (?); Sshj 10.6. Sshj 10.4 twists the theme: a poor laborer strikes a snake that has repeatedly stolen his food; as a punishment, hail begins to strike him, but he climbs a tree and upbraids the divine Duke of Thunder (*Leigong* 雷公), saying the snake is the one in the wrong for stealing his food—and with that the hail stops and the snake and its family die.

67. Yy 3.49.

son." This figure leads her up a nearby mountain, at which point the city sinks to become a lake.[68]

(4) An animal exacts revenge on behalf of its unjustly killed human benefactor. Each time she eats a meal, an old, poor, widowed woman feeds a horned snake by her bed. This snake grows large and subsequently bites and kills a prize horse owned by the prefect. Furious, the prefect demands that the snake be produced; the woman says only that it lives under the bed. The prefect has the ground dug up under the bed, but no snake is found; in his anger he kills the old woman. The snake, "having numinously learned to speak by associative resonance with a human" (感人以靈言), tells the prefect he will exact revenge on his "mother's" behalf (as would a filial son). Afterward, sounds of thunder are heard every night for forty days, and local peasants have the illusion that others are carrying fish on their heads; on the fortieth night, the area within forty *li* sinks underground to become a lake. Only the old woman's place remains intact, and it still exists today.[69]

I content myself with mentioning in passing three other motifs bearing on the moral dimensions of animal-human relations. One is that of animals parenting an orphaned or abandoned child: these narratives erode the moral distinction between human and animal by portraying both categories of beings as similarly disposed to protect and nourish the young and to value family ties.[70] Another is that of the faithful dog who saves its master from difficulty, dies sympathetically when its master dies, is buried with the rites for a human being out of gratitude for its virtue, and so on: these stories, too, erode the animal/human distinction by tacitly admitting domestic canines into the circle of human community.[71] The third is that of a person suffering the same fate (in this or in

---

68. Ssj 20.7. Similar in plot are Ssj 20.15, on which see below, and Ssj 13.8; both involve a city flooded as punishment, both involve human-animal bonds, and the human protagonist in both is an old woman. Another combination of positive and negative reciprocity is seen in Sshj 10.5.

69. Ssj 20.15; the item proceeds to describe the ongoing, subaquatic lives of the local peasants (this was why they were equipped beforehand with fish on their heads), as well as the souvenir-hunters who dive for pieces of blackened wood from the former city, which they use as pillows and give as gifts.

70. ShuyjRf 2.136 (the legend of 偃王); Ssj 14.5–6.

71. Qxj 15; Sl 1; Shuyj 15, 43, 44; Yy 3.24–25; Yml 85; Xuyj 1; Sshj 9.6–7; Ssj 9.10, 20.9–10.

the next life) as the animal he or she eats, or killing his own (transformed or reborn) relative when hunting—all of these tales cautioning against meat-eating and hunting by turning the "object" of the meal or the hunt into a moral "subject" through the narrative mechanism of role reversal.[72]

Although animal-spirits or demons are usually portrayed as either straightforwardly malevolent or as simply mischievous, a few items go so far as to explore the possibility of morally reciprocal relations between these creatures and human beings. The cases I have found all involve fox spirits that attach themselves to an official or a family and provide help (in the form of advance warning of danger, information on secret or distant affairs, and rescue from attack) in exchange for regular feeding.[73]

In the background to these narratives stand contemporaneous ideas concerning the universality of "Buddha-nature" in sentient beings as well as debates concerning karma and rebirth. We can improve our understanding of our authors' aims by briefly juxtaposing their texts against these discussions.

The term "Buddha-nature" (*foxing* 佛性) first became a fulcrum of debate in the early fifth century with successive translations of the *Mahāparinirvāna-sūtra*. Daosheng's (d. 434) extremely controversial commentary on Faxian's translation (which had reached the southern capital in 418) stressed the universality of the Buddha-nature in all sentient beings; Dharmaksema's more complete translation, which reached the south sometime around 432, explicitly confirmed Daosheng's interpretation. This *sūtra's* statement to the effect that all beings without exception would one day attain Buddhahood became the object of intense commentarial scrutiny and debate in the fifth through the seventh centuries.[74] Daosheng's influential commentary on the *Lotus Sūtra*, composed in 432, also stressed that "all beings are bound to become Buddhas," that "all living beings are [potentially] Buddhas and also are all in *nirvāna*," and that "living beings are endowed with [the faculty of] great enlightenment; all are without exception potential

---

72. Yy 5.32, 5.38, 8.37; Xuanyj 2, 10, 12, 13, 24; Mxj 6, 21, 33, 54, 67, 114; Sshj 9.12.

73. Yml 92 (TPGJ 294); Sshj 9.15; Ssj 18.12.

74. On *foxing*, Liu 1989; Sueki 1990. On the impact of Daosheng's ideas on it, Kim 1990, 35–36, 65–66; Tsukamoto 1985, 457ff. (stressing the socially egalitarian impact of his ideas); Ch'en 1964, 114–19. The essentially synonymous notion of the *tathāgatagarbha* was also introduced at around the same time or perhaps even earlier, but seems to have made much less of an immediate impact: see Liu 1989, 17; Tamaki 1961.

bodhisattvas."[75] By the late sixth century such ideas, combined with the prevalent belief that the world was in the degenerate "last age of Dharma," had been radicalized by the Three Stages sect 三階教, founded by Xinxing (540–594), into the notion that the potential buddhahood of all sentient beings should be treated as a present reality in this world, not simply as an abstract future possibility. The teachings of this sect, of which the key term was "universal" (pu 普) and of which the emphasis was on the present impossibility of making discriminations of value or status (including social and species status), entailed displays of reverence toward animals and insects and such scriptural assertions as that it was better to give one mouthful of food to an animal than to donate to all the buddhas, bodhisattvas, and *śrāvakas* in the universe.[76] All of these ideas served, among other things, to soften the ontological and moral distinctions between humans and other beings.

But the question of the moral quality of our relationship to animals was posed even more sharply by the twin Buddhist notions of karma and rebirth, which were widely discussed from the early fourth century onwards, not only in translations of *sūtras* but also in polemical writings by and for laity.[77] And, within those complex

---

75. Kim 1990, 202, 276, and 290, respectively.

76. On the *sanjiejiao* I have relied principally on Lewis 1990b and Makita 1976, 304–19. The scriptural passage mentioned occurs in T 2870 (85.1336a.24–26). I have not at this writing seen Hubbard 1986.

77. The most important of these works are listed in Zürcher 1972, 15–16, and Liebenthal 1952, 338–40; they are collected in T 2102 (v.52). For our purposes the most notable (for each I cite locations of texts in T 2102 and of Western-language trs. and discussions—in general see also Tang Yongtong 1976 [1938] and Schmidt-Glintzer 1976) are: (1) *Zhengwulun* 正誣論, author unknown, early fourth century (52.7a–9a), tr. Link 1961; Zürcher 1972, 304, 311; (2) *Gengshenglun* 更生論 by Luo Han, second half of fourth century (52.27b–c), tr. Liebenthal 1952, 343–46; Zürcher 1972, 135–36; (3) *Ming Fo lun* 明佛論 by the layman Zong Bing, written ca. 433 (52.9b–16a), tr. Liebenthal 1952, 378–94; Zürcher 1972, 20, 143, 219, 268–70; (4) *Yudaolun* 喻道論 by Sun Chuo (ca. 300–380), written middle of fourth century (52.16b–17c), tr. Link and Lee 1966; Zürcher 1972, 132–34; (5) *Ming baoying lun* 明報應論 by Huiyuan (334–416) (52.33b–34b), tr. Liebenthal 1952, 358–62; (6) *Sanbaolun* 三報論 by Huiyuan (52.34b–c), tr. Liebenthal 1952, 362–65; (7) correspondence (ca. 433) between Zong Bing and the anti-Buddhist polemicist and astronomer He Chengtian (370–447) (52.17c–21c), partial tr. Liebenthal 1952, 374–76; Zürcher 1972, 270, 305; Luo (unpublished); (8) correspondence between He Chengtian and Yan Yanzhi (384–456), including He's *Daxinglun* 達性論 (52.21c–27a); Luo (unpublished); (9) treatise by Emperor Wu of the Liang, *Li shenming chengfo yiji* 立神明成佛義記 and related documents (52.54a ff.), tr. Lai 1981.

and confusing debates, on which much ink has been spilt but which have yet to be fully and clearly interpreted, one note was sounded to which I wish to draw special attention here: namely, the affirmation or denial of the uniqueness (and hence the dignity) of humanity with respect to other beings. As was the case with regard to vexed question of the "permanence" or "impermanence" of the soul[s]" (*shenbumie* 神不滅 and *shenmie* 神滅 respectively)—with Buddhists and anti-Buddhists switching sides as the understanding of the issue and the terms in which it was framed shifted over these centuries—here too the tables turned. In the early fourth century treatise "A Rectification of Unjust Criticism" (*Zhengwulun* 正誣論), which "very probably is the oldest Chinese Buddhist treatise in existence,"[78] the pro-Buddhist author, as well as his opponent, assume that the Buddha's passing through all five courses of birth before his final birth was due to his karmic flaws. But what is most striking is that the Buddhist author—presumably hoping to win the approval of a readership he assumed would agree with him on this point and share his rhetorically floriate disgust at his opponent's position—proclaims that "among the natures of things in Heaven and Earth, that of humanity is considered most precious" 天地之性以人為貴. After alluding to a Confucian legend (of which record survives in the *Kongzi jiayu* 孔子家語) in which Confucius meets a man named Rong Qi 榮期 who discourses to him on the privilege of being human, the most precious category among all beings, the author then savages his anti-Buddhist opponent in the following terms:

> Even more: [the maligner] no longer wishes to associate himself with the human race. He does not consider birth as an animal either hateful or detestable 不醜惡於獸生; he regards grass and water as savory, and finds no disgrace in bit or bridle. If he is comfortable in this, then let him do so; there is no need for him to raise further objections.[79]

A century later, we find He Chengtian 何承天 appealing to the principle of the uniqueness and dignity of the human race—its membership, with Heaven and Earth, in the triad of the "three forces" (*sancai* 三才)—to argue the depravity of the Buddhist

---

78. Zürcher 1972, 304, assuming (rightly, in my opinion) the *Mouzi lihuolun* to be later than its purported date.

79. 52.7c.18–8a.5; I have modified the tr. in Link 1961, 150. The name of Rong Qi varies in early sources; Link cites the fourth *juan* of *Kongzi jiayu* as the source of the anecdote about his speech to Confucius.

doctrine of rebirth. It is not the metaphysical improbability of the workings of rebirth that He seizes on as most objectionable; although he does deny that the souls (*shen*) survive to receive another body, this is not the crux of his argument. He even grants (echoing certain stock passages in the classics) that the superior person shuns unnecessary violence toward animals, avoiding the kitchen and using open-weave nets when hunting. But he finds the doctrine of rebirth repugnant because it implies that humans intermix with all other kinds of beings (*zhongsheng* 眾生), and are hence no different from "things that fly, swim, and crawl."[80] His pro-Buddhist interlocutor, Yan Yanzhi, responds that the classical notion of the triad applies only, among humans, to the sages; common people are among the "mass of beings" (*zhongsheng*), sharing with them the basic conditions of life, and differing only in possessing consciousness. In thus differentiating two kinds of humans and limiting his claims to the inferior sort, Yan hopes to absolve Buddhism from the charge of "confusing moral relationships" (*luanlun* 亂倫) among different categories of beings.[81] He Chengtian replies by rejecting Yan's attempt to assimilate even common humanity to the "mass of beings," claiming that although humans share life itself (*sheng* 生) with other beings, their nature (*xing* 性) differs essentially from that of beasts; and it differs precisely because of humans' unique possession of moral faculties, which he posits in terms echoing those of Mencius.[82] Yan counters by granting He's thesis on the uniqueness of humanity but shifting its true basis not to a distinction in moral faculties but to the possession of souls (*shen*) that survive death—a position that, although retaining the post-mortem existence of the *shen* as the basis of humans' rebirth, also undermines rebirth doctrine by denying *shen* to other beings, as He did not hesitate to point out in his rejoinder.

This much suffices to make my point: that the question of whether human beings were on the same *moral* footing as other beings was a central one in early medieval discussions of the Buddhist doctrine of rebirth, although pro-Buddhist authors took different sides on this question. It is in precisely this light that the true significance of our authors' narratives on human-animal interactions can be clearly seen. Our authors weighed in heavily on the

---

80. T 2102 (52.21c–22a); I am indebted to a paper by Julia Luo (Luo [unpublished]) for this insight into He's argument.

81. T 2102 (52.22a–b); here and below I rely once more on the analysis in Luo [unpublished].

82. T 2102 (52.22b–23a).

side of the non-uniqueness[83] of humanity; they pressed the claims of a moral order that was implicate throughout Heaven, Earth, and all classes of beings in between, one that was so all-penetrating as to be capable of uniting even a man and an insect in an irrevocable moral bond. Yet, perhaps most fascinatingly, those among them who wrote from the Heaven and Humanity persuasion did not stress this theme as a way of promoting Buddhism and its notion of rebirth per se, although their writings may have had that effect (they were indeed cited by pro-Buddhist writers as evidence for their claims). They did so in order to emplace humanity in what they considered its proper station: one of respect for the limitations imposed by the authority of Heaven and Earth and, hence, by the claims posed by non-human species. They hoped not to undermine the dignity of humanity but rather to redefine it as contingent on the treatment of other species with dignity as well.

Conclusion: The Cosmic Moral Community

Why did this widening of the moral community to near-cosmic proportions occur? And why did authors of anomaly accounts portray it in the types of narratives they did? In solving this as other puzzles posed by the genre, scholars have long replied with the two-word refrain, "foreign influence," and have been quick to posit virtually all tales involving animals as having a source in the *avadāna* texts and all tales illustrating moral reciprocity as due to the influence of the idea of karma. Hence, these same scholars' propensity for labeling texts such as the Yml, Yy, Sshj, and Yhz "Buddhist" in orientation.

    Buddhist texts and ideas undeniably provided a powerful stimulus for our authors and their audience. But they do not suffice to render the evidence completely intelligible. For one thing, the themes surveyed in this chapter begin to appear already in the Ssj; in Gan Bao's day very few *avadāna* texts were available in Chinese, and even if Gan Bao had access to any of them, there is no strong evidence in the Ssj that he used them. For another, the very overlap between indigenous and Buddhist notions of reciprocity means that one cannot assume all stories of reward or retribution to be Buddhist-inspired. Finally, even if Buddhist values did stimulate a

---

83. This is not to deny, of course, that these authors still privileged the human over other conditions; but it *is* to deny that they viewed human beings as *morally unique*.

large measure of the ethical agenda of the anomaly accounts, one still wants to know why authors who were not (so far as we know) Buddhist laymen, and who did not write to promote the Buddhist cause, found these values so persuasive to write about and so good to think with.

But if we recall the analysis (in Chapter Seven) of the Heaven and Humanity persuasion, then the reasons for our texts' emphasis on cross-boundary reciprocity become clearer. One way to render that vision of the cosmos more compelling would have been to broaden and deepen the connections between humanity and other sorts of beings, by both tightening the old strands in the cosmic network of influence-response and tying new ones at new relational nodes. This tying of new strands would have been indirectly prodded (and perhaps unintentionally aided) by the third- and fourth-century renaissance of interest in the *Zhuangzi* and the rise of "dark learning," with their expansiveness of vision, although it was precisely against the anti-locativism of these currents of thought that the Heaven and Humanity authors wrote—which is why the moral structure these authors urged was one based on essentially Confucian, *li*-based values, now expanded outward in scope. For authors of this persuasion, the ever more widely accepted notions of karma, the universality of Buddha-nature, rebirth, and compassion toward sentient beings—at least to the extent that they entailed a strengthening of the ties of moral-ritual reciprocity across the boundaries of seen/unseen and human/animal—must have seemed welcome allies.

Postscript

No pat conclusions about the large and unwieldy body of texts I have been discussing would carry much weight. I close this book, however, by stepping back to cast a long look at the place of the texts in their larger historical and religious context.

In Chapter Three, I argued that, at least in the formative period studied here, authors justified the genre of anomaly accounts with reference to an older tradition of cosmographic collecting, a tradition that, so some hoped, would lend an aura of authenticity to the new genre associated with it. In light of the ensuing chapters, one can see that the authors of these accounts, for all their appeal to the classical cosmographic tradition, bent it in ways reflective of their diverse persuasive aims and interests.

If the old tradition was constituted by a specific set of dynamic relations between center and periphery, only the relatively few anomaly accounts of a Confucian persuasion continued to operate within this dyadic structure. The pro-*fangshi* and pro-Daoist authors converted it into a triad: between the ruler in the center and the periphery over which he sought dominance (symbolic and otherwise) by means of collected reports, they inserted a mediating third term. It was now the adept who, with his exclusive access to all things hidden and remote, was uniquely poised to grant or deny access to them; and it was the reporter of adepts and esoterica—the implied author—who (among others) afforded access to adepts and their knowledge and skills. Even more than the *fangshi* authors, the pro-Daoist authors claimed supreme autonomy for the adept, largely (but not quite entirely) freeing him from the bonds of the center-periphery relations seen in the cosmographic tradition as central.

Meanwhile, rather than inserting themselves and their exemplars as mediators between center and periphery as traditionally understood, writers of pro-Buddhist accounts in effect relocated the center. They documented the profound power of a new ground or field of authority to which rulers would do well to orient themselves—and to which, starting in the Liang, some did.

What, then, of those who wrote from what I have termed the perspective of Heaven and Humanity? Like the *fangshi* and Daoist but unlike the Buddhist writers, they wrote largely as a function of the old cosmographic tradition. But they did so differently. Whereas in the classical tradition the reporter of anomalies worked on behalf of the center's ongoing effort to domesticate a periphery understood as disordered and needing rectification, these writers pointed to an order already implicate in the cosmos out there. They did so, ironically, by writing about apparent disorder—beings or events whose anomalousness revealed the true, unseen order that surrounds and underlies the apparent order but actual confusion of ordinary life. It was now the "center," the locus of human life, that had come to be at risk of disorder and to need rectification. These authors cited the implicate cosmic order as a check on an increasingly unruly imperial center, and on mores seen as increasingly distant from old standards. Although they claimed to be its conservors, they in fact, perhaps unconsciously, turned the old centrist tradition of cosmographic collecting inside out.

The seeds of the genre had been planted earlier, but they flourished in the wake of the fall of the Han, the loss of the northern heartland, and the massive social dislocations and ongoing political turmoil of the ensuing centuries. I interpret the genre's flourishing as, at bottom, a creative response to—not a passive reflection of—the uncertainties of its time.

Figuratively speaking, the anti-locative, "naturalist" response to these uncertainties was a sort of flight from the center, upwards through the ceiling of mortality or outwards beyond the bounds of service to the imperial center. "Dark learning," the quest for transcendence or for mental repose and ultimate enlightenment (all such quests standing in some degree of tension with the traditional family system and the values of filiality and loyalty, even when pursued in non-monastic contexts), neo-Daoist non-conformity and Confucian-based eremeticism: these were the anti-locative options. With the important exceptions of the Daoist and some Buddhist hagiographies, and the Syj (which resorted to an intensely ironic allegory built on but subversive of the cosmographic trope of the tribute system), those who gravitated toward this response produced little in the way of anomaly accounts. Its old centrist associations probably made the genre seem unpalatable to them.

The locative, "conformist" response to the breakdown of the old order was not to flee the center but to reassert its prestige—but, typically, on new grounds. New Daoist traditions (as evidenced in texts emanating from the Celestial Master and Numinous Treasure lineages) constructed rituals and communities emphasizing the believer's locative emplacement within a new, explicitly religious network erected on the ruins of Han correlative cosmology and the lingering prestige of the cosmically resonant imperium. At the same time, karmic, *mingjiao*-style Buddhism offered an alternative network in which practitioners could find a place in the cosmos— a non-indigenous network grafted onto the Han cosmology and lashed onto the canonical traditions at various points. These new types of communities affirmed the rule-governed nature of the cosmos; they posited an unseen spiritual hierarchy to shore up or else functionally supplant the all-too-human one centered in the capital. These impressive, serene structures of immutable authority must have seemed comforting to those confident of belonging to their lower reaches, even as they held warnings to outsiders.

It was essentially these same unseen structures that the creators of the most seminal and prototypical anomaly accounts—particularly those who wrote from the Heaven and Humanity and the Buddhist perspectives—claimed to limn. The generic warrant and precedents as a function of which they wrote dictated that they limn this other world not on its own terms, not through direct divine speech, first-person visionary narration, or theological system-building, but in the case-by-case, timebound mode of history. That mode kept humanity, not the spirit-world or the marvelous periphery per se, as its constant focus. Works of the anomaly account genre proceeded to characterize the human being not by analyzing its inner nature or sorting through its dispositional types, but by charting the variety of Others against which it was liable to bump, and the relational curve traced by documented series of such bumps over time. Finding the old center's city walls in ruins, authors participated through this cosmographic genre in the much larger cultural project of locating the newly vast perimeters of a habitable zone outside the walls. They portrayed the non-human periphery, once seen as disquieting and monstrous, as marvelous for its congruities, as fundamentally—and suprisingly—like us, hence habitable. As in the old cosmographic tradition, they described this habitation by delineating its borders, but those borders had now immeasurably receded, and they had become not walls or outlying wilds but all those seams running through the midst of everyday life where the human and the non-human unexpectedly collide—or dance.

Appendix

Explanation of Conventions for the Citation of Primary Texts

The number and variety of works cited in this book perhaps makes for an appearance of confusion in the citations. My main rule of thumb is to cite texts in such a way that a reader using a different edition than mine (where it is a question of different editions of the same version of the text) can find the passages in question in his or her own edition. But different types of works are cited by different conventions.

Traditional Chinese works other than anomaly accounts are normally cited by fascicle and page number in the edition listed in the bibliography or in the body of the text; "a" and "b" denote the recto and verso sides of folio pages or else (in the Taishō canon and DKW) horizontal registers on the indicated page ("a," "b," "c," or [in DKW] "d"). When an Arabic numeral immediately follows one of these letters, it indicates the line number on the folio side or register in question. Thus, "2.17a" denotes the recto side of page 17 in the second fascicle, "10.23b2–7" indicates lines 2–7 of the verso side of page 23 in the tenth fascicle. Citations of pages in the Taishō are sometimes preceded by the volume number.

Some primary texts (other than anomaly accounts) are cited in modern, Western-formatted editions. Normally, only the page number is given in these cases, sometimes both fascicle and page number (for the convenience of readers who may be using a premodern edition of the work cited).

399

Collectanea (including both secular and canonical works) are cited by abbreviations in capital letters, and the editions used are listed in the bibliography. Citations of secular compendia such as the TPYL, TPGJ, YWLJ., etc., are by fascicle, sometimes with the addition of either (a) the number of the item in question in the consecutive series of item in the relevant fascicle (even where such numbers do not appear in the text itself) or (b) a page number. Citations of passages within texts collected in the Buddhist and Daoist canons are by fascicle and page, but the texts themselves are usually cited by their numbers in the reference works listed in the bibliography under their respective abbreviations, T and HY.

Particular hagiographic items in the Taishō edition of Huijiao's Gsz are often cited by topical section followed by the consecutive number of the item in that section. E.g., "Gsz wangshen 1" refers to the first hagiography in the *wangshen* ("Self-Immolators") section. Where Huijiao's topical section is subdivided in Gsz into more than one part—as in the case of the *shenyi* ("Wonder-Workers") section—capital letters A, B, etc., indicate the subdivisions.

Dynastic histories are cited by fascicle number followed in parentheses by the continuous page number in the modern Zhonghua shuju edition. (These editions are in all cases paginated continuously from the first through the last volume, so citation of volume numbers would be superfluous.)

Anomaly accounts have been cited as follows:

1. All works are cited by the abbreviation listed at the beginning of the bibliography. That list also indicates at a glance the edition(s) to which citations are keyed. Where two editions are listed (e.g., for Shj, Sshj), citations are to the first, not the second, unless otherwise noted.

2. Texts recompiled in LX have been cited by title and consecutive item number, although LX itself does not, unfortunately, number items. Page numbers in most cases have been omitted due to the differences in pagination among different editions of LX; item numbers should allow all readers to locate individual items accurately, although some counting may be involved for large works such as the Yml and Mxj. In these large texts, where item numbers are high the reader may find it easier to count backwards from the end, beginning with the total number of LX items I list in Chapter Two for the text in question.

3. Multi-fascicle texts in modern editions (e.g., Ssj) are cited by fascicle number and the number of the item in the series of items found in the indicated fascicle. E.g., "Ssj 15.7" indicates the seventh item of fascicle 15. (For texts with stable sequencing of items across many editions, such as the twenty-fascicle Ssj, this method should allow readers using premodern-style editions to find items just as quickly.) In the case of the Bwz I always provide both fascicle and item number (for the convenience of users of premodern editions), but to this I sometimes add the continuous item number in the *entire* text plus page number in the 1980 edition by Fan Ning. (That is, Fan Ning's item numbers run continuously across fascicle divisions. Some modern editions and studies of the Ssj also number its items this way, but, since the standard version of the Ssj contains 464 items [a very unwieldy number] I stick to the "fascicle.item" format for the convenience of readers not using one of these.)

4. Premodern-style texts not divided into multiple fascicles are cited by item number followed, in some cases, by folio page number in parentheses. E.g., "XuQxj 3 (2a)" indicates the third item in the listed edition of the XuQxj, which is found on the recto side of the second folio page. "Sxz 26" means the 26th item in the listed edition of the Sxz.

5. Premodern-style texts divided into two or more fascicles and formatted to indicate clearly the divisions between items (as are most texts) are cited by fascicle and item, sometimes followed by page number in parentheses. E.g., "ShuyjRf 1.2 (1b)" indicates the second item of the first fascicle, beginning on the verso side of the first folio page of that fascicle.

6. Premodern-style texts divided into two or more fascicles but *not* formatted to show clear distinctions between items—most notably the Syj—are cited simply by fascicle and folio page number (sometimes with the addition of the line numbers on the page in question).

7. Premodern-style texts not divided into multiple fascicles but subdivided into multiple topic sections—most notably the Shenyjing—are cited by section letter, item number, and (sometimes) folio page number. The section letter in the case of the Shenyjing corresponds to the directional topic (E = section on the East, NE = Northeast, C = Center, etc).

8. Note that where two versions of the same text are cited and where similar citation style would cause confusion, as in the case of the Sshj (of which both a two- and a ten-fascicle version are cited, both in premodern editions), letters are used to designate not sections but fascicles. E.g., "Sshj A12" means the twelfth item in the first fascicle of the two-*juan*, ZDHW edition; "Sshj 1.12" means the twelfth item in the first fascicle of the ten-*juan*, CSJC edition. Nor-

mally the ten-*juan* edition is the one cited, with the two-*juan* version cited only for comparative purposes and clearly stated to be such, so there should be no confusion.

9. Where two items found in different texts overlap to a large degree, I sometimes signal this in a string of item numbers by placing an "equals" sign (=) between the two. Note that this sign does not imply a complete, character-for-character correspondence, simply an overlap of plot and personae; the linguistic correspondence between them may or may not be close. (In such cases it is usually close but rarely complete.)

List of Works Cited (1):

Anomaly Accounts, Local Histories, and Closely Related Works, with Key to Editions Used

(Listed alphabetically by abbreviation)

Bqnz	*Biqiunizhuan* 比丘尼傳 (T 2063)	
Bwz	*Bowuzhi* 博物志 ([1] Fan Ning, ed., 1980 [2] ZDHW)	
Bzt	*Bozetu* 白澤圖 (JDJL)	
Dmj	*Dongmingji* 洞冥記 (ZDHW)	
Dxz	*Dongxianzhuan* 洞仙傳 (YJQQ 110–111)	
Fjz	SGZ, *Fangjizhuan* 三國志方技傳 (SGZ 29)	
Fslz	HHS, *Fangshu liezhuan* 方術列傳 (HHS 82A + 82B)	
Fsty	*Fengsu tongyi* 風俗通義 (Wang Liqi, ed., 1981)	
Ganyz	*Ganyingzhuan* 感應傳	
Gdt	*Guaditu* 括地圖 (HTDL)	
Gshiz	*Gaoshizhuan* 高士傳 (GJYS)	
Gslz	*Guishen liezhuan* 鬼神列傳 (LX)	
Gsy	*Guangshiyin yingyanji* 光世音應驗記 (RKKO)	
Gsz	*Gaosengzhuan* 高僧傳 (T 2059)	
Guiz	*Guizang* 歸藏 (JDJL)	
Gyz	*Guyizhuan* 古異傳 (LX)	
Gz	*Guangzhi* 廣志 (SF)	
Gzj	*Guangzhouji* 廣州記 (SF)	
Hwdnz	*Han Wu Di neizhuan* 漢武帝內傳 (ZDHW)	
Hwgs	*Han Wu gushi* 漢武故事 (LX)	
Hygz	*Huayang guozhi* 華陽國志 (Liu Lin, ed., 1984)	

403

Jingyj   *Jingyiji* 旌異記 (LX)
Jjz   *Jiujiangzhi* 九江志 (SF)
Jlj   *Jilingji* 集靈記 (LX)
Jlz   *Jinlouzi zhiguai pian* 金樓子志怪篇 (SKQS)
Jyj   *Jiyiji* 集異記 (LX)
Jzj   *Jingzhouji* 荊州記 (SF)
Jzsy   *Jizhong suoyu* 汲冢瑣語 (JDJL)
Kjj   *Kuaijiji* 會稽記 (SF)
Lgz   *Lingguizhi* 靈鬼志 (LX)
Lh   *Linhai shuitu yiwuzhi* 臨海水土異物志 (Zhang Chonggen, ed.,
                   1980)
Luyz   *Luyizhuan* 錄異傳 (LX)
Lxz   *Liexianzhuan* 列仙傳 (DZ [HY 294])
Lyz   *Lieyizhuan* 列異傳 (LX)
Mxj   *Mingxiangji* 冥祥記 (LX)
Nkj   *Nankangji* 南康記 (SF)
Nyz   *Nanyuezhi* 南越志 (SF)
Nz   *Nanzhou yiwuzhi* 南州異物志 (SF)
Pyj   *Poyangji* 鄱陽記 (SF)
Qxj   *Qi Xie ji* 齊諧記 (LX)
Sbgtl   *Ji shenzhou sanbao gantonglu* 集神州三寶感通錄 (T 2106)
Sgl   *Shenguailu* 神怪錄 (LX)
Shenyj   *Shenyiji* 神異記 (LX)
Shenyjing   *Shenyijing* 神異經 (ZDHW)
Shj   *Shanhaijing* 山海經 ([1] Yuan Ke, ed., 1980 [2] *Shj jianshu*
                   箋疏, comm. by Hao Yixing 郝懿行, 1882; rept. SBBY)
Shuis   *Shuishi* 水飾 (LX)
Shuyj   *Shuyiji* 述異記 [by Zu Chongzhi 祖沖之] (LX)
ShuyjRf   *Shuyiji* 述異記 [by Ren Fang 任昉] (ZDHW)
Sjz   *Shuijingzhu* 水經注 (Dai Zhen, ed., 1988 [1775])
Skz   *Shi Kuang zhan* 師曠占 (JDJL)
Sl   *Shenlu* 神錄 (LX)
Ssh   *Sushuo* 俗説 (LX)
Sshj   *Soushen houji* 搜神後記 ([1] CSJC [2] ZDHW)
Ssj   *Soushenji* 搜神記 (20-juan version) (Yang Jialuo, ed., 1982
                   [1959]a)
Ssj8   *Soushenji* 搜神記 (8-juan version) (ZDHW)
Ssxy   *Shishuo xinyu* 世説新語 (Yang Jialuo, ed., 1982 [1959]b)
Sxz   *Shenxianzhuan* 神仙傳 (SK)
Syj   *Shiyiji* 拾遺記 (ZDHW)
Szj   *Shizhouji* 十洲記 (ZDHW)
Wlj   *Wulingji* 武陵記 (SF)
XiGsy   *Xi Guanshiyin yingyanji* 繫觀世音應驗記 (RKKO)
Xjzj   *Xijing zaji* 西京雜記 (*Yan Danzi, Xijing zaji* [Beijing:
                   Zhonghua shuju, 1985])
Xrj   *Xiangruiji* 祥瑞記 (TPGJ 389)

Xs	*Xiaoshuo* 小説 (LX)
Xuanyj	*Xuanyanji* 宣驗記 (LX)
Xuanzj	*Xuanzhongji* 玄中記 (LX)
XuGsy	*Xu Guangshiyin yingyanji* 續光世音應驗記 (RKKO)
Xunyj	*Xunyangji* 潯陽記 (SF)
XuQxj	*Xu Qi Xie ji* 續齊諧記 (ZDHW)
Xuyj	*Xuyiji* 續異記 (LX)
Xyj	*Xiangyiji* 祥異記 (LX)
Xzj	*Xiangzhongji* 湘中記 (SF)
Yaolan	*Yaolan* 要覽 (ZDHW)
Ydz	*Yindezhuan* 陰德傳 (TPYL 556.13)
Yhz	*Yuanhunzhi* 冤魂志 (ZDHW)
Yl	*Yilin* 異林 (LX)
Yml	*Youminglu* 幽明錄 (LX)
Yslz	*Yishu liezhuan* 藝術列傳 (JS 95, pp. 2467–2506)
Ywj	*Yiwenji* 異聞記 (LX)
Yy	*Yiyuan* 異苑 (SK)
Yzgjj	*Yuzhang gujinji* 豫章古今記 (SF)
Zgc	*Cao Pi zhiguai* 曹毗志怪 (LX)
Zgj	*Zhiguaiji* 志怪記 (LX)
Zgk	*Kongshi zhiguai* 孔氏志怪 (LX)
Zgszg	*Za guishen zhiguai* 雜鬼神志怪 (LX)
Zgz	*Zu Taizhi zhiguai* 祖台之志怪 (LX)
Zyz	*Zhenyizhuan* 甄異傳 (LX)

List of Works Cited (II):

Collectanea, Series, Journals, Standard Histories, and Reference Works

(Listed by abbreviation in alphabetical order.)

(All standard histories are modern editions published by Zhonghua shuju [Beijing].)

BAS   *Bulletin of the Academica Sinica*

BBCS   *Baibu congshu jicheng* 百部叢書集成. Ed. Yan Yiping 嚴一萍. Taibei: Yiwen yinshuguan, 1966.

BEF   *Bulletin de l'École Française d'Extrême-Orient*

BH   *Baihai* 稗海. Comp. Shang Jun 商濬, printed Ming *wanli* period. Photographic rept. in 5 vols. from Zhenlutang ed. Taibei: Xinxing shuju, 1968.

BKLT   *Baikong liutie* 白孔六帖. Comp. Bai Juyi 白居易 (772–846) and Kong Chuan 孔傳 (fl. 1127–62). Ming *jiaqing* wood-block print ed., rept. 2 vols. Taibei: Xinxing shuju, 1969.

BMFE   *Bulletin of the Museum of Far Eastern Antiquities*

BQS   *Bei Qi shu* 北齊書

BS   *Beishi* 北史

BSOA   *Bulletin of the School of Oriental and African Studies*

BTSC   *Beitang shuchao* 北堂書鈔. Comp. Yu Shinan 虞世南 (558–638), collated and annotated by Kong Guangtao 孔廣陶, published in a block-print ed. re-cut from a traced Sung ed. in 1888. Facsimile rept. in 2 vols. of 1888 ed. Taibei: Wenhai chubanshe, 1962.

BZL   *Bianzhenglun* 辯正論. Comp. Shi Falin 釋法琳 (fl. 640). T 2110.

BZQS *Baizi quanshu* 百子全書. Compiler unknown. Originally printed (?) 1875.

CEA *Cahiers d'Extrême-Asie*

CGL *Chuogenglu* 輟耕錄. Comp. Tao Zongyi 陶宗儀 (fl. 1360–68). JDMS ed.

CL *Chinese Literature: Essays, Articles, Reviews*

CSJC *Congshu jicheng* 叢書集成. [1] *Chubian* 初編. Shanghai: Commercial Press, 1935–37. [2] *Xubian* 續編. Taibei: Yiwen, 1970–71.

CXJ *Chuxueji* 初學記. Comp. Xu Jian 徐堅 (659–729) et al. Modern critical recension by Si Yizu 司義祖. 3 vols. continuously paginated. Beijing: Zhonghua shuju, 1962.

DKW *Dai Kanwa jiten* 大漢和辭典. Comp. Morohashi Tetsuji 諸橋轍次. Rev. ed. Tokyo, 1984.

DZ *Zhengtong daozang* 正統道藏. Printed Shanghai, 1923–26. Rept. in photo-reduced, 60-vol. format. Taipei: Xinwenfeng, 1988.

EC *Early China*

ECT Loewe 1993

EMC "Early Middle Chinese" pronunciation as reconstructed in Pulleybank 1991

FYZL *Fayuan zhulin* 法苑珠林. Comp. Shi Daoshi 釋道世 ca. 668. T 2122.

GJSB *Gujin shuobu congshu* 古今説部叢書. Compiler and orig. publication date unknown. Printed Shanghai: Zhongguo tushu gongsi, 1915. Facsimile rept. in 5 vols. Shanghai: Shanghai wenyi chubanshe, 1991.

GJYS *Gujin yishi* 古今逸史. Comp. Wu Guan 吳琯 (fl. 1568–72). Facsimile reproduction in 6 vols. of a Ming ed. Shanghai: Commercial Press, 1937.

GSWF *Gushi wenfang xiaoshuo* 顧氏文房小説. Comp. *jiaqing* period (1522–1566). Rept. Taibei: Xinxing shuju, 1960.

GXJB *Guoxue jiben congshu* 國學基本叢書. Ed. Wang Yunwu 王雲五. Taibei: Commercial Press, 1967–68.

GYCS *Guyi congshu* 古逸叢書. Comp. Li Shuchang 黎庶昌; published 1884. BBCS ed.

GZCS *Gezhi congshu* 格致叢書. Comp. Hu Wenhuan 胡文煥; published 1596 (?).

GZJ *Ganzhuji* 紺珠集. Comp. during Sung, compiler unknown. Photographic reproduction in 13 vols. based on Ming ed. Taibei: Taiwan shangwu yinshuguan, 1970.

HHS *Hou Han shu* 後漢書

HJAS *Harvard Journal of Asiatic Studies*

HR *History of Religions*

HS *Hanshu* 漢書

HTDL Wang Mo 王謨 (*jinshi* 1778), comp., *Han Tang dilishu chao* 漢唐地理書抄. Rept. Beijing: Zhonghua shuju, 1961.

HWCS   *Hanwei congshu* 漢魏叢書. Comp. Cheng Rong 程榮, printed in 1592.
HY   *Combined Indices to the Authors and Titles of Books in Two Collections of Taoist Literature.* Harvard-Yenching Institute Sinological Index Series no. 25. Rept. Taipei: Ch'eng-wen Publishing, 1966.
IC   Nienhauser 1986
JAOS   *Journal of the American Oriental Society*
JAS   *Journal of Asian Studies*
JCR   *Journal of Chinese Religions* (formerly *Society for the Study of Chinese Religions Bulletin*)
JDJL   *Jingdian jilin* 經典集林. Comp. Hong Yixuan 洪頤烜 (1765–1837). BBCS ed.
JDMS   *Jindai mishu* 津逮秘書. Compiler unknown; a late Ming compilation. BBCS ed.
JFCS   *Jifu congshu* 畿輔叢書. Comp. Wang Hao 王灝, printed by Qiandetang 謙德堂 between 1879 and 1892. BBCS ed.
JIABS   *Journal of the International Association of Buddhist Studies*
JS   *Jinshu* 晉書
JTS   *Jiu Tang shu* 舊唐書
LeiS   *Leishuo* 類説. Comp. Zeng Zao 曾慥 (1091–1155). Photoreproduction of Ming ed. with 1626 preface. Beijing: Wenxue guji kanhangshe, 1955.
LS   *Liangshu* 梁書
LWMS   *Longwei mishu* 龍威秘書. Comp. 1794 or 1795 by Ma Junliang 馬俊良. N.p.: Shidetang 世德堂 printing house, 1796.
LX   *Guxiaoshuo gouchen* 古小説勾沈. Comp. Lu Xun 魯迅 (1881–1936). I have consulted two eds., but all page references are to the second: [1] In *Lu Xun sanshinian ji* 三十年集. N.p.: Lu Xun quanji chubanshe, 1941. [2] Beijing: Renmin wenxue chubanshe, 1954. (These eds. differ in pagination but not, so far as I have discovered, otherwise.)
LXJS   *Longxi jingshe congshu* 龍溪精舍叢書. First printed in 1918 (?); rept. Beijing: Zhongguo shudian, 1984 (?).
MCHH   *Mice huihan* 秘冊彙函, comp. Hu Zhenheng 胡震亨, Shen Shilong, et al., first printed in 1603. BBCS ed.
MQ   *Mengqiu* 蒙求. Comp. Li Han 李翰 (fl. 746 or 760). JFCS ed.
MQJZ   *Mengqiu jizhu* 蒙求集註. Ed. and comm. Xu Ziguang 徐子光 (fl. 12th c.). CSJC 51.
MS   *Monumenta Serica*
MS21Z   *Mishu ershiyizhong* 秘書二十一種. Comp. Wang Shihan 汪師韓 (late Ming?). BBCS ed.
MTB   *Memoirs of the Research Department of the Tōyō Bunkō*
NQS   *Nan Qi shu* 南齊書
NS   *Nanshi* 南史
QTW   *Qinding Quan Tang wen* 欽定全唐文. Facsimile rept. of 1814 ed. Taibei: Huiwen shuju, 1961.

RBG   *Ribenguo jianzai shumu* 日本國見在書目. Comp. Fujiwara Sukeyo 藤原佐世 (d. 898). GYCS ed.

RKKO   Makita 1970

SB   Balazs and Hervouet 1978

SBBY   *Sibu beiyao* 四部備要. Shanghai: Zhonghua shuju, 1927–1935.

SBCK   *Sibu congkan* 四部叢刊. Shanghai: Commercial Press, 1920–1922.

SDZN   *Sandong zhunang* 三洞珠囊 (DZ [HY 1131]). Comp. Wang Xuanhe 王懸和, late seventh century.

SF   *Shuofu* 説郛. Comp. Tao Zongyi 陶宗儀 (fl. 1360–1368), ed. Cheng Rong (fl. 1592) and Wang Mo (fl. 1778). Modern ed. based on six manuscripts by Zhang Zongxiang 張宗祥. Shanghai: Commercial Press, 1927. Page-number refs. to fragments of regional histories are to a 1647 ed. held by the Joseph Regenstein Library, East Asia Collection, University of Chicago.

SGZ   *Sanguozhi* 三國志

SJ   *Shiji* 史記

SJZJ   *Shijie zongjiao yanjiu* 世界宗教研究

SK   *Shuoku* 説庫. Comp. Wang Wenru 王文濡, first printed 1915. Rept. Taibei: Xinxing shuju, 1963.

SKQS   *Siku quanshu zhenben bieji* 四庫全書珍本別集. Comp. Ji Yun 紀昀 (1724–1805). Rept. Taibei: Shangwu yinshuguan, 1975.

SLF   *Shileifu zhu* 事類賦注. Comp. Wu Shu 吳淑 (947–1002); ed. Hua Linxiang 華麟祥. Rept. from 1532 ed. Taibei: Xinxing shuju, 1969.

SLJ   *Shiliju congshu* 士禮居叢書. Comp. Huang Pilie 王丕烈 (d. 1825). N.p., n.d. (copy held in Indiana University Library, East Asian Collection).

SS   *Songshu* 宋書

SSJZ   *Shisanjing zhushu* 十三經注疏. Comp. and orig. published in late Ming. Ed. and republished by Ruan Yuan 阮元, 1815. Facsimile rept. Shanghai: Shanghai guji chubanshe, 1990.

SuiS   *Suishu* 隋書

SWJL   *Shiwanjuan lou congshu* 十萬卷樓叢書. Comp. Lu Xinyuan 陸心源 (1834–94), printed 1879. BBCS ed.

T   *Taishō shinshū daizōkyō* 大正新修大藏經. Tokyo, 1922–1933. Cited by text number.

THG   *Tōhōgaku* 東方學

THGH   *Tōhō gakuhō* 東方學報

THSK   *Tōhō shūkyō* 東方宗教

TP   *T'oung Pao*

TPGJ   *Taiping guangji* 太平廣記. Comp. Li Fang 李昉 et al., completed 978. Rept. in 小説叢書大觀 series. Shanghai: Saoye shanfang yinhang, 1930.

TPHY   *Taiping huanyuji* 太平寰宇記. Comp. Yue Shi 樂史 (930–

1007). [1] Facsimile rept. Taibei: Wenhai chubanshe, 1963. [2] *Juan* 113–118 (missing from [1]): CSJC ed.

TPYL   *Taiping yulan* 太平御覽. Comp. Li Fang 李昉 et al., completed in 983. Facsimile rept. of Shangwu yinshuguan 1935 printing from a Sung copy. Beijing: Zhonghua shuju, 1992.

TR   *Taoist Resources*

TZ   *Tongzhilue* 通志略. (Treatises excerpted from *Tongzhi*.) Comp. Zheng Qiao 鄭樵 (1104–62). GXJB ed.

TZJ   *Tianzhongji* 天中記. Comp. Chen Yaowen 陳耀文 (*jinshi* 1550). SKQS ed. Facsimile rept. in 3 vols. Taibei: Taiwan Commercial Press, 1985.

WCXS   *Wuchao xiaoshuo daguan* 五朝小説大觀. Shanghai: Saoye shanfang, between 1926 and 1932.

WS   *Weishu* 魏書

XJTY   *Xuejin taoyuan* 學津討源. Comp. Zhang Pengyi 張鵬一 [Qing]. BBCS ed.

XTS   *Xin Tang shu* 新唐書

XTZ   *Xutanzhu* 續談助. Comp. Chao Zaizhi 晁載之 (11th c.). SWJL ed.

YH   *Yuhan shanfang jiyishu* 玉函山房輯佚書. Comp. Ma Guohan 馬國翰 (1794–1857), originally printed 1884. Rept. in 6 vols. Taibei: Wenhai chubanshe, 1967.

YHX   *Yuhan shanfang jiyishu xubian sanzhong* 續編三種. Comp. Wang Renjun 王仁俊 (1866–1913). Includes *Xubian* 續編, *Bubian* 補編, and *Jingji yiwen* 經籍佚文. Rept. Shanghai: Shanghai guji chubanshe, 1989.

YJQQ   *Yunji qiqian* 雲笈七籤. Comp. 1028 or 1029 by Zhang Junfang 張君房. DZ (HY 1026).

YLDD   *Yongle dadian* 永樂大典. Comp. 1408 by Yao Guangxiao 姚廣孝 (1369–1415). Rept. from various versions and parts held in Beijing Library. Beijing: Zhonghua shuju, 1960.

YWLJ   *Yiwen leiju* 藝文類聚. Comp. Ouyang Xun 歐陽詢 (557–641) et al. Modern critical recension ed. Wang Shaoying 汪紹楹. 2 vols. continuously paginated. Beijing: Zhonghua shuju, 1965.

ZDHW   *Zengding Han Wei congshu* 增訂漢魏叢書. Comp. Wang Mo 王謨 (*jinshi* 1778) based on HWCS and *Guang HWCS* (comp. He Yunzhong 何允中 [early Qing?]). Printed between 1791 and 1795; place of publication and printing house unknown. Copy held by Joseph Regenstein Library (East Asian Collection), University of Chicago.

ZH   *Zhihai* 指海. Comp. Qian Xizuo 錢熙祚 (1800 or 1801–1844). BBCS ed.

ZSBJ   *Zishu baijia* 子書百家. Hubei: Chongwen shuju, 1875.

ZYJ   *Zhouyuji* 琱玉集. Comp. during Southern Dynasties, lost. Recompiled ed. (based on Tang-period manuscript of two *juan* recovered in Japan) in GYCS.

List of Works Cited (III):

Other Works in Chinese and Japanese

A. Traditional Chinese Works

(Listed by author or title)

Bohutong 白虎通. ZDHW ed.

Cai Yong 蔡邕. *Duduan* 獨斷. ZDHW ed.

Chang Qu 常璩. *Huayang guozhi* 華陽國志. See Liu Lin 1984.

Chunqiu Zuozhuan zhengyi 春秋左傳正義. SSJZ ed.

Dong Zhongshu 董仲舒. *Chunqiu fanlu* 春秋繁露. Ed. and commentary by Ling Shu 凌曙 (1775–1829). GXJB 40.

Duan Chengshi 段成式. *Youyang zazu* 酉陽雜俎. SBCK 468–71 (case 56).

Ge Hong 葛洪. *Xijing zaji* 西京雜記. In *Yan Danzi, Xijing zaji*. Beijing: Zhonghua shuju, 1985.

———. *Baopuzi neipian* 抱朴子內篇. DZ (HY 1177).

———. *Baopuzi waipian* 抱朴子外篇. DZ (HY 1179).

Han Feizi jijie 韓非子集解. Ed. Wang Xianshen 王先慎. Originally printed 1896. Rept. Taibei: Shijie shuju, 1975.

Huainanzi 准南子. DZ (HY 1176).

Jingfa: Mawangdui Hanmu boshu zhengli xiao zubian 經法: 馬王堆漢墓帛書整理小組編. Beijing: Wenwu chubanshe, 1976.

Kongcongzi 孔叢子. SBBY ed.

Liezi jishi 列子集釋. Ed. Yang Bojun 楊伯峻. Series: Xinbian zhuzi jicheng 新編諸子集成. Beijing: Zhonghua shuju, 1979.

Liji zhengyi 禮記正義. SSJZ ed.

Liu Xiang 劉向. *Xinxu* 新序. Ed. Chen Yongguang 陳用光. GXJB ed.

Liu Xie 劉勰. *Wenxin diaolong zhu* 文心雕龍註. Ed. Huang Shulin 黃叔琳. Tainan: Weiyi shuye zhongxin, 1975.

413

Lüshi chunqiu jiaoshi 呂氏春秋校釋. Ed. Chen Qiyou 陳奇猷. Shanghai: Xinhua shudian, 1984.

Mu Tianzi zhuan 穆天子傳. SBBY ed.

Shangshu zhengyi 尚書正義. SSJZ ed.

Shiwu jiyuan 事物紀原. CSJC ed.

Taipingjing hejiao 太平經合校. See Wang Ming 1960.

Wang Chong 王充. *Lunheng jiaoshi* 論衡校釋. Ed. Huang Hui 黃暉. 4 vols. continuously paginated. Beijing: Zhonghua shuju, 1990.

Xun Yue 荀悅. *Shenjian* 申鑑. ZDHW ed.

Xunzi jijie 荀子集解. Ed. Wang Xianqian 王先謙 (1842–1917). Rept. of Shijie shuju ed. (1930s). Taibei: Yiwen yinshuguan, 1959.

Yan Zhitui 顏之推. *Yanshi jiaxun* 顏氏家訓. GXJB ed.

Yang Xiong 楊雄. *Fangyan* 方言. CSJC ed.

Yijing 易經. In *A Concordance to Yi Ching*. Harvard-Yenching Institute Sinological Index Series Supplement no. 10. Cambridge, Mass.: Harvard University Press. Rept. Taipei: Chinese Materials and Research Aids Service Center, 1966.

Zhao Ye 趙曄. *Wu Yue chunqiu* 吳越春秋. SBBY 1136 (case 132).

Zhouyi jijie 周易集解. Collated and edited by Li Dingzuo 李鼎祚. Ed. Chen Deshu 陳德述. Chengdu: Bashu shushe, 1991.

Zhuangzi 莊子. Refs. are by chap. and line numbers in *A Concordance to Chuang Tzu*. Harvard-Yenching Institute Sinological Index Series Supplement no. 20. Cambridge, Mass.: Harvard University Press, 1956.

B. Modern Chinese and Japanese Works

(Listed by author)

Chen Guofu 陳國符. 1963. *Daozang yuanliu kao* 道藏源流考. Revised ed. 2 vols. continuously paginated. Beijing: Zhonghua shuju.

Chen Pan 陳盤. 1947. "Gu chenwei shulu jieti (er)" 古讖緯書錄解題 (二). BAS 12:35–47.

Chen Yinke 陳寅恪. 1930. "Sanguo Ceng Chong Hua Tuo zhuan yu fojiao gushi" 三國曾沖華佗傳與佛教故事. *Qinghua xuebao* 清華學報 6.1:17–20.

———. 1936. "Taohuayuanji pangzheng" 桃花源記旁證. *Qinghua xuebao* 11.1:79–88.

Chen Yuan 陳垣, comp. 1988. *Daojia jinshilue* 道家金石略. Beijing: Wenwu chubanshe.

Dai Keyu 戴克瑜 and Tang Jianhua 唐建華. 1981. *Leishu di yange* 類書的沿革. N.p.: Sichuansheng tushuguan xuehui bianyin.

Fan Ning 范寧. 1957. "Lun Wei Jin zhiguai xiaoshuo di chuanbo he zhishi fenzi sixiang fenhua di guanxi" 論魏晉志怪小說的傳播和知識分子思想分化的關係. *Beijing Daxue xuebao: Renwen kexue* 北京大學學報：人文科學 1957/2:75–88.

———, ed. 1980. *Bowuzhi jiaozheng* 博物志校證. Beijing: Zhonghua shuju.

Fu Xihua 傅惜華. 1944. "Liuchao zhiguai xiaoshuo zhi cunyi" 六朝志怪小説
之存逸. *Han-hiue* 1:169–210.
Fukui Kōjun 福井康順. 1955. *Dōkyō no kisoteki kenkyū* 道教の基礎的研究.
Tokyo: Shoseki bunbutsu ryūtsūkai.
Gao Quxun 高去尋, ed. 1974. *Shanhaijing yanjiu lunwenji* 山海經研究論文
集. Hong Kong: Zhongshan.
Gu Yisheng 顧易生 and Jiang Fan 蔣凡. 1990. *Xian Qin liang Han wenxue
pipingshi* 先秦兩漢文學批評史. Shanghai: Shanghai guji chubanshe.
Guo Wei 郭為. 1979. *Yinyang wuxing jia sixiang zhi shuping* 陰陽五行家思
想之述評. Gaoxiong, Taiwan: Gaoxiong Fuwen shuju yinhang.
Guo Zhenyi 郭箴一. 1961. *Zhongguo xiaoshuo shi* 中國小説史. Hong Kong:
Taixing shuju.
Harada Taneshige 原田種成識, comp., 1983. *Sōshinki goi sakuin* 搜神記語彙
索引. N.p.: Daitō bunka daigaku bungaku-bu.
Hayashi Minao 林已奈夫. 1970. "In chūki ni yurai suru kishin" 殷中期に由
來する鬼神. THGH 41:1–70.
―――. 1974. "Kandai kishin no sekai" 漢代鬼神の世界. THGH 46:223–306.
Hihara Toshikuni 日原利國. 1972. "Saii to shin'i" 災異と讖緯. THG 43:31–
43.
Hu Daojing 胡道靜. 1982. *Zhongguo gudai di leishu* 中國古代的類書. Beijing:
Zhonghua shuju.
Hu Fuchen 胡孚琛. 1989. *Wei Jin shenxian daojiao: Baopuzi neipian yanjiu*
魏晉神仙道教: 抱朴子內篇研究. Beijing: Renmin chubanshe.
Hu Yinglin 胡應麟. 1958 [1590]. *Shaoshi shanfang bicong* 少室山房筆叢.
Beijing: Zhonghua shuju.
Huang Diming 黃滌明, ed. 1991. *Soushenji quanyi* 搜神記全譯. Guiyang:
Guizhou renmin chubanshe.
Ikeda Sueri 池田末利. 1953. "Konkaku kō" 魂魄考. THSK 3:1–14.
―――. 1956. "Kiji kō" 鬼字考. *Hiroshima Daigaku bungakubu kiyō*
10:206–48.
―――. 1970. "Kodai Chūgoku ni okeru reiki kannen no tenkai" 古代中國
に於ける靈鬼觀念の展開. *Chūo kenkyūsho shūkan* 中央研究所集刊
29:121–63.
Jiang Shaoyuan 江紹源. 1935. *Zhongguo gudai lüxing zhi yanjiu* 中國古代
旅行之研究. Shanghai: Shangwu yinshuguan.
Kamatani Takeshi 釜谷武志. 1989. "Kan Gi rikuchō ni okeru 'mei'" 漢魏六
朝における'銘'. *Chūgoku bungakuhō* 中國文學報 40:16–46.
Kang Yunmei 康韻梅. 1992. "Cong *Jingfa* deng yishu sipian yu *Han Fei zi*
sixiang di guanxi lun Han Fei zhi xue ben yu Huanglao zhi shuo"
從經法等佚書篇與韓非子思想的關係論韓非之學本於黃老之説. *Zhong-
guo wenxue yanjiu* 中國文學研究 6:1–30.
Kasuga Reichi 春日禮智. 1936. "*Zentōbun bukkyō kankei senjutsu mokuroku*"
全唐文佛教關係撰述目錄. *Nikka bukkyō kenkyūkai nenpō* 1:20–55.
Katsumura Tetsuya 勝村哲也. 1990. "*Geibun ruishū* no tōbun kōsei to rikuchō
mokuroku to no kanrensei ni tsuite" 藝文類聚の條文構成と六朝目錄
との關連性について. THGH 62:99–123.
Kawakatsu Yoshio 川勝義雄. 1970. "*Sesetsu shingo* no hensan o megutte"
世說新語の編纂をめぐって. THGH 41:217–34.

————. 1974a. *Gi Shin nambokuchō* 魏晉南北朝. Vol. 3 of *Chūgoku no rekishi* 中國の歴史. Tokyo: Kōsaidō.

————. 1982. *Rikuchō kizokusei shakai no kenkyū* 六朝貴族制社會の研究. Tokyo: Ryokugawatei.

Kominami Ichiro 小南一郎. 1966. "*Sōshinki* no buntai" 搜神記の文體. *Kyoto daigaku bungakubu Chūgoku bungakuhō* 京都大學文學部中國文學報 21:57–82.

————. 1983. "Gan Shisui 'Enkonshi' o megutte: Rikuchō shikai shōsetsu no seikaku" 顔之推'冤魂志'をめぐって: 六朝志怪小説の性格. THG 65:15–28.

————. 1984. *Chūgoku no shinwa to monogatari: Koshōsetsushi no tenkai* 中國の神話と物語リ: 古小説史の展開. Tokyo: Iwanami shoten.

Kosugi Ichio 小杉一雄. 1941. "*Sōshinki* hihan" 搜神記批判. *Shikan* 史觀 20.

Li Fengmao 李豐楙. 1986. *Liuchao Sui Tang xiandaolei xiaoshuo yanjiu* 六朝隋唐仙道類小説研究. Taibei: Taiwan xuesheng shuju.

Li Gang 李剛. 1993. "Lun *Taipingjing* wei Handai daoshu zhi heji" 論太平經為漢代道書之合集. *Shehui kexue yanjiu* 1993/3:63–68.

Li Jianguo 李劍國. 1984. *Tang qian zhiguai xiaoshuo shi* 唐前志怪小説史. Tianjin: Nankai Daxue chubanshe.

Lin Chen 林辰. 1960. "Lu Xun xiansheng 'Gu xiaoshuo gouchen' di jilu niandai ji suoshou geshu zuozhe" 魯迅'古小説鈎沈'的輯錄年代所收各書作者. *Wenxue yichan xuanji* 文學遺產選集 3:385–407.

Lin Congming 林聰明. 1977. "Balizang Dunhuangben 'Boze jingguai tu' ji 'Dunhuang ershiyong' kaoshu" 巴黎藏敦煌本白澤精怪圖及敦煌二十詠考述. *Dongwu wenshi xuebao* 東吳文史學報 2:97–116.

Lin Fushi 林富士. 1993. "Shilun *Taipingjing* de jibing guannian" 試論太平經的疾病觀念. *Zhongyang yanjiuyuan lishi yuyan yanjiusuo jikan* 62.2:225–63.

Liu Lin 劉琳, ed. 1984. *Huayang guozhi jiaozhu* 華陽國志校注. Chengdu: Bashu shushe.

Liu Wenzhong 劉文忠. 1984. "*Han Wu gushi* xiezuo shidai xinkao" 漢武故事寫作時代新考. *Zhonghua wenshi luncong* 30:291–98.

Liu Yeqiu 劉葉秋. 1959. *Gudian xiaoshuo luncong* 古典小説論叢. Beijing: Zhonghua shuju.

Lu Xun 魯迅. 1926. *Zhongguo xiaoshuo shilue* 中國小説史略. Beijing: Beixin shuju.

————. 1973. *Zhongguo xiaoshuo shilue* 中國小説史略. Rept. of Lu Xun 1926 in simplified characters. Beijing: Renmin wenxue chubanshe.

Makita Tairyō 牧田諦亮. 1970. *Rikuchō kōitsu Kanzeon ōkenki no kenkyū* 六朝古逸觀世音應驗記の研究. Kyoto: Hyōrakuji shoten.

————. 1976. *Gikyō kenkyū* 疑經研究. Kyoto: Kyoto Daigaku jimbun kagaku kenkyūjo.

Meng Sen 孟森 et al. 1974. *Yugong yanjiu lunji* 禹貢研究論集. Hong Kong: Zhongsan Book Co.

Meng Wentong 蒙文通. 1962. "Luelun *Shanhaijing* di xiezuo shidai ji qi chansheng diyu" 略論山海經的寫作時代及其產生地域. *Zhonghua wenshi luncong* 中華文史論叢 1:43–70.

Michihata Ryōshū 道端良秀. 1979. *Chūgoku bukkyō shisōshi no kenkyū* 中國佛教思想史の研究. Kyoto: Heirakuji shoten.

———. 1980. *Chūgoku bukkyō to shakai to no kōshō* 中國佛教と社會との交涉. Kyoto: Heirakuji shoten.

Mitarai Masaru 御手洗勝. 1984. *Kodai Chūgoku no kamigami: kodai densetsu no kenkyū* 古代中國の神々: 古代傳説の研究. Tokyo: Sōbunsha.

Miyakawa Hisayuki 宮川尚志. 1964. *Rikuchōshi kenkyū: Shūkyōhen* 六朝史研究: 宗教篇. Kyoto: Heirakuji shoten.

———. 1974. *Rikuchō shūkyōshi* 六朝宗教史. 2d ed. Tokyo: Kokusho kankōkai.

Morino Shigeo 森野繁夫. 1960. "Jin Hō *Jutsuiki* ni tsuite" 任昉述異記について. *Chūgoku bungakuhō* 中國文學報 13:54–68.

———. 1961. "*Ien* no tsūkōbon" 異苑の通行本. *Chūgoku chūsei bungaku kenkyū* 中國中世文學研究 1:19–31.

———. 1965. "*Sōshinki* no henmoku" 搜神記の篇目. *Hiroshima Daigaku bungaku-bu kiyo* 廣島大學文學部紀要 24.3:161–72.

Nagasawa Yōji 永沢要二. 1964. "Haku kō" 魄考. *Kangaku kenkyū* 漢學研究 n.s. 2:41–54.

———. 1977. *Kishin no genkei to sono enshin* 鬼神の原義とその演進. Tokyo.

Nishino Teiji 西野貞治. 1943. "*Sōshinki* kō" 搜神記考. *Jinbun kenkyū* (Ōsaka shiritsu daigaku) 4.8:67–84.

———. 1957. "*Tonkōhon Sōshinki* no setsuwa ni tsuite" 敦煌本搜神記の説話について. *Jimbun kenkyū* 人文研究 8.4:56–67.

Nishioka Haruhiko 西岡晴彦. 1968. "Hōyō kō" 狐妖考. *Tōkyō shinagaku hō* 東京支那學報 14:59–73.

Nishitani Toshichirō 西谷登七郎. 1951. "Gogyōshi to nijū-kanbon *Sōshinki*" 五行志と二十卷本搜神記. *Hiroshima Daigaku bungakubu kiyo* 1.1: 115–27.

Ōfuchi Ninji 大淵忍爾. 1964. *Dōkyōshi no kenkyū* 道教史の研究. Okayama: Okayama Daigaku Press.

Ouyang Xiu quanji 歐陽修全集. 2 vols. discontinuously paginated (even internally). Hong Kong: Guangzhi shudian, 1961.

Qi Zhiping 齊治平, ed. 1981. *Shiyiji* 拾遺記. Guxiaoshuo congkan. Beijing: Zhonghua shuju.

Qian Mu 錢穆. 1955. "Zhongguo sixiangshi zhong zhi guishenguan" 中國思想史中之鬼神觀. *Xinya xuebao* 新亞學報 1:1–43.

———. 1983. *Liang Han jingxue jinguwen pingyi* 兩漢經學今古文平議. Taibei: Dongda tushu gongsi yinhang.

Qing Xitai 卿希泰. 1988–. *Zhongguo daojiao shi* 中國道教史. 2 vols. to date. Chengdu: Sichuan renmin chubanshe.

Rao Zongyi 饒宗頤. 1969. "Ba Dunhuangben *Baize jingguaitu* liang canjuan" 跋敦煌本白澤精怪圖兩殘卷. BAS 41.4:539–43.

———. 1991. *Laozi Xiang'erzhu jiaozheng* 老子想爾注校證. Rev. ed. Shanghai: Shanghai guji chubanshe.

Sahara Yasuo 佐原康夫. 1991. "Kandai shitō gazō kō" 漢代祠堂畫像考. THGH 63:1–60.

Sawada Mizuho 澤田瑞穂. 1968. *Jigoku hen: Chūgoku no meikaisetsu* 地獄變: 中國の冥界説. Kyoto: Hōzōkan.

Shi Ding 施丁. 1992. "Ban Gu yu *Hanshu* de shixue sixiang" 班固與漢書的史學思想. *Lishi yanjiu* 歷史研究 1992.4:62–72.

Shimizu Eiyoshi 清水榮吉. 1955. "*Sōshinki* shiki" 搜神記私記. *Tenri daigaku gakuhō* 天理大學學報 16:105–12.

Shimizu Shigeru 清水茂. 1990. "Kami no hatsumei to Gokan no gakufū" 紙の發明と後漢の學界. THG 79:1–13.

Shimura Ryōji 志村良治. 1968. "Shōsetsu no hatsusei" 小説の發生. In *Chūgoku bunka sōsho* 中國文化叢書 5: *Bungakushi* 文學史, ed. Suzuki Shōji 鈴木修次, Takagi Masakazu 高木正一, and Maeno Naoaki 前野直彬, 97–107. Tokyo: Taishūkan shoten.

Shinohara Koichi 莊司格一. 1969. "*Meishoki* ni tsuite" 冥祥記 について. *Tōyōgaku shūkan* 22:41–65.

Shiroki Naoya 白木直也. 1953–54. "*Shōgakki* shoin shomokukō" 初學記所引書目考. *Hiroshima daigaku bungakubu* 4 (Dec. 1953):217–32 and 6 (Dec. 1954):284–323.

Sofukawa Hiroshi 曽布川寛. 1979. "Konron-san to shōsenzu" 崑崙山と昇仙圖. THGH 51:83–185.

———. 1993. "Kandai gazōseki ni okeru shōsenzu no keifu" 漢代畫像石における昇仙圖の系譜. THGH 65:23–222.

Su Baoyang 蘇抱陽. 1992. "*Taipingjing* chengshu di jige wenti" 太平經成書的幾個問題. SJZJ 1992.4:14–21.

Sueki Fumihito 末木文美士. 1990. "Bukkyō-setsu no gengen" 佛性説の淵源. *Tōyō bunka* 70:9–37.

Sunayama Minoru 砂山稔. 1975. "Kosa yōsō: nanchō ni okeru bukkyō to no hanran ni tsuite" 江左妖僧南朝における佛教徒の反亂について. THSK 46:29–62.

Takeda Akira 竹田晃. 1961. "Nijūkanbon *Sōshinki* ni kansuru ichi kōsatsu: shutoshite *Taihei kōki* to no kankei ni tsuite" 二十卷本搜神記に關する一考察: 主として太平廣記との關係について. *Chūgoku bungaku kenkyū* 中國文學研究 2:121–34.

———, tr. 1964. *Sōshinki* 搜神記. *Tōyō bunko* 東洋文庫 10. Tokyo: Heibonsha.

———. 1965. "Gan Pō shiron" 干寶試論. *Tōkyō shinagakuhō* 東京支那學報 11:23–36.

———. 1967. "Shikai, denki" 志怪, 傳奇. In *Chūgoku bunka sōsho* 中國文化叢書 4: *Bungaku gairon* 文學概論, ed. Suzuki Shōji 鈴本修次, Takagi Masakazu 高木正一, and Maeno Naoaki 前野直彬, 215–28. Tokyo: Taishūkan shoten.

———. 1970. "Rikuchō shikai ni torareru 'ningen'" 六朝志怪に語られる'人間'. *Jimbun kagakuka kiyō* 人文科學科紀要 51:95–110.

———. 1980. *Chūgoku no yūrei: Kaii o kataru dentō* 中國の幽靈: 怪異を傳る傳統. Tokyo: Tokyo daigaku shuppankai.

———. 1992. *Chūgoku no setsuwa to kōshōsetsu* 中國の説話と古小説. Tokyo: Daizō shoin.

Tang Yijie 湯一介. 1988. *Wei Jin nanbeichao shiqi di daojiao* 魏晉南北朝時期的道教. Taibei: Dongda tushu gongsi yinhang.

Tang Yongtong 湯用彤. 1976 [1938]. *Han Wei liang Jin nanbeichao fojiaoshi* 漢魏兩晉南北朝佛教史. O.p. Shanghai; rept. Taibei: Dingwen shudian.

Togawa Yoshio 戶川芳郎. 1992. "Shibu bunrui to shiseki" 四部分類と史籍. THG 84:1–21.

Uchida Michio 內田道夫. 1961. "Hōyō" 狐妖. *Tōyōgaku* 東洋學 6:12–22.

Uchiyama Chinari 內山知也. 1979. *Zui Tō shōsetsu kenkyū* 隋唐小説研究. Tokyo: Mokuji.

Wang Chang 王昶, comp. 1985 [1805]. *Jinshi cuibian* 金石萃編. Rept. (5 vols.) Beijing: Xinhua shudian.

Wang Guoliang 王國良. 1978. *Soushen houji yanjiu* 搜神後記研究. Taibei: Wenshize chubanshe.

———. 1984. *Wei Jin nanbeichao zhiguai xiaoshuo yanjiu* 魏晉南北朝志怪小説研究. Taibei: Wenshizhe chubanshe.

———. 1986. "Dunhuangben *Soushenji* kaobian" 敦煌本搜神記考辨. *Hanxue yanjiu* 漢學研究 4.2:379–87.

———. 1988. *Liuchao zhiguai xiaoshuo kaolun* 六朝志怪小説考論. Taibei: Wenshizhe chubanshe.

———. 1989. *Han Wu dongmingji yanjiu* 漢武洞冥記研究. Taibei: Wenshizhe chubanshe.

Wang Jiayou 王家祐. 1987. *Daojiao lungao* 道教論稿. Chengdu: Bashu shushe.

Wang Liqi 王利器, ed. 1981. *Fengsu tongyi jiaozhu* 風俗通義校注. 2 vols. continuously paginated. Beijing: Zhonghua shuju.

Wang Ming 王明. 1960. *Taipingjing hejiao* 太平經合校. Beijing: Zhonghua shuju.

———. 1984. *Daojia he daojiao sixiang yanjiu* 道家和道教思想研究. Beijing: Zhongguo shehui kexue chubanshe.

Wang Qing 王青. 1992. "Lun Qi Chu liang da fangshi jituan ji qi dui daojiao di yingxiang" 論齊楚兩大方士集團及其對道教的影響. SJZJ 1992.3:14–22.

Wang Qiugui 王秋桂 and Wang Guoliang, eds. 1983. *Zhongguo tushu wenxian xue lunji* 中國圖書文獻學論集. 2 vols. Taibei: Wenming shuju.

Wang Shaoying 汪紹楹, ed. 1965. *Yiwen leiju* 藝文類聚. 2 vols. Beijing: Zhonghua shuju.

———, ed. 1981. *Soushen houji* 搜神後記. Beijing: Zhonghua shuju.

Wang Yao 王瑤. 1951. "Xiaoshuo yu fangshu" 小説與方術. In *Zhonggu wenxue sixiang* 中古文學思想. Shanghai: Tangdi chubanshe.

Wu Chunshan 吳春山. "Gudai xiaoshuo di yuzhouguan: *Shanhaijing Mu Tianzi zhuan*" 古代小説的宇宙觀: 山海經穆天子傳. In *Zhongguo gudian wenxue yanjiu congkan* 中國古典文學研究叢刊 1: *Xiaoshuo zhi bu* 小説之部, 37–54. Taibei: Juliu tushu gongsi.

Wu Hongyi 吳宏一. 1979. "Liuchao guishen guaiyi xiaoshuo yu shidai beijing di guanxi" 六朝鬼神怪異小說與時代背景的關係. In *Zhongguo gudian wenxue yanjiu congkan* 中國古典文學研究叢刊 1: *Xiaoshuo zhi bu* 小說之部, 55–89. Taibei: Juliu tushu gongsi.

Xiao Dengfu 蕭登福. 1989. *Han Wei liuchao fo dao liangjiao zhi tiantang diyu shuo* 漢魏六朝佛道兩教之天堂地獄説. Taibei: Taiwan xuesheng shuju.

Xiao Difei 蕭滌非. 1944. *Han Wei liuchao yuefu wenxueshi* 漢魏六朝樂府文學史. N.p.: Zhongguo wenhua fuwushe.

Xu Yimin 許逸民. 1980. *Chuxueji suoyin* 初學記索引. Beijing: Zhonghua shuju.

Yan Gengwang 嚴耕望. 1985. "Zhonggu shidai jibu zhongyao dilishu diyi jiang: *Shuijingzhu*" 中古時代幾部重要地理書第一講: 水經注. *Hanxue yanjiu tongxun* 漢學研究通訊 4.1:145–48.

Yan Maoyuan 嚴懋垣. 1940. "Wei Jin nanbeichao zhiguai xiaoshuo shulu fu kaozheng" 魏晉南北朝志怪小説書錄附考證. *Wenxue nianbao* 文學年報 6:45–72.

Yan Yiping 嚴一萍, comp. 1976. *Daojiao yanjiu ziliao* 道教研究資料. 2 vols. Taibei: Yiwen yinshuguan.

Yang Dianxun 楊殿珣, comp. 1957. *Shike tiba suoyin (zengdingben)* 石刻題跋索引增訂本. Shanghai: Shangwu yinshuguan.

Yang Jialuo 楊家駱, ed., 1982 [1959]a. *Xinjiao Soushenji* 新校搜神記. Taibei: Shijie shuju.

Yang Jialuo 楊家駱, ed., 1982 [1959]b. *Shishuo xinyu* 世説新語. Facsimile rept. of a Sung ed. with annotations by Liu Jun. Taibei: Shijie shuju.

Yasui Kōzan 安居香山 and Nakamura Shōhachi 中村璋八. 1971–88. *Chōshū isho shūsei* 重修緯書集成. 6 vols. Tokyo: Kabushiki.

Yin Shiji 尹世積, ed. 1957. *Yugong jijie* 禹貢集解. Shanghai: Commercial Press.

Yoshioka Yoshitoyo 吉岡義豐. 1955. *Dōkyō kyōten shiron* 道教經典史論. Tokyo: Dōkyō kankōkai.

Yu Jiaxi 余嘉錫. 1974 [1937]. *Siku tiyao bianzheng* 四庫提要辨證. Vols. 9–10 of *Siku quanshu zongmu* 總目. Rept. Taibei: Yiwen yinshuguan.

Yu Mingguang 余明光. 1989. *Huang Di sijing yu Huanglao sixiang* 黃帝四經與黃老思想. Heerbin: Heilongjiang renmin chubanshe.

Yu Yingshi 余英時. 1976. *Lishi yu sixiang* 歷史與思想. Taipei: Lianjing chubanshe.

———. 1983. "Zhongguo gudai sihou shijieguan di yanbian" 中國古代死後世界觀的演變. *Lianhe yuekan* 聯合月刊 26:81–89.

———. 1986–87. "Handai xunli yu wenhua chuanbo" 漢代循吏與文化傳博. *Jiuzhou xuekan* 九州學刊 1.1:9–24, 1.2:1–22, 1.3:1–22.

Yuan Ke 袁珂. 1980. *Shanhaijing jiaozhu* 山海經校注. Shanghai: Shanghai guji chubanshe.

———. 1981 [1960]. *Zhongguo gudai shenhua* 中國古代神話. Beijing: Zhonghua shuju.

Yuan Xingpei 袁行霈. 1979. "*Shanhaijing* chutan" 山海經初探. *Zhonghua wenshi luncong* 中華文史論叢 1979/3:7–35.

Zhang Chonggen 張崇根, ed. 1980. *Linhai shuitu yiwu zhi jijiao* 臨海水土異物志輯校. Beijing: Nongye chubanshe.

Zheng Dekun 鄭德坤. 1974. *Shuijingzhu yinshukao* 水經注引書考. Taibei: Yiwen yinshuguan.

Zheng Zhiming 鄭志明. 1986. *Zhongguo shehui yu zongjiao* 中國社會與宗教. Taibei: Taiwan xuesheng shuju.

Zhong Likan 鍾利戡 and Wang Qinggui 王清貴, eds. 1991. *Da Yu shiliao huiji* 大禹史料匯集. Chengdu: Ba Shu shushe.

Zhou Cezong 周策縱. 1979. "Zhongguo gudai di wuyi yu jisi, lishi, yuewu ji shi di guanxi" 中國古代的巫醫與祭祀歷史樂舞及詩的關係. *Qinghua xuebao* 青華學報 1–2:1–60.

Zhou Yiliang 周一良. 1963. *Wei Jin nanbeichao shi lunji* 魏晉南北朝史論集. Beijing: Zhonghua shuju.

Zhou Ciji 周次吉. 1986. *Shenyijing yanjiu* 神異經研究. Taibei: Wenjin chubanshe.

List of Works Cited (IV):

Works in Western Languages

Acker, W. R. B. 1954. *Some T'ang and Pre-T'ang Texts on Chinese Painting*. 2 vols. Leiden: E. J. Brill.

Adkins, C. P. 1976. "The Supernatural in T'ang Ch'uan-ch'i Tales: An Archetypal View." Ph.D. diss., Ohio State University.

Allan, Sarah. 1991. *The Shape of the Turtle: Myth, Art, and Cosmos in Early China*. Albany: State University of New York Press.

Allen, J. R. 1992. *In the Voice of Others: Chinese Music Bureau Poetry*. Michigan Monographs in Chinese Studies 63. Ann Arbor: Center for Chinese Studies, University of Michigan.

Ames, Roger T. 1983. *The Art of Rulership: A Study in Ancient Chinese Political Theory*. Honolulu: University of Hawaii Press.

Arbuckle, Gary. 1989. "A Note on the Authenticity of the Chunqiu Fanlu." TP 75:226–34.

———. 1992. "Some Remarks on a New Translation of the *Chunqiu Fanlu*." EC 17:215–38.

Arendrup, Birthe. 1974. "The First Chapter of Guo Xiang's Commentary to Zhuang Zi." *Acta Orientalia* 36:311–415.

Ariel, Yoav. 1986. "The *K'ung-Family-Masters' Anthology* and Third-century Confucianism." In *Confucianism: The Dynamics of Tradition*, ed. Irene Eber, 39–59. New York: Macmillan.

———. 1989. *K'ung-Ts'ung-Tzu: The K'ung Family Masters' Anthology: A Study and Translation of Chapters 1–10, 12–14*. Princeton: Princeton University Press.

Audollent, A. 1903. "Devotio ou Defixio?" In *Mélanges Bossier*, 37–43. Paris: Albert Fontemoing.

———. 1904. *Defixionum Tabellae*. Paris: Albert Fontemoing.

423

Bakhtin, M. M. 1986. *Speech Genres and Other Late Essays*. Austin: University of Texas Press.

Bakhtin, M. M., and P. N. Medvedev. 1985. *The Formal Method in Literary Scholarship: A Critical Introduction to Sociological Poetics*. Tr. A. J. Wehrle. Cambridge, Mass: Harvard University Press.

Balazs, Etienne. 1964. *Chinese Civilization and Bureaucracy*. Ed. A. F. Wright. Tr. H. M. Wright. New Haven: Yale University Press.

Balazs, Etienne, and Yves Hervouet, eds. 1978. *A Sung Bibliography (Bibliographie des Sung)*. Hong Kong: The Chinese University Press.

Barnard, Noel. 1978. "The Nature of the Ch'in 'Reform of the Script.'" In Roy and Tsien 1978, 181–228.

Barrau, Jacques. 1979. "Coping with Exotic Plants in Folk Taxonomies." In Ellen and Reason 1979, 139–44.

Bauer, Wolfgang. 1965–66. "The Encyclopaedia in China." *Cahiers d'histoire mondiale* 9:665–91.

———, 1976. *China and the Search for Happiness: Recurring Themes in Four Thousand Years of Chinese Cultural History*. Tr. M. Shaw. New York: Seabury Press.

———, ed. 1980. *China und die Fremden: 3000 Jahre Auseinandersetzung in Krieg und Frieden*. München: Verlag C. H. Beck.

———. 1985. "The Hidden Hero: Creation and Disintegration of the Ideal of Eremitism." In Munro 1985, 157–98.

Beck, J. Mansveld. 1980. "The Date of the *Taiping jing*." TP 66:149–82.

Beidelman, T. O. 1973. "Kaguru Symbolic Classification." In *Right and Left: Essays on Dual Symbolic Classification*, ed. R. Needham, 128–66. Chicago: University of Chicago Press.

Berkowitz, Alan. 1991. "Hidden Spoor: Ruan Xiaoxu and his Treatise on Reclusion." JAOS 111:704–11.

Berlin, B., D. Breedlove, and P. Raven. 1974. *Principles of Tzeltal Plant Classification*. New York and London: Academic Press.

Bertholet, A. 1949. *Die Macht der Schrift in Glauben und Aberglauben*. Abhandlungen der deutschen Akademie der Wissenschaften zu Berlin, Philosophisch-historische Klasse, Jahrgang 1948 no. 1. Berlin: Akademie-Verlag.

Betz, H. D. 1986. *The Greek Magical Papyri in Translation, Including the Demotic Spells*. Chicago: University of Chicago Press.

Bielenstein, H. 1959. "The Chinese Colonization of Fukien until the End of T'ang." In *Studia Serica Bernhard Karlgren Dedicata*, ed. S. Egerod and E. Glahn, 98–122. Copenhagen: Ejnar Munksgaard.

———. 1979. *The Restoration of the Han Dynasty*. Vol. 4, *The Government*. BMFE 51:3–300.

Birch, Cyril, ed. 1965. *Anthology of Chinese Literature: From Early Times to the Fourteenth Century*. New York: Grove Press.

Birrell, Anne. 1988. *Popular Songs and Ballads of Han China*. London: Unwin Hyman.

————. 1989. "Mythmaking and Yüeh-fu: Popular Songs and Ballads of Early Imperial China." JAOS 109:223–36.

————. 1994. "Studies on Chinese Myth Since 1970: An Appraisal, Part I." HR 33:380–93.

Bleiler, Everett F. 1983. *The Guide to Supernatural Fiction.* Kent, Ohio: Kent State University Press.

Bloor, David. 1984. "Durkheim and Mauss Revisited: Classification and the Sociology of Knowledge." In *Society and Knowledge: Contemporary Perspectives in the Sociology of Knowledge,* ed. N. Stehr and V. Meja, 51–76. New Brunswick, N.J.: Transaction Books.

Bloss, Lowell W. 1971. "Ancient Indian Folk Religion as seen through the Symbolism of the Naga." Ph.D. diss., University of Chicago.

————. 1973. "The Buddha and the Naga: A Study in Buddhist Folk Religiosity." HR 13:36–53.

Boas, George. 1948. *Essays on Primitivism and Related Ideas in the Middle Ages.* Baltimore: The Johns Hopkins Press.

Bodde, Derk. 1938. *China's First Unifier: A Study of the Ch'in Dynasty as Seen in the Life of Li Ssu.* Leiden: E. J. Brill.

————. 1941. "Some Chinese Tales of the Supernatural." HJAS 6:338–57.

————. 1959. "The Chinese Cosmic Magic Known as Watching for the Ethers." In *Studia Serica Bernhard Karlgren Dedicata,* ed. S. Egerod and E. Glahn, 14–35. Copenhagen: Ejnar Munksgaard.

————. 1961. "Myths of Ancient China." In *Mythologies of the Ancient World,* ed. S. N. Kramer, 367–408. Garden City: Doubleday.

————. 1975. *Festivals in Classical China.* Princeton: Princeton University Press.

Bohannan, P., and F. Plog. 1967. *Beyond the Frontier: Social Process and Cultural Change.* Garden City: The Natural History Press.

Bokenkamp, Stephen R. 1983. "Sources of the Ling-pao Scriptures." In *Tantric and Taoist Studies in Honour of R. A. Stein,* ed. M. Strickmann, 2:434–86. Mélanges chinois et bouddhiques 21. Bruxelles: Institut Belge des Hautes Études Chinoises.

————. 1986. "The Peach Flower Font and the Grotto Passage." JAOS 106:65–77.

Boltz, Judith M. 1987. *A Survey of Taoist Literature: Tenth to Seventeenth Centuries.* China Research Monograph 32. Berkeley: Institute of East Asian Studies, University of California.

Bourdieu, Pierre. 1977. *Outline of a Theory of Practice.* Tr. Richard Nice. Cambridge: Cambridge University Press.

Brandes, S. H. 1974. "The Creation of a Mexican Memorate." *Journal of American Folk-Lore* 87:162–64.

Briggs, Charles L., and Richard Bauman. 1992. "Genre, Intertextuality, and Social Power." *Journal of Linguistic Anthropology* 2:131–72.

Brown, C. H. 1984. *Language and Living Things: Uniformities in Folk Classification and Naming.* New Brunswick: Rutgers University Press.

Brown, Peter. 1981. *The Cult of the Saints: Its Rise and Function in Latin Christianity*. Chicago: University of Chicago Press.

Bulmer, Ralph. 1967. "Why is the Cassowary Not a Bird?" *Man* n.s. 2:5–25.

———. 1979. "Mystical and Mundane in Kalam Classification of Birds." In Ellen and Reason 1979, 57–79.

Burridge, Kenelm. 1960. *Mambu: A Study of Melanesian Cargo Movements and their Ideological Background*. New York: Harper & Row.

Caillois, Roger. 1965. *Au coeur du fantastique*. Paris: Gallimard.

———. 1966. *Images, images . . . : Essais sur le rôle et les pouvoirs de l'imagination*. Paris: Librairie José Corti.

Cammann, S. 1961. "The Magic Square of Three in Old Chinese Philosophy and Religion." HR 1:37–80.

Campany, Robert Ford. 1985. "Demons, Gods, and Pilgrims: The Demonology of the *Hsi-yu chi*." CL 7:95–115.

———. 1986. "Cosmogony and Self-Cultivation: The Demonic and the Ethical in Two Chinese Novels." *Journal of Religious Ethics* 14:81–112.

———. 1990a. "Return-from-Death Narratives in Early Medieval China." JCR 18:91–125.

———. 1990b. "'Survivals' as Interpretive Strategy: A Sino-Western Comparative Case Study." *Method and Theory in the Study of Religion* 2:1–26.

———. 1991a. "Ghosts Matter: The Culture of Ghosts in Six Dynasties *Zhiguai*." CL 13:15–34.

———. 1991b. "Notes on the Devotional Uses and Symbolic Functions of Sūtra Texts as Depicted in Early Chinese Buddhist Miracle Tales and Hagiographies." JIABS 14:28–72.

———. 1991c. "Useless and Useful Survivals: A Reply to Robert A. Segal." *Method and Theory in the Study of Religion* 3:100–114.

———. 1992. "Xunzi and Durkheim as Theorists of Ritual Practice." In *Discourse and Practice*, ed. F. Reynolds and D. Tracy, 197–231. Albany: State University of New York Press.

———. 1993a. "Buddhist Revelation and Taoist Translation in Early Medieval China." TR 4.1:1–29.

———. 1993b. "The Real Presence." HR 32:233–72.

———. 1994. "Taoist Bioethics in the Final Age: Therapy and Salvation in the *Book of Divine Incantations for Penetrating the Abyss*." In *Religious Methods and Resources in Bioethics*, ed. P. Camenisch, 67–91. Dordrecht: D. Reidel.

———. Forthcoming (a). "The Earliest Chinese Tales of the Bodhisattva Guanshiyin." In *Sourcebook on Chinese Buddhism*, ed. D. S. Lopez, Jr. Princeton: Princeton University Press.

———. Forthcoming (b). "To Hell and Back: Death, Near-Death, and other Worldly Journeys in Early Medieval China." In *Death, Ecstasy, and Other Worldly Journeys*, ed. John J. Collins and Michael Fishbane. Chicago: University of Chicago Press.

———. Unpublished. "Religion on the Ground in Early Medieval China: Prolegomena." Unpublished paper.

Campbell, Mary. B. 1988. *The Witness and the Other World: Exotic European Travel Writing, 400–1600*. Ithaca: Cornell University Press.

Capon, E. 1975–77. "Chinese Tomb Figures of the Six Dynasties Period." *Transactions of the Oriental Ceramics Society* 41:279–308.

Carrasco, Davíd. 1982. *Quetzalcoatl and the Irony of Empire*. Chicago: University of Chicago Press.

Céard, Jean. 1977. *La nature et les prodiges: l'insolite au XVIe siècle, en France*. Genève: Librairie Droz.

de Certeau, Michel. 1975. *L'écriture de l'histoire*. Paris: Gallimard.

———. 1986. *Heterologies: Discourse on the Other*. Tr. B. Massumi. Minneapolis: University of Minnesota Press.

Chan, Alan K. L. 1991. *Two Visions of the Way: A Study of the Wang Pi and the Ho-shang Kung Commentaries on the "Lao-Tzu"*. Albany: State University of New York Press.

Chang, Han-liang. 1980. "Towards a Structural Generic Theory of T'ang Ch'uan-chi [sic]." In *Chinese-Western Comparative Literature: Theory and Strategy*, ed. J. J. Deeney, 25–49. Hong Kong: The Chinese University Press.

Chatman, Seymour. 1978. *Story and Discourse: Narrative Structure in Fiction and Film*. Ithaca: Cornell University Press.

Chavannes, Edouard. 1910. *Le T'ai chan: Essai de monographie d'un culte chinois*. Paris: Ernest Leroux.

———. 1910–34. *Cinq cents contes et apologues extraits du Tripitaka chinois*. 4 vols. Paris: Ernest Leroux.

Chaves, Jonathan. 1977. "The Legacy of Ts'ang Chieh: The Written Word as Magic." *Oriental Art* n.s. 23:200–215.

Ch'en, Ch'i-yün. 1975. *Hsün Yüeh (A.D. 148–209): The Life and Reflections of an Early Medieval Confucian*. Cambridge: Cambridge University Press.

———. 1980. *Hsün Yüeh and the Mind of Late Han China: A Translation of the 'Shen-chien' with Introduction and Annotations*. Princeton: Princeton University Press.

Ch'en, Kenneth. 1952. "Anti-Buddhist Propaganda During the Nan-ch'ao." *HJAS* 15:166–92.

———. 1964. *Buddhism in China: A Historical Survey*. Princeton: Princeton University Press.

———. 1973. *The Chinese Transformation of Buddhism*. Princeton: Princeton University Press.

———. 1975. "Inscribed Stelae during the Wei, Chin, and Nan-ch'ao." In *Studia Asiatica*, ed. L. G. Thompson, 75–84. San Francisco: Chinese Materials Center.

Cheng, Te-k'un. 1933–34. "The Travels of Emperor Mu." *Journal of the North China Branch of the Royal Asiatic Society* n.s. 64:124–42 and 65:128–49.

Chi, Hsien-lin. 1958. "Indian Literature in China." *Chinese Literature* 1958, issue 4:123–30.

Chin, Fa-ken. 1964. "Great Families in North China after the Yung-chia Turmoil." *Synopses of Monographical Studies on Chinese History and Social Sciences* 1:59–77.

Ch'ü, T.-t. 1972. *Han Social Structure*. Ed. J. L. Dull. Seattle and London: University of Washington Press.

Clifford, James. 1985. "Objects and Selves—An Afterword." In *Objects and Others: Essays on Museums and Material Culture*, edited by G. W. Stocking, Jr., 236–46.

Clifford, James, and George E. Marcus, eds. 1986. *Writing Culture: The Poetics and Politics of Ethnography*. Berkeley: University of California Press.

Cohen, Alvin P. 1979. "Avenging Ghosts and Moral Judgement in Ancient Chinese Historiography: Three Examples from *Shih-chi*." In *Legend, Lore, and Religion in China: Essays in Honor of Wolfram Eberhard on His Seventieth Birthday*, ed. S. Allan and A. P. Cohen, 97–108. San Francisco: Chinese Materials Center.

———. 1982. *Tales of Vengeful Souls: A Sixth Century Collection of Chinese Avenging Ghost Stories*. Variétés Sinologiques n.s. 68. Taipei: Institut Ricci.

Creel, H. G. 1970. *The Origins of Statecraft in China*. Chicago: University of Chicago Press.

de Crespigny, Rafe. 1976. *Portents of Protest in the Later Han Dynasty*. Canberra: Australian National University Press.

———. 1980. "Politics and Philosophy under the Government of Emperor Huan 159–168 A.D." TP 66:41–83.

Crowell, William G. 1983. "Social Unrest and Rebellion in Jiangnan during the Six Dynasties." *Modern China* 9:319–54.

———. 1990. "Northern Émigrés and the Problems of Census Registration under the Eastern Jin and Southern Dynasties." In Dien 1990, 171–209.

Dalby, Michael. 1982. "Revenge and the Law in Traditional China." *American Journal of Legal History* 25:267–307.

Danzel, T.-W. 1912. *Die Anfänge der Schrift*. Leipzig: R. Voigtländers Verlag.

Defert, Daniel. 1982–83. "The Collection of the World: Accounts of Voyages from the Sixteenth to the Eighteenth Centuries." *Dialectical Anthropology* 7:11–20.

Defoort, Carine. 1994. "Human Impact in the *Huang-lao Boshu*: A Case of Political Rhetoric." Paper delivered at the 1994 meeting of the Association of Asian Studies.

Dègh, L., and A. Vàzsonyi. 1974. "The Memorate and the Proto-Memorate." *Journal of American Folk-Lore* 87:225–39.

Delahaye, Hubert. 1983. "Recherches récentes sur le thème de l'ascension céleste." BEF 72:299–308.

Derrida, J. 1976. *Of Grammatology*. Tr. G. C. Spivak. Baltimore: The Johns Hopkins University Press.

———. 1978. *Writing and Difference*. Tr. Alan Bass. Chicago: University of Chicago Press.

von Dewall, Magdalene. 1976. "Grab und Totenbrauch in China." *Tribus* 25:31–81.

DeWoskin, Kenneth J. 1974. "The *Sou-shen chi* and the *Chih-kuai* Tradition: A Bibliographic and Generic Study." Ph.D. dissertation, Columbia University.

———. 1977a. "In Search of the Supernatural—Selections from the 'Soushen chi.'" *Renditions* 7:103–114.

———. 1977b. "The Six Dynasties *Chih-kuai* and the Birth of Fiction." In *Chinese Narrative: Critical and Theoretical Essays*, ed. A. H. Plaks, 21–52. Princeton: Princeton University Press.

———. 1981. "A Source Guide to the Lives and Techniques of Han and Six Dynasties *Fang-shih*." JCR 9:79–105.

———. 1982. *A Song for One or Two: Music and the Concept of Art in Early China*. Ann Arbor: Center for Chinese Studies, University of Michigan.

———. 1983. *Doctors, Diviners, and Magicians of Ancient China: Biographies of "Fang-shih."* New York: Columbia University Press.

Dien, Albert E. 1968. "The *Yüan-hun Chih* (Accounts of Ghosts with Grievances): A Sixth-Century Collection of Stories." In *Wen-lin: Studies in the Chinese Humanities*, ed. Chow T.-t., 211–28. Madison: University of Wisconsin Press.

———, ed. 1990. *State and Society in Early Medieval China*. Stanford: Stanford University Press.

Dilke, O. A. W. 1985. *Greek and Roman Maps*. Ithaca: Cornell University Press.

Diringer, D. 1962. *Writing*. London: Thames & Hudson.

Douglas, Mary. 1969. *Purity and Danger: An Analysis of the Concepts of Pollution and Taboo*. 2d ed. London: Routledge & Kegan Paul.

———. 1975. *Implicit Meanings: Essays in Anthropology*. London: Routledge & Kegan Paul.

———. 1982. *Natural Symbols: Explorations in Cosmology*. 2nd ed. New York: Pantheon Books.

Dubrow, Heather. 1982. *Genre*. London: Methuen.

Dumont, Louis. 1980. *Homo Hierarchicus*. 2d ed. Chicago: University of Chicago Press.

Durkheim, Emile, and Marcel Mauss. 1963. *Primitive Classification*. Tr. Rodney Needham. Chicago: University of Chicago Press.

Durrant, Stephen W. 1977. "The Taoist Apotheosis of Mo Ti." JAOS 97:540–46.

Dykstra, Yoshiko K. 1976. "Tales of the Compassionate Kannon." *Monumenta Nipponica* 31:113–43.

Eberhard, Wolfram. 1937. *Typen chinesischer Volksmärchen*. Helsinki: Academia Scientiarum Fennica.

———. 1942. *Kultur und Siedlung der Randvölker Chinas*. Suppl. to TP 36. Leiden: E. J. Brill.

———. 1957. "The Political Function of Astronomy and Astronomers in

Han China." In *Chinese Thought and Institutions*, ed. John King Fairbank, 33–70. Chicago: University of Chicago Press.

———. 1958. *Chinese Festivals*. London: Abelard-Schuman.

———. 1965. *Folktales of China*. London: Routledge & Kegan Paul.

———. 1968. *The Local Cultures of South and East China*. Tr. A. Eberhard. Leiden: E. J. Brill.

———. 1977. *A History of China*. 4th ed. Berkeley: University of California Press.

Ebrey, Patricia Buckley. 1978. *The Aristocratic Families of Early Imperial China*. Cambridge: Cambridge University Press.

———. 1980. "Later Han Stone Inscriptions." HJAS 40:325–53.

———. 1990. "Toward a Better Understanding of the Later Han Upper Class." In Dien 1990, 49–72.

Eichhorn, Werner. 1954. "Description of the Rebellion of Sun En and Earlier Taoist Rebellions." *Deutsche Akademie der Wissenschaften zu Berlin: Mitteilungen des Instituts für Orient-forschung* 2:325–52.

———. 1985. "Das *Tung-ming chi* des Kuo Hsien." In Naundort et al., 1985, 291–300.

Eilberg-Schwartz, Howard. 1990. *The Savage in Judaism: An Anthropology of Israelite Religion and Ancient Judaism*. Bloomington: Indiana University Press.

Eliade, Mircea. 1959. *The Sacred and the Profane: The Nature of Religion*. Tr. W. R. Trask. New York: Harcourt, Brace & World.

———. 1961. *Images and Symbols*. Tr. P. Mairet. New York: Sheed & Ward.

———. 1976. *Occultism, Witchcraft, and Cultural Fashions*. Chicago: University of Chicago Press.

Ellen, R. F., and D. Reason, eds. 1979. *Classifications in their Social Context*. London: Academic Press.

Enoki, K. 1984. "The Liang Chih-kung-t'u." MTB 42:75–139.

Fabian, Johannes. 1983. *Time and the Other*. New York: Columbia University Press.

Faure, Bernard. 1987. "Space and Place in Chinese Religious Traditions." HR 26:337–56.

Feng, H. Y., and J. K. Shryock. 1935. "The Black Magic in China Known as *Ku*." JAOS 55:1–30.

Fernandez, James W. 1986. *Persuasions and Performances: The Play of Tropes in Culture*. Bloomington: Indiana University Press.

Forke, Alfred, tr. 1962 [1907–11]. *Lun-hêng*. 2 vols. Reprint. New York: Paragon Book Gallery.

Foster, Lawrence C. 1974. "The *Shih-i chi* and its Relationship to the Genre known as *Chih-kuai hsiao-shuo*." Ph.D. diss., University of Washington.

Foster, S. W. 1982–83. "The Exotic as a Symbolic System." *Dialectical Anthropology* 7:21–30.

Foucault, Michel. 1972. *The Archaeology of Knowledge*. Tr. A. M. S. Smith. New York: Pantheon.

————. 1973. *The Order of Things*. New York: Vintage Books.

————. 1979. *Discipline and Punish*. Tr. A. Sheridan. New York: Vintage Books.

Fracasso, Riccardo. 1988. "Holy Mothers of Ancient China: A New Approach to the Hsi-wang-mu 西王母 Problem." TP 74:1–46.

Frame, Donald M., tr. 1958. *The Complete Essays of Montaigne*. Stanford: Stanford University Press.

Frazer, J. G. 1951. *The Golden Bough: A Study in Magic and Religion* (abridged edition). 2d ed. New York: Macmillan.

Frese, H. H. 1960. *Anthropology and the Public: The Role of Museums*. Leiden: E. J. Brill.

Friedrich, J. 1937. "Schriftsgeschichtliche Betrachtungen." *Zeitschrift der deutschen morgenländischen Gesellschaft* 91:319–42.

————. 1938. "Zu einigen Schrifterfindungen der neuesten Zeit." *Zeitschrift der deutschen morgenländischen Gesellschaft* 92:183–218.

————. 1941. "Noch eine moderne Parallele zu den alten Schrifterfindungen: Eine Schrifterfindung bei den Alaska-Eskimo." *Zeitschrift der deutschen morgenländischen Gesellschaft* 95:374–414.

Fung, Yu-lan. 1952–53. *A History of Chinese Philosophy*. Tr. Derk Bodde. 2 vols. Princeton: Princeton University Press.

Gardner, C. T. 1873–74. "The Tablet of Yü." *China Review* 2:293–306.

Geertz, Clifford. 1968. *Islam Observed*. Chicago: University of Chicago Press.

————. 1980. *Negara: The Theatre State in Nineteenth-Century Bali*. Princeton: Princeton University Press.

Gelb, I. J. 1963. *A Study of Writing: The Foundations of Grammatology*. 2d ed. Chicago: University of Chicago Press.

van Gennep, Arnold. 1960 [1908]. *The Rites of Passage*. Tr. M. B. Vizedom and G. L. Caffee. Chicago: University of Chicago Press.

Gernet, Jacques. 1956. *Les aspects économiques du Bouddhisme*. Publications de l'École Française d'Extrême-Orient 39. Paris: École Française d'Extrême-Orient.

————. 1959. "Écrit et histoire en Chine." *Journal de Psychologie Normale et Pathologique* 56:31–40.

————. 1963. "La Chine, aspects et fonctions psychologiques de l'écriture." In *L'écriture et la psychologie des peuples*, 29–49. Paris: Colin.

————. 1982. *A History of Chinese Civilization*. Tr. J. R. Foster. Cambridge: Cambridge University Press.

Gibbs, D. A. 1970–71. "Liu Hsieh, Author of the *Wen-hsin tiao-lung*." MS 29:117–41.

Giles, Lionel. 1921. "A T'ang Dynasty Manuscript of the *Sou Shên Chi*." *New China Review* 3:378–85, 460–68.

Girardot, Norman J. 1983. *Myth and Meaning in Early Taoism*. Berkeley: University of California Press.

Gjertson, Donald E. 1978. *Ghosts, Gods, and Retribution: Nine Buddhist Miracle Tales from Six Dynasties and Early T'ang China*. Asian

Studies Committee Occasional Papers Series no. 2. Amherst: University of Massachusetts.

———. 1981. "The Early Chinese Buddhist Miracle Tale: A Preliminary Survey." JAOS 101:287–301.

———. 1989. *Miraculous Retribution: A Study and Translation of T'ang Lin's "Ming-pao Chi"*. Berkeley Buddhist Studies Series 8. Berkeley: Centers for South and Southeast Asian Studies, University of California.

Goodman, Howard, ed. 1989. *Calligraphy and the East Asian Book*. Boston: Shambhala.

Goody, Jack. 1977. *The Domestication of the Savage Mind*. Cambridge: Cambridge University Press.

———. 1987. *The Interface Between the Written and the Oral*. Cambridge: Cambridge University Press.

Grafflin, Dennis. 1981. "The Great Family in Medieval South China." HJAS 41:65–74.

———. 1990. "Reinventing China: Pseudobureaucracy in the Early Southern Dynasties." In Dien 1990, 139–170.

Graham, A. C. 1981. *Chuang-tzu: The Seven Inner Chapters and Other Writings from the Book of Chuang-tzu*. London: Allen & Unwin.

———. 1989. *Disputers of the Tao: Philosophical Argument in Ancient China*. La Salle, Illinois: Open Court.

———. 1990. *The Book of Lieh-tzu*. New York: Columbia University Press.

Granet, Marcel. 1952. *La féodalité chinoise*. Oslo: Instituttet for Sammenlignende Kulturforskning.

———. 1973 [1953]. "Right and Left in China." In *Right and Left: Essays on Dual Symbolic Classification*, ed. R. Needham, 43–58. Chicago: University of Chicago Press. Repr. and tr. from M. Granet, *Études sociologiques sur la Chine* (Paris: Presses Universitaires de France), 261–78.

Greatrex, Roger. 1987. *The Bowu Zhi: An Annotated Translation*. Stockholm: Orientaliska Studier.

de Groot, Jan J. M. 1982 [1892–1910]. *The Religious System of China*. 6 vols. Leiden: E. J. Brill; rept. Taipei: Southern Materials Center, 1982.

Güntsch, Gertrud. 1988. *Das Shen-hsien chuan und das Erscheinungsbild eines Hsien*. Frankfurt am Main: Verlag Peter Lang.

Hanan, Patrick. 1981. *The Chinese Vernacular Story*. Cambridge, Mass.: Harvard University Press.

Hanks, William F. 1987. "Discourse Genres in a Theory of Practice." *American Ethnologist* 14:668–92.

Harbsmeier, Michael. 1985. "On Travel Accounts and Cosmological Strategies: Some Models in Comparative Xenology." *Ethnos* 50:273–312.

———. 1986. "Pilgrim's Space: The Centre Out There in Comparative Perspective." *Temenos* 22:57–77.

Harper, Donald. 1985. "A Chinese Demonography of the Third Century B.C." HJAS 45:459–98.

Harvey, P. D. A. 1980. *The History of Topographical Maps*. London: Thames & Hudson.

Hawkes, David. 1967. "The Quest of the Goddess." *Asia Major* n.s. 13:71–94.

———, tr. 1985. *The Songs of the South*. Harmondsworth: Penguin.

Hay, Jonathan. 1983. "The Human Body as a Microcosmic Source of Macrocosmic Values in Calligraphy." In *Theories of the Arts in China*, ed. Susan Bush and Christian Murck, 74–102. Princeton: Princeton University Press.

Helms, Mary W. 1988. *Ulysses' Sail*. Princeton: Princeton University Press.

Henderson, John B. 1984. *The Development and Decline of Chinese Cosmology*. New York: Columbia University Press.

Henricks, Robert G. 1983. *Philosophy and Argumentation in Third-Century China: The Essays of Hsi K'ang*. Princeton: Princeton University Press.

Herrmann, A. 1922. "Die Westländer in der chinesischen Kartographie." In *Southern Tibet*, ed. S. Hedin, 8:91–406. Stockholm: Lithographic Institute of the General Staff of the Swedish Army.

———. 1930. "Die Älteste Reichsgeographie Chinas und ihre kulturgeschichtliche Bedeutung." *Sinica* 5:232–37.

Hightower, James R. 1970. *The Poetry of T'ao Ch'ien*. Oxford: Oxford University Press.

Hobsbawm, Eric, and Terence Ranger, eds. 1983. *The Invention of Tradition*. Cambridge: Cambridge University Press.

Holcombe, Charles. 1989. "The Exemplar State: Ideology, Self-Cultivation, and Power in Fourth-Century China." HJAS 49:93–139.

———. 1992. "Liberty in Early Medieval China." *The Historian* 54:609–26.

Holzman, Donald. 1956. "Les Sept Sages de la Forêt des Bambous et la société de leur temps." TP 46:317–46.

———. 1957. *La vie et la pensée de Hi K'ang (223–262 ap. J.-C.)*. Leiden: E. J. Brill.

———. 1974. "Literary Criticism in China in the Early Third Century A.D." *Asiatische Studien* 28:113–49.

———. 1976. *Poetry and Politics: The Life and Work of Juan Chi A.D. 210–263*. Cambridge: Cambridge University Press.

Honey, David B. 1990. "Lineage as Legitimation in the Rise of Liu Yüan and Shih Le." JAOS 110:616–21.

Honko, L. 1964. "Memorates and the Study of Folk Beliefs." *Journal of the Folklore Institute* 1:5–19.

Hooke, S. H. 1937. "The Early History of Writing." *Antiquity* 11:261–77.

———. 1954. "Recording and Writing." In *A History of Technology*, ed. C. Singer et al., 1:744–73. New York: Oxford University Press.

Hou, Ching-lang. 1981. "Recherches sur la peinture du portrait en Chine, au début de la dynastie Han (206–141 avant J.-C.)." *Arts asiatiques* 36:37–58.

Howard, J. A. 1984. "Concepts of Comprehensiveness and Historical Change in the *Huai-nan-tzu.*" In Rosemont 1984, 119–32.

Hsiao, Kung-chuan. 1979. *A History of Chinese Political Thought.* Vol. 1, *From the Beginnings to the Sixth Century* A.D. Tr. F. W. Mote. Princeton: Princeton University Press.

Hsu, Cho-Yun. 1965. *Ancient China in Transition.* Stanford: Stanford University Press.

Hubbard, James B. 1986. "Salvation in the Final Period of the Dharma: The Inexhaustible Storehouse of the San-chieh-chiao." Ph.D. thesis, University of Wisconsin.

Hucker, Charles O. 1985. *A Dictionary of Official Titles in Imperial China.* Stanford: Stanford University Press.

Hume, David. 1957. *The Natural History of Religion.* Ed. H. E. Root. Stanford: Stanford University Press.

————. 1888. *A Treatise of Human Nature.* Ed. L. A. Selby-Bigge. Oxford: Clarendon Press.

Humphreys, W. C. 1968. *Anomalies and Scientific Theories.* San Francisco: Freeman, Cooper & Co.

Hunn, E. S. 1977. *Tzeltal Folk Zoology: The Classification of Discontinuities in Nature.* New York: Academic Press.

————. 1979. "The Abominations of Leviticus Revisited: A Commentary on Anomaly in Symbolic Anthropology." In Ellen and Reason 1979, 103–16.

Hurvitz, Leon. 1957. "'Render unto Caesar' in Early Chinese Buddhism." In *Liebenthal Festschrift*, ed. K. Roy, 80–114. Santiniketan: Santiniketan Press.

————, tr. 1976. *Scripture of the Lotus Blossom of the Fine Dharma (The Lotus Sutra).* New York: Columbia University Press.

Hurvitz, Leon N., and Arthur E. Link. 1974. "Three Prajñāpāramitā Prefaces of Tao-an: En hommage à M. Paul Demiéville." In *Mélanges de Sinologie offerts à Monsieur Paul Demiéville: II*, 403–70. Paris: Bibliotèque de l'Institut des Hautes Études Chinoises.

Itano, Chōhachi. 1976 and 1978. "The *T'u-ch'en* Prophetic Books and the Establishment of Confucianism." MTB 34:47–111 and 36:85–107.

James, William. 1902. *The Varieties of Religious Experience.* New York: Modern Library.

Johnson, David G. 1977. *The Medieval Chinese Oligarchy.* Boulder, Co.: Westview Press.

————. 1980. "The Wu Zixu *Pien-wen* and Its Sources." HJAS 40:93–156, 465–505.

Johnson, Mark. 1987. *The Body in the Mind: The Bodily Basis of Meaning, Imagination, and Reason.* Chicago: University of Chicago Press.

Jones, Andrew. 1987. "The Poetics of Uncertainty in Early Chinese Literature." Sino-Platonic Papers no. 2. Philadelphia: University of Pennsylvania, Dept. of Oriental Studies.

Jordan, David K., and Daniel L. Overmyer. 1986. *The Flying Phoenix: Aspects of Chinese Sectarianism in Taiwan.* Princeton: Princeton University Press.

Jordanus, C. 1863. *Mirabilia Descripta: The Wonders of the East, by Friar Jordanus*. Tr. H. Yule. London: Printed for the Hakluyt Society, ser. 1, vol. 31. Rept. New York: Burt Franklin [n.d.].

Kalinowski, Marc. 1980. "Les justifications historiques du gouvernement idéal dans le *Lü shi chunqiu*." BEF 68:155–208.

———. 1982. "Cosmologie et gouvernement naturel dans le *Lü shi chunqiu*." BEF 71:187–95.

Kaltenmark, Max. 1949. "Les Tch'an-wei." *Han-hiue* 2.4:363–73.

———. 1953. *Le Lie-sien tchouan: Biographies légendaires des immortels taoïstes de l'antiquité*. Peking: Université de Paris, Centre d'études sinologiques de Pékin.

———. 1979. "The Ideology of the T'ai-p'ing Ching." In Welch and Seidel 1979, 19–52.

Kao, Karl S. Y., ed. 1985. *Classical Chinese Tales of the Supernatural and the Fantastic: Selections from the Third to the Tenth Century*. Bloomington: Indiana University Press.

Karlgren, Bernard. 1946. "Legends and Cults in Ancient China." BMFE 18:199–365.

———. 1950. "The Book of Documents." BMFE 22:1–81.

Kawakatsu, Yoshio. 1971. "La décadence de l'aristocracie chinoise sous les Dynasties du Sud." *Acta Asiatica* 21:13–38.

———. 1974b. "Sie Ling-yun et le Che-chouo sin-yu." In *Mélanges de Sinologie offerts à Monsieur Paul Demiéville* II, 167–78. Paris: Bibliothèque de l'Institut des Hautes Études Chinoises 20.

Kee, Howard C. 1983. *Miracle in the Early Christian World*. New Haven: Yale University Press.

Keightley, David N. 1978. *Sources of Shang History*. Berkeley: University of California Press.

———. 1979–80. "The Shang State as Seen in the Oracle-Bone Inscriptions." EC 5:25–34.

———. 1983. "The Late Shang State: When, Where, and What?" In *The Origins of Chinese Civilization*, ed. D. N. Keightley, 523–64. Berkeley: University of California Press.

———. 1984. "Late Shang Divination: The Magico-Religious Legacy." In Rosemont 1984, 11–34.

———. 1988. "Shang Divination and Metaphysics." *Philosophy East and West* 38:367–97.

Kesby, J. D. 1979. "The Rangi Classification of Animals and Plants." In Ellen and Reason 1979, 33–56.

Kim, Young-Ho. 1990. *Tao-sheng's Commentary on the Lotus Sūtra*. Albany: State University of New York Press.

Kirkland, Russell. 1993. "A World in Balance: Holistic Synthesis in the T'ai-p'ing kuang-chi." *Journal of Sung-Yuan Studies* 23:43–70.

Knaul, Livia. 1985a. "Kuo Hsiang and the Chuang Tzu." *Journal of Chinese Philosophy* 12:429–47.

———. 1985b. "The Winged Life: Kuo Hsiang's Mystical Philosophy." *Journal of Chinese Studies* 2:17–41.

Knechtges, David R. 1976. *The Han Rhapsody: A Study of the Fu of Yang Hsiung (53 B.C.–A.D. 18)*. Cambridge: Cambridge University Press.

———. 1977–78. "The Liu Hsin / Yang Hsiung Correspondence on the *Fang-yan*." MS 33:309–25.

———. 1982. *Wen Xuan, or Selections of Refined Literature*. 2 vols. Princeton: Princeton University Press.

———. 1990. "A New Study of Han *Yüeh-fu*." JAOS 110:310–16.

Kuhn, Dieter. 1984. "Tracing a Chinese Legend: In Search of the Identity of the 'First Sericulturalist.'" TP 70:213–45.

Kuhn, Thomas S. 1970. *The Structure of Scientific Revolutions*. 2nd ed. Chicago: University of Chicago Press.

Lach, Donald F. 1965-77. *Asia in the Making of Europe*. 5 vols. Chicago: University of Chicago Press.

Lagerwey, John. 1981. *Wu-Shang Pi-Yao: Somme taoïste du VIe siècle*. Paris: École Française d'Extrême-Orient.

———. 1985. "The Oral and the Written in Chinese and Western Religion." In Naundort et al., ed., 1985, 301–22.

Lai, Whalen. 1979. "Limits and Failure of *Ko-I* (Concept-Matching) Buddhism." HR 18:238–57.

———. 1981. "Emperor Wu of Liang on the Immortal Soul, *Shen Pu Mieh*." JAOS 101:167–75.

———. 1987. "The Earliest Folk Buddhist Religion in China: *T'i-wei Po-li Ching* and its Historical Significance." In *Buddhist and Taoist Practice in Medieval Chinese Society (Buddhist and Taoist Studies II)*, ed. David W. Chappell, 11–35. Honolulu: University of Hawaii Press.

———. 1990. "Society and the Sacred in the Secular City: Temple Legends of the *Lo-yang Ch'ieh-lan-chi*." In Dien 1990, 229–68.

Lakoff, George. 1987. *Women, Fire, and Dangerous Things: What Categories Reveal about the Mind*. Chicago: University of Chicago Press.

Lakoff, George, and Mark Johnson. 1980. *Metaphors We Live By*. Chicago: University of Chicago Press.

Larre, Claude. 1982. *Le traité VII du Houai Nan Tseu*. Taipei: Institut Ricci.

Lascault, G. 1973. *Le monstre dans l'art occidental*. Paris: Klincksieck.

Lau, D. C., tr. 1963. *Lao Tzu: Tao Te Ching*. Harmondsworth: Penguin.

———, tr. 1970. *Mencius*. Harmondsworth: Penguin.

———, tr. 1979. *Confucius: The Analects*. Harmondsworth: Penguin.

Le Blanc, Charles. 1985. *Huai-Nan Tzu: Philosophical Synthesis in Early Han Thought*. Hong Kong: Hong Kong University Press.

Leban, Carl. 1978. "Managing Heaven's Mandate: Coded Communication in the Accession of Ts'ao P'ei, A.D. 220." In Roy and Tsien 1978, 315–46.

Ledderose, Lothar. 1984. "Some Taoist Elements in the Calligraphy of the Six Dynasties." TP 70:246–78.

Legge, James, tr. 1926. *The Sacred Books of China: The Texts of Confucianism*. Parts 3 and 4, *The Li Ki*. 2 vols. 2d ed. Sacred Books of the East, vol. 27. Oxford: Oxford University Press.

Lévi, Jean. 1977. "Le mythe de l'âge d'or et les théories de l'évolution en Chine ancienne." *L'Homme* 17:73–103.

———. 1983. "L'abstinence des céréales chez les taoïstes." *Études Chinoises: Bulletin de l'Association française d'études chinoises* 1:3–47.

———. 1986. "Les fonctionnaires et le divin: Luttes de pouvoirs entre divinités et administrateurs dans les contes des Six Dynasties et des Tang." CEA 2:81–110.

Lévi-Strauss, Claude. 1963. *Totemism*. Tr. Rodney Needham. Boston: Beacon Press.

———. 1966. *The Savage Mind*. Chicago: University of Chicago Press.

Levy, Howard. 1956. "Yellow Turban Religion and Rebellion at the End of the Han." JAOS 76:216–27.

Lewis, Mark E. 1990a. *Sanctioned Violence in Early China*. Albany: State University of New York Press.

———. 1990b. "The Suppression of the Three Stages Sect: Apocrypha as a Political Issue." In *Chinese Buddhist Apocrypha*, ed. Robert E. Buswell, Jr., 207–38. Honolulu: University of Hawaii Press.

Li, C. 1963. "The Changing Concept of the Recluse in Chinese Literature." HJAS 24:234–47.

Liebenthal, W. 1952. "The Immortality of the Soul in Chinese Thought." *Monumenta Nipponica* 8:327–97.

Lincoln, Bruce. 1989. *Discourse and the Construction of Society: Comparative Studies of Myth, Ritual, and Classification*. New York: Oxford University Press.

Link, Arthur E. 1958. "Biography of Shih Tao-an." TP 46 (2nd ser.):1–48.

———. 1961. "Cheng-wu lun: The Rectification of Unjustified Criticism." *Oriens Extremus* 8:136–65.

———. 1969–70. "The Taoist Antecedents of Tao-an's Prajñā Ontology." HR 9:181–215.

Link, Arthur E., and Tim Lee. 1966. "Sun Ch'o's 孫綽 *Yü-tao-lun* 喻道論: A Clarification of the Way." MS 25:169–96.

Liu, C. H. 1932. "The Dog-Ancestor Story of the Aboriginal Tribes of Southern China." *Journal of the Royal Anthropological Institute of Great Britain and Ireland* 62:361–68.

Liu, James J. Y. 1975. *Chinese Theories of Literature*. Chicago: University of Chicago Press.

Liu, Ming-wood. 1989. "The Early Development of the Buddha-Nature Doctrine in China." *Journal of Chinese Philosophy* 16:1–36.

Liu, Ts'un-yan. 1975. "The Compilation and Historical Value of the Tao-tsang." In *Essays on the Sources for Chinese History*, ed. Donald Leslie et al., 104–19. Columbia: University of South Carolina Press.

Loewe, Michael. 1967. *Records of Han Administration*. 2 vols. Cambridge: Cambridge University Press.

———. 1968. *Everyday Life in Early Imperial China during the Han Period*. London: B. T. Batsford.

———. 1971. "K'uang Heng and the Reform of Religious Practices (31 B.C.)." *Asia Major* n.s. 17:1–27.

———. 1973. "The Office of Music, c. 114 to 7 B.C." *Bulletin of the School of Oriental and African Studies* 36:340–51.

———. 1978. "Man and Beast: The Hybrid in Early Chinese Art and Literature." *Numen* 25:97–117.

———. 1979. *Ways to Paradise*. London: Allen & Unwin.

———. 1982. *Chinese Ideas of Life and Death*. London: Allen & Unwin.

———, ed. 1993. *Early Chinese Texts: A Bibliographical Guide*. Berkeley: Society for the Study of Early China and the Institute of East Asian Studies, University of California.

Long, Charles H. 1986. *Significations: Signs, Symbols, and Images in the Interpretation of Religion*. Philadelphia: Fortress Press.

Louton, J. 1984. "Concepts of Comprehensiveness and Historical Change in the *Lü-shih Ch'un-ch'iu*." In Rosemont 1984, 105–18.

Lovejoy, A. O., and G. Boas. 1935. *Primitivism and Related Ideas in Antiquity*. Baltimore: The Johns Hopkins Press.

Lu, Hsiao-Peng. 1987. "The Fictional Discourse of *Pien-wen*: The Relation of Chinese Fiction to Historiography." CL 9:49–70.

Lu Hsun. 1976. *A Brief History of Chinese Fiction*. Tr. Yang Hsien-yi and Gladys Yang. Peking: Foreign Languages Press. [Tr. of Lu Xun 1926; rept. of 1959 ed.]

Luo, Julia. Unpublished. "A Fifth-Century Buddhist-Confucian Debate on the Soul."

Maeno Naoaki. 1969. "The Origin of Fiction in China." *Acta Asiatica* 16:27–37.

Mair, Victor H. 1983. "The Narrative Revolution in Chinese Literature." CL 5:1–51.

———. 1989. *T'ang Transformation Texts: A Study of the Buddhist Contribution to the Rise of Vernacular Fiction and Drama in China*. Cambridge, Mass.: Harvard University Press.

———, tr. 1990. *Tao Te Ching*. New York: Bantam.

Major, John S. 1984. "The Five Phases, Magic Squares, and Schematic Cosmography." In Rosemont 1984, 133–66.

———. 1993. *Heaven and Earth in Early Han Thought: Chapters Three, Four, and Five of the 'Huainanzi'*. Albany: State University of New York Press.

Mao Han-kuang. 1990. "The Evolution in the Nature of the Medieval Genteel Families." In Dien 1990, 73–109.

Marcus, G. E., and M. M. J. Fischer. 1986. *Anthropology as Cultural Critique: An Experimental Moment in the Human Sciences*. Chicago: University of Chicago Press.

Marquès-Rivière, J. 1938. *Amulettes, talismans et pantacles dans les traditions orientales et occidentales*. Paris: Payot.

Martinson, Paul V. 1973. "*Pao* Order and Redemption: Perspectives on Chinese Religion and Society based on a study of the *Chin P'ing Mei*." Ph.D. diss., University of Chicago.

Maspero, Henri. 1948–51. "Le Ming-t'ang et la crise religieuse chinoise avant les Han." In *Mélanges chinois et bouddhiques publiés par l'Institut Belge des Hautes Études Chinoises* 9:1–71. Bruxelles: Imprimerie Sainte-Catherine.

———. 1981. *Taoism and Chinese Religion.* Tr. F. A. Kierman, Jr. Amherst: University of Massachusetts Press.

Mather, Richard B. 1961. "The Mystical Ascent of the T'ien-t'ai Mountains: Sun Ch'o's *Yu-T'ien-t'ai-shan fu* 遊天台山賦." MS 20:226–45.

———. 1968. "Vimalakïrti and Gentry Buddhism." HR 8:60–73.

———. 1969–70. "The Controversy over Conformity and Naturalness during the Six Dynasties." HR 9:160–80.

———, tr. 1976. *Shih-shuo Hsin-yü: A New Account of Tales of the World.* Minneapolis: University of Minnesota Press.

———. 1979. "K'ou Ch'ien-chih and the Taoist Theocracy at the Northern Wei Court, 425–451." In Welch and Seidel 1979, 103–122.

———. 1983. "Shen Yüeh's Poems of Reclusion: From Total Withdrawal to Living in the Suburbs." CL 5:53–66.

———. 1985. "Individualist Expressions of the Outsiders during the Six Dynasties." In Munro 1985, 199–214.

———. 1986. "Wang Jung's 'Hymns on the Devotee's Entrance into the Pure Life.'" JAOS 106:79–98.

———. 1987. "The Life of the Budda and the Buddhist Life: Wang Jung's (468–93) 'Songs of Religious Joy' (*Fa-le tz'u*)." JAOS 107:31–38.

———. 1988. *The Poet Shen Yüeh (441–513): The Reticent Marquis.* Princeton: Princeton University Press.

———. 1992. "Chinese and Indian Perceptions of Each Other between the First and Seventh Centuries." JAOS 112:1–8.

Mathieu, R. 1978. *Le Mu Tianzi zhuan.* Paris: Collège de France, Mémoires de l'Institut des Hautes Études Chinoises.

———. 1983. *Étude sur la mythologie et l'éthnologie de la Chine ancienne.* 2 vols. Paris: Collège de France, Mémoires de l'Institut des Hautes Études Chinoises.

Meyer, Andrew. 1994. "Human Beings and the Cosmos in the *Lüshi chunqiu.*" Paper delivered at the 1994 meeting of the Association of Asian Studies.

Meyer, Jeffrey F. 1978. "*Feng-shui* of the Chinese City." HR 18:138–55.

Michaud, Paul. 1958. "The Yellow Turbans." MS 17:47–127.

Miyakawa Hisayuki. 1979. "Local Cults around Mount Lu at the Time of Sun En's Rebellion." In Welch and Seidel 1979, 83–102.

Morris, Brian. 1979. "Symbolism as Ideology: Thoughts around Navaho Taxonomy and Symbolism." In Ellen and Reason 1979, 117–38.

Müller, F. Max. 1873. *Introduction to the Science of Religion.* London: Longmans, Green, & Co.

Munro, Donald, ed. 1985. *Individualism and Holism: Studies in Confucian and Taoist Values.* Michigan Monographs in Chinese Studies 52. Ann Arbor: Center for Chinese Studies, University of Michigan.

Murray, S. O. 1983. "Fuzzy Sets and Abominations." *Man* 18:396–99.

Nakamura, Hajime. 1947. "Old Chinese World Maps Preserved by the Koreans." *Imago Mundi* 4:3–22.

Naundort, G., et al., eds. 1985. *Religion und Philosophie in Ostasien: Festschrift für Hans Steininger*. Würtzburg: Königshausen und Neumann Verlag.

Naveh, J., and S. Shaked. 1985. *Amulets and Magic Bowls: Aramaic Incantations of Late Antiquity*. Jerusalem: The Magnes Press, The Hebrew University.

Needham, Joseph, ed. 1954–. *Science and Civilisation in China*. 7+ vols. Cambridge: Cambridge University Press.

Needham, Rodney. 1979. *Symbolic Classification*. Santa Monica: Goodyear Publishing.

Ngo, Van Xuyet. 1976. *Divination, magie et politique dans la Chine ancienne*. Paris: Presses Universitaires de France.

Nienhauser, William H., Jr., ed. 1986. *The Indiana Companion to Traditional Chinese Literature*. Bloomington: Indiana University Press.

Nussbaum, Martha C. 1990. *Love's Knowledge: Essays on Philosophy and Literature*. New York: Oxford University Press.

O'Flaherty, Wendy Doniger. 1980. *Women, Androgynes, and Other Mythical Beasts*. Chicago: University of Chicago Press.

———. 1984. *Dreams, Illusion and Other Realities*. Chicago: University of Chicago Press.

Ohnuki-Tierney, E. 1987. *The Monkey as Mirror: Symbolic Transformations in Japanese History and Ritual*. Princeton: Princeton University Press.

———. 1990a. "Introduction." In *Culture Through Time: Anthropological Approaches*, ed. E. Ohnuki-Tierney, 1–25. Stanford: Stanford University Press.

———. 1990b. "The Monkey as Self in Japanese Culture." In *Culture Through Time: Anthropological Approaches*, ed. E. Ohnuki-Tierney, 128–53. Stanford: Stanford University Press.

Ong, Walter J. 1981 [1967]. *The Presence of the Word: Some Prolegomena for Cultural and Religious History*. Reprint. Minneapolis: University of Minnesota Press.

———. 1982. *Orality and Literacy: The Technologizing of the Word*. London: Methuen.

Ortner, Sherry. 1973. "On Key Symbols." *American Anthropologist* 75: 1338–46.

Overmyer, Daniel. 1976. *Folk Buddhist Religion*. Cambridge, Mass: Harvard University Press.

Owen, Stephen. 1986. *Remembrances: The Experience of the Past in Classical Chinese Literature*. Cambridge, Mass.: Harvard University Press.

———. 1992. *Readings in Chinese Literary Thought*. Cambridge, Mass: Harvard University Press.

Pearson, Margaret J. 1989. *Wang Fu and the 'Comments of a Recluse'*.

Center for Asian Studies Monograph 24. Tempe, Arizona: Center for Asian Studies, Arizona State University.

Peerenboom, R. P. 1993. *Law and Morality in Ancient China: The Silk Manuscripts of Huang-Lao.* Albany: State University of New York Press.

Pelliot, Paul. 1920. "'Meou-Tseu ou Les doutes levés,' traduit et annoté." *TP* 19:255–433.

Petersen, J. Ø. 1989-90. "The Early Traditions Relating to the Han Dynasty Transmission of the *Taiping jing*." *Acta Orientalia* 50:133–71, 51:173–216.

Peterson, Willard J. 1982. "Making Connections: 'Commentary on the Attached Verbalizations' of the *Book of Change*." *HJAS* 42:67–116.

Piccaluga, G. 1974. *Terminus: I segni di confine nella religione romana.* Rome: Edizioni dell'Ateneo.

———. 1983. "La scrittura coercitiva." *Cultura e scuola* 22.85:117–24.

Pokora, Timotheus. 1975. *Hsin-lun (New Treatise) and Other Writings by Huan T'an (43 B.C.–28 A.D.).* Michigan Papers in Chinese Studies 20. Ann Arbor: Center for Chinese Studies, University of Michigan.

———. 1985. "'Living Corpses' in Early Medieval China—Sources and Opinions." In Naundort et al., 1985, 343–57.

Pollack, David. 1986. *The Fracture of Meaning: Japan's Synthesis of China from the Eighth through the Eighteenth Centuries.* Princeton: Princeton University Press.

Porkert, Manfred. 1974. *The Theoretical Foundations of Chinese Medicine.* Cambridge, Mass.: MIT Press.

Porter, Deborah. 1993. "The Literary Function of K'un-lun Mountain in the *Mu T'ien-tzu chuan*." *EC* 18:73–106.

Powers, Martin J. 1981. "An Archaic Bas-Relief and the Chinese Moral Cosmos in the First Century A.D." *Ars Orientalis* 12:25–40 + illustrations.

———. 1983. "Hybrid Omens and Public Issues in Early Imperial China." *BMFE* 55:17–55.

———. 1984. "Pictorial Art and its Public in Early Imperial China." *Art History* 7:135–63.

Przyluski, Jean. 1923. *Le légende de l'empereur Açoka (Açoka-Avadana) dans les textes indiens et chinois.* Paris: Paul Geuthner.

Pulleybank, Edwin G. 1991. *Lexicon of Reconstructed Pronunciation in Early Middle Chinese, Late Middle Chinese, and Early Mandarin.* Vancouver: UBC Press.

Rawlinson, Andrew. 1986. "Nāgas and the Magical Cosmology of Buddhism." *Religion* 16:135-53.

Remus, Harold. 1983. *Pagan-Christian Conflict over Miracle in the Second Century.* Philadelphia: The Philadelphia Patristic Foundation.

Ricoeur, Paul. 1976. *Interpretation Theory: Discourse and the Surplus of Meaning.* Fort Worth: Texas Christian University Press.

Riegel, Jeffrey K. 1986. "Poetry and the Legend of Confucius's Exile." JAOS 106:13–22.

Robinet, Isabelle. 1979a. *Méditation taoïste*. Paris: Dervy Livres.

———. 1979b. "Metamorphosis and Deliverance from the Corpse in Taoism." HR 19:37–70.

———. 1981. *Les commentaires du Tao To King jusqu'au VIIe siècle*. Mémoires de l'Institut des Hautes Études Chinoises 5. Paris: Institut des Hautes Études Chinoises.

———. 1984. *La révélation du Shangqing dans l'histoire du taoïsme*. 2 vols. Paris: Ecole Française d'Extrême-Orient.

———. 1985–86. "The Taoist Immortal: Jesters of Light and Shadow, Heaven and Earth." JCR 13-14:87–105.

Robinson, A. H., and B. B. Petchenik. 1976. *The Nature of Maps*. Chicago: University of Chicago Press.

Rosemont, Henry, Jr., ed. 1984. *Explorations in Early Chinese Cosmology*. JAAR Thematic Studies 50/2. Chico, Cal.: Scholars Press.

Roth, Harold D. 1985. "The Concept of Human Nature in the *Huai-nan tzu*." *Journal of Chinese Philosophy* 12:1–22.

———. 1991. "Psychology and Self-Cultivation in Early Taoistic Thought." HJAS 51:99–650.

———. 1992. The *Textual History of the 'Huai-nan Tzu'*. Ann Arbor: Association for Asian Studies Monograph Series.

Roy, David T., and Tsuen-hsiun Tsien, eds. 1978. *Ancient China: Studies in Early Civilization*. Hong Kong: Chinese University Press.

Rubin, V. A. 1984. "Ancient Chinese Cosmology and *Fa-chia* Theory." In Rosemont 1984, 95–104.

Ryckmans, P. 1972. "A New Interpretation of the Term *Lieh-chuan* as Used in the *Shih-chi*." *Papers on Far East History* 5:135–47.

Sage, Steven F. 1992. *Ancient Sichuan and the Unification of China*. Albany: State University of New York Press.

Sahlins, Marshall. 1981. *Historical Metaphors and Mythical Realities: Structure in the Early History of the Sandwich Islands Kingdom*. Assoc. for the Study of Anthropology in Oceania, Special Publication No. 1. Ann Arbor: University of Michigan Press.

Saso, Michael. 1978. "What Is the *Ho-t'u?*" HR 17:399–416.

Schafer, Edward H. 1951. "Ritual Exposure in Ancient China." HJAS 14:130–84.

———. 1959. "Parrots in Medieval China." In *Studia Serica Bernhard Karlgren Dedicata*, ed. S. Egerod and E. Glahn, 271–82. Copenhagen: Ejnar Munksgaard.

———. 1963. *The Golden Peaches of Samarkand: A Study of T'ang Exotics*. Berkeley: University of California Press.

———. 1967. *The Vermilion Bird: T'ang Images of the South*. Berkeley: University of California Press.

———. 1970. *The Shore of Pearls*. Berkeley: University of California Press.

———. 1977. *Pacing the Void: T'ang Approaches to the Stars*. Berkeley: University of California Press.

———. 1980a [1973]. *The Divine Woman: Dragon Ladies and Rain Maidens*. Reprint. San Francisco: North Point Press.

———. 1980b. "The Table of Contents of the *T'ai p'ing kuang chi*." CL 2:258–63.

Scharf, Robert. 1991. "The *Treasure Store Treatise* and the Sinification of Buddhism in Eighth-Century China." Ph.D. diss., University of Michigan.

Schieffelin, Edward, and Robert Crittenden. 1991. *Like People You See in a Dream: First Contact in Six Papuan Societies*. Stanford: Stanford University Press.

Schipper, Kristofer M., tr. 1965. *L'empereur Wou des Han dans la légende taoïste: Han Wou-ti nei-tchouan*. Publications de l'École Française d'Extrême-Orient 58. Paris: École Française d'Extrême-Orient.

———. 1974. "The Written Memorial in Taoist Ceremonies." In *Religion and Ritual in Chinese Society*, ed. Arthur P. Wolf, 309–24. Stanford: Stanford University Press.

Schlosser, J. von. 1908. *Die Kunst- und Wunderkammern der Spätrenaissance: Ein Beitrag zur Geschichte des Sammelwesens*. Leipzig: Verlag von Klinkhart & Bierman.

Schmidt-Glintzer, Helwig. 1976. *Das 'Hung-ming chi' und die Aufnahme des Buddhismus in China*. Münchener Ostasiatische Studien 12. Wiesbaden: Franz Steiner Verlag.

Schmotzer, J. S. 1973. "The Graphic Portrayal of 'All Under Heaven' (T'ien-hsia): A Study of Chinese World Views through Pictorial Representations." Ph.D. diss., Georgetown University.

Schutz, Alfred. 1977. "Making Music Together: A Study in Social Relationship." In *Symbolic Anthropology*, ed. J. L. Dolgin et al., 106–119. New York: Columbia University Press.

Schwartz, Benjamin. 1985. *The World of Thought in Ancient China*. Cambridge, Mass: Harvard University Press.

Seidel, Anna. 1969–70. "The Image of the Perfect Ruler in Early Taoist Messianism: Lao-tzu and Li Hung." HR 9:216–47.

———. 1978. "Der Kaiser und sein Ratgeber: Lao tzu und der Taoismus der Han-Zeit." *Saeculum* 29:18–50.

———. 1981. "Kokuhō: Note à propos du terme 'trésor national' en Chine et au Japon." BEF 69:229–61.

———. 1982. "Tokens of Immortality in Han Graves." *Numen* 29:79–122.

———. 1983. "Imperial Treasures and Taoist Sacraments: Taoist Roots in the Apocrypha." In *Tantric and Taoist Studies in Honour of R. A. Stein*, vol. 2, ed. M. Strickmann, 291–371. Bruxelles: Institut Belge des Hautes Études Chinoises.

———. 1985. "Geleitbrief an die Unterwelt: Jenseitsvorstellungen in den Graburkunden der späteren Han Zeit." In Naundort et al., ed., 1985, 161–83.

———. 1987. "*Post-Mortem* Immortality or the Taoist Resurrection of the Body." In *Gilgul: Essays on Transformation, Revolution and Permanence in the History of Religions*, ed. S. Shaked et al., 223-37. Leiden: E. J. Brill.

Shen, Chien-shih. 1936–37. "An Essay on the Primitive Meaning of the Character 鬼." MS 2:1–20.

Shepard, Roger N. 1990. *Mind Sights: Original Visual Illusions, Ambiguities, and Other Anomalies, with a commentary on the play of mind in perception and art.* New York: W. H. Freeman.

Shih, Vincent, tr. 1959. *The Literary Mind and the Carving of Dragons.* New York: Columbia University Press.

Shils, Edward. 1981. *Tradition.* Chicago: University of Chicago Press.

Shinohara, Koichi. 1988. "Two Sources of Chinese Buddhist Biographies: Stupa Inscriptions and Miracle Stories." *In Monks and Magicians: Religious Biographies in Asia,* 119–228. Ed. P. Granoff. Oakville, Ontario: Mosaic Press.

Shryock, J. K., tr. 1963. *The Study of Human Abilities: The "Jen wu chih" of Liu Shao.* Ann Arbor: University Microfilms.

Sivin, Nathan. 1969. "On the *Pao P'u Tzu Nei P'ien* and the Life of Ko Hung (283–343)." *Isis* 60:388–91.

———. 1978. "On the Word 'Taoist' as a Source of Perplexity." HR 17:303–30.

Skinner, G. W., ed. 1977. *The City in Late Imperial China.* Stanford: Stanford University Press.

Smith, Bardwell, and H. B. Reynolds, eds. 1987. *The City as a Sacred Center.* Leiden: E. J. Brill.

Smith, Jonathan Z. 1974. "Animals and Plants in Myth and Legend." *Encyclopedia Britannica (Macropedia).* 15th ed.

———. 1978a. *Map Is Not Territory: Studies in the History of Religions.* Leiden: E. J. Brill.

———. 1978b. "Towards Interpreting Demonic Powers in Hellenistic and Roman Antiquity." *Aufstieg und Niedergang der römischen Welt* 16:425–39.

———. 1982. *Imagining Religion: From Babylon to Jonestown.* Chicago: University of Chicago Press.

———. 1985. "What a Difference a Difference Makes." In *"To See Ourselves as Others See Us": Christians, Jews, "Others" in Late Antiquity,* ed. J. Neusner and E. S. Frerichs, 3–48. Chico, Cal.: Scholars Press.

———. 1987. *To Take Place: Toward Theory in Ritual.* Chicago: University of Chicago Press.

Smith, Thomas E. 1990. "Record of the Ten Continents." TR 2:87–119.

———. 1992. "Ritual and the Shaping of Narrative: The Legend of the Han Emperor Wu." Ph.D. diss., University of Michigan.

———. 1994. "The Ritual of Scriptural Transmission as Seen in the *Han Wudi neizhuan.*" Paper delivered at the 1994 meeting of the Association of Asian Studies.

———. Unpublished. "Where Chinese Administrative Practices and Tales of the Strange Converge: The Meaning of *gushi* in *Han Wudi gushi.*"

Soergel, Philip M. 1993. *Wondrous in His Saints: Counter-Reformation Propaganda in Bavaria.* Berkeley: University of California Press.

Somers, Robert M. 1986. "Time, Space, and Structure in the Consolidation of the T'ang Dynasty (A.D. 617–700)." JAS 45:971–94.

Soymié, Michel. 1956. "Le Lo-feou chan: Étude de géographie religieuse." BEF 48:1–139.

Spiro, Audrey. 1990. *Contemplating the Ancients: Aesthetic and Social Issues in Early Chinese Portraiture*. Berkeley: University of California Press.

Stein, R. A. 1979. "Religious Taoism and Popular Religion from the Second to the Seventh Centuries." In Welch and Seidel 1979, 53–82.

Stewart, Susan. 1984. *On Longing*. Baltimore: The John Hopkins University Press.

Stocking, George W., Jr., ed. 1983. *Observers Observed: Essays on Ethnographic Fieldwork*. Madison: University of Wisconsin Press.

———, ed. 1985. *Objects and Others: Essays on Museums and Material Culture*. Madison: University of Wisconsin Press.

Strickmann, Michel. 1977. "The Mao Shan Revelations: Taoism and the Aristocracy." TP 63:1–64.

———. 1978. "A Taoist Confirmation of Liang Wu Ti's Suppression of Taoism." JAOS 98:467–75.

———. 1979. "On the Alchemy of T'ao Hung-ching." In Welch and Seidel 1979, 123–192.

———. 1988. "Dreamwork of Psycho-Sinologists: Doctors, Taoists, Monks." In *Psycho-Sinology: The Universe of Dreams in Chinese Culture*, ed. C. T. Brown, 25–46. Washington, D.C.: Woodrow Wilson International Center for Scholars.

Strong, John S. 1983. *The Legend of King Aśoka*. Princeton: Princeton University Press.

Suzuki, C. 1968. "China's Relations with Inner Asia: The Hsiung-nu, Tibet." In *The Chinese World Order: Traditional China's Foreign Relations*, ed. J. K. Fairbank, 180–97. Cambridge, Mass.: Harvard University Press.

von Sydow, C. W. 1948. *Selected Papers on Folklore*. Copenhagen: Rosenkilde and Bagger.

Tamaki Kōshirō. 1961. "The Development of the Thought of Tathāgatagarbha from India to China." *Journal of Indian and Buddhist Studies* 9:378–86.

Tambiah, Stanley J. 1976. *World Conquerer and World Renouncer*. Cambridge: Cambridge University Press.

———. 1985. *Culture, Thought, and Social Action*. Cambridge, Mass: Harvard University Press.

Teiser, Stephen F. 1985. "T'ang Buddhist Encyclopedias: An Introduction to *Fa-yüan chu-lin* and *Chu-ching yao-chi*." *T'ang Studies* 30:109–28.

———. 1985–86. "Engulfing the Bounds of Order: The Myth of the Great Flood in *Mencius*." JCR 13-14:15–43.

———. 1986. "Ghosts and Ancestors in Medieval Chinese Religion: The Yü-lan-p'en Festival as Mortuary Ritual." HR 26:47–67.

―――. 1988a. *The Ghost Festival in Medieval China*. Princeton: Princeton University Press.

―――. 1988b. "'Having Once Died and Returned to Life': Representations of Hell in Medieval China." HJAS 48:433–64.

Teng, Ssu-yü, tr. 1968. *Family Instructions for the Yen Clan*. T'oung Pao Monographies 4. Leiden: E. J. Brill.

Teng, Ssu-yü, and Knight Biggerstaff. 1971. *An Annotated Bibliography of Selected Chinese Reference Works*. 3d ed. Harvard-Yenching Institute Studies II. Cambridge, Mass: Harvard University Press.

Thorndike, L. 1923–58. *A History of Magic and Experimental Science*. 8 vols. New York: Macmillan.

Till, Barry, and Paul Swart, tr. 1979–80. "Two Tombs of the Southern Dynasties at Huqiao and Jianshan in Danyang County, Jiangsu Province." *Chinese Studies in Archaeology* 1.3:74–124.

Ting, N-t. 1970. "AT Type 301 in China and Some Countries Adjacent to China: A Study of a Regional Group and its Significance in World Tradition." *Fabula* 11:54–125.

Tjan, T. S. 1949–52. *Po Hu T'ung: The Comprehensive Discussions in the White Tiger Hall*. 2 vols. Leiden: E. J. Brill.

Todorov, Tzvetan. 1975. *The Fantastic: A Structural Approach to a Literary Genre*. Tr. R. Howard. Ithaca: Cornell University Press.

―――. 1976. "The Origin of Genres." *New Literary History* 8:159–70.

―――. 1984. *The Conquest of America: The Question of the Other*. Tr. Richard Howard. New York: Harper & Row.

Tsien, T.-H. 1962. *Written on Bamboo and Silk*. Chicago: University of Chicago Press.

Tsukamoto, Zenryū. 1985. *A History of Early Chinese Buddhism*. Tr. Leon Hurvitz. 2 vols. Tokyo: Kodansha.

Tu, Wei-ming. 1979. "The 'Thought of Huang-Lao': A Reflection on the Lao Tzu and Huang Ti Texts in the Silk Manuscripts of Ma-wang-tui." JAS 39:95–110.

Turner, Victor. 1969. *The Ritual Process: Structure and Anti-structure*. Ithaca: Cornell University Press.

―――. 1973. "Center Out There: Pilgrim's Goal." HR 12.3:191–230.

Twitchett, Donald, and Michael Loewe, eds. 1986. *The Cambridge History of China*. Vol. 1, *The Ch'in and Han Empires, 221 B.C.–A.D. 220*. Cambridge: Cambridge University Press.

Unno, K. 1983. "The Geographical Thought of the Chinese People: with Special Reference to Ideas of Terrestrial Features." MTB 41:83–97.

Vande Walle, Willy. 1979. "Lay Buddhism among the Chinese Aristocracy during the Period of the Southern Dynasties: Hsiao Tzu-liang (460–494) and his Entourage." *Orientalia Lovaniensia Periodica* 10:275–97.

van der Loon, Piet. 1984. *Taoist Books in the Libraries of the Sung Period*. London: Ithaca Press.

Van Zoeren, Steven. 1991. *Poetry and Personality: Reading, Exegesis, and*

Hermeneutics in Traditional China. Stanford: Stanford University Press.

Verellen, Franciscus. 1992. "'Evidential Miracles in Support of Taoism': The Inversion of a Buddhist Apologetic Tradition in Late Tang China." TP 78:217–63.

Wagner, Roy. 1979. "The Talk of Koriki: A Daribi Contact Cult." *Social Research* 46:140–65.

Waley, Arthur, tr. 1938. *The Analects of Confucius*. London: George Allen & Unwin; rept. New York: Vintage (n.d.).

Wallacker, Benjamin E. 1962. *The Huai-nan-tzu, Book Eleven*. New Haven: American Oriental Society.

———. 1978. "Han Confucianism and Confucius in Han." In Roy and Tsien 1978, 215–28.

Wang Hsiu-huei. 1989. "Vingt-sept récits retrouvés du *Yijian zhi*." TP 75:191–208.

Wang, Yi-t'ung, tr. 1984. *A Record of Buddhist Monasteries in Lo-yang by Yang Hsüan-chih*. Princeton: Princeton University Press.

Ware, J. R., tr. 1981 [1966]. *Alchemy, Medicine and Religion in the China of A.D. 320: The Nei P'ien of Ko Hung*. Reprint. New York: Dover.

Watson, Burton, tr. 1968. *The Complete Works of Chuang Tzu*. New York: Columbia University Press.

———, tr. 1989. *The Tso Chuan: Selections from China's Oldest Narrative History*. New York: Columbia University Press.

Wechsler, Howard J. 1985. *Offerings of Jade and Silk*. New Haven: Yale University Press.

Welch, Holmes, and Anna Seidel, eds. 1979. *Facets of Taoism: Essays in Chinese Religion*. New Haven: Yale University Press.

Wheatley, Paul. 1969. *City as Symbol*. London: University College.

———. 1971. *The Pivot of the Four Quarters: A Preliminary Enquiry into the Origins and Character of the Ancient Chinese City*. Chicago: Aldine.

Wheatley, Paul, and Thomas See. 1978. *From Court to Capital*. Chicago: University of Chicago Press.

White, David G. 1991. *Myths of the Dog-Man*. Chicago: University of Chicago Press.

White, Hayden. 1972. "The Forms of Wildness: Archaeology of an Idea." In *The Wild Man Within: An Image in Western Thought from the Renaissance to Romanticism*, ed. Edward Dudley and Maximillian E. Novak, 3–38. Pittsburgh: University of Pittsburgh Press.

———. 1978. *Tropics of Discourse: Essays in Cultural Criticism*. Baltimore: The Johns Hopkins University Press.

Wiens, H. J. 1954. *China's March toward the Tropics*. Hamden, Conn.: Shoe String Press.

Wilhelm, Hellmut. 1977. *Heaven, Earth, and Man in the Book of Changes*. Seattle: University of Washington Press.

Wittkower, Rudolf. 1942. "Marvels of the East: A Study in the History of

Monsters." *Journal of the Warburg and Courtauld Institutes* 5:159–97.

Wright, Arthur F. 1948. "Fo-T'u-Têng: A Biography." HJAS 11:321–71.

———. 1954. "Biography and Hagiography: Hui-chiao's *Lives of Eminent Monks.*" In *Silver Jubilee Volume of the Zinbun-Kagaku-Kenkyusyo, Kyoto University*, 383–432. Kyoto: Kyoto University.

———. 1977. "The Cosmology of the Chinese City." In *The City in Late Imperial China*, ed. G. William Skinner, 33–73. Stanford: Stanford University Press.

———. 1990. *Studies in Chinese Buddhism*. Ed. Robert M. Somers. New Haven: Yale University Press.

Wright, John K. 1947. "Terrae Incognitae: The Place of the Imagination in Geography." *Annals of the Association of American Geographers* 37:1–15.

———. 1965 [1925]. *The Geographical Lore of the Time of the Crusades*. New York: Dover.

Wu, Hung. 1987. "The Earliest Pictorial Representations of Ape Tales." TP 73:86–112.

———. 1989. *The Wu Liang Shrine: The Ideology of Early Chinese Pictorial Art*. Stanford: Stanford University Press.

Wu, K. T. 1937. "Libraries and Book-Collecting in China before the Invention of Printing." *T'ien Hsia Monthly* 5.3:237–60.

Yang, Lien-sheng. 1957. "The Concept of *Pao* as a Basis for Social Relations in China." In *Chinese Thought and Institutions*, ed. John K. Fairbank, 291–309. Chicago: University of Chicago Press.

———. 1963a. "Hostages in Chinese History." Chap. in *Studies in Chinese Institutional History*. Cambridge, Mass.: Harvard University Press.

———. 1963b. "Notes on the Economic History of the Chin Dynasty." Chap. in *Studies in Chinese Institutional History*. Cambridge, Mass.: Harvard University Press.

———. 1968. "Historical Notes on the Chinese World Order." In *The Chinese World Order: Traditional China's Foreign Relations*, ed. John King Fairbank, 20–33. Cambridge, Mass: Harvard University Press.

Yoshikawa, Kōjirō. 1955. "The *Shih-shuo Hsin-yü* and Six Dynasties Prose Style." HJAS 18:124–41.

Yu, Anthony C. 1987. "'Rest, Rest, Perturbed Spirit!': Ghosts in Traditional Chinese Fiction." HJAS 47:397–434.

———. 1988. "History, Fiction and the Reading of Chinese Narrative." CL 10:1–19.

Yü Ying-Shih 余英時. 1964–65. "Life and Immortality in the Mind of Han China." HJAS 25:80–122.

———. 1967. *Trade and Expansion in Han China: A Study in the Structure of Sino-Barbarian Economic Relations*. Berkeley: University of California Press.

————. 1981. "New Evidence on the Early Chinese Conception of After-life—A Review Article." JAS 41:81–85.

————. 1985. "Individualism and the Neo-Taoist Movement in Wei-Chin China." In Munro 1985, 121–56.

————. 1987. "O Soul, Come Back! A Study in the Changing Conceptions of the Soul and Afterlife in Pre-Buddhist China." HJAS 47:363–95.

Zeitlin, Judith. 1993. *Historian of the Strange: Pu Songling and the Chinese Classical Tale*. Stanford: Stanford University Press.

Zürcher, Erik. 1972. *The Buddhist Conquest of China*. 2 vols. Leiden: E. J. Brill.

————. 1982. "'Prince Moonlight': Messianism and Eschatology in Early Medieval Chinese Buddhism." TP 68:1–75.

————. 1991. "A New Look at the Earliest Chinese Buddhist Texts." In *From Benares to Beijing: Essays on Buddhism and Chinese Religion in Honour of Prof. Jan Yün-hua*, ed. K. Shinohara and G. Schopen, 277–304. Oakville, Ontario: Mosaic Press, 1991.

List of Citations of Primary Texts

Only references to specific items, passages, fascicles, or (in a few cases) chapters are included; general references to texts are not (with the exception of references to Dunhuang manuscripts and inscription texts). Data given in tables in the discussion of textual history in Chapter Two are omitted here since they are easily locatable by referring to the boldfaced entries in the main index.

Citations of passages in collectanea are not listed. Official histories are listed only when specific page numbers are cited in the text.

Boldface indicates that a translation or a relatively full summary of the item or passage is given at the location specified.

Anomaly Accounts and Related Texts

Bwz

1.1	43 n. 59
1.17	222 n. 38
1.24	212 n. 20
1.32	212 n. 18, 256 n. 147
1.34	212 n. 20, 286 n. 33
1.35	212 n. 20, 286 n. 33
1.36	212 n. 20, 286 n. 33
1.37	212 n. 20, 286 n. 33
1.38	212 n. 20, 286 n. 33
1.39	212 n. 20, 286 n. 33

1.40	212 n. 20, 286 n. 33
1.41	212 n. 20, 286 n. 33
1.42	212 n. 20, 286 n. 33
1.43	212 n. 20, 259 n. 162, 286 n. 33
1.44	212 n. 18, 286 n. 33
1.45	286 n. 33
1.46	259 n. 163, 286 n. 33
1.47	286 n. 33
1.48	259 n. 163, 286 n. 33
2.1	286 n. 33
2.2	**214**, 259 n. 161, 286 n. 33
2.3	242 n. 35, 286 n. 33
2.4	286 n. 33
2.5	248 n. 88, 286 n. 33
2.6	286 n. 33
2.7	286 n. 33
2.8	286 n. 33
2.9	286 n. 33
2.10	222 n. 38, 241 n. 20, 286 n. 33
2.11	286 n. 33
2.12	248 n. 88, 286 n. 33
2.13	240 n. 13, 286 n. 33
2.14	222 n. 38, 286 n. 33
2.15	286 n. 33
2.16	240 n. 11, 286 n. 33
2.17	240 n. 11, 286 n. 33
2.18	240 nn. 8 and 11, 286 n. 33
2.19	241 n. 19, 286 n. 33
2.20	253 n. 129, 286 n. 33
2.21	259 n. 162, 286 n. 33
2.22	286 n. 33
2.23	286 n. 33
2.24	286 n. 33
2.25	251 n. 117, 286 n. 33
2.26	286 n. 33
2.27	243 nn. 46 and 50, 286 n. 33
2.28	243 n. 50, 286 n. 33
2.29	243 n. 50, 286 n. 33
2.30	243 n. 50, 286 n. 33
2.31	264 n. 209, 286 n. 33
2.32	243 n. 50, 286 n. 33
2.33	243 n. 50, 286 n. 33
2.34	242 n. 37, 286 n. 33
2.35	286 n. 33
2.36	286 n. 33
2.37	142 n. 106, 286 n. 33
2.38	286 n. 33

1.6	142 n. 107
1.7	222 n. 38
2.1	222 n. 38
2.2	243 n. 49
2.3	142 n. 107
2.4	251 n. 116
2.5	243 n. 49
2.13	243 n. 49
2.14	222 n. 38
2.16	243 n. 49
2.17	222 n. 38
2.18	142 n. 107, 243 n. 49
2.19	251 n. 116
2.20	251 n. 116
2.21	251 n. 116
2.22	251 n. 116
3.1	251 n. 116
3.4	243 n. 49
3.9	222 n. 38
3.14	251 n. 116
3.16	251 n. 116
4.1	142 n. 107, 251 n. 116

Fjz

3	187 n. 78
5	187 n. 78

Fslz (see also HHS 82A–B listings below)

1	186 n. 77
3	186 n. 77
5 (2712)	194 n. 99
9	186 n. 77
25	183 n. 66
27 (2747)	341 n. 182
30	187 n. 78

Fsty

Pref. (1–17)	**140–41**
2 (65–80)	**337**
2 (81–89)	**337**
2 (90–92)	**337**
2 (108–14)	**337**
2 (115–18)	**337–38**
6 (285–86)	40 n. 44
8 (367)	40 n. 45
8 (374)	38 n. 37
9 (388–91)	**339**

9 (388–417)	339 n. 174
9 (418)	**339**
9 (423)	**339–40**
9 (434)	**340**

Ganyz

1,2	81 n. 182

Gshiz

2.17a	251 n. 115
2.20a	189 n. 87

Gslz

1	261 n. 176

Gsy

1	326 nn. 136 and 137, 327 n. 143, 328 nn. 144 and 147
2	187 n. 78, 323 n. 129, 326 n. 138, 327 n. 139
3	187 n. 78, 323 n. 129, 326 nn. 136 and 137, 328 nn. 144 and 146
4	187 n. 78, 323 n. 129, 324 n. 132, 325 n. 133, 326 n. 136, 327 n. 140, 328 n. 148
5	187 n. 78, 323 n. 129, 326 n. 136
6	187 n. 78, 323 n. 129, 326 nn. 136 and 137, 326–27 n. 138, 327 n. 143
7	187 n. 78, 323 n. 129, 325 n. 133, 326 n. 136, 327 n. 142

Gsz: by section

shenyi A1	73, 329 nn. 150 and 151, 329–30 n. 152, 331 n. 156
shenyi A2	329 nn. 150 and 152, 330 n. 153
shenyi A3	328 n. 147, 329 n. 150
shenyi A4	329 n. 150
shenyi B1	329 n. 150, 331 n. 156
shenyi B2	329–30 n. 152
shenyi B3	326–27 n. 138
shenyi B4	327 n. 140
shenyi B5	329 n. 150
shenyi B6	327 n. 139, 328 n. 145, 329 n. 150
shenyi B7	329 nn. 150 and 151
shenyi B8	325 nn. 133–135, 326 n. 136, 329 nn. 150 and 152
shenyi B11	325 n. 134, 329 n. 150
shenyi B12	329 nn. 150 and 152
shenyi B13	329–30 n. 152
shenyi B14	331 n. 156
shenyi B15	329 n. 150
shenyi B16	328 n. 145, 329 n. 151, 329–30 n. 152
songjing 1	330 n. 153

songjing 2	329 n. 150, 330 n. 153
songjing 6	325 n. 133, 326 n. 136
songjing 7	326 nn. 136 and 138
songjing 8	330 n. 153
songjing 10	325 n. 134
songjing 13	325 n. 133, 326 n. 136, 327 n. 139
songjing 14	330 n. 153
songjing 17	325 n. 133
songjing 20	329–30 n. 152
songjing 21	330 n. 153
wangshen 1	186 n. 77, 324 n. 130, 325 n. 135, 326 n. 138, 329 n. 151
wangshen 2	329–30 n. 152
wangshen 3	325 n. 134, 329–30 n. 152
wangshen 5	325 n. 134
wangshen 6	325 n. 134, 328 n. 149, 329–30 n. 152
wangshen 7	187 n. 78, 323 n. 129, 327 n. 139, 328 n. 149
wangshen 8	325 n. 134
wangshen 9	325 n. 134
wangshen 11	329–30 n. 152

Gsz:
by *juan*, page, and register (and, in some cases, line)

6 (362b–c)	**231–32**
7 (368c.26)	345 n. 193
10 (392a)	77–78 n. 169
13 (411a)	77–78 n. 169
14 (418c)	81 n. 180

Gyz	252 n. 127, 352 n. 207

Gzj	244 nn. 63 and 64

Hygz

2 (124–25)	188 n. 83

Jingyj

3	90 n. 215
8	90 n. 215

Jlj

1	261 n. 181

Jlz

Preface	153
2	247 n. 82
3	255 n. 144
4	240 n. 13

8	243 n. 41
9	242 n. 27
10	252 n. 126, 352 n. 207
11	240 n. 13
13	259 n. 162
14	264 n. 209
15	264 n. 209
16	243 n. 42, **284**
17	187 n. 80
18	187 n. 80
21	262 n. 194, 356 n. 223
22	257 n. 150
23	42 n. 55, 262 n. 186, 356 n. 223, 361 n. 244
24	356 n. 223
30	352 n. 207
31	246 n. 71
32	241 n. 21
34	186 n. 77, 243 n. 45
38	259 n. 165
40	244 n. 56, 247 n. 87, 352 n. 205
41	252 n. 120, 255 n. 143, 352 n. 204
43	42 n. 55, 246 n. 74, 249 n. 97, 354 n. 212
51	241 n. 15
58	260 n. 175, 382 n. 50
59	353 n. 208, 385
60	258 n. 154, 357 n. 228

Jyj

1	**332–33**, 325 n. 135, 331 n. 156
2	246 n. 75, **333–34**
3	330 n. 153
4	325 n. 134, 329–30 n. 152
6	183 n. 66
7	329–30 n. 152, 331 n. 156
8	247 n. 76, 325 nn. 133 and 134, 326 n. 136, 327 n. 139, 328 n. 144
9	329–30 n. 152
10	330 n. 153

Jzj

| 1b | 222 n. 38, 244 n. 59 |
| 3a–b | 244 n. 59, 261 n. 183 |

Jzsy

9	39 n. 41
10	39 n. 41
11	39 n. 41

11	246 n. 73, 304 nn. 83 and 84, 306 n. 91
12	257 n. 152, 298–99 n. 64, 304 n. 84, 305 n. 88
13	261 n. 185, 298 n. 61, 303 n. 80, 304 n. 82
14	302 n. 76, 304 n. 82, 305 n. 89
15	304 n. 84
16	261 n. 185, 298 n. 61, 302 n. 76
17	303 n. 80, 304 nn. 83 and 84
18	244 n. 59, 299 n. 68, 304 n. 84
19	196 n. 115, 261 n. 184, 316 n. 119
20	302 n. 76, 303 n. 81, 304 n. 82, 305 n. 88
21	260 n. 171, 302 n. 76
22	304 n. 84
23	247 n. 80, 261 n. 184
25	261 n. 184, 304 n. 84, 305 n. 88
26	302 n. 76, 304 n. 84, 305 n. 88
27	260 n. 171, 261 n. 184, 302 n. 76, 304 n. 84, 305 n. 89, 306 n. 91
28	**193**, 302 n. 76, 303 n. 80
29	304 n. 84
30	302 n. 76, 304 n. 84
31	197 n. 120, 300 n. 70, 304 nn. 82 and 84
32	260 n. 171, 298 n. 61, 304 n. 84, 305 n. 88
33	304 n. 84, 305 n. 88
34	298 n. 61, 304 n. 84
35	302 n. 76, 303 n. 80, 304 nn. 83 and 84
36	303 n. 80, 304 nn. 83 and 84
38	255 n. 143, 305 n. 89
39	302 n. 76, 304 n. 84, 305 n. 88
40	304 n. 84, 305 n. 88
41	304 n. 84, 305 n. 88
42	305 n. 88
43	292, 298 n. 63, 298–99 n. 64, 302 n. 76, 305 n. 89, 329–30 n. 152
44	304 nn. 82 and 84
46	183 n. 66, 303 n. 81, 306 n. 90
47	302 n. 76
48	302 n. 76, 304 n. 84
49	302 n. 76, 304 n. 84
50	303 n. 81, 304 n. 84
52	196 n. 112, 260 n. 171, 298 n. 63, 298–99 n. 64, 302 n. 76, 329–30 n. 152
53	305 n. 89
54	196 n. 112, 303 n. 81, 304 n. 84
55	302 n. 76
57	304 n. 84
58	304 n. 84
59	304 n. 84

7	329 n. 150
8	328 n. 147, 329 n. 150
9	328 n. 145, 329 n. 150, 331 n. 156
10	325 n. 134
11	325 n. 134, 329–30 n. 152
12	326 nn. 136 and 137, 327 n. 143, 328 n. 147
13	325 n. 134, 327 n. 139
14	325 n. 134
15	325 n. 134, 329 n. 150
16	329 nn. 150 and 152
17	325 n. 134, 329 n. 150
18	325 n. 134
19	329–30 n. 152
20	79 n. 176, 187 n. 78, 323 n. 129, 327 n. 140, 329–30 n. 152
21	258 n. 159, 260 n. 170, 325 nn. 134 and 135, 327 n. 141, 332 n. 157, 389 n. 72
22	260 n. 170, 325 n. 134, 327 n. 141, 332 n. 157
23	325 n. 134, **331**
24	325 n. 134, 328 n. 148
26	328 n. 144
27	187 n. 78, 323 n. 129, 324 n. 132, 326 n. 136
28	325 n. 134
29	260 n. 170, 332 n. 157
30	187 n. 78, 323 n. 129
31	187 n. 78, 323 n. 129
32	187 n. 78, 323 n. 129, 326 n. 136, 327 n. 142
33	258 n. 159, 325 n. 135, 389 n. 72
34	260 n. 170, 332 n. 157
35	327 n. 140
36	328 n. 145
38	258 n. 159, 325 n. 135
39	198 n. 127, 329 n. 150
41	329 n. 150, 330 n. 153
43	325 n. 134, 326 n. 137, 328 n. 148
44	260 n. 170, **334**, 332 n. 157
45	260 n. 170, 332 n. 157
54	258 n. 159, 325 n. 135, 389 n. 72
55	**231–32**, 325 n. 134, 328 nn. 144 and 148, 331 n. 156
56	79 n. 176, 187 n. 78, 323 n. 129, 325 n. 134
58	260 n. 170, 332 n. 157
59	329 n. 150, 329–30 n. 152, 330 n. 153
61	326 n. 136
63	325 n. 134
64	260 n. 170, 332 n. 157
65	260 n. 170, 332 n. 157
66	324 n. 130
67	234 n. 65, 258 n. 159, 325 nn. 134 and 135, 389 n. 72

125   326 n. 136
127   327 n. 140
128   326 n. 136, 328 n. 144
129   246 n. 75, 325 n. 134, 326–27 n. 138
130   **334**, 325 n. 134

Nkj
2a   186 n. 77, 244 n. 58

Nyz   244 n. 65

Pyj
1b   183 n. 66, 265 n. 212
1b–2a   252 n. 120

Qxj
1   **385–86**
2   251 n. 117, 352 n. 204
5   251 n. 117, 352 n. 204
11   382 n. 53
15   244 n. 62, 388 n. 71

Sgl
2   260 n. 175, 382 n. 50

Shenyj
3   261 n. 183

Shenyjing
E 3   45 n. 70
E 5   282 n. 26
SW 1   248 n. 96, **281–82**
W 3   243 n. 46
W 7   262 n. 192
NW 2   222 n. 38
NW 5   240 nn. 9 and 12, 259 n. 165
NW 6   45 n. 70, 240 nn. 9 and 12
C 1   45 n. 72, 282 n. 26
C 2   281 n. 23
C 6   242 n. 28
fragment 4   **282**

Shj
194   241 n. 20
285–86   **136**
341   240 n. 11
342   240 n. 10

1.25	264 n. 206, 302 n. 79, 341 n. 183
1.27	83 n. 193
1.28	242 n. 31, 258 n. 154, 357 n. 228
1.30	263 n. 201
1.31	257 n. 149, 263 n. 201, 264 n. 205, 286 n. 32
2.1	355 n. 222
2.3	198 n. 124, 253 n. 130, 255 n. 143
2.4	198 n. 124
2.5	198 n. 124
2.7	257 n. 152
2.10	255 n. 144
2.14	355 n. 216
2.15	361 n. 244
2.17	353 n. 209, 359 n. 235, **375 n. 30**
3.1	359 n. 236
3.5	212 n. 17, 352 n. 202, 359 n. 238
3.6	359 nn. 238 and 239
3.8	260 n. 174, 261 n. 182, 362 n. 250, 378 n. 37
3.14	73
4.4	262 n. 192
4.5	262 n. 192
4.6	262 n. 192, 263 nn. 201 and 203, 264 n. 205
4.7	376 n. 34
4.8	262 n. 193, 263 n. 201, 265 n. 214, 373 n. 24
4.9	262 n. 193, 263 n. 203
4.10	262 n. 193, **376**, 373 n. 24
4.11	262 n. 193, 375 n. 30, 376 n. 34
4.12	262 n. 193
4.13	262 nn. 189 and 193, 373 n. 20
4.16	378 n. 38
4.17	257 n. 152, 359 n. 235
4.18	373 n. 24
4.19	373 n. 24
4.20	373 n. 24
4.21	257 n. 152, 359 nn. 235 and 238
5.1	257 n. 152, 359 n. 235, **375 n. 30**
5.2	**375 n. 31**
5.3	263 n. 201, 265 n. 214, **375 n. 31**
5.4	73, 263 n. 201, 375 n. 31
5.5	**376**
5.9	339 n. 177, 355 n. 222
5.10	265 n. 215, 354 n. 215
6.1	212 n. 18
6.2	212 n. 18, 256 n. 147
6.3	246 n. 68
6.4	252 n. 125, 352 n. 207
6.10	249 n. 103

7.12	257 n. 151, 359 n. 237
7.13	257 n. 151, 359 n. 237
7.17	243 n. 47
7.18	253 n. 130
7.19	249 n. 103
7.23	243 n. 47
7.24	243 n. 44
7.25	243 n. 47
7.26	248 n. 95, 257 n. 149, 353 n. 208
7.27	260 n. 172
7.31	248 n. 95, 353 n. 208
8.1	222 n. 38, 258 n. 154, 262 n. 186, 357 n. 228
8.2	258 n. 154, 262 n. 186, 357 n. 228
8.3	257 n. 149, 258 n. 154, 262 n. 186, 357 n. 228
8.4	258 n. 154, 357 n. 228
8.5	142 n. 108, 354 n. 211
8.6	258 n. 154, 264 n. 206, 357 n. 228
8.7	197 n. 122, 252 n. 120, 352 n. 204, 361 n. 243
8.8	263 n. 195, 359 nn. 235 and 238
8.10	354 n. 213
9.1	257 n. 149, 257 n. 152, 359 n. 235
9.2	257 n. 149, 257 n. 152, 359 n. 235
9.3	246 n. 74, 354 n. 212
9.4	258 n. 154, 357 n. 228
9.5	258 n. 154, 357 n. 228
9.6	257 n. 152, 359 nn. 235 and 238
9.7	256 n. 146, 257 n. 149, 354 n. 211
9.8	256 n. 146, 354 n. 211
9.9	256 n. 146, 354 n. 211
9.10	244 n. 62, 256 n. 146, 354 n. 211, 388 n. 71
9.11	256 n. 146, 354 n. 211
9.12	256 n. 146, **286**, 354 nn. 211, 213, and 214
9.13	228 n. 53, 256 n. 146, 263 n. 199, 354 n. 211
9.14	256 n. 146, 354 n. 211
9.19	257 n. 152
10.1	142 n. 108, 257 n. 148, 354 n. 213
10.2	142 n. 108, 257 n. 148, 354 n. 213
10.3	142 n. 108, 257 n. 148, 354 n. 213
10.4	142 n. 108, 257 n. 148, 258 n. 154, 354 n. 213, 357 n. 228
10.6	243 n. 45, 258 n. 154, 265 n. 215, 354 n. 215
10.7	265 n. 215, 354 n. 215
10.8	142 n. 108, 257 n. 148, 258 n. 154, 354 n. 213
10.9	260 n. 174, 265 n. 215, 354 n. 215, 378 n. 37
10.10	354 n. 213, 359 n. 238
10.11	354 n. 213
10.12	359 n. 239, 360 n. 240
11.1	252 n. 120, 352 nn. 204 and 205

19.2	250 n. 105
19.3	254 n. 138, 361 nn. 243 and 244
19.4	251 n. 118, 254 n. 136, 352 n. 204, 361 nn. 243 and 244
19.5	254 n. 139
19.6	212 n. 17, 352 n. 202
19.8	259 n. 167
19.9	359 nn. 235 and 238
20.1	251 n. 119
20.4	222 n. 38
20.6	**386**
20.7	**387–88**
20.8	**385–86**
20.9	244 n. 62, 388 n. 71
20.10	244 n. 62, 388 n. 71
20.11	187 nn. 78 and 79, **386**
20.14	**386–87**
20.15	353 n. 208, 385, **388**

Ssj8

1.7	60 n. 114
4.1	**285–86**
4.5	**285**

Sxz

Preface	**296–97**
1	222 n. 38, 304 n. 84, 306 n. 91
2	198 n. 128
3	305 n. 86
4	300 n. 72, 303 n. 80
5	300 n. 71, 303 n. 81, 304 n. 84
6	196 n. 116, 304 n. 84
7	298–99 n. 64, 299 nn. 66 and 69, 300 n. 71, 302 n. 76, 303 n. 80, 304 nn. 82 and 84
8	299 n. 66, 304 n. 84
9	298 n. 61, 300 n. 71, 303 n. 80, 304 n. 84
10	**191**, 298 n. 61, 303 n. 80, 304 n. 84
11	298 n. 61, 299 n. 66, 303 n. 80
12	304 n. 82, 304 n. 84, 305 n. 88, 306 n. 91
13	292, 298 n. 61, 300 n. 71, 303 n. 80, 304 nn. 82, 83, and 84, 306 n. 91, 362 n. 250
14	303 nn. 80 and 81, 304 nn. 82 and 84
15	299 n. 66, 303 nn. 80 and 81
16	298 n. 61, 304 n. 84
17	303 nn. 80 and 81, 304 n. 83 and 84
18	299 n. 65, 300 n. 71, 304 nn. 82 and 83
19	298 n. 61, 298–99 n. 64, 299 n. 65, 302 n. 76, 304 n. 84

20	186 n. 77, 292, 299 n. 68, 300 nn. 71 and 73, 301 n. 75, 302 n. 78, 303 nn. 80 and 81, 304 nn. 82, 83, and 84, 305 n. 88, 306 n. 91
21	300 n. 71, 302 n. 78, 303 n. 80, 304 n. 84
22	302 n. 76, 304 nn. 82 and 83
23	303 n. 81, 304 n. 84
24	303 n. 80, 304 n. 84
25	302 n. 76, 304 nn. 83 and 84
26	299 nn. 66 and 67, 302 nn. 76 and 79, 304 nn. 82 and 83, 305 n. 88, 361 n. 246
27	291, 302 n. 78, 303 nn. 80 and 81, 304 nn. 82 and 83, 305 n. 89, 341 n. 183
28	183 n. 66, 197 n. 118, 291, 298–99 n. 64, 304 nn. 82 and 83
29	291, 298 n. 61, 298–99 n. 64, 303 nn. 80 and 81, 304 n. 82
30	298 n. 61, 298–99 n. 64, 300 n. 71, 302 nn. 76 and 78, 304 n. 84, 313 n. 110
31	300 n. 70, 303 n. 80
32	186 n. 77, 298 n. 61, 303 n. 81, 304 n. 84
33	291, 304 nn. 82 and 84
34	298 n. 61, 299 nn. 65 and 66, 305 n. 89
35	302 n. 76, 304 nn. 82 and 84
36	300 n. 71, 302 n. 76, 303 n. 81, 304 n. 84
37	298 n. 61, 298–99 n. 64, 303 nn. 80 and 81, 304 nn. 83 and 84, 305 n. 88
38	303 n. 80, 304 n. 82
39	299 n. 66, 303 n. 80, 304 nn. 82 and 84
40	304 n. 82
41	303 n. 80, 304 n. 82, 306 n. 91
42	303 n. 80, 304 n. 83
43	303 n. 80
44	300 nn. 70 and 71, 303 n. 80
45	186 n. 77, 292, 298–99 n. 64, 302 n. 76, 303 nn. 80 and 81, 304 n. 82
46	178 n. 46, 298–99 n. 64, 299 n. 65, 302 n. 79, 303 n. 81, 304 nn. 82 and 83
47	303 nn. 80 and 81
48	303 n. 80, 304 n. 82, 306 n. 90
49	300 n. 71
50	303 n. 80, 304 n. 82
51	303 n. 80, 304 n. 84
52	299 n. 66, 303 nn. 80 and 81, 304 nn. 82 and 83
53	300 n. 71, 303 n. 80
54	303 n. 80
55	303 n. 81, 304 nn. 82 and 83
56	298 n. 62, 299 n. 66, 302 n. 76, 303 n. 80, 304 n. 82
57	198 n. 128, 300 n. 71, 303 n. 80, 304 n. 84
58	299 n. 66, 303 n. 80, 304 nn. 83 and 84

29	324 n. 132, 325 n. 134, 326 n. 136
30	324 n. 132, 326 n. 136
31	324 n. 132, 326 n. 136, 328 n. 144
32	324 n. 132, 325 nn. 133 and 134, 326 nn. 136 and 138, 328 n. 146
33	187 n. 78, 323 n. 129, 324 n. 132, 325 n. 133, 326 nn. 136 and 138, 328 n. 146
34	187 n. 78, 323 n. 129, 324 n. 132, 325 n. 133, 326 nn. 136 and 138, 327 n. 143
35	325 n. 133, 326 n. 136, 328 n. 148
36	325 n. 133, 326 n. 136
37	325 n. 133, 326 n. 136, 328 nn. 146 and 148
38	187 n. 78, 323 n. 129, 324 n. 132, 325 n. 133, 326 nn. 136 and 138, 327 n. 143, 328 nn. 146 and 148
39	324 n. 132, 325 n. 133, 326 n. 136, 328 n. 146
40	187 n. 78, 323 n. 129, 324 n. 132, 325 n. 133, 326 n. 136
41	326 n. 136, 328 n. 144
42	326 n. 136
43	325 n. 134, 326 n. 136, 328 n. 146
44	326 n. 136
45	326 nn. 136 and 137
46	324 n. 132, 326 n. 136, 327 n. 139
47	187 n. 78, 323 n. 129, 326 nn. 136 and 138
48	324 n. 132, 326 n. 136, 327 n. 139, 328 n. 148
49	187 n. 78, 323 n. 129, 325 n. 134, 326 n. 137, 327 n. 139
50	324 n. 132, 326 n. 136
51	326 nn. 136 and 138, 328 n. 148
52	326 nn. 136 and 137
53	187 n. 78, 323 n. 129, 326 nn. 136 and 138
54	326 nn. 136 and 137, 328 nn. 144 and 148
55	326 n. 136, 327 n. 139
56	326 n. 136
57	324 n. 132, 326 n. 136
58	326 n. 136, 328 n. 144
59	326 nn. 136 and 137, 326–27 n. 138
60	326 n. 136, 328 n. 148
61	324 n. 132, 326 nn. 136 and 138, 327 n. 143, 328 n. 148
62	187 n. 78, 323 n. 129, 324 n. 132, 325 n. 134, 326 n. 136, 327 n. 143
63	187 n. 78, 323 n. 129, 325 n. 134, 326 n. 136, 328 n. 148
64	324 n. 132, 326 nn. 136 and 138
65	325 n. 134, 326 n. 136
66	246 n. 75, 326 n. 136
67	325 n. 133, 326 nn. 136 and 137, 326–27 n. 138
68	324 n. 132, 326 n. 136, 327 n. 139
69	326 n. 136, 328 n. 148

Xs

1	264 n. 209, 378 n. 38
2	354 n. 211
5	142 n. 106, 247 n. 82
7	256 n. 146, 354 n. 211
8	247 n. 82
9	256 n. 147, 354 n. 211
11	142 n. 106
16	142 n. 106
27	**372 n. 17**
29	244 n. 64
30	196 n. 115
31	**193–94**
43	256 n. 147, 354 n. 211
54	257 n. 152, 359 n. 235
55	353–54 n. 210
61	257 n. 152, 359 n. 235
62	242 n. 33
79	257 n. 152, 359 n. 235
80	257 n. 152, 359 n. 235
85	361 n. 248
86	286 n. 32
101	353–54 n. 210
114	285
115	262 n. 192, 285
116	**286**
117	285
118	**284**
119	**286**
130	356 n. 226
131	356 n. 226

Xuanyj

1	328 n. 148, 330 n. 153
2	325 n. 135, 389 n. 72
3	77 n. 168, 324 nn. 130 and 132, 325 nn. 133 and 134, 326 n. 138, 327 n. 139, 328 n. 148
4	325 n. 135, 329–30 n. 152
5	327 n. 140, 328 n. 144
6	325 n. 134, 326 nn. 136 and 138
7	325 n. 134, 326 n. 136
8	77 n. 168, 324 n. 132, 326 n. 136, 327 n. 139
9	**334**, 325 nn. 134 and 135, 326 n. 136
10	325 n. 135, 389 n. 72
12	73, 325 n. 135, 389 n. 72
13	325 n. 135, 389 n. 72

19	244 n. 59
20	244 n. 59
21	244 n. 59, **380**
22	244 n. 59, **380**
23	228 n. 53, 244 n. 59, 263 n. 197
29	261 n. 183
30	222 n. 38
31	212 n. 20, 252 n. 122, 372 n. 17
32	76 n. 163
33	254 n. 137, 361 n. 246
34	376 n. 35
37	262 n. 187
39	183 n. 66, 265 n. 212
42	257 n. 152, 359 nn. 235 and 238
43	354 n. 213
44	142 n. 106, 246 n. 74, 354 n. 212
46	255 n. 141, 355 n. 216, 360 n. 241, 383 n. 55
49	257 n. 152, 359 n. 235, 376 n. 35
50	257 n. 152, 354 n. 211, 359 n. 235
51	257 n. 148, 354 nn. 211 and 213
52	264 n. 204, 383 n. 56
53	248 n. 93, 353 n. 208, 355 n. 217, 385
54	262 nn. 190 and 193, **375 n. 30**
55	257 n. 152, 359 n. 235
57	242 n. 33, 262 n. 189, **374**
59	**379**
60	353–54 n. 210
61	262 n. 189, 376 n. 34
63	76 n. 163, 183 n. 66, 265 n. 212, **284–85**
64	76 n. 163, 183 n. 66, 265 n. 212, **284**
65	**286**, 354 n. 211
67	261 n. 180, 353 n. 209, 353–54 n. 210
68	356 n. 226
69	263 n. 202, 361 n. 244
70	186 n. 77, 352 n. 204
71	360 n. 240
74	360 n. 240
75	257 n. 152, 354 n. 211, 359 n. 235
76	262 n. 190, 375 n. 31
77	259 n. 162
78	355 n. 219
80	254 n. 136, 353–54 n. 210
81	355 n. 220
83	258 n. 155, 324 n. 130, 330 n. 153, 357 n. 231
84	262 n. 189, 373 n. 24
85	388 n. 71
86	354 n. 213

150	247 n. 78
151	263 n. 197
152	253 n. 128, 255 n. 142, 352 n. 207
153	257 n. 152, 359 n. 235
154	246 n. 73
155	242 n. 31, 264 nn. 207 and 210, 357 n. 228
156	355 n. 220
157	353 n. 208, 385
159	**386**
160	254 n. 139, 262 n. 187, 353–54 n. 210, 361 n. 244
161	**228**, 263 n. 199
162	262 n. 190, 355 n. 222, 359 n. 238, **374–75**
163	228 n. 53, 353–54 n. 210
164	**386**
165	260 n. 175, 358 n. 234, 359 n. 239, 382 nn. 51 and 52
166	251 n. 118, 260 n. 174, 352 n. 203, 378 n. 37
167	83 n. 192, 243 n. 44, 253 n. 132, 262 n. 192, 263 n. 201, 361 n. 242
168	357 n. 228
169	261 n. 181, **385**
170	186 n. 77, 254 n. 136, 361 nn. 243 and 244
171	254 n. 136, 361 nn. 243 and 244
172	**385**
173	261 n. 178, 353–54 n. 210
176	260 n. 171, 261 n. 181, 264 n. 205
177	355 n. 216
178	357 n. 228
179	262 n. 189, **373**
180	242 n. 31
181	254 n. 134, 353–54 n. 210, 361 n. 245
182	353–54 n. 210
183	247 n. 81
184	242 n. 31
185	260 n. 175, 382 nn. 49 and 50
186	355 n. 216, 383 n. 56
187	252 n. 121, 355 n. 221
188	264 n. 207
193	263 n. 199, 264 n. 206
194	357 n. 228, **371**
195	265 n. 215, 353 n. 208, 354 nn. 213 and 215, 385
196	254 n. 135, 361 n. 245
197	251 n. 116
198	248 n. 92, **385**
199	76 n. 163, 260 n. 169, 263 n. 201
200	76 n. 163, 355 n. 222
201	355 n. 222
203	383 n. 54

2.33	78 n. 172, 259 n. 164
2.36	222 n. 38, 259 n. 164
3.1	353 n. 208, 385
3.3	**286**
3.4	184–85 n. 70, 353 n. 208, **384**, 385
3.5	353 n. 208, 385
3.6	353 n. 208, 385
3.8	185 n. 72, **384**
3.10	248 n. 93, 353 n. 208, 385
3.13	244 n. 64, 352 n. 204, 353 n. 208, 385
3.14	**384**
3.15	251 n. 117, 352 n. 204, 361 n. 243, **384**
3.20	244 n. 60
3.21	186 n. 77, 244 n. 58, **384**
3.22	187 n. 80, **384**
3.23	244 n. 61
3.24	244 n. 62, 388 n. 71
3.25	242 n. 29, 388 n. 71
3.27	243 n. 39
3.28	186 n. 77, 244 n. 58
3.29	**190**
3.32	212 n. 20, 248 nn. 89, 249 n. 98, 356 n. 223
3.33	249 nn. 98 and 99, **284**
3.34	186 n. 77, 244 n. 58, 249 n. 98, 250 n. 111
3.37	249 n. 100
3.38	248 n. 93, 384, **387**
3.39	248 n. 93, **385**, 387 n. 66
3.40	249 n. 100
3.41	387 n. 66
3.42	250 n. 110, 252 n. 124, **286**, 352 n. 207
3.43	252 n. 124, 352 n. 207
3.44	252 nn. 124 and 127, 352 n. 207
3.45	256 n. 147, 354 n. 211
3.46	185 n. 72, 259 n. 164
3.48	263 n. 198, 353 n. 208, 355 n. 220, 385
3.49	385, **387**
3.51	186 n. 77, 244 n. 58, 251 n. 118, 352 n. 204
3.52	252 n. 124, 352 n. 207
3.53	252 n. 124, 352 n. 207
3.54	246 n. 69
3.56	186 n. 77, 244 n. 58
3.57	186 n. 77, 244 n. 58
4.1–4.65	354 n. 211
4.2	228 n. 53, 357 n. 228
4.3	359 n. 236
4.4	354 n. 214
4.7	359 n. 237

9.8	248 n. 96
9.17	255 n. 144
9.18	255 n. 144
10.2	186 n. 77, 244 n. 58
10.3	247 n. 82
10.4	357 n. 228, 385
10.6	357 nn. 228 and 229
10.8	357 n. 228
10.13	262 n. 192
10.14	242 n. 34, 352 n. 206
10.15	242 n. 31
10.16	242 n. 33
10.17	352 n. 204
10.21	357 n. 228

Zgk

2	183 n. 66, 264 n. 204, 265 n. 212, 383 n. 56
5	250 n. 104
7	262 nn. 190 and 192, **375 n. 30**
8	353–54 n. 210
9	254 n. 136, 361 n. 243

Zgszg

8	262 n. 193
19	251 n. 115
20	251 n. 115

Zgz

1	262 n. 190, 372 n. 17
2	261 n. 179, 355 n. 216
3	257 n. 149
5	250 n. 104
7	248 n. 88
8	262 n. 193
9	262 n. 193
11	254 n. 136, 361 n. 243
12	261 n. 176, 362 n. 249
14	247 n. 81

Zyz

2	353–54 n. 210
3	261 n. 183
4	228 n. 53
7	353–54 n. 210
9	260 n. 169
11	260 n. 169
13	260 n. 169

Histories

27 (806)	345 n. 192
27 (820)	345 n. 192
27 (822)	345 n. 192
27 (824)	345 n. 192
27 (827)	345 n. 192
28 (850)	345 n. 192
28 (853)	345 n. 192
28 (858)	345 n. 192
29 (880)	345 n. 192
29 (896)	345 n. 192
29 (906)	345 n. 192
36 (1068–78)	172, 174 n. 24, 182 n. 60
51 (1433)	174 n. 24
72 (1899–1910)	174 n. 25
72 (1910–13)	175 n. 28
72 (1911–14)	172
82 (2150–51)	**146–49**
94 (2447–48)	184 n. 68
94 (2456–57)	68 n. 138, 172–73 n. 21, 176 n. 30
94 (2460–63)	172–73 n. 21
95 (2496–97)	66 n. 134, 172 n. 20, 175 n. 29

LS

14 (251–58)	177 n. 39, 182 n. 59
22 (348)	176 n. 36
26 (398–99)	176 n. 35
40 (572–74)	177 n. 40, 178 n. 47, 182 n. 61
41 (596)	177 n. 41
49 (698–99)	172–73 n. 21, 178 n. 46

NQS

52 (903–6)	174 n. 26

SGZ

4 (118)	44 n. 66
20 (580)	186 n. 75
29 (799–806)	186 n. 75
29 (811 ff.)	212 n. 16
29 (799–830)	340 n. 180
48 (1174 ff.)	48 n. 81

SJ

4 (116)	198 n. 125
4 (169)	103–4 n. 5
5 (185)	198 n. 125
28 (1359)	197 n. 122
28 (1365)	103–4 n. 5

Manuscript and Inscription Editions

Other Texts

Xinlun   **131**

Xu Gaosengzhuan
2.436b–439c   177 n. 38

Xunzi
16 (429)   130 n. 75

Yanshi jiaxun
6 (160)   137 n. 96
6 (161)   34 n. 25
6 (163)   194 n. 100

Yijing xicizhuan
A4.1–12   **347–48**
A8   **346–47**
A11.7   **348**

Youyang zazu, Xuji
4.7a.7–8a.2   186 n. 75

Zhen'gao
10.23b.2   299 n. 67, 302 n. 79
10.24a.2   292 n. 47

Zhuangzi
1/1–4   **151**
16/29–35   316 n. 121
26/15   **129–30**

Zuozhuan
9 (162)   106 n. 12
10 (172)   107 n. 15
21 (366)   147 n. 114
21 (368)   **103**

Index

Boldface marks the locations where the history and authorship of *zhiguai* texts are discussed.

Emperors are listed by dynasty first (e.g., Qi Emperor Wu), except ones of legend or high antiquity (e.g. Emperor Mu, Yellow Thearch).

Titles of official histories, collectanea, and editions that are mentioned in the body of Chapter Two are not indexed, nor are names of dynasties. Citations of most primary sources are indexed separately; see List of Citations of Primary Texts.

505